WITHDRAWN FROM
TSC LIBRARY

D1591917

THE COLD WAR AND THE UNITED STATES INFORMATION AGENCY

AMERICAN PROPAGANDA AND PUBLIC DIPLOMACY, 1945–1989

Nicholas J. Cull

University of Southern California

CAMBRIDGE
UNIVERSITY PRESS

CAMBRIDGE UNIVERSITY PRESS
Cambridge, New York, Melbourne, Madrid, Cape Town, Singapore,
São Paulo, Delhi, Dubai, Tokyo

Cambridge University Press
32 Avenue of the Americas, New York, NY 10013-2473, USA

www.cambridge.org
Information on this title: www.cambridge.org/9780521142830

© Nicholas J. Cull 2008

This publication is in copyright. Subject to statutory exception
and to the provisions of relevant collective licensing agreements,
no reproduction of any part may take place without the written
permission of Cambridge University Press.

First published 2008
Reprinted 2008, 2009 (twice)
First paperback edition 2010

Printed in the United States of America

A catalog record for this publication is available from the British Library.

Library of Congress Cataloging in Publication Data

Cull, Nicholas John.
The Cold War and the United States Information Agency : American propaganda and public
diplomacy. 1945–1989 / Nicholas J. Cull.
  p.   cm.
Includes bibliographical references and index.
ISBN 978-0-521-81997-8 (hardback)
1. United States Information Agency—History. 2. United States—Relations—Foreign
countries. 3. United States—Foreign relations—1945–1989. I. Title.
E840.2.C85   2008
327.1′1–dc22   2007036948

Portions of this book have appeared in other forms as follows:
"Auteurs of ideology: USIA documentary film propaganda in the Kennedy era as seen in Bruce
Herschensohn's *The Five Cities of June* (1963) and James Blue's *The March* (1964)," *Film History*,
Vol. 10, No. 3, 1998, pp. 295–310.
"Projecting Jackie: Kennedy administration film propaganda overseas in Leo Seltzer's *Invitation
to India, Invitation to Pakistan* and *Jacqueline Kennedy's Asian Journey* (1962)," in Bertrand
Taithe and Tim Thornton (eds.), *Propaganda: Political Rhetoric and Identity, 1300–2000*. Stroud,
UK: Sutton Publishing, 1999, pp. 307–26.
"The man who invented truth: Edward R. Murrow as Director of USIA," *Cold War History*,
Vol. 4, No. 1, October 2003, pp. 23–48; also published as a chapter in Rana Mitter and Patrick
Major (eds.), *Across the Blocs: Cold War Cultural and Social History*. London: Frank Cass, 2004,
pp. 23–48.
"The man in Murrow's shoes: Carl Rowan as Director of USIA," in David Welch and
Mark Connelly (eds.), *War and the Media: Reportage and Propaganda, 1900–2003*. London:
I. B. Tauris, 2005, pp. 183–203.
"Public diplomacy and the private sector: The United States Information Agency, its predecessors,
and the private sector," in Helen Laville and Hugh Wilford (eds.), *The U.S. Government,
Citizen Groups and the Cold War: The State–Private Network*. London: Frank Cass, 2006,
pp. 209–25.

ISBN 978-0-521-81997-8 Hardback
ISBN 978-0-521-14283-0 Paperback

Cambridge University Press has no responsibility for the persistence or accuracy of URLs for external or third-
party Internet Web sites referred to in this publication and does not guarantee that any content on such Web
sites is, or will remain, accurate or appropriate.

For Karen

CONTENTS

LIST OF ILLUSTRATIONS

PREFACE

This book is the biography of an idea: the idea that America needed a permanent apparatus to explain itself to the postwar world. It charts the career of the institution created around that idea – the United States Information Agency or USIA, known overseas as the United States Information Service or USIS – and its role in the Cold War. The book relates the birth, youth, midlife crisis, and mature successes of the USIA. The story of the agency's post–Cold War demise must wait for another volume. The evolution of America's approach to global public opinion remains relevant today, especially as many of the lessons learned across more than forty years of Cold War effort seem to have been forgotten.

HISTORIOGRAPHICAL CONTEXT

This book builds on the work of a number of scholars of the history of propaganda,[1] scholars of the role of culture in American foreign relations,[2] and a small group of agency veterans who have written about the USIA and gathered oral evidence from its retirees.[3] Despite these worthy antecedents, it is necessarily offered as a corrective to scholarly neglect. Not only is this is the first full and archive-based historical treatment

---

[1] The author is indebted to the pioneers of the field of propaganda history, including Philip M. Taylor, Nicholas Pronay, Robert Cole, David Culbert, Ken Short, David Welch, and Garth Jowett, who have provided intellectual models for this project and encouraged its writing, and to Donald Browne, whose work is the starting point for any scholarly engagement with international broadcasting.

[2] Emily Rosenberg and Frank Ninkovich pioneered the study of culture within American foreign policy. Allan Winkler and Holly Cowan Shulman conducted the foundational work on the Second World War period. The birth of U.S. Cold War propaganda has been eloquently covered by Walter Hixon and Scott Lucas, and the linkage between the USIA's Cold War and Civil Rights has been brilliantly explored by Mary Dudziak. Coverage of the USIA in Vietnam obviously benefits from the work of William Hammond and Caroline Page. The Voice of America has been charted by VOA veteran Alan Heil, Alexandre Laurien, and Michael Nelson and in its crucial early phase by David Krugler. Recent studies of particular elements within the U.S. international cultural program have included Penny M. Von Eschen on jazz, Naima Prevots on dance, and Michael Krenn on art. I have also benefited from the recent work of Laura Belmonte, Ali Fisher, Ken Osgood, Giles Scott-Smith, and James Vaughan. I am especially grateful to Gene Parta of RFE/RL for advance access to his monograph on radio audiences in the Cold War U.S.S.R.: R. Eugene Parta, *Discovering the Hidden Listener: An Assessment of Radio Liberty and Western Broadcasting to the U.S.S.R. during the Cold War*, Palo Alto, CA: Hoover Press, 2007.

[3] In order of publication, the key texts are Wilson Dizard, *Strategy of Truth: The Story of the U.S. Information Service*, Washington, DC: Public Affairs Press, 1961; Thomas Sorensen, *The Word War: The Story of American Propaganda*, New York: Harper & Row, 1968; Fitzhugh Green, *American*

of the agency, but also remarkably few accounts of American diplomacy even mention the USIA. This is not entirely the result of prejudice on the part of "conventional" diplomatic historians. The USIA was restricted in its self-publicity by legislation that underpinned its work, the Smith–Mundt Act of 1948, and had a rather haphazard institutional approach to its archives and record-keeping. The absence of the USIA from the historical record is a substantial omission. It was through the medium of the USIA that much of the world experienced American ideas and culture. It was the agency of "globalization" when no single private corporation could afford to disseminate information globally. It played a key part in the great events of the era, such as the Berlin crisis of 1961 and the Cuban missile crisis in 1962. World newspapers received key speeches and news stories from its offices; future leaders of the world were cultivated by its tours of the United States; millions read its books and magazines and viewed its films. From Khrushchev's Russia to Nehru's India, the world saw American life and technology firsthand in the vast spaces of major exhibitions and experienced America in the intimacy of the home, over Voice of America radio.

SOURCES

This history is based on extensive research in the system of presidential libraries, USIA and State Department holdings at the National Archives, and the USIA historical branch collection (most of which has now also been absorbed into the main National Archives holdings). Important collections further afield included the historical collection assembled by the State Department's old Bureau of Educational and Cultural Affairs, which is held at the University of Arkansas in Fayetteville. This book also makes extensive use of more than 100 of my own interviews with agency veterans and serving officers and correspondence with others. Despite the widest foundation possible, the narrative is necessarily selective, and a host of stories remain to be told in the files of the agency and U.S. missions around the world. I am particularly aware that I have privileged the story of the high politics of public diplomacy at the expense of efforts of yeomen in the field, and that I present an analysis of ideas of transient political appointees while passing over the work of thirty-year career veterans. I hope that the veterans will forgive the bias and that my fellow historians will correct it with field-centered case studies.

DEFINITIONS

The centrality of the concept of public diplomacy to this story requires a brief definition. Although an account of the coining of the term in 1965 is part of the narrative,

---

Propaganda Abroad: From Benjamin Franklin to Ronald Reagan, New York: Hippocrene Books, 1988; Allen C. Hansen, *USIA: Public Diplomacy in the Computer Age*, second ed., New York: Praeger, 1989; Hans N. Tuch, *Communicating with the World: U.S. Public Diplomacy Overseas*, New York: St. Martin's Press, 1990; and Wilson Dizard, *Inventing Public Diplomacy: The Story of the U.S. Information Agency*, Boulder, CO: Lynne Rienner Publishers, 2004. For the parallel story of the State Department's cultural work by a veteran see Richard T. Arndt, *The First Resort of Kings: American Cultural Diplomacy in the Twentieth Century*, Washington, DC: Potomac Books, 2005.

the term as understood today has helped to frame and structure the narrative. The reader must therefore tolerate my use of a twenty-first-century interpretation of a 1965 term to discuss practices in decades before the term was coined. Most simply put, if diplomacy is an international actor's attempt to conduct its foreign policy by engaging with other international actors (traditionally government-to-government contact), then public diplomacy is an international actor's attempt to conduct its foreign policy by engaging with foreign publics (traditionally government-to-people contact). It has five core components: *listening*: research, analysis, and the feedback of that information into the policy process – an example would be the commissioning of opinion polls by a foreign ministry; *advocacy*: the creation and dissemination of information materials to build understanding of a policy, issue, or facet of life of significance to the actor, which might take the form of an embassy press conference; *cultural diplomacy*: the dissemination of cultural practices as a mechanism to promote the interests of the actor, which could include an international tour by a prominent musician; *exchange diplomacy*: the exchange of persons with another actor for mutual advantage, as in the exchange of college students; and *international broadcasting*: especially the transmission of balanced news over state-funded international radio.[4] The reader will note that these components are not all one-way. Exchanges rest on a two-way flow of people and the listening process feeds data from the field to the center. This said, Cold War public diplomacy was largely characterized by a top-down dynamic whereby governments distributed information to foreign publics using capital-intensive methods such as international radio, exhibitions, and libraries. Since the end of the Cold War, the dynamic has shifted toward a more horizontal structure in which people are connecting with each other in international networks aided by new technologies; governments are joined by nongovernmental organizations, international organizations, corporations, and nonstate actors as practitioners of public diplomacy; and communication happens in real time without clear distinctions between a domestic and an international news sphere. To differentiate between this new reality and the old practices, scholars have begun to speak of the New Public Diplomacy, but this new world lies beyond the scope of this history.[5]

It should be understood that despite addressing publics, public diplomacy does not necessarily engage a mass audience. Public diplomats have always spent some – or sometimes most – of their energy focusing on significant individuals in the knowledge that they can, in their turn, either communicate to the wider public (and do

---

4 Commercial international broadcasting (IB) may still be regarded as public diplomacy (PD), but it is diplomacy for the corporate parent, not the state in which the broadcast originates. The corporate parent is free to warp the output or insist on rigid objectivity on its airwaves, according to its desired ends. Both commercial and state-funded IB can affect the terrain on which all PD is practiced: witness the rise of Al Jazeera in the late 1990s. IB work can overlap with all the other PD functions, including listening in the monitoring/audience research functions, advocacy/information work in editorials, cultural diplomacy in its cultural content, and exchange in exchanges of programming and personnel with other broadcasters. The technological requirements of international broadcasting are such that the practice has usually been separate institutionally from other public diplomacy functions, but the best reason for considering international broadcasting as a parallel practice apart from the rest of PD is the special structural and ethical foundation of its key component: news.

5 For discussion see Jan Melissen, ed., *The New Public Diplomacy*, London: Palgrave, 2005.

so more effectively because of local credibility) or become the government insiders in time. It is also worth stressing that public diplomacy is not necessarily the same thing as international communication or intercultural relations. Although international communication and intercultural relations contribute to the terrain on which public diplomacy must operate, they are not public diplomacy until they become the subject of an international actor's *policy*. An outward-bound business traveler is not always an agent of his state's public diplomacy (though he could easily be an agent of his corporation's public diplomacy if that corporation is a player in the international environment), and, similarly, an exported movie is not always part of a nation's public diplomacy. This said, a government's policy to issue the traveler with a leaflet on how to behave overseas, or its input into the making or distribution of the movie, does move these things into the realm of public diplomacy, and such cases will be seen in this history. It is also clear that when a traveler or a movie identified with a particular state offends local sensibilities, it becomes a problem for that state's diplomacy, public or otherwise.

Public diplomacy activities are neither new nor unique to the United States. Its five core practices – listening, advocacy, cultural diplomacy, exchange diplomacy, and international broadcasting – all have considerable antiquity. Sun Tzu urged his ancient Chinese readers to know an enemy's state of mind. Herodotus tells of envoys from the Persian emperor Xerxes appealing to the citizens of Argos to remain neutral during that empire's invasion of Greece. The Roman Republic extended its influence by educating the heirs to neighboring kingdoms. Celtic tribes built bonds by exchanging and fostering each other's children, and long before shortwave radio, the Holy Roman Emperor Frederick II anticipated its reach by circulating a newsletter about his activities to the courts of Europe. Similarly, at the dark psychological warfare outer edge of public diplomacy, Kautilaya urged his classical Indian audience to influence an enemy by spreading rumors in his midst.[6] America's innovation in the Cold War was to devise a single-portfolio term for all this work – "public diplomacy" – largely, as will be seen, as an alternative to the more familiar but debased word "propaganda." Whether or not we like the term "public diplomacy," the process of an actor's engagement with a foreign public to policy ends is an enduring feature of international life, and public diplomacy is as good a term for the phenomenon as any.

SCOPE AND BIASES

This book has been though a number of transformations, each of which has left its mark on the text. I originally set out in 1995 to write a history of U.S. public diplomacy during the Vietnam War, but during my preliminary research I became aware of the

---

6   For background see Harold Lasswell, "Political and Psychological Warfare," in Daniel Lerner, *Propaganda in War and Crisis*, New York: George W. Stewart, 1951, p. 261; Jarol B. Manheim, *Strategic Public Diplomacy and American Foreign Policy: The Evolution of Influence*, Oxford: Oxford University Press, 1994, p. 3; Arndt, *The First Resort of Kings*, pp. 1–23; Michael Kunczik, *Images of Nations and International Public Relations*, Mahwah, NJ: Lawrence Erlbaum Associates, 1997, pp. 152–90; and Philip M. Taylor, *Munitions of the Mind: A History of Propaganda from the Ancient World to the Present Day*, third ed., Manchester, UK: Manchester University Press, 2003.

manifest lack of a sustained scholarly treatment of the wider subject and decided to broaden my scope to include the whole story of U.S. public diplomacy. I imagined using the prism of the eight or so great crises and diplomatic set pieces of the Cold War, events such as the Hungarian rising of 1956 or the Cuban missile crisis of 1962, to tell the story. Such cases are here, but more was needed. When I commenced research, it became clear that the view of the Cold War as a series of crises, on which my plan was based, implied a crisis-driven structure of public diplomacy, and this simply did not fit the archival record of USIA. First of all, the agency had its own crises – the coincidence of the Little Rock crisis and the Sputnik launch in 1957 with serious management trouble was an especial low point – and its own triumphs, such as the Moscow Exhibition of 1959, the Dominican intervention of 1965, and the Bicentennial in 1976, all of which would have to be addressed. More importantly, I came to see the USIA's Cold War as less a succession of short, intense moments of crisis than a sustained long game of move and countermove against Moscow's propaganda machine, made for control of the contested spheres of Europe, Asia, and eventually the developing world. With this in mind, I resolved to write a seamless history of U.S. public diplomacy through the experience of the USIA. I opted to focus on the agency's administration and to explore the relationship between public diplomacy and the wider foreign policy process.

The research began at the top with the career of each USIA director and their relationships to their respective White Houses and worked outward to the USIA's media operations, paying particular attention to the Voice of America, which former USIA directors consistently cited as their single most important tool. Film also figured prominently, largely because, unlike the VOA's output, it had been archived and could be analyzed in detail, and moreover there was no shortage of archival testimony in the State Department correspondence to attest to its influence. My research then moved outward to the agency's wider activities in the field. This schema produced a narrative rather different from that which I had anticipated. Although the chronology runs seamlessly from 1945 to 1989, the focus on the view from Washington has necessarily been at the expense of the perspective from the field and the day-to-day working practices of the agency.

The available evidence – being disproportionately from the presidential libraries and the USIA Director's files – brought further bias. I have written most about the parts of the story that generated the most controversy, created the most documentation at the top, and loomed largest in the minds of my interviewees. The relationship with the VOA caused innumerable headaches and is treated in depth, and similarly the relationship with Congress and dealings with the Department of State loom large. By the same token, I have written least about the parts of the USIA that functioned best: the exchange-of-persons program seldom figures here, though the agency had a mandate from the State Department to administer that work; libraries and cultural centers attract little attention unless they are opened, closed, or burnt in a riot. I hope that there is enough detail for the reader to extrapolate an accurate picture of the whole. The USIA's research work is also underrepresented here. Although polls and survey activities appear from time to time, there is surprisingly little about the USIA's opinion research apparatus, largely because such listening activity did not figure prominently in the day-to-day administration of the agency, greatly preoccupy its leaders, or claim much of the budget. If it is absent in this book, it is because it was often absent in the agency's strategic thinking, which must be considered a major weakness within U.S. Cold War public diplomacy.

The psychological warfare activity conducted outside of the USIA by other agencies during the Cold War is dealt with only in passing. Readers seeking detailed treatments of Radio Free Europe or the cultural Cold War waged by the Central Intelligence Agency will need to look elsewhere. Similarly, although key themes in the output of overt American information, such as the civil rights issue, may certainly be traced here, this volume is not structured thematically and the thematically curious reader will need to work from the index. Finally, this volume does not probe issues of the engagement between American and local culture.[7]

TRAJECTORIES, MAPS, AND THEMES

Each of the five core elements of public diplomacy has a narrative arc that runs though this volume. They are as follows:

1) Listening: The feedback of the USIA's advice and data into the creation of U.S. foreign policy.
2) Advocacy: The ways in which the USIA was mobilized to directly advance the ends of U.S. foreign policy and the shifting approaches of its application.
3) Cultural Diplomacy: The USIA's use of cultural mechanisms including music, exhibitions, and art; its relationship with the practitioners of cultural diplomacy in the State Department; and its drive to acquire dominion over those practitioners.
4) Exchange Diplomacy: The USIA's encounter with the twin of culture, whose adherents within the State Department had their own credo of international relations based on mutuality and reciprocal exchange, and the collision between this outlook and the one-way approach of the leadership of the agency.
5) International Broadcasting: The career of the Voice of America, the development of its own ethical structure based on objective journalism, its shifting approach to America's message, and its struggle to be free from the USIA.

Besides these arcs, the reader will note geographical emphases – one might say maps – within USIA operations, which can be discerned throughout the work:

1) East–West: The role of the USIA in waging the Cold War against the Soviet Union, China, and their satellites.

---

[7] For first-rate studies of this sort see Reinhold Wagnleitner, *Coco-Colonization and the Cold War: The Cultural Mission of the United States in Austria after the Second World War*, Chapel Hill, NC: University of North Carolina Press, 1994, and Richard Kuisel's *Seducing the French: The Dilemma of Americanization*, Berkeley, CA: University of California Press, 1993.

2) West–West: The role of the USIA in sustaining and developing relationships within America's own camp in Europe and Asia.

3) North–South: The development of a role for the USIA in reaching out to the developing world, albeit with a marked obsession with the East–West context of these relationships.

Finally, there are seven essential themes within this work.

1) The relationship of the USIA to the foreign policy process: The White House and the National Security Council.

2) The development of the terminology and the idea of public diplomacy.

3) The relationships between the constituent parts of U.S. public diplomacy.

4) The domestic context of the USIA's work, its relationship with Capitol Hill (and especially the budget process), the media, the private sector, and the American public.

5) The issue of leadership in U.S. public diplomacy.

6) The development of the profession of public diplomat.

7) The changing nature of the task of public diplomacy.

The conclusion will return to these same points and seek to generate lessons from this history for America's public diplomacy today.

One book can only be a starting point. This study is offered as a framework of narrative history on which colleagues can build case by case, country by country, and element by element the next level of analysis of the role of public diplomacy in postwar American foreign relations, and – by example – begin to chart the public diplomacy of others. The significance of a such a collective project increases with each passing year. Since the end of the Cold War, international relations have moved ever more plainly into the territory of public diplomacy. America's past experience in this field stands as a guide – and a warning – to diplomats of the present and the future.

ACKNOWLEDGMENTS

This book has taken twelve years to write, and, in that time, I have contracted a long list of debts on both sides of the Atlantic. At the outset I benefited from discussions about the subject of Cold War propaganda with two remarkable teachers: Philip M. Taylor and Nicholas Pronay at the University of Leeds. I began writing a case study of the USIA's activity during the Vietnam War, but David Culbert persuaded me to broaden it into a full-scale history of the agency. The post–Cold War parts of the story will appear in a later volume.

My work began in 1995 when, while teaching at the University of Birmingham in the United Kingdom, I received the first of two grants from the British Academy to research the USIA in the United States. The Department of History at the University of Maryland at College Park provided a visiting affiliation. Here Holly Cowan Shulman took me under her wing and began introductions to veteran staff at the VOA, while Jon Tsumida provided sustaining intellectual companionship. Fellow visitor at Maryland

Mel Leffler of the University of Virginia also provided early encouragement. Martin Manning at the USIA Historical Branch initiated me into the workings of his agency and directed me to willing sources of testimony, while the VOA's head of public information, Joe O'Connell, became and has remained an invaluable point of contact with U.S. international broadcasting. At the National Archives, Sally Kuisel helped me access new sources. Much of the material used here simply could not have been opened without her intervention on my behalf.

I conducted much research at the presidential libraries and have debts at each. I am especially grateful to Denis Bilger at Truman, Jim Layerzapf at Eisenhower, Geir Gunderson at Ford, James Yancey at Carter, and the wonderful team of Jennifer Sternaman, Shelly Jacobs, Cate Sewell, and Diane Barriend at Reagan. Foundations attached to the Truman, Eisenhower, Kennedy, Johnson, and Ford Libraries provided monetary support. Friends provided accommodation during these research trips, and I am grateful to Catherine Fasbender and Louis Miller in Boston, Margit Dementi Rankin in New York, Carl Hooker and Glenn Sands in Austin, Greg Murphy in Palo Alto, and Rich Wolf in Pasadena. Lugene Whitley and Davíd Carrasco hosted me in both Princeton and Boston. Other friends who made a difference include the late Gloria Emerson, Judith Farbey, Athena Villa Gosling, Clive Kennedy, Phillip Lindley, Niall McKeown, Chris Szjeinman, and John W. Young.

The late Ken Short and David Culbert were supportive series editors. Donald Browne was a generous reader whose detailed engagement with the manuscript energized the final revisions. Beatrice Rehl at Cambridge in New York has been tolerant of delays and helped to facilitate the speedy transition of the final manuscript to print. Peter Katsirubas of Aptara and William H. Stoddard did a terrific job with the copyediting and preparation of the final version of the book.

My colleagues in the field of media history have shaped this work, especially fellow members of the International Association for Media and History, Susie Carruthers, Robert Cole, Tom Doherty, David Ellwood, Dan Leab, Michael Nelson, Tony Shaw, David Welch, and Christine Whitaker. Paul Lesch hosted me for a wonderful visit to the Family of Man exhibition. My thinking on public diplomacy has been enriched through conversation with Anne Chermak, Brian Etheridge, Ali Fisher, Joshua Fouts, Jessica Gienow-Hecht, Eytan Gilboa, Tom Goodnight, Sarah Graham, Brian Hocking, Rob Kelley, Andy McKay, Jan Melissen, Frank Ninkovich, Ken Osgood, Martin Rose, Bill Rugh, Giles Scott-Smith, Steve Seche, Nancy Snow, Jeff Taylor, Nick Waddam-Smith, Sherine Badawi Walton, and Ernie Wilson. John H. Brown has been a regular correspondent and kindly read the entire manuscript twice.

The process of writing this book has required the support of successive heads of department, and I am grateful to Richard Simmons at the University of Birmingham, Richard Bonney and Peter Musgrave at the University of Leicester, and, during the process of revision, Larry Gross and Dean Geoff Cowan at the University of Southern California's Annenberg School for Communication. All my home institutions provided financial support for research trips. I have valued feedback from my graduate students at Leicester and USC, who accepted draft sections of the book as assigned reading.

David Chang helped with the bibliography, and Andrew Sternberg copy edited an interim version of the manuscript. William A. Coger proofread the final work. The UK Arts and Humanities Research Board funded study leave to write.

This book could not have been written without the help of the people who lived the agency's history and, in some cases, work on within the Department of State. Some of these people remain anonymous. Several witnesses went on to become good friends. I owe much to Alan Heil of the VOA and Mike Schneider of the USIA, but most to the late Bernie Kamenske, who with his wife, Gloria Kamenske, became guardian angels to this work and welcomed me into their home as one of the family.

My final debt is to my family, who know that the years 1995–2007 have been something of a roller coaster ride for the author. My parents, Joan and Tony Cull, my sister Hilary O'Sullivan and her family, and my late grandfather Bernard O'Callaghan all provided vital emotional support. My sons, Sandy and Magnus, brought much good cheer to the final years of this project. Above all, my wife, Karen Ford Cull, has been *the* essential part of the completion of this book: challenging me intellectually, sustaining me personally, and holding the fort during my physical absences. This book is dedicated to my wonderful wife with much love.

Nick Cull
Redondo Beach, California, December 2007

ABBREVIATIONS

Abbreviations used in text

BBC	British Broadcasting Corporation
BBG	Broadcasting Board of Governors (parent body to RFE/RL, VOA, etc., 1994–)
BCICA	Bicentennial Committee on International Conferences of Americanists
BIB	Board for International Broadcasting (parent body to RFE/RL, 1972–94)
CAO	cultural affairs officer
CIA	Central Intelligence Agency
CPI	Committee on Public Information (in First World War)
CU	Bureau of Educational and Cultural Affairs (at Dept. of State)
ECA	(1) Economic Cooperation Administration (Marshall Plan)
	(2) Bureau of Educational and Cultural Affairs (State Dept., 1999–)
ERP	European Recovery Program (Marshall Plan)
FBIS	Foreign Broadcast Information Service
HICOG	High Commissioner for Germany
IBB	International Broadcasting Bureau (management unit for the VOA, RFE/RL, etc., 1994–)
IBS	International Broadcasting (USIA internal designation for the VOA)
IIA	International Information Administration (State Dept., 1952–53)
IIIS	Interim International Information Service (State Dept., 1945–46)
IIP	Bureau of International Information Programs (State Dept., 1999–)
IMG	Informational Media Guarantee progam
IMV	USIA designation for motion picture branch
IPI	International Public Information Group (Clinton era)
IPS	International Press Service (within the USIA)
JUSPAO	Joint United States Public Affairs Office (in Vietnam)
NSC	National Security Council
OCB	Operations Coordinating Board (in Eisenhower era)
OEX	Office of Educational Exchange (OIE/USIE/IIA subunit, 1948–53)
OIAA	Office of the Coordinator of Inter-American Affairs (Rockefeller Office)
OIC	Office of International Information and Cultural Affairs (State Dept., 1946–47)
OIE	Office of International Information and Educational Exchange (State Dept., 1947–48)
OII	Office of International Information (OIE/USIE/IIA subunit, 1948–53)
OWI	Office of War Information (World War Two)
PAO	public affairs officer

PSB	Psychological Strategy Board (in Truman era)
RFE/RL	Radio Free Europe and Radio Liberty
RIAS	Radio in the American Sector
USIA	United States Information Agency
USICA	United States International Communication Agency (in Carter era)
USIE	United States Information and Exchange (State Dept., 1948–52)
USIIA	See IIA
USIS	United States Information Service (term used for USIA posts overseas)
VOA	Voice of America

Abbreviations used in footnotes

ADST	Association for Diplomacy Studies and Training
ASoS	Assistant Secretary of State
CF	Confidential file
DASoS	Deputy Assistant Secretary of State
DDEL	Dwight D. Eisenhower Library
EF	Executive file
Emb.	Embassy
FRUS	*Foreign Relations of the United States*
GBL	George [H.W.] Bush Library
GRFL	Gerald R. Ford Library
HSTL	Harry S. Truman Library
JFKL	John F. Kennedy Library
LBJL	Lyndon B. Johnson Library
LoC	Library of Congress
NA	National Archives
NA SMPVB	National Archives Sound Motion Picture and Video Branch
OF	Official file
PPP	*Public Papers of the Presidents*
RG	Research group
RNPM	Richard Nixon Presidential Materials
RRL	Ronald Reagan Library
SoS	Secretary of State
UoA	University of Arkansas
UoC	University of Chicago
USIA HB	USIA Historical Branch
USoS	Under Secretary of State
WHCF	White House Central Files
WHORM	White House Office of Records Management

THE COLD WAR AND THE UNITED STATES INFORMATION AGENCY

PROLOGUE

The Foundations of U.S. Information Overseas

Telling America's Story to the World
            Motto of the United States Information Agency, 1953–99

In the north of Luxembourg, surrounded by the steep, wooded hills of the Ardennes, lies the small market town of Clervaux. The town is dominated by an imposing castle, one wing of which is home to a lovingly restored photographic exhibition. The show comprises 500 images made by professional and amateur photographers from around the world, documenting the breadth of the universal human experience, encompassing birth, death, love, work, faith, community, and more. Half a century ago this exhibition triumphantly toured the globe under the auspices of the United States government. Audiences from Guatemala City to Moscow waited in line for hours to view it. The exhibition's images associated its sponsors with the universal values of what the show's title called "The Family of Man" and thereby challenged the claim that any one political approach had a monopoly on the celebrating humanity. The restored exhibit is today presented as a tribute to its locally born creator – photographer Edward Steichen – but the exhibit also speaks to the best of the U.S. government's postwar cultural and informational engagement with the world and is a living memorial to the institution that brought it forth: the United States Information Agency.

   This book is a history of the U.S. government's attempts to explain itself to the world from 1945, when it considered large-scale peacetime international information for the first time, to 1989 and the heady months of political change in Eastern Europe that marked the conclusion of the Cold War, when the USIA dared to talk of victory. But the story does not begin in 1945. Since its birth, in time of crisis, the United States had sought to present its image to the world.

   It all began with the American Revolution. The United States was born from a surge of ideas and a war that demonstrated the power of propaganda to rally men and women to those ideas. The stirring prose of political writers such as Thomas Paine sustained morale in its darkest moments. Propaganda figured on the battlefield, as American forces wrote messages to encourage British troops and Hessian mercenaries to desert. The colonials even attempted what would now be termed international disinformation. During the peace talks at the end of the Revolutionary War, Benjamin Franklin arranged for a fake supplement to the *Boston Independent Chronicle* to circulate in Britain. It contained a lurid account of a shipment of American scalps collected for the English by their Seneca Indian allies.[1] Given such beginnings, with the battle won, ideological projection remained high on the agenda of the new republic.

New and radical governments have always needed to explain their politics to the world, and hence America's Declaration of Independence was crafted with an international audience in mind, and introduced its catalog of grievances against the British crown with the memorable phrase, "let facts be submitted to a candid world." As the revolution gathered momentum, Franklin led the international campaign. Franklin had spent the fifteen years leading up to the revolution working in Britain as a publicist for his home colony of Pennsylvania. As the new republic's minister in Paris from 1776 to 1784, he paid close attention to issues of image and worked to correct misunderstandings about America and its revolution. His successor in Paris, Thomas Jefferson, also spoke widely about American law and politics and wrote *Notes about Virginia* to deepen French knowledge of his homeland.[2]

Despite the achievements of Franklin and Jefferson in Paris, the revolutionary period did not lead to a permanent U.S. effort to address international opinion. For the time being, the corollary of American exceptionalism was to preserve the nation at home rather than to extend its ideas overseas. This required not only a physical but also an ideological defense. The French Revolution produced a new breed: the ideological diplomat. In 1793, the French minister, "Citizen" Edmond Genêt, scandalized America by organizing Jacobin clubs to promote the revolution, recruiting for the French army, and attempting to outfit vessels to raid British shipping. Enraged, President John Adams became the first in a long line of American leaders to move to insulate their country from the propaganda of others.[3]

The nineteenth century saw a massive expansion in the print media. In the United States, journalists urged westward expansion, opposed or defended slavery, and campaigned against corruption and office-seeking. In Europe, the electorates grew and with them both the potential and rationale for international propaganda. With the exception of religious missions, the great campaigns of the era were domestic, but the network of newspapers and political meetings provided a mechanism that could be used in an emergency. During the American Civil War both the Union and Confederacy conducted propaganda campaigns in Europe, sending out touring lecturers

---

[1]   Eric Foner, *Tom Paine and Revolutionary America*, Oxford: Oxford University Press, 1976; Carl van Doren, *Benjamin Franklin*, New York: Viking Press, 1938, p. 673; Lyman H. Butterfield, "Psychological Warfare in 1776: The Jefferson–Franklin Plan to Cause Hessian Desertions," *Proceedings of the American Philosophical Society*, 94 (1950), 233–41; and William E. Daugherty and Morris Janowitz, *A Psychological Warfare Casebook*, Baltimore: Johns Hopkins, 1958, p. 60.

[2]   Jonathan R. Dull, *Franklin the Diplomat: The French Mission*, Philadelphia: American Philosophical Society, 1982. For a text by a USIA insider claiming Franklin and Jefferson as predecessors see Fitzhugh Green, *American Propaganda Abroad: From Benjamin Franklin to Ronald Reagan*, New York: Hippocrene Books, 1988, pp. 6–10.

[3]   Harry Ammon, *The Genet Mission*, New York: Norton, 1973; Linda Frey and Marsha Frey, "'The Reign of the Charlatans is Over': The French Revolutionary Attack on Diplomatic Practice," *Journal of Modern History*, 65 (Dec. 1993), 706–44. As Linda and Marsha Frey have noted, the new diplomacy, like the radical internationalism of Republican French foreign policy, soon gave way to the familiar forms of power politics, but public opinion had moved onto the diplomatic agenda.

and placing articles in the press to rally support. The U.S. minister to Belgium, Henry Shelton Sanford, bribed journalists and even subsidized the European newspapers that supported his cause. Britain became a key theater for the Union's propaganda war with the American South, as the North, represented by Ambassador Charles Francis Adams, argued that Britain needed to defend its cotton supply and worked to hold His Majesty's government to the letter of its neutrality. The Confederate agent in London – Swiss-born Henry Hotze – being a gentleman, eschewed outright bribery. Hotze merely fed material to the British press and founded a pro-Southern journal, *The Index*, which purported to be an entirely British publication. Hotze proved a master at spreading his side's interpretation of military events, and the London *Times* obediently minimized Confederate defeats, but he was unable to persuade London editors to carry arguments in defense of slavery. The Union view of the moral case, aided by Abraham Lincoln's eloquent written appeal to the cotton workers of Manchester, prevailed and Britain remained neutral.[4]

The United States also became the focus of international image policies. The Mexican dictator Porfirio Díaz, who seized power in 1876, paid propagandists in the United States to promote his regime and encourage investment in Mexico.[5] The Ottoman Sultan Abdül Hamid II, who also came to power in 1876, sought to promote the image of Turkey in the United States and elsewhere. His tactics ranged from bribing Western journalists in Istanbul to presenting photographic collections depicting his preferred view of the modern Ottoman Empire to the Library of Congress. Turkish embassies also protested against unflattering or overly exotic representations of Turkish culture. This included objections to a Dutch skit set in a harem and the presence of a group of dervishes performing for money in the streets of New York.[6]

The clearinghouses for international image-making in the second half of the nineteenth century were the great World's Fairs, starting with the Great Exhibition in London in 1851. Here the abstract desire for prestige and the concrete quest for trade intertwined. The United States organized fairs of its own, most notably the centennial exhibition in Philadelphia in 1876 and the Chicago World's Fair of 1893. Although these reflected no shortage of American self-confidence, one had to travel to the United States to experience the emerging sense of an American global cultural mission.[7]

In the 1880s, the European states, with their more developed sense of cultural vulnerability, produced private societies committed to international cultural projection. In 1880 French citizens established the Alliance Française to teach the French

---

4   Joseph A. Fry, *Henry S. Sanford: Diplomacy and Business in Nineteenth-Century America*, Reno: University of Nevada Press, 1982; Burton J. Hendrick, *Statesmen of the Lost Cause*, Literary Guild of America, New York, 1939, pp. 389–99.

5   Later Mexican regimes followed similar policies; see John A. Britton, *Revolution and Ideology: The Image of the Mexican Revolution in the United States*, Lexington: University Press of Kentucky, 1995.

6   Selim Deringel. *The Well Protected Domains: Ideology and the Legitimation of Power in the Ottoman Empire, 1876–1909*, London: I. B. Tauris, 1998.

7   Robert W. Rydell, *All the World's a Fair: Visions of Empire at American International Expositions, 1876–1916*, Chicago: University of Chicago Press, 1984; John E. Findley and Kimberly D. Pelle, *A Historical Dictionary of World's Fairs and Expositions, 1851–1988*, Westport, CT: Greenwood, 1990.

language overseas. In 1881 private citizens in Germany established the Allgemeiner Deutscher Schulverein für das Deutschtum im Auslande (General German School Society for Germanism Abroad) to run schools overseas for expatriate Germans. In 1889 Italians founded the Dante Alighieri Society to promote Italian culture. The French foreign ministry entered the picture with the Service de Oeuvres des Français à l'Etranger (French Overseas Works Service), which originally funded schools in the Middle East and East Asia, but by 1906 extended this to French schools in Europe and the Americas.[8] In contrast, the United States trusted its international image to private enterprise, which at this time meant missionaries, touring "blackface" minstrels, and Buffalo Bill's Wild West show.[9] Even so, mounting contact around the world with American economic power carried a powerful message, prompting works such as William T. Stead's prophesy of doom from 1902: *The Americanization of the World or the Trend of the Twentieth Century.*[10]

Although the United States entered the twentieth century without an official mechanism for cultural projection or policy advocacy overseas, currents of the age laid the foundations for later developments. The nineteenth century had sharpened ideas of American exceptionalism, ethnic chauvinism, the missionary drive of the American churches, and the reformist impulse of the social campaigners. Such currents would profoundly shape American foreign policy.[11] By the 1890s these notions had coalesced with economic thinking in the United States into what the historian Emily Rosenberg has termed the ideology of liberal-developmentalism, and codified as

> 1) Belief that other nations could and should replicate America's own develop-
> mental experience; 2) faith in private free enterprise; 3) support for free or open
> access for trade and investment; 4) promotion of free flow of information and
> culture; and 5) growing acceptance of government activity to protect private
> enterprise and to stimulate and regulate American participation in international
> economic and cultural exchange.[12]

The combination of public emotion and policy logic propelled the United States into the Spanish-American War of 1898 and the acquisition of what amounted to an American empire.

The reformist impulse proved particularly significant, dominating the politics of the so-called Progressive era and reaching its apogee in the careers of Presidents

---

[8] Philip M. Taylor, *The Projection of Britain: British Overseas Publicity and Propaganda, 1919–1939*, Cambridge: Cambridge University Press, 1981, pp. 126–7. R. E. McMurray and M. Lee, *The Cultural Approach: Another Way in International Relations*, Chapel Hill, NC: University of North Carolina Press, 1947, pp. 9–15, 43.

[9] John G. Blair, "First Steps towards Globalization: Nineteenth-Century Exports of American Entertainment Forms," in Reinhold Wagnleitner and Elaine Tyler May (eds.), *"Here There and Everywhere": The Foreign Politics of American Popular Culture*, Hanover, NH: University Press of New England, 2000, pp. 17–33.

[10] William T. Stead, *The Americanization of the World or the Trend of the Twentieth Century*, London: Horace Markley, 1902.

[11] Michael H. Hunt, *Ideology and US Foreign Policy*, New Haven, CT: Yale University Press, 1987.

[12] Emily S. Rosenberg, *Spreading the American Dream: American Economic and Cultural Expansion, 1890–1945*, New York: Hill and Wang, 1982, p. 7.

Theodore Roosevelt and Woodrow Wilson. The implications for the development of U.S. cultural and political projection overseas were twofold. First, the era saw the emergence of a generation of Americans who assumed that the problems of the world were solvable and that the sort of planning and regulation that worked to fix a slum at home might also work overseas. Second, the era gave a new significance to the domestic media in the United States. The American press and progressive reform developed in tandem. Campaigning papers such as Joseph Pulitzer's *New York World* led the way in the 1880s and 1890s. In the 1900s magazines such as *McClure's* became platforms for the new breed of "muckraking" investigative journalism and demonstrated the power of the media to effect political change. At the same time, the advertising industry demonstrated the malleability of the domestic consumer. The power to persuade for profit or social progress seemed to be everywhere.[13]

The first foray of the United States government into cultural projection was in the field of international education. The nineteenth century had seen the beginnings of international educational exchange. This was not simply "thrust upon" the non-European world, but in many cases was actively sought. The case of the United States and China displays a mix of American religious zeal (a missionary brought the first Chinese students to the United States as early as 1847) and a Chinese desire for "modern" and especially military knowledge. A Chinese educational mission arrived in 1871, only to withdraw in 1881 amid fears that the students might acquire American political ideas as well as technical know-how.[14] The U.S. government did not become a significant player in educating Chinese students until the aftermath of the antiforeign Boxer Rebellion of 1900. When the great powers imposed a punitive indemnity on the Chinese, the U.S. government resolved to return its share to China in the form of scholarships to U.S. universities and funding for schools in China. President Theodore Roosevelt signed the legislation liberating some $10 million for this purpose in 1908.[15] The decision was a milestone. The Boxer scholarships did double duty for the United States, boosting America's image in China and disseminating American ideas through the returned students.

The Progressive era also saw the foundation of the first formal – if private – structures of American cultural diplomacy. The story began with the establishment of internationally minded philanthropic foundations, such as the Carnegie Endowment for International Peace, established in 1910, or the Rockefeller Foundation. These organizations supported academic exchange in the name of liberal internationalism. Particular achievements included the foundation of the Pan-American Union, which

---

[13] For growing U.S. government attention to domestic public opinion in foreign affairs see Robert C. Hilderbrand, *Power and the People: Executive Management of Public Opinion in Foreign Affairs, 1897–1921*, Chapel Hill, NC: University of North Carolina Press, 1981; on "muckraking" see Louis Filler, *The Muckrakers*, University Park, PA: Pennsylvania State University Press, 1976; on Progressive America in general see John Whiteclay Chambers, *The Tyranny of Change: America in the Progressive Era, 1890–1920*, New York: St. Martin's Press, 1992.

[14] Chih Meng, "The American Returned Students of China," *Pacific Affairs*, IV, 1 (January 1931), 1–16.

[15] Carroll B. Malone, "The First Remission of the Boxer Indemnity," *American Historical Review*, 32, 1 (October 1926), 64–8.

in turn created its own Division of Intellectual Exchange. The men behind these organizations were idealists who sought to build horizontal links with the intellectual elite of other nations. They emphasized mutual enlightenment rather than patriotic tub-thumping.[16] Theodore Roosevelt sought a wider audience with less subtle methods.

TR did much to redefine the international image of the United States. He associated the country with principles of justice and organization as expressed in the International Peace Conferences of the era, but he also understood the ideological power of the deed. In 1907, Roosevelt dispatched the "Great White Fleet" on a two-year global goodwill tour. It was the epitome of Roosevelt's motto "speak softly but carry a big stick." En route the fleet paid ceremonial visits to major ports and stopped to assist victims of an earthquake in Sicily. Humanitarian aid has since proved a perennial public relations gambit.[17] Propaganda did not fit the mood of Roosevelt's successor in the White House. William Taft never broke free from his dogmatic emphasis on international law. In contrast, concerns for international image and an intense belief in the global relevance of the American political system burned brightly in the mind of the man who sat in the White House from 1913: Woodrow Wilson.

The outbreak of the First World War in August 1914 brought a great explosion in international propaganda. The neutral United States became a major theater for the war of words and images as Britain, Germany, and the other belligerent powers struggled to secure American support. President Wilson crafted his appeals for peace and negotiation with a global audience in mind. But entry into the war in April 1917 required more. The journalistic campaigns in progress in early 1917 included one for a radical reform of American diplomatic practice. Arthur Bullard, writing in the *Atlantic Monthly* and elsewhere, demanded open American "democratic diplomacy" overseas addressed to the public and not merely professional diplomats, and a crusade to rally patriotic support for the war effort at home. Woodrow Wilson took note and acted accordingly.[18]

Woodrow Wilson swiftly established a substantial propaganda apparatus to sell the war to the U.S. public: the Committee on Public Information (CPI) under George Creel. The CPI combined the idealism of the Progressive journalists and the communication skills of the emerging advertising industry.[19] The CPI is best known for its often strident work at home, but from the autumn of 1917 the Committee also addressed world opinion. Creel called it "the fight for the mind of mankind" and characterized

[16] Frank A. Ninkovich, *The Diplomacy of Ideas: US Foreign Policy and Cultural Relations, 1938–1950*, Cambridge: Cambridge University Press, 1981, esp. pp. 8–14, 24.

[17] James R. Reckner, *Teddy Roosevelt's Great White Fleet*, Annapolis, MD: Naval Institute Press, 1988.

[18] Stephen Vaughn, *Holding Fast the Inner Lines: Democracy, Nationalism and the Committee on Public Information*, Chapel Hill, NC: University of North Carolina Press, 1980, p. 11. Arthur Bullard, "Democracy and Diplomacy," *Atlantic Monthly* CXIX (April 1917); 491–99. Bullard went on to direct CPI activities in Russia for much of the war. United States Committee on Public Information, *Complete Report of the Chairman of the Committee on Public Information 1917: 1918; 1919*, Washington, DC: Government Printing Office, 1920 (hereafter *Creel Report*) pp. 1, 212.

[19] On the CPI's link to "muckraking" see Filler, *The Muckrakers*, p. 375; on advertising see Roland Marchand, *Advertising the American Dream: Making Way for Modernity, 1920–1940*, Berkeley, CA: University of California Press, 1986, p. 6.

the effort as a response to Germany's international propaganda effort. The CPI established a Foreign Section, which successfully introduced the world to Wilson and his vision of an international order. The Foreign Section had three divisions: the Wireless and Cable Service, the Foreign Press Bureau (or Mail Feature Service), and the Foreign Films Division. The Wireless and Cable Service provided "Compub," the U.S. government's answer to allied news agencies such as Reuters and Havas. From September 1917, Compub cables carried U.S. news and presidential speeches in what Creel called "a liaison between the United States government and the peoples of the world." The wires contained both general stories and material crafted for particular audiences. The Foreign Press Bureau, under the novelist Ernest Poole, created longer features for distribution by mail, introducing U.S. law, culture, and society, by such authors as Booth Tarkington and Ida Tarbell. Later, the CPI Foreign Picture Service provided news photographs. CPI officers around the world fed this material into the local press. Newspapers that failed to carry CPI stories suddenly found it difficult to obtain supplies of paper from the United States. Creel drew U.S. businesses into his network and found that companies such as Ford and Remington Typewriters were happy to display and distribute U.S. government propaganda and to use their advertising as a lever in support of the presentation of the United States in the local press. The CPI also arranged for numerous groups of foreign journalists to visit the United States and see American military and industrial strength first hand, which Creel considered "one of the most effective ideas" for countering German propaganda about U.S. weakness. Some press delegations met Woodrow Wilson in person.[20]

The CPI's Foreign Film Division oversaw the export of the Committee's own propaganda films and in agreement with Hollywood assumed "full control of the foreign distribution of American dramatic and comedy pictures." This, Creel noted in 1919, enabled the U.S. government "to dominate the film situation in every country." Foreign distributors found that if they wanted screen Hollywood films they had to stop showing German films and also screen CPI films with titles such as *Pershing's Crusaders* and *America's Answer*. The tactic shut German films out of Norway, Sweden, and even Holland. Moreover, working through the War Trade Board, the CPI denied export licenses to films that "misrepresented" America. Characters such as Jesse James stopped at the water's edge. Creel also intervened against films likely to be offensive to allied nations, and American courts rallied to the cause. In 1917 one Robert Goldstein, an associate of D. W. Griffith, produced a virulently anti-British Revolutionary War film: *Spirit of '76*. The film passed the wartime censorship board but only because Goldstein cut a scene featuring British massacre and rape. When he restored the offending scene for release he fell foul of the Espionage Act. The U.S.

---

20 Creel supervised the CPI's foreign activity personally until January 1918 and thereafter first Will Irwin and then Edgar Sisson took charge. James R. Mock and Cedric Larson, *Words That Won the War: The Story of the Committee on Public Information*, Princeton, NJ: Princeton University Press, 1939, esp. pp. 235–47. *Creel Report*, pp. 104–8, 117. For a detailed treatment of CPI activity in Switzerland, Italy, Spain, and Russia see Gregg Wolper, "The Origins of Public Diplomacy: Woodrow Wilson, George Creel and the Committee on Public Information," Ph.D. dissertation, University of Chicago, 1991. On the journalist delegations see Creel, *How We Advertised America*, pp. 227–32, 262.

government seized the film and Goldstein received a sentence of ten years in jail. He served only one year.[21]

Closer to the battlefield, the CPI conducted operations to undermine enemy morale in cooperation with the Military Intelligence Branch (which also received CPI estimates of the state of public opinion around the world). American tactics included floating messages into enemy territory using cloth or paper balloons filled with coal gas, and innovations included water-resistant paper and ink to prevent leaflets from becoming illegible after a few hours on the damp earth of Flanders. The CPI worked hard to ensure that Germans knew exactly the terms being offered by President Wilson and not just the censored version released in the German press. The CPI also infiltrated information into Germany through its offices in Holland, Denmark, and most especially Switzerland, run by a redoubtable woman named Vira B. Whitehouse.[22]

CPI outposts developed links with local educational organizations. James F. Kerney in Paris worked closely with French universities. Elsewhere, charitable organizations including the Red Cross and the YMCA used their networks to get CPI propaganda into remote corners of China, Russia, and Latin America.[23] The CPI made excellent use of hyphenated Americans such as Fiorello La Guardia as propagandists in the ancestral homes. Other key figures included a young man who on the eve of the war had been making his way as a theatrical agent in New York: Edward L. Bernays. Born in Vienna and a nephew of Sigmund Freud, Bernays did not doubt the malleability of public opinion and after the war pioneered the field of public relations. Bernays worked in Latin America, directing CPI press work and liaison with U.S. exporters. In some countries the CPI offices became full-blown library and information centers. The best-known library was in Mexico City, where a former journalist named Robert H. Murray recruited the American expatriate community to offer English classes. As Creel recalled, the classes also "gave splendid opportunity to preach the history, aims and ideas of America."[24]

The cumulative effect of the CPI's international operation was palpable in the way in which newspapers around the world adopted President Wilson's rhetoric for the peace.[25] Even so, the CPI and its activities came to an abrupt end on 30 June

[21] *Creel Report*, pp. 140–49; Creel, *How we Advertised America*, pp. 276–7, 281; Mock and Larson, *Words That Won the War*, esp. pp.136–53. On *The Spirit of '76* see Bertil Österberg, *Colonial America on Film and Television*, Jefferson, NC: McFarland, 2001, pp. 230–31. The British were not the only race defamed by the film. As with *Birth of a Nation*, on which Goldstein had worked, *The Spirit of '76* had a racially mixed archvillain, in this case a half-Indian woman who sought to manipulate George III into making her queen of the American colonies. The film is now lost.

[22] Creel, *How We Advertised America*, pp. 283–7; Vira B. Whitehouse, *A Year as a Government Agent*, New York: Harper Bros., 1920.

[23] Creel, *How We Advertised America*, p. 294; Mock and Larson, *Words That Won the War*, esp. pp. 235–47; Rosenberg, *Spreading the American Dream*, pp. 79–81.

[24] Creel, *How We Advertised America*, pp. 245, 266, 349; Mock and Larson, *Words that Won the War*, pp. 281, 287, 321–2; Edward L. Bernays, *Biography of an Idea: Memoirs of Public Relations Counsel Edward L. Bernays*, New York: Simon and Schuster, 1965.

[25] Wolper, *The Origins of Public Diplomacy*, pp. 161, 349–50. The CPI's failures included the overselling of American friendship to Hungary. The later treatment of Hungary as an enemy power hastened the collapse of Hungarian democracy, pp. 361–2.

1919. Congress withdrew all of its funding amid allegations that the committee had been too partisan. The State Department was not sorry to see the CPI close. Yet the international operations of the CPI had shown what could be achieved by a concerted information policy and many of its activities would be recreated in later years. Half a century later, Creel's portrait hung in USIA headquarters at the start of the line of directors as the founder of American public diplomacy.[26]

*

The experience of the war changed attitudes to propaganda within the United States. Writing in 1922, the historian F. H. Hodder observed, "It is one of the minor compensations of the great war that it enriched our vocabulary by giving us new words . . . and giving new meaning to old ones." In the first category he cited "camouflage." In the second he cited "propaganda."[27] In new popular usage the word propaganda now stood in relation to information as murder to killing. As the United States struggled to come to terms with the process by which it had become involved in the war, many blamed propaganda and particularly British atrocity propaganda. Memoirs of wartime propagandists and histories alike heightened the fear of propaganda and strengthened America's determination never to be bamboozled into war again.[28] Meanwhile, the commercial power of communications became even more palpable. Advertising came of age, feeding the boom economy of the 1920s, and public relations became an industry in its own right. Edward L. Bernays showed the way with books such as *Crystallizing Public Opinion* (1923) and *Propaganda* (1928).[29]

The years following the end of the First World War display a paradox. The public reaction to Woodrow Wilson's brand of internationalism committed the United States to a policy of political isolation. The break-up of the CPI in 1919 removed the U.S. government's apparatus for both cultural projection and policy advocacy, yet the world had never seen so much of American culture, thanks to the all-pervasive medium of the motion picture.[30] The drawback, from a foreign policy point of view, was that the United States government had no control over these images of America and could not count on Hollywood to serve the subtleties of the national interest.

Those Americans who believed their country stood for more than the Keystone Cops drew comfort from the work of private international foundations. The

---

26 Creel, *How We Advertised America*, p. 427; Mock and Larson, *Words that Won the War*, p. 331; David Krugler, *The Voice of America and the Domestic Propaganda Battles, 1945–1953*, Columbia, MO: University of Missouri Press, 2000, pp. 19–22; Richard Arndt, *The First Resort of Kings*, p. 27.

27 F. H. Hodder, "Propaganda as a Source of American History," *Mississippi Valley Historical Review*, IX, 1 (June 1922), 3–18.

28 For a major analysis of intellectual responses to Great War propaganda see Brett Gary, *The Nervous Liberals: Propaganda Anxieties from World War 1 to the Cold War*, New York: Columbia University Press, 1999; also Nicholas J. Cull, *Selling War: British Propaganda and American "Neutrality" in World War II*, New York: Oxford University Press, 1995, pp. 9–10; Harold D. Lasswell, *Propaganda Technique in the World War*, New York: Knopf, 1927, p. 2.

29 Scott M. Cutlip, *The Unseen Power: Public Relations, a History*, Hillsdale, NJ: Lawrence Erlbaum, 1994; Marchand, *Advertising the American Dream*.

30 Frank Costigliola, *Awkward Dominion: American Political, Economic and Cultural Relations with Europe, 1919–1933*, Ithaca, NY: Cornell University Press, 1984.

Rockefeller Foundation and the Carnegie Endowment flourished. The Institute of International Education, founded with Carnegie money in 1919, promoted global educational and cultural exchange. Speakers traveled through the auspices of the English Speaking Union (founded in 1918) and businessmen worked for international "understanding" through the Rotary Club (founded in 1905).[31] Such organizations provided what the U.S. government did not. In May 1928 a certain Dr. Cupertino del Campo, the president of the Rotary Club of Buenos Aires, founded the Instituto Cultural Argentino-Norteamericano (ICANA). It was the first of what became known as binational centers (or binational cultural institutes). The institute funded itself by teaching the English language, but its objectives extended to a comprehensive program of cultural interchange, in accordance with a series of resolutions at recent Inter-American conferences. Many such institutes followed across Latin America along the same lines as ICANA, as joint projects of enthusiastic U.S. expatriates and local citizens.[32]

Meanwhile, other states took a more active role in international advocacy and cultural projection. The Bolshevik regime in Russia claimed the leadership of world socialism and in 1919 established Comintern to spread the word. Soviet methods included international radio propaganda. The radio battle began during the closing months of the First World War. Woodrow Wilson's "fourteen points speech" of January 1918 had been relayed internationally in Morse code. Subsequently the U.S. and Soviet Russia broadcast rival Morse messages to world news organizations about peace terms. Now, the Soviet Union embraced radio as a means both to communicate with the "masses" worldwide and to associate the Bolshevik cause with new technology. The U.S.S.R. used radio to broadcast to Romania and to striking miners in Britain in 1926 and made a series of prestige propaganda broadcasts to celebrate the tenth anniversary of the Russian Revolution in 1927. Radio Moscow began regular shortwave broadcasts in 1929. Other states, including Britain, developed major overseas services, but in the United States the private sector merely dabbled in small-scale shortwave services to Latin America.[33] This was not enough to make a difference but sufficient to ensure that commercial interests opposed later U.S. government initiatives.[34]

In the field of cultural diplomacy, the French launched an official program in 1923 with generous funding, whereas for the totalitarian regimes cultural projection was an increasingly important part of foreign policy. In 1925, the Soviet Union established the

31 On IIE see Ninkovich, *The Diplomacy of Ideas*, pp. 18–19. On the ESU see William Griffin, *Sir Evelyn Wrench*, New York: Newcomen Society, 1950; on Rotary International see Rosenberg, *Spreading the American Dream*, p. 111.

32 Martin Manning to author, 17 February 2002; J. Manuel Espinosa, *Inter-American Beginnings of U.S. Cultural Diplomacy, 1936–1948*, Washington, DC: Bureau of Educational and Cultural Affairs, U.S. Department of State, 1976.

33 For a survey see Donald R. Brown, *International Radio Broadcasting: The Limits of the Limitless Medium*, New York: Praeger, 1982, pp. 16–48. On Woodrow Wilson's use of radio to publicize his "fourteen points" in January 1918 see p. 39 and Rosenberg, *Spreading the American Dream*, p. 93.

34 USIA Historical Branch, Bruce Gregory, *The Broadcasting Service: An Administrative History*, Washington DC: USIA, 1970, sections 1 and 2. For summary see Elizabeth Fox, *Latin American Broadcasting: From Tango to Telenovela*, Luton: University of Luton Press, 1997, pp. 15–19.

All-Union Society for Cultural Relations with Foreign Countries (VOKS). In 1926, Fascist Italy opened its first Italian Cultural Institutes overseas, and even before Hitler came to power in 1933 Germany spent substantial sums on cultural propaganda. The British, who had hitherto resisted any national cultural foundation, responded in 1934 by establishing the British Council with what amounted to a plan to save democracy by teaching English and organizing lectures on Shakespeare. As investment in cultural projection spiraled, the World's Fairs of the era became vast arenas of intercultural gladiatorial combat. The new initiatives were reacting in some way to the cultural challenge of the United States. Anti-Americanism was most explicit in Nazi Germany, where Hitler launched a cultural campaign to win Latin American public opinion.[35] In such circumstances it seemed unlikely that the United States government could remain on the sidelines for long, more especially with a President with a keen eye for public opinion in the White House: Franklin D. Roosevelt.

The management of domestic public opinion was a hallmark of FDR's presidency. Whatever its economic merits, Roosevelt's New Deal was a triumph of publicity. Initiatives were unveiled in presidential "fireside chats" on the radio, launched with logos and posters, and sustained by rallies and parades. Roosevelt cultivated the press with regular press conferences. The White House press office supplied articles and even cartoons directly to rural newspapers. In 1934, the administration created an office within the National Executive Council called the United States Information Service (USIS) to help publicize the New Deal. In July 1939. Roosevelt created the Office of Government Reports (OGR), which included the USIS and a new press survey function. The new agency was variously disparaged in the Republican press as "ogre" or "Mellett's Madhouse" after its director, the former journalist Lowell Mellett.[36]

The Roosevelt administration was slower to engage in overseas information operations. In 1935, the State Department began to transmit a daily "Radio Bulletin" of information to key missions overseas. The system would in time make it possible for the U.S. government to release what amounted to global press releases. More significantly, both the Under Secretary of State, Sumner Welles, and the Secretary of State, Cordell Hull, now recognized the value of the existing system of private educational and intellectual exchanges with Latin America and moved to add a layer of federal support. On 27 July 1938, the Division of Cultural Relations at the State Department came into being. At the helm of the division was Ben M. Cherrington, a committed internationalist, who saw cultural diplomacy as a mechanism for real exchange and understanding rather than a bullhorn for the American way. The Division worked with an advisory committee appointed by the Secretary of State, which drew on leading academics,

35 Taylor, *The Projection of Britain*, pp. 136–52; McMurry and Lee, *The Cultural Approach*, pp. 63–73, 110–18.
36 Richard W. Steele, *Propaganda in an Open Society: The Roosevelt Administration and the Media, 1933–1941*, Westport, CT: Greenwood, 1985, esp. pp. 10–15; Margaret Hicks Williams, "The President's Office of Government Reports," *Public Opinion Quarterly*, 5, 4 (Winter 1941), 548–62. For sample of USIS work see Library of Congress, Robert A. Taft papers, box 844, legislative file, U.S. Information Service, Root to Taft, 18 January 1939.

presidents of the national research councils, and figures such as the director of the Institute of International Education. An associated Inter-Departmental Committee for Scientific and Cultural Cooperation oversaw exchanges and administered grants.[37]

At the very moment that the State Department was beginning its cultural outreach to Latin America, Congress moved against the threat of foreign propaganda at home. The year 1938 saw the passage of the Foreign Agents Registration Act to render all foreign information activity visible. Warnings against foreign propaganda became a major theme in the isolationist campaign to keep America neutral.

*

The outbreak of the Second World War in September 1939 transformed the neutral United States once again into an international ideological battleground. The Germans attempted a heavy-handed campaign, whereas the British developed a lower key policy, developing links with U.S. media and pressure groups and providing information on demand. Roosevelt, mindful of the impending election, stayed out of the "great debate," allowing private interventionist groups such as "Fight for Freedom" to mobilize the public. Through the efforts of the interventionists, the war against Hitler became increasingly identified with the historical mission of the United States.[38] In the summer of 1940, Roosevelt moved to address U.S. information needs overseas. In August he established the Office of the Coordinator of Commercial and Cultural Affairs between American Republics, with the young oil magnate Nelson Rockefeller as "Coordinator for Commercial and Cultural Relations." An executive order of July 1941 renamed this organization the Office of the Coordinator of Inter-American Affairs (abbreviated either as CIAA or OIIA), but most people referred to it simply as the "Rockefeller Office." Rockefeller developed the existing commercial and cultural projects in Latin America, establishing offices and libraries and coordinating and extending the network of binational centers. The office launched a host of new exchanges and lecture programs. This heavily ideological and emphatically one-way approach to information work contrasted starkly with the reciprocal nature of the cultural program initiated in 1938.[39]

In addition to the expected orchestral visits and three traveling exhibitions of contemporary art from a consortium of New York museums, the OIAA supplied news and features to the region. The office even published its own magazine, *En Guardia* (On Guard), along the lines of *Life*, which soon achieved a circulation in excess of

---

[37] Documentation: see University of Arkansas, special collections (hereafter UoA), State Department Bureau of Educational and Cultural Relations (hereafter CU); for press release on launch see CU 3/1, no. 367, 27 July 1983. For analysis see Ninkovich, *The Diplomacy of Ideas*, pp. 24–35 and Arndt, *The First Resort of Kings*, pp. 49–74.

[38] On this period see Cull, *Selling War*; Steven Casey, *Cautious Crusade: Franklin D. Roosevelt, American Public Opinion and the War against Nazi Germany*, Oxford: Oxford University Press, 2001; Mark Lincoln Chadwin, *The Hawks of World War II*, Chapel Hill, NC: University of North Carolina Press, 1968.

[39] Ninkovich, *The Diplomacy of Ideas*, pp. 36–9; Arndt, *The First Resort of Kings*, p. 89. Minutes of the Advisory Committee on Policy can be found at Joseph Regenstein Library, University of Chicago, William Benton Papers (hereafter UoC: Benton papers), box 371, 3.

half a million copies. *En Guardia*'s appeal was such that copies were stolen from the mail to be sold on the black market, and the Germans launched a "rip-off" called *De Guardia*. The OIAA also broadcast shortwave propaganda. Working with commercial U.S.-based radio networks, they trained local radio workers in U.S. methods and placed readymade programs with Latin American stations. Responses were mixed. South Americans found the news content "bombastic, sugar coated" and even "doctored" when compared to the "honest, frank and uncolored" BBC. The OIAA also encouraged "suitable" Hollywood film production – including Walt Disney's animated spectacular *Saludos Amigos* – and persuaded U.S. distributors to withhold films from theaters in the region that screened Axis newsreels. The bureau worked to develop local radio and film industries (especially in Mexico), sometimes delivering covert aid through a secret front company, founded in July 1942, called Prencinradio.[40]

The effect of so much "cultural" attention from the north was mixed. In 1941 Chancellor Oswaldo Aranha of Brazil, worn down by meeting a succession of symphony conductors, film stars, and even the "short-pants ambassador" of the Boys Club of America, quipped, "one more goodwill mission and Brazil will declare war on the U.S.A." But such work blunted Axis propaganda in the region and, in the case of Brazil at least, nurtured a public sentiment that led that country into war alongside the United States.[41] The work continued throughout the war, though from 1944 on, Rockefeller himself moved to the State Department as Assistant Secretary of State for American Republic Affairs, leaving his friend the architect, Wallace Harrison, as director of the OIAA.

By the beginning of 1941, Roosevelt, now safely reelected, felt able to initiate large-scale Lend Lease Aid to the beleaguered allies. America's world role was changing. The year also provided a vision of what that new role might be. In his famous *Life* magazine editorial, the Republican publisher Henry Luce presented his vision of "the American Century," in which the United States would "assume the leadership of the world" and serve "as the powerhouse of the ideals of Freedom and Justice." Liberals recoiled, but a conservative alternative to liberal internationalism was taking shape. This vision would require not only military involvement in the world but also a cultural involvement overseas far beyond the gentle bilateralism of the State Department's Division of Cultural Relations.[42]

Meanwhile, the United States moved belatedly to develop the apparatus necessary for global warfare in the mid-twentieth century, including a capacity for propaganda overseas. On 11 July 1941, Roosevelt created the Office of the Coordinator of Information under the war hero Col. William "Wild Bill" Donovan. This new agency

[40] Cary Reich, *The Life of Nelson A. Rockefeller, Worlds to Conquer, 1908–1958*, New York: Doubleday, 1996, pp. 214–60; USIA Historical Branch, *History of the Office of the Coordinator of Inter-American Affairs*, Washington, DC: GPO, 1947; Barrett, *Truth Is Our Weapon*, pp. 21–5, 51–3; Robert William Pirsein, *The Voice of America: An History of the International Broadcasting Activities of the United States Government 1940–1962*, New York: Arno Press, 1979, pp. 7–36; Fox, *Latin American Broadcasting*, 1997, pp. 19–24; Rosenberg, *Spreading the American Dream*, pp. 206–8.
[41] Frank D. McCann Jr., *The Brazilian–American Alliance*, pp. 247–9.
[42] W. A. Swanberg, *Luce and His Empire*, New York: Scribners, 1972, pp. 180–83.

included intelligence and special operations activities (it later became the famous Office of Strategic Services) and a Foreign Information Service. The FIS had headquarters in New York under the direction of the interventionist playwright and Roosevelt speech-writer Robert Sherwood. Sherwood's recruits to FIS shared his left-of-center, antifascist "Popular Front" political outlook: journalists Joseph Barnes of the *New York Herald Tribune* and Edd Johnson of the *New York World*, and as deputy director for policy planning the financier, political writer, and interventionist campaigner James Warburg.[43] His approach rested heavily on the image of FDR as a symbol of peace and postwar idealism. "All U.S. information," Sherwood argued, "should be considered as if it were a continuous speech by the president."[44]

It has often been said that the British were midwives at the wartime birth of the American international intelligence apparatus; the same midwife delivered the new U.S. propaganda apparatus. Sherwood worked closely with Britain's Special Operations Executive and Political Warfare Executive, which both maintained missions in New York. In September 1941, Sherwood visited London and arranged for the short-wave radio component of this work to use transmitters provided by the British Broadcasting Corporation. Moreover, Sherwood, like MacLeish at the OFF, subscribed to the British idea of a "Strategy of Truth," holding that the best way to manage information in war was to aim for credibility and conduct propaganda with facts.[45] The methods road-tested by the British in 1940 and 1941 became a model for the United States for the rest of the war.

Sherwood's FIS swiftly opened a chain of ten information offices around the world, which used (or reused) the title United States Information Service. These handled press relations and acted as a distribution point for FIS propaganda. The FIS radio propaganda began in January 1942 with the relay over the BBC of fifteen-minute news broadcasts in German, Italian, and French. On 24 February 1942, nearly three months after the attack on Pearl Harbor, the FIS formally launched their radio station: initially known informally by the plural "Voices of America," the station soon became the Voice of America (VOA). The first broadcast – in German – included the promise: "The news may be good or bad. We shall tell you the truth."[46]

The VOA boasted an able and committed staff. Its first director (though the title was not used) was John Houseman, who had built a formidable reputation with the Federal Theater Project in the 1930s. Working closely with Orson Welles, Houseman had co-founded the Mercury Theater and produced the radio adaptation of *War of the Worlds* that famously sent some Americans into panic on Halloween 1938.

---

43 Holly Cowan Shulman, *The Voice of America: Propaganda and Democracy, 1941–1945*, Madison, WI: University of Wisconsin Press, 1990, pp. 13–23; Winkler, *The Politics of Propaganda*, pp. 74–6.

44 Winkler, *The Politics of Propaganda*, p. 27.

45 Cull, *Selling War*, p. 144; interview: Leonard Miall (PWE New York, 1943–1945), 20 July 1987; Shulman, *The Voice of America*, esp. 46, 71; on the links between British intelligence and the private U.S. shortwave station WRUL see Nigel West (intro.), *British Security Coordination: The Secret History of British Intelligence in the Americas, 1940–1945*, New York: Fromm International, 1999, pp. 59–65.

46 Pirsein, *The Voice of America*, pp. 57–8 (re the debate over the exact words broadcast); Shulman, *The Voice of America*, pp. 25–9.

Like Sherwood's, Houseman's politics were left of centre. The VOA also employed a talented array of émigrés. The largest branch – the French service – founded by Pierre Lazaroff, included the surrealist writer André Breton, the anthropologist Claude Lévi-Strauss, and a young actor named Yul Brynner.[47]

As Houseman later recalled, the new radio station set about the search for a signature tune and had fixed on the "Battle Hymn of the Republic," "until an observant British advisor pointed out that that was the tune of the German army's marching song 'Laura, Laura.'" The Americans hastily settled on "Yankee Doodle" instead and commissioned the composer Virgil Thompson to orchestrate a rousing version for use on air. The choice was well made, as "Yankee Doodle" proved particularly well suited to cutting through static and, during the Cold War, the sound of Soviet jamming.[48]

At first the Voice of America relied on borrowed time on BBC medium- and longwave transmitters and a slot on the U.S. shortwave station WLWO Ohio, but it developed rapidly. By April 1942 the VOA offered a twenty-four-hour service with programs in German, French, Italian, and English. By the end of the year the VOA was able to transmit on all of the American-based, largely commercial, shortwave transmitters. Its targets were principally European. Asian broadcasters were handled by a separate structure within the OWI and from transmitters on the west coast. Programs at the Voice of America went beyond news. With the encouragement of their resident BBC advisor at Britain's Political Warfare Executive office in New York, Leonard Miall, the VOA developed a cultural strand in its programming. This added considerable value to the VOA's output, as the time problems in broadcasting from the United States ensured that the news component was frequently stale by the time that the broadcasts aired in Europe.[49] The VOA's output included broadcasts made under the nom de guerre Commander Norden, aimed at German U-boat crews. The broadcasts mixed tabloid gossip about the German fleet and its commanders with material calculated to undermine the credibility of U-boat claims of success and undermine the confidence of crews. The VOA knew from POW interviews that they had an audience and "a crushing effect on morale."[50] Curiously, given its later currency, the name "Voice of America" was not officially used, and within the bureaucracy its title was the dry "International Broadcasting Division of the Office of War Information."

The multiple efforts of the Roosevelt administration in the field of propaganda meant that the United States joined the Second World War without a coherent structure. Journalists, including Elmer Davis of CBS, argued that the time had come for the unification of the U.S. news and information apparatus. On 13 June 1942, Roosevelt created the Office of War Information. Elmer Davis served as director. The FIS became the Overseas Branch of the OWI, with Sherwood at the helm. It operated the VOA and coordinated propaganda policy with allied nations; it distributed American news and information overseas and expanded its chain of USIS offices across Europe, Africa,

[47] Shulman, *The Voice of America*, pp. 25–9.
[48] Alan L. Heil, Jr., *The Voice of America: A History*, New York: Columbia University Press, 2003, p. 38.
[49] Shulman, *The Voice of America*, p. 71.
[50] Barrett, *Truth Is Our Weapon*, pp. 8–10.

and East Asia. Davis later wrote of the numerous flaws in this structure. He felt that he never had the necessary authority over the parallel information operations, particularly those run by the military. He recommended at the war's end that any future domestic wartime operation be located under the White House Press Secretary, who, in addition to enjoying the confidence of the President, would need "the varied abilities of a lobbyist, a traffic policeman, and the impresario of an opera company. . . ."[51] Rockefeller's Inter-American bureau remained outside of the structure. It helped to be a friend of the President.

The OWI's activities included the publication and distribution of books and magazines, from the newspaper for France *l'Amérique en Guerre* to the life story of Franklin Roosevelt in cartoon strip form. Magazines included *Victory*. In January 1945, after over a year of negotiations, the OWI launched a Russian-language pictorial magazine in the same format as *Life*, entitled *Amerika*. Leaflets showcasing the American way of life included *Small Town U.S.A.*, a portrait of Alexandria, Indiana. The OWI also initiated an exchange program for journalists, acknowledging that the most persuasive newspaper copy was that written by correspondents from the target countries rather than Americans, however well-meaning.[52]

Elsewhere within the bureaucracy, Lowell Mellett headed the OWI's Bureau of Motion Pictures in Los Angeles, which sought to steer Hollywood motion picture production to serve war policy and, to some extent, foreign policy.[53] The office also commissioned documentary films of its own. Domestic audiences saw shorts with succinct titles such as *Salvage, Fuel Conservation*, or *Troop Train*, while overseas OWI released more elaborate products such as its monthly *Magazine of the Screen* and films that introduced the American way of life to neutral, allied, and newly liberated countries. OWI films for export included *The Town* (1944), introducing a typical American small town, and *The Cummington Story* (1945), which documented the process by which four immigrant families were assimilated.[54] Particular hits included the light-hearted short *Autobiography of a Jeep* (1943), in which a jeep "narrated" its own career from design through testing to war service as "pal" of the American soldier. It remained a staple of USIA film shows for decades to come. *The True Glory*, a compilation of combat footage documenting the European campaign made in collaboration with Britain's Ministry of Information, received an Academy Award for best documentary

51 Winkler, *The Politics of Propaganda*, also Harry S. Truman Library (HSTL), OF 74, box 420, Elmer Davis, Report to the President: The Office of War Information, 13 June 1942–15 September 1945.

52 Daugherty and Janowitz (eds.) *A Psychological Warfare Casebook*, p. 589–97; Ninkovich, *The Diplomacy of Ideas*, p. 117; Winkler, *The Politics of Propaganda*, pp. 70–80, 154.

53 Clayton R. Koppes and Gregory D. Black, "What to Show the World: The Office of War Information and Hollywood, 1942–1945," *Journal of American History*, 64, 1, 1977, 87–105; Theodore A. Wilson, "Selling America via the Silver Screen? Efforts to Manage the Projection of American Culture Abroad, 1942–1947," in Reinhold Wagnleitner and Elaine Tyler May (eds.), *"Here, There and Everywhere*," pp. 83–100.

54 Richard Dyer MacCann, *The People's Films: A Political History of US Government Motion Pictures*, New York: Hastings House, 1973, pp. 129–72; Richard Barsam, *Nonfiction Film: A Critical History*, Bloomington, IN: Indiana University Press, 1973, pp. 218–23.

feature in 1946. The VOA inherited the statuette and fifty years later it still stood sentinel in the trophy cabinet outside the director's office.[55]

Like the CPI in the First World War, the OWI developed a presence on the battlefield, where the British and United States combined to form a joint Political Warfare Branch. The work began in Algiers in late 1942. In 1944, in preparation for D-Day, the effort was coordinated by the war department under the aegis of the Political Warfare Division (PWD) of the Supreme Headquarters Allied Expeditionary Force (SHAEF), administered by General Robert McClure, a visionary officer now revered as the father of U.S. army "special warfare." The leading lights of these battlefield campaigns stood in stark contrast to the "popular front" journalists who prevailed in New York. Influential figures included C. D. Jackson of *Life*, Edward Barrett of *Newsweek*, and William S. Paley, the chairman of CBS. C. D. Jackson would emerge as the key figure in U.S. propaganda in the early 1950s.[56]

PWD methods included leaflet drops and loudspeaker appeals for desertion and surrender, nicknamed "hog calling" by the army. PWD used their radio facilities, which included those of the ABSIE (American Broadcasting Station in Europe) and transmitters captured from Radio Luxembourg, for appeals to particular towns or groups of enemy soldiers. Success stories included the surrender of German forces in Cherbourg after a leaflet drop.[57] Eisenhower was profoundly impressed by the contribution of psychological warfare to victory in Europe. At the war's end he wrote: "Without doubt, psychological warfare has proved its right to a place of dignity in our military arsenal."[58]

Controversy dogged the OWI. The office fought a turf war with the Office of Strategic Services over responsibility for psychological warfare and was frequently subject to criticism in the U.S. press for being "partisan." Southern politicians bitterly resented OWI pamphlets endorsing black rights. The OWI's enemies in Congress included Representative John Taber (R-NY), who led a massive assault on the OWI budget in 1943 that resulted in the reduction of its domestic operations to a mere coordinating role. The Overseas Division seemed likely to be the next target, as the presence of a significant number of foreign nationals on the staff begged for criticism.[59] Internally the OWI leadership in Washington had grave concerns about its lack of policy control over the Overseas Division in New York. In the course of 1943

---

55 MacCann, *The People's Films*, pp. 144–5, 171–2. For archive copy of *Autobiography of a Jeep* see NA (SMPB) RG 208 300.

56 Barrett, *Truth Is Our Weapon*, p. 27; Shulman, *Voice of America*, p. 82; Winkler, *The Politics of Propaganda*, pp. 127–30. On Paley see Sally Bedell Smith, *In All His Glory: The Life of William S. Paley*, New York: Simon & Schuster, 1990, pp. 207–27. On McClure see Alfred H. Paddock Jr., *US Army Special Warfare: Its Origins* (revised ed.), Lawrence, KS: University of Kansas Press, 2002.

57 Daniel Lerner, *Psychological Warfare against Nazi Germany: The Sykewar Campaign from D-Day to VE Day*, Cambridge, MA: MIT Press, 1971, pp. 47–59; Max W. Kraus, *They All Come to Geneva and Other Tales of A Public Diplomat*, Cabin John, MD: Seven Locks Press, 1988.

58 Paddock, *US Army Special Warfare: Its Origins*, p. 20.

59 Winkler, *The Politics of Propaganda*, p. 44, notes that of 2,885 employees in the Overseas Branch, 493 were "alien" (around 17%). For an account of troubles in Congress see Krugler, *Voice of America and the Domestic Propaganda Battles*, pp. 31–3.

the *New York Times* began monitoring the international output of the OWI, eager for a scalp at the expense of the administration. The ploy paid off in July when, at a time of delicate negotiations between the post-Mussolini Italian government and the Department of State, the Voice of America English language broadcast repeated a piece of news commentary on the fall of Mussolini by Samuel Grafton of the *New York Post*. Grafton decried the remaining powers in Italy as "the moronic little king" (Victor Emmanuel III) and "a Goering-like . . . Fascist" (Marshall Pietro Badoglio). A VOA commentary by James Warburg (using a pseudonym) reflected similar views. On the morning of 27 July 1943, the front page of the *New York Times* carried a story by Arthur Krock attacking the OWI for the broadcasts. Roosevelt strove to distance himself from the story, which the *New York Times* interpreted as evidence that the OWI was running its own idiosyncratic left-wing foreign policy. The criticism was not wholly unjustified. Warburg made no secret of his wish to use the broadcasts to deter the British government particularly from compromise with former fascists in Italy. Other newspapers and hostile legislators seized on the story and cast the OWI as the soft pink underbelly of Roosevelt's New Deal.[60]

The "Moronic Little King" incident brought major changes to the Voice of America. Barnes, Warburg, and Johnson all lost their jobs. Sherwood, for his part, took up duties in London before leaving the OWI to work on Roosevelt's electoral campaign in September 1944. In Sherwood's place at the helm of the Overseas Branch, Elmer Davis appointed Edward W. Barrett, formerly the associate editor of *Newsweek*. Barrett had served with both the COI and the OWI (for which he worked in North Africa) and was an enthusiast of the strategic value of propaganda. Ed Barrett worked well with Davis and went on to become an important architect of U.S. propaganda in the early years of the Cold War. At the VOA John Houseman had also left the directorship in July 1943 to become a producer for Paramount Studios in Hollywood. His replacement, Louis G. Cowan, had a background in public relations and broadcasting, being best known as the creator of the radio program *The Quiz Kids*, which ran from 1940 to 1953. With Barrett in charge of the Overseas Branch, the OWI settled into place with the United States war effort, while Lou Cowan's VOA provided coverage of the Allied advance through Europe and U.S. plans for the postwar world.[61] By August 1945, with the benefit of advance copy and pretransmission of programs to their BBC relay stations, it was possible for the VOA to carry the text of a presidential speech in French and German more or less as it was actually being delivered and then follow up in twenty-two other languages.[62]

[60]   James P. Warburg, *Unwritten Treaty*, New York: Harcourt, Brace and Co., 1946, pp. 106–11. Shulman, *Voice of America*, pp. 98–102 gives an account of the incident that includes the memories of the *Times* employee who heard the broadcast, which is at odds with Warburg's account of organized monitoring. See also Winkler, *The Politics of Propaganda*, pp. 94–5.

[61]   Winkler, *The Politics of Propaganda*, p. 109; Barrett, *Truth Is Our Weapon*. Cowan (1909–76) was president of Louis G. Cowan Public Relations before the war and Louis G. Cowan Inc. Radio and Television Production from 1955 to 1958. He then served as president of CBS Television.

[62]   HSTL OF 74-B, box 420, Barrett (OWI) to Ross (White House), 14 September 1945: "Overseas Coverage of President Truman's Speech, Thursday August 9, 1945."

In contrast to the VOA in New York, no one paid much attention to the State Department's programs, which continued to develop during the war years with money from a President's Emergency Fund. The Division of Cultural Relations extended its activities to include language teaching and to embrace new areas, including China on 1942 and the Middle East in 1943. The division opened cultural centers to promote knowledge of U.S. history and literature and from mid-1941 began assigning members of the new Foreign Service Auxiliary to cultural duties. In 1941 and 42, it worked with the Rockefeller Office to establish special reception centers for distinguished foreign visitors in Washington, New York, Miami, and eventually New Orleans, San Francisco, Honolulu, and for a short time Seattle. It assumed responsibility for the Rockefeller Office program of aid to schools in Latin America. In the course of 1943, the formal title of cultural relations attaché first appeared on State Department diplomatic lists. The first appointments included a cultural attaché in Ankara. In 1944, it launched exchanges with India, Afghanistan, Iran, Egypt, and Ethiopia.[63]

Despite the attempt of its staff to insulate themselves from the overtly ideological agenda of the OWI, by the end of the war the Division of Cultural Relations found itself drawn into the policy structure, while the OWI moved increasingly into cultural territory. In 1944 the Division of Cultural Relations moved into the State Department's new Office of Public Information under the administration of the newly created Assistant Secretary of State for Public and Cultural Relations, Archibald MacLeish. The move suggested a mounting acceptance that cultural diplomacy had something to contribute to the future of American foreign policy, albeit with a broader audience and higher policy content than seen in the Division of Cultural Relations to date. Problems included limited legislative authority for the program. Finance for the new programs came from the President's emergency fund. In 1944, Representative Sol Bloom (D-NY), who chaired the House Foreign Affairs Committee, twice introduced legislation to permit the permanent funding of U.S. cultural programs overseas. Both bills withered in the committee stage.[64]

The State Department also operated an International Information Division, which worked to facilitate the distribution of U.S. media around the world, including documentary films, newsreels, and some specially created radio programs. The International Information Division arranged for the continued distribution of the Swedish edition of *Reader's Digest* by flying copies at high level over German-occupied Norway. This assistance gave the State Department a measure of control over the magazine's content, though as the division chief from 1944 to 1946, John M. Begg recalled they only killed a story outright on one occasion: it was critical of the Soviet Union.[65]

---

[63] For a survey see UoA CU 2–3, J. Manuel Espinosa, "Landmarks in the history of the Cultural Relations program of the Department of State, 1938–1976," 1978, p. 3.

[64] Ninkovich, *The Diplomacy of Ideas*, pp. 39, 53, 63–71, 114–17, 121; Rosenberg, *Spreading the American Dream*, p. 208. Under the OPI the DCR became first the Division of Science, Education and Art and then the Division of Cultural Cooperation. The creation of the Assistant Secretary of State for Public and Cultural Relations was authorized on 8 December 1944 under P.L. 78–472; 58 Stat. 798. The post became Assistant Secretary of State for Public Affairs in 1946.

[65] ADST Oral History, Adamnson; HSTL Oral History Begg, p. 11.

As the Allied armed forces advanced into Germany in 1945, the psychological warriors took on a new challenge: reeducation and the process now termed "de-Nazification." General McClure's Political Warfare Division now became the Information Control Division (ICD) of the military occupation. The ICD ran radio stations. It took over Nazi printing presses and began to produce newspapers for the local population. On 18 May, the allies launched a weekly newsreel called *Welt im Film*. Its fifth issue was devoted to horrific film evidence of the mass exterminations in Nazi concentration camps. The U.S. and the British had no intention of allowing future generations in Germany to deny the fact of the Holocaust.[66]

Thus, the United States entered the final months of the war with a mighty global apparatus of advocacy and cultural projection. The OWI had outstripped its equivalent in the First World War. At home it had ensured the circulation of Allied news, images, and ideas, such as the need for a United Nations organization. Its broadcasts overseas could be heard in forty languages. It represented a formidable resource for U.S. foreign policy during postwar reconstruction, but its enemies had no intention of allowing it to live on beyond victory. In May 1945, Elmer Davis pleaded to the House Subcommittee on Appropriations for funding to continue the OWI's work in peacetime. The committee remained unmoved and slashed $17 million from the agency's budget on the grounds that because Germany had surrendered, its operations would now be limited to the Pacific theatre. Further uncertainty came from events in the White House. The sudden death of Franklin D. Roosevelt in April meant that a new and untried President would decide the future of American propaganda: Harry S. Truman.[67] The OWI responded by compiling a film profile of the new President and splicing it into footage of Roosevelt's funeral in its United Newsreel, which it distributed worldwide in seventeen languages.[68]

The OWI ended the war on a note of triumph. In August 1945, the office conducted what the chief of its Overseas Branch, Edward W. Barrett, considered to be one of its most valuable operations of the entire war. On 10 August, the Japanese government gave its first indication of an intention to surrender. U.S. radio began broadcasting the news immediately and the OWI's Japanese branch created a leaflet in a matter of hours documenting the Japanese government's readiness to surrender and the U.S. government's willingness to accept such a move. By the miracle of "radio-photo" OWI transmitted this leaflet to the Pacific theater printing presses on Saipan. Three million copies fluttered down on Japanese cities over the next few days. Japanese officials later acknowledged that this act prevented hardliners in the Japanese cabinet from changing their minds and precipitated the Emperor's final announcement of

[66] Nicholas Pronay and Keith Wilson (ed.) *The Political Re-education of Germany and Her Allies after World War II*, London: Croom Helm, 1985; James F. Tent, *Mission on the Rhine: Re-education and De-Nazification in American Occupied Germany*, Chicago: University of Chicago Press, 1982; Jessica C. E. Gienow-Hecht, *Transmission Impossible: American Journalism as Cultural Diplomacy in Post-war Germany, 1945–1955*, Baton Rouge, LA: Louisiana State University Press, 1999.

[67] Krugler, *Voice of America*, pp. 33–4; Ninkovich, *The Diplomacy of Ideas*, p. 117; Shulman, *Voice of America*, p. 174.

[68] HSTL OF 74, OWI, box 420, Klauber (OWI) to Daniels (White House), 20 April 1945.

surrender on 14 August.[69] The "I" bomb of information had worked in tandem with the "A" bombs dropped on Hiroshima and Nagasaki to reach the desired end.

But the OWI's triumph in Japan blended with profound uncertainty. With the OWI scheduled to be dissolved with the end of the war, it seemed that the United States would enter the postwar world with no apparatus of international propaganda. For the outgoing Assistant Secretary, Archibald MacLeish, this was a foolhardy way to approach the postwar world. On 9 August, he wrote to the Secretary of State, noting that the French, British, and Russians all planned to sustain their wartime information work. "If the United States is not to be at a hopeless disadvantage," he concluded, "plans must be made now to enable the United States government to conduct that part of international affairs which are discussed through public channels at least as effectively as other nations are able to conduct them."[70] But the fate of U.S. information overseas rested with one man – the still largely untried President, Harry S. Truman.

---

69 Barrett, *Truth Is Our Weapon*, pp. 12–15, confirmed from Japanese sources in Robert J. C. Buttow, *Japan's Decision to Surrender*, Stanford, CA: Stanford University Press, 1954, pp. 205–9, which cites, for English text of the leaflet, U.S. Navy Department, *Psychological Warfare*, supplement no. 2 (15 August 1945), leaflet #2117.
70 NA RG59, Files of the Assistant Secretary of State for Public Affairs, 1945–50, Box 11, Correspondence, 1945–8, MacLeish to SoS, 9 August 1945.

1 Getting the Sheep to Speak

THE TRUMAN YEARS, 1945–53

The nature of present-day foreign relations makes it essential for the United States to maintain informational activities abroad as an integral part of the conduct of our foreign affairs.

Harry S. Truman, 31 August 1945.[1]

The engineers at the Voice of America (VOA) loved to tell a story from later in the Truman years. It arose from the U.S. effort to establish a network of high-powered transmitters around the Soviet sphere. When the French gave the VOA the use of transmitters at Tangier, VOA managers decided to allow local farmers to graze their sheep in the antenna field. Sometimes animals rubbed against the supporting structure. One unfortunate animal's curiosity or itch coincided with a "hot spot" of accumulated power in the transmitter's guy wires. To the astonishment of watching shepherds, the sheep attracted a sudden arc of energy. It was neither the flash nor the speed of the animal's demise that impressed the audience but the fact that at the moment of its death the sheep was clearly heard to utter the words "Harry Truman."

VOA engineers could easily explain the quirk of physics that could turn a Moroccan sheep momentarily into a radio receiver.[2] It is harder to explain exactly how the United States, which had historically been so skeptical of the idea of peacetime propaganda, became so committed to overseas propaganda as to set high-powered propaganda signals coursing through cables in distant places. In August 1945 – given feeling in Congress – this would have been unthinkable. The change came only as a result of the perceived threat from the U.S.S.R. and at the end of a prolonged tussle between vision on one side and politicking and intransigence on the other. Truman himself did not always help matters.

The story of U.S. information in the Truman presidency falls into four phases, each with its own leader and – confusingly – a different name for the information program. The first phase, from 1945 to mid-1947, saw the State Department's pro tem Interim International Information Service (IIS) and then the Office of International Information and Cultural Affairs (OIC) struggle into life as Assistant Secretary of State William Benton swam against the stream, arguing for readiness in the emerging Cold

---

[1] From text of Executive Order no. 9608, 31 August 1945.
[2] ADST Oral History: Edgar T. Martin, 24 May 1988. Martin's explanation was, "when you draw an arc under modulation it sort of rectifies and you get the audio component."

War. During the second phase, from late 1947 to 1949, the administration applied itself to rapid preparation for the Cold War but neglected key aspects of the information program. The work developed as the Office of International Information and Educational Exchange (OIE) under Assistant Secretary George V. Allen. In the third phase, from 1950 to 1951, Truman at last led the way with a major overseas propaganda drive, which he called "the Campaign of Truth." Edward W. Barrett directed what was now called the United States International Information and Educational Exchange Program (USIE). The final year of the Truman administration saw a belated effort to respond to the mounting pressure to remove U.S. information from the Department of State and into its own agency. Truman tried the "semi-autonomous" U.S. International Information Administration (IIA or USIIA), but more was clearly needed. Eisenhower successfully drew the strands begun under Truman into the coordinated fabric of the United States Information Agency in August 1953, and the agency's success hence owes something to Truman as well. Yet Truman's legacy in international information was mixed. Moscow successfully linked its foreign policy with peace and tarred the United States as a warmonger. Washington allowed opportunities to correct its image to slip by. Most seriously of all, U.S. public diplomacy never recovered from design flaws built into the system during the Truman years. By 1953 these flaws were too entrenched to change.

1) SURVIVING THE PEACE
BILL BENTON LAYS THE FOUNDATIONS, 1945–47

On 31 August 1945, President Truman signed Executive Order 9608, winding up the Office of War Information (OWI), but he did not demolish the wartime propaganda machine in the manner of 1919. Truman had read a report on postwar information by management expert Arthur W. MacMahon. "Modern international relations," MacMahon maintained, "lie between peoples not merely governments." He argued,

> International information activities are integral to the conduct of foreign policy. The object of such activities is, first to see that the context of knowledge among other peoples about the United States is full and fair, not meager and distorted and, second, to see that the policies which directly affect other peoples are present abroad with enough detail as well as background to make them understandable.

Accordingly he recommended that the wartime information apparatus be retained as a resource for postwar U.S. foreign policy.[3] Truman accepted MacMahon's report and

---

[3] Harry S. Truman Library (hereafter HSTL), Charles Hulten papers, box 8, file: "State Dept. Study of postwar international information programs." Arthur MacMahon, "Memorandum on the postwar international information program of the United States," 5 July 1945, p. 1. Although MacMahon believed that "The portrayal of the United States must be accompanied substantially by the normal currents of private interchange through the media of the printing press, radio, camera and screen and others," he also argued that the U.S. government needed to take a vital "facilitative and supplementary role."

ordered that the overseas information activities of the OWI and Rockefeller's OIAA be transferred into the State Department and join with the existing information and cultural apparatus to form an Interim International Information Service (IIIS), pending review. Lifting words directly from MacMahon, Truman described this agency's brief as "to see to it that other people receive a full and fair picture of American life and the aims and policies of the United States government." "Full and fair" became the ruling principle for U.S. information overseas for the immediate postwar period. But executing this policy would not be easy.[4]

As the IIIS began its uncertain life, key figures from the OWI returned to civilian life. Ed Barrett went back to *Newsweek*; VOA director Lou Cowan resumed his commercial broadcasting career. Archibald MacLeish returned to his poetry by way of UNESCO. The newly formed postwar international information agency needed a leader.[5]

In late August 1945 the Secretary of State, James F. Byrnes, persuaded his friend William B. Benton to accept the post of Assistant Secretary of State for Public and Cultural Relations. A new outlook and expertise came with him. Whereas journalists had dominated the wartime OWI, Benton came from the world of advertising. Born in Minneapolis in 1900, he was dapper, fast-talking, and highly ambitious. The son of a missionary, he had inherited his share of proselytizing zeal. After graduating from Yale in 1921, he turned down a Rhodes scholarship to work first in the innovative sales department of National Cash Register and then as an advertising executive for Lord and Thomas of Chicago. In 1929, Benton moved to New York, where he and Chester Bowles founded their own advertising agency, Benton and Bowles. B&B proved a runaway success, leading the way with customer research and lively copy, and pioneering the use of radio soap operas.[6] By the mid-1930s Benton craved fresh challenges. He "retired" in 1937 and became vice president of the University of Chicago, where his projects included the purchase of the *Encyclopaedia Britannica*. Around the same time, he bought the Muzak Corporation and revived its fortunes by selling its unique brand of aural wallpaper to new types of customers, including department stores and banks.

Benton was no stranger to political propaganda. In 1940, he aligned with America First to preserve U.S. neutrality in World War Two, but his isolationism was no bar

---

[4] The quotation is from Truman's executive order of 31 August. See also HSTL, Hulten papers, box 7, OWI: State Department take-over of OWI, Klauber (acting director OWI) to Truman, 17 August 1945.

[5] Shulman, *Voice of America*. p. 184.

[6] A summary of Benton's career can be found in the finding aid to the William Benton papers at the Joseph Regenstein Library, University of Chicago (hereafter UoC); also Alden Whitman, "William Benton Dies Here at 72," *New York Times*, 19 March 1973, p. 73. For a full biography see Hyman, *The Lives of William Benton*, esp. pp. 5, 123–42, 234–6; on the Benton and Bowles agency see Marchand, *Advertising the American Dream*, pp. 46, 310. Benton was not Secretary of State James Byrnes' first choice for the post. Hyman, p. 308, notes that the administration first approached Benton's old business partner, Chester Bowles. B&B's variety program *The Maxwell House Showboat* introduced such staples of American broadcasting as a live studio audience led by queue cards to laugh or applaud. B&B was also first to use sound effects in radio advertising.

to his contributing to "hemisphere defense." In the summer of 1940, Benton became a consultant to Nelson Rockefeller's Inter-American office. Compulsively gregarious, he could not help but bring his salesman's drive to bear with his broad social circle in support of his causes. As assistant secretary, Benton worked not only to sell America to the world, but also to sell the idea of overseas information to the American elite. It remained to be seen whether Benton's version of American information would be as multifaceted as the University of Chicago or as anodyne as Muzak. The State Department's cultural diplomats feared the worst.[7]

His responsibilities were enormous. More than half of State's employees worked under Benton, including more than five hundred people inherited from the OWI and the Rockefeller Office. He held sway over existing U.S. information outlets; he shared responsibility for "re-education" in Japan and Germany, and full responsibility for U.S. involvement in UNESCO. He had to accomplish this by working with an often isolationist Congress and press. Above all, Benton had to overcome America's prejudice against propaganda, which was nowhere more keenly felt than within the State Department itself.[8]

Benton's first priority was improving the State Department's domestic media relations. Problems ranged from the press dislike of departmental secrecy to press panic over links between the Department and the radical journal *Amerasia*.[9] Benton steered directly into these storms, launching a State Department "Office of Public Information" – eventually known as the Office of Public Affairs (PA) – to operate domestically. He failed to recruit Edward R. Murrow of CBS to head the unit.[10] Benton handled links with senior figures in the U.S. media personally, maintaining relationships with publishers including Henry Luce. In his bid to promote the idea of international information, he worked closely with the network of the OWI and Rockefeller alumni.

---

7 On Benton's isolationism see James C. Schneider, *Should America Go to War? The Debate over Foreign Policy in Chicago, 1939–1941*, Chapel Hill, NC: University of North Carolina Press, 1989, esp. pp. 191–5. With America First, Benton wrote the committee's advertising copy and managed links between the group and a key academic supporter: President Robert Hutchins of the University of Chicago. Also on America First see UoC Benton papers, box 254/1. On the Rockefeller Office see box 371/3–15. For negative assessments of Benton see Ninkovich, *The Diplomacy of Ideas*, pp. 118–19 and Arndt, *First Resort of Kings*, p. 163.

8 Hyman, *The Lives of William Benton*, pp. 307–16; UoC Benton papers, box 375/1 and 375/2. Benton arranged with Eisenhower for the costs of enemy reeducation to be covered by the budget appropriation of the U.S. military occupation and not the State Department; see UoC Benton papers, box 375/2, Benton to President Truman, 7 January 1946. For a summary of press attitudes to propaganda see Benton papers, box 375/16, Benton to George C. Marshall, 13 June 1947.

9 In June 1945 the FBI arrested six people associated with the journal and charged them with spying for the Chinese Communists. As *Amerasia* reproduced documents leaked from the State Department, the story boiled over into a hunt for enemies within the U.S. bureaucracy. Distinguished "China Hands" such as Robert Service fell under public suspicion. Other targets included the acting head of Benton's Office of International Information and Cultural Cooperation, William Stone, UoC Benton papers, box 376/2 and 375/9, Benton to Byrnes, 8 December 1945. For an account of the *Amerasia* case see Harvey Klehr and Ronald Radosh, *The Amerasia Spy Case: Prelude to McCarthyism*, Chapel Hill, NC: University of North Carolina Press, 1996.

10 UoC Benton papers, box 375/1. Benton to Stone, Kuhn, Howe, and Lasswell, 11 December 1945; 375/2, Benton to Murrow, 15 January 1946. The responsibilities of PA included public studies, public liaison, historical policy research, and publications.

Obvious allies included the three villa-mates from wartime Algiers: C. D. Jackson at Time–Life, Ed Barrett at *Newsweek*, and Bill Paley, president of CBS. Benton pandered to the alumni by producing certificates honoring their wartime service.[11]

As an advertising executive, Benton knew the power of a name. By 1945, the State Department used the name "Voice of America" intermittently and then only as a title for certain broadcasts in Europe. The bureaucracy preferred to speak of the "Office of War Information Broadcasting," and it seemed that any postwar radio work would be called "State Department Broadcasting." After noticing the title "Voice of America" on a schedule, Benton embraced it as his key "brand." He also renamed his own job "assistant secretary of state for public affairs," borrowing the term from Canada. He feared that "Public and Cultural Relations" would be too easily linked to propaganda. Both names hit their mark.[12]

*

In one area the U.S. government remained confident that propaganda could make a difference: the reeducation of former enemies. Allied occupation forces in Germany, Austria, and Japan maintained control over the media and education and worked hard to inculcate the positive message of democracy and the warning that "war doesn't pay." In Germany, the work devolved to two key offshoots of SHAEF: the Information Control Division (ICD) and the Educational and Religious Affairs Section (E&RA). E&RA officers scrambled to recover suitable Weimar-era textbooks from libraries in the United States and to weed out Nazis from the available pool of teaching staff, while the ICD began the process of licensing new publications to replace the U.S. military's emergency newspapers. They started in July with the *Frankfurter Rundschau*. These new papers were frequently staffed by returned refugees from Nazi Germany and edited by veterans of U.S. psychological warfare. The best-known U.S.-sponsored publication was the newspaper *Neue Zeitung* (New Times). In Austria the U.S. occupation Information Services Branch founded a highly successful newspaper, *Weiner Kurier*. In November 1945, the ICD launched a news agency to serve the U.S. zone in Germany, called DANA. The ICD licensed Radio Frankfurt to resume its broadcasts with a staff of returned refugees, while in Berlin, where the radio tower was in the Soviet sector, the United States began *Drahtfunk*, a system for transmitting

---

11   Other helpful war propaganda veterans included Wallace Carroll of the Washington bureau of the *New York Times*; Jim Linen, publisher of *Time*, who had run the OWI in Italy; and Don Francisco of J. Walter Thompson advertising, who had directed Nelson Rockefeller's radio propaganda to Latin America. UoC Benton papers, box 375/10, Benton to Byrnes, 22 February 1946; box 375/16, Benton to George Marshall, 13 June 1947; also correspondence in box 376/1; box 523/5, Benton interview, 23 January 1960, p. 8. For memos from alumni calling for expanded postwar information see NA RG59, Records of Assistant Secretary of State William Benton, Memoranda 1945–7, Box 14, "William Benton 1945," untitled memo by C. D. Jackson, 27 September 1945; Don Francisco to Benton, 5 November 1945. Other supporters included the inveterately political Hollywood producer Walter Wanger, who wrote to Benton in September 1945 calling for a major U.S. initiative in the field of radio propaganda. NA RG59, Records of Assistant Secretary of State for Public Affairs, 1945–57, Box 13, correspondence, 1945–8, Wanger to Benton, 18 September 1945.

12   UoC Benton papers, box 523/5, Benton interview, 23 January 1960; Hyman, *The Lives of William Benton*, pp. 323, 332.

radio signals over telephone wires. In Austria the United States operated a radio station named for the colors of the Austrian flag: *Rot, Weis, Rot*. The crown jewels of the occupation were the *Amerika Häuser* (America Houses), a network of libraries across the U.S. zone in Germany and Austria. By November 1948, some 2,700,000 Germans regularly used these facilities. Cynics noted that the *Amerika Häuser* were always warm in winter, but there was no shortage of useful literature to peruse while thawing out.[13]

In Japan the U.S. occupation lacked the ex-refugees and returning Americanized immigrants who aided the occupation of Germany and Austria, but many Japanese people proved eager to adapt themselves to the new political circumstances. The U.S. occupation – operating through the Civil Information and Education Section of the U.S. General Headquarters in Tokyo – revised Japanese textbooks and used their powers of film censorship to clamp down on the genres that had fueled Japanese militarism, such as samurai epics. They released American films and encouraged the Japanese film studios to show more progressive images, including scenes of public kissing, unthinkable under the old regime.[14]

In retrospect, the United States misread reeducation – overestimating the role of Allied cultural intervention and underestimating the contribution of preexisting liberal traditions within the occupied countries – but the experience contributed to the sense of the value of information and cultural activity. The reeducation apparatus of the postwar occupations would, in time, be reoriented to become part of America's response to the Cold War.[15]

*

On 1 January 1946, the IIIS became the State Department Office of International Information and Cultural Affairs (OIC), incorporating some sixty-two USIS posts and the VOA into State.[16] The OIC structure mirrored the desks of the State Department, with five area divisions and a further five "operating divisions" comprising International Broadcasting; International Press and Publications; Libraries and Institutes; International Exchange of Persons; and International Motion Pictures,

13 For a summary of this activity see Lucius D. Clay, *Decision in Germany*, London: Heinemann, 1950, pp. 281–7. See also James F. Tent, *Mission on the Rhine: Re-education and De-Nazification in American Occupied Germany*, Chicago: University of Chicago Press, 1982. For a sustained treatment of Austria see Wagnleitner, *Coca-Colonization and the Cold War*. For memories of participants see ADST Oral History: Denise Abbey, Arthur A. Bardos.

14 Kyoko Hirano, *Mr. Smith Goes to Tokyo: Japanese Cinema under the American Occupation*, Washington, DC: Smithsonian, 1992; Gordon Daniels, 'The Re-education of Imperial Japan,' in Nicholas Pronay and Keith Wilson (eds.), *The Political Re-education of Germany and Her Allies after World War II*, London: Croom Helm, 1985, pp. 203–18.

15 For an excellent revisionist work on the occupation see Jessica C. E. Gienow-Hecht, *Transmission Impossible: American Journalism as Cultural Diplomacy in Post War Germany, 1945–1955*, Baton Rouge, LA: Louisiana State University Press, 1999.

16 UoC Benton papers, box 375/1, Byrnes to President Truman, 31 December 1945. The OIC also included U.S. libraries overseas, *Amerika* magazine (which now sold 50,000 copies in Russia), and the production of a daily 7,000-word "Wireless Bulletin" of articles and current information about the United States for release to local press around the world

which commissioned or purchased documentaries for use overseas. Most embassies included an OIC representative. Although the staff of under 3,000 people represented a reduction from more than 11,000 employed by the wartime OWI and the Rockefeller office, opponents of international information were not appeased.[17]

Benton's first challenge came from the news agencies on which the VOA relied for its raw material. Early in 1946, first the Associated Press and then the United Press suspended their newswire service to the Voice on the grounds that if the VOA used their service and credited it on the air, it would tar AP and UP news as propaganda. In reality, they feared that if foreign customers could hear their news for free, they would not subscribe. Benton hit back, noting that the AP was happy to sell news to the U.S.S.R., but the agencies remained unmoved. The VOA soldiered on, using the International News Service alone.[18] Meanwhile, Republicans in Congress alleged that the peacetime VOA would be biased toward the Democratic administration. As a rash of spy scandals provoked fears about an enemy within, the Voice dismissed all but a handful of "alien" staff and begin loyalty checks. Unimpressed, the House cut the proposed OIC budget for fiscal year 1947 from 19 to 10 million dollars. There were further troubles to come. The Bloom Bill, which contained the legislative authority to maintain the VOA and the OIC outside of the Americas, died when Senator Robert A. Taft (R-OH) manipulated the timetable on the floor of the Senate to keep the bill from a final vote in the closing hours of the Senate session. U.S. information was running on empty.[19]

Although disappointed by the Hill, Benton was encouraged by growing sympathy in the American press. In spring 1946, Benton persuaded the American Society of Newspaper Editors to establish a committee to investigate U.S. international information. Their report recognized that the "present uncertainties in international relations justify an effort by the United States government to make its activities and its policies clear to the people of the world. . . ."[20] Benton recognized the wider need for

[17]   UoC Benton papers, box 491/2, Benton, "What's Ahead for Our Peace-Time International Information Service?" *Democratic Digest*, November 1946; box 376/3, fact sheet on OIC circa spring 1947. A typical post had a public affairs officer in charge, a cultural relations officer, an information officer, and a librarian (all of whom were listed in either the Foreign Service Reserve or the Foreign Service Staff Corps rather than the regular Foreign Service). Of the 372 OIC staff overseas in 1946, 105 were women. The OIC also engaged 1,400 translators and assistants locally. Staff in the United States stabilized at around 400 employees in Washington and 600 in New York (mostly VOA).

[18]   UoC Benton papers, box 523/5, Benton interview 23 January 1960, p. 8; NA RG59, Assistant Secretary of State for Public Affairs, 1945–50, box 7, Subject file, 1945–50, file "Associated Press"; Barrett, *Truth Is Our Weapon*, p. 60; Hyman, *The Lives of William Benton*, pp. 332–48; Krugler, *Voice of America*, pp. 40–51; Shulman, *Voice of America*, p. 118. Benton argued that his tough response to AP deterred similar objections to OIC operations from CBS and Twentieth Century Fox. For pro-VOA press comment see William L. Shirer, "AP and UP Ban on News for U.S. Radio Hit," *New York Herald Tribune*, 17 February 1946.

[19]   On Taft and the Bloom bill see LoC Robert A. Taft papers, box 809, legislative file: State Department propaganda, 1946 & 47, Benton to Taft, 26 August 1946. On press comment see UoC Benton papers, box 375/16, Benton to George C. Marshall, 13 June 1947. On staff reductions see box 382/1 Benton to Representative Taber, 9 February 1948.

[20]   UoC Benton papers, box 375/16, Benton to George C. Marshall, 13 June 1947, and for report of 1 October 1946 see HSTL OF 20E, box 166, Interim Information Service # 1, Benton to Ross

influential figures in the media to understand the information program and to this
end established two permanent committees loaded with OWI veterans: an Advisory
Committee chaired by Ed Barrett that included John Hay Whitney, Ferdinand Kuhn
of the *Washington Post*, and advertising executive Don Francisco, and a Radio Advisory
Committee chaired by Mark Ethridge (publisher of the *Louisville Courier*) and including Francisco, Gardner Cowles Jr. (publisher of the *Des Moines Register*), Edward R.
Murrow, and propaganda guru Professor Harold Lasswell of Yale. These two advisory committees became the prototypes for the President's Advisory Commission on
Information, established in 1948, which became an invaluable resource for U.S. information.[21]

*

Benton made his institutional changes with an eye to mounting propaganda
from Moscow. In May 1945, the Soviet Union launched an Arabic news feed; in
June 1945 it began shipping propaganda about Soviet life and prosperity to Brazil
and unveiled plans for four new French language periodicals; in September the U.S.
embassy in Prague reported a city awash with "photographs of Stalin, flags, motion
pictures, press and dissemination of rumors."[22] The only counterweight was the information apparatus left over from the OWI. The U.S. ambassador to Czechoslovakia
reported that 1,000 people a day still used the OWI's reading room, and patrons
queued outside until spaces became free. Only "effective U.S. information work," he
wrote, could challenge the mounting influence of Moscow.[23]

In early October 1945, Benton received a draft analysis of "Information Policies Concerning Russia" from Professor Harold Lasswell. Although swiftly filed with
the annotation "discard," this document reveals just how much of the coming storm
was apparent by the autumn of 1945. Lasswell began by predicting that "The dominant structure of world politics is the two-power system. America and Russia will
confront one another on practically every question throughout the globe. This multi-
plies opportunities for friction and for anxiety neuroses on both sides." Lasswell saw
multiple problems for U.S. information. Benton had to clarify U.S. objectives and
justify Stalin's expansion in Eastern Europe to an unsympathetic domestic American

(White House), 6 January 1947. The committee, which included George Cornish, managing editor
of the *New York Herald Tribune*, N. R. Howard, editor of the *Cleveland News*, and Edwin L. James,
managing editor of the *New York Times*, noted that OIC channels dramatically extended the reach of
American news and information. The simple expedient of passing the text of a presidential address to
the British press in advance of its delivery increased the amount of space devoted to that address by
a factor of 6 against speeches for which this was not done. However, as this was done for the more
important speeches, news value might also have entered into the equation.

21 UoC Benton papers, box 375/16, Benton to George C. Marshall, 13 June 1947.
22 NA RG59, Assistant Secretary of State for Public Affairs, 1945–50, box 13, Correspondence, 1945–
     8, undated Secret memo "Broadcasting Overseas," cites 320 from Prague embassy, 7 September
     1945.
23 NA RG59, Assistant Secretary of State for Public Affairs, 1945–50, box 13, Correspondence, 1945–8,
     Summary of comment from foreign service establishments indicating need for continuance of U.S.
     information program, Confidential, 3 October 1945. The Czech telegrams quoted are 327 of 10
     September 1945 and 377 of 21 September 1945.

audience. Benton had to work in a world that retained a wealth of admiration for the wartime efforts of the U.S.S.R. He also had to remember the weaknesses of the U.S. image. As Lasswell noted, "The Russians have the reputation of being remarkably free of racial prejudice. We, on the contrary, are vulnerable in this respect. Abroad we must play up our progress; and at home we must continue to lose racial biases." Lasswell's suggested policy was to step up U.S. information worldwide and "present a full and truthful picture of life in the United States." Lasswell's final paragraph was especially prescient:

> There is a danger of a cultural armaments race between America and Russia in countries lying between them, – in the form of scientific, artistic and educational expenditure. Furthermore there is danger of aggressive psychological warfare through mass media of communication. *We should undertake to obtain joint declarations of policy condemning cultural armaments races and aggressive psychological warfare.*[24]

Events unraveled much as predicted by Lasswell.

In early 1946, mistrust between the Anglo-American allies and the Soviet Union over the postwar settlement spilled into a war of words. On 9 February 1946, Stalin made his "election speech," declaring an ideological opposition between the Soviet and Western systems. On 22 February 1946, George F. Kennan wrote his famous "long telegram" from the U.S. embassy in Moscow counseling the policy of containment. On 5 March, Churchill declared that an Iron Curtain had fallen across Europe. The U.S. embassy in Moscow called for an active response. The U.S. might yet need a global propaganda apparatus.[25]

The Moscow embassy called for a Voice of America Russian Service. Benton had already noted the absence of such broadcasts from both VOA and BBC schedules as a wartime concession to Russian sensibilities. He moved swiftly to correct the lack (though not as swiftly as the BBC, which launched its Russian Service in March 1946). He negotiated with the U.S. occupation force in Germany for the use of old Nazi radio transmitters in Munich. General Lucius Clay initially objected on the grounds that such broadcasts would be "inconsistent with the spirit of quadripartite government." Infrastructure in New York followed, and in the autumn of 1946 the VOA established a Russian branch under the energetic leadership of diplomat Charles Thayer. Early plans called for such luminaries as Brooks Atkinson of the *New York Times* to advise the VOA and for George Kennan himself to deliver a regular broadcast commentary. In the event, Atkinson declined on the grounds that "his bosses" felt he would lose his "professional independence," whereas Kennan tried a microphone test but, alarmed by his exaggerated accent, recommended that Benton look elsewhere

---

[24] NA RG59, Assistant Secretary of State for Public Affairs, 1945–50, box 13, Correspondence, 1945–8, Lasswell to Benton, Information policies concerning Russia (rough draft), 22 October 1945. Emphasis in original. Lasswell ended by remarking that "It should be obvious that we are determined, if necessary, to out compete whatever efforts Russia makes in the area we decide to regard as our security zone."

[25] For Kennan's Long Telegram see Kennan to State Department, 22 February 1946, *FRUS 1946, Vol. VI*, pp. 696–709.

for a vibrant Russian voice. The service went on the air without Kennan in early 1947.[26]

During the spring of 1946, Benton developed an audacious plan to reform the VOA. He concluded that the best way to neutralize the hostility of the commercial radio sector was to create an independent Voice of America under a new "International Broadcasting Foundation of the United States." The foundation's board would include the Secretary or Assistant Secretary of State and fourteen private citizens. The foundation would, he imagined, take over U.S. government–controlled radio transmitters and VOA broadcasts would be subject to a charter that defined the VOA's role as "to disseminate information pertaining to American life, policy, industry, techniques, culture and customs." Benton presented this scheme to Secretary of State Byrnes on 24 September 1946 and nursed it throughout the following year, even drafting a bill for Congress. The bill slipped from the agenda when Benton left office in September 1947, and the commercial radio networks proved happy to snap up contracts to make programs for the VOA as it stood. Benton felt disappointed and betrayed, but his idea that the VOA might somehow become an independent body protected by a charter lived on.[27]

Benton believed that U.S. film had a vital role to play in any global information campaign. In the autumn of 1945, the newsreel companies agreed to a deal whereby the State Department distributed a United Newsreel (to which they all contributed) in countries such as Czechoslovakia and Holland where they had no commercial interest. State conceded a free rein for the commercial newsreels elsewhere. The deal expired in 1946. Benton's advisor on film matters was John Hay Whitney, who had acted as the wartime liaison officer between Nelson Rockefeller's bureau and the studios, encouraging sensitive representation of Latin America. Whitney now recommended expanding that "sensitivity" worldwide. Benton could also count on the help of a second wartime colleague, Eric Johnston, who had headed the Chamber of Commerce of the United States and was now president of both the Motion Picture Association of America and the Motion Picture Export Association. In March 1946, Benton traveled to Hollywood and successfully brokered a deal whereby the Motion Picture Association acquired the research files of the Rockefeller Bureau's Hollywood office, and the studios agreed to a voluntary system of consultation with the State Department in their representation of international matters. Benton impressed upon the Assistant

---

26 UoC Benton papers, box 375/3 Stone to Benton, 24 July 1946 and Benton to Stone, 4 November 1946; box 375/10, Benton to Byrnes, 21 August 1946; box 523/5 Benton interview 23 January 1960, p. 13. On the BBC Russian Service see Asa Briggs, *The History of Broadcasting in the United Kingdom. Vol. IV, Sound and Vision*, Oxford: Oxford University Press, 1979, p. 513.

27 HSTL Charles Hulten papers, box 15, Voice of America, 1946–7, Origins of International Broadcasting Activities of the US, folder 1 & 3; esp. Benton to Weiner et al., 28 March 1946; Bracken to Benton, 28 March 1946; Benton to SoS (Byrnes), 24 September 1946; Benton to SoS (Byrnes), 4 January 1947; Benton to Hulten, 10 June 1948, also NA RG59, Assistant Secretary of State for Public Affairs, 1945–50, box 9, Subject file: Radio Foundation No II, from 1-1-47 and box 8, Subject file: IBD, Benton to Rep. Karl Steffans, 9 June 1948, in which he blames Senator Joe Ball (Minn., Rep.) for the decision to assign so many contracts to CBS and NBC. For press comment see *New Republic*, 2 December 1946.

Secretary of State for Economic Affairs, Will Clayton, the political value of helping Hollywood export movies.[28]

Benton shared his greatest success with a young Senator named William Fulbright (D-AR). On 1 August 1946, Congress passed "an act to amend the Surplus Property Act of 1944," authorizing an expanded program of educational exchanges. The act had begun life in September 1945, when Fulbright proposed that funds generated from the sale of war surplus should be used to fund international education. Fulbright, a former president of the University of Arkansas, had studied in Britain as a Rhodes scholar. Now he proposed a scheme whereby Americans could study and teach in countries that signed on to the program and – in the scheme's ultimate form – foreign students and faculty be eligible for scholarships in the United States. The element of reciprocity enhanced the plan. Benton immediately recognized the value both of the idea and of Fulbright's name as a "brand." He threw his support behind the bill, and to Fulbright's surprise, Benton immediately began to speak of the "Fulbright program," "Fulbrighters," and other variations of the name. He stood beside Fulbright when Truman signed the bill into law. The first agreement was signed in November 1947 with China. The first Fulbrighters left for Burma in the fall of 1948.[29] Projects closely tied to the Fulbright program included promoting the new discipline of American studies. Here, milestones included the foundation of the Salzburg Seminar in American studies in Austria in 1947, which evolved into a major resource for universities across the continent.[30]

*

In the summer of 1946, President Truman commissioned a survey of U.S.– Soviet relations from his Special Council, Clark Clifford, and young speechwriter George Elsey. Their report confirmed the alarm sounded by Kennan. Clifford and Elsey noted "constant" Soviet propaganda denouncing U.S. aid programs as "imperialism."

---

28 Hyman, *The Lives of William Benton*, pp. 352–3; see also UoC Benton papers, box 75/2. Johnston also wrote *America Unlimited*, Garden City, NY: Doubleday, Doran, 1944, a book extolling the American system with a chapter entitled "The People's Capitalism," a term later used widely in USIA propaganda. For background to the visit see box 375/10, Benton to Byrnes, 22 February 1948. An example of this connection can be found in *FRUS 1952–1954, Vol. II, pt. 2*, Meeting with the Secretary, item 4, 5 May 1952, re concern over negative impact of gangsters and racial discrimination in U.S. movies overseas. The newsreel deal ended in 1946; see NA RG 59, Assistant Secretary of State for Public Affairs, 1945–50, box 2, Office Symbol Files, 1945–50, "IMP," Benton to Stone, 16 July 1946 and attached correspondence re Jock Whitney.

29 Randall B. Woods, *Fulbright: A Biography*, New York: Cambridge University Press, 1995; Hyman, *The Lives of William Benton*, p. 335; Ninkovich, *The Diplomacy of Ideas*, pp. 140–44; also Harry P. Jeffrey, "Legislative Origins of the Fulbright Program," *Annals of the American Academy of Political and Social Science*, 491 (May 1987), 11–35. For a detailed discussion of the program's working and history see Arthur Power Dudden and Russell R. Dynes, *The Fulbright Experience*, New Brunswick, NJ: Transaction, 1987 and Richard T. Arndt and David Lee Rubin, *The Fulbright Difference*, New Brunswick, NJ: Transaction, 1996.

30 UoA CU 2–3, Espinosa, "Landmarks in the history of the Cultural Relations program of the Department of State, 1938–1976," 1978, p. 4. On Salzburg and American studies see Timothy W. Ryback, *The Salzburg Seminar: The First Fifty Years*. Salzburg: Salzburg Seminar in American Studies, 1997; also Elaine Tyler May, "The Radical Roots of American Studies: Presidential Address to the American Studies Association," *American Quarterly*, 48, 2 (June 1996), 179–200.

They called for a "determined effort . . . to expose the fallacies of such propaganda." Within the Soviet Union, America's problem lay with a "small ruling clique" – hence they called for the United States to "distribute books, magazines, newspapers and movies to the Soviets, beam radio broadcasts to the U.S.S.R., and press for exchange of tourists, students and educators" and to correct the misinformation being fed to the masses by their Communist rulers and build a foundation for coexistence.[31] But before Benton could build on the memorandum, a fresh storm hit.

In early 1946, an OIC divisional assistant named J. LeRoy Davidson used surplus OWI funds to purchase seventy-nine modern paintings, including works by Ben Shahn, Jacob Lawrence, and Yasuo Kuniyoshi, to create a touring exhibition. The idea built on the wartime Rockefeller office exhibitions, which toured Latin America in an initiative suggested by Benton himself. The OIC exhibition, "Advancing American Art," received rave reviews at its preview at the Metropolitan Museum of Art in New York and as part of a UNESCO event in Paris in October 1946. State then divided the collection and sent it to Prague and Port-au-Prince, Haiti, at the start of regional tours. But news of the exhibition enraged conservatives. On 18 February 1947, *Look* magazine ran reproductions of the more provocative images – such as Kuniyoshi's voluptuous seminude *Circus Girl Resting* – with the caption, "your money bought these pictures." The Hearst press and Republicans in Congress protested loudly against wasting taxes on a "Communist plot to warp the natural perceptions of youth." Congressman Karl Stefan (R-NE) called for the export of food to halt the spread of communism rather than "words, music, art and what-not." The exhibition became a soft target for those who wanted to score points against the Democrats. President Truman responded by distancing himself. "If that's art," he told a press conference, "then I'm a Hottentot." Benton did not defend the enterprise. He withdrew the paintings and abolished the art specialist position at State, but Benton's detractors had their fun regardless. Stefan demolished Benton in hearings on the exhibit. Ironically, the available evidence suggests that the show was an effective piece of propaganda. Art lovers in Prague remarked on the exhibition's superiority to the bland and ideologically rigid rival show mounted by the Soviet Union. The message was not lost on Benton's successors.[32]

---

[31] The report is reproduced in Arthur Krock, *Memoirs*, New York: Funk & Wagnalls, 1968, pp. 419–82, see esp. 479–81.

[32] UoC Benton papers, box 378/3; NA RG59, Assistant Secretary of State for Public Affairs, 1945–50, box 7, Subject file, 1945–50, file "Art"; Hyman, *The Lives of William Benton*, pp. 387–95; Frank Ninkovich, "The Currents of Cultural Diplomacy: Art and the State Department, 1938–1947," *Diplomatic History*, 1 (Summer 1977), 215–38; Rosenberg, *Spreading the American Dream*, p. 216; Serge Guilbaut, *How New York Stole the Idea of Modern Art: Abstract Expressionism, Freedom and the Cold War*, Chicago: University of Chicago Press, 1983. Much of the *Advancing American Art* exhibition, including *Circus Girl Resting*, was purchased by Auburn University in Alabama and remains on display in the university gallery. For reproductions of the paintings and a first-rate essay on the affair, see Taylor D. Littleton and Maltby Sykes, *Advancing American Art: Painting, Politics and Cultural Confrontation at Mid-Century*, Tuscaloosa: University of Alabama Press, 1989. The story and subsequent use of art in U.S. Cold War cultural propaganda is treated at length in Michael Krenn, *Fall-Out Shelters for the Human Spirit: American Art and the Cold War*, Chapel Hill, NC: University of North Carolina Press, 2005.

The early preparations for an ideological confrontation with the Soviet Union were taken against an increasingly uncertain domestic political background. The midterm elections of November 1946 brought Republican control to both houses for the first time since the 1920s. The old enemy, John Taber, now chaired the House Appropriations Committee, and the Republican Campaign Committee had made overseas information the focus of party's entire assault on the Truman administration. Undeterred, Benton lobbied hard. His tactics included shameless bribery with gifts of encyclopedias and losing heavily in the poker circle run by Representative Eugene Cox (D-GA) of the House Rules Committee. Benton's converts included Karl Mundt (R-SD), who proved a vital ally for the future.[33]

*

In early 1947, the Truman administration began active preparations for a prolonged confrontation with the Soviet Union. In February, the White House introduced a National Security Bill to establish a Central Intelligence Agency, a National Security Resources Board, a Joint Chiefs of Staff, and a single Defense Department. Above it all a National Security Council (NSC), made up of the key senior figures in foreign and defense policy, would meet to coordinate the U.S. approach to the world.[34] As the VOA launched its overdue Russian service,[35] the OIC detected an ominous rise in Soviet activity. One policy officer went so far as to argue that the U.S.S.R. had "declared psychological warfare against the United States, and that Soviet propaganda is likely to be effective during the next few years."[36]

In February 1947, Benton received a detailed intelligence report on the prevalence of "stereotyped concepts about the United States presented in selected foreign

[33] Barrett, *Truth Is Our Weapon*, p. 58; Hyman, *The Lives of William Benton*, p. 350; Krugler, *Voice of America*, pp. 42–54. UoC Benton papers, box 523/5, Benton interview, 23 January 1960.

[34] For summary see Charles E. Nue, "The Rise of the National Security Bureaucracy," in Louis Galambos (ed.), *The New American State: Bureaucracies and Policies since World War Two*, Baltimore: Johns Hopkins University Press, 1987; for the creation of the national security state see Melvyn P. Leffler, *A Preponderance of Power: National Security, the Truman Administration and the Cold War*, Palo Alto, CA: Stanford University Press, 1992.

[35] VOA Russian began modestly with a single hour of music, U.S. and world news, and features. Concerns on the eve of the first transmission had included the best way to translate the title of Cole Porter's "I've Got You under My Skin" for Russian listeners. The embassy wired congratulations, noting, "Russian people are starved for humor, bright music, folk songs and any form of entertainment which offers an escape from [the] grim reality of daily existence," *FRUS 1947, Vol. IV, Eastern Europe; The Soviet Union*, pp. 531–3, Smith (Moscow) to Secretary of State, 15 February 1947. See also HLST Charles Thayer papers, box 5, "alpha cones: Voice of America." For a summary of embassy reactions to a sample script (requesting the dropping of "Yankee Doodle") see NA RG59 Assistant Secretary of State for Public Affairs, 1945–50, box 8, subject file 1945–50, filed in "German radio 1946," Neal (OIC) to Delgado (VOA, New York) et al., 15 October 1946. By mid-March the Embassy felt able to report that the "this program has corrected certain misconceptions regarding the U.S.A." The State Department had no lack of testimony as to the value of equivalent broadcasts to Bulgaria, Hungary, Poland, and Yugoslavia. *FRUS 1947, Vol. IV, Eastern Europe; The Soviet Union*, p. 541, Smith (Moscow) to Benton, 16 March 1947; also, pp. 168, 395–6, 468, 824, 808.

[36] NA RG59, Assistant Secretary of State for Public Affairs, 1945–50, box 3, office symbol files, 1945–50, "PEB-Victor Hunt, 1946," Hunt to Stone, 10 January 1947.

countries." These stereotypes focused on the idea of a concerted drive by the United States for global domination and could be found in rough proportion to the influence of the Soviet Union over the country in question.[37] Benton felt that the time had come for a concerted initiative to repay the U.S.S.R. in kind. On 7 March, he wrote a secret memorandum to the new Secretary of State, George C. Marshall, posing the question "how directly should we counter Soviet psychological warfare against the US?" Benton noted that the output of the OIC had to this point emphasized the virtues of America rather than the vices of the U.S.S.R. Policy had begun to shift in December 1946. First the OIC issued a directive to the Information Control Division in Germany permitting the correction of Communist misrepresentation of American life. In its wider output the OIC selected "subjects about which Soviet propaganda is most misleading." There was now scope to go further and engage the flaws in Soviet ideology. Benton acknowledged that such a step constituted full-fledged psychological warfare.

Marshall refused to cross this line. Replying from Moscow on 15 April, he confessed a little insultingly that he had "not considered your proposals thoroughly," but argued,

> The use of propaganda as such is contrary to our generally accepted precepts of democracy and to the public statements I have made. Another consideration is that we could be playing directly into the hands of the Soviets who are masters in the use of such techniques. Our sole aim in our overseas information program must be to present nothing but the truth, in a completely factual and unbiased manner. Only by this means can we justify the procedure and establish a reputation before the world for integrity of action.

Marshall's only concession was to recommend enlarged activities in "the so-called satellite states such as Hungary, Romania, Poland and so forth, and in those countries where Communist influence and representation are increasing."[38]

Meanwhile, the overseas information program remained under attack. In March, Karl Stefan launched congressional hearings on the choice of books for USIS libraries, making particular capital out of the alleged presence of Edmund Wilson's sexually frank novel of life in the New York suburbs, *Memoirs of Hecate County*, in seventy U.S. government collections. His charges were discredited when it emerged that the books had not actually been sent. In April, Taber attacked the VOA for its sympathetic treatment of the controversial liberal politician Henry A. Wallace in a book review for the Austrian service. Moreover, Benton still lacked the budget authority that he needed. Yet the spring of 1947 also presented opportunities.[39]

---

[37] HSTL Charles Hulten papers, box 9, Dept. of State Info Programs, 1947, Stereotyped concepts of US, Intelligence Research Report OCL 4242, 5 February 1947.

[38] UoC Benton papers, 375/16, Benton to Marshall, 7 March 1947; Marshall to Benton, 15 April 1947.

[39] UoC Benton papers, box 373/4, outline of testimony to House Appropriations Subcommittee 20 and 21 March 1947; Benton to Carter, 5 May 1947; Sargeant to Benton, 2 June 1947. On the budget crisis see Anthony Leviero, "House Group kills Program of U.S. Broadcasts Abroad," *New York Times*, 24 April 1947.

On 12 March 1947, President Truman redefined American foreign policy. Addressing a joint session of Congress, he called for massive aid to Greece and Turkey to assist their struggle against revolution. He revealed the "Truman Doctrine" that the United States would help states facing subversion from internal or external sources. Although he did not name that external source, the President plainly intended his words to rally opinion behind the confrontation with Stalin. The Moscow embassy reported that the speech "clearly captured the political warfare offensive and put Soviet propaganda machinery on the defensive." The foreign policy of containment had arrived.[40]

"Containment" provided a clear logic to retain and expand U.S. information. Benton immediately stepped up information programs in Greece and Turkey and resumed VOA broadcasts to Greece. A comprehensive plan for an expanded program followed, in the form of the Informational and Education Exchange Bill introduced by Karl Mundt in May. The bill proposed funding mechanisms to spread "information about the United States, its peoples, and policies." The bill faced stiff opposition. Some congressmen opposed all state-funded publicity overseas. John Bennett (R-MI) argued, "For more than 200 years – even in the remotest corner of the earth – people have known that the United States meant freedom in the fullest connotation of the term. Things which are self evident require no proof."[41]

Senator Alexander Smith (R-NJ) cosponsored Mundt's bill. Benton worked hard to generate press support. He mobilized OWI alumni and arranged for their favorable editorials to be read into the *Congressional Record*. He scored a major success when the American Society of Newspaper Editors endorsed the bill.[42] Benton and Mundt brought impressive witnesses to testify in support of the bill. General Eisenhower noted the "appalling ignorance that exists throughout the world about the United States," while Walter Bedell Smith, then ambassador to Moscow, noted the danger of leaving world opinion to the mercy of the Soviet propaganda machine. Secretary of Commerce Averell Harriman stressed the value of the information program to U.S. trade. The approach paid off. On 24 June the House approved Smith–Mundt by 272 to 97. Now the bill faced the challenge of the Senate.[43]

Meanwhile, Benton worked to restructure the State Department's information apparatus to cope with the painfully small budget.[44] In order to conform to the language of Smith–Mundt, the Office of International Information and Cultural Affairs

40 *FRUS 1947, Vol. IV, Eastern Europe; The Soviet Union*, pp. 562–4, Dubrow (chargé, Moscow) to Secretary of State, 22 May 1947.
41 For narrative of these debates see Belmonte, "Defending a Way of Life: American Propaganda and the Cold War, 1945–59," Ph.D. dissertation, University of Virginia, 1996, pp. 63–7; Krugler, *Voice of America*, pp. 57, 66–9; Ninkovich, *The Diplomacy of Ideas*, pp. 124–5, 130.
42 UoC Benton papers, box 375/16, Benton to George C. Marshall, 13 June 1947. He concluded, "we should remember that the press is much more literate, because more experienced, on issues involved in OIC – than Congress at this time can be expected to be."
43 Hyman, *The Lives of William Benton*, pp. 381–3; see also Shawn J. Parry-Giles, *Exporting America's Cold War Message: The Debate over America's First Peacetime Propaganda Program, 1947–1954*, Ph.D. dissertation, Indiana University, 1992, pp. 38–66.
44 UoC Benton papers, box 489/13, Benton Press Release # 618, 31 July 1957. Although Congress had been generous in its support for UNESCO and Latin American exchanges, the OIE would receive only

(OIC) became the Office of International Information and Educational Exchange (OIE). With his funding at sixty percent, Benton cut operations dramatically, slashing expenditures on motion pictures, and closing USIS offices across the British Common-wealth and elsewhere. Benton drew hope from the appointment of a joint subcommittee of the House and Senate to travel overseas in search of evidence to help them weigh the Smith–Mundt Bill: he knew that they would find hostile foreign propaganda and widespread misperceptions of the United States.[45]

On 3 September 1947, Benton resigned. He had not worked well with Marshall and now felt that he could do more for the cause of international information through external lobbying. As a leaving gift, his staff presented him with a screen to which they pasted some of the twenty-five thousand letters received each month from VOA listeners. An inscription read, "To Bill Benton without whose valiant fight there would be no Voice of America."[46] He returned to influence far more swiftly than anyone imagined, as a senator for Connecticut.

2) WAGING COLD WAR
GEORGE V. ALLEN HOLDS THE FORT, 1947–49

Benton's successor as Assistant Secretary of State for Public Affairs – George V. Allen – did not take up the post until March 1948. Despite the able service of Benton's deputy Howland Sargeant in the interim, the emerging U.S. information machine suffered from the absence of a "big hitter." As propaganda initiatives sprang from diverse corners of the bureaucracy, there was a desperate need for someone to speak for the interests of the State Department's information effort at the highest level. This was not done and U.S. overt information overseas never quite recovered from its exclusion from the foreign-policy-making structures created in these months. The most ambitious new initiative began on 5 June 1947, when Secretary of State George C. Marshall announced a massive program of economic aid for European recovery. The "Marshall Plan" or European Recovery Program (ERP) included an informational dimension. The plan itself had a strong propaganda value, but its home agency – the Economic Cooperation Agency (ECA) – had an explicit mandate for publicity. The relevant legislation passed in October 1949. Marshall Plan publicity began as

---

$12.4 million. Running costs topped $20 million a year and Benton had requested $25 million. The budget for all overseas operations fell from $6,200,000 (1947) to $2,462,000 (1948). In domestic expenditure motion pictures fell from $2,700,00 to $400,000; press and publications from $1,400,000 to $800,000; and VOA from $7,800,000 to $6,200,000.

45   UoC Benton papers, box 489/13, Benton Press Release # 618, 31 July 1957. In addition to the British Commonwealth, other closures were in Afghanistan, Portugal, El Salvador, Honduras, Nicaragua, and the Dominican Republic.

46   UoC Benton papers, box 523/5, Benton interview 23 January 1960, p. 4; HSTL OF 20E box 166, Voice of America 3, note on Benton to Truman, 5 May 1947. Admiring comments on his service included kind words from congressional foes and press skeptics such as Arthur Krock of the *New York Times*. Ben Cherrington, who, as a founder of the original State Department Cultural Program, was no friend of Benton's salesman approach, confessed that he had "done a whale of a job" as Assistant Secretary of State. UoC Benton papers, box 376/4–6; 376/7 Cherrington to Howe, 9 October 1947; Hyman, *The Lives of William Benton*, pp. 386–7.

an effort to ensure that Europe understood the U.S. role in the reconstruction, but soon expanded into a large-scale attempt to project the American way of life and the virtues of the free enterprise system. The ECA program surpassed State's efforts in scale, budget, and ambition, more especially as most of the work was paid for by the European host governments in "counterpart funds" – local currency generated by the sale of Marshall Plan goods.[47]

The Soviet Union also worked to extend its influence, launching a new Communist propaganda agency to replace Comintern, which Stalin had dissolved as a good will gesture in 1943. The new organization – Cominform – was created at a conference of Communist parties held in Poland at the end of September 1947. Cominform claimed independence from the Soviet state. Meanwhile Moscow prepared to crack down on U.S. propaganda in Russia. Readers of the U.S. magazine *Amerika* experienced harassment, and the prominent Soviet writer Ilya Ehrenburg denounced the VOA. The U.S. embassy in Moscow read both developments as a testament to the effectiveness of U.S. information work.[48]

Back in Washington, preparations for the Cold War proceeded apace. The National Security Act passed both houses in July and came into force in September 1947. But the act included a flaw destined to haunt U.S. international information in years ahead. The new National Security Council – nerve center of U.S. foreign and defense policy – had no seat for a propaganda or information expert. Planners assumed that the U.S. government's senior propagandist would have nothing to say to the nation's service chiefs, senior diplomats, or strategists. As if to bear out the point, the NSC immediately began to consider overt propaganda as a method of waging the Cold War and to debate which arm of the government was best suited to conduct such a campaign. No representative of the OIE was present. The consequences of this omission echoed down the decades like Original Sin. What would eventually be known as U.S. public diplomacy would always tend to be seen as a tool for the enactment of foreign policy rather than a dimension of foreign-policy-making as a whole.[49]

The new mood of confrontation brought marked changes to the U.S. military information work in Germany and Japan. In October 1947, the U.S. reeducators in Germany launched "Operation Talk Back," a policy of presenting facts to counter Soviet propaganda and to warn against totalitarianism. The editors of *Neue Zeitung* increased the paper's ideological content and serialized translations of the two books that became holy writ of the cultural Cold War against communism: George Orwell's

47 For legislative authorization for ECA publicity see PL 327, 6 October 1949, 63 Stat. 709. On Counterpart Funds, which were also used to underwrite inter-European trade, for modernization, and later for military expenditure, see Michael J. Hogan, *The Marshall Plan: America, Britain and the Reconstruction of Western Europe, 1947–1952*, Cambridge: Cambridge University Press, 1987, esp. pp. 85–6 and p. 388. Wagnleitner, *Coca-colonization*, p. 57.
48 Daugherty and Janowitz (eds.), *A Psychological Warfare Casebook*, pp. 738–9; *FRUS 1947, Vol. IV, Eastern Europe; The Soviet Union*, pp. 604–5, Smith (Moscow) to Secretary of State, 31 October 1947.
49 *FRUS 1945–1950, The Emergence of the Intelligence Establishment*, Washington, DC: USGPO, 1996, pp. 615–21.

Animal Farm and Arthur Koestler's *Darkness at Noon*.[50] In Berlin the U.S. occupation had established RIAS – "Radio in the American Sector" – a radio station with a German staff under U.S. direction, initially for the portion of Berlin ruled by the U.S. but eventually aimed at the entire city and its surrounding region. It began using the Nazi-era wire system, but soon shifted to the airwaves. It is difficult to overestimate the contribution of RIAS to the morale of Berlin. Its news became the life-blood of the city, its comedy programs provided light relief, and its resident orchestra – the RIAS symphony orchestra – helped revive cultural life, becoming famous in the 1950s under the baton of Ferenc Fricsay.[51] RIAS was also an invaluable propaganda tool and from October 1947 the station's director, William F. Heimlich, had authorization to explicitly attack the Communist system taking shape in the Soviet zone. RIAS had become the prototype for America's "surrogate" broadcasters seen later in the Cold War, providing a free medium for those living under censorship.[52]

As the occupation in Germany shifted over to Cold War priorities, a similar shift took place in Japan. Early in 1948, George Kennan (now head of State Department planning) recommended a reverse course in the occupation, turning away from liberalization and aiming to build an anti-Communist bastion in East Asia.[53]

On 17 December 1947, the National Security Council approved a "report on coordination of foreign information measures" or NSC 4. The report began with an account of Moscow's "intensive propaganda campaign" and "coordinated psychological, political and economic measures designed to undermine non-Communist elements in all countries." NSC 4 stressed the need for a coordinated U.S. response to this threat and authorized the Assistant Secretary of State for Public Affairs as the appropriate person to conduct this coordination.[54] It was a major milestone in the development of U.S. propaganda. It meant the end of both the old concept of U.S. cultural diplomacy as a conversation between countries and the "full and fair" policy enunciated by Truman in August 1945. The Truman administration now saw such overseas information activities as a one-way sales pitch. No one doubted that the United States was now engaged in a propaganda war; it merely lacked the apparatus to do the job.[55] Fortunately, the Smith–Mundt Bill was making significant progress on Capitol Hill. The subcommittee toured Europe in September and October 1947. They were, as Benton predicted, appalled by what they found and delivered unequivocal support for the bill, which cleared the Senate on 16 January 1948. Truman signed the

50   Gienow-Hecht, *Transmission Impossible*, pp. 121–39.
51   For an introduction to RIAS see Brown, *International Broadcasting*, pp. 132–5. The RIAS Symphony Orchestra was later known as the *Berlin Radio symphonie-orchester* and now the *Deutsches symphonie-orchester*.
52   Clay, *Decision in Germany*, pp. 284–5.
53   For Kennan's account of this see George F. Kennan, *Memoirs, 1925–1950*, Boston: Atlantic, Little, Brown, 1967, pp. 368–96; David Mayers, *George Kennan and the Dilemmas of U.S. Foreign Policy*, New York: Oxford University Press, 1988, pp. 162–70.
54   *FRUS 1945–1950, The Emergence of the Intelligence Establishment*, USGPO, doc. 252, NSC 4, 17 December 1947.
55   For further comment see Krugler, *Voice of America*, pp. 78–9.

Smith–Mundt Act on 27 January. Large-scale U.S. information overseas had legislative authority at last.[56]

The rough passage through Congress had left its mark on the final Smith–Mundt Act. By design and as a result of amendment, the act included multiple safeguards on the operation of U.S. information programs. Benton added a provision requiring that the FBI approve all personnel appointments, to head off charges of a "fellow-traveling" staff. Carefully chosen language specified that the Smith–Mundt programs were to operate *overseas*. In later years lawyers interpreted this language as a ban on any of the materials created under that law being available in the United States. It was the information equivalent of *posse comitatus*, the law forbidding domestic deployment of the U.S. military, and touched similar nerves. For the public good, Congress would not tolerate a federal agency either competing with the commercial media or promoting an incumbent President. There would be no domestic broadcasts by the VOA or domestic circulation of OIE publications. By the early 1960s, the act was interpreted as meaning that films produced by the USIA required an act of Congress before they could be shown within the United States. From 1972 onward, the act underwent a series of revisions to make this ban explicit.[57]

The Smith–Mundt act appeased the commercial media by requiring that information work be subcontracted to the private sphere "to the maximum extent practicable" and that the Secretary of State "reduce such government information activities whenever corresponding private information dissemination is found to be adequate." The commercial networks NBC and CBS now provided two-thirds of VOA broadcasts. Amendments empowered Congress to compel the VOA to present scripts for review and to cut the funding for any activity it disliked.

Finally, Smith–Mundt created two advisory commissions (similar to the two advisory committees created by Benton in 1946) – a United States Advisory Commission on Information and a United States Advisory Commission on Educational Exchange. These would be composed of five leading figures in the U.S. media and, for the exchange commission, education. A Radio Advisory Committee was formed under the auspices of the Information Commission to guide the VOA. The President would appoint the commissioners, and no more than three could come from any one party. The chairman of the 1946 Radio Advisory Committee, Mark Ethridge, became chair

[56] *United States Information and Educational Exchange Act of 1948*, PL 80–402, 27 January 1948. An account of the signing can be found in UoC Benton papers, box 378/1, Sargeant to Benton, 6 February 1948; also Benton interview of 23 January 1960 (box 523/5). For the subcommittee report see Committee on Foreign Relations, *The United States Information Service in Europe*, 80th Congress, 2nd session, 1948, S. Rept. 855. For Benton's encouraged reaction see HSTL PPF 1971, box 540, Benton to Truman, 25 October 1947 and Truman to Benton, 28 October 1947. Benton notes that John Taber had not been outside the United States before this point. For press comment see "Victory for the Voice," *New York Times*, 18 January 1948.

[57] PL 80–402; the restrictive section is 501. For an analysis of the evolution of the law see Allen W. Palmer and Edward L. Carter, 'The Smith–Mundt Act's Ban on Domestic Propaganda: An Analysis of the Cold War Statute Limiting Access to Public Diplomacy," *Communication, Law and Policy*, 11 (2006): 1–34. The Smith–Mundt Act would also mean that until the 1990s USIA sources were largely closed to scholars as well. This seriously hampered private academic study of the USIA.

of the Advisory Commission on Information. The advisory commissions were required to report to Congress twice a year.[58] Both could be counted on to support the cause of overseas information on Capitol Hill and do a little to counter the fact that such activities lacked a coherent domestic constituency.[59]

*

In January 1948, Truman nominated diplomat George V. Allen to fill the vacant post of Assistant Secretary of State for Public Affairs. This came as balm to State Department traditionalists who had been rubbed raw by Benton's Madison Avenue ways. George V. Allen was born in North Carolina in 1903. His service included time as ambassador to Iran. Although he later quipped he had no idea why he was appointed, he had as a young man worked as a journalist at both the *Ashville Times* and the *Durham Herald-Sun*. He had also served as advertising manager of the *Foreign Service Journal.* He took office on 31 March.[60] With Allen in post the State Department began major adjustment of the OIE's internal structure, erecting a firewall between its cultural activities and its political advocacy work overseas. Veterans of the cultural program saw the linking of culture and propaganda in the Smith–Mundt structure as a major flaw. Now, the OIE split into an Office of International Information (OII), which looked after what were termed the "fast media" of radio, press, and motion pictures, and a parallel Office of Educational Exchange (OEX) that administered the "slow media": exchanges, libraries, and links to institutes around the world. Both, like the domestically oriented Office of Public Affairs, remained under Allen's direction.[61]

The VOA also experienced a stronger diplomatic influence. In December 1947 the chief of the International Broadcasting Division, Kenneth D. Fry, resigned in protest against Congressional "hamstringing" of the Voice. In his place, Marshall appointed the former chief of the VOA Russian desk, Charles Thayer. Thayer knew the Eastern bloc well. He had served in the U.S. embassy in Moscow in the 1930s and as OSS liaison officer to Tito in wartime Yugoslavia. But rather than engaging the

---

[58]   PL 80–402; UoC Benton papers, box 379/8, Hulton to Howe, 5 May 1952; Barrett, *Truth is Our Weapon*, pp. 58–9; Krugler, *Voice of America*, pp. 62–3, 73, 78. For documentation on the setting up of the advisory commission see HSTL OF 20R, box 167, U.S. Advisory Commission on Information file.

[59]   ADST Oral History: Olom. Olom recalled that the Commissions were the result of Harold Lasswell's suggestion of Benton. He also noted that Philip D. Reed (a commissioner from 1948 to 1961) and Sigurd S. Larmon (1954–60) met socially most weeks with President Eisenhower and could easily turn the conversation around to the agency. Their intervention brought Eisenhower to the agency to address the staff, which proved a great boost to morale.

[60]   ADST Oral History: Robert F. Woodward and Walter Roberts; Dennis Merrill, "Allen, George V.," *American National Biography*, Vol. 1, New York: Oxford University Press, 1999, pp. 317–19; Piersin, *The Voice of America*, p. 143.

[61]   *Subcommittee on Overseas Information Programs of the United States, Staff Study No. 4, Organization of United States Overseas Information Functions*, Washington, DC: USGPO, 1953, p. 5. For full details of changes see HSTL Howland Sargeant papers, box 20, W. Benton file, State Departmental Announcement 70, June 1948. For criticism of the old OIC structure see UoC Benton papers, box 376/4–6; 376/7 Cherrington to Howe, 9 October 1947.

Soviets, Thayer found himself fending off an enemy closer to home: Representative John Taber.[62]

In February 1948, Taber used the Smith–Mundt Act to obtain a selection of VOA scripts including a translation of "Know North America," a series produced by NBC and broadcast to Latin America in 1947. The program introduced U.S. geography through dialogue between imaginary travelers. Unfortunately the dialogue did not flatter the United States. In one script a speaker quipped that "New England was founded by hypocrisy and Texas by sin." Another spoke of naked Indian girls racing in Wyoming and claimed that congressmen left office as millionaires. "One could almost suspect . . . " he raged, "a Machiavellian plot to ridicule the American people and present them to the rest of the world as morons and neurotics." The House Committee on Expenditures swooped into the fray to pour scorn on broadcasts suggesting that Russian women might try using beer to rinse and set their hair. Following a damning report from this committee, it came as little surprise when in October 1948 the VOA parted company with NBC and CBS. Whatever the future held for the VOA, Capitol Hill wanted to control its output. The Voice proceeded cautiously, aware that too much coverage of a controversial story such as Communist successes in the Chinese Civil War could land the VOA in the midst of controversy.[63]

While legislative headaches proliferated, George V. Allen also faced a challenge from within the executive branch. The NSC approved NSC 4-A, authorizing the newly formed CIA to conduct "covert psychological operations designed to counteract Soviet and Soviet inspired activities." Marshall had been keen to distance the State Department from such work, but Allen took a different line. He argued that the State Department should retain authority over such work in peacetime. The compromise came in June 1948 when NSC 10/2 created an Office of Special Projects (later the Office of Policy Coordination or OPC) within the CIA. The Secretary of State was given the authority to nominate its director (the job went to Frank Wisner) and representatives from the State and Defense Departments figured in the organizational structure. Wisner's proposed methods included clandestine broadcasting, a subsidy for anti-Communist and refugee organizations, and such imaginative enterprises as spreading rumors, arranging defections, and encouraging the black market.[64]

[62] ADST Oral History, Amb. William E. Schaufele, Jr. Thayer (1910–69) moved in 1950 to Germany, first as U.S. political liaison officer to the West German government and then as consul general in Munich; he resigned from the foreign service in 1953 after being asked about an illegitimate child during Congressional loyalty hearings. Charles Thayer, *Bears in the Caviar*, Philadelphia, PA: J. P. Lippincott Company, 1951. For a study of Thayer see Thomas George Corti, "Diplomat in the Cavier, Charles Wheeler Thayer, 1910–1969." Ph.D. dissertation, St. Louis University, 1988.

[63] NA RG59, Assistant Secretary of State for Public Affairs 1945–50, box 8, subject file 1945–50, file: "Know North America" series. For script samples see "The Abstracts of Voice Broadcasts Describing Six States," *New York Times*, 26 May 1948. On the end of the contract see "Farming Out of Voice Scripts to End Oct. 1," *Washington Post*, 12 July 1948. For comment see Belmonte, "Defending a Way of Life," pp. 79–81; Krugler, *Voice of America*, pp. 81–95; Pirsein, *Voice of America*, pp. 145–6.

[64] *FRUS 1945–50, The Emergence of the Intelligence Establishment*, Docs. 241, 250, 252, 253, 257, 264, 291–3, 306. For discussion see Lucas, *Freedom's War*, p. 61 et seq. and Peter Grose, *Operation Rollback: America's Secret War behind the Iron Curtain*, Boston and New York: Houghton Mifflin, 2000.

The policy makers in Washington had no shortage of evidence that overt U.S. propaganda was hitting home in the Eastern bloc. During 1948 the Soviet and satellite governments took measures against the organs of Western information. In Hungary the government prosecuted VOA listeners.[65] That spring the Soviet Union began its first major experiments in jamming the BBC and VOA by broadcasting unpleasant noise on their frequencies. The U.S. embassy in Moscow argued against any counter jamming of Radio Moscow "in view of the unfavorable effect it would have on world opinion regarding the unequivocal traditional American stand on freedom of information." The embassy also hoped that the jamming would go away if they ignored it. It did not.[66]

*

The year 1948 brought the Communist seizure of power in Czechoslovakia in February, which was swiftly followed by the first set-piece ideological battle of the early Cold War: the Italian election campaign. The overt and covert agents of U.S. propaganda worked hard to ensure the defeat of Communists at the ballot on 18 April. The campaign included high policy nuggets for Italy, such as the Allied pledge to return the disputed city of Trieste. The CIA made hefty donations of cash and newsprint to the Christian Democratic Party. With official encouragement, Italian-American groups organized a letter-writing campaign so that thousands of Italians received letters from friends and relatives in the United States warning against communism. The USIS organized exhibitions to show the conditions enjoyed by workers in America. The VOA carried news stories reflecting U.S. interest in Italian affairs and especially a drive among Hollywood celebrities to raise money for Italian orphans. Hollywood studios flooded the country with feature and documentary films on a not-for-profit basis. American films had been unavailable under Mussolini. Most presented a vision of everyday prosperity under capitalism, but some went further. Ernst Lubitsch's anti-Soviet satire *Ninotchka* (1939) had Greta Garbo as a Russian diplomat delivering lines such as "the last mass trials were a great success . . . there are going to be fewer but better Russians." This was comedy with a sting. The Christian Democrats won 48.5 percent of the vote. Raking through the ashes of the defeat, one Italian Communist mourned, "what licked us was *Ninotchka*."[67]

[65] *FRUS 1948, Vol. IV Eastern Europe; Soviet Union.* p. 365.
[66] *FRUS 1948, Vol. IV*, Smith (Moscow) to Marshall, 20 April 1948. For a history of jamming see HSTL PSF box 257, intelligence, OSI reports 1950, OSI-1-50, Historical Developments in the Jamming of VOA by the U.S.S.R., 20 January 1950. This report notes that postwar jamming began with Franco's Spain jamming Soviet broadcasts by the *Independent Spain* station in 1946. When Franco launched retaliatory broadcasts these were jammed in response by the U.S.S.R.
[67] Daugherty and Janowitz (eds.), *A Psychological Warfare Casebook*, pp. 322–6; Arnaldo Cortesi, "Report from Italy," in Lester Markel, *Public Opinion and Foreign Policy*, New York: Harper Bros., 1949. For background see James E. Miller, *The United States and Italy, 1940–1950*, Chapel Hill, NC: University of North Carolina Press, 1986; John Lamberton Harper, *America and the Reconstruction of Italy, 1945–1948*, Cambridge: Cambridge University Press, 1986, and for detailed discussion see Wendy L. Wall, "'America's Best Propagandists': Italian Americans and the 1948 'Letters to Italy' Campaign," in Christian G. Appy (ed.), *Cold War Constructions: The Political Culture of United States Imperialism, 1945–1966*, Amherst, MA: University of Massachusetts Press, 2000, pp. 89–109.

The Italian election demonstrated the value of cooperation with private enterprise. The State Department accordingly moved to build closer links with U.S. industry. The principal channel for the contact was the Advertising Council, a group formed by the U.S. advertising industry in 1942 to create and place advertisements on behalf of the government. The council had continued this work into peace at an estimated one-third of the wartime level, which translated into an annual commercial value of $100 million a year.[68] Cold War projects on the home front included the Freedom Train, a rolling exhibit of the most treasured documents of American political history, which toured the United States between 1947 and 1949.[69]

In the spring of 1948, the State Department consulted the Advertising Council on the best way to promote the Marshall Plan. In March 1948, Allen and the leading lights of the council agreed on a basic theme of the U.S. approach to Europe: "The United States is helping Europe to economic recovery – to promote the cause of peace and to protect the liberty of the individual – the freedom of European states – and thus keep our own liberty." A further afternoon meeting on 1 April 1948 at Washington's Statler Hotel brought together the Under Secretary of State, Robert A. Lovett, Allen, and his senior staff with the leaders of the Advertising Council and representatives of the biggest American corporations. They produced a Marshall Plan steering committee.[70] By May, Allen's staff had produced a succinct two-page guidance document for American corporations advertising in Europe. The "lines to stress" included the classlessness, prosperity, and rights enjoyed in American civic life, and a note that "Big business is only big in its aggregate. In general, it is owned by thousands of small investors." "Lines to avoid" were counterproductive boastful superlatives or copy that created the impression that the U.S. government served the interests of business. The State Department guidance also warned that: "The richness of America is distasteful to many . . . In many countries men work harder and live more modestly than do Americans, without consequent reward" and suggested that advertisers "Avoid themes which, by emphasis on free enterprise in the American system give the impression that we seek to impose our system on the rest of the world."[71]

---

[68] The administration kept the Council abreast of its broad policy needs by running an annual conference with members at the White House. Its peacetime creations included Smokey the Bear and the slogan "Friends don't let friends drive drunk." The figure comes from HSTL OF 73-A, box 420, White House Motion Picture Conference, remarks by John R. Steelman, director of war mobilization and reconversion, 20 November 1946.

[69] For background see Richard M. Fried, *The Russians Are Coming! The Russians Are Coming! Pageantry and Patriotism in Cold War America*, Oxford: Oxford University Press, 1998.

[70] The views of the industrialists on their potential role in U.S. information and the best response to Soviet propaganda were mixed. Harry Bullis of General Mills Inc. argued, "We have got to impress the common man over there [in Europe] that our system is a lot better, and our propaganda could stir up a revolution in Russia." Representatives of Coca-Cola and Standard Oil were equally enthusiastic. The representative from General Electric, however, urged caution, whereas Neil McElroy of Procter and Gamble, whose advertisements were only seen in Britain, warned, "Procter and Gamble does not want to be thought of, in England, as an American firm." HSTL Charles W. Jackson, box 11, OGR: Overseas Information Meeting, 1 April 1948; State Department Overseas Info. file 1, Notes of discussion period, Washington Meeting. 1 April 1948.

[71] NA RG 59, Records relating to International Information, 1938–55, box 8, file: ECA-OII overseas, Allen to Repplier, 25 May 1948 and attached documents.

The first European Recovery Program (ERP) legislation passed in mid-1948. Marshall Plan propaganda began forthwith. Soon ERP information offices in each participating country commissioned and distributed films and press stories documenting America's generosity and the wider benefits of the American economic system. These offices were typically staffed locally but headed by American journalists. Star performers included Andrew Berding, formerly a journalist for the Associated Press, who ran the office in Rome. In addition to the usual output of films and exhibitions, Berding's office sponsored essay and art contests, radio variety programs, ERP ceremonies, and a touring ERP train exhibit. In Sicily the ERP used a traveling puppet show to bridge the literacy gap for children and their parents.[72] Marshall Plan publicity proved astonishingly effective. As early as 1947, research in Norway reported ninety-four percent awareness of the plan, eighty-seven percent knowing that it was in operation, and seventy-four percent able to answer "technical questions" about its workings.[73]

Back in Washington, the OIE established an office for liaison with the private sphere and commissioned a study on the potential for commercial propaganda by the editor of *This Week* magazine, William I. Nichols. Nichols concluded that the weakness of European currency severely limited the scope for commercial distribution of U.S. films and other materials. The Marshall Plan addressed this through what became known as the Informational Media Guarantee (IMG). This program allowed selected foreign countries to pay for U.S. films and books with their own currency, so that they could consume U.S. culture without worrying about depleting their limited dollar reserves. The first agreements, concluded in 1949, covered media exports to Germany, Austria, Norway, and the Netherlands. Italy followed in 1950 and France in 1951. The IMGs were renewed under the Mutual Security Acts of 1951 and 1952, at which point a rider was added to require that materials exported "reflect the best elements of American life and shall not be such as to bring discredit upon the United States." The program soon extended into the developing world and even, following the upheaval of 1956, into Poland.[74] The first German IMG of December 1949 included prints of Disney's *Snow White and the Seven Dwarves* (1937) and *Fantasia* (1940),

72 David W. Ellwood, "From Re-education to the Selling of the Marshall Plan in Italy," in Pronay and Wilson (eds.), *The Political Re-education of Germany and Her Allies after World War II*, pp. 227–36. For ECA in Italy see Ellwood in Luciano Cheles (ed.), *The Art of Persuasion: Political Communication in Italy from 1945 to the 1990's.* Manchester, UK: Manchester University Press, 1999. On the ECA in France see Kuisel, *Seducing the French*, pp. 70–102. In March 1957 the Eisenhower administration appointed Berding Assistant Secretary of State for Public Affairs, an office that by that stage focused on the domestic media.

73 HSTL Hulten box 9, file: "Dept. of State Information Programs," report: Marshall Plan in Norway, 1947, p. 4.

74 On Nichols see UoC Benton papers, box 375/5, Nichols to Sargeant (acting dir. OIE), 18 October 1947. For an overview of the IMG program see NA RG 306, A1 (1070) USIA historical reports and studies, 1945–94, box 29, "A History of the IMG program," 25 July 1971 and UoA CU box 10/7, "History of the Informational Media Guaranty program," April 1972; also Curtis G. Benjamin, *U.S. Books Abroad: Neglected Ambassadors*, Washington, DC: Library of Congress, 1984. The program covered 21 countries over the course of its life. The European IMGs ended in the 1950s; the program expired in 1968.

twelve Disney shorts, and eighty-seven feature films from other studios, as approved by the occupation government.[75]

With its restored budget OIE resumed making documentary films. The International Motion Picture Division budget returned to its 1947 level (exceeding two million dollars). The chief of division, Herbert T. Edwards, had long experience making and distributing documentary films. His previous posts included director of motion picture distribution for the Republican National Committee in 1936. Edwards' staff was divided between administration offices in Washington and the Production Branch in New York City. The division now produced some forty reels of film itself and released a further sixty reels of commercially produced material each year, in fourteen language versions and two hundred prints. By 1950, the estimated audience for OIE film topped 125 million worldwide.[76]

*

The second great propaganda battle of 1948 took place in Berlin. On 24 June 1948, the Soviets blocked all land routes to West Berlin. The allies responded by launching the Berlin Airlift, flying thousands of tons of supplies into the city to preserve the enclave of Western control in the midst of the Soviet zone. It was propaganda by deed. The apparatus of U.S. publicity swung into action to maximize the impact of the airlift. The VOA mounted broadcasts; the U.S. Information Service distributed newsreels and circulated stories about pilots dropping sweets for children. RIAS radio kept up its flow of news during the power shortage by touring the streets in an old U.S. military vehicle and delivering the news over a loudspeaker. Edward W. Barrett later wrote that the airlift not only lifted the spirit of Berlin: "It left millions of free people elsewhere with new hope and new confidence."[77]

During the early months of the airlift, the State Department increased the ideological content of the VOA.[78] But key restrictions remained. In June 1948 Marshall forbade the use of refugees on the Voice, citing "resentment often felt against refugees by people remaining in their own country."[79] The VOA's reach was never so clear as on 12 August 1948, when Oksana Kasenkina, a Soviet schoolteacher on a visit to the United States, leapt to freedom from the third floor of her country's consulate in New York. The VOA had her story on the air just five minutes later. Within hours U.S. diplomats heard the incident being discussed all over Moscow.[80] On 9 October, two

---

[75] NA RG59 Assistance Secretary of State for Public Affairs, 1945–50, box 1, Office Symbol files, 1945–50, envelope: IMG, Mellen (IMG branch ECA to Begg, 16 Feb 1950).

[76] HSTL Charles Hulten papers, box 10, Dept. of State Info Programs, 1948, OII organization, International Motion Picture Division, esp. budget and program comparison. The figures quoted are for FY 1949.

[77] Barrett, *Truth Is Our Weapon*, pp. 65–6. The RIAS story is mentioned (and illustrated) in NA RG 306, USIA Historical Branch papers, 01–1, 13, box 18, Photos *USIA World*, file May/June 1986.

[78] *FRUS 1948, Vol. IV*, Smith (Moscow) to Marshall, 4 November 1948.

[79] *FRUS 1948, Vol. IV*, circular by Marshall, 16 July 1948, p. 425, Smith (Moscow) to Marshall, 22 July 1948, p. 246.

[80] Barrett, *Truth Is Our Weapon*, pp. 116–17. Walter Bedell Smith, the U.S. ambassador in Moscow, later suggested that it was this incident that prompted the Soviet regime to step up its jamming program.

Soviet pilots – Lt. Anatoli Barsov and Guard Lt. Piotr Pirogov – crash-landed their aircraft near Linz in the U.S. zone of Austria. They explained that they had decided to defect after hearing a VOA story about the Virginia State Fair some years before. Their story suggested that the details of American life could be more potent than ideological diatribes.[81]

By the fall of 1948, the VOA was displaying the unmistakable symptoms of an emerging news culture. VOA coverage of the presidential election proved an important test case. In covering the campaign, the Voice of America had not only noted that Truman was lagging behind Thomas Dewey but also reported a stinging attack on U.S. foreign policy as "imperialistic" by the third party candidate Henry Wallace. A VOA official explained to the newspapers that "the spectacle of a Government broadcast carrying an attack on that Government's foreign policy must be electrifying to listeners behind the iron curtain." Such coverage could not but "raise the prestige of the 'Voice' as a factual reporter of news." It was an early display of the commitment to balanced reporting that would later come to define the VOA.[82]

The weeks following Truman's election victory opened questions about the future. On 23 November the NSC approved NSC 20/4. The directive formally refined the objectives of U.S. Cold War policy as "To reduce the power and influence of the U.S.S.R. to limits where it will no longer constitute a threat to peace, national independence and stability of the world family of nations." The United States was now explicitly working to roll back Soviet power. The only practical means of working toward this goal was through a massive campaign of covert psychological warfare and overt information. The business of U.S. information now sat at the core of the central project of U.S. foreign policy.[83] At the same time that the goals of U.S. foreign policy shifted into high gear, the entire executive branch was undergoing a major investigation chaired by ex-President Hoover to determine the best structure for its future operation. In November 1948 a two-man Task Force on Foreign Affairs, composed

81 In Barsov's case the reality of life in the United States was not enough. After touring the United States (including a visit to the VOA's studios in New York), he became homesick and requested repatriation. He served five years in a labor camp. For background see "Two Who Fled Russia Taken to Virginia: Happy to Tour State Depicted by 'Voice,'" *New York Times*, 5 February 1949, p. 4; "Two Russians Visit 'Voice' Studio Here: Flyers Who Escaped Soviet Area Hear Program That Originally Lured Them," *New York Times*, 18 February 1949, p. 12; Walter H. Waggoners, "US Deports Flyer Who Fled Russia," *New York Times*, 31 August 1949, p. 1; HSTL Sargeant papers, box 4, press cutting from *Life*, n/d, late 1949, "The Gloomy Diary of a Russian Deserter"; Max Frankel, "Soviet Produce Former Defector Reported Shot on Return in 1949," *New York Times*, 16 May 1957, p. 8; for a postscript on the case see Clyde H. Farnsworth, "Where the Spies Are . . .," *New York Times*, 14 November 1985, p. B.14. For comment see Belmonte, "Defending a Way of Life," pp. 87–8. In 1951 the VOA and RFE were cited as inspiration by a Czech engineer, Jaroslav Konvalinka, who drove his train with 108 passengers aboard across the frontier into West Germany. Thirty-one people chose to defect with him. "Czechs Tell Story of Flight by Train.," *New York Times*, 16 September 1951, p. 31; Walter Hixson, *Parting the Curtain: Propaganda, Culture, and the Cold War, 1945–1961*, New York: St. Martin's Press, 1997, pp. 49, 66.
82 "Truman Outpaced in Campaign, State Department's 'Voice' Says," *New York Times*, 11 October 1948; "'Voice of America' Tells World Truman Lags behind Dewey," *Washington Post*, 11 October 1948.
83 *FRUS 1948*, Vol. 1, NSC 20/4, "US Objectives with Respect to the U.S.S.R. to Counter Soviet Threats to U.S. Security," 23 November 1948, pp. 662–9.

of two Hoover-era assistant secretaries of state, James Grafton Rogers and Harvey H. Bundy, delivered a stunning recommendation: that the entire information program be transferred to a new government corporation, merely steered by State Department policy guidance.[84]

Despite the Rogers/Bundy proposal, the full Hoover Report, presented in early 1949, recommended that such work remain at State under the Assistant Secretary of State for Public Affairs. Hoover's only suggested reform was to create a new post of General Manager with operational authority to coordinate all information activities and to execute policy. The State Department followed this recommendation, appointing Charles M. Hulten to the post of General Manager.[85] Hoover's reform also placed public affairs experts within each of the regional bureaus of the State Department.[86] At this point the overall structure of State Department overseas information became known as the United States International Information and Educational Exchange Program (USIE).[87]

Although the Hoover Commission rejected the notion of an independent information agency, the idea of independence remained nagging in the background for the rest of the Truman years. The President's Advisory Commission on Information spoke up loudly on behalf of the program in its first semiannual report, published in March 1949. They stressed the need for the full integration of information issues into policy-making as well as policy exposition and called for USIE input into policy planning. The report spurred the NSC to issue its own report calling for "a vigorous coordinated foreign information program."[88]

The next move came from the Soviet Union. On 24 April 1949, both American and British diplomats in Moscow reported that their respective Russian language

84 *Subcommittee on Overseas Information Programs of the United States, Staff Study No. 4, Organization of United States Overseas Information Functions*, p. 5. Also Acheson to Benton, 24 January 1951, *FRUS 1951*, vol. 1, p. 909. "Report on the Organization of the Government for the Conduct of Foreign Affairs" for Foreign Affairs Task Force of the Commission on Organization of the Executive Branch of the Government. Nelson Rockefeller had floated the same idea of an independent information agency in the autumn of 1945; see NA RG59, Assistant Secretary of State for Public Affairs 1945–50, box 13, correspondence, 1945–50, file "Information – Overseas Program," esp. Ferdinand Kuhn to Benton, 8 October 1945.
85 Hulten had proved himself as assistant director for management for the wartime OWI and more recently as a deputy assistant secretary of state, first for public affairs and then for administration.
86 This move proved counterproductive, as rather than increasing awareness of the importance of international information, it tended to dissipate the influence of the Assistant Secretary. For full details see *Subcommittee on Overseas Information Programs of the United States, Staff Study No. 4, Organization of United States Overseas Information Functions*, p. 5. Also Acheson to Benton, 24 January 1951, *FRUS 1951*, vol. 1, p. 909, "Report on the Organization of the Government for the Conduct of Foreign Affairs" for Foreign Affairs Task Force of the Commission on Organization of the Executive Branch of the Government.
87 The Office of International Information (OII) and Office of Educational Exchange (OEX) remained as subunits. This structure is described in *The Campaign of Truth: The International Information and Educational Exchange Program, 1951*, Washington, DC: Department of State, 1951, copy filed in SD PDHC, Campaign of Truth file.
88 HSTL Democrat National Committee clipping file, Box 159, United States Advisory Commission on Information. Semiannual report to the congress, March 1949; *FRUS 1949, Vol. 1*, Draft report by National Security Council Staff, 30 March 1949, "Measures Required to Achieve U.S. Objectives with Respect to the U.S.S.R.," pp. 271–8.

broadcasts were inaudible: large-scale Soviet jamming had begun.[89] Unlike the experiments of the previous year, this time the jamming signals stayed. Moscow now regarded Western broadcasting as such a threat that it was prepared to devote millions of rubles to operating powerful transmitters for the sole purpose of broadcasting noise on Western frequencies. From August 1949 the Communist Bloc also jammed VOA services to Czechoslovakia, Hungary, Greece, and China. The VOA and the BBC cooperated to confound the jammers. Methods included subtle changes of frequency that left the Soviets obstructing dead air. The Italian, Greek, and Canadian governments cooperated to maximize the number of frequencies available at any one time, carrying the same signals simultaneously. Even with the jamming, some broadcasts still got through. The VOA boasted that it could be heard twenty-five percent of the time in downtown Moscow and from sixty to eighty percent of the time in the provinces. They estimated an audience in excess of ten million. Some results were physically apparent. Defectors and escapees from the east routinely cited Voice coverage of other defections as instrumental in their decision to leave the U.S.S.R. Ironically, jamming also played into the hands of the VOA by implying that Stalin had something to hide.[90]

The prominence of radio drew forth pressure for the VOA's Russian branch to deliver a more politically pointed service. The heads of the branch – Alex Frenkley and émigré General Alexander Barmine – wrote a joint memo to the VOA director in July 1949 counseling against such a course and insisting that VOA Russian broadcasts were committed to "an objective presentation of the news without editorializing." "To start on the path of editorialized news . . ." they argued, "would certainly affect our reputation for objectivity, therefore of credibility."[91] Although the news remained sacrosanct, the commentaries became ever more strident. In later years, Allen regretted this: "Looking back, perhaps our tone wasn't justified. A calm persuasive tone is much better than a mere calling of names."[92]

Even as the Voice pondered the conflicting demands of the Cold War and journalistic integrity, an initiative approved elsewhere in the State Department opened an ingenious solution. On 21 June 1949 the acting Secretary of State gave an unofficial nod to a new venture that would extend the capacity of the United States to act in the Cold War without compromising either the government or the credibility of the Voice of America. A group of prominent internationalists combined to form the

---

[89] *FRUS 1949, Vol. 5, Eastern Europe; The Soviet Union*, Kohler to Acheson, 24 April 1948, p. 609.

[90] For a full report on the extent of jamming see HSTL Hulten box 16, VOA 1950, Program Evaluation Branch, Report No. A-62, "Indications of VOA Penetration of Soviet Jamming," 15 May 1950; Briggs, *Sound and Vision*, p. 513 cites British Parliamentary discussion of VOA/BBC cooperation: *Hansard*, Vol. 467, cols. 2960–1, 30 July 1949. For listener estimates see Foy D. Kohler, "Effectiveness of the Voice of America," *Department of State Bulletin*, 14 May 1951, p. 781.

[91] HSTL Charles W. Thayer papers, box 5, "alpha – Voice of America," Barmine and Frenkley to Thayer, 25 July 1949 and attachments. A study of the VOA by New York University's Research Center for Human Relations in April 1950, called *Speaking with Many Voices*, noted that the Russian and other Eastern bloc services had a much higher percentage of news in their output, as against feature material, which predominated elsewhere.

[92] Pirsein, *Voice of America*, p. 156: citing his interview with Allen, 1965. Allen continued, "This is one of the advantages of the BBC – they always seem to present their views in a calm, persuasive way."

National Committee for a Free Europe (NCFE) and planned a radio station – Radio Free Europe (RFE) – to use refugee voices to broadcast anti-Communist propaganda into the Eastern bloc.[93] Although publicly private, RFE was not independent of the U.S. government. The inspiration and most of its funding came secretly from the CIA. RFE did not begin operation till July 1950.[94]

The year 1949 saw further solidification of the battle lines of the Cold War. In April, the United States and its European allies signed the North Atlantic Treaty. A large-scale U.S. program of Mutual Defense Aid began that autumn. The coordination of information policy with allies became an element in the planning of the North Atlantic Treaty Organization (NATO). The United States took care to avoid the appearance of a Western Cominform. There would be no central propaganda structure beyond a basic NATO Information Service. Instead, the democracies agreed to exchange information and guidance in order to coordinate their individual responses. At the London meeting of foreign ministers held in May 1950, Acheson, Bevin, and Schuman agreed to work together to create a "sharper, more effective psychological effort."[95] The closest working relationship developed between Britain and the United States. Major areas of cooperation included pooling resources to overcome Soviet jamming.[96]

In May 1949, Stalin lifted the Berlin blockade; in the following months the rival zones of Germany became full-fledged West and East German states. Responsibility for the U.S. media program in Germany passed from the military to the High Commissioner for Germany (HICOG) under the State Department, and the program increased its scope to cover all of West Germany.[97] RIAS in Berlin proved its worth, broadcasting appeals for citizens to vote.[98] The HICOG came to believe that its most effective tool was the system of exchanges that allowed young Germans to visit the United States. A HICOG survey of 1952 asking "What do Germans consider the most reliable source

---

[93] *FRUS 1949*, vol. V, Acting SoS Memo, 21 June 1949, p. 289.

[94] On the history of Radio Free Europe see Sig Mickelson, *America's Other Voice: The Story of Radio Free Europe and Radio Liberty*, New York: Praeger, 1983 and Arch Puddington, *Broadcasting Freedom: The Cold War Triumph of Radio Free Europe and Radio Liberty*, Lexington, KY: University of Kentucky Press, 2000; also Lucas, *Freedom's War*, pp. 67, 101.

[95] *FRUS 1950, Vol. IV*, "US Views on Capturing Initiative in the Psychological Field," circulated 14 April 1950, p. 296; NSC 59/1, 9 March 1950, pp. 298–9, and note p. 306. For NATO coordination procedures see *FRUS 1950, Vol. III*, p. 1 et seq. On the NATO Information Service (NATIS), see *FRUS 1951, Vol. 1*, NSC114/1, Annex 5, 8 August 1951. On U.S.–U.K. relations in the propaganda field see *FRUS 1950, Vol. III*, esp. U.S. delegation at tripartite preparatory meeting, London to SoS, 25 April 1950, p. 868 and 20 April 1950, p. 890.

[96] *FRUS 1950, Vol. IV*, Circular by Acheson, 15 July 1950; notes on Barrett/Warner meetings, 22 May 1950, pp. 1641–8; U.S.–U.K. memo of discussions on the present world situation, 25 July 1950, p. 1668. For a detailed treatment of this relationship see Andrew Defty, *IRD: Britain, America and Anti-Communist Propaganda, 1945–1953*, London: Frank Cass, 2004 and NA RG 59, Records relating to International Information, 1938–45, box 15, file: "Cooperation with British." Relations with Canada began later. For summary see RG 306, Office of Administration, 1952–55, box 3, file: "Other Governments 1952–1953."

[97] Expenditure authorized under PL 759, 6 September 1950, 64 Stat. 595. A similar program was attached to the office of the U.S. High Commissioner for Austria. These programs became fully part of the global USIE program from fiscal year 1953. For a summary of this activity see *FRUS 1951, Vol. 1*, NSC 114/2, 12 October 1951, items 22, 26, 27, pp. 949–50.

[98] *FRUS 1950, Vol. IV, FRUS 1950, Vol. IV*, HICOG Berlin to High Commissioner, Germany 29 November 1950, p. 901.

of information about America" reported that fifty percent of respondents said "Other Germans who have visited." German books, newspapers, and radio scored nine, eight, and six percent. The VOA got six percent, whereas only three percent said "Americans" and only two percent endorsed U.S. films.[99] The subsequent investment in the West German exchange program was such that ten years later nearly a third of the Bundestag, over half of the Bundesrat, and over two-thirds of the cabinet had visited the United States on an exchange. No other country had been so cultivated.[100]

Elsewhere, USIE initiatives included a series of bilateral schemes to aid students from strategically significant areas: Finland, Nationalist China, and Iran.[101] The department launched a new Exchange-Visitor Program accompanied by a special exchange visa to facilitate overseas travel to American universities, hospitals, businesses, and foundations. By the 1970s, around 50,000 people a year entered the country under 1,700 programs authorized under the scheme.[102] Meanwhile, the VOA added new languages, including Persian in March 1949, Turkish in December 1949, Arabic on New Year's Day 1950, and Vietnamese in August 1950.[103]

Despite these innovations, the autumn of 1949 presented a bleak prospect. First the Soviet Union exploded an atomic bomb, and then Mao Zedong proclaimed the People's Republic of China. The one point of light was Yugoslavia. The Tito regime had split from the mainstream of the Communist Bloc in the course of 1948, suggesting a model that U.S. propaganda could exploit. Yugoslavian developments had unexpected consequences for USIE. The United States needed new outreach to Tito, and so on 27 October 1949, Truman nominated George V. Allen to serve as ambassador to Belgrade. His left his post on 28 November. The USIE needed a replacement and quickly.

3) THE CAMPAIGN OF TRUTH
EDWARD BARRETT MAKES PROGRESS, 1950–51

Just before Christmas 1949, Secretary of State Dean Acheson approached the wartime director of the OWI's overseas branch, now editorial director of *Newsweek*,

99 UoA CU box 336/15, HICOG study as cited in 1960 Review of Evaluation Studies, p. 6. The full set of responses (with second choice in brackets) were Germans who have visited 50% (16%); no opinion 11% (14%); books by German authors 9% (26%); German newspapers 8% (8%); German radio 6% (9%); the VOA 6% (8%); books by American authors 4% (7%); Americans 3% (4%); American films 2% (4%); Other 1% (1%).
100 UoA CU box 332/23 Dept. of State: Mutual Educational and Cultural Exchange activities, background paper, FY 1963, see also 335/17.
101 Finnish Exchange Program, PL 265, 24 August 1949, 63 Stat. 630; Chinese Student Aid Program, PL 327, 6 October 1949, 63 Stat. 709; Iranian Student Aid Program, PL 861, 64 Stat. 1081. Iran did not develop as the United States hoped. A U.S. attempt to use propaganda to warn Iran away from the Soviet embrace failed to prevent a Soviet–Iranian trade agreement on November 1950. *FRUS 1950, Vol. V, The Near East, South Asia, and Africa*, Washington DC, GPO 1978. State Dept. Memo UM D-97, "The Present Crisis in Iran," c. 21 April 1950, p. 517; minutes of Under Secretary's Meeting, 26 April 1950, p. 520; SoS to Embassy, Iran, 20 November 1950, p. 615–16.
102 UoA CU 2–3, Espinosa, "Landmarks in the History of the Cultural Relations Program of the Department of State," 1978, p. 5.
103 HSTL OF 20E, box 165, Voice of America file 1, VOA to White House, 15 March 1949, 15 December 1949, 19 December 1949, 9 August 1950.

Edward Barrett, and offered him the post of Assistant Secretary of State for Public Affairs. Born into wealth in Alabama in 1910 and educated at Princeton, Edward Ware Barrett had built a distinguished career as a journalist. He believed in the information program. He had chaired the prototype Advisory Committee set up by Benton in 1946 and been vice chairman of the U.S. National Commission to UNESCO.[104] His loyalty to the cause of information was such that in September 1947 he had passed information to Benton on the likely source of leaks to the press from within the Department of State.[105] Acheson invited Barrett for an off-the-record meeting with the President on 20 December 1949 during which Truman stressed the importance of the job. Impressed, Barrett noted that Truman "clearly understood the problem of international information work far better than Roosevelt ever had." Barrett accepted the post for a two-year term but warned Truman that he had not voted for him. The President cheerily replied: "Oh, that's all right Mr. Barrett, between us, we've run out of good Democrats." Barrett took up his duties in February 1950.[106]

President Truman had hitherto been absent from the battles over propaganda, but he did not disappoint Barrett. Truman finally brought the full weight of his political muscle to bear in the cause of U.S. information overseas.[107] Barrett's appointment coincided with a major statement of U.S. policy toward the Eastern bloc. NSC 58/2 of 13 December 1949 held that the policy of the U.S. would be "to keep alive the anti-Communist sentiment and hope of the non-Communist majorities" and promote what was termed "deviationism" from the Soviet line. The obvious method for achieving this was radio.[108] On hand to carry it out was a new director of the Voice of America, Foy Kohler, who like his predecessor had first-hand knowledge of the Soviet Union. He was much admired by his staff.[109]

For their part, Soviet propagandists also stepped up their campaign against the United States. Barrett estimated that the U.S.S.R. now spent an estimated $1.5 billion each year on overseas propaganda: a sum equivalent to 2 percent of Soviet national income and sixty times the U.S. information budget. In January 1950, Moscow

---

[104] HSTL Oral History Edward W. Barrett, p. 19; jacket notes, Barrett, *Truth Is Our Weapon*.
[105] NA RG59, Assistant Secretary of State for Public Affairs, 1945–50, box 4, Office Symbol File, 1945–50, file: Secretary of State, Benton to Lovett, 22 September 1945. Barrett told Benton: "The Secretary's own office is the worst sieve in the entire Department and people down the line get blamed for it." Benton duly informed the Secretary of State.
[106] Barrett, *Truth Is Our Weapon*, pp. 74–5; HSTL Oral History Barrett, p. 27.
[107] Barrett noted that propaganda concerns had a role in policy-making for the Korean War, Truman's disarmament proposals, and the appointment of Eisenhower to take command of U.S. forces in Europe in the spring on 1951; see *FRUS 1951, Vol. 1*, Barrett to Webb, 13 November 1951, p. 959; also Barrett, *Truth Is Our Weapon*, p. 16.
[108] See *FRUS 1950, Vol. IV, Central and Eastern Europe; The Soviet Union*, progress reports by Webb to NSC, 2 February 1950 and 26 May 1950, pp. 8, 31.
[109] Kohler (1908–90) left the VOA in September 1952 to serve on the State Department's planning staff. His later career included a period as ambassador to the Soviet Union. Kohler's immediate successor at the VOA was Alfred Morton (1897–1974), a radio and television executive who had worked at RCA and NBC and was director of television at Twentieth Century Fox between 1948 and 1950. ADST Oral History: Edward Alexander and Barry Zorthian.

launched their "Hate America" campaign, which emphasized the Soviet wish for "peaceful coexistence" and identified the United States with warmongering. The Soviet Union sponsored peace petitions, peace conferences in Stockholm, Bombay, New York, Tunis, and Montevideo, and in 1951 a World Peace Council. Offshoots of this campaign included attempts to nurture anti-Americanism in Europe. Communists in France worked to associate U.S. business with strategic ambition, coined the term "coca-colonization," and launched a campaign against the local production of that most iconic of American drinks.[110] But Truman also faced propaganda closer to home, that of the junior senator from Wisconsin: Joseph McCarthy.

On 9 February 1950, speaking in Wheeling, West Virginia with an eye to reelection, McCarthy launched his scare campaign around the danger of communism and the failure of the Truman administration to police its own bureaucracy. He selected the usual weak spot – Truman's foreign policy – but with the instinct of a true bully, he probed for a weak spot within that weak spot. His eye fell on the information program. On 20 February 1950, speaking in the Senate, McCarthy linked thirty employees of the information program to Communism and singled out the VOA as a nest of subversives. The administration commissioned Senator Millard Tydings (D-MD) to investigate. Tydings failed to find any disloyalty at the VOA or elsewhere. But McCarthy's attack was an ill omen for the future.[111]

Not all the news from the Senate was bad. In December 1948, Senator Vera C. Bushfield (R-SD) resigned, providing a seat for information advocate Karl Mundt. Then, in late 1949, the resignation of Raymond E. Baldwin (D-CT) created another unexpected vacancy. The governor of Connecticut, Chester Bowles, offered the seat to his old business partner Bill Benton, who successfully defended it in 1950 in a close and rather dirty fight with Prescott Bush, father and grandfather of Presidents Bush. With Fulbright still on hand and also winning a second term in the autumn of 1950, the cause of international information had never been so well supported in the Senate. From the moment he took office, Benton lost no time in preparing a campaign of support. With the ad man's eye for a slogan, Benton dubbed his campaign for an expanded information program "The Marshall Plan of Ideas."[112]

Truman was open to a new initiative in U.S. propaganda. On 1 March, he wrote to Acheson, suggesting a new committee to improve the VOA.[113] In response, Barrett suggested "a Presidential directive to put top priority of the agencies of government into immediate exploration of *all* techniques and resources for communication of

[110] For a full treatment of leftwing anti-Americanism in France see Kuisel, *Seducing the French*, pp. 37–69; Barrett, *Truth Is Our Weapon*, p. 183.
[111] *Congressional Record*, 20 February 1950, Vol. 96, pt. 2, 1952–81; for Barrett's rebuttals see NA RG 59, Assistant Secretary of State for Public Affairs 1945–50, box 8, Subject files, 1945–50, file: "Department's Answers to McCarthy's Attacks (Loyalty)." Also box 1, Office Symbol files, 1945–50, file: "1950 ARA" and box 8, Subject file, 1945–1950, "Loyalty Working File."
[112] Hyman, *The Lives of William Benton*, pp. 408–11; on the election see pp. 435–42.
[113] *FRUS 1950, Vol. IV*, Truman to Acheson, 1 March 1950, p. 271. Truman suggested Barrrett, David Sarnoff of RCA, Senators McMahon and McFarland (who sat on the Subcommittee on Communication), the Under Secretary of Defense, and FDR's press secretary, Stephen Early.

ideas behind the Iron Curtain, including the use of radio broadcasting."[114] The NSC seemed sympathetic and on 10 March approved NSC 59/1, calling for expanded propaganda, though this still fell short of the full presidential directive suggested by Barrett.[115] On 22 March 1950, Benton introduced Senate Resolution 243 proposing that "the international propagation of the democratic creed be made an instrument of supreme national policy – by the development of a Marshall Plan in the field of ideas." The twelve cosponsors included Fulbright and Mundt. Hearings on the Marshall Plan of Ideas followed that summer.[116] In April the National Security Council approved NSC 66 on "Support for the Voice of America in the fields of intelligence and of research and development," a bid to overcome the Soviet jamming. In the scare language typical of the era, the paper predicted that, unchecked, the Soviets might in time be able to disrupt all radio communications "worldwide." The NSC established a special planning project to investigate possible responses.[117] There was more to come.

Early in 1950, Truman asked the key departments in Washington to generate an integrated strategy for the Cold War. On 7 April 1950, the planners, led by Paul Nitze, presented the strategy: NSC 68. Although best known for advocating a massive military build-up, this document had great implications for overseas information because, as Barrett's assistant put it, "for the first time the United States government officially recognized psychological activities as one of the four basic means of influencing foreign affairs – military, economic, diplomatic and psychological" and "specifically stated that all of these four means were to be used in concert." NSC 68 called for "an affirmative program" to "wrest the initiative" from the Kremlin. Its acceptance sealed a fundamental shift in U.S. strategic thinking. U.S. foreign policy had become a zero-sum game in which any advance for the U.S.S.R. represented a defeat for the United States and the credibility of American power became a vital national interest.[118]

Meanwhile, the Bureau of Public Affairs pondered the best response to the mounting restrictions on USIE information activities across the Eastern Bloc. The bureau surmised that the Soviets hoped that by cutting off the flow of U.S. information, they could create the impression that the United States had abandoned Eastern Europe.

---

[114]   *FRUS 1950, Vol. IV*, Barrett to Acheson, 2 March 1950, p. 272.

[115]   *FRUS 1950, Vol. IV*, Barrett to Webb (Under Secretary of State), 6 March 1950, pp. 274–5. Barrett also suggested a series of fifteen-minute special broadcasts created in conjunction with the BBC in London to be called "the Voice of Freedom." This was never followed up. See also "US Views of Capturing the Initiative in Psychological Field," *FRUS 1950*, 4, pp. 296–302, and for Truman's endorsement see HSTL Acheson papers, box 66, Memoranda of conversation, 6 March 1950, item no. 4, Barrett propaganda proposal.

[116]   The resolution called for diplomatic pressure for worldwide freedom of information; support for UNESCO; more educational exchanges; an expanded radio network; cooperation with the rest of the non-Communist world for a "better understanding on common themes"; and the creation of a "non-governmental agency to help inspire and guide the efforts of the millions of private American citizens who might use their talents and resources and contacts overseas in furtherance of the programs and objectives of this resolution." S.Res. 243, 81st Congress, 2nd session; Hyman, *The Lives of William Benton*, pp. 428–9.

[117]   *FRUS 1950, Vol. IV*, NSC 66, 4 April 1950, pp. 285–9.

[118]   *FRUS 1950, Vol. 1, National Security Affairs; Foreign Economic Policy*, Washington, DC: GPO 1977, pp. 234–92; SDPDC, "Campaign of Truth" file, Oren Stephens to Barrett, 28 November 1951.

As in the matter of jamming, the State Department resolved not to retaliate in kind, but to use the evidence of such restrictions in its anti-Soviet propaganda directed at the region.[119]

On 20 April 1950, Barrett got the full presidential endorsement he needed. Speaking to the Annual Convention of the American Society of Newspaper Editors, Truman called for an integrated program of government and private outreach:

> We must make ourselves known as we really are – not as Communist propaganda pictures us. We must pool our efforts with those of other few peoples in a sustained, intensified program to promote the cause of freedom against the propaganda of slavery. We must make ourselves heard round the world in a great *campaign of truth*.[120]

Coverage of the speech dominated the news in all twenty-four VOA languages.[121]

The Campaign of Truth needed a massive emergency budget.[122] But before Congress could hold hearings, events underlined the need to act. On 25 June, Communist North Korea invaded non-Communist South Korea. The United States immediately prepared a military response, but clearly would also need battlefield propaganda and an explanatory information campaign around the world. The crisis confirmed Truman's Cold War policy and spurred the approval of NSC 68, with its emphasis on the psychological dimension in international politics. U.S. propaganda about the Korean War was much aided by Truman's success on 27 June in obtaining – thanks to the absence of the Soviet delegation – a UN resolution supporting action against North Korea. With this in mind, the USIE immediately created a special newsreel called *United Nations Aids the Republic of Korea*, emphasizing that the war was a coalition

---

[119] *FRUS 1950, Vol. IV*, Memo Bureau of Public Affairs, 6 April 1950, p. 290. The Polish government was sufficiently suspicious of the USIS wireless file to attempt to disrupt its distribution. *FRUS 1950, Vol. IV*, Department of State Policy Statement on Poland, 27 November 1950, pp. 1040–42. In August 1951 the Polish government forced the closure of the USIS operations in their country: *FRUS 1951, Vol. IV*, doc. 751, Department of State Wireless Bulletin, 10 August 1951.

[120] *PPP Truman, 1950*, pp. 260–64; Barrett, *Truth Is Our Weapon*, pp. 73–4; *FRUS 1950 4*, pp. 271–6. The speech included mention of the role of ASNE members such as Mark Ethridge on the U.S. Advisory Commission on Information. For further background see HSTL WHCF, CF, box 4, State Dept. Corresp. 1950, file 5, Acheson to Truman, "Measures to Strengthen Voice of America and Our Total Information Efforts Abroad," 3 April 1950. Also HSTL WHCF CF box 41, State Dept. Corresp. 1950, file 5, Barrett to Truman, "Proposals for a Total Information Effort Abroad," n.d. For positive press response see Anne O'Hare McCormick, "When Words Have Spoken Louder Than Action," *New York Times*, 22 April 1950.

[121] HSTL PPF, 200 Speeches, box 332, ASNE Washington DC, 4/20/50, Barrett to Ross (White House), 24 April 1950.

[122] On 26 May 1950, Under Secretary of State James Webb – an enthusiast for propaganda whom Barrett recalled as more sympathetic to his project than Secretary of State Dean Acheson – presented the NSC with the State Department's estimate of funds necessary "to win the Cold War or be ready to deal with the alternative." He proposed spending $82.3 million for new operations and $47.6 for transmitter construction. The memo, drafted by Barrett, included a list of the twenty-eight priority countries for the coming struggle, arranging them under four convenient headings, from "Hard Core" (Russia only) and "Iron Curtain" (Albania, Bulgaria, and so forth) through the "Crucial Periphery," which included Burma and Indochina, to the "Danger Zone" of places such as France and India. *FRUS 1950, Vol. IV*, Webb to NSC, 26 May 1950, pp. 311–13. On Webb see HTSL Oral History Barrett, p. 31.

response to a northern invasion. By 18 July, this film was ready and the USIE shipped nearly one thousand prints in twenty-two languages to the field, where the immediate audience was estimated at thirty million.[123]

The Korean War dominated the Senate hearings on the Campaign of Truth and Marshall Plan of Ideas in July. Marshall, with none of his old diffidence, called for a "dynamic procedure . . . in this conquest of the mind"; Eisenhower spoke of the decisive "value of morale" and called truth "our T-bomb," whereas a rising star, Acheson's Special Consultant John Foster Dulles, went so far as to argue, "the question of whether we have a general war or not may hinge, very largely upon the relative effectiveness of the Communist propaganda and the Free World propaganda."[124] On 13 July, Truman appealed for $89 million in additional funds for information overseas. Newspaper editorials surged behind Truman's plea. Only the *Chicago Tribune* objected. The syndicated columnist Drew Pearson even took up the idea of creating an entirely new agency dedicated to overseas propaganda. Congressional support was a different matter. The Campaign of Truth budget passed on 27 September, but only after Congress had trimmed $10,000. This appropriation fell some 50 percent short of the budget requested by the State Department. Benton and others renewed calls for more.[125]

As the Campaign of Truth captured public attention, the architects of U.S. propaganda found themselves able to draw on support from private industry. The USIE's contact with the private sphere was the responsibility of the small Office of Private Enterprise and Cooperation, directed by John M. Begg (formerly associate editor of the Pathé newsreel and veteran of the State Department's wartime information work). Starting with a staff of just four divided between Washington and New York, the office worked hard to involve U.S. charities, corporations, and publishers in USIE work and liaised with the Advertising Council to develop ideas and shape U.S. commercial advertising overseas in useful directions.[126]

123 NA RG 59, Assistant Secretary of State for Public Affairs, 1945–50, box 2, Office Symbol files, 1945–50, "IMP 1950," Edwards to Barrett, 27 July 1950. USIE struck 437 35-mm prints and 506 16-mm prints in the United States. Additional prints of this film were later struck in Germany, Austria, Italy, and Britain.
124 UoC Benton papers, box 492/12, press release #711, 5 July 1950.
125 UoC Benton papers, box 460/16, Office of Public Affairs "special report on American opinion," 21 July 1950 also noting growing criticism of "ineffective" use of existing resources in overseas publicity. Box 479/11, Benton Senator McKellar (D-TN) as per press release, 2 September 1950. On budget see *FRUS 1950, Vol. IV*, pp. 313–17; also HSTL DNC clipping file, Box 159, United States Advisory Commission on Information, second semiannual report to the Congress, September 1949.
126 HSTL Charles W. Jackson papers, box 30, State Dept. Overseas Info. File 2, John M. Begg, Cooperation with Private Enterprise, 6 October 1948; see also HSTL Oral History: Begg. Begg created a guide to enable U.S. corporations to shape their advertising copy in Europe in politically valuable directions, extolling the virtues of the American way. This booklet, *Advertising a New Weapon in the World-Wide Fight for Freedom: A Guide for American Business Firms Advertising in Foreign Countries* was pictured and praised in the United States Advisory Commission on Information, 1st semiannual report to Congress of March 1949. Subsequent initiatives included a campaign over Christmas 1951, to get U.S. businesses to mark envelopes bound for Europe, "Listen to special year-end Voice of America programs," HSTL Charles W. Jackson papers, box 31, 1948–52, Voice of America, Advertising Council Radio Fact Sheet, December 1951, including a striking Advertising Council cartoon.

The office was well placed to capitalize on the swelling of American public feeling around the issue of the Cold War. Begg and his colleagues appealed to publishers to donate leftover textbooks for use overseas. In two years they obtained 134,000 books either as gifts or sold at token rates. The office persuaded the charity CARE to appeal for funds to ship books as "food for thought." As the campaign gathered momentum, *Time*, *Life*, and other major magazines gave their unsold editions. The office also cooperated with the King Features Syndicate to insert "information themes" into its comic strips for export. In similar spirit, the office persuaded companies to loan exhibits to the USIE's exhibitions that showcased American material prosperity, such as "America 1950," which toured Britain. The office also encouraged grass-roots links between Americans and the rest of the world, advising Rotary, Kiwanis, and Lions clubs in developing international projects. They encouraged some 128 U.S. communities to "adopt" a foreign town. They persuaded the creators of internationally syndicated newspaper features, including *Believe It Or Not* and King Features Syndicate cartoon strips, to integrate anti-Communist messages into their output. They enrolled the American Heritage Foundation and the *New York Herald Tribune* as sponsors for a guide to appropriate behavior for American tourists in Europe, called *What Should I Know When I Travel Abroad?* Issued in 1952, the book recommended answers to commonly asked questions about the United States.[127]

The office also encouraged the sort of private letter-writing work that had proved so useful during the Italian election in 1948. In partnership with the Common Council for American Unity (an organization set up during the First World War to promote the political education of recent immigrants into the United States), the office developed the Letters from America Campaign: a plan to stimulate and then influence letters sent overseas by members of some sixty non-English language communities across America. The USIE provided the Common Council with a survey illustrating the extent and nature of common European misconceptions about the U.S. – an uncultured land of materialism, racial injustice, and economic exploitation – and steered the Common Council in the creation of regular editorials, placed in some 260 foreign language papers and 195 radio programs, encouraging letters home to the old country and suggesting politically helpful themes. By the end of 1952, the first- and second-generation immigrant community (around thirty-five million people) had written over one billion such letters (an average of over twenty-eight letters

---

127 SD PDHC Campaign of Truth file, booklet: *The Campaign of Truth: The International Information and Educational Exchange Program 1951*, 15 November 1951; NA RG306, Office of Administration, 1952–5, box 2, file "Private Enterprise and Co-operation, 1952–3," "IE/PR projects in cooperation with private enterprise … July 1 to December 31, 1951" (for *Believe It or Not* and King Features see p. 9). A useful statement of office projects can also be found in UoC Benton papers, box 378/7, 31 December 1950. For a summary of IOP activity in the second half of 1952 see DDEL USPCIIA (Jackson Committee) Box 2, file: correspondence B (8), reports filed under "Begg." On the guide for American tourists abroad drawn up in discussion with the Young and Rubicam advertising agency, the 1953 edition was sponsored by the Common Council for American Unity and *American* magazine; see NA RG 59, Bureau of Public Affairs, Office files of Edward W. Barrett, 1950–51, box 2, file "L," memo of conversation, 3 February 1951 and DDEL WHCF OF 247, box 909, Streibert (USIA) to C. D. Jackson (White House), 20 October 1953.

each).[128] Such programs proved such a success and at a tiny cost that the Private Enterprise and Cooperation office opened regional branches in San Francisco and New Orleans.[129]

Sometimes the flow of information ran from the private sphere to the USIE. In 1951 the American Federation of Labor created a map to illustrate the location of gulags in the Soviet Union and promised a substantial cash reward for anyone able to disprove its claims. The map transformed an obscure litany of names into a tangible portrait of human rights abuse. The VOA described the map on the air to Latin America and shortly thereafter received thousands of requests for copies. USIS offices also distributed the map to student and labor organizations that found themselves in competition with Communists.[130]

Hollywood also helped. In April 1950, Barrett, Acheson, and the administrator of the Marshall Plan, Paul Hoffman, met Eric Johnston, the president of the Motion Picture Association of America. The agenda combined the specifics of getting Hollywood's aid to make documentary shorts with Marshall Plan counterpart funds to "mobilizing the motion picture industry in this cold war much as was done in the last war." Johnston was eager to be of service but noted that one of Hollywood's contributions to the Cold War had already encountered diplomatic problems overseas. When, in mid-1948, Twentieth Century Fox released *The Iron Curtain*, a treatment of the Gouzenko spy case, directed by William A. Wellman, the U.S. embassies in Paris, Oslo, and elsewhere blocked local distribution on the grounds that "it would stir up too much hostility towards the U.S." Acheson apologetically pledged in the future to wire each embassy as necessary, requesting cooperation with the release of such films.[131] By 1951, the State Department was proposing to underwrite the losses for Hollywood studios agreeing to produce politically useful feature films for overseas distribution.[132] Meanwhile, the USIE's Herbert T. Edwards helped MGM make a documentary called

[128] SD PDHC Campaign of Truth file, booklet: *The Campaign of Truth: The International Information and Educational Exchange Program 1951*, 15 November 1951; UoC Benton papers, box 378/7, 31 December 1950. For more detail on Letters from America (though without any mention of an official connection to the office) see HSTL OF 20S, box 167, Campaign of Truth, Barrett to Henry Lee Muson, Associate Dir. Common Council, 24 October 1950. Also HSTL Hulten papers, box 14, Dept of State Information programs, 1953-general, "Letters from America Campaign, Progress Report for 1952 to Friends and Supporters," 24 March 1953.

[129] Begg's staff also advised the National Committee for a Free Europe on its appeal for funding for Radio Free Europe. SD PDHC Campaign of Truth file, booklet: *The Campaign of Truth: The International Information and Educational Exchange Program 1951*, 15 November 1951; planners suggested that the State Department might also work to stimulate "public utterances by American government officials and leading personages in civic labor, religious and other fields, in order to promote established propaganda themes and create source material for propaganda." See *FRUS 1951, Vol. 1*, NSC 114/1, annex 5, 8 August 1951.

[130] William R. Young, "Gulag-Slavery Inc: The Use of an Illustrated Map in Printed Propaganda," Daugherty and Janowitz (eds.), *A Psychological Warfare Casebook*, pp. 597–602.

[131] HSTL Acheson papers, box 66, memo of conversation, 26 April 1950, 5 pm, "Film Projects for ECA and the Cold War." Johnston also requested and obtained the cooperation of State in the renegotiation of the 1948 regulations about foreign currency. *FRUS 1951, Vol. 1*, program as summarized in NSC 114/1, annex 5, 8 August 1951 notes that the State Department planned to underwrite losses for Hollywood studios that agreed to produce politically useful feature films for overseas distribution.

[132] *FRUS 1951, Vol. 1*, program as summarized in NSC 114/1, annex 5, 8 August 1951.

The Hoaxsters. The film exposed Communist and Nazi propaganda techniques and was released in January 1953.[133] Hollywood sometimes reciprocated. In 1950, Cecil B. DeMille offered assistance with the domestic promotion of the VOA.[134] In 1952, MGM created a short film called *The Million Dollar Nickel* endorsing the Letters from America scheme, in which foreign-born stars appealed to potential correspondents in their own languages.[135] Finally, the 1952 B-movie *Red Planet Mars* actually showed the VOA bringing about the collapse of communism in Russia, although the scenario – relaying of a message from "God," discovered in a radio transmission from Mars – was unlikely to be repeated in the real world.[136]

Not all America's private initiatives were as private as they claimed. The most spectacular private enterprise that summer was actually the result of CIA funding: the launch of Radio Free Europe. RFE began in Czech on 4 July 1950. Broadcasts in Romanian, Hungarian, Polish, and Bulgarian followed. The idea worked so well that the CIA developed sister projects: the short-lived Radio Free Asia aimed at China, which went on the air in May 1951, and Radio Liberation, aimed at Russia, which went on the air in March 1953.[137] Despite help from the CIA, the National Committee for a Free Europe worked hard to muster private funding and turned to the legendary public relations skills of General Mills for help. The result was a campaign dubbed the Crusade for Freedom, organized by Abbott Washburn and Nate Crabtree, who were General Mills men destined to play a role in the birth of the USIA.[138] The CIA's other

---

[133]   NA RG 59, Bureau of Public Affairs, Office files of Assistant Secretary of State, Edward W. Barrett, 1950–51, box 2, file "L," correspondence with Victory Lasky, producer, MGM. The working title for *The Hoaxsters* was *The Big Lie.*

[134]   NA RG59 Assistance Secretary of State for Public Affairs, 1945–50, box 1, Office Symbol files, 1945–50, file "IBD-de Mille, VOA broadcasts." Cecil B. de Mille's idea was a radio domestic series funded by his foundation. A thirteen-part series was made available in 1952, but without a direct link to de Mille; see HSTL Elsey papers box 65, "foreign relations-VOA," "Your Voice of America," press release 7, 5 January 1952.

[135]   The stars were Pier Angeli in Italian, Ricardo Montalban in Spanish, Leslie Caron in French, and Zsa-Zsa Gabor in Hungarian. HSTL Hulten papers, box 14, Dept. of State Info. 1953-general, "Letters from America Campaign, Progress Report for 1952 to Friends and Supporters," 24 March 1953 (erroneously crediting Eva Gabor).

[136]   Harry Horner (dir.), *Red Planet Mars*, Mealby Pictures Corp., 1952.

[137]   Puddington, *Broadcasting Freedom*, pp. 20–21; Nelson, *War of the Black Heavens*, pp. 46–7; and Mickelson, *America's Other Voice*, pp. 30–42. For parallel projects and context see *FRUS 1952–54, Vol. 2, Part 2*, Jackson Committee report, 30 June 1953, pp. 1831–4. Radio Free Asia closed in 1953 because too few mainland Chinese owned shortwave radios. The name was revived in the 1990s.

[138]   The Campaign for Freedom initially favored a searchlight as their emblem until Crabtree hit on the idea of a bell. Shortly thereafter it occurred to Washburn and Crabtree to physically create such a bell and install it in the tower above the town hall in West Berlin, where it could ring out across the Eastern zone. They commissioned a sculptor to create a magnificent relief for the outside with allegorical images of the five races of the world and a paraphrase of Lincoln's Gettysburg address: "that this world, under God should have a new birth of Freedom." A British foundry cast the bell over the summer of 1950. The bell soon became the focus for the campaign to rally American support for the cause. Following a grand launch of the Crusade for Freedom on 4 September 1950 (Labor Day) with a speech from General Eisenhower, the bell made a tickertape parade along Broadway and began a nationwide tour aboard the "Freedom Train." The campaign raised 16 million signatures (each with a donation) on what were called "Freedom Scrolls," petitions that would be kept alongside the bell. Each Freedom Scroll bore a pledge and the banner headline "Enroll in the Crusade for Freedom, Help Lift the Iron Curtain Everywhere." Then, on 24 October 1950, the "Freedom Bell"

major gambit was the launch of an ostensibly private coalition of anti-Communist intellectuals – the Congress for Cultural Freedom (CCF) – with a first meeting in Berlin in June 1950. Its leading lights included Melvin Lasky, Arthur Koestler, and Arthur Schlesinger Jr. In the years to come the CIA secretly funded a number of the CCF's journals, including the British journal *Encounter*.[139]

One final element of genuine private involvement in the Campaign of Truth came with the recruitment of university academics as consultants. Webb and Barrett asked President Robert Killian of the Massachusetts Institute of Technology to investigate means for the VOA to overcome jamming. This swiftly developed into a grand review of all U.S. psychological operations. With Killian's assistance they put together a team of twenty top brains in physics, engineering, and other disciplines, including social science under the chairmanship of John Ely Burchard, dean of social science at MIT. Members included physicist Edward M. Purcell, Hans Spier of the RAND corporation, Elting E. Morrison of Harvard's history department, and Max Millikan, who went on to found MIT's Center for International Studies. The State Department named the exercise Project TROY, equating American propaganda with the famous wooden horse. The TROY report, presented on 1 February 1951, endorsed two major VOA initiatives: the Ring Plan to encircle the U.S.S.R. with a belt of fourteen one-megawatt medium-wave radio transmitters (but conveniently devised by an engineering consultant named Andrew Ring), and a plan called "Operation Clipper" for the deployment of an electronic device to boost signal strength tenfold by "clipping" unnecessary portions of the signal being transmitted. The report also suggested developing cheap transistor radios to equip the next generation of VOA listeners.[140]

The report had insightful recommendations for broadcasts to Russia: "Do not give great emphasis to comparisons between material conditions in the United States and the U.S.S.R. The contrast should be between what *is* and what *could be in the U.S.S.R.*" European conditions were a different matter, and TROY suggested encouraging defections by publicizing the economic opportunities in the West. The team gave strict warnings against support for separatist movements in places like Ukraine,

made its way through the streets of Berlin to its new home. Half a million Berliners (of whom an estimated third came from the East) turned up to see General Clay dedicate the bell. As he did so he declared: "We are your friends and always will be." The German postal service responded by featuring the bell on its stamps in 1951 and 1952 and Berlin named its highest cultural award after the bell. RIAS carried the daily striking on the bell live to the city and beyond. Interview: Abbott Washburn (1/12/95). See also Veronika Liebau and Andreas W. Daum, *The Freedom Bell in Berlin*, Berlin: Jaron, 2000.

139   On the CIA and the CCF see Francis Stonor Saunders, *Who Paid the Piper: The CIA and the Cultural Cold War*, London: Granta, 1999; Giles Scott-Smith, *The Politics of Apolitical Culture: The Congress for Cultural Freedom, the CIA, and Postwar American Hegemony*, London: Routledge, 2002; Hugh Wilford, *The CIA, The British Left, and the Cold War: Calling the Tune?* London: Frank Cass, 2003.

140   For report see NA RG59, lot 52–283, IIA records relating to Project TROY, box 1; Allan Needell, "Truth Is Our Weapon: Project TROY, Political Warfare and Government -Academic Relations in the National Security State," *Diplomatic History*, 17 (Summer 1993), pp. 399–420; also Barrett, *Truth Is Our Weapon*, pp. 118–23.

which would provoke a "Mother Russia" anti-reaction, and recommended against anything that could "encourage hopeless acts" of resistance.[141]

Part of Project TROY involved analysis of the State Department's "brain-wave" files: home to the more extreme suggestions for getting messages into the Soviet bloc. In New York the VOA staff had allowed their imaginations free rein. Their proposals ranged from the obvious – bigger transmitters and black propaganda stations along the border – to the bizarre. Propaganda messages could be flown in by kites or floated to their audience in bottles (a plan weakened by the fact that the United States had ready access to the estuaries rather than the sources of Eastern bloc rivers). Messages could even carried by "individuals with exceptional hypnotic powers" who could be "smuggled behind the iron curtain." The most picturesque plan focused on skywriting aircraft, which one staffer suggested could place a VOA schedule in the sky above the border.[142] TROY approved the idea of floating messages into Communist territory by balloon, as suggested by Barrett back in March. The most far-fetched plans received short shrift, but an annex by Robert S. Morrison of MIT on Asia suggested recruiting a body of young Americans to conduct humanitarian projects in the region as a means for communicating U.S. values "face to face." It has been suggested that this was the germ from which Morrison's colleague Max Millikan developed the idea of the Peace Corps.[143] The most significant element in the TROY report for the future of U.S. propaganda was its endorsement of the entire field of "political warfare": the coordination of a range of U.S. efforts against the U.S.S.R. into a "well rounded and coordinated whole." The report argued that this necessitated a "single authority" to direct the effort. The academic experts had added to the mounting pressure for a major review of the structure of U.S. propaganda, more especially as they predicted that a reformed effort could turn the tide of the Cold War.[144]

Meanwhile, the war in Korea ground on. In the early autumn of 1950, UN forces seemed to have the upper hand. USIE did more for the war effort than just disseminate information. Barrett's staff monitored Communist propaganda in the region and extracted valuable intelligence data. On 3 November, Barrett delivered a warning derived from this work that the token force of 18,000 Chinese "volunteers" currently engaged in Korea could soon multiply. Mao's government was clearly preparing its population for all-out war with the United States. Barrett urged the UN to brace for the entry of hundreds of thousands of Chinese soldiers into the Korean War.[145] The warning went unheeded. On 26 November, UN forces experienced the full force of the predicted Chinese onslaught and fell back. Panic spread fast from the battlefield

---

[141] NA RG59, lot 52–283, IIA records relating to Project TROY, box 1, Vol. I, pp. 48, 75. This policy of restraint was carefully followed by RIAS in its broadcasts during the 1953 disturbances in Berlin but, as will be seen, seems to have slipped in certain broadcasts to Hungary in 1956

[142] SD PDHC, Campaign of Truth file, Robert Ross (VOA NY) to Davidson Taylor (Special Consultant, P, State Dept.) 25 October 1950; Barrett, *Truth Is Our Weapon*, pp. 119–20.

[143] NA RG59, lot 52–283, IIA records relating to Project TROY, box 1, Vol. II, annex 2 & 3 and Vol. II annex 9; Needell, "Truth Is Our Weapon," pp. 399–420.

[144] NA RG59, lot 52–283, IIA records relating to Project TROY, box 1, vol. 1, p. ix, pp. 80–81.

[145] *FRUS 1950, Vol. VII*, Barrett to Rusk (ASS for Far Eastern Affairs), 3 November 1950, p. 1030.

to the White House. Truman feared that incautious press speculation could further erode the U.S. position and on 5 December – after consulting Barrett – he issued an order requiring extreme caution in all public statements on foreign or military affairs by the military and senior members of the executive branch. New protocols required statements to be cleared with the State Department or Pentagon.[146] By 6 January 1951, the military situation in Korea had deteriorated to the point that the USIE mission had fled from the capital and reestablished operations in Pusan in the extreme South.[147] The crisis underlined the need for an effective information effort.

*

The State Department entered 1951 with bold ambitions for its information program toward the Soviet bloc. The VOA and other media would seek to "capitalize on every vulnerability of the Soviet thought control system," emphasizing the benevolence of the United States and the possibility of alternatives to the Soviet way and quite simply delivering "accurate information" about the United States, its allies, and world events in general.[148] RFE also helped. Its private status made it easy for the station to hire refugees and, as Barrett put it, "many things could be said by Radio Free Europe which we could not say since they do not openly reflect government policy." Behind the scenes the State Department provided "guidance" to RFE. Its future looked bright, more especially after the appointment of a dynamic new head for the National Committee for a Free Europe: Barrett's old housemate from wartime Algiers, C. D. Jackson.[149] Under Jackson's leadership, the committee launched a new initiative called "Winds of Freedom," releasing some 15,000 balloons on the Czech–German border in August 1951 loaded with propaganda leaflets. A small radio on the balloons allowed RFE to track their progress and to trigger the drop at an appropriate location. "Winds of Freedom" worked well enough to receive the blessing of the Secretary of State to continue as an element in the U.S. "overall psychological effort" behind its private cover.[150]

146 *FRUS 1950, Vol. VII*, Memorandum of Conversation by Dir. of Executive Secretariat, 3 December 1950 and editors note, pp. 1335–6.
147 *FRUS 1951, Vol. VII*, Ambassador Muccio to Secretary of State, 6 January 1951, pp. 30–31.
148 *FRUS 1951, Vol. IV*, doc. 767, Draft State Dept Policy Notice c. January 1951, esp. pp. 1539–40. The United States also prepared to overcome Soviet barriers to this message. On 19 January 1951 the NSC approved NSC 66/1, to provide intelligence support for the Voice of America with regard to Soviet jamming. See *FRUS 1951, Vol. IV*, doc. 602, NSC 66/1, 19 January 1951, p. 1202.
149 *FRUS 1951, Vol. IV*, doc. 605, Memo on RFE, 24 January 1951, doc. 611. Report by Barrett, 2 February 1951, p. 1206. See also doc. 658, circular 14, 24 December 1951, "Relationship of USIE to Radio Free Europe and Similar Activities," p. 1315.
150 *FRUS 1951, Vol. IV*, doc. 636, Deputy Assistant Secretary of State for Public Affairs (Sargeant) to UsoS (Webb), 17 August 1951; doc. 656, Memo by Barrett, 20 November 1951. Each "Winds of Freedom" operation had to be approved by both the appropriate geographical bureau and the Public Affairs structure within State. For later operations see Hixson, *Parting the Curtain*, p. 66 and for technical details see David L. Hollyer, "Winds Aloft: When Radio Free Europe Flew Balloons," *QST* (official journal of the Amateur Radio Relay League), April 2001, pp. 49–52.

With RFE carrying the burden of confrontational propaganda, the way was clear for the Voice of America to develop along more news-based lines.[151] As early as February 1951, Assistant Secretary of State for European Affairs George W. Perkins wrote in a top secret cable to the Secretary of State: "in regard to the Soviet Union, it is necessary to lay even greater stress in VOA programs on building reputation for credibility through calm dispassionate recital of fact. This lays [a] sound basis for combating Communist propaganda and for weakening [the] position of [the] Soviet state with [the] Russian people."[152] Barrett supported this approach in a "statement of basic policy" for the VOA drawn up in May 1951. He noted that the VOA needed credibility and had to report the news "fairly and honestly," including reverses in Korea and lynching in the American South. He insisted that political argument belonged on the air only when clearly flagged as opinion in the VOA's commentaries.[153]

In March 1951, a committee chaired by Barrett delivered an "Emergency Plan for Psychological Offensive (U.S.S.R.)." It called for VOA commentaries to emphasize the "reckless nature of Soviet policy and its consequences."[154] New initiatives within the plan included vigorous negative attacks on Stalin and Marxism rather than the presentation of the positive virtues of the American way. Themes included exposing the vast gap between Soviet propaganda promises and reality and pandering to Russian sensibilities: "Since the less educated Russian likes to regard himself as *khitri* (clever–sly–hard to dupe), it might be a useful technique in exposing Soviet propaganda lies to imply that we understand that the listener is too smart to have been taken in by the trick." The State Department agreed that the more aggressive approach should be shared with key allies. Paul Nitze recommended writing speeches in keeping with the theme and passing them to selected congressmen.[155]

The aggressive approach clearly aggravated the Kremlin. Soviet bloc newspapers began to run cartoons denouncing the VOA. Given the double meaning of the French word *canard*, used in Poland and Hungary, as both a "lie" and a "duck", the Eastern bloc press adopted the duck as the standard visual image for the VOA. There were other examples that the VOA was finding its mark. On 8 November 1951, the

151 NA RG 59, Assistant Secretary of State for Public Affairs, 1949–53, box 1, Subject files, 1949–53, file: "A–B"; the idea that RFE and VOA were "complimentary to each other" was confirmed from the field. See Sargeant, memo re conversation for Ambassador Ellis Briggs (Prague), secret, 18 June 1952.

152 *FRUS 1951, Vol. IV*, doc. 610, Perkins to SoS, 2 February 1951.

153 NA RG59, Bureau of Public Affairs, Office files of Edward W. Barrett, 1950–51, box 6, file "P–Mr. Schwinn," Barrett to Schwinn, "Proposed Statement on our Basic Policy," 31 May 1951: "We do not suppress news of a lynching, but it in reporting it, we do point out that it is the first lynching in so many years, and we point out how sharply the rate of lynchings has declined in recent years."

154 *FRUS 1951, Vol. IV*, doc 618, Emergency Plan for Psychological Offensive (U.S.S.R.), 9 March 1951, pp. 1232–3. For calls for such a policy see doc. 668, Ambassador to Czechoslovakia (Briggs) to SoS, 2 March 1951.

155 *FRUS 1951, Vol. IV*, doc 620, Record of the Under Secretary's Meeting, 28 March 1951, p. 1238. For detailed plans see HSTL PSF box 164, Subject files: foreign affairs, Russia, State Dept., "Plan for Psychological Offensive (U.S.S.R.)." With cover memo by Barrett, 11 April 1951; see esp. "An analysis of principal psychological vulnerabilities in the U.S.S.R. and of the principal assets available to the U.S. for their exploitation."

Soviet representative at the United Nations general assembly in Paris, Andrei Vishinsky, denounced Western disarmament proposals as a "dead mouse" and claimed a sleepless night from laughing about the plan. Moscow detected a potential *faux pas* and deleted the remarks from the transcript of the speech printed in *Pravda*. The VOA noted the omission and broadcast a tape of the offending remarks in Vishinsky's own voice, which compelled Vishinsky to come clean in a subsequent speech.[156] Similarly, when in February 1952 Congress began an inquiry into the massacre of Polish officers in the Katyn forest in 1940 and began to present evidence of Soviet guilt, the VOA gave the story saturation coverage in its broadcasts to Poland. The state-controlled Polish media attempted to remain silent, but ten days into the inquiry, with Warsaw abuzz, they began a rather feeble countercampaign of denials. The VOA duck could bite.[157]

During the spring of 1951, the White House pondered further intensification of "political warfare." Advisors, including White House Special Counsel Charles S. Murray and George Elsey, warned that the administration's foreign policy had not been effectively "packaged," and Truman remained vulnerable to critics at home offering easy solutions. The critic of the hour was General Douglas MacArthur, dismissed from his command in Asia by the President in April 1951 and now speaking widely against Truman's approach. Elsey and his colleagues recommended a counterattack including explicit discussion of working for the overthrow of the Soviet regime and the liberation of the Eastern bloc. The State Department moved to rein in such enthusiasm, leaving this "rollback" approach to be picked up the following year by the Republicans.[158] The MacArthur affair also became a prime example of the VOA's even-handedness in its presentation of domestic criticism of the President. The Voice carried MacArthur's address to Congress live.[159]

---

[156]   HSTL Hulten papers, box 18, VOA 1951, Program Evaluation Branch, VOA highlights, December 1951; for a compendium of VOA cartoons see Hulten papers, box 19, VOA 1952, World Wide Communist Reaction to VOA, Program Evaluation Branch report A-101, The VOA as Communists Picture It, 31 January 1952. Examples include a cartoon by the Hungarian Laszlo Egri, exhibited in October 1951, showing a fat businessman hurling dollar bills at a microphone, which metamorphose into quacking ducks in midair, whereas the Polish journal *Kurier Codzienny* of 6 October 1951 showed a listener slowly mutating into a donkey while a duck perched on the radio set quacks, "This is the Voice of America." Sometimes Polish mockery of the VOA took poetic form. On 28 June 1953 *Radio i Swiat* (Warsaw) published a poem called "Culinary recipes from the Atlantic radio cookery." The first stanza, "*Bigos* a la Wall Street" ran, "Two kilos of lies, one kilo of nonsense,/ A pound of provocations and a deca of facts,/ dilute with 'national' wash/ in the Atlantic Pact pail;//To sharpen the appetite/ a pinch of atom – instead of paprika./ Do you know this recipe? 'Voice of Wall Street'/ Under the firm 'Voice of America.'" The second stanza was "Duck a la BBC": "Take an event, eviscerate it of truth/ And fill it with stuffing made of duck's feathers,/ Moisten the 'objectiveness' with troubled gravy –/ this is a recipe from the yapping English cuisine." Other stanzas addressed RFE and German radio. DDEL C D Jackson papers, box 79, NCFE Black Book file 1, The Black Book, vol. iv, pp. 6–7.

[157]   HSTL Hulten papers, box 19, VOA 1952, Div. of Radio Program Evaluation, VOA highlights, No. 17, 15 May 1952.

[158]   *FRUS 1951, Vol. 1*, Shulman (Special Asst to SoS) to Acheson, 15 May 1951.

[159]   NA RG59, Bureau of Public Affairs, Office files of Edward W. Barrett, 1950–51, box 6, "White House 1951," Memo of telephone conversation, Barrett/Joseph Short (White House), "Handling of MacArthur speech on VOA," 19 April 1951.

In Korea, McArthur's replacement, General Ridgeway, paid increased attention to psychological factors. The U.S. embassy noted that most of the Chinese "volunteers" were veterans of the Nationalist army and open to desertion given the right stimulus from defeats and propaganda appeals.[160] Similar effort went into presenting the U.S. effort at home and to the world at large, with an emphasis on America's willingness to negotiate.[161] The North Koreans responded with a devastating propaganda gambit: they stated that the United States had deployed bacteriological weapons in Korea. Ridgeway dismissed the claim, but the story lived on to become one of the most enduring propaganda canards of the Cold War.[162]

Throughout 1951, the United States attempted to gain some sort of propaganda initiative over the U.S.S.R. In June 1951, the administration arranged for Senator Brian McMahon (D-CT) and Representative Abraham Ribicoff (D-CT) to sponsor a "Friendship resolution" on Capitol Hill that emphasized American goodwill toward the Soviet people. Truman signed it on 7 July 1951. When the Soviets declined to make the text public, it naturally became a staple of Voice broadcasts. But one resolution could not wrest the concept of peace from Soviet hands. Truman tried again with a disarmament proposal in November 1951.[163]

The Campaign of Truth soldiered on with its reduced budget. In August 1951, a State Department report took stock. Achievements were mixed. The USIE had created new information centers and opened Regional Service Centers in London and Manila to mass-produce propaganda literature close to where that material would be used. This worked well, and the report proposed a further center for the Middle East. The VOA had expanded its output, with twenty-one new languages (making a total of forty-five) and thirty-one extra hours of programming (making a total of sixty-one hours per day).[164] The State Department felt that the VOA was working well, encouraging "Titoism" in the Eastern bloc.[165] Conversely, the State Department worried that the increasing emphasis on U.S. military strength in many of the administration's public statements now detracted from U.S. psychological objectives and warned that "military power dissociated from a persuasive idea may neither deter an enemy nor persuade

---

[160]   *FRUS 1951, Vol. VII*, Muccio (ambassador in Korea) to Secretary of State, 21 April 1951, pp. 374–5; JCS to Ridgeway, 1 May 1951, p. 397.

[161]   *FRUS 1951, Vol. VII*, Austin to ASoS for UN Affairs (Hickerson), 23 May 1951, pp.451–4.

[162]   *FRUS 1951, Vol. VII*, editorial note, p. 581; see also Barrett, *The Strategy of Truth*, pp. 177–9, and on the persistence of the story, *FRUS 1952–1954, Vol. XV*, Korea, pp. 308–10.

[163]   The resolution had its origin in a suggestion by Barrett from January 1951; see *FRUS 1951, Vol. 1*, Barrett, "Combating the Crisis of Confidence," 29 January 1951, p. 516 and note; *FRUS 1951, Vol. IV*, doc. 788, Truman to President of the Presidium of the Supreme Soviet of the U.S.S.R. (Shvernik), 7 July 1951 and doc. 813, Memo of conversation by Sargeant, 5 October 1951.

[164]   *FRUS 1951, Vol. 1*, NSC 114/3, annex 5, 8 August 1951. The RPC were capable of producing in excess of 60 million booklets a year. Manila's output included a magazine, *Free World*, issued in 11 languages and 400,000 copies; a wall newspaper called "*World Photo Review*" issued in an edition of 250,000 in 13 languages and displayed in such locations as temple walls in Cambodia; and a cartoon book telling the story of a convert away from Communism told in strip cartoon form: *The Story of Dr. Liang*. Daugherty and Janowitz (eds.), *A Psychological Warfare Casebook*, pp. 150–53.

[165]   *FRUS 1951, Vol. IV*, doc 630, Progress report on NSC 58/2, Under Secretary of State (Webb) to NSC, 22 May 1951, p. 1258.

an ally." Time, it warned, had been wasted: "A gun not produced today can still be produced next month. A psychological attitude not created or supported today may never be brought into being."[166]

A further State Department review of 12 October 1951 identified five essential tasks facing the USIE: "to multiply and intensify psychological deterrents" to Communist aggression; to build confidence and unity in the Free World; to combat extremism in non-Communist Asia and the Middle East; to stress the interdependence of the U.S. and its traditional allies, especially in Latin America; and to maintain the hope of liberation for those dominated by the U.S.S.R.[167] With these objectives in mind, in the late autumn of 1951 the State Department circulated its propaganda agenda for the coming year. The key theme would be "progress through strength towards peace and freedom." Barrett planned special leaflets and VOA broadcasts to recapture the theme of peace for the Christmas season, many emphasizing Truman's disarmament speech of 7 November.[168] Negatively themed leaflets included "Beware, the Red Dove of Peace" which promised "the facts behind the Kremlin's phony peace." The cover carried an image of a bird of prey, composed of a hammer and sickle, perched on the Kremlin wall and holding a pistol in one wing and an olive branch in the other. The copy inside began, "Stalin has disguised the Communist vulture of conquest and terror as a red dove of peace," and concluded, "STALIN'S RED DOVE OF PEACE IS A BIRD OF PREY." The USIE transmittal slip for this leaflet included a recommendation that the leaflet be printed on cheap paper to avoid a "slick" appearance and stressed that "USIS attribution is NOT to be used" and "no intimation is to be given as to the source of this material." Despite new NSC guidelines, the USIE was straying into gray propaganda.[169]

---

[166] *FRUS 1951, Vol. 1*, NSC 114/3, annex 5, 8 August 1951. Suggestions for further expansion included increased exchange programs for opinion makers from countries in the front line of Communist expansion.

[167] *FRUS 1951, Vol. I*, NSC 114/2, annex 5, 12 October 1951. At the same time, the NSC drafted objectives for the entire U.S. psychological approach to the world (draft NSC 114/2): "We shall seek to convince all peoples of the world – great and small – that we are dedicated to maintaining without resort to general war, a world at peace and in that world an economy of plenty; and that there is need for each of them in the common struggle for this goal. A) We shall seek affirmative ways by which to deter the Soviet Union from undertaking a global war and to deny to the Soviet Union the capability of achieving its aims by measures short of war. Thus, we shall operate against the vulnerabilities of the existing Communist regimes in the Soviet Union and in areas now under its control, and seek to create conditions under which those areas may be freed from the Kremlin's grip. B) We shall reduce Communist strength in the free world and build up the will of the free world to resist both Communist influence and Communist aggression. We shall undertake these courses of action as integral parts of an over-all strategy." Draft NSC 114/2 as quoted in HSTL SMOF PSB files, box 15, 091.412–2, Browne to Allen, "Preliminary Evaluation of Our National Psychological Strategy," 7 May 1952.

[168] *FRUS 1951, Vol. 1*, Webb (Action SoS), Quarterly Propaganda Emphases, 17 November 1951, pp. 961–5. The United States also recommend this approach to its allies; see for example *FRUS 1951, Vol. IV, Europe, Political and Economic Development*. doc. 311, Conversation between Secretary of State and PM of Italy, 24 September 1951 (including Barrett), in which Acheson stresses need to appeal to European youth with the idea of European unity and peace, p. 685.

[169] SD PDHC, Campaign of Truth file, Transmittal slip, 25 January 1952; "Stalin's Red Dove of Peace." In November 1951 the NSC moved sought to clarify lines of responsibility between the USIE and

At the end of 1951, as Barrett approached the end of his tenure, he could look back over the first eighteen months of the Campaign of Truth and draw satisfaction from some impressive statistics. The number of individuals being brought to the United States in leadership exchanges had increased from 3,900 in 1950 to 10,000 in 1951, whereas the department's output of documentary films had increased three hundred percent. The USIS had created 125 million printed items for the campaign and book and magazine circulation increasing from 1.5 million to 3.7 million items from 1950 to 1951.[170] But Barrett knew this was a mere whisper of what was needed to win the Cold War.

4) THINGS LEFT UNDONE

THE INDEPENDENCE DEBATE, 1950–53

For all its many flourishes, by 1952 all intelligence estimates suggested that the "Campaign of Truth" had achieved little. Two years into the Campaign, Moscow still held the propaganda initiative. One obvious weakness lay in a lack of policy coordination. The period of the Campaign of Truth saw an intense debate in Washington over the future structure of U.S. propaganda overseas. The debate followed three – sometimes parallel, sometimes overlapping – lines. There was the question of management and the need for a "national psychological strategy"; there was the question of whether overt information should be the responsibility of a new and separate agency; and there was the issue of the VOA and whether it should bludgeon the Soviet bloc with ideology or work more subtly through balanced news.

In March 1950, on the eve of his Campaign of Truth speech, Truman authorized a basic structure to facilitate interdepartmental cooperation under NSC 59/1. This established a small Interdepartmental Foreign Information Office and an Interdepartmental Foreign Information Staff. The key players knew that the big prize was the direction of the psychological warfare machine in wartime and maneuvered accordingly.[171] Just six months later, on 17 August 1950, Truman announced the creation of a National Psychological Strategy Board, which reconfigured the NSC 59/1 structure.

"other U.S. information activities." Black propaganda and operations, which could prove controversial if they were disclosed, were placed firmly outside the remit of the USIE. A memorandum specifically forbade the USIE or the ECA (Marshall Plan) to provide covert subsidies to foreign news media outlets or "labor, youth or women's groups" and to conduct "propaganda campaigns designed to influence foreign political elections." Such "Black Propaganda" operations were, of course, the responsibility of the Office of Policy Coordination at the CIA. A hardened Cold Warrior such as the OPC's director, Frank Wisner, had no desire to have amateurs on his patch. See *FRUS 1951, Vol. 1*, Foreign Service Information and Educational Exchange Circular No. 4, 1 November 1951, pp. 954–6, which includes definitions of white, gray, and black propaganda.

170   *FRUS 1951, Vol. I*, NSC 114/2, annex 5, 12 October 1951; HSTL Sargeant papers, box 4, Corresp., Asst. Sec. of State for Public Affairs, Barrett to Sargeant et al., 18 January 1952, attachment: "Statement of Achievements of Campaign of Truth." Thanks to close cooperation with commercial film distributors and the deployment of 350 mobile cinema vans to the field, State now estimated its film audience at 400 million per year. The number of registered borrowers at U.S. information libraries had risen from 283,000 in 1950 to 417,000 in 1951.

171   In the summer of 1950, Under Secretary of State Webb produced a "Plan for National Psychological Warfare" in the event of a general war with the Soviet Union: NSC 74. This document called for

With Ed Barrett as director, this new board coordinated the information activities of the State Department with other key agencies. Its members included "consultants" Brig. Gen. John Magruder from the Pentagon, Vice Admiral Leslie C. Stevens from the JCS, and Frank Wisner from the CIA. Representatives from the Defense Resources Board and European Cooperation Agency sat in as needed.[172] Early decisions included the stockpiling of balloons on the frontier between East and West for future use in propaganda. A meeting in November considered unconventional channels for getting information across the "Iron Curtain," including "Moslems," migrant clergy, criminals, imitation newspapers, and intriguingly *"frauleins."* Unfortunately the document did not explain the role German women might play in the great propaganda game.[173] Barrett's own priorities included coordinating the USIE with the ECA, which now had an explicit mandate "to promote understanding of the nature of Soviet communism and to encourage attitudes hostile to it. . . ."[174] The ECA and the USIE worked well together, sharing both key committees and operations. Barrett noted with satisfaction that "the over-flamboyance of many ECA operatives and over cautiousness of the State operators have tended to neutralize the other, with generally healthy results." But the wider question of the structure remained.[175]

Early in 1951, Truman moved to resolve the deadlock between State and the rest of the bureaucracy over the direction of psychological warfare.[176] On 4 April 1951, Truman created the Psychological Strategy Board (PSB), made up of the deputy Secretary of Defense, the director of the CIA, and the Under Secretary of State: "for the formulation and promulgation, as guidance to the departments and agencies responsible for psychological operations, of over-all national psychological objectives, policies

America to match the perceived readiness of the U.S.S.R. to fight a propaganda war and set out the ground rules for any U.S. campaign. These included "The maintenance of the credibility of our overt psychological warfare through factual accuracy, plausibility, and objectivity." The USIE and VOA would retain their "white propaganda" missions. NSC 74 also proposed that the Secretary of State take charge of wartime psychological operations. The Joint Chiefs of Staff howled in protest and the NSC never accepted the report as policy. HSTL PSF, box 210, 77th NSC meeting, NSC 74, 10 July 1950. HSTL SMOF PSB files, box 9, PSB 091.412, W. K. Scott to USoS (Webb), 20 February 1951.

172 For an overview of the bureaucratic realignments see HSTL SMOF PSB box 15, 091.412–2, memo by Edward P. Lilly (PSB), Psychological Operations, 1945–51, 4 February 1952 and NA RG59 Records relating to International Information, 1938–45, box 15, National Psychological Strategy Board, "Proposed Steps for Strengthening the Present Interdepartmental Foreign Information Organizations, Secret," 11 August 1950; also Barrett, *Truth Is Our Weapon*, p. 301; Gregory Mitrovich, *Undermining the Kremlin: America's Strategy to Subvert the Soviet bloc, 1947–1956*, Ithaca, NY: Cornell University Press, 2000, p. 6.

173 NA RG59 Records relating to International Information, 1938–45, box 15, National Psychological Strategy Board, Barrett to Nitze, 15 September 1950; Davidson Taylor to members of [N]PSB, "Penetration Devices for Possible Discussion at PSB Meeting on Monday, 27 November 1950," 27 November 1950.

174 *FRUS 1950, Vol. 1, National Security Affairs; Foreign Economic Policy*, NSC. 68/3, annexes, 8 December 1950, p. 448.

175 *FRUS 1951, Vol. 1*, Barrett to Webb/Humelsine, 5 January 1951, pp. 902–4.

176 On 4 January he referred the deadlock for adjudication by the Bureau of the Budget and a "special consultant," Admiral Sidney Souers, who was the former director of Central Intelligence and the first executive secretary of the NSC. On 18 January Souers delivered his recommendation, proposing a board "under the NSC" with a chairman appointed by the President. HSTL SMOF PSB files, box 9, PSB 091.412, W. K. Scott to USoS (Webb), 20 February 1951.

and programs, and for the coordination and evaluation of the national psychological effort." The board had a staff of seventy-five or so and an office just a block and a half from the White House. At the same time, Barrett's National Psychological Strategy Board became known as the Psychological Operations Coordinating Committee and moved over to the PSB.[177] In June, Truman named a director for the PSB: former Secretary of the Army Gordon Gray. Divided by turf wars and lacking political clout, the board never really worked properly, but it was a start.[178]

While Truman worked to strengthen the center of U.S. propaganda, Benton worked at the periphery. Benton had returned to the view that for the Voice of America's news to be credible the Voice would need to be separate from the political work at State; to this end he revived the issue of an independent propaganda agency. In December 1950 he announced his intent to sponsor legislation to "take propaganda operations out of the State Department."[179] Benton's proposal troubled Ed Barrett. Barrett's fears were not solely based on a desire to preserve "turf." He warned that an independent agency would face the same troubles as the OWI in getting its voice heard in policy making. He also noted that any information agency would need jurisdiction over USIS posts overseas and that this would challenge the authority of ambassadors and the regional bureaus of the State Department: the United States risked "having more than one United States' story in each country." With this in mind, he recommended a less radical solution: strengthening the information program within State by subsuming the publicity functions of the Economic Cooperation Administration (Marshall Plan) and the new Mutual Defense Assistance Program.[180] The ECA took an opposite view. Roscoe Drummond, the director of the Information Division at the ECA's headquarters in Paris, contested State's ability to run "aggressive and effective propaganda" and backed the idea of a new agency. Both parties agreed to allow the Bureau of the Budget to arbitrate a compromise, but meanwhile the Senate initiative remained in play.[181]

[177] *FRUS 1951, Vol. 1*, Truman, directive, 4 April 1951, p. 58 and note p. 921; *FRUS 1951, Vol. IV*, pp. 58–60; also HSTL SMOF, box 25, PSB, file 334–1, Webb to Marshall, 2 May 1951, and for dissent from the new structure memo by Frank Wisner for Assistant Dir. CIA, 28 May 1951.

[178] HSTL OF, box 1656, 1290-D, Barrett to Short (White House), 25 June 1951, with press release 20 June attached. Examples of NSC use of the PSB include a move in February 1952 to clear up confusion over the discussion of the new and more powerful atomic weapons. The problem was that the official statements on U.S. strength necessary to deter Moscow created complacency at home and an image of U.S. bullying elsewhere in the world. PSB guidelines suggested that all U.S. officials issuing statements on nuclear weapons ask, "Will this statement create a fear that the U.S. may act recklessly in the use of these weapons." *FRUS 1952–1954, Vol. II, pt. 2*, Lay (NSC) to Raymond Allen (PSB), 27 February 1952

[179] See *FRUS 1951, Vol. 1*, editorial note p. 907.

[180] *FRUS 1951, Vol. 1*, Barrett to Webb, 12 January 1951, pp. 904–7; also NA RG59, Bureau of Public Affairs, office files of Edward W. Barrett, 1950–51, box 6, Sargeant to Barrett, "personal and confidential," 5 February 1951

[181] *FRUS 1951, Vol. 1*, Memorandum of Conversation: State-ECA Information Program, 27 January 1951, pp. 911–12 and note. The Bureau of the Budget report, 1 October 1951, recommended against a merger of the two programs but called for the State Department to lead in planning joint activities. As European reconstruction advanced, the priorities of U.S. aid shifted more explicitly into the military field. On 30 December 1951, before any new structure had been agreed upon with the State Department, ECA programs, including information activity, passed to the new Mutual Security Agency; PL 165, 10 October 1951, 65 Stat. 373.

On 19 February 1951, Benton presented his resolution to the Senate (SR 74) calling for a full investigation of the international information apparatus. He questioned the content of U.S. propaganda with its emphasis on American achievement, noting, "like good salesmen we must talk to them [the rest of the world] in terms of their interests and not primarily ours." He suggested discussion of industrial and agricultural methods, health, sanitation, and other "down to earth problems." Most importantly, he stressed the need for VOA independence and asked whether the time had come for an independent information agency of cabinet rank.[182] Benton's speech drew widespread approval. Edward Bernays wrote a letter of support, with the important rider that to avoid the image of an "American Goebbels" any new agency director be of cabinet rank but not actually sit in the cabinet.[183] The State Department responded with a transparent attempt to appease Benton by suggesting a semiautonomous "Foreign Information Administration" within State. The Senator was unimpressed.[184]

Benton's proposed Senate investigation into the best structure for U.S. information prompted the State Department to begin an internal quest to the same end. This made sense given that one-half of all State employees worked for the information program. In the summer of 1951, Under Secretary of State Webb commissioned a special task force to consider the question. In July, Deputy Under Secretary of State for Administration Carlisle H. Humelsine argued that the best solution was to create a semiautonomous Foreign Information Administration within the State Department.[185] More detailed plans, presented in September and October, developed Humelsine's idea, suggesting that an administrator with rank equivalent to deputy under secretary direct the program and that semi-independence would increase the perceived significance of overseas information within the bureaucracy. Senior observers expressed doubts. Assistant Secretary of State for Far Eastern Affairs Dean Rusk saw the plan as strengthening the hands of those who wished for a wholly independent information agency. It was a risk that Barrett was prepared to take.[186]

Benton's doubts over the standing of the U.S. information program proved well founded. The budget issue had still not been resolved. In January 1951, President

182 UoC, Benton papers, Box 347/6 "VOA" file, including C. P. Trussell, "Independence for the Voice Is Urged: Benton Asks Senate Study of Shift of Foreign Appeals from State Department," *New York Times*, 20 February 1951; also box 378/5, Benton to Heimlich, 9 March 1951. Mundt also endorsed a commission, but felt that the VOA should stay in State; see transcript of MBS-WDC "Reporters Round-Up" 15 March 1951 in UoC Benton papers, box 347/8.

183 UoC Benton papers, box 347/9, Bernays to Benton, 28 February 1951. Bernays cited the example of President Wilson and his famous political fixer Colonel House as his model.

184 *FRUS 1951, Vol. 1*, Humelsine (DUSoS for Administration) to Webb (USoS), 8 February 1951, pp. 917–18.

185 Humelsine believed that this would maximize flexibility of operations while still providing for "close integration" of information activities "within our overall conduct of foreign relations" and a role "in proper measure in the formulation of our foreign policy." SD PDHC Campaign of Truth file, Humelsine to Secretary of State (Acheson), 23 July 1951.

186 *FRUS 1951, Vol. I*, Under Secretary's Meeting, 10 October 1951 and notes, pp. 934–8. The planners proclaimed that "the functional approach to information is better than the geographic approach" and accordingly diminished the role of regional bureaus of State in executing policy, allowing orders to go direct to embassies. They took care, however, not to diminish the authority of ambassadors in the field.

Truman had requested $115 million for the entire program. In March, he submitted yet another request for a further $97.5 million to build the Ring Plan transmitters. But on 6 April, an unsympathetic House Committee on Appropriations, convinced that money had been wasted, slashed the Ring Plan request to a mere $9.5 million. Charges of extravagance and mismanagement abounded. Critics pointed to nine-dollar-a-head lunches and confusion in the bidding process for new transmitters. Truman protested and Benton spoke of the United States slashing its own throat, but to their horror the revised bill passed in June. Barrett tried to salvage the situation by appointing a subcommittee of the Radio Advisory Committee to investigate the whole question of VOA administration and planning, but to little avail. The budget cuts continued. The House Committee on Appropriations cut Truman's main request from $115 to $85 million. In August the Senate attempted a further cut to just $63 million. Benton and Mundt's counterattack restored the budget to the $85 million level.[187]

The man behind the budget cut was Senator Pat McCarran (D-NV). He sought to build political capital at the expense of the Campaign of Truth and in the summer of 1951, as chair of the Appropriations Subcommittee, he held joint, closed session hearings on the VOA with the Senate Internal Security Subcommittee. Witnesses included former VOA employees of Eastern European extraction eager to settle scores. The hearings never moved beyond hearsay and innuendo and soon descended into absurdity as one witness, a Slovak nationalist, denounced the national heroes of Czechoslovakia, Benes and Masaryk, as "Communists at heart." No Communists were found, but McCarran slashed the VOA budget anyway.[188]

*

On 18 January 1952, the State Department unveiled its response to Benton: the "semiautonomous" United States International Information Administration (IIA). Building on the former idea of a General Manager, operational authority rested with the new IIA Administrator, Wilson Compton. Unfortunately, more than sixty years old, Compton did not exude the sort of energy necessary to invigorate U.S. propaganda. The administration probably hoped that as a Republican he would draw less fire from Capitol Hill. They hoped in vain.[189] Compton's early blunders included

187 HSTL OF 20S, box 167, Campaign of Truth, including Truman to Speaker of HoR, 5 March 1951; for legislative summary see editorial notes in *FRUS 1951* vol. 1, pp. 919 and 933; also *Public Papers of the Presidents: Harry S. Truman, 1951*, pp. 218, 475–7. A detailed USIE rebuttal, "comments on charges that have been made against the Campaign of Truth," 29 March 1951, can be found in SD PDHC, Campaign of Truth file. For Benton's protest see "US Would Cut Own Throat by Stifling 'Voice,' Says Benton," *Washington Post*, 4 April 1951; for the report of the subcommittee of the Radio Advisory Committee of the U.S. Advisory Commission on Information, see HSTL, OF 20E, box 165, VOA [2], Barrett to Elsey, 12 July 1951.
188 "Senators Told Reds Infiltrate Voice Program," *New York Herald Tribune*, 10 July 1951; Marquis Childs, "Mishmash Heard by Red Probers," *New York Post*, 13 July 1951; "Truman Plea to Restore Funds for 'Voice' Rejected in Senate," *New York Herald Tribune*, 22 August 1951.
189 *FRUS 1952–1954, Vol. II, pt. 2*, Dept. of State announcement no. 4, 16 January. 1952; Subcommittee on Overseas Information Programs of the United States, Staff Study No. 4, Organization of United

insensitive handling of the VOA. Although VOA director Foy Kohler did not personally favor the "divorcement" of the VOA from the USIE, he took offense when Compton rejected an Advisory Committee paper on the idea without consulting him.[190] For his part, Compton dismissed Kohler's vision for the future as just "more voices on air in more and more languages." Kohler left the VOA in September 1952.[191]

Under the new structure, the Assistant Secretary of State for Public Affairs still provided policy guidance and had input into policy formation, but lost all remaining operational responsibility for information work. Barrett completed his agreed two years in office and, in poor health and financial difficulty, returned to private life on 20 February 1952. The post now passed to Howland Sargeant. Born in 1910 and educated at Dartmouth and Oxford (as a Rhodes scholar), Sargeant had been the deputy assistant secretary since Benton's time. Although Sargeant had much to commend him, the press fixated on one detail of his private life. In June 1951 he married movie star Myrna Loy.[192] But this was the least of his worries.

Reviewing the progress of the national psychological strategy in May 1952, a top secret PSB report presented stark conclusions. The writer, one Mallory Brown, observed that in Western Europe, although "not losing the Cold War, we are not yet winning it"; in Latin America there were growing signs of danger, but in the Middle East and south and east Asia, the United States was "in real and imminent danger of losing the Cold War." The successes – Brown named the Voice of America, the Marshall Plan, and the Mutual Security Program – were tactical victories, but "the over all psychological strategy is not as effective as it must become if we are to win the Cold War." The United States had effectively failed to counter the Soviet tactic of persistently identifying the United States with war and the Soviet Union with peace and economic development. It seemed unclear exactly what the United States stood for. Despite the creation of the Psychological Strategy Board, the United States had yet to

States Overseas Information Functions, p. 6. Also HSTL SMOF Charles W. Jackson, box 30, OGR file, State Dept. Overseas Info, 1; Press Release No. 43, 17 January 1952. For press comment see "New U.S. Office Due to operate 'Voice,'" *New York Times*, 13 January 1952, noting that Paul G. Hoffman, formerly of the ECA, has endorsed Benton's call for full independence. Born in 1890, Wilson Compton was a scion of a famous academic family. His brothers were Dr. Karl Compton, chairman of the board at MIT, and Dr. Arthur H. Compton, Nobel Laureate in Physics and chancellor of Washington University, St. Louis. After a Ph.D. from Princeton, he served as general manager of the National Lumber Association (1918–44) and as a professor of economics, rising to the post of president of Washington State College at Pullman (now Washington State University). Compton's previous government work had included service on numerous advisory committees; representing the United States at various UN meetings, including the 4th General Assembly in 1949, and membership of the special U.S. educational mission to Japan in 1946. Now Compton's responsibilities included input into the execution of policy across departmental lines as chairman of the Psychological Operations Coordination Committee.

[190] NA RG 306, Office of Administration, box 1, broadcasting service 1951–2, Kohler to Compton, 25 February 1952.

[191] Pirsein, *Voice of America*, p. 229.

[192] NA RG 59, Assistant Secretary of State for Public Affairs, 1949–53, box 1, Subject files, 1949–53, file "A-B," Barrett to Truman, 5 December 1951 and Acheson, 5 December 1951; Barrett, *Truth Is Our Weapon*, p. 97; *FRUS 1952–1954, Vol. II, pt. 2*, Humelsine to Regional Bureau executive directors, 30 January 1952, p. 1597. Sargeant and Loy divorced in 1960.

generate a clear and achievable psychological strategy. Two years into the Campaign of Truth, the PSB was still arguing that the United States needed to go onto the offensive in the global war of ideas.[193]

The PSB identified regional difficulties especially in the Middle East, where the United States had lost much ground since sponsoring the creation of Israel in 1948. Now the United States had to rebuild its relationship with Arab populations and challenge the Soviet presentation of its system as the wave of the future.[194] In February 1951, U.S. ambassadors from across the Middle East met for a weeklong conference in Istanbul. They praised the value of new USIS mobile film units but raised major criticisms of the VOA. They spoke of "irrelevant and ill chosen programs" flawed by "high pressure" tactics, which, they added, could not even be heard properly because of the lack of medium-wave transmitters.[195] The United States stepped up its work in the region. USIS posts created posters and pamphlets, screened films, and subsidized translation and publication of politically helpful books through Franklin Publications Inc., founded by the State Department in 1952 and subsidized by IIA. Among the first books translated was Orwell's *Animal Farm*.[196] Meanwhile, the NSC called for politically targeted development aid. The benefits of the "Point IV" program became a key element in the output of USIS posts across the region. The embassy in Iraq reported considerable success with a poster series depicting Soviet Communists as pigs (with hammer and sickle tails). There were, however, obvious problems in applying the usual "Campaign of Freedom" material to a region characterized by absolute

193 HSTL SMOF PSB files, box 15, 091.412–2, Mallory Browne to Raymond B. Allen (PSB director), "Preliminary Evaluation of our National Psychological Strategy," 7 May 1952. A detailed intelligence addendum to this report (Tab A: Intelligence summary and analysis of Soviet power position & of position of Western Powers vis-à-vis Soviet Communism, esp. p. 19, item 40) expanded on particular weaknesses in the U.S. approach to the world. One paragraph even identified ethical contradictions within U.S. policy that left it vulnerable to Soviet propaganda: "Can the United States at the same time it proclaims its moral superiority also engage in immoral operations designed to reduce the impact of communism. Can the United States, while proclaiming its economic altruism, impose economic controls over the other countries? Can the United States while proclaiming its belief in economic freedom, social justice, and political self-determination, insist on a partial or complete sacrifice of sovereignty among its allies? And, having done so, can the United States believably proclaim its ideology to the Soviet orbit?"

194 HSTL SMOF PSB files, box 15, 091.412–2, Browne to Allen, "Preliminary Evaluation of our National Psychological Strategy," 7 May 1952: Tab A: Intelligence summary and analysis of Soviet power position & of position of Western Powers vis-à-vis Soviet Communism, esp. p. 19, item 40.

195 *FRUS 1951, Vol. V, The Near East and Africa*, Washington DC: GPO, 1982. Agreed conclusions and recommendations of the conference of Middle Eastern Chiefs of Mission, Istanbul, 14–21 February 1951, pp. 73–5. The assembled ambassadors also considered the best structure for U.S. propaganda. As might be expected, the group "strongly recommended that the public information program remain under the policy control of the [State] Department, in the interests of its effective integration with United States foreign policy objectives."

196 On books see UoA Fulbright papers, box A 143, BCN30-F20, "Books Published Abroad, July 1, 1950–Dec. 31, 1950," Department of State, 1954. At around this time the U.S. government also paid for translations of Orwell's *Animal Farm* into Greek, Indonesian (both in 1952), and two Indian languages, Marathi (1952) and Bengali (1953). Other widely translated titles included testimonials by the defectors Kravchenko and Barmine. The subsidy to Franklin is noted in DDEL OSANA NSC/Subject files, box 4, OCB progress report to NSC on implementation of the recommendations of the Jackson Committee, 30 September 1953, Annex B, p. 6.

monarchies and dictatorships.[197] One success came in 1952. When a local airline overbooked and left 3,800 Muslim pilgrims stranded in Beirut, the U.S. embassy arranged for the U.S. Air Force to airlift the pilgrims to Mecca in "Operation Magic Carpet." When the airline reimbursed the U.S. government for the face value of the tickets, the government donated the money to charity. Such a story turned on American compassion and respect for Islam. A shared respect for God in the face of godless communism became the default message of U.S. Cold War propaganda in the Middle East.[198]

The PSB call for a more assertive approach coincided with the feeling of a meeting convened by C. D. Jackson of the National Committee for a Free Europe in Princeton in May 1952. The delegates were thirty prominent private citizens and government officials (operating in a private capacity) interested in propaganda. Officials present included Charles E. Bohlen from the State Department, Allen Dulles and William H. Jackson from the CIA, and George Morgan from the PSB.[199] C. D. Jackson set the ball rolling by speaking about the failure of the government to exploit the psychological blows struck in the Soviet bloc by RFE. Speaker after speaker called for the United States to go onto the ideological offensive and to replace passive containment with an explicit agenda to liberate Eastern Europe. The meeting ended with a call for a new program of political warfare against the U.S.S.R. The Truman administration failed to respond, but the Princeton agenda would find its champion in presidential candidate Dwight D. Eisenhower.[200]

In August 1952, the NSC's Reporting Unit examined the achievements of the PSB from its foundation in April 1951 to June 1952. It noted that only the broadest interdepartmental priorities had been agreed upon. Looking out into the world, the report bemoaned the rash of neutralism and rejection of U.S. aggressiveness. Europe questioned the military nature of U.S. aid; the Islamic world questioned U.S. support for Israel; for the developing world present or remembered white colonialism seemed

---

[197]   On U.S. propaganda in the early Cold War Middle East, James Robert Vaughan, *The Anglo-American Relationship and Propaganda Strategies in the Middle East, 1953–1957*, Ph.D. dissertation, University College London, 2001, (esp. on Point IV aid, pp. 62–70); also the National Security Archive briefing book edited by Joyce Battle. For overview essay see http://www.gwu.edu/~nsarchiv/NSAEBB/ NSAEBB78/essay.htm – esp. doc. 21: Crocker to State, 10 March 1951; doc. 33, U.S. embassy, Jidda, to State, 2 October 1951; and doc. 46, U.S. embassy, Saudi Arabia to State, 8 January 1952.

[198]   Daugherty and Janowitz (eds.), *A Psychological Warfare Casebook*, p. 337; also HSTL, PSF, box 219, 126th meeting of NSC, PSB D-34, "Progress Report on the National Psychological Effort for the Period July 1 1952, through September 30, 1952," 30 October 1952. For a policy paper on religion in USIE output see HSTL, Elsey papers, box 65, foreign relations VOA (info progs. 1950) paper, "The Recognition of Moral and Religious Factors in the USIE Program," UM D-143, 29 May 1951.

[199]   HSTL SMOF PSB files, box 27, 337 staff meetings, 1952-Jan. '53, file 3, PSB Staff Meeting, 12 May 1952; DDEL CD Jackson papers, box 83, Princeton Meeting. C. D. Jackson's notes on the meeting list the following: "Frank Altschul; Lloyd V. Berkner (Pres. Associated Universities Inc); Adolf A. Berle; Cyril Black (History, Princeton); Charles E. Bohlen; Tom Braden; Howard Chapin; John Devine; Commander Dickson (MIT); Frederick R. Dolbeare; Allen W. Dulles; Lewis Galantiere; Joseph C. Grew; William E. Griffith; John C. Hughes; C.D. Jackson; Robert Joyce; R. E. Lang; John Leich; Admiral H. B. Miller; George Morgan (PSB); DeWitt C. Poole; Walter Rostow (MIT); Levering Tyson; Alan Valentine (CFA); Abbott Washburn; J. B. Wiesner (MIT)."

[200]   DDEL CD Jackson papers, box 83, Princeton Meeting; esp. Galantiere to Jackson, 6 June 1952 with transcript and Jackson to Lucius D. Clay, 5 September 1952 with attachments.

far more potent than the U.S. depiction of the Soviet threat, whereas the British questioned the U.S. policy toward China. Domestic politics cast a shadow overseas. The NSC cited "race relations; the restrictive immigration policy...and tariff laws." The only bright spot seemed to be the success of the VOA and RFE in reaching audiences behind the "Iron Curtain."[201]

Meanwhile, the budget crisis raged on. The IIA failed to secure additional funding from Congress in 1952, while familiar rumors of disloyalty among its staff promised problems for the future.[202] In the summer of 1952 the FBI began investigating the alleged disloyalty of VOA employees in New York City. Charges focused on alleged toning-down of VOA content and the "sabotage" of propaganda messages. Unimpressed, the FBI passed the investigation to the State Department's Division of Security, which assigned four agents to advance the enquiry. They found that some of the complaints related to "moral deviation" of staff rather than any political offense. They dismissed the individuals concerned.[203]

The USIIA had been created to blunt Benton's attempt to restructure U.S. overseas information. It failed. On 30 June 1952 the Senate adopted SR 72, a resolution presented by Bill Benton and Alexander Wiley (R-WI), authorizing "a full and complete study and investigation of the existing overseas information programs of the United States government." The resolution created a subcommittee of the Committee on Foreign Relations. Fulbright chaired and Wiley, Guy Gillette (D-IA), and Bourke B. Hickenlooper (R-IA) served, while Mundt and Benton were coopted. The subcommittee meant business, and promptly commissioned comparative staff studies on overseas information in the United States, Britain, and the U.S.S.R.[204]

Meanwhile, the beleaguered IIA did its best to cope with war in Korea. Projects included attempts to expose Communist propaganda techniques. In June 1952 Wilson Compton instructed all key officers in the IIA to read Edward Hunter's book *Brain Washing in Red China* and recommended a special effort to discreetly pass evidence of the power of Communist indoctrination techniques to press contacts around the world.[205] Chinese sources continued to give great play to claims of American "germ

201 *FRUS 1952–1954, Vol. II, pt. 1, National Security Affairs*, NSC Key Date book, as transmitted 5 August 1952, pp. 178–9. A parallel review of activity directed specifically at the Soviet Union called for the United States to intensify "positive political, economic propaganda and paramilitary operations" within the Soviet orbit. See *FRUS 1952–1954, Vol. II, pt. 1*, NSC 135/1, 15 August 1952.
202 *FRUS 1952–1954, Vol. II, pt. 2*, Report by the administration of the USIIA (Compton) to the Secretary of State (Acheson), transmitted 29 July 1952.
203 *FRUS 1952–1954, Vol. II, pt. 2*, DASoS for Admin (Scott) to Administrator IIA (Compton), Investigation at VOA, 12 September 1952.
204 Subcommittee on Overseas Information Programs of the United States, Staff Study No. 1, 2, 3, 17 November 1952, Washington, DC: USGPO; see also note in *FRUS 1952–1954, Vol. II, pt. 2*, p. 1627.
205 *FRUS 1952–1954, Vol. II, pt. 2*, Acheson to all diplomatic offices, 17 June 1952. For background on Brainwashing see Susan L. Carruthers, "*The Manchurian Candidate* (1962) and the Cold War Brainwashing Scare," *Historical Journal of Film, Radio and Television*, 18, 1 (March 1998), 75–94.

warfare" in Korea. The press in Asia seemed all too willing to believe it.[206] In the spring the Chinese broadened their claims, adding that there had been an American bacteriological air raid on the Chinese city of Tsingtao on 6 March using infected fleas, ants, beetles, and flies.[207] As such claims sometimes cited the discovery of mysterious empty canisters on the battlefield, the USIIA released photographs showing these canisters in legitimate use as leaflet bomb casings for U.S. propaganda. The United States asked the Red Cross to investigate and introduced a UN resolution condemning the charges, which the U.S.S.R. vetoed in July.[208] The State Department also developed strategies to speed the truce negotiations at Panmunjom. Ideas included attempting to push the Chinese into making panicked demands on the U.S.S.R. by spreading of rumors of an imminent UN amphibious landing or political pressure to use the atomic bomb. The rumors were circulated, but the conflict remained locked in stalemate.[209]

Beyond Korea, the IIA's theme for the first half of 1952 was the second phase of the general "Progress though strength towards peace with freedom" campaign. Assuming that the United States would have recaptured the notion of "peace" from Soviet propagandists by that point, the State Department prepared material around the theme of *Strength* with the subthemes "Aggression has been stopped"; "The Free World is Invincible"; and "The Slave system is doomed." Materials distributed during this phase included a booklet called *Consumer Capitalism in Action*; another, called *The Deadly Parallel*, presented "a 16-page comparison of the similarity between Nazism and Communism." The IIA began to address America's reputation for racism. A documentary film called *Workers for Peace* presented Nobel Peace Prize winners and highlighted the most recent recipient, African-American Ralph Bunche.[210] Black American athletes figured prominently in IIA publicity relating to the Helsinki Olympics.[211] Book translations included numerous versions of the biography of the black agricultural scientist George Washington Carver,[212] and the administration created a glossy booklet presenting a range of black American achievements angled to balance the image of an impermeable color bar: *The Negro in American Life*.[213]

206   *FRUS 1952–1954, Vol. XV*, Memo of conversation by DASoS Far Eastern Affairs (Johnson) w. Tomlison (British Embassy, Washington), 3 March 1952, pp. 73–4.
207   *FRUS 1952–1954, Vol. XV*, Memo re JCS/State Dept. meeting, 19 March 1952, p. 101.
208   *FRUS 1952–1954, Vol. XV*, editor's note, pp. 343–4; for a PSB paper on the allegations see DDEL NSC Staff, OCB Secretariat Series, box 3, Ideological documents, file 2, PSB-D-25 a, draft, 24 July 1952.
209   *FRUS 1952–1954. Vol. XV*, DASoS for Public Affairs (Phillips) to Special Assistant to SoS for Public Affairs (MacKnight), 3 September 1952, p. 484.
210   *FRUS 1952–1954, Vol. II, pt. 2*, Quarterly Propaganda Emphases, 15 February 1952, pp. 1616–25. The centerpiece of the film campaign was a three-part documentary called *Peace with Freedom*. The three episodes were *Peace Worth Having, Keeping the Peace*, and *Defending the Peace*.
211   NA RG 306, Office of Administration, 1952–5, box 4, file "private enterprise and co-op," Walsh to Barrett, "1952 Olympics Progress Report no. 4." ND circa December 1951. Other strategies connected to the Olympics included emphasis on the presence of one official minder for each Eastern bloc athlete at the Oslo Winter Olympics; see Walsh to Compton, 3 April 1952.
212   UoA Fulbright papers, box A 143, BCN30-F20, "Books Published Abroad, July 1, 1950–Dec. 31, 1950," Department of State, 1954.
213   Filed at HSTL Sargeant papers, box 4, Corresp, ASoS for Public Affairs, 1952, Barrett to Sargeant, 21 January 1952.

It is fitting, given Compton's cerebral background, that the most enduring initiative of 1952 was an academic journal called *Problems of Communism*. Inspired by the HICOG's German journal *Ost-Probleme* (Eastern Problems), *Problems of Communism* sought to supply the world's intellectuals with "high-quality, well documented materials on communism." Appearing bimonthly, the journal presented articles, book extracts, and reviews. Its illustrations regularly included cartoons from the Soviet satire journal *Krokodil*. The pilot issue offered an article by Franz Borkenau, "Double Purge in Czechoslovakia"; a review of a monograph on the Hitler–Stalin Pact; an *Izvestia* piece in which the newspaper tied itself into knots trying to explain the absence of the "withering of the state" predicted by Lenin; and a delicious *Krokodil* cartoon in which an artist responds to a party directive by simply renaming all his paintings (a view of a goat on a farm called "Dusk Is Falling" becomes "Future Site of Agrogorod"). The journal found its way into libraries around the world and ran until 1992.[214]

Compton's public relations problems included management of world reaction to the Rosenberg Case. Scientists Julius and Ethel Rosenberg had been convicted of betraying atomic secrets to the U.S.S.R. in January 1951 and sentenced to death. As their case moved into a succession of appeals, it became a *cause célèbre* for the U.S. left. Soviet propaganda presented the Rosenbergs as persecuted Communists who also happened to be Jewish and stepped up this attack at the time of the purge trial of their own Communist who happened to be Jewish, Rudolph Slansky in Czechoslovakia. The IIA responded by transmitting full details of the Rosenberg court proceedings to posts, including a report by the American Civil Liberties Union. The VOA covered both the Rosenberg and Slansky cases in depth and used the rigorous procedure of the former as a potent contrast to the show-trial tactics in Czechoslovakia.[215]

The Communist germ warfare libel sparked internal pressure on Compton to reply in kind with his own "big lie." He set his face firmly against such a course, arguing, "We have said that the Voice of America will not be the voice of Americans unless it is the voice of truth; and if we were to seek to model after international Communists, that we would lose even if we won."[216] Compton's emphasis on credibility was born out by audience research. A University of Chicago study comparing the VOA and BBC broadcasts to Germany in 1948 and 1949 noted that the British were thought more credible. The study also remarked on the success of the BBC strategy of avoiding excessive "self projection" and paying attention to the problems of the listener's own country.[217]

[214] NA RG 306–93–0134, *Problems of Communism*, box 1, vol. 1.

[215] *FRUS 1952–1954, Vol. II, pt. 2*, Deputy ASoS for Public Affairs (Phillips) to USoS (Bruce), 11 December 1952, pp. 1640–41. For a report comparing VOA and RFE coverage of the Slansky case (compiled by RFE with VOA help), see DDEL WHCF, OF 133-M-1, box 673, Jan Stransky (RFE) to CD Jackson, 28 January 1953, noting that both stations mounted effective coverage; though the VOA had a more satiric tone, RFE gave move attention to the issue of anti-Semitism.

[216] *FRUS 1952–1954, Vol. II, pt. 2*, Report by the administration of the USIIA (Compton) to the Secretary of State (Acheson), transmitted 29 July 1952.

[217] HSTL Hulten papers, box 17, VOA 1951, program evaluation branch, report no. A-93, VOA & BBC broadcasts to Germany in 1948–9; 15 March 1951. The report also asked a further important question: "From the standpoint of appearing to be objective and not giving the impression of boastfulness, should the VOA increase its attention to American problems and deficiencies?"

Meanwhile the VOA worked to extend its reach. Innovations in 1952 included the deployment of *Courier*, a former coastguard ship refitted to carry a 150-kilowatt medium-wave radio transmitter, two 35-kilowatt shortwave transmitters, and enough stores to operate self-sufficiently for six months. A helium balloon held the main antenna aloft. Truman personally inaugurated the vessel, making a dramatic broadcast speech in praise of its "Cargo of Truth" on 4 March 1952.[218] The inauguration of *The Courier* caught the imagination of newspapers around the world. On 1 April, *El Tiempo* in Bogota, Columbia carried a cartoon of the ship punching a hole in a riveted iron curtain, while Stalin clung helplessly above and quaintly dressed peasants labeled Hungary, Bulgaria, China, and so forth applauded from the shore. The Communist press fulminated against the increased flow of lies. Listeners as far away as India heard the test broadcast.[219] On 7 September, *The Courier* began its regular broadcasts from its anchorage in Rhodes Harbor. It carried short- and medium-wave transmissions in nine languages: Turkish, Persian, Hebrew, Arabic, English, Armenian, Georgian, Azerbaijani, and Tartar. Monitors reported excellent reception; however, the VOA's budget did not permit the creation of sister ships. *Courier* remained unique.[220]

The year 1952 was a presidential election year and the campaign proved an invaluable source of positive stories for the U.S. information apparatus. A VOA commentary in May contrasted Stalin's ever-tightening hold on power with the decision taken by Truman that it would be inappropriate to run again. Truman himself read the script and communicated his approval.[221] The IIA took care to make clear that U.S. foreign policy was based on the will of the people and was unlikely to shift as a result of the coming election.[222] But the election soon developed particular implications for U.S. propaganda policy. When Dwight D. Eisenhower announced that he was seeking the Republican nomination, there was suddenly an excellent chance that the next man to sit in the White House would be an outspoken advocate of international information. The Republican Convention of July 1952 provided poetic revenge for U.S. information. Its friend, Eisenhower, received 845 votes, whereas its detractor, Robert A. Taft of Ohio, netted only 280 votes. Eisenhower's staff included a number of enthusiasts for propaganda, among them C. D. Jackson and Abbott Washburn. It was Jackson who presented Eisenhower with his winning campaign promise: "I will go to Korea."[223]

[218]   On speech see HSTL OF 20E box 165, VOA file 2; On the background to the *Courier* Barrett, *Truth Is Our Weapon*, p. 127, and Pirsein, *Voice of America*, p. 174. The project had the codename VAGABOND.

[219]   HSTL Hulten papers, box 19, VOA 1952, Div. Of Radio Program Evaluation, VOA highlights, No. 17, 15 May 1952

[220]   HSTL, PSF, box 219, 126th meeting of NSC, PSB D-34, "Progress Report on the National Psychological Effort for the Period July 1 1952, through September 30, 1952," 30 October 1952, Annex A, p.8.

[221]   HSTL PSF general, box 121, Voice of America, Commentary # 173 by Howard Maier, "Pravda Enters the American Election." 26 May 1952; HSTL Acheson memos of conversations, box 71, June 1952, memo of conversation with the President, 5 June 1952.

[222]   HSTL WHCF CF box 43, State Dept. 1952, Sargeant to Short (White House), 11 July 1952 with attachment: IA special instruction, 1952 U.S. presidential campaign, 8 July 1952.

[223]   Dwight D. Eisenhower, *Mandate for Change, 1953–1956*, New York: Doubleday & Co., 1963, pp. 72–3

In August 1952, Jackson and Washburn briefed Eisenhower on the conclusions of the Princeton Conference.[224] Eisenhower took the recommendations on board, and reform of the U.S. information apparatus became a major issue in the campaign. On 8 October he told an audience in San Francisco: "The present administration has never yet been able to grasp the full import of a psychological effort put forth on a national scale." He developed his theme: "While we have been dozing at the gate, the psychological strategists of communism have crept into our citadel." Eisenhower proposed a concerted national psychological effort under "men of exceptional qualifications" and called for Americans to "realize that as a nation everything we do, and everything we fail to say or do, will have its impact on other lands. It will affect the minds and wills of men and women there."[225] With a pledge to trade containment for decisive action, Eisenhower swept to victory in November.

The coming of Eisenhower meant the departure of the key figures in Truman's information policy, although many remained active in the cause of U.S. information. Bill Benton lost his Senate seat and returned to Chicago to run the *Encyclopaedia Britannica*. He advised his successors, testified to the Senate, served on a variety of panels, and represented Presidents Kennedy and Johnson as U.S. ambassador to UNESCO. He died in 1973.[226] Edward W. Barrett wrote a rousing book in defense of the information program, called *The Truth Is Our Weapon*. He went on to work in public relations as executive vice president of Hill and Knowlton and then served as dean of the Columbia Graduate School of Journalism, where his initiatives included a scheme to teach U.S. journalistic ethics to overseas students and, with ex-VOA director Lou Cowan, the foundation of the *Columbia Journalism Review*. He died in 1989.[227] Howland Sargeant left office frustrated that he had not been able to advise the Secretary of State on domestic or foreign public opinion. From 1954, he presided over the new radio station aimed at Russia, named Radio Liberation, and at a more genteel end of international cultural relations, from 1980 he directed the Harkness Fellowships of the Commonwealth Fund of New York, bringing students from the British Commonwealth to American universities. He died in 1984.[228] George V. Allen returned to play a key role in the later Eisenhower years. The lackluster Wilson Compton remained in office.

224 DDEL CD Jackson papers, box 83, Princeton Meeting, Washburn to Eisenhower, c. August 1952.
225 DDEL presidential (Ann Whitman) speech series, box 2, file 3, "Text of address . . . October 8 1952." Looking back on the election, the *Economist* observed, "Belief in the powers of psychological warfare became, during the election, almost an article of faith for Republicans, often perverted into a simpleminded conviction that a blast on a high-frequency shortwave trumpet would bring down the walls of the Soviet Jericho. The myth that there was a new secret weapon, which had been overlooked by the Truman administration in its lackadaisical fumbling, was on the way to being born." "Psychological Discords," *The Economist*, 21 March 1953.
226 Alden Whitman, "William Benton Dies Here at 72," *New York Times*, 19 March 1973, p. 73.
227 UA Fulbright papers, box A571, Barrett to Fulbright, 9 October 1957; Glen Fowler, "Edward W. Barrett, 79, Ex-journalism Dean dies," *New York Times*, 25 October 1989, p. D.29.
228 Joan Cook, "Howland Sargeant, State Dept. Official from 1947 to 1952," *New York Times*, 2 March 1984, p. B.5; HSTL Sargeant papers, box 5, corresp. misc. 1953, Sargeant to Acheson, 16 January 1953 (which also deals with Sargeant's concerns over UNESCO); Sargeant also served as president of the trustees of Radio Liberation (later known as Radio Liberty) from 1954 to 1975.

Truman left a mixed legacy in the field of propaganda. His policies had opened as many questions as they had answered. With multiple initiatives, the structure of U.S. propaganda had operated in a permanent state of flux, as revealed by its bewildering succession of acronyms. It was a mercy that the name on the door overseas remained United States Information Service. Essential questions of structure, division of labor, and the role of the Voice of America remained unanswered. The key new structure in U.S. foreign policy making – the National Security Council – had no seat for a senior representative of the information program, thus building a future role for information as a tool rather than a dimension of U.S. foreign policy. Some of the best aspects of the programs that Truman had inherited were sacrificed to Cold War expedience. The old ideas of reciprocity and mutual exchange that underpinned the original State Department cultural initiatives were superseded by what one historian has termed "the pursuit of power."[229] Finally, although the Truman years saw an expansion of U.S. information overseas, this was not because Benton, Barrett, and its other advocates had won their debate and convinced Capitol Hill that sound information policies should be an essential component of twentieth-century foreign policy. Congress accepted their program only as an adjunct of the Cold War, and many legislators were hostile despite this. The international information program was built on inherently unstable foundations. Any future thaw in the Cold War would leave U.S. information vulnerable and exactly where it began in August 1945: fighting for its life.

[229] Ninkovich, *Diplomacy of Ideas*, p. 168.

2 Mobilizing "the P-Factor"

EISENHOWER AND THE BIRTH OF THE USIA, 1953–56

> It is not enough for us to have sound policies, dedicated to the goals of universal peace, freedom and progress. These policies must be made known to and understood by all peoples throughout the world.
>
> Dwight D. Eisenhower, 30 July 1953.[1]

President Eisenhower took office with an unequivocal pledge to wage the Cold War. "Freedom," he declared in his inaugural address, "is pitted against slavery, lightness against the dark."[2] Although he soon backed away from early talk of actually liberating the Communist bloc, Eisenhower worked consistently to reinvigorate U.S. information. As a soldier he had learned the value of the psychological dimension of power – "the P-factor" as he called it – on the battlefield. As President he promptly launched two inquiries into U.S. information overseas: the President's Committee on International Information Activities, chaired by William H. Jackson,[3] and the President's Advisory Committee on Government Organization, chaired by Nelson Rockefeller.[4] Meanwhile, the Senate Foreign Relations Committee continued its investigation of information initiated by Benton and chaired by Fulbright under the new chairmanship of Bourke Hickenlooper (R-IA).[5] The net result of these three

---

[1] Quoted in *USIA 1st Review of Operations, August–December 1953.*

[2] *Public Papers of the Presidents: Dwight D. Eisenhower, 1953.* (*PPDDE*) Washington DC: GPO, 1960, pp. 1–8; for overseas information instructions see *FRUS 1952–1954, Vol. 2, Part 2,* Acheson, InfoGuide Bulletin 237, 19 January 1953.

[3] *PPDDE*, p. 8, noting that the decision was taken in cabinet on 23 January 1953. For advanced news of the Jackson Committee see James Reston, "Eisenhower plans key staff to guide 'Cold War' policy," *New York Times*, 11 January 1953, quoting heavily from Eisenhower's San Francisco speech of 8 October 1952.

[4] Reich, *The Life of Nelson Rockefeller*, pp. 500–505. The Rockefeller committee promised to pick up where the Truman-era Hoover Commission had left off. Although it was not restricted to information, this was a major element in its brief. Of its three members, Nelson Rockefeller (the chairman), Milton Eisenhower (youngest brother of the President), and Arthur S. Flemming, both Rockefeller and Eisenhower had worked in wartime propaganda. Milton Eisenhower was president of Penn State University and Arthur S. Flemming president of Ohio-Wesleyan University, and later served (1953–7) as Eisenhower's director of the Office of Defense Mobilization.

[5] The Senate subcommittee's agenda included the possible removal of information activities from the State Department. Members were Fulbright (former chair, D-AR), Lister Hill (D-AL), who replaced Benton, William F. Knowland (R-CA), and Theodore Francis Green (D-RI). DDEL Jackson Committee, box 1, "Congress," "Overseas information programs of the United States, Interim report of the committee on foreign relations pursuant to the provisions of S. Res. 74, 82nd Congress, 2nd

committees would be the creation of the United States Information Agency in August 1953.

The idea that information needed an independent agency came from three key sources: Eisenhower's adviser on matters of propaganda, C. D. Jackson; Nelson Rockefeller; and the new Secretary of State, John Foster Dulles. Jackson and Rockefeller both believed that information needed its own agency and Dulles plainly wished to jettison the controversial apparatus from his State Department so that he could focus on traditional diplomacy. Unfortunately this new consensus coincided with a challenge that stopped the U.S. information machine dead in its tracks. It was the fourth major investigation of 1953: hearings on the VOA and the State Department overseas library program mounted by the Permanent Subcommittee on Investigations of the Senate Committee on Government Operations, chaired by Senator Joseph McCarthy.

McCarthy moved against the Voice of America in late February 1953. Although there had been a flurry of subpoenas and newspaper articles in the weeks before, the attack still came as a shock. On 20 February 1953, a knot of staff in the VOA newsroom clustered around a loudspeaker listening to the first day of the public hearings live over a line to Washington. They caught the name of Virgil Fulling, a colleague on the Latin America desk, in the flow of proceedings and called for Fulling to come and listen. With a chill the newsroom suddenly became aware that Fulling's chair was empty. He was McCarthy's next witness. As they listened, Fulling mumbled out a tale of news copy manipulated to blunt its anti-Communist content. He named the guilty parties: VOA news editors Robert Goldmann and Donald Taylor and their chief, Hal Berman. "Do you think they were Communists?" asked Democrat Senator Henry M. Jackson. Fulling replied with well-practiced ease: "I would not like to state my opinion on that, senator. I would be very glad for the committee to determine." A nightmare had begun.[6]

1) THE ORDEAL
THE MCCARTHY CRISIS AND THE CREATION OF THE USIA, JANUARY–JULY, 1953

Eisenhower trusted one man to steer his approach to U.S. propaganda overseas: Charles Douglas Jackson, known to all as "C. D." Born in New York City in 1902 and the heir to a marble import business, C. D. Jackson spent much of his youth in Europe. He graduated from Princeton in 1924, where he hoped to teach French literature, but the death of his father forced him to take over the family firm. When the depression killed America's demand for marble he found a new niche as assistant to the publisher Henry Luce. Here Jackson shone. As general manager of *Life*, he steered that

session." Also box 11, "Hickenlooper Subcommittee." Marcy (Subcommittee staff) to Washburn, 10 April 1953; also *FRUS 1952–1954, Vol. II, pt. 2*, p. 1627.
[6] Interview: Robert B. Goldmann, 26 December 1996; Robert B. Goldmann, *Wayward Threads*, Evanston, IL: Northwestern University Press, 1997, pp. 164–5.

magazine to phenomenal success.[7] Jackson's career as a propagandist began during
the period of American neutrality before Pearl Harbor. In the summer of 1940 he
founded the interventionist pressure group the Council for Democracy. In the war he
served successively as special assistant to the U.S. ambassador in Turkey, deputy chief
of the OWI Overseas Division for North Africa and the Middle East, and from January
1944 to July 1945, deputy chief of the Political Warfare Division of SHAEF, where he
earned the enduring respect of General Eisenhower.[8] Not all his wartime adventures
were strictly military. He pursued a relationship with the wife of the British Foreign
Secretary, Anthony Eden. Beatrice Eden filed for divorce and moved to New York in
1945 hoping to marry Jackson. She was disappointed.[9]

After the war, Jackson returned to the Luce empire as managing director of Time–
Life International and then as publisher of *Fortune* magazine. In February 1951 he
took leave to head the National Committee for a Free Europe and campaign for
Eisenhower, stressing the need to prepare U.S. propaganda to exploit the "coming
crisis" in Soviet power. With the White House secure, Eisenhower asked Jackson to
draft his inaugural address and then to coordinate the U.S. psychological approach
to the world in the new post of special assistant for psychological warfare, known
colloquially as the "special assistant for the Cold War."[10]

Jackson's early duties included representing John Foster Dulles on the President's Committee on International Information Activities, known by the name of
its chair, William H. Jackson (an investment banker, former deputy director of the
CIA and no relation). Abbott Washburn served as the committee's executive secretary.[11] The Jackson Committee consulted 250 witnesses, including senior staff
from the International Information Administration and the Marshall Plan, as well
as such well-informed outsiders as Ed Murrow. The committee's background reading

---

[7] An outline biography for Jackson prepared by *Time* at the time of his death in September 1964
     can be found with the C. D. Jackson papers at the Dwight D. Eisenhower library, Abilene, Kansas.
     For essays on Jackson see Blanche Wiesen Cook, "First Comes the Lie: C. D. Jackson and Political
     Warfare," *Radical History Review*, no. 31 (1984), 42–70; H. W. Brands, "C. D. Jackson: Psychological
     Warriors Never Die." in H. W. Brands, *Cold Warriors: Eisenhower's Generation and American Foreign
     Policy*, New York: Columbia University Press, 1988, pp. 117–37; Valur Ingimundarson, "Containing
     the Offensive: The 'Chief of the Cold War' and the Eisenhower Administration's German Policy."
     Presidential Studies Quarterly, 27, 3 (Summer 1997), 480–96.
[8] On C. D. Jackson and the Council for Democracy see Chadwin, *The Hawks of World War II*,
     p. 114.
[9] The relationship is noted in D. R Thorpe, *Eden: The Life and Times of Anthony Eden, First Earl of
     Avon, 1897–1977*. London: Chatto & Windus, 2003, pp. 311, 338; David Dutton, *Anthony Eden: A
     Life and Reputation*. London: Arnold, 1997, pp. 232, 469–70.
[10] Eisenhower, *Mandate for Change*, p. 100; on the coming crisis of Soviet power see DDEL CD Jackson
     papers, box 79, NCFE Operation Marshmallow, Jackson to Dulles, 18 April 1952.
[11] DDEL Jackson Committee, box 1, White House press release #6, 26 January 1953. The other com-
     mittee members were Robert Cutler (Eisenhower's special assistant for national security affairs), the
     advertising executive Sigurd Larmon (who served on the Advisory Commission on Information, but
     here represented the Mutual Security Agency), Gordon Gray (the first director of the PSB), John
     C. Hughes (chair of the executive committee of the National Committee for a Free Europe), and
     a businessman (and sometime CIA consultant), Barklie McKee Henry. Deputy Secretary of Defense
     Roger M. Kyes joined the team in February.

included the Fulbright committee's staff studies of British and Soviet information programs.[12] The Jackson Committee also kept a weather eye on the parallel investigations of U.S. propaganda. The views of the Rockefeller committee members were soon well known.[13] In mid-February, C. D. Jackson called on Hickenlooper to see how his deliberations might interlock. Hickenlooper confided that he thought the VOA "a dangerous mess" that had "materially contributed to the toboggan slide" of U.S. prestige, but Jackson was relieved that the Senator at least had a constructive response: "the solution is not to kill information activities but to set up some good ones."[14]

Hickenlooper's witnesses included a delegation from Hollywood, led by Eric Johnston, president of the Motion Picture Association of America, who gave a fascinating account of Hollywood's informal system of cooperation with the State Department. He and fellow witness George Weltner (president of Paramount and chairman of the foreign managers' committee of the Motion Picture Export Association) stressed the film industry's commitment to spreading images of democracy and cited research to refute the European claim that Hollywood films promoted crime. They also set out the role of the Production Code Administration (or more specifically one Addison Durland) in advising Hollywood on the implications of particular elements in their scripts for foreign audiences. Weltner explained the system at Paramount where a multilingual Italian-American named Luigi Luraschi "screens every script before it goes on the set...battles with the directors and the script writers with regard to scenes that he thinks will either offend a foreign nation or be offensive from the standpoint of placing America in a wrong light." Weltner reported daily contact with Luraschi. He did not mention (or perhaps did not know) that Luraschi also reported to the CIA. But whatever the new structure, Hollywood was ready to play its part.[15]

While the investigations rolled forward, the IIA remained hard at work. Initiatives in 1953 included a new response to the Soviet "Hate America" campaign: presenting such attacks as "a general assault on non-Communist governments and peoples."[16]

12 DDEL Jackson Committee, box 13, misc. PCIIA reading material; box 12, "Labor Info in Europe," report 2 February 1953; box 13, MSA, report n/d; box 1, "Bibliography, PCIIA" "Reading Materials Available to the Committee."
13 See DDEL Jackson Committee, box 1, file "Bearing on Report 4," U.S. Advisory Commission on Information, 7th semi annual report to Congress, January 1953. Washburn annotations as recorded above.
14 DDEL Jackson Committee, box 11, CD Jackson to Washburn, 19 February 1953.
15 *Hearings before a Subcommittee of the Committee on Foreign Relations United States Senate, Eighty-Third Congress, First Session on Overseas Information Programs of the United States*, Washington: GPO, 1953, pp. 231–98, esp. pp. 235, 292. Luraschi's role is also documented in David N. Eldridge, "'Dear Owen': The CIA, Luigi Luraschi and Hollywood, 1953," *Historical Journal of Film, Radio and Television*, 20, 2 (June 2000), 149–98. The Jackson Committee also made contact with Hollywood; see DDEL Jackson Committee, box 4, DeMille, Interview 23 April 1953 and box 11, Zanuck, report 20 April 1953. For background on Addison Durland see Brian O'Neil, "The Demands of Authenticity: Addison Durland and Hollywood's Latin Image during World War Two," in Daniel Bernardi (ed.), *Classic Hollywood, Classic Whiteness: Race and the Hollywood Studio System*, Minneapolis: University of Minnesota Press, 2000.
16 *FRUS 1952–1954, Vol. 2, Part 2*, InfoGuide Bulletin 241, 26 January 1953, pp. 1654–5.

Sensitive issues that spring included Eisenhower's decision to sustain the death sentence on the spies Julius and Ethel Rosenberg. IIA directives urged "matter-of-fact treatment" of this case and suggested that USIS posts contrast the due process seen in the United States with "travesties of justice" in the Soviet sphere. The IIA provided documents to support foreign press coverage of the Rosenbergs up to and following their execution in June.[17]

All hope that the IIA might operate normally during the period of the reviews vanished when Senator McCarthy launched his attack on the VOA. McCarthy found a quick route to the heart of the Voice. He recruited disgruntled employees, eager to testify against their bosses. Grouses and gripes that would have otherwise remained at the level of stairwell mutterings became the raw material for McCarthy's tale of Communist conspiracy. The Senator's chief source was a Romanian-born broadcaster called Paul Deac who styled himself leader of a "Loyal American Underground" at the VOA. He had no shortage of stories of how his colleagues had mismanaged the Voice in ways that served Stalin's grand design. Deac did not testify himself. He delivered a succession of witnesses eager to serve his agenda, including an engineer named Lewis J. McKeeson. Employed at the VOA from December 1949 to November 1952, McKeeson had resigned because he believed that the two relay stations servicing the Ring Plan, code-named Baker East and Baker West, were being built too far north. The same magnetic forces that created the aurora borealis would, McKeeson claimed, ruin the VOA's signal. McCarthy smelled a Communist rat.[18]

Word of the McCarthy investigation reached Secretary of State John Foster Dulles on 12 February 1953 in a telephone call from the Senator's associate, columnist George Sokolsky. Dulles raised no objections and added that the investigation might be "helpful" so long as it did not "unfairly try to blame" Dulles himself for things he "had nothing to do with." The Secretary of State seemed willing to use McCarthy as a peasant farmer uses fire, to burn away unwanted foliage and prepare the ground for the new crop. The hearings would also justify his new security procedures at State.[19] McCarthy's assault began on 13 February with a round of closed hearings on the Voice and lurid claims in the *Chicago Tribune*. The public hearings began on 20 February 1953.[20] McCarthy's team included two young zealots: his chief counsel, Roy Cohn, prosecuting attorney from the Rosenberg trial, and chief consultant G. David Schine,

---

[17] *FRUS 1952–1954, Vol. 2, Part 2*, InfoGuide Bulletin 260, 11 February 1953, pp. 1668–70; see also InfoGuide Bulletin 378, 13 June 1953, and Info Attaché Embassy Netherlands to SoS, 18 August 1953.

[18] Pirsein, *The Voice of America*, pp. 239–74.

[19] *FRUS 1952–1954, Vol. 2, Part 2*, Dulles telephone conversation with George Sokolsky, 12 February 1953, pp. 1670–71. The VOA director only heard of the impending inquiry on 9 February; see NA RG 306 Office of Administration, box 1, file: McCarthy, Kimball, Memo for the record, "New York Investigation . . ." 11 February 1953; Compton to Dulles, 13 February 1953. For detailed discussion of Dulles' motives see Krugler, *The Voice of America*, pp. 200–202.

[20] See *Executive Sessions of the Senate Permanent Subcommittee on Investigations of the Committee on Government Operations*, 83rd Congress, 1st session, made public January 2003, Washington DC: GPO, 2003, vol. 1, pp. 457 et seq. Also *Senate Committee on Government Operations, State Department Information Program – The Voice of America: Hearings before the Permanent Subcommittee on Investigations*, 83rd Congress, 1st session, Washington, DC: GPO, 1953.

heir to a hotel fortune. In preparation for their attack on the VOA, Schine made his family's suite at New York's Waldorf Astoria available as a headquarters. During early February, Cohn and Schine subpoenaed potential witnesses to the suite and cross-examined them. VOA staff spoke with a chill of "going to the Waldorf."[21]

With a spate of negative press stories, by mid-February 1953 the tide of anti-VOA feeling was such that some in the administration considered simply pulling the plug on the Voice. C. D. Jackson wrote to Dulles on 19 February opposing the "immediate liquidation of VOA" on the grounds that this would "almost inevitably be interpreted as evidence of panic" and would shake the confidence of friends overseas.[22] But Jackson did not deny the need to reform the VOA, as he wrote to the IAA administrator a month later: "it is an equally dangerous oversimplification to say, 'kill the Voice' as it is to say, 'the Voice must not be touched.'"[23]

The VOA had few defenders. Neither IIA administrator Wilson Compton nor Alfred Morton, the VOA director appointed in October 1952, stood up to McCarthy. Morton, a former vice president of NBC, urged VOA colleagues in New York to "keep your tailboards up," which earned him the nickname "Tailboard Morton." One colleague recalled: "He wouldn't dare come out of his office, the guy was so scared."[24] Compton did little better. In testimony he conceded waste in the VOA's transmitter projects and promptly resigned.[25] Bereft, the VOA newsroom sought to mount its own defense. The chief of VOA News, an energetic Armenian-American ex-Marine named Barry Zorthian, resolved to appeal directly to the senator's staff and engineered an invitation to the Waldorf. But any confidence Zorthian had as he knocked on the suite door evaporated when a VOA engineering colleague, Howard Hotchner, opened it for Cohn and Schine. Zorthian had underestimated their reach within the Voice. He tried explaining that his newsroom colleagues were loyal. Cohn and Schine cut him off: "Have you ever made a mistake? We want to hear about mistakes," they barked: "Testify about errors." In later years Zorthian recalled that nothing, whether in his service in World War Two or later work in Vietnam, was as terrifying as that encounter. Cornered, Zorthian now knew that the VOA was facing an attack from fanatics.[26]

[21] Interview: Zorthian, 4 December 1995; Thomas C. Reeves, *The Life and Times of Joe McCarthy*. New York: Stein and Day, 1982, p. 489.
[22] DDEL Dulles papers, Telephone calls series, box 1, file 1, Jackson to Dulles, 19 February 1953. At the cabinet meeting on 25 February C. D. Jackson spoke about the problems facing U.S. psychological warfare. DDEL, DDE Cabinet, box 1, minutes of cabinet meeting, 25 February 1953.
[23] NA RG 306, Office of Administration, box 1, McCarthy, C. D. Jackson to Robert Johnson, 17 March 1953.
[24] ADST Oral History: Zorthian.
[25] Pirsein, *The Voice of America*, pp. 239–43. The extent to which Compton jumped or was pushed is unclear. He told the press that, as a loyal Republican, he had told Dulles in December that he was at his disposal and willing to remain in office. He submitted his resignation as a formality and was rather surprised to have it accepted. See "Wilson Compton Quits 'Voice'; Dulles to Pick New Director" (sic), *Washington Star*, 19 February 1953; C. P. Trussell, "Dr. Compton Quits as Head of 'Voice,'" *New York Times*, 19 February 1953.
[26] Interview: Zorthian, 4 December 1995; ADST Oral History: Zorthian. Author conversation with Zorthian, 26 April 2007.

*

Compton's successor was another college president, Robert Livingston
Johnson of Temple University in Philadelphia. Born in 1894, and a co-founding vice
president of Time Inc., Johnson became a millionaire by the age of forty. He headed
the Pennsylvania Relief Administration during the Depression and had recently lobbied
for the reorganization of the executive branch of government. As part of the recruitment process, first Dulles and then Eisenhower assured Johnson that the IIA would
soon be independent of the State Department. Reassured, Johnson accepted what he
thought was an interim commission to investigate the future of the IAA from within.
Johnson was hence somewhat surprised when on 24 February the administration simply announced him as the new administrator of the IAA.[27] The press responded with
just one question: what did he think of McCarthy's inquiry into the VOA? Johnson's
executive assistant, Martin Merson, recorded his boss' carefully worded reply in his
diary for 26 February: "I think he [McCarthy] is a good American who wants to see
the Voice works properly. So do I."[28] Johnson not only revised this judgment but also
became convinced of the existence of a wider conspiracy within the Republican Party
to sabotage the information program. He was too much of a gentleman to publicly
name names.[29]

Johnson brought much to the IIA. He focused on "the expression of American religion" to demonstrate that "the strongest bond between freedom-loving peoples on both sides of the Iron Curtain is their *shared* faith in spiritual values." Johnson doubled the VOA's religious output and shipped a range of religious books to
U.S. libraries overseas under the guidance of a special advisory panel of two bishops
and the U.S. Navy's senior rabbi.[30] Johnson also recruited the man with the best
claim to being God's personal moviemaker, Cecil B. DeMille, to the honorary post
of Chief Consultant for Motion Pictures. DeMille spoke supportively of the IIA's
film in public and private, and hoped that his own output would help. He thought
his remake of *The Ten Commandments* might bring together Christians, Jews, and
Muslims.[31]

Unlike DeMille, Johnson had to work with a cripplingly small budget. The IIA
lost 997 jobs, a disproportionate 403 of which were at the Voice. The VOA's Spanish,

[27] Martin Merson, *The Private Diary of a Public Servant*, New York: Macmillan, 1955, pp. 2–7. See also
FRUS 1952–54, Vol. 2, Part 2, Dulles to Eisenhower, 27 June 1953, pp. 1715–16, and Reich, *The
Life of Nelson Rockefeller*, p. 499.

[28] Merson, *The Private Diary of a Public Servant*, p. 9.

[29] For a retrospective view see DDEL DDE President, Administrative files, box 22, file: R. L. Johnson,
Johnson to Eisenhower, 15 June 1955.

[30] DDEL WHCF, CF, subject files box 99, USIA, file 1, Johnson, "Report on Operations of IIA March
3 to July 31, 1953."

[31] DDEL Jackson Committee, box 4, DeMille, Interview 23 April 1953. IIA also established a Motion
Picture Subcommittee of the U.S. Advisory Commission on Information. Prominent members
included producer Frank Capra and representatives of two Hollywood studios and the educational
film world, under the chairmanship of Mark May. DDEL Jackson Committee, box 12, Misc. file: G–L
[1], Loomis to Washburn, Membership of Motion Picture Subcommittee of IIA Advisory Committee
(sic), 2 April 1953. This did not last.

Portuguese, and Malay services disappeared, while Italian and French suffered major reductions. The VOA's English-language output shrank from nearly six hours a day to a scant thirty minutes. Johnson offset the impact of these cuts by increasing local placement of VOA programs. He also took steps to improve the quality of VOA news, cutting back drastically on argumentative commentaries and focusing on "straight and unbiased news reporting."[32] But it was McCarthy rather than Johnson who defined the era at the IIA.

Before Robert Johnson arrived in Washington, McCarthy opened a second front in his attack on the information machine: U.S. libraries overseas. McCarthy had acquired IIA documents that suggested that, despite a purge in 1952, works by known Communist authors such as Howard Fast could still be found on their shelves. An IIA policy order of 3 February (Order No. 5) recommended evaluating texts by "usefulness" but, realizing the potential for misinterpretation, a second order of 8 February (Order No. 9) banned all works by Communists and fellow travelers. A further order (InfoGuide 272) of 19 February went beyond this, ordering that "librarians should at once remove all books and other materials by Communists, fellow travelers etc., from their shelves and withdraw any that may be in circulation." Lacking storage space, some librarians burnt the offending books. The policy had implications for the Voice of America. Director Alfred Morton wired the State Department to say the VOA "will still quote Stalin . . . and other Communists to the extent that the use of such material advances our cause." When this telegram also found its way to McCarthy, the senator complained. On 24 February, Under Secretary of State Walter Bedell Smith suspended Morton, only to reinstate him the following day. Morton did not stick his head above the parapet again.[33]

While Johnson found his feet in Washington, the rank and file of the VOA in New York prepared a counterattack against McCarthy. The accused editor Harold Berman had family reasons for not wanting to expose himself to McCarthy's inquisition and resigned, but his colleagues Goldmann and Taylor resolved to fight. Fulling's accusation rested on an account of a demonstration in support of the inauguration of Eisenhower held outside of the U.S. embassy in Guatemala on 21 January 1953. As copy editor, Goldmann had removed a particularly repetitious adjective "anti-Communist" and substituted the synonyms "citizens" and "democratic elements." Fulling claimed that the word "democratic" had now become code for "Communist" in a Latin American context, and that hence Goldmann's edits were "softening

---

32   DDEL WHCF, CF, subject files box 99, USIA, file 1, Johnson, "Report on Operations of IIA March 3 to July 31, 1953"; also Murray Marder, "US Information Service Cuts Out 997 Jobs . . . ," *Washington Post*, 23 April 1954. A deal with Associated Broadcasters, Inc. of San Francisco allowed a continued private Spanish language service for Latin America, with some content commissioned by the IIA. See HSTL, Hulten papers, box 15, Dept. of State Info Programs – 1953, press release No. 297, 28 May 1953.

33   Merson, *The Private Diary of a Public Servant*, pp. 12–18; see also *FRUS 1952–54, Vol. 2, Part 2*, IIA (Connors) to DASoS for Admin. (Scott), 20 February 1953, p. 1673. For later policy see InfoGuide 303, 17 March 1953, pp. 1686–7. On burning see Evans (PAO Sydney) to State, 30 April 1953, p. 1709; for further documentation see NA RG 306 Office of Administration, box 1, file: McCarthy.

language to support communism." Goldmann and Taylor assembled documents to demonstrate that they used tough language to talk about communism. The whole newsroom pitched in to help. With the approval of Morton, Taylor and Goldmann asked McCarthy for the right to reply. Goldmann suspected that McCarthy would summon him on short notice. He took to carrying his whole set of defense documents with him at all times.[34]

Meanwhile, McCarthy broadened his approach to smear the VOA with any evidence of deviation from the American mainstream. He hounded the VOA's head of religious broadcasting, Roger Lyons, because an ex-girlfriend claimed he was an atheist. In reality Lyons was a practicing Reformed Jew. In McCarthy's hands an innocent invitation extended by one colleague in the French branch to another to join a house share became a lecherous proposition to join a Marxist sex commune. As the witnesses had been schooled at the Waldorf and then cross-examined in closed session, McCarthy knew exactly the moment to cut off testimony to accentuate a negative impression for the television cameras. Between 3 and 5 March, McCarthy's committee cross-examined the IIA deputy administrator, Reed Harris. Harris' "crime" was cutting the Hebrew service of the VOA in 1952, which Cohn construed as aiding the Communists at a time of anti-Semitic purges in the Eastern bloc. McCarthy's real interest in Harris was his past. While a student at Columbia in 1932 he had written a book called *King Football: The Vulgarization of the American College*, which McCarthy revealed with much camped up horror, included a passage berating that university for dismissing two teachers "for being too radical." Other writings had been reprinted in the *Daily Worker*. Harris explained that he had long held different beliefs, but to no avail. Reed Harris became a veritable Trotsky in McCarthy's version of the VOA. He resigned on 24 April.[35]

On the afternoon of 5 March, McCarthy's committee wired Goldmann and Taylor, demanding that they appear in Washington first thing the next day. The two men jumped onto the night train and braced themselves for battle. Taylor was rather subdued in his testimony, but Goldmann took his seat fired up with indignation. Robert Goldmann had come to the United States as a German-Jewish refugee from Nazi persecution and, although alarmed to see a tyrant in his new homeland, he recognized that the American system afforded him something that the German system had not. "In America," he wrote in his memoirs, "we could fight." He gave the performance of his life. Goldmann eloquently disputed Fulling's claim that "democracy" had become a Communist term. "I think," Goldmann argued, "we should never let the Communists steal that word from us and use it for their own big lie campaigns." After batting the issue back and forth for some forty minutes, McCarthy lost interest. It was a small

---

[34] Interview: Goldmann, 26 December 1996; Goldmann, *Wayward Threads*, pp. 167–9; Interview: Zorthian, 4 December 1995; ADST Oral History: Zorthian. Berman had never married his partner, and wished to spare her and their son humiliation at the hands of McCarthy.

[35] Pirsein, *The Voice of America*, pp. 287–9; Executive Sessions of McCarthy Hearings, Vol.1, pp. 660–712; for Cohn and the Hebrew Service see 704 et seq. The offending pages of Reed Harris, *King Football*. New York: Vanguard Press, 1932, are on pp. 150–51.

victory. Following Goldmann's testimony, McCarthy switched his attention entirely
to the network of U.S. libraries overseas.[36]

*

On 5 March, as the hearings on the VOA reached their climax, Joseph Stalin
died. VOA coverage of his death followed a tough line, dwelling on Stalin's tyranny
and international aggression.[37] The White House, in contrast, appeared rather more
circumspect, as Eisenhower was unsure how to respond. C. D. Jackson and a young
consultant from MIT named Walt Rostow saw the Soviet dictator's demise as "the
first really big propaganda opportunity offered to our side for a long time." They
recommended a dramatic presidential appeal for peace as a first move. John Foster
Dulles, in contrast, favored caution and squashed the idea of an immediate speech.
In the event the new Soviet premier, Georgi Malenkov, preempted any U.S. appeal
with a peace offensive of his own.[38] Eisenhower's counterthrust came on 16 April in
a speech developed by Rostow and Jackson entitled "The Chance for Peace." Seeking
to contest Moscow's hold on the vocabulary of "peace," Eisenhower dwelt on the
word as he urged the Soviet Union to match its fine words with constructive action in
Korea, Germany, and arms control.[39] This "Chance for Peace" speech became a key
element in IIA propaganda that season. The IIA printed three million copies for use in
Europe and Latin America and created a short documentary film version called *Path
to Peace*. The IIA screened the film in its libraries, released it theatrically worldwide
through MGM, and placed the kinescope of the speech on infant television systems
around the world. Its audience in Britain topped six million. "Peace" was no longer
the Kremlin's word alone.[40]

*

On 9 April 1953, Rockefeller's Committee on Government Organization
delivered its recommendation for U.S. information. As expected, it urged a presidential reorganization plan to "Establish a new foreign information agency, in which
would be consolidated the most important foreign information programs and cultural

---

[36] Interview: Goldmann, 26 December 1996; Goldmann, *Wayward Threads*, pp. 167–9.

[37] *Subcommittee on Overseas Information Programs of the United States, Staff Study No. 8, the Voice of
America Broadcasts on the Death of Stalin, Printed for the Use of the Committee on Foreign Relations,*
83rd Congress 1st Session, Washington, DC: GPO, 1953. For IIA preparation for Stalin's death see
FRUS 1952–1954, Vol. VIII, Eastern Europe; Soviet Union, Mediterranean, doc. 545, Revey (Policy
and Plans) to Connors (Ast. Administrator IIA), 25 February 1953, pp. 1080–82.

[38] For PSB contingency planning see *FRUS 1952–1954, Vol. VIII*, doc. 532, PSB D-24, 1 November
1952, pp. 1059–60 and doc. 550, NSC discussion, 4 March 1953, pp. 1091–5. For a full account of
the response to Stalin's death see W. W. Rostow, *Europe after Stalin: Eisenhower's Three Decisions of
March 11, 1953*. Austin, TX: University of Texas Press, 1982; for further comment Hixson, *Parting
the Curtain*, pp. 88–90.

[39] Rostow, *Europe after Stalin*; Brands, *Cold Warriors*, pp. 122–3; *PPPDDE, 1953*, pp. 179–88; *FRUS
1952–1954, Vol. 2, part 2*, InfoGuide Bulletin 342, 22 April 1953, pp. 1699–1706.

[40] DDEL, C. D. Jackson, box 5, movies, Guarco (IMS) to C. D. Jackson, 11 May 1953; Cook, "First
Comes the Lie," p. 56.

and educational exchange programs." The VOA would be part of this new agency.[41] In the Senate, Fulbright maneuvered to ensure that "his" scholarships remained at the State Department.[42] On 23 April, the principal players in the Jackson and Hickenlooper committees and the IIA met at the White House and struck a compromise around the Rockefeller plan. Hickenlooper agreed to accept an independent information agency on condition that educational exchanges could stay at State. C. D. Jackson reluctantly conceded the point as the price of the Senator's acquiescence.[43]

On 1 June 1953, Eisenhower sent Congress Reorganization Plan No. 8, "Relating to the establishment of the United States Information Agency." In an accompanying statement, Eisenhower argued that the new agency was "the one sound way to provide real unity and greater efficiency" in U.S. information. In accordance with Fulbright's wishes, the exchange program would remain at the State Department under the Assistant Secretary of State for Public Affairs but would be administered overseas by USIA personnel. The State Department also retained the UNESCO national commission. The plan imaged two levels of policy coordination: a lateral flow of guidance across from the State Department and integration of the director into the policy-making. The plan made no concrete provision for the USIA director to join the NSC; rather, Eisenhower ordered, "The director of the United States Information Agency shall report to and receive instructions from me through the National Security Council or as I may otherwise direct."[44]

---

[41] DDEL, Presidents Advisory Committee on Government Organization, box 79, No. 91, International Affairs 1953, memorandum for President Eisenhower, #14, Foreign Affairs Organization, 9 April 1953. Rockefeller suggested that the "Hereafter the term 'the Voice of America' should be applied only to statements of the official United States' positions." This idea soon fell by the wayside.

[42] DDEL, papers of John Foster Dulles, telephone call series, telephone conversation with Sen. Hickenlooper, 28 April 1953. Dulles agreed to meet the senators on 29 April to discuss the problem.

[43] Merson, *The Private Diary of a Public Servant*, p. 81. Jackson's daily log indicates a subsequent doubt over John Foster Dulles' position recording a meeting of W. H. Jackson, Dulles, Beedle Smith (USoS), Don Lourie (USoS for Admin), and John Hughes (MSA) "to find out how Foster really wants IIA, in or out. He wants out." DDEL C. D. Jackson papers, box 68, log 1953 [1], 30 April 1953. Eisenhower's own views emerge from a letter to William Benton, who opposed the plan. Eisenhower explained, "My own personal viewpoint is that the Voice of America belongs to the State Department. I personally think that all other activities would be best operated outside the State Department. . . . " Eisenhower felt that the government role in information should be either minimal or covert. He stressed that the "job of presenting the American story throughout the world" should be handled as much as possible by "privately operated enterprises" or through "clandestine arrangements" with foreign publishers. Both types of operation should be "carefully segregated from the official statement of the American position before the world." He also emphasized the value of "deeds" such as the U.S. overseas aid program. Eisenhower concluded, however, "I by no means intend to impose my own individual views upon a program that has been devised by a whole group of devoted people." His implication was clear: if the President could go along with C. D. Jackson and Nelson Rockefeller then so could Benton. DDEL DDE Papers as President, (Ann Whitman File), DDE Diary Series, box 3, President to Benton, 1 May 1953 (also UoC Benton papers, box 384/1).

[44] For text of the relevant messages see *PPPDDE, 1953*, pp. 342–54; for full documentation and administrative diagrams see NA RG 306, Office of Administration, box 1, file: Reorganization Plan – Laws, Executive Orders and Regulations. The State Department and USIA did not finalize their division of labor over the exchange programs until 24 June 1955. For correspondence about this see UoA CU 1–6, 1–7, and 1–8.

*

While Eisenhower planned the future of U.S. information, McCarthy continued to cut a swath though its present operation. His hearings on U.S. libraries overseas had begun on 24 March.[45] But the best-known episode of this inquiry did not take place in Washington but in Europe. On Easter Day (4 April 1953), McCarthy's assistants Cohn and Schine appeared in Paris at the start of a whirlwind tour of U.S. information centers. In ten days the two also visited Bonn, Frankfurt, Munich, Vienna, Belgrade, Athens, Rome, and London in search of waste, subversion, and any left-wing library books. Chaos followed in their wake. Their main victim was Theodore Kaghan, from the office public of affairs at the HICOG in Bonn, who defiantly referred to the pair as "junketeering gumshoes." Summarily recalled to the United States to answer to McCarthy for youthful radicalism, Kaghan resigned. But the real casualty was the image of the United States in Europe.[46] The library hearings continued sporadically through April and May with three sessions in July. U.S. information braced itself for the senator's next sortie.[47]

For the staff of the IIA, one of the bewildering features of McCarthy's inquisition was the failure of Eisenhower to halt it. Jackson blamed the President's "passion" not to offend anyone in Congress.[48] On 14 June Eisenhower broke his silence. In a speech at Dartmouth College he condemned censorship of libraries: "Don't join the book burners . . . How will we defeat Communism unless we know when it is and what it teaches . . . ?"[49] Dulles immediately back-pedaled, claiming (apparently accurately) that the President did not mean U.S. libraries overseas. When the press lauded an American Libraries Association resolution against the IIA blacklist, it seemed clear that the purge had become a major embarrassment. Dulles suspected that some IIA librarians had burned books in "a deliberate effort to discredit the anti-Communist policy."[50] On 1 July, the Psychological Strategy Board noted "the serious effects on world opinion produced by reports of "book burning . . . " and recommended that IIA libraries operate with "the same basic policy with respect to freedom of reading as are

---

45 For full text see *State Department Information Program – Information Centers.* Hearing before the Permanent Subcommittee on Investigations of the Committee on Government Operation, United States Senate, 83rd Congress, 1st session pursuant to S. Res. 40, Washington, DC: GPO, 1953 and Executive Sessions, McCarthy Hearings, Vol. 2.

46 Rovere, *Senator Joe McCarthy,* pp. 199–205; Reeves, *The Life and Times of Joe McCarthy,* pp. 489–91; Nicholas von Hoffman, *Citizen Cohn: The Life and Times of Roy Cohn,* New York: Doubleday, 1988, pp. 144–67. For McCarthy's bulletin to Dulles on the tour see *FRUS 1952–54, Vol. 2, Part 2,* McCarthy to Dulles, 7 April 1953, pp. 1697–8; for documentation on the tour see *FRUS 1952–54, Vol. 1, Part 2,* pp. 1379 et seq. Murray Marder, "McCarthy's 'Junketeering Gumshoes' Flayed by U.S. official Admitting Red Ties in Youth." *Washington Post,* 30 April 1953, p. 7.

47 For full text see *State Department Information Program – Information Centers.* Hearing before the Permanent Subcommittee on Investigations of the Committee on Government Operation, United States Senate, 83rd Congress, 1st session pursuant to S. Res. 40, Washington DC: GPO, 1953 and Executive Sessions, McCarthy Hearings, Vol. 2.

48 Merson, *The Private Diary of a Public Servant,* p. 73.

49 *PPSDDE, 1953,* p. 104.

50 Merson, *The Private Diary of a Public Servant,* pp. 100–126; *FRUS 1952–54, Vol. 2, Part 2,* Dulles to Eisenhower, 27 June 1953, pp. 1715–16.

American libraries in this country."[51] On 8 July the IIA issued new guidelines ending the purge.[52]

The final phase of the drama focused on the IIA administrator, Robert L. Johnson. On 30 June 1953, McCarthy challenged Johnson to answer questions on the IIA's "failure to utilize the writings of proven anti-Communists and ex-Communists to expose communism for what it is."[53] But Johnson now had free hand. On 3 July, he informed Eisenhower that he needed to resign on doctor's orders.[54] Realizing that Johnson could now attack McCarthy, Senator Karl Mundt tried to trade approval of the information budget for a pledge of restraint. Johnson testified regardless, denouncing McCarthy without naming him. "It is one of the tragic ironies of our time," he told the press, "that some of those who are in the forefront of the fight against communism are among those who are damaging the actions of programs that do battle against it." Johnson left office on 29 July.[55]

Sensing that his library investigation had also now run its course, McCarthy set his sights elsewhere. He had found no Communists in the VOA or IIA, but his investigation had damaged the U.S. information effort, bringing morale to an all-time low. Staff resigned not only because of past radicalism, but also out of a simple reluctance to be dragged through the mud. The resignations included Herbert T. Edwards of the Motion Picture Branch, whose crimes included "widespread waste" and the use of "Communist propaganda." McCarthy never explained how else Edwards could obtain footage of life inside the Soviet bloc. The IIA cancelled plans to build the Baker East and Baker West relay stations, setting back VOA modernization by almost ten years. Some paid an even higher price. On 5 March 1953, Raymond Kaplan, a VOA engineer on the Baker project, threw himself under a speeding truck in Boston. His suicide note included the line, "You see, once the dogs are set on you, everything you have done

---

51 *FRUS 1952–54, Vol. 2, Part 2*, memo by acting dir. PSB (George A. Morgan) to USoS (Smith), 6 July 1953.

52 Merson, *The Private Diary of a Public Servant*, p. 126. The new guidelines were hardly liberal and did not represent a commitment to restore purged texts; rather, as *USIA 1st Review of Operations, August– December 1953*, p. 8, noted, "This directive orders that books shall be selected primarily on the basis of their content and value to the information program. It excludes from the shelves, however, the works of avowed Communists, of persons convicted of crimes involving a threat to the security of the United States, and of persons who publicly refuse to answer questions of congressional committees regarding their connections with the Communist movement. No books in those three proscribed categories are currently in our libraries." Many controversial books remained on a restricted list and could only be supplied if necessary for a particular policy objective. Restrictions also remained in the field of music. The agency archives reveal that it was not until 1958 that the agency allowed the completely free use of work by Leonard Bernstein and Aaron Copland. See NA RG 306 64-A-0536, Director's Office Subject files, 1957–8, box 6, file: Security-General, 1958, Walsh to Washburn & media/area directors etc., 20 January and 14 February 1958.

53 NA RG 306 Office of Administration, 1952–5, box 1, McCarthy, McCarthy to Johnson, 30 June 1953.

54 HSTL Sargeant papers, box 5, IIA, 1953–4 [2], White House press release 6 July 1953.

55 Merson, *The Private Diary of a Public Servant*, pp. 100–126; Reeves, *The Life and Times of Joe McCarthy*, p. 491; *FRUS 1952–54, Vol. 2, Part 2*, editorial note pp. 1722–3. For press coverage of Johnson's departure see Paul Healy, "House Oks Voice Cut; Johnson Slaps Joe," *New York Daily News*, 16 July 1953 and Philip Potter, "Head of IIA Hits Critics of Program," *Baltimore Sun*, 16 July 1953.

since the beginning of time is suspect." The friendly witness, Virgil Fulling, resigned and also later took his own life.[56] McCarthy, never one to be restrained by shame, fancied that his hearings had helped to create the independent USIA.[57]

*

The Jackson Report arrived on Eisenhower's desk on 30 June 1953. At its core the report asserted a great and often forgotten truth of information in foreign policy, that "psychological activity is not a field of endeavor separable from the main body of diplomatic, economic, and military measures by which the United States seeks to achieve its national objectives. It is an ingredient of such measures."[58] With this in mind the committee recommended abolishing Truman's Psychological Strategy Board, with its loose connection to the highest tier of policy making. Instead a new body, the Operations Coordinating Board (OCB), would coordinate this area, fully integrated within in the structure of the National Security Council. As with the PSB, the OCB's brief was to integrate the psychological aspects of U.S. foreign and defense policy, but the OCB had a higher-powered membership, including the Under Secretary of State as chair, the director of the CIA, deputy directors from Defense and agencies, and a representative of the President, C. D. Jackson. Eisenhower called the new board into life on 2 September 1953.[59] Its innocuous name was deliberate. The committee felt that "Psychological Warfare" and "Cold War" were both "unfortunate terms" that failed to describe the U.S. effort to "build peace and freedom" and hence should be discarded.[60]

The body of the Jackson Committee report contained the expected plan to create a "consolidated" U.S. information service including the VOA.[61] The report stressed the

56 Heil, *The Voice of America*, pp. 53–5; Goldmann, *Wayward Threads*, p. 167; Merson, *The Private Diary of a Public Servant*, p. 69; Executive Sessions, McCarthy hearings, Vol. 1, p. 769–70. Edwards' immediate successor as head of motion pictures was J. Cheever Cowdin (chairman of Universal Pictures from 1936 to 1949 and later chairman of Ideal Chemicals Inc.), recruited with the help of Cecil B. DeMille – see HSTL, Hulten papers, box 15, Dept. of State Info. Programs – 1953, Press Release No. 325, 17 June 1953. He did not last long in the job.

57 Senate Permanent Subcommittee on Investigations, Annual Report of the Committee on Government Operations, 83rd congress, 2nd session, Rept. No. 881, Washington, DC: GPO, 1954.

58 *FRUS 1952–54, Vol. 2, Part 2*, Jackson Committee to Eisenhower, letter of transmittal, 30 June 1953, p. 1796.

59 DDEL WHCF OF 133-M-1, box 674, press release, 8 July 1953; *FRUS 1952–1954, Vol. II, Pt. 1*, note 455. In his end-of-year report, C. D. Jackson noted with satisfaction that the OCB was working "fast and well" and had "miraculously avoided becoming tagged as the new octopus or Public Enemy Number One." The flow of policy from the OCB to the NSC Planning Board to the NSC to the President and then back to the OCB for "allocation of responsibility, coordination of action plans, and follow through on action" was also "working well," thanks to the cooperation of Robert Cutler at NSC. DDEL DDE President, Administrative files, box 22, file: C. D. Jackson (3), Jackson to Eisenhower, 6 January 1954. A USIA representative attended all NSC Planning Board meetings as an observer; see NA RG 306 Office of Administration, box 4, memo by Washburn, "USIA relationships with the NSC and OCB, 8 September 1954."

60 DDEL WHCF OF 230, box 894, Gray to W. H. Jackson, 10 March 1953. When pondering alternative names for the Psychological Strategy Board, Gordon Gray suggested "Security Strategy Board" as "each of these three words is meaningful and has a connotation . . . of something solid"; WHCF OF 133-M-1, box 674, press release, 8 July 1953.

61 DDEL WHCF OF 133-M-1, box 674, press release, 8 July 1953.

need for "a clear line of demarcation" between the VOA and Radio Free Europe and Radio Liberation (an RFE sister station aimed at Russia, which went on the air on 1 March 1953), noting that as "the official voice of the United States Government" the VOA should broadcast with "restraint and dignity," whereas "All material intended for psychological warfare should be diverted to Radio Liberation or other nonofficial stations."[62] Accordingly, the Jackson committee called for "objective, factual news reporting" as the core of the VOA's output but noted that satire, humor, music, and entertainment also had their place. The committee even suggested renaming the Voice of America as a response to the recent tide of criticism.[63]

The Jackson Committee recommended that the new information agency adapt all broadcasting and information activities to the needs of each target country. It noted that local production of propaganda would save on staffing in the United States and avoid annoying audiences around the world with inappropriate material. "Not all the free world is prepared to view its problems in the context of the struggle between the United States and the Soviet Union," the report noted. "The note of self-praise and the emphasis on material achievements by the United States frequently creates envy and antagonism."[64] The report also suggested another mechanism for minimizing hostility to U.S. propaganda: nonattribution. "As a general rule," the report argued, "information and propaganda should only be attributed to the United States when such attribution is an asset." The committee also suggested use of private U.S. organizations overseas, such as missionaries or labor groups.[65]

Like the Advisory Commission before it, the Jackson committee recommended ending the Smith–Mundt ban on the domestic circulation of IIA material. This was not acted on and would still be raised as a hindrance to U.S. information fifty years later. On the matter of books and libraries, the committee declared that although the U.S. government should not distribute subversive material, it "should not hesitate to distribute books and publications just because they contain criticism of American life." The program as a whole should give "greater attention" to "fundamental beliefs and values" shared with millions of people around the world.[66] The Jackson report stopped short of stating that this new conglomerate should be independent. William H. Jackson and C. D. Jackson agreed to differ on that point, but the findings of the Rockefeller report had already closed the matter.[67]

The reorganization opened the issue of who should preside over the new agency. C. D. Jackson's first choice was Philip D. Reed, chairman of General Electric and

---

[62] *FRUS 1952–54, Vol. 2, Part 2*, Jackson Committee report, pp. 1826–7.
[63] *FRUS 1952–54, Vol. 2, Part 2*, Jackson Committee report, pp. 1846–7, and for the rejection of "re-naming" see OCB progress report, 30 September 1953, p. 1883.
[64] *FRUS 1952–54, Vol. 2, Part 2*, Jackson Committee report, p. 1841.
[65] *FRUS 1952–54, Vol. 2, Part 2*, Jackson Committee report, p. 1841.
[66] DDEL WHCF OF 133-M-1, box 674, press release, 8 July 1953, which defined these values as "belief in God, belief in individual and national freedom, belief in the right to ownership of property and a decent standard of living, belief in the common humanity of all men and in the vision of a peaceful world."
[67] Interview: Washburn, 1 Dec. 1995.

a member of the Advisory Commission. Although not refusing outright, Reed suggested, "No one in his right mind would take the job."[68] The search for a director continued as the deadline for announcing the appointment approached. Hope dawned on the morning of 27 July in the form of a radio executive named Theodore Streibert. Jackson sweetened the USIA directorship by promising top-quality staff including his own deputy, Abbott Washburn, as Streibert's deputy. With all parties satisfied, the White House announced that it had found its man. The first director of the United States Information Agency would be Ted Streibert.[69] With the appointment settled, the USIA came into being on 1 August 1953.[70] In a gesture of solidarity, Eisenhower held Streibert's swearing-in ceremony in the Oval Office.[71]

2) STREIBERT TAKES CHARGE
THE STRUCTURE OF THE USIA IN 1953

Born in Albany, New York, in 1899, Theodore Cuyler Streibert was a former assistant dean of Harvard Business School and a successful broadcasting executive. He was no stranger to the U.S. information program, having worked on the Radio Advisory Committee of the Advisory Commission on Information and advised Robert L. Johnson. He sat on an IIA committee, chaired by former Under Secretary of the Army Tracy S. Voorhees, that had formulated a blueprint for an independent information agency. He had also advised the U.S. High Commissioner in Bonn on restructuring the HICOG's information program.[72] Streibert had an abrasive style. He pinned his staff down to short-term and annual targets and gave a rough ride to any who fell short. Posts soon learned to devise impressive-sounding goals that they knew could be accomplished. Streibert was not without flair. He changed the number of the agency's headquarters from 1778 to 1776 Pennsylvania Avenue, to inspire staff with their connection to the mission of the American Revolution.[73]

Streibert had an excellent staff, beginning with his deputy, Abbott Washburn, the USIA's link to the White House and the NSC. His Assistant Director for Policy and Programs, Andrew Berding (former head of information first for the Marshall Plan in Italy and then for the entire Mutual Security Program), oversaw the delicate process

68 DDEL DDE Papers as President, (Ann Whitman file), Administration Series, box 21, C. D. Jackson 1953, file 2, C. D. Jackson to President, 3 July 1953.

69 DDEL C. D. Jackson papers, box 68, log 1953 (3), 27 and 28 July 1953.

70 For executive order 10477 "Authorizing the Director of the United States Information Agency to Exercise Certain Authority Available by Law to the Secretary of State and the Director of the Foreign Operations Administration," 1 August 1953, see DDEL WHCF, OF247, box 909

71 DDEL WHCF, OF247, box 909, Streibert swearing-in ceremony, 5 August 1953.

72 DDLE OH-153: Oral History interview with Theodore Streibert, 10 December 1970; for the report of the subcommittee of the Radio Advisory Committee of the U.S. Advisory Commission on Information, see HSTL, OF 20E, box 165, VOA [2], Barrett to Elsey, 12 July 1951; on the Voorhees committee see *USIA 1st Review of Operations, August–December 1953*, p. 1, and for report NA RG 306, A1 (1070) USIA historical reports and studies, 1945–94, box 6; HSTL, Hulten papers, box 15, Dept. of State Info. Programs – 1953, press release no. 323, 17 June 1953.

73 ADST Oral History, Adamson; Kraus, Ryan.

of transmitting policy guidance from the State Department to the USIA. Berding and his successors attended the Secretary of State's morning meeting and directed the political output of the USIA and VOA accordingly. The system did not always please the State Department, but it allowed the USIA the dignity of thinking for itself. Streibert's third key man was his special assistant, Henry Loomis, formerly an aide to the president of MIT, a staffer to the PSB, and the CIA representative on the Jackson committee. Loomis founded the USIA's Office of Research and Intelligence in late 1954; this was one of the jewels of the new agency, providing detailed analysis of particular trends in world opinion and responses to major events, and synthesizing the wisdom of agency staff in the field for further dissemination within the wider apparatus of U.S. foreign policy making. His products found their way to the White House; on one occasion, President Eisenhower reportedly waived a text under the nose of John Foster Dulles, exclaiming, "But Foster, you forget the human side." Loomis went on to direct the VOA and serve as deputy USIA director in the Nixon years.[74]

Robert L. Johnson had already made two other important appointments. The new director of the VOA would be Leonard F. Erikson, vice president of the New York advertising agency McCann–Erickson, Inc., and former general sales manager of CBS. No less importantly, given the reputation of information work as a magnet for "radicals," Johnson had, at J. Edgar Hoover's suggestion, recruited a former FBI agent named Charles M. Noone to head the USIA's Office of Security. Noone had a staff of seventy-one and a brief to ensure the security of documents and personnel. In his first six months he sacked thirty-one members of staff for "security reasons." He found no Communists.[75]

The head recruiter for the USIA in the early days was Washburn's old colleague from General Mills, Nate Crabtree. When Crabtree found somebody he wanted for the agency he drove mercilessly for a swift security clearance, demanding and sometimes getting a clearance within forty-eight hours. For years thereafter the USIA staff called obtaining a quick security clearance "doing a Crabtree."[76] For lesser recruits, the USIA's tight security procedures came as something of a surprise to new staff. A young recruit to the Voice of America in 1955, Bernie Kamenske, recalled that shortly after his successful interview, two earnest black-suited security officers toured his Boston Jewish neighborhood asking questions about him. His elderly neighbors mistook them for marriage brokers. All their answers were therefore angled to impress a potential spouse with Kamenske's virility. Given the security office's underlying worries about

74 Interview: Abbott Washburn, 1 December 1995; Thomas Sorensen, *The Word War*, p. 83.

75 Interview: Abbott Washburn, 1 December 1995. For biographies of top USIA staff, see *USIA 2nd Review of Operations, January–June 1954*, pp. 29–32. For Johnson press releases see HSTL, Hulten papers, box 15, Dept. of State Info. Programs – 1953, press releases no. 324, 17 June 1953 and no. 349, 1 July 1953; *USIA 1st Review of Operations, August–December 1953*, p. 5.

76 Interview: Abbott Washburn, 1 December 1995; Burnett Anderson in Hans N. Tuch and G. Lewis Schmidt, *Ike and USIA: A Commemorative Symposium*, Washington, DC: USIA Alumni Association/Public Diplomacy Foundation, 1991, p. 24.

staff sexuality the misunderstanding probably helped his case.[77] But tight security made it hard to hire foreigners. The VOA noted that the BBC had no such trouble.[78]

There was one further dimension to staffing: the possibility that the USIA could be used as cover for the CIA. Here Streibert took an emphatic line. Noone's successor as chief of the office of security, Joseph C. Walsh, had the message drilled into him by his boss: Under no circumstances was the agency to be used as cover for any CIA personnel, as exposure would destroy the USIA's credibility. Streibert warned that if any "CIA type, by whatever method" got into the agency, it would cost Walsh his job. Walsh remained appropriately watchful. Rumors that the USIS staff were actually CIA agents recurred regardless. In early-sixties Tanzania the Public Affairs Officer found that the swiftest way to scotch such stories was to hire the mistress of the brother of that country's president as a secretary. In Vietnam just a few years later – and in one or two other times and places – such rumors were true.[79]

For its overseas operations the USIA retained the name United States Information Service, as the acronym "USIS" was now so well known. Members of the USIS field staff were veterans of the IIA, ECA, and even OWI programs. Most senior staff had been journalists. A compendium of biographical sketches of the nineteen key public affairs officers assembled for Congress in 1955 gave journalistic backgrounds for PAOs in Argentina, Brazil, Britain, Egypt, Germany, Japan, India, Italy, Korea, Spain, and Thailand. Six had attended Ivy League universities and all were white males with Anglo-Saxon surnames.[80]

The USIA's field staff included a small number of black Americans, whose presence did something to counteract America's deserved reputation for bigotry. In the spring of 1955 the White House requested a full list of such personnel to appease the African American congressman from New York, Adam Clayton Powell, who had begun to agitate for black Americans to be sent overseas. The agency listed eleven men, the most senior being Frank Snowden, Cultural Affairs Officer in Rome, and Lemuel Graves, chief of the editorial branch in Paris. The list included a press officer in New Delhi and PAOs in Lagos, Nigeria; Medan, Indonesia; and two PAOs in Accra, on

[77] Interview: Bernie Kamenske, 6 December 1995.
[78] NA RG 306 250/67/04/07, ORI Report S-23–53, The Philosophy of the BBC, 30 November 1953, noted that "The BBC has the advantage over the VOA in not having any laws against hiring aliens. It is able to get people who know the particular audience immediately – somebody who knows every street, every store, every hotel in a particular city." As cited in Vaughan, *The Anglo-American Relationship and Propaganda Strategies in the Middle East, 1953–1957*, p. 34.
[79] ADST Oral History: Joseph C. Walsh and Charles Robert Beecham. Burnett Anderson, who was agency liaison with the CIA in the early 1960s, also maintained a firewall (interview: Anderson, 14 December 1995). In a press interview in 1992, agency veteran Walter Roberts conceded that "occasionally in the beginning" CIA agents had used the USIA for cover; see David Binder, "American Voice of Cold War Survives, but in Different Key," *New York Times*, 4 February 1992, A.8. Some CIA agents were apparently integrated into the Joint United States Public Affairs Office apparatus with a USIA affiliation.
[80] *USIA 4th Report to Congress, January to June 1956*: The PAO in Pakistan had mixed journalism with a stint as publicity director for the CIO. Other exceptions were the president of a private art company who ran Tehran; a radio scriptwriter in Taipei; the former "assistant to the director of research at the Industrial College of the Armed Forces" in Manila; a college "instructor in languages" in Paris; and a "college professor in public relations" who ran USIS Vienna.

the Gold Coast. The agency clearly understood the value of nonwhite staff in the developing world. The White House thought the list "very impressive," but in reality, the USIA, like the rest of the government, had a long way to go.[81] The only mention of women in early USIA reports was a feature in a report to Congress on the voluntary contributions of "USIS wives" to the communities in which their husbands served.[82] Subsequent generations at the USIA would reflect much greater diversity, including two African-American directors, a host of senior women, and strong representation from first and second generation Americans with a keen appreciation for the values they and their families had found in their new home.[83]

*

Streibert took charge of the USIA at an auspicious moment: an armistice in Korea, riots in East Germany, and the fall of the left-leaning Prime Minister of Iran, Mohammed Mossadegh, as a result of a combined operation by the CIA and British intelligence all suggested an upturn in America's fortunes abroad. The CIA's campaign in Iran included much covert propaganda, including faked documents to establish Mossadegh as an irreligious dupe of Moscow. The USIA was marginal to the plan, but following the coup, USIS Tehran launched a vigorous campaign to boost the restored regime of Shah Mohammed Reza Pahlavi. Streibert ordered flat denials of any U.S. involvement in the coup and, noting the growing myth around Mossadegh, also ordered that the agency "neither originate nor pick up comment" on the deposed leader, except when absolutely necessary "for credibility." In October 1953, Streibert ordered the embassy in Tehran to send copies of its materials supporting the Shah to "help create reaction favorable [to the] new regime [and] U.S. aid effort" at home. The request breached the Smith–Mundt Act, but no one minded.[84] Events in Iran taught the administration to trust covert action. It proved a dangerous precedent.

The unrest in East Berlin began on 17 June and soon spread across the country. The image of a worker's paradise disintegrated in the face of the brutal repression.[85] RIAS, now the USIA's radio station in Berlin, cautioned against violence but sent reporters onto the streets to collect eyewitness accounts from key flash points. West German radio relayed RIAS reports as the core of its coverage. More than this, as

---

81 DDEL WHCF OF 247, box 910, Kieve (USIA) to Rabb (White House), 25 May 1955; Rabb to Kieve, 26 May 1955.

82 *USIA 6th Report to Congress, January–June 1956*, pp. 26–30.

83 First-generation officers serving in junior capacities at the start of the USIA included the Hungarian-born Arthur Bardos and Tibor Borgida and the German-born Hans N. Tuch and Max W. Kraus. ASTL Oral History: Bardos, Borgida, Tuch & Kraus.

84 For documentation of this campaign see National Security Archive electronic briefing book. U.S. propaganda in the Middle East: http://www.gwu.edu/~nsarchiv/NSAEBB/NSAEBB78/docs.htm, documents 106 to 114, esp. 106, 111. For the CIA and analysis see Vaughan, *The Anglo-American Relationship and Propaganda Strategies in the Middle East, 1953–1957*, p. 108. A 200-page CIA history of its role in Iran may be read at http://www.nytimes.com/library/world/mideast/041600iran-cia-index.html.

85 *FRUS 1952–54, Vol. 2, Part 2*, SoS to certain diplomatic posts, 24 July 1953, pp. 1726–7. For a detailed treatment see Christian F. Ostermann (ed.), *Uprising in East Germany, 1953*. Budapest: Central European University Press, 2001.

C. D. Jackson put it in a report to Congressman John Taber, "Short of inciting violence, RIAS worked to encouraged the continuation of demonstrations and gave moral support and highly complementary treatment to the actions of the East Zone populace." The station had proved its worth.[86]

But the USIA faced problems also. In its dying weeks the Psychological Strategy Board noted an "intensification of anti-American feeling among significant elements of European opinion" and blamed Europe's reaction to America's "anti-Communist hysteria," trade policies, and the end of U.S. economic assistance.[87] On 31 July, Vice President Nixon told the NSC of his concerns with the decline in U.S. prestige overseas. John Foster Dulles blamed twenty years of Democratic propaganda smearing Republicans as isolationists. All that the new administration needed to do to win back Europe, so Dulles said, was to wait until the superiority of the new U.S. foreign policy became obvious.[88]

Streibert faced these challenges with a budget of only $86 million. In his first six months he dismissed some 2,849 members of staff, of whom 763 were American. The information program had already lost 1,985 people in the first half of the year, and would lose a further 293 in the first half of 1954. Streibert cut the number of USIS posts from 255 in eighty-five countries to 217 in seventy-six countries. Major casualties included the Marshall Plan information apparatus in Paris. The reduction in force at least answered complaints about deadwood from the war period.[89] Other staffing problems arose from the removal of USIA staff from the State Department. USIA officers were now ineligible for diplomatic passports, although the State Department belatedly granted diplomatic status to senior agency staff in June 1954. Similarly, although USIA staff could be drawn from Foreign Service Reserve, Foreign Service Staff, and Foreign Service Local categories, they could not come from the career stream of foreign service officers (FSOs), who remained at the exclusive disposal of the Secretary of State. FSOs were assigned to the USIA for tours of duty; the system made it difficult to accumulate real experience. USIA officers were second-class citizens with limited promotion prospects and lacking tenure or pension rights. Although Eisenhower introduced legislation for a USIA career service in 1956, the plan bogged down in committee. This problem was not solved until 1967, when President Johnson finally authorized a Foreign Service Information Officer career stream.[90] The USIA at

[86] DDE C. D. Jackson papers, box 5, file: RFE, Jackson to Taber, 22 July 1953; Partridge (AcoS, G2) to Allen Dulles (CIA), 3 August 1953. For a discussion see Hixson, *Parting the Curtain*, pp. 73–7. McCarthy responded to the newfound fame of the RIAS by alleging that it was full of communists and demanding an investigation.

[87] DDEL Office of Special Assistant for National Security Affairs (OSANA), NSC/Status of Projects, box 4, file: NSC 161, PSB report no. 8, 30 July 1953.

[88] DDEL DDE Papers as President NSC box 4, discussion at the 157th NSC, 30 July 1953. For a report commissioned as a result of this meeting see *FRUS 1952–1954*, Vol. 1, pp. 1480–1525.

[89] HSTL DNC box 158, foreign affairs file: USIA replaces IIA, Washburn to Jack Martin (White House), 11 May 1954; *USIA 1st Review of Operations, August–December 1953*, p. 1; ADST Oral History: Hemsing.

[90] For early comments on the limits of the USIA career structure see the U.S. Advisory Commission on Information, 9th semiannual report to the congress, January 1954; the *USIA 2nd Review of Operations*,

least began to train its own specialists. Washburn swore in the first class of fifty junior officer trainees in September 1954.[91]

Streibert managed to integrate the USIA into policy-making. Although not of cabinet rank and initially only an observer in the Operations Coordinating Board, within a year Streibert moved to full participation in the OCB. The USIA received all NSC agenda papers and agreed on policy documents, and a USIA observer attended the NSC planning board when directly relevant.[92] Streibert soon sat in on most NSC meetings. The minutes of Eisenhower's NSC reveal abundant contributions from successive USIA directors. This would not be sustained in subsequent administrations.[93]

Eisenhower extended one further channel to the new agency by inviting Streibert to a monthly meeting at the White House, from 9:00 to 9:30 a.m. on the last Tuesday of each month. As Washburn recalled, the President explained, "I want to see you every month, whether you have something to ask or not. I want to know what you are doing." Washburn, who either accompanied the director or substituted for him, found the meetings invaluable. At Eisenhower's suggestion, he used to bring agency section heads with him. Eisenhower knew that such visits were "good for morale."[94] Streibert's access notwithstanding, it was still C. D. Jackson who brought information issues onto the highest levels of policy making.

With the new machinery of information in place, the administration had to clarify its objectives. After some discussion, the NSC agreed to a mission for the USIA on 24 October:

1. The purpose of the U.S. Information Agency shall be to submit evidence to peoples of other nations by means of communication techniques that the objectives and policies of the United States are in harmony with and will advance their legitimate aspirations for freedom, progress and peace.
2. The purpose in paragraph 1 above is to be carried out primarily:

JanuaryJune 1954, p. 4. For correspondence on the progress of career legislation see NA RG 306 64–A-0536, Office of the Director, subject files, 1957–8, box 1, file: Administration – Personnel – Foreign Service, 1957, DuVal (IGC) to Larson (director), "Points Previously Made by Mr. Vorys in Opposition to Our Career Service Legislation," 11 March 1957 and file: Administration – Personnel – Foreign Service, 1957, Washburn to Allen (director), 22 October 1957.

91 *USIA 3rd Report to Congress, July–December 1954*, p. 8; *USIA World*, Vol. 12, No. 4, 1993, p. 7. For discussion see Arthur Larson, *Eisenhower: The President Nobody Knew*, New York: Scribners, 1968, p. 24.
92 DDEL NSC-PSB, CF, box 10, PSB 040 USIA, esp. Cutler to Streibert, 26 October 1953. The OCB's first plans included a "National Operations Plan to Exploit Communist BW [Bacteriological Warfare] Hoax, Mistreatment of POWs and Other Atrocities Perpetrated by Communist Forces during the Korean War." *FRUS 1952–54, Vol. 2, Part 2*, OCB National Operations plan . . . 14 October 1953, pp. 1739–50; NA RG 306 Office of Administration, box 4, memo by Washburn, "USIA Relationships with the NSC and OCB," 8 September 1954. The director's membership of the OCB was formalized under Executive Order 10958 of 28 February 1955.
93 DDLE OH-153: Oral History interview with Theodore Streibert, 10 December 1970.
94 Interview: Washburn, 1 December 1995; also DDEL WHCF OF 247, box 909, "Memorandum for Mr. Stephens," 18 June 1954.

a. By explaining and interpreting to foreign peoples the objectives and policies of the United States Government.

b. By depicting imaginatively the correlation between U.S. policies and the legitimate aspirations of other peoples in the world.

c. By unmasking and countering hostile attempts to distort or to frustrate the objectives and policies of the United States.

d. By delineating those important aspects of the life and culture of the people of the United States which facilitate understanding of the policies and objectives of the Government of the United States.[95]

Following the Jackson Committee, the NSC noted that the USIA (but not the VOA) "is authorized to communicate with other peoples without attribution to the United States Government on matters for which attribution could be assumed by the government if necessary."[96]

Streibert saw the mission statement as a great foundation. He wrote to Eisenhower: "Under this new mission, avoiding a propagandistic tone, the Agency will emphasize the community of interest that exists among freedom loving peoples and show how American objectives and policies advance the legitimate interests of such peoples." To this end the agency would "concentrate on objective, factual news reporting and appropriate commentaries, designed to present a full exposition of important United States actions and policies, especially as they affect individual countries and areas." Streibert had no doubt that this fact-based approach would hit home: "Facts, and comment associated with facts, are more compelling than accusations and unsupported assertions on a wide variety of issues."[97]

Although these principles were consistent with the evolution of the Voice of America as an organ of news rather than advocacy, Streibert took care to fix the VOA firmly within his structure. Picking up on a suggestion made by Robert L. Johnson, he planned to relocate the VOA from eight sites around New York City to Washington DC and place the newsroom and administration inside USIA headquarters. The studios and technical facilities would be installed in the Health, Education, and Welfare building, located over a mile away on the south side of the National Mall on Independence Avenue. Because of the technical demands of creating new studio facilities, the move would take a full year. Many staff chose not to relocate, which proved a useful way of pruning back the VOA.[98] The VOA also suffered a major budget cut. Its output fell back from thirty-three hours of programming a day in forty languages to twenty-eight hours in thirty-four languages. But at least the new operating procedures enabled the VOA to make the most of its money.[99]

---

[95] *FRUS 1952–1954, Vol. 2, Part 2*, NSC action no. 936, 22 October 1953 and Mission of the USIA, approved as NSC 165/1, 24 October 1953, pp. 1750–55.

[96] *FRUS 1952–1954, Vol. 2, Part 2*, Mission of the USIA, p. 1753.

[97] *FRUS 1952–1954, Vol. 2, Part 2*, Streibert to Eisenhower, 27 October 1953.

[98] For comment see *FRUS 1952–1954, Vol. 2, Part 2*, NSC 5430, part 7, I, 18 August 1954, p. 1781. On Johnson see DDEL WHCF, CF, subject files box 99, USIA, file 1, Johnson, "Report on Operations of IIA March 3 to July 31, 1953."

[99] *USIA 1st Review of Operations, August–December 1953*, pp. 9–10.

Streibert structured the USIA's day-to-day operations along the lines suggested by the Voorhees Committee, with initiatives coming from USIA staff on embassy country teams rather than the center. Streibert conceived of the USIA's media staff in the International Press Service, Motion Picture Service, and Information Center Service in Washington as serving the needs of the field. In order to coordinate the relationship between the field and USIA headquarters, Streibert appointed four area assistant directors for each region. The shape of the four USIA "areas" and their budgets reveal the agency's priorities: Europe and the British Commonwealth was served by 3,500 staff with a budget of $22.5 million, around half of which was committed to Germany; American republics, in comparison, had only 500 staff and a budget of $1.5 million. The Far East, focus of so many fears for the spread of communism, had 1,300 staff and a budget of $2.7 million. Fourth, the Near East, South Asia, and Africa, a curious regional amalgam that united twenty-five countries from Greece east to India and south to the Belgian Congo, commanded 1,200 staff and a budget of $2.9 million. The area directors were required to spend as much time as possible visiting posts, with appearances in Washington expected at sixty-day intervals. Lacking USIS operations on the ground in the Soviet Union bloc, USIA policy to the "Soviet Orbit" was part of the VOA director's brief as "assistant director for radio and Soviet orbit." His budget fell just short of $18 million.[100]

Under the new system the objectives for any country were determined in the first place in the field by the senior public affairs officer in any country, who generated an annual country plan in collaboration with his ambassador. The PAO then cleared his country plan with the relevant area assistant director, the USIA administration, and the State Department and either requested the appropriate publicity materials from Washington to fulfill the country plan or created the necessary items in the field.[101] This decentralization did not preclude the use of grand themes by the agency. Initially Streibert took his lead from the Jackson report. USIA materials produced in 1953 emphasized the religious and economic values that America broadly shared with millions of people around the world.[102]

The new structure for the USIA included an Office of Private Cooperation. The idea of drawing on links to the private sphere appealed to both Streibert and the President and hence the office became the only unit within the agency to benefit materially from the transition from the IIA: its budget doubled to $182,000. It employed nineteen staff in offices in Washington, New York, Chicago, and San Francisco. When Eisenhower called on all Americans traveling overseas to recognize that "Each of us, whether bearing a commission from his government or traveling himself for pleasure or for business is a representative of the United States of America," Streibert lost no time in forwarding examples of the office's ongoing attempts to steer U.S. travelers in the right direction, noting that *What Should I Know When I Travel Abroad?*, the guide for visitors to Europe published in 1952, was now being revised for travelers to

---

[100]　*USIA 1st Review of Operations, August–December 1953*, p. 4.
[101]　*USIA 1st Review of Operations, August–December 1953*, p. 4.
[102]　*FRUS 1952–1954, Vol. 2, part 2*, Streibert to Eisenhower, 27 October 1953.

Latin America. An updated European edition followed in 1955, paid for by Republic Steel and the Common Council. Twenty-one of the country's leading travel organizations distributed hundreds of thousands of copies. The Office of Private Cooperation developed a similar document for corporate travelers and worked with the World Affairs Council of Northern California to produce a television program to raise the awareness of Americans going overseas about their responsibilities as "unofficial ambassadors."[103]

As the USIA's first Christmas neared, C. D. Jackson suggested that the administration attend to the question of agency morale. "USIA has been the lowest form of Government life," he wrote on 9 November; "Ted Streibert has done an almost miraculous job in the three months he has been around, and done it virtually single handed, and he deserves a pat on the back." Eisenhower responded by appearing at a grand USIA staff meeting on 10 November and pledging the administration's support to the agency. The President angled his words to underscore that the era of McCarthy's purge had ended: "No one who serves in this organization with what his chiefs or associates say is decency and to the best of his ability is ever going to suffer if I can help it. On the contrary I shall try to do my best to pin the accolade of a 'well done' to every such person." The President concluded in cheerful fashion, "Good luck to each of you, and this administration is with you." The USIA had the President's word that its nightmare had ended.[104]

3) FROM "ATOMS FOR PEACE" TO "PEOPLE'S CAPITALISM"
THE USIA'S OUTPUT, 1954–56

Although the Jackson report design for the USIA emphasized local messages rather than a central script, the Eisenhower administration proved adept at generating campaigns with universal appeal. The slogans of the Eisenhower years resonated like no others in the history of the agency. Eisenhower launched the first such campaign in a speech to the United Nations on 8 December 1953: its title was Atoms for Peace. Atoms for Peace began on 8 May 1953 when the NSC Planning Board's ad hoc Committee on Armaments and American Policy delivered a secret report calling for "candor" at home and overseas regarding the atomic arms race. The government needed U.S. public support for its nuclear arms expenditure. It also needed to present enough details of its nuclear arsenal to deter enemies and make friends feel safe. The plan, accepted as NSC 151, included discussion of the "constructive aspects of our atomic energy program."[105]

---

103 DDEL WHCF OF 247, box 909, Streibert to C. D.Jackson, 20 October 1953; *USIA 1st Review of Operations, August–December 1954*, p. 3; *USIA 4th Report to Congress, January–June 1955*, p. 14; NA RG 306 A1 (1072) USIA historical collection, box 14, file: Office of Private Cooperation, History 1971, Krill to Newpher, 29 January 1971, with "Brief History of the Office of Private Cooperation" attached.
104 DDEL WHCF OF 247, box 909, Jackson to T. E. Stephens (White House), 9 November 1953; PPPDDE 1953, Remarks to the staff of the USIA, 10 November 1953, pp. 753–5.
105 *FRUS 1952–1954, Vol. 2, Part 2*, NSC 151, 8 May 1953, pp. 1150–60.

On 30 July, the NSC discussed the best method of implementing this "candor." C. D. Jackson proposed that Eisenhower should deliver a speech on the subject and work began on drafts. The writers had trouble striking a balance between boring and terrifying the audience. A simple account of the Soviet power to strike and the U.S. ability to counterstrike was too gloomy; as one staffer put it: "bang-bang, no hope, no way out at the end." The answer came when Eisenhower hit on the notion of proposing a pool of fissile material, donated by the U.S. and U.S.S.R., that could be shared between nations. Jackson and the chairman of the Atomic Energy Commission, Lewis L. Strauss, developed the idea over the next months. Finally, they ran the plan past the British during the Bermuda Conference in December. Eisenhower, Strauss, Jackson, and John Foster Dulles worked on a final draft of the speech on the plane home from Bermuda on 8 December 1953. Jackson kept the plane circling so that the finished document could be handed to the press as soon as they landed. That same day Eisenhower delivered his speech at the United Nations.[106]

The Atoms for Peace speech was a splendid piece of political theater. Eisenhower declared, "The United States pledges its determination to help solve the fearful atomic dilemma – to find the way by which the miraculous inventiveness of man shall not be dedicated to death, but consecrated to his life." The entire UN General Assembly rose in ovation. The United States stood to gain from this proposal whether the U.S.S.R. accepted the idea of an international pool of nuclear resources or not. In one case the United States had led the way and in the other the Soviets were the spoilers. C. D. Jackson worked to ensure that the USIA and other overseas agencies made maximum use of the "Atoms for Peace" theme. On 9 December, he set up a special interdepartmental working group at the OCB to oversee the effort.[107]

On the eve of the speech the USIA sent out instructions to maximize the impact of Eisenhower's dramatic offer.[108] The VOA carried the speech live in English and broadcast thirty foreign-language versions within half an hour. The USIA transmitted its full text around the world, arranged translations, created leaflets, and distributed a film version. Many foreign newspapers ran the speech verbatim. "Never before in history," Streibert wrote to Eisenhower, "have the words of the President of the United States been so widely disseminated to all the peoples of the earth – or more welcomed by them." In the following weeks PAOs received an Atoms for Peace kit containing photographs, background information, and display material. The USIA's Office of Private Cooperation arranged for 266 U.S. firms to distribute 300,000 translations of highlights of Eisenhower's speech in their outgoing international correspondence. The USIA added an Atoms for Peace page to the *What Should I Know When I Travel Abroad?* guide for tourists to Latin America and encouraged Rotary, the Lions, and

106   *FRUS 1952–1954, Vol. 2, Part 2*, Memo of discussion at NSC, 30 July 1953, pp. 1184–5; Memo by Robert Cutler, 10 September 1953; Chronology, Atoms for Peace project, 30 September 1954.
107   *FRUS 1952–1954, Vol. 2, Part 2*, Jackson to OCB, 9 December 1953, pp. 1293–4; Smith (Acting SoS) to certain missions, 11 December 1953, pp. 1294–5.
108   *FRUS 1952–1954, Vol. 2, Part 2*, Washburn (Acting Dir.), Usito 164, 8 December 1953.

other such organizations to include the Atoms for Peace message in their international materials. In 1954, the agency sent touring exhibitions to Italy, Germany, Spain, the Netherlands, and Britain. The exhibit reached India and Pakistan in 1955. In São Paulo, Brazil, 400,000 people visited it during its first six months. The USIA's Atoms for Peace films included *A Is for Atom, The Atom in Industry, The Atom and Agriculture*, and *The Atom and the Doctor*.[109] Jackson complained that Atoms for Peace lacked concrete "follow-through." Eisenhower blamed the length of time that it had taken to get the Russians to formally reject his proposal, but assured Jackson that the United States planned to deliver soon.[110] Any doubt as to the value of the program vanished when Russia launched a copycat campaign.[111]

In March 1954, C. D. Jackson informed Eisenhower of his intent to return to Time–Life. This, he explained, had always been his plan. Assessments of Jackson's work for Eisenhower have dwelt on his role as the great prophet of rollback and spokesman for the foreign policy path not taken. Such an interpretation obscures Jackson's effectiveness as the architect of both the "Chance for Peace" speech in April 1953 and Atoms for Peace. As the energizing force behind the creation of the USIA and OCB he brought much-needed order to the U.S. psychological approach to the world. He proved a hard man to replace.[112]

*

The VOA spent most of 1954 preoccupied with the move to Washington. In April, VOA director Erikson resigned, claiming, somewhat fancifully, that he had "accomplished his mission of reorganizing the Voice."[113] He did at least rid the VOA of McCarthy's chief "stool pigeon": Paul Deac. When Erikson demoted Deac as a "disruptive element" whose work was "not up to standard," Deac resigned. He continued to snipe at the Voice as a leading light of the "National Confederation of American Ethnic Groups."[114]

[109] *FRUS 1952–1954, Vol. 2, Part 2*, Progress Report of the Working Group of OCB, 30 April 1954, pp. 1403–12; *USIA 1st Review of Operations, August–December 1953*, p. 3; *USIA 3rd Report to Congress, July–December 1954*, pp. 1–3; *USIA 5th Report to Congress, July–December 1955*, p. 5. DDEL DDE Papers as President (Ann Whitman file), Administrative Series, box 37, USIA (2), Streibert to Eisenhower, 27 February 1954; DDEL OSANA, NSC/Status of Projects, box 6, NSC 5525, The USIA program, 11 August 1955.

[110] DDEL DDE Papers as President (Ann Whitman file), diary series, box 3, August 1954 (3), entry for 11 August 1954.

[111] *USIA 3rd Report to Congress, July–December 1954*, p. 3.

[112] DDEL, DDE Papers as President (Ann Whitman file), Administration series, box 22, file: C. D. Jackson (2), Jackson to Eisenhower, 3 March 1954; "C. D. Jackson Will Leave His Post as Presidential Advisor 1 April," *New York Times*, 4 March 1954, p. 15; also Ingimundarson, "Containing the Offensive," n. 85. The "path not taken" is particularly clear in Brands, *Cold Warriors*, pp. 117–37. In contrast, Blanche Wiesen Cook, "First Comes the Lie," draws a direct line from Jackson to U.S. covert operations overseas in the 1980s.

[113] "Leonard F. Erikson Resigns as the Voice of America Chief," *Washington Post*, 19 April 1954.

[114] "Denies Critics Charges: Ex-official of "Voice" Says He Was Forced Out by Leftists," *New York Times*, 3 February 1954, p. 12. On Deac's later activities see NA RG 306, ZZ entry 1 (formerly 1006), Director's Chronological Files, 1953–64, box 2, microfilm reel 31, Memo for the files by Eugene S. Staples (director's office), "Conversation with Paul M. Deac," 15 January 1959.

Erikson's successor, J. R. Poppele, had worked for Streibert in commercial broadcasting. As the first president of the Television Broadcasters' Association, he was well qualified to lead the VOA into that new world. By the summer of 1954 the VOA had increased its daily output of programs to thirty-and-one-half hours and had invested in English. In the autumn of 1954 the VOA added new languages: Hindi, Urdu, Tamil, and Bengali.[115] By the time Poppele left the VOA in 1956, the VOA had forty-six languages and created an astonishing seventy-six hours of original programming each day, with repeat broadcasts totaling eighty-six hours.[116] The move to Washington allowed the VOA to carry more direct comment from U.S. foreign policy makers. New programs included *Foreign Policy Review*, a fifteen-minute compilation of the week's most significant statements of U.S. foreign policy, and *Press Conference U.S.A.*, in which three journalists cross-examined officials and politicians in a manner impossible in most other countries at that time.[117]

The VOA's plans for 1955 included a "disk jockey program ostensibly aimed at Scandinavia but reaching the U.S.S.R.," originally proposed by the U.S. embassy in Moscow.[118] Listeners in Europe on the evening of 6 January 1955 heard the exhilarating strains of Duke Ellington's "Take the A-Train" signature tune followed by the resonant, tobacco-deepened voice of host and jazz expert Willis Conover. Although jazz had aired on the VOA earlier in the decade on Leonard Feather's *Jazz Club*, Conover's program, *Music U.S.A. – Jazz Hour*, broadcast six nights a week, captured the audience's imagination. A second hour of *Music U.S.A.* covered other genres. In 1956, with *Music U.S.A.* averaging 1,000 fan letters a month, the VOA began transmitting the program worldwide.[119]

For the next forty years, Conover remained the best-known broadcaster on the VOA. In order to retain a political distance, he was always a contractor rather than an employee of the VOA. He had no doubt of the political value of the music he broadcast. Writing in *Jazz Forum* in 1988, he observed,

> Jazz is the musical parallel to our American political system and social system. We agree in advance on the laws and customs we abide by, and having reached agreement, we are free to do whatever we wish within these constraints. It's the same with jazz. The musicians agree on the key, the harmonic changes, the tempo and the duration of the piece. Within these guidelines, they are free to play what

[115] *USIA 2nd Review of Operations, January–June 1954*, pp. 10–11, 30; *USIA 3rd Report to Congress, July–December 1954*, p. 9.
[116] *USIA 7th Report to Congress, July–December 1956*, pp. 35–6.
[117] *USIA 4th Review of Operations, January–June 1955*, pp. 12–13; *USIA 5th Review of Operations, January–June 1956*, p. 12.
[118] NA RG 306 Office of Administration, 1952–5, box 2, file: Committee, Area Directors, Minutes of Area directors meeting 9 December 1954.
[119] *USIA 5th Review of Operations, January–June 1956*, p. 8. On the career of Leonard Feather see "Music Is Combating Communism: The Voice of America Shows Bring Universal Harmony," *Down Beat*, 8 October 1952; also Leonard Feather, *The Jazz Years: Eyewitness to an Era*, New York: Da Capo, 1987. For a full treatment of the use of jazz by the State Department and VOA in the Cold War see Penny M. Von Eschen, *Satchmo Blows Up the World: Jazz Ambassadors Play the Cold War*. Cambridge, MA: Harvard University Press, 2004.

they want. And when people in other countries hear the quality in the music, it stimulates the need for freedom in their lives.

Conover also hoped that jazz might show America to be a melting pot of opportunity. He knew from his tangles with segregation laws during his career as a jazz promoter that the African-American inventors and exponents of jazz faced all manner of obstacles in their own country. In an era of prejudice he believed that black American culture had something to say to the world and belonged on the Voice of America.

Testaments to Conover's impact in the Eastern bloc abounded. Although jazz had taken root in the region in the 1920s, by the 1950s it was suppressed by the Communist regimes. Conover kept the flame alive. Improvised recordings of his and other broadcasts made on x-ray plates circulated between dedicated fans in the growing *Stiliagi* (style-hunter) subculture. The cultural attaché at the U.S. Embassy in Moscow reported that young Russians not only learned their English from Conover, but also spoke it in a laidback drawl in imitation of him. When he visited Poland in 1959 Conover was greeted as a musical messiah.[120]

Around the time of the launch of *Music U.S.A.*, the National Security Council debated the effectiveness of the VOA in the Eastern bloc. Arthur Flemming, director of the Office of Defense Mobilization and a member of the Rockefeller Committee, complained that the BBC "was having much better results in these regions because of its high reputation for objectivity," and demanded an investigation. Eisenhower opposed any new inquiry but argued that it was "an impossibility to combine factual reporting and propaganda. If propaganda entered in, people simply would not believe what was truth in factual reporting." He went on to note that the VOA "should never permit itself to be caught in errors of fact, if for no other reason than if it ever should become necessary in an emergency to broadcast something which was not factual, such broadcasts would not be believed." The President was determined to place the VOA on a path to balance and objectivity.[121]

*

Streibert worked to develop the USIA's output in film and television. By the end of 1953, USIA film claimed an annual audience worldwide of 500 million. The USIA served 210 U.S. film libraries around the world. USIS posts had a total stock of 6,000 projectors and 350 mobile motion picture units equipped to take film to the people. Regular products included *Our Times*, a monthly twenty-minute newsreel of "events bearing on U.S. policies," launched in July 1954 and soon shown in thirty-one

120 Nicholas J. Cull, obituary, "Willis Conover," *Independent*, 11 May 1996; Interview: Tuch, 15 November 1995; Heil, *the Voice of America*, p. 288; S. Frederick Starr, *Red and Hot: The Fate of Jazz in the Soviet Union*, New York: Limelight Editions, 1994, pp. 236–51. The Jazz Journalists Association present an annual Willis Conover award in memory of his work. In 2001 Russian fans marked the fifth anniversary of his death with a three-day jazz festival. Conover's papers and recordings are held at the University of North Texas, Denton, Texas. For a biography see Terence M. Ripmaster, *Willis Conover: Broadcasting Jazz to the World*. Lincoln, NE: iUniverse Inc., 2007.

121 DDEL DDE Papers as President (Ann Whitman file), NSC Series, box 6, Memo: Discussion at the 235th meeting of NSC, 3 February 1955 (Washburn present representing the USIA).

language versions in eighty-four countries. The USIA also distributed film of presidential press conferences. Streibert determined that all USIA films should be either "hard hitting anti-Communist films calculated to expose Communist lies and distortions" or "designed to support and clarify American foreign policy." He steered the agency away from Americana. Typical USIA films were tales of Communist oppression such as *My Latvia*, using actual film of the Communist takeover, *Poles Are a Stubborn People*, telling the stories of the two defectors Korowics and Hajdukiewics, or *An Unpleasant Subject*, which documented Communist atrocities during the Korean War.[122]

USIA filmmakers produced much material locally. By 1954, more than two-thirds of USIA's anti-Communist films were made in the field, with local settings and local talent. In the first half of 1956, USIS posts created sixty-five documentary and feature films and 100 newsreel releases, whereas only nine documentaries were created centrally. The USIS made films in France, Italy, and especially South East Asia. Film box office successes released without USIA attribution included *Kampong Sentosa*, a two-hour feature film made in Singapore about the impact of Communist guerrillas on a single village, and *Huk*, a feature film about international Communist control of the Philippine Communist movement. USIS films in Asia were not all anti-Communist blood and thunder. USIS offices in Burma, the Philippines, and Thailand created films to communicate basic ideas about citizenship and democracy.[123]

Film is a slow medium, and despite Streibert's ruling against Americana, the USIA found itself releasing projects commissioned under the old regime. Among the most interesting was a documentary about Mexican-American shepherds in New Mexico called *And Now, Miguel* (1953), directed by Joseph Krumgold. The film depicted life through the eyes of a Mexican-American boy, as he longs to play a full role in the life of the farm and learns the necessity of his brother leaving home to fight in the Korean War. It was not until the Kennedy administration that USIA filmmakers again tackled so ambitious a project.[124]

122   DDEL WHCF CF subject files, box 99, USIA (1), Washburn to Streibert/Jackson, 19 January 1954; *USIA 2nd Review of Operations, January–June 1954*, p. 16; *USIA 3rd Report to Congress, July–December 1954*, p. 13.

123   DDEL OSANA NSC/Subject files, box 4, OCB progress report to NSC on implementation of the recommendations of the Jackson Committee, 30 September 1953, Annex B, p. 6; DDEL WHCF CF subject files, box 99, USIA (1), Washburn to Streibert/Jackson, 19 January 1954; *USIA 3rd Report to Congress, July–December 1954*, p. 13. Local production of films did not always guarantee audience satisfaction. An IIA film for Iraq in which puppets performed anti-Communist versions of traditional "Hoja" stories left audiences confused and appalled; see Joyce Battle essay http://www.gwu.edu/~nsarchiv/NSAEBB/NSAEBB78/essay.htm re doc 101. Undeterred, the USIA produced fresh language versions of these films in 1956. *USIA 5th Review of Operations, January–June 1956*, pp. 9–10.

124   Krumgold turned his documentary into a novel for children, which won the 1954 Newbery medal as the year's "most distinguished contribution to American literature for children." It remains in print. Translations and other novels followed. In 1966 *And Now Miguel* became a feature film by Universal Pictures. Joseph Krumgold, dir., *And Now, Miguel*, USIA, 1953; Joseph Krumgold (with Jean Charlot, illustrator), *And Now, Miguel*, New York: Crowell 1953; James B. Clark (dir.), *And Now, Miguel*, Universal Pictures, 1966. HSTL Hulten papers, box 15, Dept. of State Info. Programs, 1953, Motion Pictures, brochure *"The Film Program of the United States Information Agency,"* c. 1955.

More explicitly political USIA films included a forty-minute drama-documentary called *Dance to Freedom*. Produced in Germany in 1954 by the HICOG's film unit, *Dance to Freedom* told the story of the Hungarian husband and wife ballet stars, Istvan Rabovsky and Nora Kovach, who defected in May 1953. The two re-created their escape for the cameras. Cecil B. DeMille facilitated theatrical distribution overseas, while Washburn arranged for the film to be screened at the White House.[125] Despite the restrictions later read in Smith–Mundt, *Dance to Freedom* also played at home on the CBS arts show *Omnibus* on 17 October 1954.[126]

The USIA developed its plans for closer relations with Hollywood. Its method would be voluntary cooperation administered from Washington by the new director of the USIA's motion picture branch, Andrew W. Smith Jr. (formerly general manager of 20th Century Fox and general sales manager of United Artists and RKO, appointed to the USIA at the suggestion of Eric Johnston). Smith's key contacts in Hollywood would be Cecil B. DeMille and a "special West coast representative," the veteran MGM producer and president of the Motion Picture Producers Guild Carey Wilson. Smith would keep in regular contact with both Carey Wilson and Addison Durland of the Production Code Administration, and these men would visit Washington for briefings with the State Department and the USIA and be supplied with a full set of the annual "country plans." The USIA decided to start by encouraging positive representations of the United States and "let the negative or censorship aspect develop later." DeMille was eager for censorship, declaring *From Here to Eternity* "a terrible thing to export," but was successfully reined in. By January 1954 the chief problem facing Abbott Washburn was how to best launch the scheme. He planned a grand White House dinner for all the major studio bosses, as he wrote to C. D. Jackson, "Unless the idea is presented to all these prima donnas at the same time and at the highest level, they will not all cooperate." The grand launch never happened but the system apparently worked. The exact details of script changes made at the request of the USIA are now obscure, but the Sprague Committee, which investigated the USIA in 1960, had no doubt of its effectiveness.[127]

Hollywood certainly helped distribute USIA material. Agency films released theatrically overseas in early 1954 included *Atomic Power for Peace* (through Universal), *The Korea Story* (through Warner Brothers), and *The Life of Eisenhower* (through RKO).[128] Initiatives maintained from the IIA period included "Project Kingfish," the

---

[125]   DDEL WHCF OF111-J-1, box 555, Washburn to Mrs. Whitman (White House), 12 April 1954 and attachments.

[126]   NA RG 306 Office of Administration, 1952–5, box 2, file: Committee, Directors Staff, Acting Director's staff meeting, 12 October 1954; see also Anna McCarthy, "Television, Culture and Citizenship at the Ford Foundation," Working Paper No. 13, International Center for Advanced Studies, New York University, November 2003, on-line at http://www.nyu.edu/gsas/dept/icas/Anna#20McCarthy.pdf. The screening included credit to and a discussion of the work of the USIA.

[127]   DDEL WHCF OF 247, box 909, Jackson to Sherman Adams (White House), 19 January 1953 (dating the initiative to Daryl Zanuck's testimony to the Jackson Committee); Washburn to Jackson, received 21 January 1954 with attachments, and the account of the Sprague committee in the next chapter.

[128]   DDEL WHCF CF subject files, box 99, USIA (1), Washburn to Streibert/Jackson, 20 January 1954.

covert subsidy of a newsreel, created by Associated Newsreel, Inc. "Kingfish" brought images of world news from a U.S. point of view to more than half a million viewers in the Middle and Far East who were simply not a viable audience in commercial terms alone. The subsidy of $309,759 each six months represented about a sixth of the USIA's total motion picture budget. The subsidy ran until 1967. The USIA also had strong editorial input into the Fox Movietone newsreel *News of the Day*, which also appeared without attribution. Country-specific newsreels followed.[129]

The USIA handled television separately from film under the auspices of the VOA. The Voice's television initiative began in 1952 with the establishment of a small TV Development Branch in the Central Program Services Division headed by veteran OWI radio producer Jack Gaines. Early successes included an agreement to distribute material from NBC's prestigious *Firestone Hour* internationally. The unit spent its time not so much selling the United States as selling the very idea of television around the world.[130] In January 1953, the VOA oversaw the distribution of television images of the presidential inauguration. Its only customers for full coverage were the Netherlands, which received the images just twenty-four hours after the ceremony, and Japan, which used the inauguration broadcast to launch its TV service. The USIA found wider audiences for a weekly newsreel of events in U.S. business called *Industry on Parade*. The scarcity of programming material gave the USIA a wonderful opportunity.[131] During its early life, the USIA supplied many of its propaganda films for unattributed use on television around the world. The agency gladly assisted countries to develop their television capacity, knowing that opportunities for further discreet program placement would follow.[132]

By the summer of 1954, television placement included *This Is the United States*, a series introducing U.S. landscape and history, and nearly two hours of news and feature material a week. The agency's list of clients now covered twenty-four stations in nineteen countries.[133] In 1955 the VOA upgraded its television operation to the level of an office (designated IBS/T). By 1956, the USIA supplied 460 programs

129 NA RG 306, Office of Administration, 1952–5, box 2, files: "Reprogramming," "Proposed New Projects – FY 1954 and 1955," and "Proposal for New or Extended Project or Activity FY 1954," 11 February 1954. See also DDE, NSC Staff Papers, 1948–61, OCB Central Files series, OCB 091/4, Near East (#4) (2), OCB Memo "USIA Information Programming to the Middle East in Present Crisis," 10 December 1956 as cited in Vaughan, *The Anglo-American Relationship and Propaganda Strategies in the Middle East, 1953–1957*, p. 40.

130 NA RG 306–01–1 USIA Historical Branch, item 15, box 30 (Motion Pictures), Jack De Viney, *History (of USIA TV and Film Service)*, Ch. 1.

131 DDEL Jackson Committee, box 6, correspondence file H (10): evidence of Richard Hubbell, head of television desk, IBS New York, 9 April 1953. Originally produced by NBC for the National Association of Manufacturers, the IIA placed thirty-eight episodes of *Industry on Parade* in Cuba, thirty-two in Brazil, thirty-one in Venezuela, and smaller numbers of episodes in ten other countries including the United Kingdom, Italy, and France.

132 DDEL OSANA NSC/Subject files, box 4, OCB progress report to NSC on implementation of the recommendations of the Jackson Committee, 30 September 1953, Annex B, p. 6; placements in the United Kingdom in 1953 included the screening of the film *UN Report on Prisoners of War*, refuting a Communist atrocity story, screened on 18 April to an audience of eight million. See DDEL, C. D.Jackson, box 5, movies, Guarco (IMS) to C. D. Jackson, 11 May 1953.

133 *USIA 2nd Review of Operations, January–June 1954*, pp. 12–13.

(including thirty-four original productions) to 150 stations and an audience estimated at forty million. *Report from America*, a series of monthly programs profiling American life and politics created in conjunction with the BBC, proved sufficiently popular in Britain to move into a prime Sunday evening slot in early 1956.[134]

Of the other media services at the USIA, the Information Center Service (ICS) worked to rebuild after the devastating McCarthy investigation. By 1955, the 160 USIS libraries estimated their annual turnover at thirty-eight million users borrowing eleven million books. The network of binational centers expanded in Latin America, with similar institutions opening in Austria and Vietnam. English language classes prospered. By the end of 1956 the USIA either operated or assisted 120 separate English teaching programs in fifty-five countries. The ICS also oversaw the translation program (which in December 1955 published its 2,500th book since the project began in 1950). Its "bestseller," with 219,000 copies in twenty languages, was a work of economic history, Frederick Lewis Allen's *The Big Change: America Transforms Itself, 1900–1950*. The ICS also arranged small-scale exhibitions. Subjects featured during this period included Benjamin Franklin.[135]

The International Press Service (IPS) produced news and background material at the rate of 7,000 words a day and forwarded it in the wireless file to sixty-six countries. New projects in 1954 included a special collection of fifty-four books exposing the dark side of communism with titles such as *Forced Labor in Soviet Russia* and *The Communist War on Religion*. The IPS catered for the mass market with widely syndicated newspaper cartoon strips. *True Tales*, supplied to 869 newspapers in forty-six countries, featured the story of Abraham Lincoln and other uplifting American sagas. Parallel series depicted U.S. athletes and satirized life in the Communist Bloc.[136] The IPS's journal *Problems of Communism* went from strength to strength. Articles in 1953 included Alan Little on Soviet propaganda techniques and a terrific series on the warping of culture in the U.S.S.R.[137] The USIA launched a Spanish version for Latin America. French, Portuguese, Japanese, and Italian versions followed.[138]

---

[134] NA RG 306–01–1 USIA Historical Branch, item 15, box 30 (Motion Pictures), Jack De Viney, *History* (of USIA TV and Film Service), Ch. 1; *USIA 6th Report to Congress, January–June 1956*, pp. 6–7, cites the *London Sunday Times*: "What is finest about these reports is the integrity that is written all over them. America speaks for herself, through un-doctored pictures of her streets and the untrained voices of men in them."

[135] *USIA 4th Review of Operations, January–June 1955*, pp. 9–11; *USIA 5th Report to Congress, July–December 1955*, pp. 15, 31; *USIA 6th Report to Congress, January–June 1956*, p. 14.

[136] *USIA 2nd Review of Operations, January–June 1954*, pp. 8–9, 31; *USIA 4th Report to Congress, January–June 1955*, pp. 7–8; *USIA 5th Report to Congress, July–December 1955*, p. 10.

[137] Alan M. G. Little, "Pavlov and Propaganda," *Problems of Communism (POC)*, 2, 2 (1953), 14–21; Jacob Landy, "Soviet Painting and Socialist Realism," *POC*, 2, 3–4 (1953), 15–25; Peter Willen, "Soviet Architecture, Progress and Reaction," *POC*, 2, 6 (1953), 24–33 (noting how Bolshevik modernism has now been squashed by "wedding cake monumentality").

[138] For sample copies see NA RG 306–93–0134, *Problems of Communism*, box 2. *Problemas del Communismo* spent its last two years as *Problemas Internacionales*. The French version ran from July 1954 to the end of 1956; the Italian version ran from 1955 through to 1957. See also DDEL C. D. Jackson papers, box 89, Quantico Meetings 24, OCB progress report on the U.S. ideological program, 16 August 1955.

The USIA did whatever it could to downplay America's reputation for racism. It helped when the agency had good news to report. In the spring of 1954 the Supreme Court had ruled against segregation in public schools in the landmark case of Brown v. Board of Education of Topeka, Kansas. Within minutes of the decision USIS posts had the text in full. Every VOA language carried a commentary on the decision, and the wireless file provided daily features about the decision to fifty-six countries for the next two weeks. It was, the USIA administration felt, "one of the severest blows to Communist propaganda in recent years."[139] Other IPS efforts on the subject of race included a report commissioned from the South African novelist Alan Paton, called *The Negro in America Today*.[140] Printed material could only be the raw material for the campaign. The accurate reporting of the U.S. race issue overseas relied on USIS staff in the field painstakingly building links with journalists and providing the sort of background material, photographs, and statistics that they needed for their stories. A clutch of formerly skeptical left-wing newspapers shifted to a more positive line as a result: the USIA noted feature stories on integration in *Le Populaire* of Martinique and positive editorials in *Arbeiderbladet* in Oslo and *The Times* in Rangoon. It was a start.[141]

Like Robert L. Johnson before him, Streibert emphasized religion in the USIA's output. On 8 March 1954, the USIA appointed its first chief of religious information, a theologian named D. Elton Trueblood, who immediately launched a special VOA program called *The Life We Prize* about American religion. Features on the Gideons and other religious charities followed. Trueblood also designed a touring exhibition called "The Church in America." With all USIA outlets emphasizing American observance and the contrasting Soviet repression of religion, the agency felt sure it had struck a winning formula. Confirmation came in November 1954 when Moscow suddenly began to "soft pedal" attacks on religion. The USIA deduced "a ban on jibes at religion, at least for ears outside the Soviet Orbit."[142]

*

Obvious challenges for the USIA included America's lackluster showing at international trade fairs. The Soviet display of consumer goods had won first prize at the Bangkok Constitution Fair of 1953, whereas the United States had not even been officially represented. Under Streibert things were different. A joint effort between the USIA, the Department of Commerce, and 100 U.S. corporations prepared a lavish exhibit for the 1954 Bangkok fair called "The Fruits of Freedom." At the Damascus Trade Fair in September 1954 the agency unveiled a secret weapon, a film exhibit, that proved a powerful draw for the rest of the decade: *This is Cinerama*. Cinerama was a super-widescreen film process by which three electronically

---

139 *USIA 2nd Review of Operations, January–June 1954*, pp. 7–8.
140 *USIA 3rd Report to Congress, July–December 1954*, p. 12.
141 *USIA 7th Report to Congress, July–December 1956*, p. 15.
142 *USIA 2nd Review of Operations, January–June 1954*, p. 8; *USIA 3rd Report to Congress, July–December 1954*, pp. 3–4.

synchronized projectors threw sections of an image onto a vast curved screen. The film included such spectacular sequences as a rollercoaster ride. The crowds surging around the entrance to the Cinerama show in Damascus blocked access to the Soviet pavilion. The Russians muttered about unfair competition and a superior Soviet invention along the same lines created fifteen years earlier. Whether because of Cinerama or the advance word of the "Fruits of Freedom" exhibit, the Soviets withdrew from the 1954 Bangkok fair just ten days before the opening. The U.S. exhibit took first prize.[143]

In the summer of 1954, Eisenhower rescued the USIA from a serious set back. Although Streibert had requested $89 million for fiscal year 1955, Congress only authorized $77.1 million.[144] Eisenhower softened the blow by raising a $5 million special President's Emergency Fund for International Affairs to assist the State Department, the USIA, and the Department of Commerce, with the USIA as the body "charged with action as executive agent."[145] In designing content for the trade fairs, the USIA emphasized America's commitment to peace and freedom and its willingness to use bilateral trade as a tool to this end, but the products on display spoke loudest of all. The fairs of the 1950s became – in art historian Robert H. Haddow's memorable phrase – "pavilions of plenty," showcasing American abundance. Highlights in 1955 included the "America at home" exhibit at the Frankfurt fair in March, which included a "completely furnished full-scale five room modern house with actors impersonating an American family and demonstrating the various elements of the home." But the agency did not have unlimited funds. A fair in Utrecht got an off-the-peg Atoms for Peace show and the fair in Izmir, Turkey got a simple trade information booth.[146]

The President's Emergency Fund kick-started major cultural work overseas. As the reorganization of 1953 had left much of the U.S. cultural apparatus at the State Department, this cultural campaign had to be interdepartmental. The OCB established a working group to oversee the initiative. Individual USIS posts mounted "American Cultural Weeks" of sponsored concerts and lectures. The agency also began to assign eminent scholars to embassies as cultural affairs officers or consultants to the PAOs.[147] In July 1954 Streibert instructed posts, "We must develop an understanding and appreciation of the culture of our people, as a people. A realization of American cultural achievement and aspirations can influence political attitudes and aspirations."[148]

The State Department initiated the major events of the cultural program, whereas the USIA managed the in-country administration and supporting publicity. A *Music*

[143] *USIA 3rd Report to Congress, July–December 1954*, pp. 5–6; Robert H. Haddow, *Pavilions of Plenty: Exhibiting American Culture Abroad in the 1950s*, Washington, DC: Smithsonian Institution Press, 1997, pp. 41–2.

[144] *USIA 2nd Review of Operations, January–June 1954*, p. 5.

[145] *FRUS 1952–54, Vol. II, pt. 2*, Eisenhower to Pres. of Senate, 27 July 1954, pp. 1776–7; Eisenhower to Dulles, 18 August 1954, pp. 1790–91; also Haddow, *Pavilions of Plenty*, pp. 40–41.

[146] DDEL WHCF OF 247, box 910, Streibert to Eisenhower, 6 May 1955; Haddow, *Pavilions of Plenty*, p. 12.

[147] *USIA 4th Report to Congress, January–June 1955*, pp. 2–3; DDEL OSANA, NSC/Status of Projects, box 6, NSC 5525, The USIA Program, 11 August 1955, pp. 4–5.

[148] *FRUS 1952–54, Vol. II, pt. 2*, Streibert to all USIS posts (USIA CA-8, 6 July 1954).

in America exhibit toured India, Great Britain, and Sweden; a *Highlights of American Painting* show visited twenty-two venues from Norway to Ethiopia; the U.S. government created an entire "Salute to France" music season with multiple visitors to that country. The José Limón Dance Troupe toured South America, assisted by the fact that its star was a Mexican-American and fluent in Spanish. The U.S. track and swimming teams from the Mexico Pan-American games toured Central America. The violinist Isaac Stern played to rapt audiences in Iceland and Yugoslavia. But one event above all others spoke of the power of culture in the international sphere: the triumphant Mediterranean tour of George Gershwin's *Porgy and Bess*.[149] The opera opened to packed houses in Zagreb and Belgrade, Yugoslavia, in December 1954. It progressed to Alexandria and Cairo, Athens, Tel Aviv, and Barcelona, challenging stereotypes of U.S. culture as it went, and closing in Naples in February.[150]

Flushed with these successes, the USIA commissioned films on cultural subjects. *William Faulkner in Japan* proved a particular hit. Meanwhile the State Department and the USIA laid plans to send *Oklahoma* around the world and began to discuss the possibility of some sort of cultural agreement with the U.S.S.R. and Soviet bloc.[151] The range of activities paid for by the President's Emergency Fund proved such a success that, in 1956, Congress passed an International Cultural Exchange and Trade Fair Participation Act to make them permanent.[152]

*

In 1955 the agency unveiled a major tool of cultural diplomacy: *The Family of Man*, a magnificent photographic exhibition originally developed for the Museum of Modern Art in New York. Created by the legendary American photographer Edward Steichen, *The Family of Man* comprised 503 pictures by 273 photographers, both professional and amateur, from sixty-eight countries including the Soviet Union. Engagingly hung in three-dimensional space, the pictures provided multifaceted glimpses of human life in all its diversity. It was, as the *Philadelphia Inquirer* put it, "The whole story of mankind."

After a swirling image of a galaxy, the show began with images of courtship from around the world. This being the 1950s, pictures of marriages properly preceded the images of birth and motherhood. Then the exhibition moved onward and outward

---

[149] *USIA 4th Report to Congress, January–June 1955*, pp. 2–3; DDEL OSANA, NSC/Status of Projects, box 6, NSC 5525, The USIA program, 11 August 1955, pp. 4–5. For a detailed discussion of the role of dance in the cultural program see Naima Prevots, *Dance for Export: Cultural Diplomacy and the Cold War*, Middletown, CT: Wesleyan University Press, 1998.

[150] DDEL DDE Papers as President (Ann Whitman file), Administrative Series, box 37, USIA (2), Streibert to Goodpaster (White House), 20 December 1954 with telegram 473 from Belgrade, 17 December 1954.

[151] *USIA 6th Report to Congress, January–June 1956*, p. 10; DDEL WHCF OF 247, box 910, Streibert to Eisenhower, 6 May 1955; OSANA, NSC/Status of Projects, box 6, NSC 5525, The USIA program, 11 August 1955, pp. 4–5; NA RG 306 Office of Administration, 1952–5, box 2, file: Committee, Area Directors, Minutes of Area directors meeting 9 December 1954. ADST Oral History: Schmidt.

[152] UoA CU 2–3, J. Manuel Espinosa, "Landmarks in the History of the Cultural Relations Program of the Department of State, 1938–1976," 1978, p. 8.

through childhood to the adult world of work, the land, learning, exuberant self-expression, and beyond. Some pictures were rendered on a giant scale. Some were built into pillars or alcoves, or in a moving display of democratic practice around the world, a ballot box. Images of children abounded in the show, lending energy and playfulness. The show's numerous references to the human religious experience (rather than any one religion) fitted with the USIA's output in the 1950s. Short religious texts taken from the world's great holy books and a range of other writers from Jefferson to Anne Frank accompanied the pictures. The ballot box bore a Sioux Indian text: "Behold this, also love it! It is very sacred and you must treat it as such."

Some images had explicit political resonance. Visitors saw a snapshot of the Warsaw ghetto; a photograph of rioters confronting tanks in Berlin in 1953; pictures of apartheid in South Africa; a dead soldier in Korea; and a glorious giant panorama of the general assembly of the United Nations as the exhibition reached its end. The images were honest about America, depicting the dust bowl of the 1930s through the eyes of Dorothea Lange. Seen as a whole, the entire show glowed with life-affirming energy. By sponsoring such an exhibition the USIA became a bridge, introducing the individual viewer to the rest of the planet.[153]

Within months of the exhibition opening in New York City, the USIA created two touring editions and sent one to Berlin and the other to Guatemala City. In Berlin, crowds three and four abreast flocked to see what one paper called the "miracle at the Steinplatz." Many came from the eastern sector, wearing sunglasses to avoid being recognized. In Guatemala, the weekly *Lunes* praised *The Family of Man* as "one of the greatest artistic accomplishments of our century." The show moved on to similar acclaim in Munich and Mexico City. The USIA created further editions and a film narrated by Steichen and scheduled visits to Asian and European capitals for 1956. London's socialist *Daily Worker* spoke of "the most moving collection of photographs ever seen." In India, a quarter of a million people queued in a monsoon to view the show.[154] In Paris, Roland Barthes raised a rare voice of opposition, attacking the show in his seminal book *Mythologies* for presenting images without reference to history. This was – of course – the point, because history meant either the dialectic of class conflict peddled by Moscow or the local national experiences that held human beings apart.[155]

By 1962, when it stopped touring, the exhibition had visited ninety-one locations in thirty-eight countries, including Moscow. In 1965, the U.S. government presented

153 Edward Steichen, *The Family of Man*, New York: The Museum of Modern Art, 1956. For background see Eric J. Sandeen, *Picturing an Exhibition: The Family of Man and 1950s America*, Albuquerque: University of New Mexico Press, 1995. For recent scholarship see Jean Black and Viktoria Schmidt-Linsenhoff (eds.), *The Family of Man, 1955–2001: Humanism and Postmodernism, A Reappraisal of the Photo Exhibition by Edward Steichen*, Marburg, Germany: Jonas Verlag, 2004.
154 *USIA 4th Report to Congress, January–June 1955*, pp. 9–10; *USIA 5th Report to Congress, July–December 1955*, pp. 5–6; *USIA 7th Report to Congress, July–December 1956*, p. 17. HSTL Hulten papers, box 15, Dept. of State Info. Programs, 1953, Motion Pictures, brochure *"The Film Program of the United States Information Agency,"* c. 1955.
155 Roland Barthes, "La Grande Famille de Hommes," in *Mythologies*, Paris, 1957, reproduced in Jean Black and Viktoria Schmidt-Linsenhoff (eds.) *The Family of Man, 1955–2001*, pp. 275–6.

the entire exhibit to Steichen's birthplace, Luxembourg, where, following restoration in the 1990s, it remains on display in the magnificent Château de Clervaux in the north of the Grand Duchy. In 2004, it won a place on UNESCO's Memory of the World register. Half a century after the opening, Steichen's book based on the exhibition remains in print.[156]

The USIA's other great success in these years also had roots outside the agency: the theme of People's Capitalism created by Theodore Repplier, president of the Advertising Council. Repplier had spent the first six months of 1955 touring the world as an Eisenhower Fellow, comparing USIA work with what he saw of Communist propaganda. He realized that the USIA had already achieved much, but now needed to move beyond talk of gulags and purges and recognize "that communism in theory is idealistic and moralistic." The United States needed to project its own ideals. To this end Repplier devised a new way to present the U.S. economic system.

Repplier realized that Communist parties around the world painted an outdated picture of the capitalist system based around the pictures of bloated mill owners in top hats current when Karl Marx wrote. A People's Capitalism campaign would set the record straight and show the economic system that had brought prosperity to the many. Repplier's use of the term "People's" was deliberate. "No word is more American," he argued; "It is high time we liberated this noun from the Russians."[157] Replier pointed out that under U.S. People's Capitalism the "means of production" belonged to every American who paid into a pension fund or insurance fund that then purchased stock. Bank investments came from ordinary people's deposits. All Americans had a stake in this system. On top of this, the rewards of the free market had drawn forth ingenuity, boosted productivity, and brought higher wages for all. Capitalism had actually done what communism promised. Repplier presented his idea to the President in August 1955 along with a plan for more overseas aid. Eisenhower commended the scheme to Streibert and "People's Capitalism" entered the vocabulary of the USIA.[158]

In January 1956, the USIA launched its People's Capitalism campaign and suggesting that all PAOs use the concept. The USIA HQ supplied monthly updates on key indicators of American prosperity, a color film called *Our Productive Industry*, and a VOA radio series.[159] In February the USIA unveiled the exhibition "People's

---

156 Sandeen, *Picturing an Exhibition*, esp. Ch. 3, http://www.luxembourg.co.uk/clervaux.html. For a Luxembourgian take on Steichen and his show see Rosch Krieps, *Steichen – Story I/II, Er Umarte die Menschheit*, Luxemburg: Selbstverlag, 2004. In Luxemburg the show is presented as a celebration of humanity on a par with Goethe's writings or Beethoven's symphonies and advances the cosmopolitan image of its new home country by association.

157 DDEL C. D. Jackson papers, box 111, Washburn, (4), Speech by Repplier, 27 October 1955; on background see Haddow, *Pavilions of Plenty*, pp. 48–53.

158 DDEL WHCF CF subject, box 99, USIA (2), Lambie (White House) to President, 3 August 1955 with Repplier, "Some Thoughts about American Propaganda," 17 June 1955; interview: Washburn, 1 December 1995. For comment see Hixson, *Parting the Curtain*, pp. 133–40.

159 DDEL C. D. Jackson papers, box 111, Washburn (4), USIA CA-1244, 10 January 1956, Streibert to all country public affairs officers with attachments.

Capitalism – A New Way of Living," designed by the Advertising Council to travel to trade fairs around the world. Covering over 7,000 square feet, the exhibit both explained the structure of American capital ownership and displayed U.S. material progress. The exhibition set a full-size reconstruction of a typical home from 1776 next to a furnished American home of 1956; it placed a machine from 1775 capable of producing sixteen nails an hour next to its sixteen-thousand-nails-an-hour modern-day descendant. Films illustrated the progress from homespun to nylon. The show opened for a test run at Washington's Union Station in February 1956. Eisenhower toured the show on its first day. The press hailed a great addition to the U.S. ideological arsenal.[160] People's Capitalism proved its worth. The USIA noted excellent responses to the show at the Bogotá Trade Fair in Colombia in November and December 1956 and the use of the term by the center party in the Chilean election that year.[161] In the longer term, the agency acknowledged limits. In May 1958, then USIA director George V. Allen told the NSC that the exhibit had prompted "considerable grumbling and disapprobation" in Latin America, where in the absence of their own People's Capitalism many saw only "old fashioned capitalist imperialism."[162] One group at least reacted most encouragingly. In the U.S.S.R., the editor of *Pravda* (and soon-to-be foreign minister) Dimitri Shepilov fumed that "People's Capitalism" made as much sense as "fried ice," and in the summer of 1956 the Kremlin commissioned economist Eugene Varga to refute the concept in two five-thousand-word articles for its international journal *New Times*. Moscow was worried.[163]

*

The final worldwide slogan coined in the USIA's early years was "People-to-People." This grew from a suggestion by Abbott Washburn, transmitted via Streibert at one of his White House meetings, that the USIA coordinate links between ordinary Americans and their counterparts around the world. Eisenhower liked the idea and proposed personally leading a recruitment drive "for increased participation of nongovernment groups and individuals in telling America's story overseas." In the summer of 1955, Eisenhower proposed a speech inviting all Americans to work with him to "create worldwide understanding of U.S. aims and to help build a climate for

---

160   Interview: Washburn, 1 December 1995; "People's Capitalism: This is America," *Collier's Magazine*, 6 January 1956; DDEL WHCF, OF247, box 910, Repplier to Eisenhower, 1 February 1956; *USIA 6th Report to Congress, January–June 1956*, p. 6. The preview enabled the USIA to fine-tune the show. When the executive secretary of the OCB, Elmer Staats, noted the absence of nonwhite faces in the scenes of prosperity, the USIA introduced a suitable crowd photo illustrating U.S. diversity. By the end of the decade, such inclusiveness had become second nature to the USIA. See DDEL WHCF OF 247, box 910, Staats to Washburn, 14 February 1956; Haddow, *Pavilions of Plenty*, p. 54.

161   *USIA 7th Report to Congress, July–December 1956*, p. 6. For an anthology of reactions see NA RG 306, 64-A-0536, Office of the Director, Subject files, 1957–8, box 2, file: People's Capitalism: Editorial Comments, 1955–7.

162   *FRUS 1958–1960, Vol. V., American Republics*, doc. 56, 366th NSC meeting, 22 May 1958, pp. 239–46.

163   Interview: Washburn, 1 December 1995; DDEL DDE Papers as President (Ann Whitman file), Administrative Series, box 37, USIA (1), Streibert to Eisenhower, 13 September 1956 with Henry Hazlitt "Business Tides: People's Capitalism," *Newsweek*, 17 September 1956.

enduring peace."[164] Streibert's first step was to invite the nineteen most significant U.S. corporations with personnel overseas to join an Industrial Cooperation Council, launched with a conference at the White House in November 1955.[165] The USIA's Office of Private Cooperation looked for more. Other ideas included letter writing, more leaflets for American travelers, work though women's and labor groups, and even films.[166]

Streibert and Eisenhower planned for these public-private initiatives to come together in the grand campaign to enlist private citizens to work for information goals under the banner title – devised by Eisenhower – of "People-to-People." They planned an announcement for June 1956 but the President's heart attack delayed this.[167] On 11 September 1956, Eisenhower launched People-to-People at a large White House reception. By the end of the year private interests had rallied to create twenty-eight People-to-People committees in areas of civic life as diverse as farming and sports. The Industrial Cooperation Council became the Business Council for International Understanding, embracing fifty corporations with substantial staff. The Council members mounted exhibitions, film shows, and even English classes. Other initiatives included the collection of old textbooks for donation overseas.[168] It would be a major theme in the second Eisenhower administration.

*

The obvious achievements of the young USIA did not deter critics. In early 1955, a Republican nontheatrical film distributor and self-styled propaganda expert named Eugene W. Castle published an "exposé" of the USIA entitled *Billions, Blunders and Baloney*. Despite outrageous distortions, U.S. newspapers took note.[169] The USIA prepared a careful defense, compiling a detailed rebuttal for use by a sympathetic representative, Hugh D. Scott Jr. (R-PA). But the USIA also had public supporters. In October 1954 Edward Bernays launched a National Committee for an Adequate Overseas Information Program, which united gurus in the field such as Harold Lasswell, George Gallup, and Ted Repplier with such old hands as Edward W. Barrett and Robert L. Johnson. In December 1954 a conference held at MIT generated recommendations for the USIA's future development, including increased cultural interchange. In 1955 the committee mounted a campaign to counteract Castle's book, but

164 For Washburn's account see Tuch and Schmidt, *Ike and USIA*, p. 12; DDEL DDE Papers as President (Ann Whitman file), Administrative Series, box 37, USIA (2), quoted in Washburn to Eisenhower, 20 December 1955. According to *FRUS 1954–57, Vol. IX*, McCardle (AsoS for PA) to Murphy (DUSoS) n.d., p. 583, the context of Eisenhower's suggestion was Steibert's budget request in autumn 1955.
165 DDEL WHCF OF 247-B, box 912, Streibert to Adams, 21 October 1955 and attachments.
166 DDEL DDE Papers as President (Ann Whitman file), Administrative Series, box 37, USIA (2), quoted in Washburn to Eisenhower, 20 December 1955. The USIA talked to Walt Disney about an Atoms for Peace cartoon and asked Eric Johnston and Cecil B. DeMille to stimulate a Hollywood film that could address the theme of peace as eloquently as William Wyler's *Best Years of Our Lives* had addressed the issue of postwar readjustment back in 1946. Neither film proved forthcoming.
167 *USIA 6th Report to Congress, January–June 1956*, p. 15.
168 *USIA 7th Report to Congress, July–December 1956*, pp. 19–20.
169 Eugene W. Castle, *Billions, Blunders and Baloney*, New York: Devin Adair Co., 1955.

more than this, it organized campus conferences promoting the USIA as a career.[170] The USIA had arrived. Predators in search of easy meat had to look elsewhere.

4) THE USIA AND COLD WAR GEOPOLITICS
1954–56

The USIA increasingly played a key tactical role supporting U.S. diplomacy. In Europe the agency promoted European integration. Material created for this included a film called *Tom Schuler, Statesman, Cobbler*, which used the story of the union of the thirteen original American colonies to demonstrate the advantages that could flow from the removal of trade and political barriers.[171] Germany remained the center of the USIA's European work as the agency strove to ease the path to West German reintegration into Europe. The agency also worked against the Communist Party in Italy by aiding the "free trade unions" and managed the media events around the signing of the Austrian treaty.[172]

In Latin America, the USIA's approach owed much to a report on the region by President Eisenhower's youngest brother, Milton, which included a call for expanded agency work in the region.[173] The NSC defined six priority countries – Brazil, Chile, Bolivia, Mexico, Guatemala, and Argentina – but the agency expanded across the region to meet the challenge from both home-grown nationalism and imported Marxism. Regional emphasis included the theme of the U.S. and Latin America as "partners in progress." The USIA publicized a good will mission by Vice President Nixon and exposed several "youth educational conferences" planned for the region as Communist front activity. Governments including Brazil and Chile revoked authorizations for or denounced these events. Life was getting harder for Soviet propagandists. The USIA challenged the Soviet monopoly on labor politics in Latin America, emphasizing the role of free trade unions in American life with projects such as outdoor film shows for workers in Quito and a monthly journal launched in Mexico City, called *El Obrero*, dedicated to news of labor in the United States. After five months its circulation reached 27,000.[174]

---

[170] DDEL WHCF OF 247, box 910, Bernays to Rockefeller, 2 February 1955 and 3 March 1955. For detailed refutation of Castle see DuVal (USIA general counsel) to Masterson (White House), 30 March 1955. Rep. Scott prepared his rebuttal for the American Legion magazine in response to an article by Castle summarizing his book. For the archive of the NCAOIP see Library of Congress, Edward Bernays papers, pt. I, boxes 278 to 284. Proceedings of the MIT conference, which was attended by Streibert, may be found in box 1. The NCAOIP suggested that "The government should act as a broker stimulating private activities promoting cultural interchange," thus anticipating the "people-to-people" concept. Associated correspondence may be found in UoA Fulbright papers, A538, Bernays to Fulbright, 10 April 1956 etc.

[171] *USIA 1st Review of Operations, August–December 1953*, p. 20.

[172] *USIA 4th Report to Congress, January–June 1955*, pp. 17–18.

[173] *USIA 1st Review of Operations, August–December 1953*, p. 18.

[174] *USIA 4th Report to Congress, January–June 1955*, p. 5; *FRUS 1955–1957, Vol. VI, American Republics; Multilateral; Mexico; Caribbean*, doc. 8, NSC Progress Report, Latin America, 28 March 1956, pp. 46–57. Global labor projects included fraternal greetings broadcast by U.S. labor leaders to the world on May Day 1955 over the VOA.

Guatemala proved a particular preoccupation. In 1950, a socialist named Jacobo Arbenz Guzmán won the presidential election and embarked on a radical campaign of land reform, confiscating some of the land owned by the American owned United Fruit Company and awarding it to peasants. Washington detected the hand of Moscow. In 1952, Truman authorized a plan to overthrow Arbenz. In August 1953, flushed with success in Iran, Eisenhower approved a revised plan.[175] In the closing months of 1953, as the CIA prepared to move against Arbenz, the USIA developed a supporting media effort. The agency sent a new PAO to Guatemala City with a brief to play down talk of United Fruit imperialism and create and place unattributed articles in the country's media "labeling certain Guatemalan officials as Communists and also labeling the Guatemalan government as Communist inspired." The USIA reinforced its facilities in Mexico to mass-produce leaflets and, in May 1954, went into overdrive publicizing news of a shipment of Eastern European arms to Arbenz. In the next four weeks the USIA created 200 articles, backgrounders, and scripts for placement with foreign media and distributed 27,000 anti-Communist posters or cartoons.[176]

In June 1954, a CIA-backed army of rebels entered Guatemala from Honduras. Buoyed by a clandestine CIA radio station and timely improvised air support, they overthrew the Arbenz government and installed General Carlos Castillo Armas. USIA coverage of events stressed "Kremlin coordination" of Arbenz's diplomatic moves and his contempt for the Organization of American States. The USIA then worked to bolster the new anti-Communist government by playing up the misdeeds of the Arbenz regime. Two USIA cameramen toured the country to collect evidence of Communist atrocities. Documentary films followed.[177] The IPS included a cartoon strip, "the liberation of Guatemala," in its *True Tales* strip, then seen in forty-six countries. The USIS used radio, touring exhibits, film shows, press, and pamphlets to "re-educate those sectors formerly most exposed to Communist propaganda." They also worked closely with the education ministry to purge Communist influence from textbooks and staged events for Guatemalan teachers though the Binational Center. The USIS produced a special film to celebrate the first anniversary of the overthrow of Arbenz "illustrating a year of progress under freedom." The film played commercially across the country. Guatemala was the first port of call in the hemisphere for both *The Family of Man* and *Porgy and Bess*.[178]

While the USIA trumpeted Guatemalan freedom, the Castillo regime suspended civil liberties, cancelled the election scheduled for 1955, and showed no mercy to its opposition. Torture and political murders abounded. The Castillo regime did not

---

175   For a complete history of the coup see Stephen Schlesinger and Stephen Kinzer, *Bitter Fruit, The Story of the American Coup in Guatemala*, Harvard University Press, 1999. Kate Doyle and Peter Kornbluh, *National Security Archive Electronic Briefing Book No. 4, CIA and Assassinations: The Guatemala 1954 Documents*, on line at http://www.gwu.edu/~nsarchiv/NSAEBB/NSAEBB4/.

176   *FRUS 1952–1954, Guatemala*, doc. 280, "Report on actions taken by USIA in Guatemalan situation," 27 July 1954.

177   *FRUS 1952–1954, Guatemala*, docs. 236, 237, and 280; ADST Oral History, Adamson. For an internal CIA history see http://www.gwu.edu/~nsarchiv/NSAEBB/NSAEBB4/cia-guatemala5_a.html.

178   DDEL OSANA, NSC/Status of Projects, box 6, NSC 5525, The USIA program, 11 August 1955; *USIA 5th Report to Congress, July–December 1955*, p. 10.

endure long, but its successors – also supported by the United States – were cut from the same cloth. Civil war broke out in 1962. In the forty years following the overthrow of Arbenz over 200,000 people died in political violence in Guatemala. An estimated ninety-three percent were victims of the military dictatorships.[179]

*

The USIA's approach to the Middle East emphasized respect for Islam. USIS posts gave intensive coverage to a colloquium of Islamic and American scholars held at Princeton, in September 1953, under the auspices of the Library of Congress. While USIA cameras whirred, delegates visited the White House.[180] Cultural activities flourished, the State Department expanded its educational exchange program for study in the United States, U.S. sports teams visited, and musicians toured, the most successful being Dizzy Gillespie in the spring and summer of 1956. USIS posts cultivated Middle Eastern journalists in their home countries. PAOs would have liked to bring them to the United States on exchanges, but knew that U.S. visa restrictions simply would not allow left-wing journalists to enter the country. The USIA was always on the lookout for new strategies and USIS Iraq helped circulate host government leaflets linking communism with Zionism. The theme failed to generate much excitement. The Baghdad embassy did better criticizing communism as antinationalistic.[181]

In Egypt, USIS Cairo achieved a number of remarkable coups in its relations with the government of Nasser. By 1955, a visit to the USIS library had been written into the curriculum for Egyptian high school students. Nasser wrote the introduction to a USIS book, *The Truth About Communism*. Even so, the United States saw Nasser as a threat, especially after he purchased a sizeable shipment of arms from Czechoslovakia in the autumn of 1955. In March 1956, the State Department joined the British Foreign Office in developing a covert propaganda strategy to undermine Nasser's standing in the Arab world and boost their preferred client, Iraq. USIS posts took up the necessary themes. In July 1956, Nasser nationalized the Suez Canal and set his policy on a collision course with Britain and France. As conflict loomed, the United States distanced itself from London and Paris. Anglo-American propaganda cooperation withered. Guidance to USIS posts emphasized upholding international law, with a caveat to avoid any linkage between Suez and the U.S. role in Panama. When Britain, France, and Israel launched their military expedition against Egypt in October, the VOA stepped into the breach as an authoritative news source, scheduling extra

---

[179] The statistics come from the conclusion of the Comisión para Esclarecimiento Histórico (Historical Clarification Commission) established in 1994 by the Oslo peace process. For text in English version see http://shr.aaas.org/guatemala/ceh/report/english/toc.html. Eighty-three percent of the victims were Mayan.

[180] *USIA 1st Review of Operations, August–December 1953*, p. 15.

[181] Vaughan, *The Anglo-American Relationship and Propaganda Strategies in the Middle East, 1953–1957*, pp. 53–61, 70–78. On Dizzy Gillespie see also Penny M. Von Eschen, "Who's the Real Ambassador: Exploding Cold War Racial Ideology," in Christian Appy (ed.), *Cold War Constructions: The Political Culture of United States Imperialism, 1945–1966*, Amherst: University of Massachusetts Press, 2000. On Iraq see http://www.gwu.edu/~nsarchiv/NSAEBB/NSAEBB78/docs.htm, doc. 22.

bulletins to cover the crisis. Although Nasser emerged from the Suez crisis as the propaganda victor, Eisenhower won friends by engineering a ceasefire through the UN, and the USIA believed that its even-handed output during the crisis enhanced their standing in the region.[182]

*

The USIA's output in Asia focused on the containment of China. Its first major campaign seized on the story of 14,000 "Communist" prisoners of war, held in South Korea at the time of the armistice of 1953, who asked not to be repatriated to the People's Republic of China. Treatment included news material generated by the agency's press service and intensive coverage on the VOA.[183] Propaganda to China itself fell under "Operation Discord": a plan to promote a Sino–Soviet split. As the only channel open to the USIA was the VOA, the agency developed commentaries to sow distrust of the Russian ally.[184] The confrontation with China created problems for the USIA elsewhere in the world. When in 1955 the Chinese attempted to militarize the strategically valuable islands of Quemoy and Matsu, the Eisenhower administration used the threat of a nuclear strike to hold the line. Although Asian audiences understood the stakes, they suspected an ethnic bias in America's readiness to use such weapons in their region just ten years after Hiroshima and Nagasaki. Europeans were simply appalled that the United States would risk war over two small islands.[185]

In South Korea, the USIA recognized that public democratic messages would irritate the government, and so the agency began to target opinion-formers directly through books, motion pictures, and personal contact. The USIA set up an Information Policy Coordinating Committee to coordinate the work of all U.S. agencies in the country. Joint programs ranged from documentary films to stenciling "Strength for Korea from America" on all shipments of aid. Overseas the USIA attempted to steer world reporting of the negotiations over Korea "with the aim of fixing the blame for failure to reach agreement squarely on the Communist side."[186]

During the early 1950s, Indochina emerged as the preeminent focus of U.S. concern in Asia. Truman had initiated aid to the French in their war against the

---

[182]　Vaughan, *The Anglo-American Relationship and Propaganda Strategies in the Middle East, 1953–1957*, esp. pp. 84, 184–91, 247–59. See also http://www.gwu.edu/~nsarchiv/NSAEBB/NSAEBB78/ docs.htm, doc. 131. Despite Suez, Harold Macmillan swiftly concluded an agreement with Eisenhower to establish a small number of Anglo-American working groups to help coordinate policy in "political, economic, defense, scientific and psychological warfare fields." DDEL DDE Papers as President (Ann Whitman), Administrative Series, box 37, USIA file 1, Eisenhower to Washburn, 5 November 1957; also NA RG 306 64-A-0536, Director's Office Subject files, 1957–1958, box 1, file: Field – British relations, 1957, Memorandum of Conversation 20 December 1957, "US–UK information and psychological activities," – joint activities included British monitoring of VOA reception in countries where the U.S. had no embassy and exchange of policy guidance.

[183]　*USIA 1st Review of Operations, August–December 1953*, pp. 12–13; *USIA 2nd Review of Operations, January–June 1954*, p. 22. With funding from the government of the Republic of China (Taiwan), a group of these soldiers toured Asia lecturing on their experiences.

[184]　DDEL OSANA, NSC/Status of Projects, box 6, NSC 5525, The USIA program, 11 August 1955.

[185]　DDEL OSANA, NSC/Status of Projects, box 6, NSC 5525, The USIA program, 11 August 1955.

[186]　*FRUS 1952–1954, Vol. XV*, 2nd OCB progress report on NSC 170/1, 29 December 1954, pp. 1952–3.

Communist-led Viet Minh in 1950. In that same year a USIS post opened in Saigon to service the local press and steer the swelling corps of international correspondents. USIA staff in Saigon included a young ex-journalist named Howard R. Simpson, who later wrote a vivid memoir of his futile attempts to teach the Bao Dai government the basics of Western press relations and develop the psychological warfare capacity of the French and their Indo-Chinese allies. By 1954, as the French war ground toward defeat, Eisenhower spoke with increasing anxiety about the need to contain communism in the East. At a press conference on 7 April 1954, he used the famous metaphor of falling dominoes and speculated that the loss of Indochina might start a chain reaction of catastrophe for U.S. interests. The USIA had an obvious role to play in holding the line.[187] The agency did much to support the "domino" immediately next to Indochina: Thailand. In 1954, the USIA began a major anti-Communist indoctrination program, opening three information centers in the northwest of the country, near border areas where Viet Minh troops had been active. The USIA also planned a program for the Thai army focusing on the benefits of democracy. By 1955, participants included Buddhist priests who had hitherto remained aloof from politics. The USIA reported a positive response in Thai editorials and official denunciations of communism.[188]

Then came the Geneva Conference. In the early summer of 1954 the great powers agreed upon the future of Indochina. Laos and Cambodia would be separate states and Vietnam would be temporarily divided into a Communist-dominated North and an anti-Communist South. The United States saw South Vietnam and its new leader Ngo Dinh Diem as ideal candidates for nation-building and deployed the USIA as one of the major tools to this end. Before the Geneva talks concluded, the USIA created new posts at Battambang in Cambodia and Svannakhet in Laos. The USIA used mobile units, including special sampans on the Mekong River, to carry the anti-Communist message inland. Posts created and screened the first movies with Lao or Cambodian soundtracks and the first moving images of the Laotian king. In Vietnam the USIA braced for the expected wave of Communist infiltration.[189]

The key figure in the USIA's post-Geneva work in South Vietnam was the new PAO in Saigon, George Hellyer, appointed in 1953. He began with a psychological warfare course for the Vietnamese armed forces and government.[190] In March 1954, the President's Special Committee on Indochina, which included Jackson, Streibert, and Allen Dulles, called for an expansion of overt and covert propaganda.[191] The

---

187   Howard R. Simpson, *Tiger in the Barbed Wire: An American in Vietnam, 1952–1991*, Washington, DC: Brassey's, 1992.

188   *USIA 2nd Review of Operations, January–June 1954*, p. 21; DDEL OSANA, NSC/Status of Projects, box 6, NSC 5525, The USIA program, 11 August 1955, p. 15.

189   *USIA 2nd Review of Operations, January–June 1954*, p. 21; *USIA 4th Report to Congress, January–June 1955*, p. 16.

190   *FRUS 1952–1954, Vol. XIII, Indochina, Part 1*, pp. 256–9 for early work of USIS Saigon; Heath (Saigon) to State, 15 February 1954, pp. 1046–9; ADST Oral History: Robert Chatten; Howard R. Simpson. Also Simpson, *Tiger in the Barbed Wire*, pp. 65, 84–5.

191   *FRUS 1952–1954, Vol. XIII*, Report of President's Special Committee on Indochina, 2 March 1954, pp. 1109–16.

CIA's campaign began that summer under the leadership of an Air Force Colonel now seconded to the CIA, Edward G. Lansdale, a counterinsurgency expert who had made his reputation in the Philippines. Lansdale arrived in June. As well as organizing teams of saboteurs for infiltration into the North, Lansdale set about a major psychological campaign. He found a keen ally in Hellyer, who shared his desk and served as Lansdale's translator in meetings with Diem. Both men tried to convince Diem of the importance of good press conferences. This proved an uphill struggle.[192]

Lansdale's set piece campaign was a bid to panic as many Vietnamese as possible into fleeing to the south during the ten-month relocation window agreed upon at Geneva.[193] Eight hundred thousand people relocated.[194] Black propaganda rumors of a coming persecution of Catholics proved especially powerful.[195] USIS staff in Saigon worked closely with Lansdale in three areas. The first was stimulating the movement in the first place by promoting the virtues of life in the free South; techniques included leaflets and posters issued as though by the Diem government. One colleague recalled Hellyer delivering such leaflets himself, tossing them out of planes while lying on the floor. Next, the USIS had to keep the refugees informed and counter Communist messages during their actual migration, touring refugee camps with special films and sound recordings. Finally, the USIS tried "to counter . . . disillusionment" when the refugees actually arrived in the South. This last task proved to be the most difficult. The South Vietnamese regime proved a tricky commodity to sell.[196]

In October 1955, Diem moved to consolidate his power, calling a snap election (in which he "won" more than 98 percent of the vote) and proclaiming the Republic of South Vietnam with himself as president. Washington accepted his fait accompli and settled into the business of touting Diem around the world as a paragon of democratic virtue. By the end of the year, the USIS had twenty-three branch offices in Vietnam and suffered its first hand grenade attack at its Saigon headquarters. The USIA's Vietnam War had begun.[197]

[192] *The Pentagon Papers: The Defense Department History of United States Decisionmaking in Vietnam, Vol. 1 (The Senator Gravel Edition)*, Boston: Beacon Press, 1971, "Lansdale team's report on covert Saigon mission in 1954 and 1955," pp. 573–83; ADST: Oral History, Robert Chatten; Howard R. Simpson; James J. Halsema; Cecil B. Currey, *Edward Lansdale: The Unquiet American*, Washington, DC: Brassey's, 1998, pp. 140–52; Simpson, *Tiger in the Barbed Wire*, p. 115.
[193] *The Pentagon Papers, Vol. 1 (Gravel Edition)*, pp. 573–83; Currey, *Edward Lansdale*, pp. 156–63; Simpson, *Tiger in the Barbed Wire*, pp. 118–22.
[194] Ronald H. Spector, *Advice and Support: The Early Years of the U.S. Army in Vietnam, 1941–1960*, New York: Free Press, 1985, pp. 225–7.
[195] Bernard Fall, *The Two Vietnams: A Political and Military Analysis*, New York: Praeger, 1964, pp. 153–4.
[196] William Conrad Gibbons, *The U.S. Government and the Vietnam War: Executive and Legislative Roles and Relationships, Part 1, 1945–1960*, Princeton, NJ: Princeton University Press, 1986, p. 266; *USIA 3rd Report to Congress, July–December 1954*, p. 19. The USIS role in Lansdale's campaign is recalled by Everet Bumgardner in Neil Sheehan, *A Bright Shining Lie: John Paul Vann and the American Experience in Vietnam*, New York: Random House, 1988, pp. 135–6; also ADST Oral History: Burnett; Halsema.
[197] *USIA 4th Report to Congress, January–June 1955*, p. 17; *USIA 5th Report to Congress, July–December 1955*, p. 22.

*

In April 1955, the leaders of twenty-nine emerging nations of Africa and Asia
met in Bandung on the coast of Indonesia. Although the neutralism at the heart of
the conference ostensibly offered a bleak prospect to the USIA, the agency turned the
conference to modest advantage, largely by helping to prepare sympathetic delegations
and their home audiences for the conference. The PAO in Libya actually briefed that
country's delegation before their departure for Bandung. When, discreetly encouraged by the United States, any delegates expressed anti-Communist or pro-Western
sentiments, the two USIA officers assigned to the conference relayed the text back to
Washington, where it was speedily given global distribution over the VOA and the
USIA's wireless file.[198]

The USIA's approach to the emerging nations had its pitfalls. In May 1955,
the Secretary General of the Indian Ministry of Foreign Affairs summoned the U.S.
ambassador to New Delhi, John Sherman Cooper, to an uncomfortable interview.
Prime Minister Nehru had heard rumors about USIA "subsidies of Indian newspapers
and individuals." Nehru felt undermined. The Foreign Ministry cited the appearance
of the same article attacking China in both a Pakistani and an Indian newspaper on the
same day, under different local bylines, as evidence of American intrigue. The USIA
concluded that the coincidence was probably the result of lazy journalists passing off
a USIS handout as their own composition. Ambassador Cooper assured Nehru that
the USIA did not subsidize newspapers and reminded him of its record of support
for the government of India. He even offered to allow the Indians to review USIS
operations in the country. Nehru appeared placated but maintained obvious doubts
about "other agencies." Cooper tactfully suggested a review of the CIA's work in
India.[199]

*

The shift of the Cold War into the new theater of the developing world
during the early Eisenhower years did not mean that the administration took its
eye off the Kremlin. Washington read the host of small confrontations around the
world as evidence of a great animating design initiated by Moscow. Soviet propaganda
rallied behind a new slogan: "Peaceful coexistence." Eisenhower believed that their
budget topped $2 billion. Unfortunately, since the departure of C. D. Jackson, the

---

[198] DDEL OSANA, NSC/Status of Projects, box 6, NSC 5525, The USIA program, 11 August 1955
p. 4.

[199] *FRUS 1955–1957, Vol. VIII, South Asia*, doc. 145, Cooper to State, 23 May 1955, pp. 279–81; doc.
146, Cooper to State, 25 May 1955, pp. 281–3; doc. 147, Hoover (USoS) to Cooper, 25 May 1955,
pp. 284–6; doc. 148, Cooper to State, 1 June 1955, pp. 286–8. Indian interference with the USIS
continued. The agency's annual report to the NSC in June 1957 cited as typical the GOI attempt to
withhold an exhibition license for the Amalgamated Clothing Workers film *With These Hands*, used by
the USIS for some time, unless a scene dealing with attempted communist infiltration were deleted.
The USIS refused to be strong-armed and to the plaudits of many in the local press withdrew the
film entirely. See DDEL OSANA, NSC/Status of Projects, box 7, NSC 5611 part II (3), Status of
National Security Program on 30 June 1957, part 6, p. 13.

United States had no single psychological strategist to match the Soviets in the great game.[200] At the close of 1954, Eisenhower belatedly appointed Nelson Rockefeller as his replacement special assistant for psychological warfare. The brief had shifted somewhat from the confrontational strand in Jackson's understanding of the post. Eisenhower spoke of Rockefeller giving "advice and assistance in the development of increased understanding and cooperation among all peoples." Rockefeller began by revising the structure of the OCB. He also addressed the knot of ever-chafing interests around planning for psychological warfare in wartime and took charge of a secret interdepartmental program developed by the Pentagon in collaboration with the State Department, CIA, and USIA called "Militant Liberty," a plan to train a new generation of anti-Communist leaders for the developing world, which came to nothing.[201]

In February 1955, the OCB approved a new interdepartmental initiative to reinvigorate the projection of U.S. ideology, coordinated by a special Ideological Working Group. Much of the program fell under the brief of the State Department, where projects included the further encouragement of American studies in universities in Europe and elsewhere. The USIA's contribution included two illustrated books, *What Is Democracy?* and *What Is Communism?*, and an unattributed journal called *Under Scrutiny*, which examined political developments in the Communist bloc. The USIA's chief of religious information, Trueblood, put together a packet of thirty-two books for USIS posts "emphasizing the spiritual and religious foundations of freedom," including a volume of his own lectures entitled *Declaration of Freedom*. The USIA also expanded magazine article and book translation programs and continued a scheme to subsidize the export of selected books through the charity CARE.[202]

Other new initiatives in 1955 included a significant contribution from the new USIA Office of Research and Intelligence. Work included publication of a single-page update on the Soviet line and propaganda activity, called *Soviet Orbit Propaganda*, three times a week; the compilation of an annual survey of Soviet propaganda; and translation of the official *Soviet Encyclopedia*. When entries revealed criticism of a prominent person or organization outside the Soviet bloc, the USIA sent the translation to the press in the country mentioned, thereby stirring anti-Soviet feeling.[203]

[200] For a review to 31 December 1954 see *FRUS 1955–1957, Vol. IX, Foreign Economic Policy; Foreign Information Program*, doc. 185, NSC 5509, 2 March 1955, pp. 504 et seq. Eisenhower cites the $2 billion figure in doc. 186, Hagerty diary entry, 22 March 1955 p. 521–2.

[201] Rockefeller created a new Planning Coordination Group in March 1955 under his chairmanship "to aid in developing planning and to infuse dynamic, new and imaginative ideas in plans and programs to implement national security policies." It did not work as Rockefeller hoped, and at the close of 1955 he initiated a second round of reform of the OCB, including a shift in the chairmanship from the Under Secretary of State to the special assistant for national security affairs. Reich, *The Life of Nelson A. Rockefeller*, pp. 551–60; DDEL WHCF CF subject, box 49, OCB (3), Rockefeller to Eisenhower, 22 December 1955.

[202] DDEL C. D. Jackson papers, box 89, Quantico Meetings 24, OCB progress report on the U.S. ideological program, 16 August 1955.

[203] *USIA 4th Report to Congress, January–June 1955*, pp. 6–7. In its approach to the U.S.S.R., the USIA had also to head off a Soviet campaign to encourage its citizens to redefect. Emphasis on the conditions enjoyed by escapees from the Eastern bloc proved an effective counterblow. DDEL OSANA, NSC/Status of Projects, box 6, NSC 5525, The USIA program, 11 August 1955.

These initiatives coincided with a marked thaw in Soviet–American relations. During the course of 1955, the United States and U.S.S.R. agreed to recommence cultural exchange. At the end of 1955, the United States began cultural operations on Soviet territory with a visit of *Porgy and Bess* to Leningrad. The USIA revived *Amerika* magazine (last seen in 1952) as *America Illustrated*. Moscow agreed to allow the sale of 50,000 copies on newsstands and the magazine duly reappeared in 1956. Despite the thaw, an OCB report of 1955 stressed the need for the United States to continue its psychological support for the "satellite" nations of the Eastern bloc. The VOA and RFE/RL ensured that Eastern Europe did not feel forgotten.[204]

In the summer of 1955, Rockefeller made two great strides in revitalizing U.S. propaganda. First, he persuaded Eisenhower to revisit an old theme with a startling new initiative. On 11 June 1955, the President announced that the United States would provide all the fuel and half the funding necessary to create nuclear research reactors for any free country wishing to develop an atomic power program.[205] Next, Rockefeller assembled an impressive range of academic experts for a secret conference at the U.S. Marine base at Quantico, Virginia. He sought a range of fresh policy options to deal with the recent developments in the Cold War, not the least being the Soviet development of ballistic missiles. Participants included C. D. Jackson and Henry Kissinger. Streibert and Washburn joined the final sessions. The Quantico Panel made a number of fascinating suggestions, including a plan from Max Millikan of MIT for a major disarmament initiative based around mutual inspection from the air. Eisenhower picked up this ball at his Geneva meeting with the new Soviet leader Nikita Khrushchev. On 21 July 1955, he stunned the world with what the press dubbed his "Open Skies" proposal. The United States and U.S.S.R. should, Eisenhower proposed, exchange blueprints on their key technical facilities and each allow the other to overfly and photograph its nuclear installations. Eisenhower realized that much of the instability around nuclear weapons came from uncertainty over the scale and readiness of the opponent's nuclear arsenal.[206]

The USIA did much to publicize "Open Skies." The VOA carried Eisenhower's words in English and thirty-seven other languages; the wireless file transmitted full details both of Eisenhower's proposal and UN reactions. The agency worked with the Air Force to create an exhibit in New York (and brochure for worldwide use) called *Mutual Inspection for Peace* in which fantastic aerial photographs showed just how much could be learned by a reconnaissance aircraft. Versions of this exhibit toured the world in 1956 and 1957. By December 1957 more than 1.5 million people had seen the exhibit. In a similar vein, all USIS posts received a dramatic set of images of Rome taken from high altitude by the Italian air force. In many places around the world,

[204] DDEL NSC staff, OCB/Central files, box 68, OCB091.4 Eastern Europe, file # 4 (3), OCB paper "Psychological implications of Geneva for U.S. information programs," 7 September 1955.

[205] Reich, *The Life of Nelson A. Rockefeller*, pp. 561–8.

[206] For a narrative of this episode DDEL, C. D. Jackson papers, box 56, "Log-1955," C. D. Jackson, "From Quantico to Geneva, June–July 1955"; W. W. Rostow, *Open Skies: Eisenhower's Proposal of July 21, 1955*; also Reich, *The Life of Nelson A. Rockefeller*, pp. 577–608.

pictures of the Vatican struck a chord that images of Manhattan could not. The USIA also created an Open Skies documentary film, *Sentinels of Peace*, released in thirty-two languages in seventy-eight countries. Open Skies did not lead to an agreement with Moscow, but it reaffirmed Eisenhower's image as a man of peace.[207]

Nelson Rockefeller supported the USIA bid for an expanded budget of $150 million for FY 1957 (which would have nearly doubled the $85 million voted for FY 1956). He proposed spending the money on a "Free World Crusade" with more People's Capitalism work, an increased program in Latin America, and expansion of the weekly service of free material to television stations around the world to serve 200 rather than just 40 stations. The eventual appropriation for FY 1957 of $113 million represented a significant breakthrough, but it stung Rockefeller as a defeat.[208] Rockefeller had one major problem: John Foster Dulles. Rockefeller never mastered the art of dealing with Dulles, who for his part resented the notion that someone outside of the State Department could generate ideas in foreign policy and did his best to erode Rockefeller's standing. By December 1955, Rockefeller had had enough and resigned. He was a great loss to the administration. Many of his observations proved prophetic, but none more so than his warning in May 1955 that the U.S. decision to develop separate systems for ballistic missiles and space launch vehicles might delay the development of both to such an extent that the U.S.S.R. could become the first nation to launch a satellite into space. "The sake of prestige," he wrote, "makes this a race we cannot afford to lose." Ignored in 1955, his warning was remembered in October 1957.[209]

Following Rockefeller's departure, Eisenhower persuaded William H. Jackson to serve as special assistant for psychological warfare during 1956 and 1957 but increasingly recognized the persistence of "resentment in the State Department." Eventually he "thought it best to abolish the office" and create a new position called Special Assistant to the President for Security Operations Coordination, who would also be vice-chairman of OCB.[210]

*

The year 1956 began quietly enough for the USIA. The agency had four key objectives for the year: promoting the unity of the free world; exposing local

---

207 *USIA 5th Report to Congress, July–December 1955,* pp. 1–3; *USIA 6th Report to Congress, January–June 1956,* p. 3; *USIA 7th Report to Congress, July–December 1956,* p. 7; *USIA 9th Review of Operations, July 1–December 31, 1957,* p. 7.

208 DDEL WHCF, OF 247, box 910, Rockefeller to Eisenhower, 30 November 1955; *USIA 6th Report to Congress, January–June 1956,* p. 37; Reich, *The Life of Nelson Rockefeller,* pp. 629–31. On the budget issue see also *FRUS 1955–1957, Vol. IX,* doc. 186, Hagerty diary, 22 March 1955, in which Eisenhower tells key senators that "appropriations for USIA were very close to his heart"; doc. 195, memo of meeting of President and legislative leaders, 13 December 1955, pp. 562–4 and doc. 196, memo of meeting between President and Republican leaders, 13 March 1956, pp. 564–5.

209 Robert S. Rosholt et al., *An Administrative History of NASA, 1958–1963,* Washington, DC: 1966, pp. 4–5, cited in Rostow, *Open Skies,* p. 77. On Rockefeller's resignation see Reich, *The Life of Nelson Rockefeller,* pp. 631–4.

210 DDEL OSANA – OCB/subject, box 1, Coordination of information and public opinion aspects of National Security Policies, esp. President to Secretary of State, 21 July 1959.

Communist parties as expressions of global "Red Colonialism"; communicating the message that "The United States champions peace and progress through peaceful change"; and publicizing Atoms for Peace.[211] But the next few months saw dramatic new opportunities.

It began at midnight on 24–5 February 1956. In a seven-hour secret session speech to the Twentieth Communist Party Congress in Moscow, Khrushchev made a full and damning case against Joseph Stalin. The U.S. ambassador in Moscow, Bohlen, picked up a rumor of the speech at a French embassy reception on 10 March. Allen Dulles briefed the NSC on its likely contents on 22 March. While the CIA tried frantically to get hold of the complete text, the beginnings of a de-Stalinization campaign around the Eastern bloc – including the dissolution of COMINFORM – gave the USIA more than enough material to exploit the growing crisis in communism. In May the Operations Control Board urged the VOA and the USIA to use broadcasts and unattributed press articles to ridicule the Soviet campaign and "sow confusion and doubt." The OCB hoped that de-Stalinization would unleash popular pressure for reform.[212]

By June the CIA had obtained a copy of the speech from Israel. It appeared in the *New York Times* on 5 June. Now the campaign began in earnest. On 7 June, Streibert instructed USIS posts to argue, "We can believe [that the] present regime has repudiated Stalinism only when it supplants [the] denunciation [of] certain Stalin excesses by cessation [of] methods of Stalin['s] dictatorship." VOA broadcasts and USIS press releases gave maximum publicity to the story, including the text of Khrushchev's remarks and the reactions of leaders around the world to them (but avoided U.S. comment). Eastern bloc silence gave the USIA's material all the more impact. The Italian Socialist Party leader, Pietro Nenni, remarked on the irony that it was "through the press section of USIS that the Communist parties themselves represented at the Moscow Congress have come to know one of the most serious and dramatic documents in the Communist literature of the world."[213]

The changes in Eastern Europe were initially most pronounced in Poland, where Khrushchev's speech caused the Secretary General of the Polish Communist Party, Bolesław Bierut, to drop dead of a heart attack. The new leader, Edward Ochab, announced a program of reform and the State Department began overtures toward cultural exchange. On 28 June, pressure for further liberalization and anger at food shortages boiled over in riots in Poznán. Targets included a radio jamming station. The USIA responded by circulating accounts of violent repression of the riots by Polish troops and revealing the secret arrival of Soviet food aid, hoping to anger ordinary

[211] DDEL OCB Secretariat series, box 3, Ideological documents, file 7, Lilly (OCB) to Staats (OCB), 17 January 1956.
[212] *FRUS 1955–1957, Vol. XXIV, Soviet Union; Eastern Mediterranean*, doc. 44, OCB Special Working Group Report, 17 May 1956, pp. 99–103; Bohlen, *Witness to History*, pp. 397–8; *FRUS 1955–1957, Vol. XXV, Eastern Europe*, doc. 50, 280th NSC, 22 March 1956, p. 128; *FRUS IX*, doc. 197, circular airgram USIA to all missions, 11 April 1956; doc. 198, Report of OCB special working group, 17 May 1956, pp. 578–82.
[213] *FRUS 1955–1957, Vol. XXIV*; doc. 50, circular to certain missions, 2 June 1956, pp. 109–10; doc. 51, Bohlen to State, 2 June 1956; *FRUS 1955–1957, Vol. IX*, editorial note, p. 582; *USIA 7th Report to Congress, July–December 1956*, p. 1; Hixson, *Parting the Curtain*, p. 78.

Russians, who knew their country had little to spare.[214] By the end of October the crisis had passed. A new government headed by Władysław Gomułka had sidestepped a planned Soviet military intervention, restored stability, and set course toward an idiosyncratically Polish brand of communism. Gomułka's changes included a greater openness to information from the West. In November 1956 the new government suspended its jamming of the Voice of America, thereby saving $17.5 million. Polish television began to screen USIA programs, including a documentary on the presidential election. But the parallel developments in Hungary ended very differently.[215]

On 23 October 1956, Hungary erupted. Demonstrators, inspired by the Polish protests, demanded reform in their own country. On 24 October, the moderate Imre Nagy became Prime Minister. Ordinary people turned against the Russian troops in their streets and threw down the symbols of Soviet power. On 28 October, the Soviet occupiers fell back. On 1 November, Nagy withdrew Hungary from the Warsaw Pact and declared his country's neutrality. But any sense of a new dawn was cruelly premature. Knowing that the Western powers were preoccupied with the simultaneous Suez crisis, Moscow launched a swift and bloody counterattack.[216] The assault on Budapest began at dawn on 4 November. Hungarian citizens armed with hunting rifles and Molotov cocktails fought the mechanized might of the Red Army for three days. They had no chance. Thousands died. For an old Cold Warrior such as C. D. Jackson the spectacle of U.S. impotence as the Soviet tanks rolled on Budapest was too much to bear. He wrote to Eisenhower urging decisive action in support of the rebellion, but to no avail. His time had passed.[217] Hungary exposed what Washington had acknowledged privately for a long time: there would be no immediate liberation of Eastern Europe. The two systems, each now armed with a massive nuclear arsenal, would have to play a different game, sparring for influence in the developing world.

The USIA seized on the events in Hungary as a source for anti-Soviet copy. The VOA reported the story round the clock. The International Motion Picture Service created a documentary film – *The Hungarian Fight for Freedom* – using the first actual footage brought out of the country and released the film in twenty-four languages to eighty-one countries. USIS posts publicized U.S. aid to the thousands of Hungarian refugees and displayed a dramatic set of pictures illustrating the street fighting carried across the Austrian border by an escapee. [218]

But the role of the USIA during the Hungarian crisis soon became a major issue in its own right. Had the United States, as Tito and some German newspapers claimed, fomented the revolt with radio propaganda, only to then stand back while the Soviet

214 *FRUS 1955–1957, Vol. XXV, Eastern Europe*, doc. 51, State to Embassy Warsaw, 28 March 1956; doc. 67, Sec of State Staff Meeting, 29 June 1956, p. 187; doc. 81, Meeting of OCB, 18 July 1956, p. 222. For Polish background see Adam Zamoyski, *The Polish Way*, London: John Murray, 1987, pp. 379–80.

215 *USIA 7th Report to Congress, July–December 1956*, pp. 2–4.

216 The USIA responded to Suez by expanding VOA Arabic from 1.5 to 14.5 hours daily. *USIA 7th Report to Congress, July–December 1956*, p. 3

217 Brands, *Cold Warriors*, pp. 132–4.

218 *USIA 7th Report to Congress, July–December 1956*, p. 2; *FRUS 1955–1957, Vol. XXV*, doc. 175, 303rd NSC, 8 November 1956.

tanks did their worst? The U.S. press soon asked the same question. Within days of the invasion, Washburn gave President Eisenhower a full report on VOA broadcasting to Hungary, including sample scripts. At this time the VOA carried an hour of programming each day in Hungarian from the Washington studio and forty-five minutes more from Munich (both heavily jammed) with a half hour of English (unjammed). Half of this material was news and the rest split evenly between commentary or editorial roundups and features. The broadcasts held fast to a policy outlined by Streibert back on 27 October 1953 of emphasizing "truth, objective news coverage and commentary from the U.S. policy viewpoint." Washburn noted, "Stridency and inflammatory content have been avoided." Over recent years, he reported, the VOA had sought to preserve "the idea of hope and freedom" and even to foster nationalisms in Eastern Europe, but the Voice had avoided talk of liberation. When the riots began on 22 October 1956, the VOA pointedly limited its output to keeping the Hungarian people informed about the events and the world's reaction. Some programs explicitly urged caution. The VOA even took the decision to "omit material, although verified, which might have an incendiary effect on the Hungarian audiences such as stories concerning Soviet atrocities."[219]

The VOA's restraint stood in marked contrast to the behavior of Radio Free Europe. For the political exiles who broadcast over RFE, the rising was an answer to their prayers and they did whatever they could to cheer on Hungarian resistance. An internal review conducted in December 1956 revealed that during the days leading up to the Soviet invasion, some RFE broadcasters had flouted policy guidance and suggested that NATO aid was imminent. The message to Hungary was to keep fighting and wait for liberation. Earlier broadcasts included instructions on guerrilla warfare techniques. Even programs that followed policy guidelines were "over-excited" and flawed by "too much rhetoric, too much emotionalism." The review concluded that although RFE had not instigated the revolution, it had at least failed to deter it and at times had inflamed matters. RFE's system of policy control had failed.[220]

Eisenhower responded to the controversy on 14 November by issuing a press statement that "the United States doesn't now, and never has, advocated open rebellion by an undefended populace against force over which they could not possibly prevail." The State Department noted that because RFE was a nominally independent operation,

---

[219] DDEL NSC staff, OCB/Central Files, box 68, OCB 091.4, Eastern Europe (5), Washburn to Eisenhower, "the Voice of America broadcasts to Hungary," 19 November 1956; see also Bundy (USIA) to Staats (OCB) 3 December 1956 inc. USIA paper: "Policy Control of VOA Output to Eastern Europe." Reproduced as doc. 197 in *FRUS 1955–1957, Vol. XXV, Eastern Europe*, pp. 470–71; see also doc. 185, 46th meeting of Special Committee on Soviet and Related Problems, OCB, 13 November 1956. This analysis is borne out by the case study by Garry D. Rawnsley; see Rawnsley, *Radio Diplomacy and Propaganda: The BBC and VOA in International Politics, 1956–64*, New York: St Martin's Press, 1996, pp. 67–108.

[220] For documentation on RFE and Hungary see Csaba Békés, János Rainer, and Malcolm Byrne (eds.), *The 1956 Hungarian Revolution in Documents*, Budapest: Central European University Press, 2002, online at http://www.gwu.edu/%7Ensarchiv/NSAEBB/NSAEBB76/doc10.pdf; Policy Review for Voice of Free Hungary programming, 23 October—23 November 1956; William Griffith, 5 December 1956; see also *FRUS 1955–1957, Vol. XXV*, doc. 214, Wailes (Budapest) to State, 18 December 1956, pp. 520–22.

this statement did not apply. The statement did not appease the administration's ene-
mies. In mid-December, Senator Hubert Humphrey called for an investigation of the
VOA's broadcasts during the uprising. Both RFE and the VOA carried the lesson of
Hungary forward into the future.[221]

In the midst of the Hungarian crisis, Eisenhower won a second term as President.
The USIA publicized the election campaign as a shining example of democracy in
action, but the election meant trouble. The Democrats retained the control of the
Senate and House that they had won in 1955, which left the USIA beholden to the
tough-minded Senate majority leader, Lyndon Baines Johnson of Texas. With Eisenhower's reelection secure, Streibert returned to private life. Accepting his resignation
on 8 November 1956, Eisenhower wrote, "You and your colleagues have developed
the United States Information Agency into a strong arm of our country in our struggle
for world freedom . . . You have every reason to be proud of your accomplishments."[222]
Streibert moved to an executive position at Time–Life broadcasting. He maintained a
keen interest in Cold War propaganda and from 1962 to 1965 served as president of
Radio Free Europe. He died in 1987.[223]

Under Streibert's leadership the USIA had indeed achieved much, helping Eisenhower to recapture the initiative in the ideological Cold War. But the agency also still
had obvious limitations. The director of the USIA lacked the advisory functions seen in
the old office of Assistant Secretary of State for Public Affairs or maintained by the CIA
director. The role of injecting the psychological dimension into foreign policy planning had remained with the special assistant for psychological warfare. The demise
of this position left room for an expanded role for Streibert's successors. Although
the USIA did not have a monopoly over U.S. programs reaching out to the world's
public – the exchange and cultural programs remained at the State Department –
the agency led the way in the field. Moreover, the post-rollback approach fitted both
the USIA's flexibility and the emerging news agenda of the VOA. The agency had the
global reach necessary to carry the message of reconciliation into the Eastern bloc and
to fight the Cold War in the emerging theater of the newly decolonized world.

---

[221] *FRUS 1955–1957, Vol. XXV*, doc. 213, Hoover (USoS to Hagerty (White House)), 15 December
       1956, p. 518; doc 216, 58th meeting of the Special Committee on Soviet and Related Problems, 19
       December 1956.
[222] DDEL WHCF OF 247, box 910, Eisenhower to Streibert, 8 November 1956.
[223] Aubin Krebs, "Theodore Streibert, First Director of USIA," *New York Times*, 22 January 1987,
       p. B.20.

3 In the Shadow of Sputnik

THE SECOND EISENHOWER ADMINISTRATION, 1957–61

> Whether you like it or not, history is on our side. We will bury you.
>
> Nikita Khrushchev, 18 November 1956[1]

The USIA began Eisenhower's second term warmed by the glow of accomplishment. The agency's managers felt that their staff had worked well in the field, and the USIA director increasingly shared in foreign policy-making. On 25 February 1957, a presidential executive order mandated the director's full membership of the Operations Coordinating Board and located the board within the framework of the NSC. The agency's place within the foreign policy structure was secure. On that same day, Eisenhower celebrated the fifteenth anniversary of the VOA by becoming the first President to address the world directly from its studios. The USIA estimated the audience at around 350 million.[2] But unlike the first term, the course of U.S. information in the second Eisenhower administration would not be defined by initiatives from Washington. The terrain of Cold War propaganda was changed utterly by a beeping 22-inch metal sphere from the Soviet Union, weighing around 183 pounds, trailing four antennas, and named "traveling companion," or in Russian, "Sputnik."

The Soviet launch of Sputnik, on Friday 4 October 1957, pitched humanity headlong into the Space Age. The news broke at around six in the evening Washington time. "Sputnik Night" became one of those news events so potent as to print itself indelibly on the memory of those who lived through it. America responded as to a mixture of Lindbergh flying the Atlantic and Pearl Harbor. The country's wonder at the breakthrough was tinged with the sting of being bested by a rival and a chill awareness of the vulnerability of the United States to missile attack. Sputnik had passed across the United States quite undetected twice before Moscow announced its presence. Democrats had a field day scoring points against an administration caught napping. G. Mennen Williams, the Democratic governor of Michigan, expressed his response in verse: "Oh little Sputnik, flying high, with made-in-Moscow beep,/You

---

[1] Quoted in "Ambassadors Walk Out," *Times* (London), 19 November 1956, p. 8.
[2] *USIA 8th Review of Operations, January 1–June 30, 1957*, p. 19; NA RG 306, ZZ entry 1 (formerly 1006), Director's Chronological files, 1953–64, box 2, microfilm reel 16, Larson (USIA director) to President, 26 February 1957. Washburn to Stanley, 23 February 1957, notes Larson wrote this address for Eisenhower. For text see *PPPDDE, 1957*, pp. 158–61.

tell the world it's a Commie sky, and Uncle Sam's asleep."[3] Along similar lines, at the time of Sputnik's reentry, English children devised a parody of the Perry Como hit "Catch a Falling Star": "Catch a falling Sputnik,/Put it in a basket,/Send it to the U.S.A./They'll be glad to have it,/Very glad to have it,/And never let it get away."[4]

The USIA's Office of Research and Intelligence hurried to take stock of the damage done by Sputnik. Surveying world opinion, they found wide acceptance of Soviet claims to technological superiority over the United States, a sense in Western Europe that the military balance must also have shifted in Moscow's favor, and a general enhancement of Soviet prestige. The USIA had no doubt that Sputnik would lend credibility to the economic system that had created it and be especially potent among "those least able to understand it" – the "backward, ignorant and apolitical" citizens of the developing world.[5] Suddenly the United States was on the ropes. Eisenhower's second term would be dominated by talk of "gaps" in space, prestige, and missiles.[6] Unfortunately, by October 1957, the USIA was in no shape to respond. The air of self-confidence seen at the close of 1956 had been transformed to profound uncertainty by a year of political difficulties at home. The root of these difficulties was simple: Eisenhower's decision to appoint Arthur Larson to the office of USIA director.

1) "EGGHEAD WITH TROUBLES"
ARTHUR LARSON AND THE USIA IN 1957[7]

When Eisenhower selected Arthur Larson to head the USIA, he chose a man whose political affiliation was far more obvious than that of Ted Streibert. Born in Sioux Falls, South Dakota, on 4 July 1910, and described in the press as handsome and well dressed with an "oddly hopeful look," Arthur Larson had a glowing vita. A Rhodes scholar at Oxford in the early 1930s, he practiced labor law in Tennessee, held a chair of law at Cornell by 1945, and was dean of law at the University of Pittsburgh from 1953. Larson served as Under Secretary of Labor during Eisenhower's first term. His books included the path-breaking treatise *The Law of Workmen's Compensation* (1952). In the early summer of 1956, Larson published a surprise bestseller, *A Republican Looks at His Party*, in which he developed a notion of "New Republicanism." The book called for Republicans to claim the political middle ground. "In politics – as in chess," Larson

3   Roger D. Launius, Sputnik and the Origins of the Space Age, http://www.hq.nasa.gov/office/pao/History/sputnik/sputorig.html#visions.
4   Quoted in DDEL PCIIA (Sprague Committee), box 22, report no. 23, "The Impact of achievements in science and technology upon the image abroad of the United States," 6 June 1960, Section III.1. The original song *Catch a Falling Star*, written by Lee Pockriss and Paul Vance, was released in the United Kingdom in February 1958.
5   DDEL OSANA, OCB/Subject, box 8, Space, Satellites, Rockets etc., file 1, USIA ORI, "World Opinion and the Soviet Satellite," 17 October 1957, P-94–57; also DDEL WHCF, OF 247, box 911, USIA ORI, "The Impact of Sputnik upon the Press of Western Europe," 18 October 1957, P-92–57.
6   For a full treatment of Eisenhower's response see Robert A. Divine, *The Sputnik Challenge: Eisenhower's Response to the Soviet Satellite*, New York: Oxford University Press, 1993.
7   The title comes from a press profile of Larson: "Egghead with troubles," *New York Times*, 11 May 1957, p. 11.

wrote, "the man who holds the center holds a position of almost unbeatable strength." Even before publication Eisenhower brought Larson into the inner circle of his 1956 presidential campaign, commissioning him to write his nomination acceptance. As the race gathered momentum, the press hailed Larson as the Republican Party's "No. 1 Egghead" and "GOP find of the year." Once Ike had won again, it seemed logical to redeploy the architect of that victory in a global campaign through the USIA.[8]

William Benton, who kept a fatherly eye on the USIA, approved of the appointment. "Arthur Larson is a smart propagandist," he wrote, "perhaps the smartest that the Republicans have developed."[9] But Larson foundered precisely because of his party role. As the brains behind "New Republicanism," Larson was doomed to draw fire on himself and his agency from Democrats with their own designs on the political center, and to muster no sympathy from traditionalists within his own party. Washington's newest political target sat naked at the helm of a perennial whipping boy activity, with predictable results.[10] To make matters worse, since the spring of 1956 the press magnate Roy Howard had been lobbying against the USIA, claiming that it competed unfairly with his United Press. The Scripps–Howard newspaper chain launched a "vicious campaign" alleging waste and mismanagement at the USIA. Larson's enemies on the Hill did not have to look far to find ammunition.[11]

Arthur Larson began his tenure at the USIA with a flourish. He assured the press that he would not be "preaching," "bragging," or "selling America." He pledged to develop the USIA and VOA as bastions of factual reporting with material about America crafted to meet the needs of the overseas audience, not the creator's pride.[12] With this in mind he discontinued use overseas of the agency's slogan "telling America's story to the world."[13] The USIA also ceased using religious programming on the VOA for propaganda purposes, halting the broadcast of Orthodox services to Russia and the practice of reading from the Koran before news in Arabic.[14]

8 Arthur Larson, *A Republican Looks at His Party*, New York: Harper & Bros, 1956, p. 19. On Larson's background and appointment see Marquis Childs, "Ike's Team Plans New Look for GOP," *Washington Post*, 29 August 1956, p. 10; Edward T. Follard, "Larson Rated GOP's 'Find of the Year,'" *Washington Post*, 30 September 1956, p. E.1; Gardner L. Bridge, "Larson Named to Head USIA," *Washington Post*, 11 November 1956; George Dixon, Washington Scene . . . , "Be-Beastly-to-USIA-Week," *Washington Post*, 10 June 1957, A.13; Bruce Lambert, "L. Arthur Larson Is Dead at 82; Top Eisenhower Aide and Writer," *New York Times*, 1 April 1993, p. D.24.
9 UoC Benton papers, box 380/1, Benton to Howe, 20 November 1956.
10 For an example of Larson's partisan speeches see "New GOP Unified says USIA Head," *Washington Post*, 15 March 1957, p. C.5.
11 DDEL DDE Cabinet, box 8, minutes 18 January 1957. For a summary of this affair see NA RG 306 64-A-0536, Director's Office Subject files, 1957–8, box 5, file: Public Info/Press, Cushing (I/R) to Allen (USIA director), 7 May 1957; also "USIA as a Scapegoat," *Washington Post*, 19 May 1957. AP and INS executives testified during the hearings of 1957 that the USIA was not unfair competition.
12 Dana Adams Schmidt, "Voice Chief Sees U.S. Opportunity," *New York Times*, 24 December 1956, p. 6; Ruth Montgomery, "Larson Ends Bragging as USIA Policy," *Washington Post*, 29 December 1956, p. B.14.
13 NA RG 306, ZZ entry 1 (formerly 1006), Director's Chronological files, 1953–64, box 2, microfilm reel 17, Washburn to Dennis (IOP/L) 29 March 1957.
14 NA RG 306 64-A-0536, Director's Office Subject files, 1957–8, box 1, Broadcasting Service – Programs, 1957, Oren Stephens to Washburn, "Preliminary Report on Religious Broadcasting by VOA," 29 January 1957.

Unlike his predecessor, Larson made a point of attending all cabinet meetings whenever he was in Washington. Larson relished the fact that only he and the CIA director were part of the cabinet, the NSC, and the OCB.[15] On 18 January, Larson briefed the entire cabinet on the agency's work, showing film clips and a succession of charts. Larson told the cabinet that the U.S. message "can succeed only to the extent if everybody in America, both in public and private life, becomes acutely and automatically conscious of the impact of his every action on world opinion." He proposed that every department establish a "watchdog" to act as liaison with the agency, transmitting USIA themes and consulting on the public relations dimension of major initiatives. The cabinet endorsed the plan.[16]

A step toward this integrated approach Larson desired came in April 1957 with the establishment by the Postmaster General of a stamp advisory committee, which included a seat for the USIA to propose themes for stamps used on international mail. The agency, represented by deputy director Washburn, immediately suggested a series of stamps entitled "Champions of Liberty" featuring portraits of Filipino leader Ramon Magasaysay, Kossuth of Hungary, Masaryk of Czechoslovakia, Garibaldi of Italy, and Mannerheim of Finland. The first (the Magasaysay stamp) appeared on 31 August 1957. Stamp design remained in the USIA's brief for the rest of the Eisenhower years. Subsequent agency designs included arctic exploration, "World Peace through World Trade," NATO, and an "American Credo" series in 1960, featuring famous phrases from the great men of U.S. history.[17]

Larson's USIA mixed old hands with new blood. Of Streibert's key lieutenants, Abbott Washburn and Henry Loomis remained on hand. Andrew Berding moved to the post of Assistant Secretary of State for Public Affairs at the State Department. Larson's staff included a number of relatively recent additions to the senior management team. 1956 had brought new directors to the VOA, the Motion Picture Service, and the Office of Private Cooperation: Robert Button, Turner B. Shelton, and Conger Reynolds. All had ample experience. The new VOA director, Button, had served as a lieutenant colonel in signals intelligence on Eisenhower's staff in the war and as a

---

15 Larson, *Eisenhower: The President Nobody Knew*, p. 17.
16 DDEL DDE Cabinet, box 8, minutes 18 January 1957; record of action RA-57–65, 22 January 1957; text of Larson presentation. On the operation of the Watchdog system see NA RG 306, ZZ entry 1 (formerly 1006), Director's Chronological Files, 1953–64, box 2, microfilm reel 25, Allen to Secretaries of Agencies, 9 May 1958, and box 3, microfilm reel 31, Payne to Patterson (White House), 25 March 1959, which cites the example of the CIA providing advance copies of its director's speeches to the USIA as an example of effectiveness. Also NA RG 306 64-A-0536, Director's Office Subject Files, 1957–8, box 4, file: Government – Watchdog.
17 NA RG 306 64-A-0536, Director's Office Subject files, 1957–8, box 3, file: Stamp Committee: General Corresp, esp. Minutes, 30 April, 1957; press release, 30 April 1957; Briefing Paper n/d. Also box 1, file: Advisory Group – Stamps and box 3 Advisory Group – Stamps/Advisory Committee, 1958; also NA RG 306, ZZ entry 1 (formerly 1006), Director's Chronological Files, 1953–64, box 2, microfilm reel 32, C. R. Payne (director's office) to O'Conner (IOPP "Usage of U.S. stamps for Propaganda Purposes," 6 May 1959 and box 3, film reel 34, Washburn memo "U.S. Postage Stamp Program for 1961," 12 November 1959, etc. For a retrospective view of the committee's work see box 3, reel 39, C. R. Payne, "Observations and Recommendations of Postmaster General Arthur E. Summerfield's Citizens' Stamp Advisory Committee," 15 December 1960.

senior executive at NBC before joining the VOA as deputy to J. R. Poppele. Turner B. Shelton had run his own television production company, served as assistant director of the Treasury Department's Motion Picture Division during the war, and advised the IIA. Conger Reynolds was a journalist and former Foreign Service officer who since 1930 had directed public relations for Standard Oil. The highest profile USIA initiative of the second Eisenhower administration fell into Reynolds' bailiwick: the People-to-People program.[18]

Under Conger Reynolds' direction, the Office of Private Cooperation swelled to meet the needs of People-to-People. Its budget grew from $205,000 in 1956 to $573,000 in 1960 and the staff swelled to forty. Although the People-to-People committees became the "primary mechanism" for contact with the public, the office provided a vital support and coordination role.[19] In the year following Eisenhower's launch of People-to-People in September 1956, the Office of Private Cooperation helped muster some forty-one People-to-People committees, each representing an aspect of American life and dedicated to reaching out to their equivalents overseas. A committee of lawyers reached out to lawyers, artists to artists, farmers to farmers, and cities reached out to cities in a program of civic twinning that became known as Sister Cities. Committee representatives received a weeklong agency training course before traveling overseas. Particular successes included a shipment of free medicine to fight Asian flu in the Philippines and a new pamphlet called *Make a Friend This Trip* produced by the transportation and public relations committees for departing American tourists. The nationalities committee, which mobilized the "hyphenated" Americans around the country, organizing such events as a taped message of greeting from the Polish-American community of Cleveland to the people of Poznań. But there were setbacks too. The White House had difficulty launching a parent corporation for People-to-People (with former Secretary of Defense Charles E. Wilson as president) to distance the program from the government. The big charitable foundations did not warm to the idea.[20]

The U.S. information program used its advisory commission as a mechanism for keeping on good terms with men of influence in the field of communications and

18 *USIA 7th Report to Congress, July–December 1956*, p. 8; "Voice Director Named," *New York Times*, 18 July 1956, p. 13. After joining the USIA Shelton switched onto a Foreign Service career path and eventually became U.S. ambassador to Nicaragua in 1970.

19 NA RG 306 A1 (1072) USIA historical collection, box 14, file: Office of Private Cooperation, History 1971, Krill to Newpher, 29 January 1971, with "Brief history of the Office of Private Cooperation" attached.

20 NA RG 306 64-A-0536, Director's Office Subject files, 1957–8, box 2, file: Private Enterprise – People to People Committees, 1957, esp. Larson to Adams (White House), "People-to-People Corporation," 12 October 1957; *USIA 8th Review of Operations, January 1–June 30, 1957*, pp. 20–21. International civic twinning agreements had existed before People-to-People. The movement began with a wave of Franco-German twinning agreements following the Second World War. The first link to America came in 1953 with the twinning of Arles in Provence with York in Pennsylvania; Montpellier and Louisville, Kentucky followed. All American twinning was subsumed within People-to-People, which headed off some of the radical impetus in the European initiatives. For a full discussion see Antoine Vion, "Europe from the Bottom Up: Town Twinning in France during the Cold War," *Contemporary European History*, II, 4 (2002), pp. 623–40.

public relations. A new activity with the same potential developed from Eisenhower's Executive Order No. 10660 of 15 February 1956, "Providing for the Establishment of a National Defense Executive Reserve." This order created a framework for all federal agencies, including the USIA, to assemble teams of private citizens who either had served at a senior level in that agency or possessed specialist knowledge of the agency's field of activity. In the event of a nuclear war, these reservists would be gathered at the emergency centers of government to assist the federal government once the mushroom clouds over America's cities had dispersed. Larson created a reserve of 125 advisors. They included such senior figures from the postwar information program as Bill Benton, Ed Barrett, Ted Streibert, and C. D. Jackson. He also recruited senior public relations executives from such companies as Ford Motors, United Fruit, and Monsanto Chemicals and George Murphy of MGM. Other luminaries, with what amounted to a USIA ticket to survive Armageddon, included Edward Bernays, Ted Repplier, George Gallup, and Cecil B. DeMille. The USIA's reservists met for annual briefings and a four-day simulation exercise known as "Operation Alert" held each summer at the agency's emergency location near Greenville, North Carolina. Exercises included live broadcasts of the VOA to Poland and Czechoslovakia and a worldwide press exercise, to test the workability of backup systems and contingency plans. It was never clear exactly what these advisors would be able to contribute to the USIA in time of crisis, but that did not cause much worry. Washburn reminded Bill Benton, after a meeting of the reserve in November 1957: "Our greatest need is still for support and understanding both from the public and from the Congress. If you, Bernays, and the others can help us on this score that would be a magnificent contribution."[21]

*

Larson continued the cultural work begun under Streibert. Exhibitions of U.S. art, photography, and design toured and the agency continued to act as the operational arm of the President's Special International Program. Highlights of the 1957 program included an Asian tour by the San Francisco Ballet and a return visit to Burma by the Native American dancer and lecturer Tom Two Arrows. The VOA supported this cultural effort by launching an American Theater of the Air – the brainchild

21 NA RG 306, 64-A-0536, Office of the director, Subject Files, 1957–8, box 1, file Administration: Emergency Planning 1957 and box 3, files Emergency Planning and Personnel: Executive Reserve, 1958; NA RG 306, ZZ entry 1 (formerly 1006), Director's Chronological files, 1953–64, box 2, microfilm reel 16, 18, 19, and 20, and box 3, reel 35 (Washburn to Kenin, 11 February 1960). The quotation is from reel 20, Washburn to Benton, 7 November 1957. Correspondence from Abbott Washburn in March 1960 (see for example box 3, reel 36 Washburn to Romney Wheeler, ITV, 26 March 1960, secret) reveals that the USIA also planned to have a separate staff of 35 allocated to the U.S. government's emergency seat of nonmilitary government, the "Office of Civil Defense Mobilization Classified Location" – also known as "High Point." These men – director, area directors, and media directors – would generate policy while Washburn directed operations in Greenville. The State Department had an allocation of 300 places at High Point. For the files of an individual reservist see UoC Benton papers, box 382/7. The agency ceased this exercise and dissolved its reserve early in the Kennedy administration. The wider concept survives within the Federal Emergency Management Agency.

of the new program manager Barry Zorthian – beginning with an acclaimed broadcast of Thornton Wilder's *Our Town* in June. Jazz music remained a staple of USIA programming. The year 1957 brought Benny Goodman to Japan. As the U.S. ambassador to Rio noted in December 1957, "One Satchmo Armstrong is sometimes worth five art exhibits."[22] The USIA's bureaucracy developed to support this new emphasis. In late 1956, the agency established a Cultural Operations Division to administer State's cultural campaign. For guidance the Division could look to a special Advisory Committee on Cultural Information, chaired by Mark May and including the president of the Museum of Modern Art.[23]

The political output of Larson's USIA was dominated by the events in Hungary in 1956. The agency sought to keep the story "alive and in the forefront of world opinion." Agency materials stressed the democratic nature of the rebellion and the brutality of Soviet repression. The agency purchased thousands of copies of a *Life* magazine special issue called *Hungary's Fight for Freedom* in both English and Spanish and created a string of documentary films on the subject including *A Nation in Torment* and *Now We Are Free*.[24] The publications service translated books dealing with the story, including James A. Michener's novel *The Bridge at Andau*. In the summer the USIA publicized the United Nations special report on Hungary; the VOA transmitted daily readings at dictation speed, and the motion picture branch created a film about the report, called *Document A/3592*. The agency marked the first anniversary of the rising with a traveling exhibit, a television documentary for Latin America, and an anthology of writing on the events by dissident authors.[25] The message did not always get through. In May 1958, Larson's successor told the NSC that "It has been next to impossible to keep the Hungary story vivid in the minds of these Frenchmen. When our people brought up Hungary, one Frenchman had replied, 'Why not talk about the Punic Wars?' "[26]

Following the political reforms of the previous year, Poland now figured prominently in the USIA's activities. The agency treated Poland as a second Yugoslavia. A conference of diplomats and U.S. government–funded broadcasters even noted that

[22] NA RG 306 64-A-0536, Director's Office subject files, 1957–8, box 5, President's Emergency Fund, Inter-Agency Committee on Presentation, 1958, OSB "Report on Activities of the Cultural Presentation Committee," 20 August 1958; on the cultural budget see NA RG 306, 64-A-0536, Office of the director, Subject Files, 1957–8, box 1, Larson to Dulles, Allocation Letter No. 35–7, 20 June 1957; *USIA 8th Review of Operations, January 1–June 30, 1957*, p. 23; Richard F. Shepard, "Drama by Shortwave; Voice of America to Do 'The Glass Menagerie,'" *New York Times*, 8 December 1957, p. D.15; *FRUS 1955–1957, Vol. VII*, Briggs to State, 31 December 1957, Doc. 375, p. 775.

[23] *USIA 7th Report to Congress, July–December 1956*, pp. 17–18, 34. This board retained most of the members of the Committee on Books Abroad, which it replaced. The USIA retained its main Advisory Committee (also still chaired by May) and a Broadcast Advisory Committee.

[24] NA RG306 64-A-0536, Director's Office, Subject Files, 1957–8, box 1, file: field-Hungary, IOP Dennis/Revey to Larson, "USIA Coverage of the Hungarian Story," 7 January 1957; Shelton to Larson, "Motion Picture Service Output on the Hungarian Revolt," 7 January 1957.

[25] *USIA 8th Review of Operations, January 1–June 30, 1957*, pp. 14–15; *USIA 9th Review of Operations, July 1–December 31, 1957*, p. 18.

[26] *FRUS 1958–1960, Vol. V, American Republics*, doc. 56, 366th NSC meeting, 22 May 1958, pp. 239–46.

the country was now "in many ways no longer a totalitarian state."[27] The year 1957 saw a lavish U.S. contribution to the Poznań trade fair, stuffed with the bounty of American consumerism. Seventy thousand Poles viewed the USIA's traveling "Built in the U.S.A." exhibition featuring current U.S. architecture.[28] Poland received visits from the Glenn Miller band, the Cleveland Orchestra, and the José Limón dance troupe in 1957 and looked forward to visits from the Dave Brubeck Jazz Quartet, the American Ballet Theater, and the Philadelphia Orchestra in the first half of 1958.[29] In February 1958, Poland gained access to U.S. films and books through the Informational Media Guarantee program. By the end of 1958, $1 million of American materials had entered the country. In May 1958, the Poles agreed to the publication of *Ameryka*, a Polish language version of *America Illustrated*. The magazine launched in early 1959. The Ford and Rockefeller Foundations set up programs to bring Polish students to the United States as early as 1957, and from 1960, Poland joined the Fulbright program.[30]

The USIA's growing program required funding, and Larson approached the budget round in 1957 with a sense of urgency. Suez and Hungary, so the agency's budget memorandum argued, had left the United States as "the principal force for peace with justice in the world" and presented an immense opportunity for the USIA. Larson requested $144 million, an increase of $31 million on FY 1957, but the hearings on the Hill did not go well. The appropriations subcommittee, chaired by Democrat John Rooney of New York, charged that the USIA had wasted money. Rooney claimed that the USIA had secretly subsidized a Hollywood flop. The *Chicago Daily News* identified the film as the adaptation of George Orwell's *1984* released in September 1956, to which the USIA had contributed $100,000 on top of the producer's $500,000. Unimpressed, the House cut the USIA's budget from $113 million to $106 million.[31] Worse came in the Senate.

Larson's unraveling began in March when his staff suggested that he visit Hawaii to speak in support of statehood and thereby show the race-blind nature of American

27 DDEL U.S.PCIIA (Sprague Committee), box 1, Radio and Television File 6, Report of Chairman, Fourth Annual Conference on Broadcasting to the Soviet Orbit, September 1957, p. 2.
28 *USIA 8th Review of Operations, January 1–June 30, 1957*, p. 21; NA RG 306, ZZ entry 1 (formerly 1006), Director's Chronological files, 1953–64, box 2, reel 19, Washburn to Dept. of Commerce, 1 July 1957; On the Poznań trade fair see Haddow, *Pavilions of Plenty*, p. 63.
29 NA RG 306 64-A-0536, Director's Office subject files, 1957–8, box 5, President's Emergency Fund, Inter-Agency Committee on Presentation, 1958, OSB "Report on Activities of the Cultural Presentation Committee," 20 August 1958.
30 DDEL OSANA NSC/Status of Projects, box 8, NSC 5819 (5) Status of National Security Projects on 30 June 1958, pt. 6, The USIA program, p. 15; *USIA 11th Review of Operations, July 1–December 31, 1958*, pp. 4–5; Yale Richmond, *U.S.–Soviet Cultural Exchanges, 1958–86: Who Wins?* Boulder, CO: Westview, 1987, pp. 114–15.
31 Warren Unna, "Appeal Made by Ike for USIA Support," 17 April 1957, *Washington Post*, p. A.13; Robert E. Hoyt, "*1984* Named as Movie USIA Aided," *Washington Post*, 6 July 1957. Larson praises the unnamed film in Serm Williams, "USIA Money Well Spent, Says Chief," *Honolulu Advertiser*, 16 April 1957, p. 1 as "the most effective anti-Communist film ever made." For the background to Rooney's views on the USIA see "Rep. Rooney blasts USIA as Futile," *Washington Post*, 26 October 1955, p. 15. For Agency preparation for the hearings see NA RG 306 64-A-0536, Director's Office subject files, 1957–8, box 1, Administration – Budget – 1957.

democracy. Larson obtained an invitation to deliver a belated Lincoln Day speech to the islands' Republican Party, on 16 April, at a $100-a-plate dinner. His speech strayed into issues of Republican ideology. Only Hawaiian papers reported the speech and this might have been the end of the matter had not a Democratic Representative named Abraham J. Multer (NY) been passing through Honolulu that same week. Noting some unusual phrases, he clipped the coverage and forwarded it to John Rooney. The clips arrived too late to be part of Rooney's hearings but would be grist to the Senate's mill.[32]

On 2 May, Larson presented his case for extra funds at a hearing of the Senate appropriations subcommittee. The Democrats lost no time raising the Hawaii speech. Senator Allen Ellender of Louisiana quoted Larson's saying, "Throughout the New and Fair Deals, this country was in the grip of a somewhat alien philosophy imported from Europe." Was this, the Senator asked, any way to win friends in Europe? Larson attempted to explain that the "alien philosophy" was merely the elevation of the executive branch derived from the writings of the British political scientist Harold Laski. The committee was unconvinced. They painted Larson as a Democrat-hater peddling partisan propaganda at federal expense in a vacation spot. Senator Lyndon B. Johnson, the subcommittee's chairman, presided over the slaughter. While Fulbright and others poured scorn on agency expenditure in friendly European countries, Johnson scored cheap points by asking Larson to answer detailed operational questions off the top of his head. In the end Johnson bluntly told Larson that "in my opinion more money is wasted by this agency than by any other agency I know of" and cut the budget back to just $89 million. "Seldom," the columnist Marquis Childs noted, "has a witness been so neatly fried on both sides as was the hapless Larson."[33]

Larson and his team fought a gallant rearguard action. Washburn revealed that the agency would have to close half its operations in Western Europe, the target for sixty percent of Moscow's propaganda effort, and the USIA television could disappear altogether. They could do little to divert the onslaught. In a blatant bid to "steamroller" the budget through the Senate, Johnson released the 1,200-page volume of hearings only twenty-four hours before the Senate vote. John F. Kennedy interrupted Johnson's rambling speech in support of the reduced budget to complain about the Senate leader's scant supporting evidence. Their acrimonious exchange had to be

[32] NA RG 306, ZZ entry 1 (formerly 1006), Director's Chronological Files, 1953–64, box 2, microfilm reel 17, Berg to Washburn, 14 March 1957; Sherm Williams, "Isle Statehood Would Make USIA's Job Easier," *Honolulu Advertiser*, 17 April 1957, p. 1; on Multer see "Post Scripts: Target Larson," *Washington Post*, 20 May 1957, p. A.2.

[33] For hearings see Departments of State, Justice, the Judiciary, and related agencies appropriations, 1958, Hearings before the subcommittee of the committee on appropriations United States Senate, 85th Congress, 1st session, on HR 6871, pp. 488 et seq. Richard L. Lyons, "Democrats Attack USIA Chief on Speech," *Washington Post*, 3 May 1957, p. A 9; Richard L. Lyons, "Larson Tries to Convince Senators He Needs More to Convince World," *Washington Post*, 9 May 1957, p. A.2; "Johnson Assails U.S. News Unit as the Most Wasteful of Agencies," *New York Times*, 9 May 1957, p. 14; Marquis Childs, "Larson in Charge of Sputnik Talks," *Washington Post*, 11 November 1957, p. A.16. For associated recollections by colleagues see ADST Oral History: Kendall; Martin; Pike.

edited for the *Congressional Record* for the sake of propriety. But Kennedy and other Democratic critics of Johnson's methods fell into line for the vote.

Subsequent wrangling in the committee brought a compromise budget of around $95 million, but this still fell short of Larson's needs. In the following weeks Johnson, ever the political operator, offered a route to full funding. He suggested trading the budget for the USIA's return to the State Department. As Eisenhower recalled in his memoirs, John Foster Dulles had no desire to regain responsibility for overseas information and, with the President's agreement, refused the initiative. The affair had left the USIA underfunded, with key figures on the Hill pressing for its return to State. As a *New York Times* profile put it, Larson was now an "egghead with troubles."[34]

Larson did his best to take the budget cut in his stride. The agency reduced expenditure in Western Europe by twenty-seven percent and cut seventy-five percent from television work.[35] Larson worked to ensure the efficiency of all expenditure. Looking at the VOA, Larson resolved that credibility was the key to maximum effectiveness and took steps to ensure that the Voice continued to develop as a provider of news rather than rhetoric. The President and Secretary of State concurred. In June, Dulles wrote to Larson stressing that he and the President believed that "Voice of America is destroying a great deal of its own usefulness when it engages in the field of propaganda." This was the task of the CIA and its outlets. "Voice of America," Dulles asserted, "ought to be known as a completely accurate dispenser of certain information." In an enclosed note, Eisenhower suggested that the core of that information be "news of a character that has world interest and the dissemination of which can assist other peoples to understand better the aims and objectives of America and the progress of the world's ideological struggle." Although agreeing that VOA Washington already followed such a policy, Dulles worried that commentaries from the Munich Radio Center seemed too "propagandistic."[36]

Larson responded by initiating "Project Credibility" at the Voice. He created a new Central News Desk at the VOA to "eliminate practically all of the uncertainty as to policy and tone which has resulted in the past from leaving considerable editorial discretion to the various language desks." Now VOA language branches would receive a single master news script of a "model broadcast" from Central News. Their only element of freedom in the news was selecting which of these stories they wished

34 DDEL WHCF, OF 247, box 911, esp. Memorandum regarding the current legislative needs of the USIA, n.d.; Washburn to A. M. Gruenther (Red Cross), 20 May 1957, also NA RG 306, ZZ entry 1 (formerly 1006), Director's Chronological files, 1953–64, box 2, reel 18, Washburn to C. D. Jackson, 20 May 1957, etc.; on JFK and LBJ see Drew Pearson, "Washington Merry-Go-Round: Johnson Rushes USIA Funds Cut," *Washington Post*, 25 May 1957, p. D.11; on Dulles see DDEL John Foster Dulles, General Correspondence and Memoranda, box 1, memo of conversation with Senator Lyndon Johnson, 14 June 1957; for Eisenhower's account see Dwight D. Eisenhower, *Waging Peace*, Garden City, NY: Doubleday & Co., 1965, pp. 136–8; for Larson's account of Dulles see Larson, *Eisenhower: The President Nobody Knew*, p. 77; "Egghead with Troubles," *New York Times*, 11 May 1957, p. 11.
35 *FRUS 1955–1957, Vol. IX, Foreign Economic Policy; Foreign Information Program*, doc. 207, NSC 5720, 11 September 1957, pp. 594–612; Richard L. Lyons, "Truth Stressed by USIA Chief," *New York Times*, 23 July 1957, p. A9.
36 NA RG 306 64-A-0536, Director's Office Subject files, 1957–1958, box 1, file: Broadcast Service – General, 1957, and *FRUS 1955–1957, Vol. IX*, doc. 204, Dulles to Larson, 27 June 1957, p. 590.

to translate and use and arranging their running order within the bulletin. Larson also ordered the VOA to increase its output of news rather than commentaries. The remaining commentaries would be closely tied to specific statements by policy makers rather than the commentator's own whim.[37] With these changes under his belt, Larson informed Congress that he was "eliminating from USIA output anything that could be interpreted as 'propaganda.'"[38]

Larson found a sympathetic audience in the Voice newsroom. "Project Credibility" fitted the sort of agenda that VOA Program Manager Barry Zorthian had been pursuing over the past year. On 22 July 1957, Larson issued a set of guidelines to VOA director Button, intended to serve as a foundational document for a news-driven agenda at the VOA:

> The best rule of thumb to follow is this: Will the tone and content of this broadcast in the ears of the particular listening audience establish a reputation for believability? In other words we are striving to reach the day when no one, at home or abroad, will say, "they are dishing out propaganda."[39]

At the same time, representatives of the USIA and the CIA met on an Inter-Agency Broadcasting Committee and agreed to a clearer delineation of role between the news-driven VOA and the more polemic RFE and RL. "It will be the usual rule," the committee agreed, "that VOA will not broadcast commentary originated by it on the internal affairs of countries to which RFE broadcasts." Exceptions required rigid adherence to official guidance.[40] News could still have an impact, as the VOA demonstrated in July by announcing major changes to the Soviet cabinet ten hours before the Kremlin.[41]

Larson continued to believe that the USIA as a whole should move away from propaganda. In an effort to codify this into agencywide practice he drew up – in consultation with Eisenhower and Dulles – "the USIA Basic Guidance Paper." The document, finished by October 1957, made clear what the USIA would not be doing:

> Any material whose appeal is based not on facts but on emotion or rhetoric is outside our statement of purpose. This ban extends to all kinds of polemics and denunciation, to any tone which is sarcastic or boastful or self-righteous, and

[37] NA RG 306 64-A-0536, Director's Office Subject files, 1957–8, box 1, file: Broadcast Service – General, 1957, Bradford to Larson, 2 July 1957 & 11 July 1957; Larson to Bradford, 10 July 1957; Dulles to Larson, 9 August 1957; *FRUS 1955–1957, Vol. IX*, doc. 205, Larson to Dulles, 23 July 1957, pp. 592–93.

[38] *USIA 8th Review of Operations, January 1–June 30, 1957*, p. 5.

[39] NA RG 306 64-A-0536, Director's Office Subject files, 1957–8, box 1, file: Broadcast Service – General, 1957, Button to Larson, 22 July 1957; Dulles to Larson, 9 August 1957; Ewing to Larson, 29 August 1957.

[40] NA RG 306 64-A-0536, Director's Office Subject files, 1957–8, box 1, file: Broadcast Service – General, 1957, Bradford to Larson, "Delineation of Broadcasting Roles and Its Relation to MRC," 29 August 1957.

[41] *USIA 9th Review of Operations, July 1–December 31, 1957*, p. 17. DDEL U.S.PCIIA (Sprague Committee), box 19, USIA 2, undated secret memo (c. 1960), "The U.S. Information Program since July 1953," p. 4.

to any style which employs loaded phrases and purple adjectives. E.G., "bloody hands."

The document also warned against "drawing obvious morals" in presenting policy. "Give your audience credit for enough intelligence to form its own judgment," Larson wrote. He insisted that the USIA present the U.S. cause with dignity and meet hysteria with "calmness and confidence." He recommended that the USIA focus on the "opinion formers" in any country rather than aiming for the masses. He recommended what he termed "the Mutuality Theme." The USIA's output should be tied to the needs of its audience: "The aspirations of the other country for freedom, progress and peace are the beginning-point of our content." To this end he ended the document with a set of key principles, which he termed "What we are FOR," urging the agency to "accentuate the positive," to build on the "broad common bond" of a shared quest for freedom, justice, individual dignity, property, and religious faith, and to look together toward a better future. The paper was apparently shown to journalists and officials as necessary to refute the charge that the USIA was "in the 'propaganda' business."[42]

*

Johnson's budget cut forced Larson to reduce expenditure in every region except one. Africa received a small increase. Larson made this money go a long way. Posts opened in Dakar and Mogadishu. Agency projects included a monthly newsreel of U.S. and African events, created in Arabic, French, and English versions called *Today*, a magazine called *American Outlook*, and numerous leaflets explaining U.S. policy on decolonization with titles such as *The Future Belongs to Freedom*. The State Department organized a good will tour by the black American athlete Mal Whitfield.[43] The remaining colonial governments looked on with suspicion.[44]

The USIA's output for the Middle East focused on spreading the Eisenhower doctrine, enunciated by the President in a joint session of Congress on 5 January. USIS Cairo enlisted the city's army of newsboys to distribute pamphlets about the speech. The agency also gave wide coverage to the visit of King Saud of Saudi Arabia to the United States.[45] In September 1957, Larson urged USIA missions to step up their campaign against Syria and portray the country as increasingly Communist-dominated. The agency re-released its films about Communist takeovers and published alarming testimony from a Czech diplomatic defector named Richard Sedlacek who had been privy to Communist plans in the Levant. The USIA also attempted to combat America's image as the sponsor of Israel by playing up support for Arab regimes and

---

42   NA RG 306 64-A-0536, Director's Office Subject files, 1957–8, box 1, file: Director-General, USIA basic guidance paper; Larson to Berding (ASoS), 4 October 1957; Saxton Bradford (IOP – deputy director policy & plans) to all PAOs "Transmitting USIA guidance paper," 22 October 1957.
43   *USIA 9th Review of Operations, July 1–December 31, 1957*, pp. 12–16
44   *FRUS 1955–1957, Vol. XVIII, Africa*, doc. 104, Leopoldville Embassy to State, 21 March 1957, pp. 310–12; doc. 106, Leopoldville Embassy to State, 27 August 1957, pp. 314–19.
45   *USIA 8th Review of Operations, January 1–June 30, 1957*, pp. 9–13.

stressing points at which the U.S. had gone against Israeli wishes, as in the extension of aid to Arab countries.[46]

In Asia, Vietnam remained the major focus of agency work. In the summer of 1957, the USIA characterized its role in South Vietnam as "verbal protagonist for the Diem government in its search for mass support."[47] But there were doubters. In August a two-man team from the International Cooperation Administration of James S. Killen and former VOA director Foy Kohler studied the U.S. program in Vietnam and questioned the "showcase theory" that "the 'Miracle of Vietnam' be converted into the prime example in Asia that loyal cooperation with the West pays, and pays handsomely." Killen and Kohler observed that, rather than boosting the country, the scale of U.S. aid was "a disincentive to development of the country's own resources."[48]

In approaching their greatest challenge – the Eastern bloc – Larson's USIA faced a rapidly shifting situation. In September 1957, representatives of U.S. embassies in the region, State, and the USIA, the VOA, RIAS, RFE, and RL all met at the U.S. embassy in Paris for their five-day "Fourth Annual Conference on Broadcasting to the Soviet Orbit" under the chairmanship of Stanford University's professor of communications Wilbur Schramm. The conference heard that the political changes in Poland and influx of refugees from Hungary had dramatically enhanced U.S. knowledge of its radio audience in the East. Intelligence estimated ownership of shortwave radios in the "Soviet orbit" at around twenty million sets. The conference noted a hardening of anti-Soviet attitudes and a marked rise in the readiness of Russian intellectuals to criticize their government. The conference sensed that the time had come to seek the face-to-face approach of cultural exchange and participation in events like the Moscow Youth Congress.[49] In February 1957, with Britain opening its own doors to the U.S.S.R., Ambassador Bohlen formally suggested that the United States resume cultural exchanges with the Soviet Union.[50]

*

By the summer of 1957, two major issues had emerged to challenge the good image of the United States in all regions. The first was the conduct of U.S. servicemen overseas. A spate of manslaughter and murder cases perpetrated by GIs in South and East Asia proved especially challenging for the USIA. USIS posts begged the army to restrain its personnel. In the Philippines, pressure from USIS Manila persuaded the

---

[46] *FRUS 1955–1957, Vol. XIII, Near East: Jordan-Yemen*, State/USIA circular to certain missions, 25 September 1957, p. 404; DDEL DDE Papers as President (Ann Whitman file) Administrative Series, box 31, USIA (1), Larson to President, 28 September 1957; NA RG 306 64-A-0536, Director's Office Subject Files, 1957–8, box 1, file: Near East, Huntington Damen (Asst. Dir. NE) to Larson, "Psychological campaign in regard to Syrian developments," 14 October 1957.

[47] DDEL OSANA, NSC/Status of Projects, box 7, NSC 5611 part II (3), Status of National Security Program on 30 June 1957, part 6, p. 15.

[48] DDEL C. D. Jackson papers, box 109, USIS surveys, Vietnam Report No. 17, c. April 1958.

[49] DDEL U.S.PCIIA (Sprague Committee), box 1, Radio and Television file 6, Report of Chairman, Fourth Annual Conference on Broadcasting to the Soviet Orbit, September 1957.

[50] *FRUS 1955–1957, Vol. XXIV*, doc. 110, Bohlen to State, 28 February 1957, pp. 256.

army to surrender a sergeant who had killed a priest in a hit and run for local trial.[51] The second issue was nuclear testing. Although the U.S.S.R. and United Kingdom both pursued active test programs, U.S. tests seemed uniquely controversial. The USIA's senior policy officer, Saxton Bradford, blamed the fact that the United States had been the first nation to develop nuclear weapons and the only nation to use them. In April 1957, Nobel Peace Prize winner Albert Schweitzer appealed to the world to stop nuclear testing, boosting anti-nuclear protest movements. A West German poll revealed that opposition to tests had increased from two-to-one to ten-to-one. Rejection of nuclear weapons was no longer just the province of elderly Quakers and vegetarians. Larson urged a major U.S. initiative on disarmament, but was ignored.[52]

Just when Larson believed his job could not get any harder, it did. On 4 September 1957, nine African American schoolchildren attempted to enroll at Central High School in Little Rock, Arkansas. The Arkansas National Guard barred their way. Newspapers around the world printed pictures of black American children facing white American soldiers with loaded rifles. No one in Washington doubted that the international image of the United States was at stake, and, with world opinion in mind, Eisenhower deployed federal troops to resolve the matter.[53]

Larson's USIA did not shrink from reporting Little Rock, but stressed peaceful school desegregation seen elsewhere in the South. The USIA distributed pictures illustrating integrated schools and trumpeted the achievements of particular African Americans. Black Americans traveling as part of the cultural program were called on to testify at press conferences about the changing picture of race relations. Star performers in this work included the singer Marian Anderson, during her concert tour of Asia. USIS posts were generally satisfied by the restrained and balanced coverage given to the Little Rock story in all but Communist newspapers around the world.[54]

On 30 September, Larson wrote to Eisenhower recommending that the President write an open letter to the students of Little Rock, appealing for them to act in a democratic manner. This, Larson believed, could ease the crisis and "show the world that freedom and equality not only are enshrined in our laws but also dwell in the

51 NA RG 306 64-A-0536, Director's Office Subject files, 1957–8, box 2, file Research and Intelligence, 1957; Loomis (IRI) to Larson, "U.S. troop incidents," 14 June 1957. For background on cases see Foster Hailey, "Girard Is Guilty; Term Suspended by Court in Japan," *New York Times*, 19 November 1957, p. 1; Associated Press, "U.S. Flag Trampled by Rioters in Taiwan," *New York Times*, 24 May 1957, p. 1; E. W. Kenworthy, "Cases of 2 GI's Raise Questions," *New York Times*, 25 May 1957, p. 3. In 1958 USIA director George V. Allen wrote to the Secretary of the Air Force, James H. Douglas, commending the positive work done by Maj. Gen. John B. Ackerman, commander of the XIII Air Force in the Philippines, to ensure better behavior and understanding of U.S. policies. In associated correspondence he offered to help the Army achieve the same results. NA RG 306, ZZ entry 1 (formerly 1006), Director's Chronological files, 1953–64, box 2, microfilm reel 25, Allen to Douglas, 5 March 1958 et seq.
52 NA RG 306 64-A-0536, Director's Office Subject files, 1957–1958, box 1, file: Policy and Plans: General, 1957, Bradford to Larson, "Nuclear Tests," 29 May 1957; Larson to Dennis (IOP), "Disarmament Program," 3 September 1957.
53 For a detailed treatment of the crisis, the role of world opinion, and the response of the executive branch including the USIA see Mary Dudziak, *Cold War Civil Rights: Race and the Image of American Democracy*, Princeton: Princeton University Press, 2000, pp. 115–51.
54 *USIA 9th Review of Operations, July 1–December 31, 1957*, p. 5.

hearts of our people." Eisenhower declined to appeal, presumably suspecting that the student reaction might demonstrate something rather different.[55]

As the Little Rock crisis subsided from the headlines, the USIA's Office of Research and Intelligence conducted detailed research into Western European reactions to the events. To their surprise, the agency found that the crisis had not produced a great swing in European attitudes. Unfortunately, the reason for this was that while many Europeans believed that the United States had made progress in racial matters over the past decade, they still saw U.S. race relations as a "disgrace." The only "good news" was that negative opinions on race did not interfere with the general good opinion in which Europe held the United States.[56]

Larson had barely caught his breath from Little Rock when the Sputnik shock hit on 4 October. In the NSC, Allen Dulles contextualized the launch as the last in a trilogy of Soviet propaganda moves. The U.S.S.R. had also just tested a large-scale hydrogen bomb and an intercontinental ballistic missile. Larson warned the NSC: "If we lose repeatedly to the Russians as we have lost with the earth satellite, the accumulated damage would be tremendous." The United States had to aim higher and "accomplish some of the next great breakthroughs first." Larson recommended launching a manned satellite or "getting to the moon." Eisenhower took Larson's basic point about the risk to U.S. prestige but was wary of competing with the U.S.S.R. in "areas about which we don't know anything." The President emphasized that above all the United States must retain "a military posture that the Soviets will respect."[57]

The Eisenhower administration responded to Sputnik with a frenzy of activity. Although initially shy of a space race, the President reinstated the post of government science adviser, called an emergency NATO summit, and instituted an annual naval exercise off the Philippines to display U.S. military technology to East Asian ministers of defense and chiefs of staff.[58] The President also sought to reinvigorate the USIA. This required moving Larson to other duties. On 16 October, the White House announced that Larson was to become the President's special assistant for "international information matters" with a brief to advise on responding to Soviet propaganda. In Larson's place (and apparently at his suggestion), Eisenhower recalled the Truman-era Assistant Secretary of State, George V. Allen.[59]

[55] Dudziak, *Cold War Civil Rights*, pp. 137–8.

[56] DDEL, WHCF CF subject box 99, USIA (3), "Post-Little Rock Opinion on the Treatment of Negroes in the U.S.," PMS no. 23, ORI, January 1958. The agency ran polls in its regular barometer countries, Britain, West Germany, Italy, and France, and added Norway.

[57] DDEL, DDE Papers as President (Ann Whitman file), NSC series, box 9, 339th NSC meeting, 11 October 1957. Larson later wrote to Eisenhower suggesting that an easier and cheaper alternative might be to use a "clean" nuclear bomb to "create a harbor where none existed before." He repeated his Moon idea as just "hitting the moon" with a rocket, which reveals it as less ambitious than the eventual Project Apollo. See DDEL, DDE Papers as President (Ann Whitman file), Administrative Series, box 37, USIA file 1, Larson to President, 15 October 1957.

[58] ADST Oral History: Loomis; Marshall Green; Joseph Green.

[59] Chalmers M. Roberts, "Report Says Larson Will Quit USIA but He Denies It in Reply to Word Spread by Officials," *New York Times*, A.1, 16 October 1957; DDEL WHCF, OF 247, box 911, Larson to President, 16 October 1957; Jay Waltz, "Envoy to Succeed Larson at USIA," *New York Times*, 17 October 1957, p. 1; Carroll Kilpatrick, "Ike Names Larson as Special Aide; Allen to Take Over as

Larson went to the White House hoping to apply the lessons he had learned at the USIA to the President's domestic and international image. He planned a new genre of presidential statement, crafted for film and supported by images and music. Eisenhower's stroke and subsequent speech problems ruled out anything so novel. Larson became just another speechwriter. Disillusioned with Washington, he accepted the chair of law at Duke University and resumed his academic career in August 1958.

Larson's contribution to the USIA was not quite over. He drew together his thoughts about core American values treated in outline in the "What we are FOR" section of his "USIA Basic Guidance Paper" of October 1957 and created a succinct book also called *What We Are For*, published in early 1959. The book was favorably reviewed in the *New York Times* by Senator John F. Kennedy. Larson acted as a consultant to the Johnson administration in matters of international law. His 1968 memoir *Eisenhower: The President Nobody Knew* caused a stir by revealing Eisenhower's lack of personal commitment to civil rights. Larson died in 1993.[60] Larson's demise obscured his successes, but he had cleared the way for the Voice of America charter of 1960, strengthened the hand of objective information at the USIA, and also added a women's affairs advisor to the agency's staff. Several of his successors would bequeath much less to the agency's future. As a *Washington Post* editorial noted at the time of his return to private life, "Arthur Larson deserved better than the political buffeting he received in Washington."[61]

2) BREAKING THE "MILWAUKEE EFFECT"
THE RETURN OF GEORGE V. ALLEN

George V. Allen was ideally qualified for the directorship of the USIA. As Assistant Secretary of State for Public Affairs from March 1948 to November 1949, he had more or less done the job before. His career in the Foreign Service had given him a truly global perspective. His postings included Jamaica, China, and Egypt and serving as ambassador to Iran, Yugoslavia, and India. In January 1955 he became Assistant Secretary of State for Near Eastern, South Asian, and African Affairs and held the post until mid-1956 when, following a falling out with Dulles, he became ambassador in

Head of USIA," *Washington Post*, 17 October 1958, p. A1. For Larson's role in the nomination of Allen see Larson, *Eisenhower: The President Nobody Knew*, p. 158.

60 Edward T. Folliard, "Larson, 'Egghead' Aide to Ike Resigns for University Post," *Washington Post*, 12 August 1958, p. A.2; NA RG 306 64-A-0536, Office of the director, subject files, 1957–58, box 4, file: International Cultural Centers – books, Washburn to Hawley (ICS), 31 December 1958; John F. Kennedy, "If the World's to Know Us Better: We Must Show Ourselves as We Are Urges One-Time Eisenhower Aide," *New York Times*, 8 February 1959, p. BR 1 (Kennedy argued that Larson was "perhaps too worried about America's image abroad" and "What really matters is whether our policies and actions in the world appear to overlap significantly with the aspirations of other people"). Bruce Lambert, "L. Arthur Larson Is Dead at 82; Top Eisenhower Aide and Writer," *New York Times*, 1 April 1993, p. D.24. Larson, *The President Nobody Knew*, pp. 124–9.

61 Editorial "Egghead's Reward," *Washington Post*, 16 August 1958; on the women's affairs advisor see Haddow, *Pavilions of Plenty*, p. 141.

Athens. His expertise in Africa and the Middle East fitted the emerging priorities of the USIA. Moreover, just as Truman had needed his brand of level-headed professionalism in 1948 to reassure the State Department traditionalists after the Madison Avenue flourishes of Bill Benton, so now Eisenhower needed it to reassure Capitol Hill after the partisan hiccup of Larson. Allen did not disappoint. Many who served under him considered him the best director the USIA ever had.[62]

Reactions to Allen's appointment were muted. Many saw only a caretaker. The *New York Times* called Allen's post the "least sought-after and most inglorious" job in Washington. The new director faced the enmity of Congress, the civil rights crisis, and the aggressive personal diplomacy of the Secretary of State. The *Times* quoted an "embittered official" at the USIA complaining, "All we ever do is mop up the mess after Dulles spills the gravy."[63] In the event, Dulles proved broadly supportive of Allen and his old bellicosity was blunted by his struggle with terminal cancer. Unfortunately his successor, Christian Herter, proved less sympathetic.[64] The external challenge of Moscow towered over all other problems. In the wake of Sputnik, the U.S.S.R. launched a campaign to sell itself as overwhelmingly strong but committed to peaceful progress. Memories of Hungary faded when the Soviets unveiled a unilateral nuclear test ban in March 1958. USIA analysts reported that such moves worked to "inhibit America's allies and reinforce the stand of neutrals."[65]

Even before Allen could be sworn in, U.S. prestige took a second blow. On 3 November 1957, the Soviets launched Sputnik II with the dog Laika on board. The satellite circled the earth, sending back a stream of data and anxious woofing sounds. The agency took care not to belittle the Soviet achievement but, while waiting for the first U.S. launch, stressed the broader context of technological advances of the era.[66] Unfortunately, U.S. attempts to match Sputnik did not go to plan. The launch of the first American satellite, the Navy's Vanguard, which was scheduled for 4 December, had to be postponed at the last moment. Eager to maximize the utility of the mission to the International Geophysical Year, the United States had given scientists around the world plenty of notice of their intent to launch. The delay seemed all the more humiliating. On 5 December, George V. Allen and Allen Dulles urged the President to order future launchings to be secret until their success was ensured. The NSC

62 Dennis Merrill, "Allen, George V.," *American National Biography*, Vol. 1, New York: Oxford University Press, 1999, pp. 317–19; Russell Baker, "Allen Shoulders USIA Troubles," *New York Times*, 16 November 1956, p. 6. Interview: Walter Roberts, 10 November 2001. Arndt, *First Resort of Kings*, p. 289.

63 NA RG 306 64-A-0536, Office of the director, subject files, 1957–58, box 1, file: Administration – Personnel – Foreign Service, 1957, U[nited] P[ress] story 17 October 1957 appended to Washburn to Allen, 22 October 1957; Wallace Carroll, "U.S. Propaganda Post Called Thankless Job," *New York Times*, 20 October 1957, p. E.9.

64 NA RG 306 64-A-0536, Office of the director, subject files, 1957–58, box 1, Administration, Budget – 1959, Washburn (acting director) to Adams (White House), 13 November 1957; see also Washburn to Berding (ASoS) 2 November 1957.

65 DDEL OSANA NSC/Status of Projects, box 8, NSC 5819 (5) Status of National Security Projects on 30 June 1958, pt. 6, The USIA program, p. 2.

66 *USIA 9th Review of Operations, July 1–December 31, 1957*, p. 2.

commissioned a study to consider the feasibility of such a policy.[67] On 6 December, the Navy attempted to launch Vanguard once again. The rocket proudly rose four feet, sank back, and exploded in a fireball. The *New York Times* conceded a "blow to U.S. prestige," while the Soviet delegation to the UN mischievously offered the United States aid under the U.S.S.R.'s program of technical assistance to backward nations.[68]

The NSC saw no alternative to public launches, and although success came soon, the world's newsreels accumulated a collection of launch-pad booms, fizzes, flips, and flops. In the midst of space triumphs in the 1960s, USIA filmmakers recycled images of the early American rocket failures as evidence that openness was more important to a free society than success. At the time those failures hurt. Audience reaction overseas made it worse. Allen was particularly struck by an account of a newsreel audience in Toronto greeting scenes of Vanguard exploding with riotous cheers. This response set Allen thinking about the degree to which the world had tired of American preeminence. When briefing the National Security Council on this problem on 2 October 1958, Allen drew on a baseball metaphor and spoke of the "Milwaukee Effect." That week the giants of the sport, the New York Yankees, found themselves pitted against the Milwaukee Braves in the World Series. Milwaukee attracted, as Allen put it, "many friends whose only interest in the contest is to see the leading team brought down to size." Like the Yankees, the United States suffered from having "dominated the big leagues for a number of years." Allen did not propose that the United States become weak in order to win friends, but U.S. behavior had to change:

> Our chief problem is to grow up psychologically. We boast about our richness, our bigness, and our strength. We talk about our tall buildings, our motor-cars, and our income. Nations, like people, who boast can expect others to cheer when they fail. The first part of Teddy Roosevelt's dictum, speak softly, has even more applicability today than when he made it, for we carry a very big stick.[69]

Allen guided the USIA accordingly.

Allen saw two problems facing the USIA. "The first," he wrote to Sigurd Larmon of the Advisory Commission, "is the suspicion – this is particularly acute in Congress – that there is something fundamentally evil and un-American about a propaganda agency." His answer to this was to increase the agency's long-term programs and ensure that the VOA, the press service, and other fast operations dealt in "a straight story." The second problem was a basic failure to understand the limitations of information policy. "I do not believe," he continued, "that, if we had the best, most expensive equipment in the world and the shrewdest experts in the United States, we could make a foreign people believe that a policy is really in their best interest when it

---

67   DDEL DDE Papers as President (Ann Whitman file), NSC series, box 9, 347th NSC, 5 December 1957.

68   Constance Mclaughlin Green and Milton Lomask, *Vanguard: A History, NASA SP-4202,* Washington, DC: NASA, 1970, Chapter 11.

69   DDEL OSANA OCB/Subject, box 3, "The Image of America," 23 October 1958.

obviously is not." The USIA did not have "a magic wand which can transmute lead into gold." Even so, Allen was determined to restore America's flagging image.[70]

In early 1958, Allen presented his key recommendation for "regaining the initiative in the post-Sputnik situation" to the Operations Coordinating Board: remove America's space program from the military and create "a U.S. Government Space Agency for basic research on Outer Space for peaceful purposes." This idea coincided with an initiative from an emergency committee led by Lyndon Johnson in the Senate and suggestions from the American Rocket Society and interagency Rocket and Satellite Research Panel. By April, Eisenhower was committed to the idea. The National Aeronautic and Space Administration sprang into life on 1 October 1958.[71]

Science and technology loomed large in the USIA's output in 1958. In the State of the Union address on 9 January, Eisenhower had broadened his Atoms for Peace initiative into Science for Peace and proposed that the United States and U.S.S.R. begin by pooling efforts to wipe out malaria and then move on to cancer, heart attacks, and even hunger. The OCB arranged a Science for Peace conference in the United States to lay the foundations.[72] On 17 January 1958, USIA staff voted Science for Peace as their priority theme for the coming year.[73]

On 31 January 1958, U.S. science had something to celebrate. A U.S. Army team successfully launched the satellite Explorer I and in the process discovered a belt of radiation around the earth, which was soon named after the satellite's designer, James Van Allen, as the Van Allen belt. The USIA publicized the achievement. The VOA gave the story maximum play and reported that a number of European networks picked up their feeds on the story. USIS posts created explanatory exhibitions. The USIS post in Korat, Thailand produced a leaflet with the news, which they dropped on less accessible villages from a police helicopter. The agency sent full-size models of the satellite around the world and created a ten-minute documentary film called *The Explorer in Space.* Further films celebrated the belated launch of Vanguard in March 1958 and the voyage of the nuclear submarine U.S.S. *Nautilus* beneath the North Pole.[74] But Soviet successes continued to seize the headlines. In January 1960,

70   NA RG 306, ZZ entry 1 (formerly 1006), Director's Chronological Files, 1953–64, box 2, microfilm reel 27, Allen to Sigurd Larmon, 15 September 1958.
71   DDEL OSANA OCB/Administrative, box 5, Melborne (Dep. ExO, USIA) to Dearborn (OCB), 24 January 1958; also Special OCB Committee (1) agenda for 24 February 1958. See also James M. Grimwood, *Project Mercury: A Chronology*, NASA SP-4001, Washington, DC: NASA, 1963, and for background House Report 67, 87th Congress, 1st session. George V. Allen and the chairman of the National Advisory Committee for Aeronautics can be found in common cause in the NSC on 3 July 1958; see DDLE, DDE Papers as President (Ann Whitman file), NSC series, box 10, memo of discussion at 371st Meeting of NSC 3 July 1958, 5 July 1958, item 2, re. NSC 5814, p. 3. On USIA liaison with NASA see NA RG 306 64-A-0536, Director's Office Subject files, 1957–1958, box 5, file: Policy & Plans – General, 1958, Bradford to Allen/Washburn, "USIA–NASA relationship," 31 October 1958.
72   DDEL, WHCF CF subject box 99, USIA (3), USIA to Adams (White House), 22 March 1958.
73   NA RG 306, ZZ entry 1 (formerly 1006), Director's Chronological Files, 1953–64, box 2, microfilm reel 24, Washburn to Allen, 17 January 1958. The priority themes in order were (1) Science for Peace; (2) Americana; (3) Disarmament; (4) Anti-Communist Information.
74   DDEL OSANA NSC/Status of Projects, box 8, NSC 5819 (5) Status of National Security Projects on 30 June 1958 pt. 6, The USIA program, p. 10; *USIA 10th Review of Operations, January 1–June*

Allen warned the House Science and Astronautic Committee of the danger to U.S. prestige if the Soviet Union maintained its preeminence in space. "Regardless of how Americans may feel about it," Allen declared, a space race had begun.[75]

*

Each director of the USIA had a particular enthusiasm, and for George V. Allen it was the spreading of the English language. Allen had noted the demand for English language classes while ambassador in Greece. At the USIA, Allen immediately launched a program to develop English language teaching around the world.[76] When he joined the agency, the USIA had 110,000 language students enrolled in fifty-two countries. By the end of 1959, the USIA estimated total enrollment at 175,000 (a figure that represented a sevenfold increase over the decade). The USIA also launched a series of seventy-five seminars across thirty-two countries to train local English language teachers. By the end of 1959, the enrollment had passed 6,000. The USIA was particularly gratified to find many of its patrons "emphatic and even insistent in their demand to be taught and to be able to hear American as distinguished from British English." The agency played to this interest by launching "Easy English" editions, a range of inexpensive paperback versions of contemporary U.S. literature with simplified vocabulary. The campaign brought a bonus. Language programs were found to be "often acceptable to and sometimes even welcomed by governments which clamp down tightly on media operations."[77]

Allen also emphasized the power of English language broadcasts on the VOA. In Athens he noted that even the most anti-British Greek politicians tuned in to the BBC World Service News in English, whereas they dismissed the BBC's Greek language broadcasts as mere propaganda. As incoming USIA director, he saw increased broadcasting in English as a vital element of any wider drive to advance the credibility of the VOA. As he wrote in September 1958, "we will never throw off the stigma of being merely a propaganda outfit . . . until we put emphasis on our own language." He also saw an emphasis on English as essential if the Voice was to develop a constituency on Capitol Hill. In the past the VOA had relied on fragmented, ethnically based support for each individual language. In the future, Allen believed, the VOA could appeal to any politician with a desire to see American culture and influence extended.

 30, 1958, pp. 8–10. On the voyage of the nuclear submarine U.S.S Nautilus below the North Pole see "The Nautilus Crosses the Top of the World," *USIA 11th Review of Operations, July 1–December 31, 1958*, p. 16.

75 John W. Finney, "Congress Warned on Space Prestige: George V. Allen Says Soviet Gains Harm U.S. Position – Fears Threat to Peace," *New York Times*, 22 January 1960, p. 1.

76 *USIA 9th Review of Operations, July 1–December 31, 1957*, p. 3; Pirsein, *The Voice of America*, pp. 380–88.

77 *USIA 9th Review of Operations, July 1–December 31, 1957*, p. 3; DDEL OSANA NSC/Status of Projects, box 8, NSC 5819 (5) Status of National Security Projects on 30 June 1958 pt. 6, The USIA program, pp. 3, 11; see also *USIA 10th Review of Operations, January 1–June 30, 1958*, p. 5 and *USIA 14th Review of Operations, January 1–June 30, 1960*, pp. 17–18; DDEL U.S.PCIIA (Sprague Committee), box 19, USIA 2, undated secret memo (c. 1960), "The U.S. Information Program since July 1953," p. 13; DDEL OSANA, NSC/Status of Projects, box 9, NSC 6013 (5), p. 9 (the report mentions Cambodia particularly).

Hence, in June the VOA began English language broadcasts to Europe. By October 1958, VOA English could be heard sixteen hours a day in Eastern Europe and the Middle East; fourteen hours a day in East Asia; eleven hours a day in Africa; nine hours a day in India; and three in Latin America.[78]

Allen's enthusiasm for English matched the central recommendation of the 1958 Ewing Report on the VOA's language priorities. Unsurprisingly, it also fitted the priorities of the new VOA director, Henry Loomis. Loomis had already proved his value to the agency as founding head of its research arm. In November 1957, he moved out of the USIA to a post in the Office of the Science Advisor. Allen was keen to engineer his return, if only, as Loomis recalled, because the science advisor, Jim Killian, was an old college rival. Loomis returned in May 1958. His tenure would see the transformation of the VOA. Projects included the use from 1959 of "Special English" for certain news broadcasts: a system for communicating to populations with a limited knowledge of the English language using a vocabulary of around 1,000 words delivered at a slow speed.[79] English was emerging as the new language of global communication and the USIA would work to further facilitate that rise.

Allen placed particular emphasis on the USIA's cultural activities. In January 1958, his staff voted for "Americana" to be the agency's second priority (after Science for Peace).[80] In the field this meant that USIS posts were actively engaged in things such as nurturing the development of American studies at European universities. Posts worked to establish chairs in the subject, sometimes with the help of U.S. foundations such as the Ford Foundation.[81] Music also remained a staple of USIA cultural activity. In France alone, in 1958, the USIS sponsored sixty-one live concerts of American and French music in thirty-eight towns and cities around the country. The motion picture service made *Symphony across the Land*, a film celebrating the great American orchestras. In November 1958, the Voice of America mounted a three-day season of special programs to mark the seventieth birthday of Irving Berlin. The VOA's own Willis Conover narrated and produced the programs, which included a host of Irving Berlin's hit songs and interviews with and comments from prominent performers of his work and well-wishers, including President Eisenhower.[82]

Some musical elements in the cultural program attracted criticism. The conservative press found it easy to snipe at public money being used to send Dizzy Gillespie

[78] NA RG 306 64-A-0536, Director's Office Subject files, 1957–8, box 3, file: Broadcasting Service – programs, 1958, Allen to Loomis, 8 September 1958.

[79] Allen further explains his views about English broadcasting in DDEL NSC special staff file series, box 8, (USIA), Notes on "The Image of America," a presentation by Mr. George V. Allen director of USIA, at the [NSC] planning board, 30 September 1959. "Loomis Heads Voice; White House Aide, 39, Named to Succeed Button," *New York Times*, 22 May 1958, p. 30; *USIA 9th Review of Operations, July 1–December 31, 1957*, p. 3; Pirsein, *The Voice of America*, pp. 380–88.

[80] NA RG 306, ZZ entry 1 (formerly 1006), Director's Chronological files, 1953–64, box 2, microfilm reel 24, Washburn to Allen, 17 January 1958.

[81] DDEL OSANA, NSC/Status of Projects, box 9, The USIA, status on June 30, 1960, NSC 6013 (5), pp. 6, 11. The report mentions USIA support for developments at Johns Hopkins, Bologna, Leeds, and the University of London; the Ford chairs were established in Germany.

[82] *USIA 11th Review of Operations, July 1–December 31, 1958*, p. 13.

to Greece. The agency had also noted hostility to jazz in some quarters in Western Europe. One West German told a USIA pollster bluntly, "we aren't Negroes and don't want to listen to aborigine music." In August 1958, an OCB report pondered the problem and noted,

> Requests for jazz groups from all geographic areas continue to be received. It is recognized that jazz is an especially controversial element in the program. It is without equal, however, in appealing to youth groups abroad. It is planned to continue programming about one jazz group per area each year.[83]

It should also be noted that not everyone in the jazz world was delighted to be coopted by a government that had yet to throw its full weight behind civil rights. Little Rock so enraged Louis Armstrong that he pulled out of a tour of the Soviet Union in protest. He later mocked official appropriation of jazz in a musical review, "The Real Ambassadors," written by Dave and Iola Brubeck for the Monterey Jazz Festival in 1962.[84] Jazz remained a mainstay of the cultural program.

*

Allen maintained excellent relations with Capitol Hill. He had no difficulty in being confirmed by the Senate. He knew how to speak to their priorities and conceded the need to eliminate waste from the USIA.[85] In April 1958, he arranged an evening of USIA films at the White House for senior figures from the key committees, including Johnson, Mundt, and Fulbright. The show included *Washington Mosque*, a twenty-minute documentary displaying freedom of religion in the United States, and the CBS *See It Now* documentary *The Lady from Philadelphia* on Marian Anderson's tour of Asia.[86] Allen survived the round of appropriation hearings in May largely unscathed. The House trimmed the budget back from the $110 million requested to $100 million, but did so without vitriol. In the Senate, Lyndon Johnson merely suggested that the VOA's lusty theme music – "Columbia, the Gem of the Ocean" – might betray clandestine listening habits of the audience behind the Iron Curtain.[87]

---

[83] For poll see NA RG 306, 64-A-0536, Office of the director, Subject files, 1957–1958, box 2, Wanda Allender (IRI) to Washburn, "Western European Reactions to American Jazz," 11 September 1957; NA RG 306 64-A-0536, Director's Office subject files, 1957–1958, box 5, President's Emergency Fund, Inter Agency Committee on Presentation, 1958, OSB "Report on Activities of the Cultural Presentation Committee," 20 August 1958. For domestic criticism of jazz see "USIA the Entertainers," *Wall Street Journal*, 15 June 1959, p. 10.

[84] For a discussion of U.S. jazz diplomacy in Africa see Penny M. Von Eschen, "Who's the Real Ambassador? Exploding Cold War Racial Ideology" in Appy (ed.), *Cold War Constructions*, pp. 110–31 and Louis Armstrong, "Cultural Exchange," on Dave and Iola Brubeck, *The Real Ambassadors*, New York: Columbia Records, 1994 and sleeve notes p. 7.

[85] Associated Press, "Director Admits Waste in USIA but Says He's Going to Tighten Up," *Washington Post*, 20 January 1958, p. A.2.

[86] NA RG 306, ZZ entry 1 (formerly 1006), Director's Chronological files, 1953–64, box 2, microfilm reel 25, Washburn to Bryce Harlow (White House), 14 April 1958.

[87] William F. Arbogast, "House Cuts USIA, State Cash $15.4 Million," *Washington Post*, 10 May 1958, p. A,1; Russell Baker, "Johnson Says Music on 'Voice' Traps Eastern European Listeners," *New York Times*, 28 May 1958, p. 12.

Allen also worked to maintain the wider public profile of the USIA. He gave numerous speeches describing the agency and spoke eloquently on such television programs as NBC's *Meet the Press*.[88] He extended the system of advisory committees with a new public relations advisory committee.[89] He worked behind the scenes to ease the USIA's relationship with the broadcast media. His particular targets for cultivation included the president of CBS, Frank Stanton.[90] Stanton eventually became one of the most eloquent advocates of the USIA's cause.

Allen's priorities within the agency included better evaluation of USIS work in the field. In 1958, the agency began a major series of in-depth investigations, including – where the budget permitted – a nongovernment member on the team. The program of reviews began with surveys of USIS operations in South Vietnam and the increasingly awkward ally, France. The report on South Vietnam found something to commend in the way in which the USIA had gotten the Vietnamese Information Service (VIS) up and running and helped to train the Vietnamese army, but much of the report made for difficult reading. Besides predictable examples of inefficiency and interagency overlap, it appeared that elements in the USIS program had backfired. The massive amount of publicity around Diem had apparently gone to the President's head. His regime was so authoritarian that the report recommended "[t]hat USIS rigorously avoid any pushing of 'democracy,' 'freedom of the press' or related topics." Diem's emphasis on strength at the expense of reform threatened to increase domestic opposition, and the Vietnamese people now displayed "growing resentment of American largesse." The report recommended that the "American presence" in South Vietnam "must now be reckoned with as a negative factor" and U.S. aid programs in the country be presented with care.[91]

There was one innovation attributed to USIS Saigon that proved particularly enduring. The United States had long sought to weaken the anti-Diem insurgents by tarring them all as Communists. Around 1956, someone in the USIS post had the idea of promoting an alternative name for the enemy. Rather than the nationalist title Viet Minh, which was apparently enhancing the image of communism among the wider population, the USIS dubbed them *Viet Cong* (translating roughly as Vietnamese Commies). As Everet Bumgardner, who became one of the USIA's most respected Vietnam specialists, recalled, USIS Saigon worked long and hard to get this phrase

88   Dana Adams Schmidt, "USIA Head Chides America for Gloom in Propaganda War," *New York Times*, 7 April 1958, p. 1.
89   NA RG 306 64-A-0536, Director's Office Subject files, 1957–1958, box 3, Advisory Groups – Public Relations; for first meeting see NA RG 306, ZZ entry 1 (formerly 1006), Director's Chronological files, 1953–64, box 2, microfilm reel 32, Washburn to Shelton, 17 June 1959.
90   In December 1959 Allen observed, "Stanton is rather like Roy Howard – suspicious of USIA as a government operation which might lead to government competition with or perhaps control of private TV. Moreover, he, like the press services, wants to stay as far away as possible from any contact with USIA which might give any possible grounds for suspicion that CBS is a tool or organ of U.S. propaganda. However, he and I are good personal friends of long standing, and I think we can gradually bring him round." See NA RG 306, ZZ entry 1 (formerly 1006), Director's Chronological files, 1953–64, box 3, reel 34, Allen to Wheeler (ITV), 22 December 1959.
91   DDEL C. D. Jackson papers, box 109, USIS surveys, Vietnam Report No. 17, April 1958.

into Diem's speeches and the statements of the U.S. mission. By 1958 it had taken hold in U.S. government circles in both Saigon and Washington, although it did not figure in U.S. press coverage until the 1960s. In the long run the phrase "Viet Cong" also proved counterproductive: it conceded the Vietnamese identity of the insurgents, who were only too ready to play the nationalist card against their foreign enemy.[92]

*

Allen's entry into the USIA coincided with mounting concern over the growth of anti-American feeling in Latin America. The United States faced a lively Soviet campaign emphasizing the benefits of a neutral foreign policy. In May 1958, the principal advocate of an improved U.S. response, Vice President Richard Nixon, experienced a vivid demonstration of South American hostility toward the United States when a Venezuelan mob attacked his motorcade during a visit to Caracas. In June 1958, Nixon pressed the NSC for expanded links with the region's journalists and universities. By the end of the year, the NSC had authorized millions of dollars for extra exchanges. The USIA opened branches of binational centers on selected campuses and expanded a program to distribute textbooks in the region. Cultural exchanges abounded as part of the bid to increase the prestige of the United States among intellectuals. Other target groups included the non-Communist left and labor. An NSC policy statement of February 1959 committed the United States to maintaining links with opposition parties in Latin America, while taking care to avoid the impression that the United States supported "authoritarians of the right or left." The OCB's objectives for Latin America emphasized the creation of "mutual understanding" and getting the region to accept responsibility for its own progress. Tools included use of national commissions, made up of local opinion leaders, to direct cultural exchange.[93]

In Cuba, the USIA sought to counter the growing anti-Americanism of the new leader, Fidel Castro. In the spring of 1960, the NSC discussed strategies to communicate with the Cuban people, including the idea of broadcasting television programs into the country from a specially equipped aircraft, or using radio to relay baseball games with news inserted into the pauses in play. Allen counseled against both strategies, arguing that Castro could claim to be a victim of "television aggression" and that

92 Sheehan, *A Bright Shining Lie*, p. 189; see also Library of Congress, Neil Sheehan papers, box 120, folder 15, Bumgardner interview notes. The term was used in a contribution by a Vietnamese letter writer to the *Washington Post* in March 1956, Hoai Quoc, "Vietnam's Multiparadox," *Washington Post*, 10 March 1956, p. 14, and its first use in the *New York Times* appears to be in a quotation from Diem in an AP story, "Saigon Calls for Unity," *New York Times*, 27 October 1960, p. 6. It first appeared in the body of a story in Robert Trumbull, "Red Guerrillas War on South Vietnam," *New York Times*, 16 March 1961.

93 *FRUS 1958–1960, Vol. V, American Republics*, doc. 4, 369th meeting of NSC, 19 June 1958, pp. 27–32; doc. 5, editorial note; doc. 7, OCB report to NSC, 26 November 1958, pp. 36–60; doc. 11, NSC 5902/1, 13 February 1959, pp. 91–103; doc. 12, OCS Regional Operation Plan for Latin America, 1 July 1959, pp. 117–34. See also DDEL OSANA NSC/Status of Projects, box 8, NSC 5819 (5) Status of National Security Projects on 30 June 1958, pt. 6, The USIA program, pp. 24–6. A detailed study of binational centers in Latin America and elsewhere can be found in NA RG 306, ZZ entry 1 (formerly 1006), Director's Chronological Files, 1953–64, box 3, microfilm reel 38, Scherbacher to Washburn, "The Status of Binational Center Grantees," 1 September 1960, and associated documents.

baseball was "not sufficiently dignified for a U.S. program." In the end the CIA led the way, placing a covert anti-Castro radio station on Swan Island off Honduras and working with the USIA and State to create and distribute a daily bulletin of unattributed material about Cuba in Latin America.[94]

The Middle East caused Allen particular concern. Pan-Arab nationalism gained momentum as Egypt and Syria formed a United Arab Republic in February 1958. In July 1958, a bloody coup overthrew the pro-Western regime in Iraq. Friendly governments in Lebanon and Jordan suddenly also seemed in danger. The Lebanese president, Chamille Chamoun, appealed to Eisenhower for military support. On 15 July the United States sent in a sizeable force to prop up Chamoun's government, while the British deployed troops to protect the rule of King Hussein of Jordan. The Americans remained in Lebanon until October. The USIA worked hard to allay suspicion of U.S. motives, while the U.S.S.R. unloaded an unprecedented volume of propaganda to nurture it. USIS countermeasures made particular use of Eisenhower's statement on the intervention. In Lebanon, the U.S. air force dropped a million copies of a USIS leaflet featuring the President's picture and an Arabic translation of his words. The USIS information officer in Beruit, Granville Austin, gave two press conferences a day, giving particular attention to journalists from the developing world.[95]

The VOA rose to the challenge of the Lebanon crisis by tripling its broadcasts to the Middle East and switching to an all-news format. The VOA could now be heard twenty-four hours a day, with half an hour of English news "on the hour" and half an hour of Arabic news "on the half hour." The crisis provided a political rationale for Allen's planned expansion of the World Wide English schedule. Eisenhower was particularly impressed when, in August, the VOA cleared its schedule to carry a special session of the UN General Assembly on the Lebanon crisis live in all five official UN languages.[96] When the Soviet Union intensified its jamming to blot out the UN relay, the VOA broadcast samples of the interference to the world.[97]

The Lebanon crisis had a big payoff for the VOA. Eisenhower approved a $22.3 million supplemental budget request for new transmitter construction to boost VOA signal strength to the Middle East and Africa. Although the Senate trimmed this to $15 million, the budget included $10 million to build a new transmitter in North Carolina, at last plugging the gap left by the abandonment of the Baker project in 1953.[98] The

---

[94] *FRUS 1958–1960, Vol. VI, Cuba*. doc 443, Washburn to Amb. Bonsal (Havana), 29 January 1960, pp. 773–6; doc. 505, 441st NSC meeting, 14 April 1960, p. 893; doc. 524, Rubottam (ASoS) to Bonsal pp. 932–3; doc. 545, 450th NSC meeting, 7 July 1960, p. 989.

[95] *USIA 11th Review of Operations, July 1–December 31, 1958*, p. 17 and NA RG 306 64-A-0536, Office of the director, subject files, 1957–8, box 4, file: Middle East Situation, 1958.

[96] DDEL WHCF OF 247-D, box 912, President to Allen, 21 August 1958; DDEL OSANA NSC/Status of Projects, box 8, NSC 5819 (5), Status of National Security Projects on 30 June 1958, pt. 6, The USIA program, p. 2.

[97] *USIA 11th Review of Operations, July 1–December 31, 1958*, p. 19.

[98] DDEL OSANA OCB/Subject, box 4, Near East Radio Broadcasting (1), esp. Allen to Senator Carl Hayden, 29 July 1958. Plans included new MW transmitters in Liberia, Iran, and Cyprus and a SW transmitter in Liberia; DDEL WHCF OF 247-D, box 912, Harry Tyson Carter (USIA deputy general counsel) to Jack Z. Anderson (White House), 18 August 1958.

USIA's follow-up projects in the Middle East included the launch in October 1959 of a bimonthly magazine called *Al Hayat Fi America* (American Life).[99]

The USIA's work gathered pace in Africa. New libraries and information centers sprang up. The agency's newsreel *Today* reached 200 theaters. The Agency puffed U.S. diplomatic initiatives and the visits of African leaders such as Ghana's Prime Minister Kwame Nkrumah to the United States. Although unable to provide much evidence of effectiveness, the USIS at least seemed welcome in the emerging nations of Africa. In 1959 the agency proudly reported that the PAO in Uganda had been made an honorary elder of the Luo tribe in recognition of the agency's work.[100] In 1960, Africa finally became an "area operation" in its own right within the USIA structure, under an assistant director for Africa. Even so, USIS posts emphasized the need for large-scale investment in the region. The battle for Africa was only just beginning.[101]

In Western Europe, Allen worked to claw back ground lost by the budget cuts of 1957. Allen did not doubt the need to maintain USIS operations in "friendly countries," not least in the United Kingdom. Two alarm bells sounded in the course of 1958. In January, the agency received a report compiled by public relations pioneer Edward L. Bernays during a holiday in Britain over the summer of 1957 called "What the British Think of Us." The report told a sorry story of rising anti-Americanism. Allen forwarded the document to the White House, blaming British resentment of America's power and sponsorship of colonial peoples for the problem.[102] In May 1958 Britain's senior psychological warrior, Ralph Murray of the Foreign Office Information Research Department, wrote warning of mounting concern in the British government over the deployment of U.S. bombers armed with H-bombs and the clumsy language used in associated statements from a Washington on defense matters. Examples of Pentagon ineptitude included the publication of an army report on chemical and biological warfare at the height of disarmament talks in London. Allen raised the matter at the interdepartment watchdog committee. If British opinion could waiver then no ally could be taken for granted.[103]

The USIA had a marginal role in the most spectacular piece of U.S. propaganda in Europe in 1958: the pavilion at the Brussels World's Fair. In October 1956, the

---

99 *USIA 13th Review of Operations, July 1–December 31, 1959*, pp. 6–7.

100 *USIA 11th Review of Operations, July 1–December 31, 1958*, pp. 14–15.

101 DDEL OSANA, NSC/Status of Projects, box 9, The USIA, status on June 30, 1960, NSC 6013 (5), p. 7; NA RG 306, ZZ entry 1 (formerly 1006), Director's Chronological files, 1953–64, box 3, microfilm reel 39, Allen to Satterthwaite (ASoS African Affairs), 22 November 1960.

102 For report see NA RG 306 64-A-0536, Director's Office Subject files, 1957–8, box 7; for correspondence see NA RG 306, ZZ entry 1 (formerly 1006), Director's Chronological files, 1953–64, box 2, microfilm reel 24, Allen to Sherman Adams (White House), 5 February 1958.

103 NA RG 306 64-A-0536, Director's Office Subject files, 1957–8, box 4, file: Government – Watchdog, Bundy (IOP) "Illustrative statements or actions for possible use at 'Watch Dog' meeting on Friday May 16, 1958," 14 May 1958. Eisenhower had raised concerns about British and French press "abuse" of "the U.S. and U.S. political personalities" in a meeting with British PM Harold Macmillan on 20 March 1957; see NA RG 306 64-A-0536, Director's Office Subject files, 1957–8, box 1, file: Government Agencies – State, Dept. of, 1957, Secret memorandum of dinner conversation at the mid-ocean club, 20 March 1957.

Department of State established an Office of the United States Commissioner General under the direction of stage impresario Howard Cullman to plan the exhibit. Its attractions included Circarama, a 360-degree film presentation featuring a tour of spectacular American sites created by Walt Disney; Rogers and Hammerstein's *Carousel*; an RCA color television; and an IBM "electronic brain" – the 305 RAMAC computer with the first ever "hard drive."[104] Despite its popularity with visitors, the U.S. pavilion received negative attention back home. Critics focused on a special exhibit called "Unfinished Work" on America's social challenges, which included images of racial segregation. Even before the opening day, Southerners howled on Capitol Hill. The press also objected to a display of modern art and a large etching of a bare-breasted Indian maiden, copied from a renaissance woodcut, presented as an image of the New World. On 7 May, Eisenhower suggested that Allen inspect the fair, make his own assessment, and advise.[105]

On 26 June, Allen reported back to Eisenhower, recommending that the racial element in "Unfinished Work" be diluted by including material on public health[106] The fair team overreacted and redesigned the entire exhibit to focus solely on public health. A squall of liberal protest greeted its reopening in mid-August, but the black American press and the U.S.S.R. largely ignored the story. Ironically, all evidence suggested that the original exhibition had made a positive impression on visitors. The USIA had remained peripheral to the debacle, but memories of Brussels loomed large as the agency stepped up its representation of the civil rights question.[107]

*

The ultimate focus of Allen's work at the USIA was, of course, the Soviet Union. In his testimony on Capitol Hill and public speaking engagements, he emphasized the scale of the resources that the U.S.S.R. poured into its propaganda. In a speech to the Overseas Press Association on 21 September 1958, he estimated the combined overseas propaganda budget for the Soviet bloc for 1957 at between $500 million and $750 million, excluding the cost of radio jamming. The Soviet bloc was engaged in "the greatest propaganda effort history has ever known." He pleaded with

104 For end of fair reports see NA RG 306 64-A-0536, Director's Office Subject files, 1957–8, box 4, file: Information Centers Service – Exhibits 1958 – Brussels World Fair – from August. The fair is a major element in Haddow, *Pavilions of Plenty*, esp. pp. 70–111; see also Michael L. Krenn, "'Unfinished Business': Segregation and U.S. diplomacy at the 1958 Brussels World's Fair," *Diplomatic History*, 20, 4 (Fall 1997), 591–612.
105 DDEL DDE Papers as President (Ann Whitman file), Ann Whitman diary series, box 10, May 1958 file 2, Allen and Goodpaster, Memorandum of Conversation with the President, 7 May 1958; NA RG 306 64-A-0536, Director's Office Subject files, 1957–1958, box 5, Brussels Fair – Allen Report and Recommendations; Michael L. Krenn, *Black Diplomacy: African Americans and the State Department, 1945–1969*, Armonk, NY: M. E. Sharpe, 1999, pp. 106–8; Krenn, "Unfinished Business," pp. 599–605; Krenn, *Fall-Out Shelters of the Human Spirit*, pp. 142–6; also Haddow, *Pavilions of Plenty*, pp. 169–200.
106 DDEL DDE Papers as President, Administrative, box 2, George V. Allen, Allen to President, 26 June 1958. NA RG 306, ZZ entry 1 (formerly 1006), Director's Chronological files, 1953–64, box 2, microfilm reel 25, Washburn to Allen, 25 June 1958; Allen to Cullman, 26 June 1958.
107 Krenn, *Black Diplomacy*, p. 108; Krenn, "Unfinished Business," pp. 608–11.

Congress to halt baseless attacks on the VOA and provide the necessary resources to respond.[108]

In confronting the U.S.S.R., Allen's USIA hit on familiar themes. The shock execution of the Hungarian "deviationist" leader Imre Nagy in June 1958 justified the reuse of materials about 1956.[109] Allen worked hard to learn the lessons of Hungary. He reminded the NSC on 24 May 1958 that the VOA needed clear policy guidelines in its dealings with the Eastern bloc. The VOA would only pursue "discreet encouragement of dissent and non-cooperative attitudes" if this was national security policy.[110] Chastened by memories of 1956, the NSC now emphasized promoting gradual change in the East and looked to cultural tools as the best way to promote that change. Remarkably, by January 1958, the Soviets themselves were also open to exchange. A new phase in the cultural Cold War was about to begin.[111]

3) CRUSADING WITH CULTURE
THE CULTURAL PROGRAM IN THE U.S.S.R., 1958–60

Given Eisenhower's appreciation of the power of culture in international affairs, it was only to be expected that any opportunity to gain a foothold in the U.S.S.R. would be seized. As early as the Geneva Summit of 1955, the United States, the United Kingdom, and France proposed a seventeen-point program of Soviet concessions to allow such things as freer exchange of information, tourism, and an end to jamming. The Soviets rejected any multilateral accord on culture but seemed open to bilateral agreements. They showed themselves willing by inviting *Porgy and Bess* to Moscow and Leningrad. The United States codified its wish for cultural exchange as a method of influencing Soviet society in the policy document NSC 5607 of 29 June 1956. In that year the Soviets renewed the exchange of *Amerika* magazine for *Soviet Life*, permitted tours by the Boston Symphony Orchestra, and signed exchange agreements with Belgium and Norway. The violinist Emil Giels became the first Soviet artist since the war to perform in the United States. A door was opening.[112]

Eisenhower now saw large-scale cultural exchanges with Russia as a priority. When he appointed Arthur Larson in November 1956, he urged the USIA director to "offer [the U.S.S.R.] unlimited access to America in exchange for same" in a broad range of fields including "publications, visitors, cultural, broadcasts etc." Larson worked accordingly. The United States proposed an exchange of television and radio news coverage in June 1957, and during Larson's final months at the USIA, the agency

---

108 "Red Propaganda Placed at Record," *New York Times*, 24 September 1958, p. 6; "U.S. Losing Broadcast War, 'Voice' Chief Says," *Washington Post*, 23 September 1958, p. A.2.

109 *USIA 10th Review of Operations, January 1–June 30, 1958*, p. 15.

110 *FRUS 1958–1960, Vol. X, Part 1, Eastern Europe Region; Soviet Union; Cyprus*, doc. 5, 366th NSC, 22 May 1958, pp. 12–18

111 *FRUS 1958–1960, Vol. X, Part 1*, doc. 6, NSC 5811/1, 24 May 1958, pp. 18–31; doc. 18, OCB operational plan for Soviet dominated nations of Eastern Europe, 2 July 1959, pp. 79–84

112 For background including NSC 5607 see Yale Richmond, *U.S.–Soviet Cultural Exchanges, 1958–1986: Who Wins?* Boulder, CO: Westview, 1987, pp. 133–9. The U.S.S.R. concluded a cultural agreement with France in 1957.

helped persuade Congress to amend the chief obstacle to large-scale exchange with the Soviet Union: the 1952 immigration act. Full-scale negotiations began in Washington at the end of October 1957. The Soviets proved tough negotiators, whose prime interest appeared to be "acquiring American industrial know-how." The United States worked to ensure that any "know-how" bought access to the Soviet public. On 27 January 1958, the countries signed a two-year "Agreement . . . in the Cultural, Technical, and Educational Fields." The road to large-scale exchange was clear.[113]

In the spring of 1958, the two countries exchanged a handful of students for the first time. U.S. airports saw the spectacle of wispy Soviet dancers, brooding concert virtuosi, implausibly enormous wrestlers, and earnest scientists bound for academic conferences. Delegations from the American steel and plastics industries, the Philadelphia Orchestra, and assorted U.S. athletes toured the U.S.S.R. The first American to really make a splash was a young pianist from Texas named Van Cliburn, who won the Tchaikovsky International Piano competition. Cliburn then toured the U.S.S.R., inspiring rave reviews from hard-to-please critics and the passionate devotion of a host of Russian women of all ages.[114] Both sides worked for more. Eric Johnston of the Motion Picture Association of America negotiated a film exchange, but an even more dramatic proposal came from the Soviet side.[115]

In the early summer of 1958, the Soviet Union proposed an exchange of exhibitions in 1959. The United States had a chance to mount a "national exhibition showing the progress of science, technology and culture in the U.S." in the heart of the Soviet capital. With just a year to organize an exhibit, and no buildings or contents planned, the offer presented a formidable challenge. But Eisenhower had no doubt that the United States had to accept. "It must be done," he told Allen and Washburn; "this will be the first time since the Bolshevik revolution that we'll be able to meet a mass of Russians face to face." The two nations signed a preliminary agreement on 10 September 1958. The USIA would organize the exhibit, with Washburn coordinating.[116]

The agency appointed a businessman from California named Chad McClellan to serve as general manager of the exhibit. Harold C. McClellan was president of the Old Colony Paint and Chemical Company of Los Angeles and had already distinguished

---

[113] Larson, *Eisenhower: The President Nobody Knew*, p. 82.; *FRUS 1958–1960, Vol. X, Part 2, Eastern Europe; Finland; Greece; Turkey*, doc. 2, Policy Information Statement: U.S.–Soviet Exchange Agreement, 29 January 1958, pp. 2–6; for text see *Department of State Bulletin*, 17 February 1958, pp. 243–7; Hixson, *Parting the Curtain*, pp, 151–5. For USIA congressional correspondence in 1957 see NA RG 306, ZZ entry 1 (formerly 1006), Director's Chronological files, 1953–64, box 2, microfilm reel 16.

[114] *FRUS 1958–1960, Vol. X, Pt. 2*, doc. 5, Lacy (Special Assistant to SoS for East–West Exchanges), to Dulles, 25 July 1958, pp. 10–13; doc. 29, U.S. embassy Moscow, No. 45, 18 July 1960, drafted by Hans N. Tuch, pp. 67–70.

[115] "U.S.–Soviet Pact on Films Nearer," *New York Times*, 1 May 1958, p. 35, and on the conclusion of the deal see Max Frankel, "U.S., Soviet Agree to Film Exchange," *New York Times*, 10 October 1958, p. 36.

[116] Interview: Washburn, 1 December 1995; NA RG 306, ZZ entry 1 (formerly 1006), Director's Chronological files, 1953–64, box 2, microfilm reel 27, Washburn to Allen, "Moscow Exhibit," 29 August 1958, and reel 28, Washburn to Crabtree (General Mills Inc.), 15 December 1958.

himself in the field of international exhibitions as Assistant Secretary of Commerce for International Affairs. He had many qualities that contributed to his success in the U.S.S.R., including tenacity in negotiation and an ability to drink his Russian counterparts under the table. He left for Moscow in mid-October 1958.[117]

The opening of cultural relations between the United States and the U.S.S.R. did not preclude Cold War sparring. In autumn 1958, Khrushchev began to press on West Berlin. The USIA responded by contrasting this threatening behavior with the official Soviet espousal of "Peaceful Coexistence." The crisis demonstrated the value of the agency's newly enhanced teletype network. USIS posts around the world received prompt and ample documentation on the crisis, including translations of the State Department's analysis of Khrushchev's ultimatum and Eisenhower's address on the crisis in March 1959. USIS Paris published a French text of this speech in booklet form in just thirty hours. The International Press Service created a picture story called *A Tale of Two Cities* contrasting life in East and West Berlin, whereas the Motion Picture Service created a ten-minute documentary on the crisis called simply *Berlin*. The broadcasts of the RIAS remained a key element in maintaining the morale of West Berlin and informing East Berlin of the U.S. position.[118]

While the Berlin Crisis smoldered, McClellan pressed ahead with negotiations. His first problem was the venue. He soon realized that the original site in Gorki Park was unsuitable, but secured an admirable alternative in the middle of Sokolniki Park, just a fifteen-minute subway ride from Red Square. The Soviets eventually offered to landscape the park, to install the necessary utilities, and to purchase the 80,000-square foot exhibition building at the end of the season. December saw a second major hitch, as the Soviets attempted to exclude cultural elements such as film and live performances from the exhibition. McClellan stuck to his guns and threatened to withdraw altogether. The Soviets yielded. Live components in the eventual exhibition included concerts by Leonard Bernstein and the New York Philharmonic, a fashion show, and a special variety show hosted by Ed Sullivan. The two powers signed the final exhibition agreement on 29 December 1958. American expectations for the show were now sky high. Llewelyn Thompson, the U.S. ambassador in Moscow, went so far as to say that the exhibition would be "worth more to us than five new battleships" and "may well have an impact on the whole course of the future Soviet American relations."[119]

Then came the matter of planning the content of the exhibition. McClellan and the USIA worked hard to avoid anything smacking of ideological confrontation and to allow America's goods and culture to speak for themselves. The White House

---

[117] Interview: Washburn, 1 December 1995; "Team Leaves for Russia to Set Up U.S. Exhibit," *Washington Post*, 19 October 1958, p. B.12.

[118] *USIA 11th Review of Operations, July 1–December 31, 1958*, p. 2; *USIA 12th Review of Operations, January 1–June 30, 1959*, pp. 7–9.

[119] NA RG 306, ZZ entry 1 (formerly 1006), Director's Chronological files, 1953–64, box 2, microfilm reel 28, Washburn to Crabtree (General Mills Inc.), 15 December 1958; NA RG 306 A1 (1061) USIA historical collection misc. files, 1940s–1990s, box 12; Harold C. McClellan, *A Review of the American National Exhibition in Moscow*, December 1959, esp. pp. 14–17.

assistant for religion, Frederic Fox, worried that the emphasis on U.S. consumer goods would play into the Communist critique of Western materialism and lobbied to inject God into the exhibition. The USIA remained content to showcase Mammon.[120] The Moscow exhibition took shape as the apotheosis of all that the United States had achieved in its international exhibition program to date. The USIA's "Greatest Hits" from earlier shows formed the backbone to the Moscow exhibition, including the entire *Family of Man* exhibit, Disney's Circarama, RCA's color television, and IBM's RAMAC computer, now programmed with the answers in Russian to 3,500 questions about the United States. Frequently asked questions included "What is the meaning of 'the American Dream?'"[121] To adapt the *Family of Man* to Moscow, the USIA tactfully dropped the image of East Berliners throwing rocks at a Soviet tank and added dates to contextualize the images of poverty in the Dust Bowl. The agency also added a photograph of the death mask of Russia's favorite president – Lincoln – with an appropriately rousing quotation. The Russians demanded the removal of an image of a famine victim in China in 1946.[122]

The central structure of the exhibit would be a large geodesic dome. This revolutionary design by Buckminster Fuller, with its interlocking segments, was propaganda for American ingenuity in its own right. Geodesic domes had stunned Soviet rivals at the Kabul trade fair of 1956 and wowed Polish fair-goers in Poznań in 1957. The USIA hoped that a still larger, golden dome would work the same magic in Moscow. Under the geodesic dome, fairgoers would find a magnificent exhibit designed by Jack Masey: a shining cornucopia of American consumer goods, food and clothing, a model house, and at its heart a kitchen fully fitted with all modern conveniences in which demonstrators prepared a range of Bird's Eye frozen ready-meals. In an exhibit created by the legendary designers Charles and Ray Eames, vast screens showed slides of a day in the life of America: streets full of happy, well-fed people; highways teeming with magnificent cars; and lush college campuses alive with eager, well-groomed youths. The surrounding area would contain a children's playground, an exhibition of American cars and boats, and a stand distributing free samples of America's second most characteristic beverage, Pepsi-Cola, which was one of the few products to gain access to the Soviet market as a result of the exhibition.[123]

Washburn traveled to Moscow to oversee progress. He watched as cheerful Soviet workers labored round the clock in three competing shifts to build the exhibition space and raise the seventy-eight-foot-high dome.[124] Encouraged, he invited the Vice

---

[120] DDEL OSANA, OCB/Subject, box 2, exhibits/fairs, Fox to Karl Harr, 25 February 1959, etc.; also Hixson, *Parting the Curtain*, pp. 166–8.

[121] *USIA 12th Review of Operations, January 1–June 30, 1959*, p. 13

[122] NA RG 306, ZZ entry 1 (formerly 1006), Director's Chronological Files, 1953–64, box 2, microfilm reel 31, Washburn to Sivard (ICS/E), 19 March 1959; *FRUS 1958–1960, Vol. X, Pt. 2*, doc. 16, INR report 8100.3, U.S.–Soviet exhibits a successful exchange, Washington, August 1959, p. 39

[123] Interview: Washburn, 1 December, 1995; Tuch, 16 November, 1995; Hixson, *Parting the Curtain*, pp. 174–5.

[124] NA RG 306, ZZ entry 1 (formerly 1006), Director's Chronological files, 1953–1964, box 2, microfilm reel 32, Washburn to Allen quoted in Payne to Roberts, 30 April 1959; on the geodesic dome see Haddow, *Pavilions of Plenty*, p. 61.

President to open the exhibition. Nixon readily agreed.[125] Meanwhile, the Soviets maneuvered to diminish the appeal of the exhibition. In May, they forbade live jazz and the distribution of cosmetics, toy cars, and most printed materials at the fair. McClellan had to fight hard to retain the right to serve samples of Pepsi. Although unable to hand out books, exhibition staff found a strategically turned back to be a wonderful encouragement to the disappearance of any pamphlet, book, or other item that was not fixed down. Bibles and Sears Roebuck catalogs vanished particularly swiftly.[126] As opening day neared, the Communist Party launched a desperate counteroffensive claiming that the show would not represent the reality of American life. The regime showed more entertainment on television to keep people at home and even opened a rival "Exhibition of the People's Economic Achievement" nearby. Finally, they attempted to keep tickets in the hands of party members. But the campaign could not dim the allure of the marvel taking shape in Sokolniki Park.[127]

As usual, the exhibit had its critics on Capitol Hill. They focused on the exhibition of American art since World War One. On 1 July the House Committee on Un-American Activities, now chaired by Frances E. Walter (D-PA), opened hearings on the art show. Walter claimed that more than half of the artists featured in the exhibition were Communist sympathizers. Controversial pictures included "Welcome Home" (1946) by Jack Levine, an angry expressionist work showing a bloated general gorging himself at a victory dinner. The press asked amateur artist Eisenhower to comment. The President wisely explained that a jury of four experts had selected the art and that the paintings were, in any case, just a small part of the whole exhibit. While Ike conceded that "Welcome Home" looked more "like a lampoon than art" he refused to play censor. He did suggest that a future exhibit jury pay attention to "what America likes" and quietly withdrew one of his own pictures from display in McClellan's office.[128]

As the American art world rallied to support Eisenhower's refusal to censor, the USIA pondered its policy with regard to the controversial pictures. Washburn noted that "one *sure* way to draw undue attention to them would be to withdraw them from the exhibit." The agency decided to adjust its planned exhibit by extending the chronological range of paintings on display, with masterpieces from the earlier ages of American art: Copley, Eakins, Whistler, Remington, and their ilk. At

[125]   Richard M. Nixon, *Six Crises*, Garden City, NY: Doubleday & Co., 1962, p. 255.

[126]   *FRUS 1958–1960, Vol. X, Pt. 2*, doc. 16, INR report 8100.3, U.S.–Soviet exhibits a successful exchange, Washington, August 1959, p. 40; Hixson, *Parting the Curtain*, pp. 187–92; NA RG 306, ZZ entry 1 (formerly 1006), Director's Chronological Files, 1953–64, box 3, microfilm reel 33, Allen to Curtis Benjamin (American Book Publisher's Council), 28 September 1959; Interview: Abbott Washburn, 1 December 1995 and NA RG 306 A1 (1061) USIA historical collection misc. files, 1940s–1990s, box 12; Harold C. McClellan, *A Review of the American National Exhibition in Moscow*, December 1959.

[127]   *FRUS 1958–1960, Vol. X, Pt. 2*, doc. 16, INR report 8100.3, U.S.–Soviet exhibits a successful exchange, Washington, August 1959, p. 38–9; Hixson, *Parting the Curtain*, pp. 185–7, 192–3.

[128]   "President Favors Art Liked by U.S." and "Transcript of the President's News Conference," *New York Times*, 2 July 1959, pp. 3, 10; Hixson, *Parting the Curtain*, pp. 172–3; and for a full treatment of art at the exhibition, Krenn, *Fall-Out Shelters of the Human Spirit*, pp. 155–78.

Eisenhower's personal suggestion, the agency also affixed labels to the paintings to pin down the artist's intent. In Ike's book an uncategorized work of art was a hostage to fortune.[129]

The final days before opening saw a frenzy of last-minute activity. Russian and American builders and fitters swarmed over the site. The corps of seventy-five Russian-speaking American exhibition guides – mostly graduate students – bridged the language gap with running translations and helped out with the last-minute painting.[130] There was one last political hitch. On 6 July the House passed a resolution calling on the President to proclaim the third week of July as a Captive Nations Week, dedicated to prayer for liberation from communism. The first Captive Nations Week coincided exactly with the opening of the exhibition in Moscow. Frustrated, Washburn stressed the need to avoid such mistiming in the future.[131]

On 23 July, Vice President Nixon arrived in Moscow to open the exhibition. Other distinguished Americans present for the opening included Walt Disney, Buckminster Fuller, Edward Steichen, William Randoph Hearst, and senior executives from contributing private companies including Pepsi-Cola, Eastman Kodak, and Macy's. The U.S. press also arrived in force, eager to record the meeting of East and West. Neither the exhibition nor its opening day disappointed.[132]

Nixon began the opening day badly. During an impromptu tour of a market, he tried to give money to a citizen who said he could not go to the fair. The embarrassed Russian explained that he lacked a ticket, not the money to buy it. Nixon then met Khrushchev at the Kremlin and endured dressing down over the Captive Nations Resolution before proceeding to Sokolniki Park, where the two men toured the exhibit. The respective security details scuffled as the two men moved around the pavilion. Khrushchev badgered Nixon with anti-American quips as they went. Embracing a nearby worker he taunted, "Does this man look like a slave laborer?" Eventually the pair reached the heart of the show: the high-tech model kitchen. Here Nixon at last hit back, delivering the opening salvo of what became known as "the Kitchen Debate." Surrounded by the material evidence of American prosperity, Nixon explained that the house on display was within the reach of all ordinary Americans. Khrushchev parried by claiming that the Soviet state provided the same but as a right to all citizens, and added that Soviet houses lasted longer than just twenty years. When Nixon then stressed the role of the free marketplace in advancing prosperity, Khrushchev roared back a defense of the command economy, and bragged about Soviet military strength. After some

[129] NA RG 306, ZZ entry 1 (formerly 1006), Director's Chronological Files, 1953–64, box 3, microfilm reel 33, Washburn to Bryce Harlow (White House), 6 July 1959; also Sanka Knox, "Eisenhower Wins More Art Backing," *New York Times*, 4 July 1959, p. 17; Hixson, *Parting the Curtain*, pp. 172–3.

[130] Edmund K. Faltermayer, "U.S. Fair in Moscow Gets Finishing Touch as Confusion Abounds," *Wall Street Journal*, 22 July 1959.

[131] *FRUS 1958–1960, Vol. X, Part 1*, doc. 21, Washburn (as acting director OCB) to OCB, 29 July 1959, pp. 99–100; Nixon, *Six Crises*, pp. 251–22.

[132] *FRUS 1958–1960, Vol. X, Part 1*, editorial note p. 329; NA RG 306, ZZ entry 1 (formerly 1006), Director's Chronological files, 1953–64, box 2, microfilm reel 32, Washburn to Allen, "VIPs to Sokolniki," 4 June 1959.

minutes toe to toe and apparently on the verge of blows, the two politicians relaxed and broke off to complete their tour and formally open the event. For the USIA, the Vice President's feisty response had global value. The agency circulated the full text of the Kitchen Debate to all posts. The quintessential setting of domestic American Cold War "containment culture" – the kitchen – had inspired a defining moment in the ideological clash between East and West.[133]

From the first day, the exhibition was a runaway success. Despite the ticket controls and police at the gates of Sokolniki suggesting that visitors might prefer the rival Soviet show, Muscovites flocked to the exhibition. They viewed the gleaming automobiles, watched the films and kitchen demonstrations, and sipped Pepsi from disposable cups. The pavilion staff handed out a million souvenir pins and over two million brochures, which immediately became prized items on the Soviet black market and turned up in every corner of the country. Visiting Russia in later years, Washburn was touched by how many people still treasured their pins from 1959.[134]

One element of the fair attracted praise above all others: the exhibit guides. USIA had selected the guides with care, whittling 1,000 hopefuls down to the final twenty-seven women and forty-eight men. The recruitment criteria specified that they be "between the ages of twenty and thirty-five, fluent in the Russian language, well adjusted, well educated and of good appearance." The group included four African Americans. All worked as volunteers for a per diem of $16 a day. Their training included preparation to answer difficult questions about American life, and especially the question of U.S. economic and racial inequalities. Moscow's exhibition-goers relished the chance to chat with open and informed American youths. Although Communist Party agitators mingled with the ordinary fair-goers to challenge the guides, they proved well able to rise above heckling.[135]

Ten days into the fair's run, Soviet disruption suddenly subsided. It was a symptom of yet another warming of Soviet–American relations. At 10.30 on the morning of Monday, 3 August 1959, Eisenhower announced that he had invited Khrushchev to visit the United States, in September 1959, and that he in turn would be visiting the Soviet Union. The announcement caused considerable disquiet at the

---

[133] Nixon, *Six Crises*, pp. 150–60; *USIA 13th Review of Operations, July 1–December 31, 1959*, p. 9; Interview: Tom Tuch, 16 November 1995; for comment see Ellen Tyler May, *Homeward Bound: American Families in the Cold War Era*, New York: Basic Books, 1988, pp. 16–18; Hixson, *Parting the Curtain*, pp. 178–81; Haddow, *Pavilions of Plenty*, pp. 216–17. The scuffles between the secret service and KGB were noted and dodged by Reuters correspondent Bob Elphick. Interview: Robert Elphick, 24 July 2005.

[134] *FRUS 1958–1960, Vol. X, Pt. 2*, doc. 16, INR report 8100.3, U.S.–Soviet exhibits a successful exchange, Washington, August 1959, pp. 38–9; doc. 25, USIA Exhibit Program for 1960–61 for the Soviet Area, 21 March 1960, p. 58. Interview: Washburn, 1 December 1995; Interview: Tom Tuch, 16 November 1995.

[135] Interview: Washburn, 1 December 1995; Interview: Tom Tuch, 16 November 1995; NA RG 306 A1 (1061) USIA historical collection misc. files, 1940s–1990s, box 12, Harold C. McClellan, *A Review of the American National Exhibition in Moscow*, December 1959, pp. 28–9; Hixson, *Parting the Curtain*, pp. 171, 185–7, 192–3; *FRUS 1958–1960, Vol. X, Pt. 2*, doc. 16, INR report 8100.3, U.S.–Soviet exhibits a successful exchange, Washington, August 1959, p. 39.

agency, as the USIA knew nothing of the announcement until half an hour before-hand when the news ticker spoke of simultaneous press conferences in Moscow and Washington. Washburn, who was acting director at that time, reached the White House press secretary Jim Hagerty and obtained the story at around 10.15, which meant that the VOA and the other agency news channels were alerted with only "a few seconds to spare."[136] The visit would at least provide an opportunity for the USIA to build on the success of Moscow by negotiating directly for further exchanges.

Back in Moscow, Khrushchev returned twice more to the exhibition, making his final unscheduled visit on the penultimate day of business. On this occasion Khrushchev paid particular attention to the art on show. As his official translator had been lost in the crowd, the USIA's Tom Tuch was called on to translate. To Tuch's horror, the Soviet premiere proclaimed that John Marin's "Sea and Sky" looked "as though a little boy peed on the floor" and then demanded an accurate translation of the remark. He raged on through the gallery, ending outside with a nude sculpture by Lachaise, declaring that "only a homosexual could have done such a statue since he obviously didn't think much of womanhood." Khrushchev's opprobrium was an excellent sign that the U.S. art exhibition had hit the mark.[137]

By the time the American National Exhibition in Moscow closed on 4 September 1959, some 2.7 million Soviet visitors had passed through its gates. No one doubted that it had been a runaway success. The reciprocal Soviet exhibit at New York's Coliseum – with its Sputnik replicas, giant worker sculpture, and laughably dated committee-made fashions – was a very damp squib in comparison. McClellan immediately began to lobby for a follow-up exhibition in 1962, but the United States never again mounted an exhibit on the scale of the American National Exhibition.[138]

Some in the USIA regretted that Russia's enthusiasm had so clearly been for the material benefits rather than the underlying values of the American system, yet this had its value. The USIA soon became aware of Soviet attempts to increase the availability of consumer goods. Just as Sputnik had forced the United States into a space race, so the American Exhibition forced the U.S.S.R. to attempt to deliver the chrome-plated

136 Washburn complained to Under Secretary of State for Political Affairs Robert Murphy, "We felt like orphans on this one . . . the information media must be cut in earlier if they are to do their best work. I do hope nothing remains of the old feeling that because we *are* a propaganda department we are ipso facto somehow less trustworthy to keep a secret until the moment of agreed-upon release." Murphy blamed ironclad instructions from the White House. NA RG 306, ZZ entry 1 (formerly 1006), Director's Chronological files, 1953–64, box 3, reel 33, Washburn to Murphy, 5 August 1959; Washburn to Allen, 6 August 1959.

137 Interview: Tom Tuch, 16 November 1995; Tuch and Schmidt, *Ike and USIA*, p. 38; Hixson, *Parting the Curtain*, pp. 208–9. For Soviet reaction to the art exhibit see Osgood Caruthers, "Russians at U.S. Fair Debate Abstract Art and Right to Like It," *New York Times*, 4 September 1959, p. 3.

138 Osgood Caruthers, "U.S. Fair in Soviet Jammed at Close," *New York Times*, 5 September 1959, p. 3; *FRUS 1958–1960, Vol. X, Pt. 2*, doc. 16, INR report 8100.3, U.S.–Soviet exhibits a successful exchange, Washington, August 1959, pp. 38–9; Hixson, *Parting the Curtain*, p. 210; NA RG 306, ZZ entry 1 (formerly 1006), Director's Chronological files, 1953–64, box 3, microfilm reel 34.

gadgets and gizmos of modern American life. A time bomb of expectation was ticking within the U.S.S.R. As the historian Walter Hixson has noted,

> The images and symbols of American life had made a profound impression. Most Soviets, it seemed, were still willing to be patient and give the socialist system the time it needed to catch up with the West. Thirty years later, their patience would come to an end.[139]

*

In September 1959, Khrushchev visited the United States. He parlayed in Washington, loved San Francisco, hated Hollywood, and was disappointed not to see Disneyland. His party included Yuri Zhukov, the chairman of the Council of Ministers State Committee on Cultural Relations with Foreign Countries, and the round of talks in Washington included discussion of cultural matters. Issues included radio jamming. Khrushchev offered to cease jamming the VOA if the Voice ceased hostile broadcasting. Allen reported to Eisenhower that he had "taken steps to be certain that the general tone of Voice of America broadcasts are not such as to give cause for legitimate objection" but concluded: "We have continued to report the news, factually and in a straightforward manner, as calmly and objectively as possible."[140] Two of the CIA's clandestine stations, Radio Caucasus and Radio Baikal, went off the air in a reciprocal gesture of conciliation. By the end of October, the Soviet Union only jammed VOA programs dealing with the troubled relationship of China and the U.S.S.R. and news of the Sino-Indian border dispute. BBC and Radio Liberation broadcasts remained completely jammed.[141]

In the optimistic postvisit atmosphere, the United States and U.S.S.R. began the exchange of films agreed in 1958. On 10 November 1959, various dignitaries, including Eric Johnston and George V. Allen, attended premieres in two Washington venues of the Soviet wartime drama *The Cranes Are Flying*, one of seven Soviet films received in the United States. That same night Russian audiences viewed the 1955 romantic comedy *Marty*, starring Ernest Borgnine, which was one of ten films sent by the United States. The Soviet films attracted a small flurry of attention before sinking onto the art house circuit, but American films became a real part of Soviet

---

[139] Hixson, *Parting the Curtain*, pp. 210, 213.

[140] *FRUS 1958–1960, Vol. X, Pt. 2*, doc. 18, Memorandum of Conversation, "Exchanges of Information," 15 September 1959, pp. 41–6; DDEL DDE Papers as President, Administrative, box 2 (George V. Allen), Allen to President, "Discussions with Soviets re Jamming and Other Radio Matters," 5 November 1959. An earlier memo by Allen to the President on 5 October 1959 noted that "VOA has been particularly circumspect since full jamming was lifted. Broadcasts to the Soviet Union carry news, editorial roundups, features on various aspects of life in America, and occasional political commentaries which carefully expound the U.S. position on major international affairs. All programs are supervised by senior officers of USIA." VOA broadcasts in Czechoslovakian, Hungarian, Romanian, and Bulgarian, and RFE/RL broadcasts continued to be jammed. Allen to President, 23 September 1959, noted that the BBC remained jammed. For press coverage see UPI, "10-Year Red Jamming of "Voice" Is Halted," *Washington Post*, 16 September 1959, p. A.4.

[141] DDEL DDE Papers as President, Administrative, box 2 (George V. Allen), Allen to President, "Discussions with Soviets re Jamming and Other Radio Matters," 5 November 1959.

popular culture. As Yale Richmond has noted, the Soviet Union attempted to skew the representation of the United States toward the negative through their selection of films, but such movies as *Twelve Angry Men, Some Like It Hot,* and *To Kill a Mockingbird* transcended such intent and spoke exuberantly for the culture that created them.[142]

Negotiations bore further fruit when, on 21 November 1959, Ambassador Thompson signed "an agreement . . . for cooperation in exchanges in the scientific, technical, educational, and cultural fields in 1960 and 1961." The changes in word order in the title from the 1958 agreement reflected Soviet hopes for more science and less culture. On 24 November, accords signed in Washington provided for exchanges in the field of atomic energy.[143]

The year 1960 brought the second wave of U.S. exhibitions in the U.S.S.R., showcasing U.S. technology, beginning with Plastics U.S.A., a 5,000-square foot traveling show about the past, present, and future of this rapidly evolving industry crafted to "increase Russian consumer pressures on the Soviet economy." Plastics U.S.A. reflected lessons learned at the Sokolniki exhibit, which in essence meant excellent guides and plenty of souvenirs. At Plastics U.S.A. the souvenirs were actually produced by the machinery on display. Every visitor received a bag, button, and plastic cup to remind him or her of the experience. The exhibit brought the eye-popping colors of U.S. plastics to a utility-gray country. The agency followed up with a Medicine U.S.A. show.[144]

Suddenly, on 1 May 1960, it all seemed in jeopardy. Soviet missile batteries in the vicinity of Sverdlovsk shot down an American high-altitude reconnaissance plane. The hope of the Cold War thaw plunged to earth with the U-2. When Eisenhower attempted to cover American tracks by speaking of a missing weather plane, Khrushchev produced the aircraft's captured pilot, Gary Powers. He raged against American bad faith and pulled out from the projected Paris peace summit. Eisenhower cancelled his planned trip to Russia. The crisis showed flaws in the policy links between State and the USIA. In an ABC television interview on 15 May, Allen denied that Christian Herter supported continued U-2 flights. The State Department contradicted this and argued that Allen was speaking for himself.[145]

The U-2 crisis reflected poorly on both the United States and the U.S.S.R. USIA polls found that Europeans blamed both the Soviets and the United States. Britain and France now seemed as skeptical of the U.S. capacity for world leadership as they

[142] "Capital Theaters Show Soviet Film," *New York Times*, 11 November 1959, p. 40; Marie McNair, "Soviet Film Makes Double Debut," *Washington Post*, 11 November 1959, p. C.1; Richmond, *U.S.–Soviet Cultural Exchanges, 1958–1986*, pp. 63–5.

[143] Richmond, *U.S.–Soviet Cultural Exchanges, 1958–1986*, p. 2; *FRUS 1958–1960, Vol. X, Pt. 2*, editorial note, p. 51.

[144] *FRUS 1958–1960, Vol. X, Pt. 2*, doc. 25, USIA Exhibit program for 1960–61 for the Soviet Area, 21 March 1960, pp. 55–9.

[145] "U-2 Pilot Is Up held as Obeying Orders," *New York Times*, 16 May 1960, p. 1; "Powers Told to Confess if Caught," *Washington Post*, 16 May 1960, p. A.3; "Ike Halted Spy Flights Two Days before Trip," *New York Times*, 17 May 1960, p. A.4. For policy statement see NA RG 59 State CPF 1960–63, box 1045, 511.00/6–760, CA-10186, Herter to all posts 10 May 1960.

were doubtful of U.S. technological or military superiority. Some in the administration hoped that news of the U-2 overflights might boost the standing of U.S. technology. It did not.[146] The USIA worked to minimize the damage by feeding the world's opinion makers materials including the text of the UN debate on the U-2, in which Ambassador Lodge delivered a stinging attack on the Soviet record of international intrigue. The VOA carried the UN debate live. The flow of USIA information gave added weight to the U.S. case during the trial of Garry Powers.[147]

The U-2 crisis damaged but did not destroy East–West cultural exchange. While the U.S.S.R. resumed jamming of the VOA, Russia's blossoming passion for things American remained. American films could still be seen in over half of Moscow cinemas. Soviet audiences still gave rapturous receptions to stage performances of *My Fair Lady* and recitals by Isaac Stern and their beloved Van Cliburn. Plans remained for the next round of American exhibitions in 1961.[148] Cultural exchanges had become as much a part of the Cold War world as spy trials and defections.

4) ALLEN'S USIA TO JANUARY 1961
THE VOA CHARTER AND THE SPRAGUE COMMITTEE

The cultural work in the Soviet Union was only a small portion of USIA activity in the final years of the Eisenhower administration. The USIA developed new initiatives and fought fresh battles across familiar terrain. Allen's tenure reached its conclusion with two documents. The first – the VOA Charter – was succinct and resonated for decades. The second – the report of the President's Committee of International Information Activities, known as the Sprague Committee – was a weighty document with multiple annexes, which stalled plans to restructure the agency. The Sprague Committee members knew that the reception of their report depended on the result of the 1960 presidential race. Little did they guess that the USIA and its work would be an issue in that election.

High points of the later years of Allen's tenure included the 150th anniversary of the birth of Abraham Lincoln, celebrated in 1959. Lincoln presented a positive channel into the discussion of civil rights, setting a white man and his federal government in the position of honor, which was much more comfortable than straight reporting of the civil rights issue. The USIA created a host of special exhibitions, pamphlets, and lectures and a color documentary film. The VOA mounted a one-hour radio

---

146 JFKL Pierre Salinger papers, box 132, "USIA 1961," ORA WE-64, Post-Summit Trends in British and French Opinion of the U.S. and U.S.S.R., June 1960: The agency's "barometer" of British opinion recorded an unprecedented slip, but even so 38% of the country still held favorable views of the United States. Polled in May 1960, 55% of Britons and 40% of French people asked rated the U.S.S.R. "ahead" of the U.S. "in total military strength." Continued Soviet success in space produced an even more marked perception of Soviet superiority in that sphere. In May 1960, 81% of Britons and 74% of French rated the U.S.S.R. as "ahead in space developments."

147 DDEL OSANA, NSC/Status of Projects, box 9, The USIA, status on June 30, 1960, NSC 6013 (5), pp. 4–5; also *USIA 14th Review of Operations, January 1–June 30, 1960*, pp. 2–4.

148 *FRUS 1958–1960, Vol. X, Pt. 2*, doc. 29, U.S. embassy Moscow, No. 45, 18 July 1960, pp. 67–70.

tribute called *In Search of Lincoln*, which featured contributions from Eisenhower and a line-up of world statesmen including Adenauer, Macmillan, Nehru, Nkrumah, and, rather out of his class, Diem of South Vietnam.[149]

Successes for the International Press Service included a lively line in newspaper strip cartoons. In April 1958, the IPS launched "Visit to America," a strip detailing the experiences of a South Asian student in the U.S. By 1959, this strip appeared in 3,000 newspapers across forty-eight countries, making it the world's most widely circulated cartoon strip.[150]

Allen's tenure at the USIA saw the evolution of television. In 1958, he established a separate television service, and in 1960, he opened a studio equipped with the latest videotape equipment. Successful programs included a series of fifteen-minute documentaries called *The American Scene*, episodes of which included "Cowboy Legend" on the realities of ranch life and treatments of the Supreme Court and the presidential electoral system. Other major projects included a weekly news series called *Panorama Panamericano*, exported to twenty-four cities in fifteen countries across Latin America. Only Cuba, the Dominican Republic, and Haiti declined to screen the program.[151]

The People-to-People program continued to flourish. By 1959, Allen noted that the phrase "People-to-People" had taken off in popular usage in the United States and in Britain too; he also reported that a number of communities overseas had formed counterpart committees. Although some U.S. committees had fallen away by 1958, Allen's annual report for that year listed thirty-six.[152]

By January 1959, the book committee had shipped 100,000 volumes, and seventy U.S. cities had affiliated with sister cities in nineteen countries, with a further seventy-three affiliations pending. Forty-three U.S. universities had launched international twinning schemes. The more innovative elements included the Armed Services

---

[149] *USIA 12th Review of Operations, January 1–June 30, 1959*, pp. 15–18; *USIA 13th Review of Operations, July 1–December 31, 1959*, p. 19.

[150] *USIA 10th Review of Operations, January 1–June 30, 1958*, p. 7; *USIA 13th Review of Operations, July 1–December 31, 1959*, p. 6.

[151] *Presenting America Abroad through Television*, Washington, DC: USIA, 1960, copy in UoC Chicago, Benton papers, 386/11; *USIA 14th Review of Operations, January 1–June 30, 1960*; *USIA 15th Review of Operations, July 1–December 30, 1960*: for plans see NA RG 306, ZZ entry 1 (formerly 1006), Director's Chronological files, 1953–64, box 3, microfilm reel 36, Corrigan to Washburn, 22 March 1960.

[152] The committees were Advertising Organizations, Armed Services, Banking, Books, Business Activities, Cartoonists, Civic, Education, Farms, Fine Arts, Foreign Affairs Societies, 4-H clubs, Fraternal Organizations, Handicapped (to pool information on rehabilitation techniques), Hobbies, Hotel Industry, Insurance, Labor, Legal Societies, Letter-Writing, Magazines, Motion Pictures, Medicine and Health, Music, Nationalities (to work with first generation Americans), Public Relations, Religion, Scientists and Engineers, Service Organizations, Speakers, Sports, Transportation Industries, Travelers, Veterans, Women's Organizations, and Youth. DDEL DDE Papers as President, Administrative, box 2, George V. Allen, Allen to President, 25 February 1959, Annual Survey of People-to-People Activities, January 1959; also Allen to President, 15 October 1959, noting use of term "People to People" by British Prime Minister Harold Macmillan and Leader of the Opposition Hugh Gaitskell. On the redesign of the less successful committees see NA RG 306, ZZ entry 1 (formerly 1006), Director's Chronological Files, 1953–64, box 2, microfilm reel 32, Allen to Reynolds, 23 April 1959.

Committee, which encouraged enlisted men serving overseas to see themselves as ambassadors and enroll in volunteer work. The Hobbies Committee covered 110 distinct leisure activities, but stamp collecting loomed especially large. The committee distributed 30,000 first day covers of the USIA-inspired stamps honoring international champions of liberty. Other People-to-People projects included material targeted at pet owners and hikers and a scheme from the magic subcommittee to work with European magicians to use sleight of hand as a form of therapy for the disabled. The cartoonists' committee, co-chaired by Al Capp, produced 40,000 copies of a 100-page booklet called *You Don't See These Sites on the Regular Tours*, showing through cartoons how American tourists ought not to behave overseas. The Travelers Committee continued to guide Americans leaving the country. The Motion Picture committee built links with film industries around the world and sent out producers as guest speakers. The actor Yul Brynner provided an exhibit of his work as an amateur photographer for USIS Vienna. The Nationalities Committee held a gala dinner to honor foreign-born scientists Wernher von Braun and Edward Teller.[153]

The most successful People-to-People initiative of the era came from the medical committee. Following Eisenhower's heart attack in 1955, he met an energetic young cardiologist named William B. Walsh. The President persuaded Walsh to participate in People-to-People and Walsh became co-chair of the medical committee. In 1958, Walsh proposed Project HOPE (the acronym stood for Health Opportunities for People Everywhere), by which he would take over a mothballed naval hospital ship, staff it with one hundred volunteer doctors, and sail wherever it was invited. The USIA supported the scheme, but the navy dragged its feet. Six months after Walsh and Washburn first put the idea to Eisenhower, it still remained just an idea. Years later Washburn vividly recalled Eisenhower's anger at learning of the bureaucratic delays. Fixing the responsible parties with his piercing blue eyes, he snapped, "I want this done." So it was. The navy gave Walsh an old hospital ship named the U.S.S. *Constellation*, which he refitted and renamed the S.S. *Hope*. Hundreds of doctors and nurses volunteered for the project and the pharmaceutical industry donated medicines. The USIA and its allies were never far in the background. C. D. Jackson sat on the board of governors, and where charity fell short, the USIA picked up the bill. On 22 September 1960, the *Hope* set sail on its maiden voyage to Indonesia and South Vietnam. The USIA provided the necessary cultural orientation for the crew.[154] There was no doubt that People-to-People had taken off.

[153] DDEL DDE Papers as President, Administrative, box 2, George V. Allen, Allen to President, 25 February 1959, Annual Survey of People-to-People Activities, January 1959.

[154] Interview: Washburn, 1 December 1995; NA RG 306 64-A-0536, Director's Office Subject files, 1957–8, box 5, file: People to People Committee, Reynolds to Allen, "Project of Dr. William B. Walsh . . . ," 28 November 1958; NA RG 306, ZZ entry 1 (formerly 1006), Director's Chronological files, 1953–64, box 3 microfilm reel 34, Allen to C.D. Jackson, 13 October 1959; reel 35, Allen to Reinhardt (State), 15 January 1960, and reel 36, Goodfriend (Special Asst. to Dep. Dir.) to C. D. Jackson, 4 October 1960. For further background on Project HOPE see http://www.projecthope.org/ and http://americanhistory.si.edu/hope/.

*

In early 1959, the agency launched "Books from America." This scheme involved an appeal in U.S. newspapers for citizens to donate unwanted American histories, biographies, or textbooks to the USIA, which undertook to ship them overseas, labeled as "a gift from an American." It proved an innovative way to cope with the constraints on the budget.[155] The USIA continued its program of book translation. Favorites included Senator John F. Kennedy's Pulitzer Prize-winning study *Profiles in Courage*, first published in 1956. By 1960, the USIA had arranged publication in Vietnamese, Spanish, four Indian languages (Gujarati, Hindi, Marathi, and Telugu), Indonesian, Japanese, Arabic, and German. The list was a geography lesson in the agency's priorities. "Your book," Allen wrote to Kennedy in August 1960, "has proved to be one of the best vehicles we have found in our efforts to bring basic concepts of American history to foreign peoples." Kennedy, by this time the Democrat Party's nominee for President, had already begun to show his value to the U.S. image.[156]

USIA literary propaganda gambits included efforts to publicize the censorship decisions of others. The agency made particular use of the publication in the West of Boris Pasternak's novel *Doctor Zhivago*.[157] Conversely, the USIA had literary problems of its own. In the autumn of 1958, Deputy Director Washburn questioned the use of Jack Kerouac's *On the Road* in a VOA feature introducing the Beat Generation. Washburn doubted the artistic value of the Beats. "The middle-aged delinquents of the 'beat' cult have no message," he wrote to Zorthian, "no solid emotion; they are protoplasm; they are there, lying limp and soggy in the bottom of the dish." Moreover, the USIA had placed *On the Road* on its "conditional list," meaning that it could only be supplied to U.S. libraries overseas if the post could make a request based on a compelling policy reason. It was possible that the broadcast might encourage a demand that USIS libraries could not meet. Washburn suggested that in the future the VOA check the "library approved" list before producing a feature on a book.[158]

A further literary problem arose from the phenomenal success of the novel *The Ugly American* by William J. Lederer and Eugene Burdick. The book criticized the cultural ignorance of the U.S. Foreign Service. Opinion within the USIA was divided as to the novel's suitability for inclusion on the Informational Media Guarantee program, whereby the U.S. government underwrote the convertibility of foreign funds

155   Editorial, "Any Old Books?" *New York Times*, 12 March 1959, p. 30; Letter by Curtis G. Benjamin, "To Send Books Abroad," *New York Times*, 3 April 1959, p. E.8.
156   NA RG 306, ZZ entry 1 (formerly 1006), Director's Chronological Files, 1953–64, box 3, microfilm reel 37, Allen to Kennedy, 18 August 1960.
157   NA RG 306 64-A-0536, Director's Office Subject Files, 1957–8, box 4, file: Information Centers Service – Books, Reed to Stephens, "Current USIA action on ideas for promoting *Doctor Zhivago*," 24 November 1958; Evidence of CIA/USIA liaison can be found in NA RG 306, ZZ entry 1 (formerly 1006), Director's Chronological Files, 1953–1964, box 2, microfilm reel 28, Washburn to Allen Dulles, Secret, 12 November 1958. See also Pirsein, *The Voice of America*, p. 399.
158   NA RG 306 64-A-0536, Director's Office Subject files, 1957–8, box 3, file: Broadcasting – programs, Washburn to Zorthian, "VOA feature on the Beat Generation," 14 October 1958.

used to purchase the book. Mindful of the budget, Allen ruled that the USIA should focus its resources on the publications that were "most useful in building international understanding" and kept the novel off that autumn's list of approved books. On 29 November, a Manila paper claimed that the book had been "banned in the Philippines" and other IMG countries. To avoid public accusations of censorship, Allen swiftly reversed course and approved the sale of the book under the IMG. The announcement came just in time to head off an NBC interview with the authors. The authors were dismayed that their novel had caught the imagination of the American right as a critique of the U.S. Foreign Service. Burdick, a liberally minded professor from California, wrote to the USIA and requested guidance on how respond constructively to the press requests for criticisms.[159]

Although book problems largely escaped the notice of critics on Capitol Hill, the USIA was not so lucky in the matter of film. During the appropriations hearings for 1959, Representative John Rooney forced the publication of the list of motion pictures barred from export under the IMG program. The titles included such classics as *All Quiet on the Western Front* (1930) and *All the King's Men* (1949) and more recent hits such as *The Sweet Smell of Success* (1957) and *Somebody Up There Likes Me* (1956). Others in the House railed against the export of films that showed problems in the United States, such as the exposé of conditions in inner city schools, *Blackboard Jungle* (1955), or the controversial account of capitalist oppression and worker resistance amongst Mexican-American miners and their families, *Salt of the Earth* (1954), created by a team of radical filmmakers who had been blacklisted in Hollywood. Although little seen at home, this film had won the 1955 International Grand Prize from the Académie du Cinéma de Paris. Testifying in defense of the agency, the head of the Motion Picture Service, Turner Shelton, stated the limits of the IMG program and disclaimed responsibility for commercial releases elsewhere. As so often, the agency found itself in a no-win situation. The USIA placed *Salt of the Earth* on its blacklist.[160]

*

Allen's tenure at the USIA saw the final phase in a decade-long transformation of the VOA. The Voice now estimated its audience at fifty million people a day, of

---

[159] NA RG 306, ZZ entry 1 (formerly 1006), Director's Chronological Files, 1953–64, box 2, microfilm reel 28, GVA minute to Hawley, 19 November 1958; NA RG 306 64-A-0536, Director's Office Subject files, 1957–8, box 4, file: Information Centers Service – Books, esp. Storer Lundt (chairman, WW Norton & Co.) to Allen, 5 December 1958; Allen to Lunt, 8 December 1958; Esterline to Hoofnagle, (IOA) 15 December 1958. The IMG program at this time covered Poland, Yugoslavia, Spain, Israel, Turkey, Pakistan, Burma, Indonesia, Taiwan, Philippines, Vietnam, and Chile. In August 1958 Congress cut the agency's budget for this work from $7 million to just $2.5 million. For press comment see "USIA in Reversal on 'Ugly American,'" *New York Times*, 6 December 1958, p. 10.

[160] UPI, "U.S. Lists Movies It Limits Abroad," *New York Times*, 24 March 1959, p. 46. For previous discussion of the issue see AP, "Censoring Conceded: USIA Rejects Some Movies and Books for Program," *New York Times*, 26 April 1958, p. 23. On the case of *Salt of the Earth* see James J. Lorrence, *The Suppression of* Salt of the Earth: *How Hollywood, Big Labor and Politicians Blacklisted a Movie in Cold War America*, Alberquerque, NM: University of New Mexico Press, 1999, esp. p. 153.

whom – if the CIA's interviews with refugees were to be believed – ten million lived in the Eastern bloc. Jamming remained only partial and continued to lend the VOA the air of forbidden fruit.[161] VOA director Henry Loomis and Program Manager Barry Zorthian shared a determination to build the Voice into a major international news provider to match the BBC's international broadcasting. Further support for this came from the new chief of the VOA newsroom, Robert B. Goldmann. Goldmann visited the BBC early in 1958 and was simply astonished by the absence of policy pressure from the British Foreign Office. They knew that George V. Allen shared their admiration for the BBC. As Goldmann recalled, Allen never made an appointment for 9 a.m., a time that he reserved for listening to the news from London. Allen was sympathetic to reform.[162]

There was a final force pushing for continued change at the VOA, and a force not typically acknowledged within the VOA in the creation of its charter: President Eisenhower himself. On 3 June 1958, Eisenhower made his views on the VOA clear to Allen, who passed them on to Loomis that same day in a secret memorandum:

> At a meeting at the White House this morning, the president expressed himself once more, very forcefully, on the subject of the Voice of America. He said he had been trying for twelve years to urge that the Voice consist of straight factual reporting without any propaganda. During the last war everyone listened to the BBC because they thought it reported straight news. He could not understand why the Voice could not build up a similar reputation.

Eisenhower was not turning his back on psychological warfare. He understood the value of a firewall between the covert and overt elements in America's information apparatus. Allen reported, "The president recognized that propaganda type of broadcasting might sometimes be needed but he thought we should supply information and facilities to local broadcasters in countries like Libya and Ethiopia and allow them to 'do the talking.'" Eisenhower was heartened to be told that the USIA had loaned $35,000 worth of television equipment to help India begin a television service. In response to the President's exposition, Allen explained his intent to link a push for credibility with a new emphasis on English as the flagship language of the VOA. Allen Dulles endorsed the approach and told the President that although "he was trying to make Radio Free Europe and Radio Liberation do as little of the emotional type of broadcasting as possible," he agreed with Allen's view "that any broadcasting of this nature that might be needed should be left to RFE and RL." Eisenhower ended the meeting commenting that "he hoped now, for the first time in twelve years, that something might be done about his views concerning VOA."[163]

[161] Pirsein, *The Voice of America*, p. 398.
[162] Interview: Goldmann, 26 December 1996.
[163] NA RG 306 64-A-0536, Director's Office Subject files, 1957–8, box 3, file: Broadcasting Service – General, 1958. Allen to Loomis, Secret, 3 June 1958. The meeting lasted 20 minutes.

Something was done. Allen moved the newsroom out of the USIA headquarters at 1776 Pennsylvania Avenue and relocated it with the rest of the VOA in the Health, Education, and Welfare building on the south side of the Mall. The source of VOA news now sat close to its end users, the broadcasters, and further from the source of policy pressures. With Allen's blessing, the power of the newsroom grew relative to that of the language services. Credibility remained the Holy Grail. Goldmann usually demanded two sources before the VOA would broadcast a story, although seeking to compete with the BBC's speed, he would on occasion commit to a story from a single report, knowing that the wires sometimes did the same.[164]

Allen presided over the redesign of the Munich Radio Center, which had created much of the VOA's most politically aggressive material. In the course of 1958, the center stopped originating news and commentaries and became a "special events servicing unit." This required the dismissal of all non-American staff. Allen contacted the CIA to suggest a recruiting opportunity for RFE and RL.[165]

Such could only be the beginning. VOA director Henry Loomis knew that, despite Larson's directive of 1957, the VOA lacked a succinct foundational document equivalent to the USIA's general mission statement of 1953.[166] Loomis felt there was a need for a final statement of whether the VOA was a tactical instrument of U.S. propaganda or strategic. "If strategic," he argued, "it must build respect for its credibility and therefore report items temporarily troublesome for our side – Little Rock, riots against the Shah in Iran, etc." The worst situation was "oscillation from one concept to another and back again."[167]

Barry Zorthian agreed. The experience of being assistant program manager for policy during and after the Hungarian rising had convinced him of the need for a foundational document. Loomis, with Allen's support, summoned Zorthian and all his heads of division to a "pajama party" at his house in Middleburg, Virginia. Talking deep into the night, he outlined the VOA's need for a charter and invited his senior staff to design a document that both fitted their identity as a government agency and allowed them to operate in the manner they believed to be right. As a result of this and subsequent meetings, numerous senior VOA staff created drafts. Their initial effort – dated 2 March 1959 – ran for eight pages. Zorthian recalled penning a version that ran over five pages. All bogged down in Cold War detail.[168]

---

[164] Goldmann once personally typed coverage of a De Gaulle press conference while the conference was still in progress and rushed into the studio to hand over the copy during the broadcast. He established the model of what a VOA news chief should be. Interview: Goldmann, 26 December 1996; Kamenske to author, 6 October 1997; see also Pirsein, *The Voice of America*, p. 397.

[165] NA RG 306, ZZ entry 1 (formerly 1006), Director's Chronological Files, 1953–64, box 3, microfilm reel 26, Allen to Allen Dulles, secret, 16 July 1958.

[166] This case is argued in DDEL U.S.PCIAA (Sprague), box 1, Radio and Television (11), Len Reed and Barry Zorthian, "VOA directive," 22 April 1960, attached to Gullion to Hare et al., 3 May 1960.

[167] DDEL U.S.PCIAA, box 12, Chron file – official (1), 23 February 1960, Waldemar Nielsen, Memorandum of Conversation [with Loomis], 23 February 1960.

[168] ADST Oral History: Klieforth, Zorthian; Pirsein, *The Voice of America*, p. 406.

In 1959, Loomis assigned his new deputy, a Foreign Service Officer named Jack O'Brien, to sift through the ten-inch stack of drafts and produce a synthesis that would please both the VOA and Capitol Hill. O'Brien took a day away from the office to read the various drafts. He found that the desire to emulate the BBC dominated. In producing his own condensed version, he stood back from the Cold War context and pictured the VOA's work in its essence. Both Loomis and Allen were delighted with the result, though Allen suggested that for the time being it should not be called a charter for fear of alarming Capitol Hill. The document became known for the time being as the VOA "directive."[169] By January 1960, the draft document was ready for consideration by the agency as a whole.[170] On 1 November 1960, Allen issued the VOA charter as a formal statement of mission. It ran as follows:

> The long-range interests of the United States are served by communication directly with the peoples of the world by an official radio, the Voice of America. To be effective the Voice of America must win the attention and respect of listeners. These principles will govern VOA broadcasts:
>
> 1. VOA will establish itself as a consistently reliable and authoritative source of news. VOA news will be accurate, objective, and comprehensive.
> 2. VOA will represent America, not any single segment of American society. It will therefore present a balanced and comprehensive projection of American thought and institutions.
> 3. As an official radio, VOA will present the policies of the United States government clearly and persuasively. VOA will also present responsible discussion and opinion of these policies.

Allen and Loomis lost no time in applying it to the management of the Voice.[171]

It is difficult to overestimate the role of the charter in the history of the Voice of America. The charter gave a shape and substance to a news culture that had gained momentum throughout the 1950s. Its birth was facilitated by a coincidence of views. It certainly helped that the President and the USIA director saw eye to eye with the lowliest newsroom minion on this issue at least. Those in the language services who preferred an activist line were caught in a pincer movement. It is also plain that the VOA's news culture was only possible because of the parallel existence of RFE

---

169   ADST Oral History: O'Brien.
170   DDEL U.S.PCIAA (Sprague), box 1, Radio and Television (3), Loomis to Allen et al., "Director to VOA," 21 January 1960. This draft differed from the eventual charter in two minor regards. Here the "official radio" line is point 1 whereas the VOA's sense of its priority meant that news became point 1 on the eventual charter, and "American thought and institutions" in the final document was originally rendered as "American political, economic, cultural, social and scientific thought and institutions." This version was submitted to the Sprague Committee on 9 May 1960; see box 20, PCIAA-5.
171   ADST Oral History: O'Brien; Heil, *Voice of America*, p. 65. For recirculation of the VOA charter see NA RG 306, 89.0180, director's chronological file, 1969–70, box 17, reel 34, Murrow, "Voice of America Policy," 4 December 1962 attached to Shakespeare, "Instructions to the Voice of America...," 9 June 1970. The date for the issue of the charter is noted in *USIA World*, vol. 12, no.4, p. 12.

and RL with their distinct mission. Given the bitter rivalry between the VOA and
RFE/RL in the 1980s and 90s this interdependence is somewhat ironic. But the VOA
had reached a defining moment. Henceforth, the charter strengthened the VOA's hand
against policy interference from the State Department, Congress, an unsympathetic
future director of the USIA, or a President who did not see the need to separate news
from psychological warfare.

*

Allen's years as the USIA director saw a reemergence of questions over the
best location for the agency and its work within the foreign policy bureaucracy. During
the budget debate of 1957, Lyndon Johnson had proposed that the USIA be returned
to the jurisdiction of the State Department. Senator Mike Mansfield of Montana maintained pressure for this idea and it resurfaced in the deliberations of the President's
Advisory Committee on Government Organization, now chaired by Arthur S. Flemming. Under Secretary of State Christian Herter, suspecting that the proposal might
attract widespread support, approached George V. Allen to establish a working group
to establish the position of State and the USIA on such a proposal and consider how
it might work. Herter suggested that should the USIA rejoin State, the entire cultural
apparatus would come under one roof. Even Dulles, in his last month as Secretary of
State, seemed amenable. Washburn was appalled and rallied the Advisory Group to
defend the USIA, but Allen agreed to participate in the working groups. He saw the
debate as an opportunity to place his vision "that Voice of America be established as
a separate entity" on the agenda of a meeting between Flemming's committee, the
USIA, State, and the Bureau of the Budget on 9 April 1959.[172]

On 8 June 1959, Flemming presented his proposals for the "Reorganization of
the Department of State" to enable "a meaningful integration of the psychological
and information aspects of foreign policy with the Department's politico-economic-
diplomatic activities." This required an enhanced role for both the Secretary of State
and his ambassadors and the integration of the USIA back into the State Department
structure as the U.S. Cultural and Information Administration, arranged in parallel
with the apparatus of U.S. aid overseas, the International Cooperation Administration. The ICA and the USCIA would be run by two administrators, each paid at the
level of an under secretary of state.[173] But Eisenhower was swayed by the unanimous
support of the Advisory Commission on Information for continued independence

172 For Mansfield on USIA's return to State see Warren Unna, "Appeal Made by Ike for USIA Support," 17 April 1957, *Washington Post*, p. A.13; DDEL President's Advisory Committee on Government Organization (PACGO) box 17 [#124 (2)], Memo for the record "Foreign Affairs Organ-
isation," Kimball, 20 March 1959; Herter to Allen, 18 March 1959; DDEL WHCF OF 247, box
911, Washburn to Persons (White House), 17 March 1959, and minute by Ferne (White House),
18 March 1959. The period is summarized in the Stanton Panel report of 1975; see GRFL WHCF
OA 2272.
173 DDEL PACGO box 17 [#124 (2)], Memorandum for the President, Reorganization of the Department of State, 8 June 1959.

for the USIA. He asked Flemming to consider reorganizing State without moving the USIA.[174]

By the summer of 1959, a draft bill to return the USIA to the State Department existed, but the White House delayed submitting it to Capitol Hill. In October the Advisory Commission set out their case for opposing the move. In a letter to the Secretary of State, Chairman Mark May defended the agency's achievement and emphasized Allen's role as "international public opinion counselor to the president, the National Security Council, and the Operations Coordinating Board." He also noted that "the Agency has performed better outside the State Department than it did within it." Replying, Christian Herter, now Secretary of State, accepted May's points but remained committed to the reorganization. He assured May that "we have taken every appropriate measure that has been suggested to ensure for the information program retention of the values of autonomy and independence."[175]

Rather than fold the USIA into State, Eisenhower conceded the need to update the U.S. approach to propaganda and resolved to create a committee to "review the findings and recommendations" of the Jackson Committee of 1953 in the light of "changes in the international situation." Mansfield D. Sprague, former Assistant Secretary of Defense for International Affairs and president of the American Machine and Foundry Company, agreed to chair. Other members included Allen Dulles from the CIA and C. D. Jackson, who had been pressing for exactly such a review for some months. George V. Allen represented the USIA, with Philip Reed on hand from the Advisory Commission on Information. The Sprague Committee had its own staff, led by executive director Waldemar A. Nielsen, on loan from the Ford Foundation. The staff included two USIA officers and one member of staff each from the CIA, State, and the White House. The State staffer was a FSO named Edmund A. Gullion, who would eventually coin the phrase "Public Diplomacy" to describe the USIA's activity.[176]

The Sprague committee held its first meeting on 1 March 1960.[177] It consulted policy makers, officials, and external experts and commissioned studies on subjects such as "Agricultural Technical Assistance and the American Image."[178] Evidence

---

[174]   DDEL PACGO box 17, [#124 (2)], Meeting...with the President to discuss the reorganization of the Department of State, 12 June 1959.

[175]   DDEL PACGO box 17 [#124 (1)], May to Dillon & Herter, 19 October 1959; Herter to May, 27 October 1959.

[176]   DDEL WHCF OF 133-M-1, box 673, Eisenhower to Sprague, 2 December 1959. The details of the committee are from DDEL DDE Papers as President (Ann Whitman file), Administrative Series, box 37, Sprague Committee file 2. The CIA, State, the Pentagon, and the USIA also all provided alternates for occasions when their representatives were indisposed. Abbott Washburn deputized for Allen. Other members were Gordon Gray, the special assistant to the President for national security affairs; Karl G. Harr Jr., the special assistant to the President for security operations coordination; John N. Irwin II, Assistant Secretary of Defense for International Security Affairs; and Livingston T. Merchant, the Under Secretary of State for Political Affairs.

[177]   DDEL U.S.PCIIA (Sprague Committee), box 12, Committee Meeting 1 (3), minutes 1 March 1960.

[178]   DDEL NSC staff/registry, box 14, "PCIAA study #39, Agricultural technical assistance and the American Image" prepared by the University of Michigan, 8 August 1960.

included testimony from Washburn outlining problems for the future of the U.S. image including the impatience of the developing world for change, the identification of the U.S. with dictatorships and the status quo, and "the negative image of the U.S. as projected by many U.S. films, TV programs, comic books, and rock-and-roll music." Against this, Washburn stressed the freedom, creativity, and openness of American society and obvious contradictions within communism.[179] Other moot subjects included the proposed VOA charter.[180]

The committee did not include the question of the USIA returning to the State Department within its brief, but even as it prepared to convene the debate raged on. Secretary of State Herter endeavored to keep his plan to recapture the USIA alive.[181] His case was weakened by reports from the Brookings Institution and the Advisory Commission recommending not only the continued independence of the USIA but also its elevation to cabinet level with total responsibility for the cultural functions still held by the State Department.[182] Herter was able to accomplish one reform at least. In 1959 he removed cultural work from the jurisdiction of the Bureau of Public Affairs and established a new Bureau of International Cultural Relations, designated by the letters CU, as a home for the department's cultural, exchange, and exhibitions work. In 1960 CU was reorganized again and became the Bureau of Educational and Cultural Affairs. CU's early projects included support for a new East–West Center, established by Congress in Hawaii, to promote Transpacific understanding and exchange. Congress also passed a Special Currency Program that provided a special fund of $40 million to promote American Studies around the world. These reforms laid the foundation for cultural work overseas in the decade ahead.[183]

*

During the summer of 1960, the question of U.S. information and prestige in the world became a surprise issue in the presidential race between Vice President Richard Nixon and the energetic Democrat challenger John F. Kennedy. Neither was a stranger to the U.S. information program overseas. Kennedy's standard campaign speech hammered away at four key points: "America cannot stand still;

179 DDEL U.S.PCIIA (Sprague Committee), box 27, Minutes (13), Memo for the record re USIA presentation by Abbott Washburn, 14 March 1960.
180 C. D. Jackson noted "an almost neurotic search on the part of VOA for purity" and suggested that an ideal directive for VOA would require the station to "establish and maintain credibility" but also allow "leeway for dirty tricks" but "not get caught telling lies." In the end – mercifully for the future of the VOA – the committee declined to offer amendments to the proposed document; see DDEL U.S.PCIAA (Sprague), box 1, Radio and Television (7), Committee discussion on a directive for the Voice of America, 10 May 1960.
181 DDEL PACGO box 17, file #124 (1), Herter to President, 5 February 1960.
182 DDEL PACGO box 13, file #92, International Affairs, "United States Foreign Policy: The Formulation and Administration of United States Foreign Policy," Study prepared at the request of the committee on Foreign Relations United States Senate by the Brookings Institution, no. 9, 13 January 1960, and Lewis Gulick (AP), "Agency on Information at Cabinet Level Urged," *Washington Post*, 4 April 1960; "Information Post in Cabinet Urged," *New York Times*, 4 April 1960.
183 UoA CU 1–13, Departmental Circular No. 355, 26 April 1960. The special funding could be carried over from one year to another and the funds were not exhausted until 1966.

her prestige fails in the world; this is a time of burdens and sacrifice; we must move."[184] The decline in U.S. prestige became an equivalent of the so-called "missile gap" used by the Democratic Party to berate the Eisenhower administration. But this was no imagining. The Kennedy team had seen a number of classified USIA reports. An internal campaign briefing document cited studies called "U.S. or U.S.S.R., which is the wave of the future?" "Image of America," and "U.S. prestige" and pointed out that "these are all known to Nixon and Lodge, of course, who nevertheless insist, their better knowledge to the contrary, that U.S. prestige was never higher."[185]

In his second televised debate with Nixon, on 7 October, Kennedy confronted the Vice President with the evidence of America's perceived decline. Nixon rebutted by rebuking Kennedy for "running America down and giving us an inferiority complex." Unfortunately for Nixon, the *New York Times* obtained copies of the USIA polls and ran their findings in a front-page story on 25 October, vindicating Kennedy. On 27 October the White House attempted to combat the leak by pushing Allen to state that "the prestige and position of the United States in the world is unmatched by any other nation." Allen refused on the grounds that this would "inject the agency into politics." The issue did not go away. On 2 November, the *New York Times* published an alarming USIA survey of "Free World Views of the U.S.–U.S.S.R. Power Balance" from August 1960. The "international prestige issue" duly became another element in Kennedy's wafer-thin victory on 8 November. Kennedy, like Eisenhower, came into office with a commitment to address the international image of the United States.[186]

Presidential elections had long been a boon to the USIA, and the nail-biting climax to the election of 1960 proved a particular gift. The agency had whetted global appetites through its worldwide distribution of the Kennedy–Nixon debates. Now the USIA provided a wealth of support for election night coverage around the world. Events at USIS posts drew excited responses. In Dacca, Pakistan the entire editorial staff of one paper decamped to the USIS office and worked from there as the results came in; USIS Rio allowed a local station to anchor its broadcast directly from the post and use the ambassador as a commentator. One Southeast Asian post reputedly displayed the results on a giant scoreboard to a wildly cheering crowd gathered in the street outside the office. But the waves of ecstasy were

---

[184]   Theodore H. White, *The Making of the President, 1960*, London: Jonathan Cape, 1961, p. 256.

[185]   JFLK, JFK prepresidential papers, 1960 campaign files, position and briefing paper: briefing book, box 993A, file: "Decline of U.S. Prestige," memo, Elizabeth Farmer to Mike Feldman, 4 October 1960. The memo also cites alarming opinion polls from "the UK, our chief ally."

[186]   DDEL DDE Papers as President (Ann Whitman file), Administrative Series, box 37, USIA file 1, memo for the record, Wilton B. Persons (White House), 19 January 1961; "Partial Text of Information Agency's Report of Aug. 29 on U.S. Prestige," *New York Times*, 2 November 1960, including polls in which majorities of British, Arab, Brazilian, Italian, French, and Turkish citizens endorsed the U.S.S.R. when asked, "If the U.S. and U.S.S.R. settle down to competition without war for the next twenty to twenty-five years, which of the two do you think will end up as the stronger?" Also White, *The Making of the President, 1960*, p. 304; Mark Haefele, "John F. Kennedy, USIA and World Opinion," *Diplomatic History*, 25, 1 (Winter 2001), 69.

not necessarily for the fresh-faced Kennedy and the spectacle of democracy. Industrious bookies were found moving amongst the crowd taking bets on the next number to appear.[187]

*

On 23 December, Sprague submitted his report to Eisenhower. The report noted increasing effectiveness of U.S. information over the previous decade and the success of the OCB as a tool of management. It also noted the limited resources that the United States committed to international information. The grand total for all information work across all agencies for fiscal year 1960 reached $300 million out of a total national security budget of $50 billion (or 0.6 percent). The committee stressed the continued challenge of communism and effectiveness of Communist propaganda. This challenge required the continued improvement of U.S. information. This was not just a job for the USIA. The report stressed the need for American diplomats, soldiers, economists, and scientists to be trained in international communication. It spoke of the need for their efforts to be coordinated in what it termed "total diplomacy" to defeat communism.[188]

The Sprague report was a wake-up call to the new demands of conducting foreign policy in the age of public opinion and mass communication.[189] The report urged major expansion of USIA work in Latin America, where information activity had lagged behind U.S. economic policy, and most critically in Africa, where "the pace of political developments has outstripped our informational preparations." Other regions – even Western Europe, where the bulk of recent budget cuts had fallen – also needed a bigger information effort. The only potential slack identified in the information and exchange budget lay in the educational exchanges with Western Europe, where private schemes stood ready to fill any gaps.[190]

---

[187] NA RG 306, ZZ entry 1 (formerly 1006), Director's Chronological files, 1953–64, box 3, microfilm reel 38, Washburn to all principal USIS posts, "Kennedy–Nixon TV discussions," 9 September 1960; Washburn to C. D. Jackson, 26 September 1960, thanks Jackson for a quantity of booklets on the election created by *Time–Life* and donated to the agency. *USIA 15⁻ Review of Operations, July 1– December 30, 1960*, pp. 10–11.

[188] DDEL DDE Papers as President (Ann Whitman file), Administrative Series, box 33, Sprague Committee file 1, Conclusions and Recommendations of the President's Committee on Information Activities Abroad, December 1960, Section II.2, II.16–18; DDEL C D Jackson papers, box 104, Sprague Committee, file 1, Sprague to Eisenhower, 23 December 1960 as released to press, 12 January 1961.

[189] DDEL C D Jackson papers, box 104, Sprague Committee, file 1, Extracts from the Conclusions and Recommendations of the President's Committee on Information Activities Abroad, as released to press, 12 January 1961, p. 2. Also p. 13: "In both the new countries and the older ones going through the crisis of modernization, formal and traditional diplomacy of the predominantly government-to-government type often plays a limited role. This means that our diplomacy increasingly must understand public opinion in all countries, open and closed, old and new, and must give greater emphasis to this factor in the handling of conferences and negotiations, in the selection and training of members of the foreign services, and in our treatment of foreign visitors."

[190] DDEL C D Jackson papers, box 104, Sprague Committee, file 1, Extracts from the Conclusions and Recommendations of the President's Committee on Information Activities Abroad, as released to press, 12 January 1961, pp. 3–4.

The committee placed particular emphasis on the growing importance of "Educational, Cultural and Exchange" activities. It called for massive expansion, especially in Africa and the Soviet bloc, and a nationwide system of organized hospitality for foreign visitors. It noted the "vast and spontaneous demand for learning English" and emphasized the need to further encourage the international role of the English language. Methods suggested included diplomatic pressure to see English accepted as an official second language in certain countries, promoting the teaching of English, and greater cooperation with the British Council and other bodies promoting English around the world.[191]

The Sprague Committee confronted what it called "The problem of countering the fact of our present inferiority in the field of exploring space" and the need to "counter the Soviet propaganda effort to translate this specific inferiority into an image of general scientific and educational inferiority."[192] The committee took a broad approach considering the full range of U.S. science and technology and asked "whether the pattern of government support for basic research should be directly influenced by psychological considerations?" While accepting that breakthroughs were unpredictable, the committee recommended that the President stress the psychological dimension to those who controlled the purse strings in scientific research. The committee also stressed the need to "dramatize" U.S. achievements in science and for competent information experts and enhanced international exhibits.[193] A committee study pondered the scientific breakthroughs most likely to restore the international image of the United States. This study doubted that the manned space mission planned for 1961 – Project Mercury – would accomplish the task, but had high hopes for a manned mission to the moon or Mars.[194]

The Sprague Committee noted the contribution of commercial channels to the U.S. information effort. Hollywood films now commanded a weekly overseas audience of 150,000,000. Although noting the concern in Washington over the more extreme representations of U.S. life in some Hollywood films, the Committee endorsed the USIA's informal relationship with the studios over shaping content. Its remarks

---

[191] DDEL DDE Papers as President (Ann Whitman file), Administrative Series, box 33, Sprague Committee file 1, Conclusions and Recommendations of the President's Committee on Information Activities Abroad, December 1960, Section VI.15.

[192] DDEL U.S.PCIIA (Sprague Committee), box 12, Committee Meeting 1 (3), minutes 1 March 1960. For evidence of post-Sputnik opinion see box 6, Science and Technology #23, file 3 (5), USIA ORA report, Public Opinion abroad and U.S. and Soviet science and technology, 15 April 1960; for detailed committee discussion see box 27, minutes (5), Meeting no. 7, 20 June 1960.

[193] DDEL DDE Papers as President (Ann Whitman file), Administrative Series, box 33, Sprague Committee file 1, Conclusions and Recommendations of the President's Committee on Information Activities Abroad, December 1960, Section IV. On the working group see DDEL U.S.PCIIA (Sprague Committee), box 6, Science and Technology #23, file 3 (9).

[194] DDEL PCIIA (Sprague Committee) box 22, report no. 23, "The Impact of achievements in science and technology upon the image abroad of the United States," 6 June 1960. Other projects that the committee considered to have prestige potential included the quest to create a sustained thermonuclear reaction, a cure for cancer, drilling a hole in the earth's crust (Project MoHole), building a cheap flying car, or the creation of an interplanetary space vehicle powered by successive nuclear explosions (Project Orion).

constitute one of the few concrete indications yet to surface of the USIA's input into Hollywood filmmaking in this era:

> The present voluntary arrangements between the government and the film industry appear to have worked reasonably well, at least in modifying some types of objectionable material while films are still in the production stage. The difficulties and dangers which would be involved in going beyond such arrangements do not seem justified in terms of the probable gains to be realized. Present cooperative arrangements should be strengthened where possible and the situation kept under review.[195]

The committee's briefing documents include a more detailed description of the nature of these informal contacts between the USIA and Hollywood as of 1960. A secret USIA summary of U.S. information since the Jackson Committee noted,

> The Agency has given much attention to the task of maintaining liaison with the U.S. motion picture industry in efforts to reduce the negative impact abroad of U.S. commercial films and to improve their positive impact. Efforts along these lines, as the [Jackson] committee recommended, have been strengthened and are believed to have been increasingly effective over the years. The relationship between the Agency and the industry is delicate and highly confidential. This relationship works best with the more responsible producers and producing organizations. However, means have been developed to exercise influence on almost all elements of the theatrical motion picture industry.
>
> On the whole, the Agency's influence with the industry in regard to specific films has been greater in regard to film sequences having foreign policy and foreign relations implications then in regard to aspects of American life depicted. On these matters the industry prefers to be guided largely by its own domestic code and by moral standards established by importing countries.

The agency told the committee that in the four countries where they now operated Informational Media Guaranty agreements with major U.S. film companies – Poland, Yugoslavia, Turkey, and Vietnam – the USIA was "in a position to exert somewhat more control on the totality of U.S. films shown."[196]

In addition to its praise for Hollywood, the Sprague committee was taken with the potential of television as a means of international communication. It called for further U.S. aid to assist developing nations in their attempts to acquire television and a U.S. role in preparing the way for the regulation of international television broadcasting.[197]

---

195   DDEL DDE Papers as President (Ann Whitman file), Administrative Series, box 33, Sprague Committee file 1, Conclusions and Recommendations of the President's Committee on Information Activities Abroad, December 1960, Section VI.14–15: For polling data on reception of Hollywood films in Europe see DDEL U.S.PCIIA (Sprague Committee), box 4, Western Europe #17 (1), The Image of America in Western Europe, draft, October 1959.
196   DDEL U.S.PCIIA (Sprague Committee), box 19, USIA 2, undated secret memo (c. 1960), "The U.S. Information Program since July 1953," pp. 12–13:
197   DDEL DDE Papers as President (Ann Whitman file), Administrative Series, box 33, Sprague Committee file 1, Conclusions and Recommendations of the President's Committee on Information Activities Abroad, December 1960, Section IV.15.

The Committee did not express an opinion of the future disposition of the USIA, and merely observed that the present arrangement had worked well. Philip Reed of the Advisory Commission on Information, however, recorded his personal view that the USIA should both remain independent and acquire the Cultural and Exchange apparatus from State.[198]

By the time the Sprague Committee had presented its findings, the Eisenhower administration had run its course. The Sprague report was intended to be a resource for the incoming administration, but in the event, the Democrats commissioned their own Task Force to plan the future of the USIA. Even so, the findings of the Sprague Committee had an impact.[199] The report certainly influenced the Democratic Task Force and prepared the way for the Fulbright–Hays Act in the summer of 1961. The central vision of the Sprague Committee – that a new era had dawned in international relations and that this required a new type of diplomacy – would be animated later in the decade by Gullion. Its notion of "total diplomacy" anticipated his notion of "public diplomacy."

The Sprague Committee marked the last hurrah of that central figure in Eisenhower era propaganda, C. D. Jackson. Sprague told Jackson, "You continually strengthened my right arm when the battle of words began to wear down my fortitude." Jackson managed to get a memo to Kennedy urging the preservation of the OCB. But Kennedy would find his own gurus in men like Maxwell Taylor. The new President had more of a taste for counterinsurgency than Jackson's brand of psychological warfare. Jackson died in 1964.[200]

*

On 11 November 1960, the White House announced that USIA director George V. Allen intended to resign from the agency to become president of the Tobacco Institute Inc. of North Carolina. President Eisenhower thanked Allen for "the effort you have devoted to bringing the vital work of the agency to the highest possible effectiveness." Propaganda loomed large in Allen's new job. He spent much of the early 1960s defending the tobacco industry against mounting evidence of a link between smoking and cancer. One may ask why perhaps the most effective director in the history of the USIA should devote his skills to such a tawdry cause. Perhaps it was the lure of a prestigious job in his home state or simply the eloquence of a corporate paycheck. Allen himself did not smoke and urged his son to break the habit. Later, from 1966 to 1969, he directed the U.S. government's Foreign Services Institute, a post with rank equivalent to assistant secretary of state. He died in July 1970. Duke University established a chair in international affairs in his memory.[201]

---

[198] DDEL C D Jackson papers, box 104, Sprague Committee, file 1, Extracts from the Conclusions and Recommendations of the President's Committee on Information Activities Abroad, as released to press, 12 January 1961, p. 18.

[199] Felix Belair Jr., "U.S. Urged to Act for Raise Prestige," *New York Times*, 12 January 1961, p. 1.

[200] DDEL C D Jackson papers, box 104, Sprague, 1, Sprague to Jackson, 10 January 1961; Jackson to Sprague, 16 January 1961.

[201] Felix Belair Jr., "Allen Quits as Head of Information Unit," *New York Times*, 12 November 1960, p. 1; "George V. Allen Is Dead at 66," *New York Times*, 12 July 1970, p. 64; Dennis Merrill,

Henry Loomis remained in post as VOA director and continued to build the Voice along the lines set down in the VOA charter. Abbott Washburn remained as acting director until Kennedy's director had received Senate confirmation. Washburn then returned to private life and the practice of public relations. He was public relations director of Citizens for Nixon in the 1968 election and represented both the Nixon and Reagan administrations in international discussions of satellite broadcasting, with the rank of ambassador. He served as a commissioner on the Federal Communications Commission from 1974 to 1982. Washburn remained an advocate for the USIA and the achievement of the Eisenhower years. He died in 2003.[202]

As an ex-President, Eisenhower continued to support U.S. information overseas. His influence would be felt during the Johnson administration. Eisenhower and his family maintained close links with the People-to-People program, which incorporated as a private organization called People to People International (PTPI) in 1961, and established a headquarters in Kansas City, Missouri. The privatization greatly diminished the role of the USIA's Office of Private Cooperation, which finally folded in June 1967. As a private group PTPI flourished. By the end of the twentieth century PTPI had developed particular strength in youth work and regional strength in the Americas. Its major initiatives included World Wide Conferences to promote cultural exchange; the home hosting of International Visitors; pen pals for children under thirteen; student, artistic, and sports ambassadors; and a committee on disability, which has lobbied for international disabled rights and against landmines. Twenty thousand schoolchildren, students, and adults each year participated in international exchanges under its auspices. Eisenhower would have been very proud.[203]

The Eisenhower administration had transformed U.S. information around the world. As of 1960 the USIA had 202 posts in eighty-five countries. It employed 3,771 Americans and a further 6,881 foreign nationals. The VOA had a daily audience of fifty million. The IPS produced a daily wireless file of 40,000 words; USIA films reached an audience of around 500,000 each year, and USIA television programs were seen in forty-seven countries. The USIA director sat on the NSC, attended cabinet meetings,

"Allen, George V.," *American National Biography*, Vol. 1, New York: Oxford University Press, 1999, pp. 317–19. Documentation on Allen's tenure at the TI may be found at the Tobacco Documents Online Web site; the quotation comes from the Hill and Knowlton informational memorandum, PR 23–63, 10 October 1963: http://tobaccodocuments.org/pm/1003542928–3301.html#p10, and Clyde Osborne, "Tobacco Institute's Chief Asks Respite for Product," *Charlotte Observer*, 24 September 1963. See also http://tobaccodocuments.org/pm/2025028740–8836.html#p1. For Allen's out-of-office view of the USIA see George V. Allen, "USIA: The Big Problem Is Belief," *New York Herald Tribune*, Sect. 2, pp. 1, 8.

202 "Abbott Washburn, 88, Dies; USIA Official and FCC Member," *Washington Post*, 19 December 2003, p. B.8

203 For up-to-date information on PTPI see http://www.ptpi.org/about_us/index.jsp. NA RG 306 A1 (1072) USIA historical collection, box 14, file: Office of Private Cooperation, History 1971, Krill to Newpher, 29 January 1971 with "Brief history of the Office of Private Cooperation" attached. The business advisory function, with its brief to encourage U.S. business to promote American values overseas, passed to the USIA Office of Policy and Research, the Information Center Service took over the acquisition of books and other materials from private donors, and the State Department's Bureau of Educational and Cultural Affairs took on liaison with People-to-People and the parallel Sister City organization.

and by 1960 was meeting the President at the White House every three weeks.[204] But challenges remained. Moscow and Beijing and Cairo all surpassed the VOA in terms of hours broadcast, and in Cuba, Fidel Castro worked to export his revolution to his neighbors. The VOA countered by resuming its direct Spanish broadcasts to that region in March 1960.[205] The USIA faced a challenge in the developing world that would stretch the resources of the USIA and the incoming Kennedy administration to the full.[206]

[204] DDEL U.S.PCIIA (Sprague Committee), box 27, Minutes (13), Memo for the record re USIA presentation to Sprague Committee by Abbott Washburn, 14 March 1960. DDE WHCF OF 247, box 911, Abbott Washburn, "Accomplishments of the Eisenhower administration in the field of international information, July 1960," as forwarded to Eisenhower on 26 November 1960; *USIA 14th Review of Operations, January 1–June 30, 1960.* For a detailed briefing on the USIA director's access see NA RG 306 64-A-0536, Director's Office Subject files, 1957–8, box 3, file: Administration, budget 1958, Washburn to Allen, 4 November 1957. This document lists monthly meeting with President (and emergency access at any time); fortnightly meeting with Secretary of State; NSC meetings (director sits at table); Cabinet meetings (director not at table); OCB meetings (1 p.m. lunch every Wednesday). Washburn suggested that Allen also attend SoS's daily staff meeting (which Streibert and Allen had not).

[205] DDEL OSANA, NSC/Status of Projects, box 9, NSC 6013 (5); *USIA 14th Review of Operations, January 1–June 30, 1960*, pp. 5–7. Also on Cuba see NA RG 306, ZZ entry 1 (formerly 1006), Director's Chronological files, 1953–64, box 3, microfilm reel 33, Washburn to William Rogers, Attorney General, 24 July 1959, in which Washburn argues on information grounds against the issuing of a visa to the deposed Cuban dictator, Batista.

[206] Michael R. Beschloss, *The Crisis Years: Kennedy and Khrushchev, 1960–1963.* New York: Harper Collins, 1991, pp. 60–63.

4 Inventing Truth

THE KENNEDY ADMINISTRATION, 1961–63

American traditions and the American ethic require us to be truthful, but the most important reason is that truth is the best propaganda and lies are the worst. To be persuasive we must be believable; to be believable we must be credible; to be credible we must be truthful. It is as simple as that.

Edward R. Murrow, May 1963.[1]

In January 1961, two speeches vied for world headlines. The first was made in secret on 6 January to a select group of Soviet propagandists and released to the press twelve days later. In it Nikita Khrushchev formally declared his intention to extend the Communist revolution and sponsor "wars of National Liberation" around the world. He spoke intending to pull Mao's China into line, but his words terrified the United States. The second speech was delivered in public, a little after noon on 20 January, on the steps of the Capitol in Washington, DC. In it the newly inaugurated President John F. Kennedy matched the Soviet Union with a global commitment of his own, to "pay any price, bear any burden, meet any hardship, support any friend, oppose any foe, in order to assure the survival and the success of liberty." Mutually alarmed, Soviet and American propagandists broadcast these words around the globe. An ideological duel followed, fought in the newspapers, classrooms, airwaves, and cinema screens of the developing world. The USIA sat at its heart.[2]

The USIA transmitted the Kennedy inaugural live over the VOA in English, and beamed it to Africa in French, Arabic, and Swahili, and fifty-six countries received a thirty minute "videotape or kinescope" of the inauguration. A film version attracted large audiences in Jordan especially. Hundreds of thousands of books and pamphlets and even a comic book about Kennedy were translated and distributed in the opening shots of the agency campaign.[3]

Kennedy knew that he needed to deliver on his campaign promise to rebuild the international image of America. He selected the journalist Edward R. Murrow to lead

---

[1] Edward R. Murrow, testimony to Congressional Appropriations Committee, quoted at http://www.publicdiplomacy.org/1.htm and in Alexander Kendrick, *Prime Time: The Life of Edward R. Murrow*, Boston: Little, Brown and Co., 1969, p. 466.

[2] William J. Thompson, *Khrushchev: A Political Life*, London: Macmillan, 1995, pp. 232–3; Michael R. Beschloss, *The Crisis Years: Kennedy and Khrushchev, 1960–1963*, New York: HarperCollins, 1991, pp. 60–63.

[3] *USIA 16th Review of Operations, 1 January–30 June 1961*, pp. 5–6.

the effort as his USIA director. Murrow embraced the challenge with a pledge to paint America "warts and all." He worked to make the USIA an integral part of the making as well as the execution of American foreign policy. As Murrow himself was fond of saying, his USIA needed to be "in on the take offs as well as the crash landings."[4] Murrow's great legacy at the USIA would flow from the broadcaster's ability to distill the accumulated wisdom of the agency in a few telling phrases. "We cannot judge our success by sales," he warned; "no cash register rings when a man changes his mind." Still more famously he argued that "the really crucial link in the international communication chain is the last three feet, which is bridged by personal contact, one person talking to another." These aphorisms were destined to remain agency lore for the next forty years.[5]

The Murrow years brought many achievements. The USIA played a role in the major foreign policy stories of the era: Berlin, Cuba, Vietnam. The agency's research department rode high under Leo Crespi, with its polls finding wide circulation. President Kennedy made it his first order of business each day to read the USIA's digest of world editorials. In 1963, the agency initiated a running world opinion survey and immediately found an eager reader in the Oval Office.[6] But beneath the achievements lay serious weaknesses. The Murrow era demonstrated the growing incompatibility between the USIA and VOA. Murrow spoke of the VOA as an organ of truth, but expected to be able to manipulate its content as policy dictated. Within weeks of Murrow's arrival, Bernie Kamenske in the VOA newsroom had ironically dubbed the new director "The man who invented truth."[7]

Although Murrow disappointed the VOA, he too had reason to feel betrayed. On the morning of 5 April, his deputy, Don Wilson, stopped in Georgetown for a casual breakfast with his old journalist friend Tad Szulc of the *New York Times*. Szulc had traveled up from an assignment in Miami and was staying at the home of his uncle, former Ambassador John C. Wiley. Over toast and coffee Szulc alluded to an administration plan to support an invasion of Cuba by an army of American-trained anti-Castro exiles. Szulc was just about to publish a story on the build-up to the invasion. He estimated that it would take place on 19 April and wondered how the USIA would be supporting press coverage. Szulc realized from Wilson's expression that this was the first he had heard of the plan. Wilson dashed over to Murrow's office

---

[4] This quote is a much repeated piece of agency lore, recalled by virtually all the Kennedy-era staff interviewed for this book. For a print version see Kendrick, *Prime Time*, p. 456.

[5] Kendrick, *Prime Time*, p. 490. For use recent use see Arthur Bardos, "Public Diplomacy, an Old Art, a New Profession," *Virginia Quarterly Review*, Summer 2001. For recent use of the "last three feet" quotation see Ramona Harper, "The Art of Public Diplomacy," 2003, on line at http://www. ketchum.com/DisplayWebPage/0,1003,1171,00.html; William A. Rugh in Adam Garfinkle, *A Practical Guide to Winning the War on Terrorism*, Palo Alto, CA: Hoover Press, 2004, p. 155; and in the United Kingdom Peter Aspden, *Selling Democracy? The Past and Future of Western Cultural Relations and Public Diplomacy*, London: Counterpoint/British Council, 2004, p. 9, online at http://www.counterpoint-online.org/download/216/Selling-Democracy-report-FINAL.pdf.

[6] For a full treatment of polling in the Kennedy-era USIA see Mark Haefele, "John F. Kennedy, USIA and World Opinion," *Diplomatic History*, 25 (2001), 63–84.

[7] Interview: Bernie Kamenske.

to confirm the story. Murrow was equally astonished and the two men raced to a hastily scheduled meeting with Allen Dulles at the CIA. Dulles refused to confirm the plan and merely sat nonchalantly smoking his pipe. Twenty minutes later Murrow received a summons to the White House from the special assistant to the President for National Security Affairs, McGeorge Bundy, who laid out the entire background to the story. The plan appalled Murrow. Invading Cuba, he warned, would be a psychological disaster, but the wheels were in motion. The USIA had been left "out of the loop" on one of the biggest American foreign policy decisions of the decade: the landings at the Bay of Pigs. Murrow spent much of the next three years recovering from the implications of that single decision. This was not the approach that the new President had promised.[8]

1) FACING KHRUSHCHEV
MURROW'S USIA TO DECEMBER 1961

John F. Kennedy had an instinctive understanding of the power of the image. He won the election with the help of television. His next campaign would be global. On 18 November 1960 the President-elect described the U.S. task in Latin America as being "to catch the imagination of the people living there." In Africa, he was concerned that the American propaganda effort should match the Soviet, Chinese, and Egyptian campaigns.[9] Kennedy established five foreign policy Task Forces to report on the immediate needs of American foreign policy, covering Africa, disarmament, economic foreign policy, the State Department, and the United States Information Agency. In a little over a month the USIA Task Force consulted twenty-two leading academics, journalists, and experts in international affairs, including Ed Murrow at CBS.[10]

The Task Force report accepted the premise of a crisis in American standing in the world and understood the limits of propaganda:

> We cannot put a good face on unsound or inadequate policies or unwise actions by information or cultural operations, let alone by slogans or propaganda gimmick . . . Fundamentally, the decline in United States prestige can be arrested only by more dynamic presidential leadership, a much clearer sense of our national

---

[8]   Interview (telephone) Tad Szulc, 30 October 2000 and Donald Wilson, 2 July 1996; *FRUS 1961–1963*, Vol. X, *Cuba, 1961–1962*, doc. 231, Memo 1. Cuba Study Group to President, 13 June 1961, items 39, 40; Peter Wyden, *Bay of Pigs: The Untold Story*, New York: Touchstone, 1979, pp. 144–5. Wilson has on several occasions (including a JFKL oral history interview) misdated these events to Saturday 15 April, only two days before the invasion; hence the error in Sperber, pp. 623–4, and Persico, p. 475. Szulc's story appeared in the *New York Times* in much eviscerated form on 7 April 1961.

[9]   Arthur M. Schlesinger, Jr., *A Thousand Days: John F. Kennedy in the White House*. Boston: Houghton Mifflin Co., 1965, pp. 157–9.

[10] JFKL Pre-presidential papers, box 1074. Summary of Recommendations, 31 December 1960. Other consultants included veteran propagandists like Edward W. Barrett and Wallace Carroll; public opinion experts Hadley Cantril and George Gallup; Hans Speier at the Rand Corporation; and Robert Carlson, vice-president of Standard Oil.

purposes, sound substantive policies and better coordinated programs for accomplishing them.[11]

Even so, there was much scope for the USIA to act, especially by working to "identify" the U.S. with "the revolution of rising expectations" across the globe. American propaganda needed to do more than just snipe at Communism; it needed to play a role in the global development of "free governments," to engage with accusations of racism, and to "come to terms with the spirit of nationalism" at work in the emerging nations of Africa and Asia. Although much of this fitted the recommendations of the Sprague Committee, the Task Force report was much more explicit in its recommendations for the USIA. The agency should remain independent, with an expanded cultural function (acquiring some responsibility from the State Department) and twenty percent more money for existing work. The director of the USIA should be an ex officio member of the National Security Council and regularly present in cabinet meetings as "chief advisor to the president and members of the Cabinet on the psychological aspects of international problems." The USIA seemed on the verge of becoming a major player in the formation as well as the execution of U.S. foreign policy.[12]

With the pathway for a revised USIA emerging, Kennedy now needed to select a suitable director for the agency. His first choice was CBS president Frank Stanton. Stanton declined, but suggested that Kennedy consider "someone like Ed Murrow" instead. Although the administration also considered two other mainstays of CBS news, Sig Mickelson and Fred Friendly, and Phil Graham, publisher of the *Washington Post*, Murrow had special appeal.[13]

Born Egbert Roscoe Murrow in North Carolina in 1908, and raised in the state of Washington, Murrow was trained not in journalism but in speech – his passion as a high school debater and his major at Washington State College. Many of his professional achievements lay in the field of rhetoric and flowed from his keen understanding that presentation was half of any battle. At a personal level, he recognized the value of changing his name and was not above padding his curriculum vitae or adding a couple of years to his age to help his progress. The young Murrow shone in student politics and, in 1929, was elected president of the National Student Federation of America. From 1932 to 1935, he worked as assistant director of the International Institute for Education, playing a role in the private sector side of what would later be called public diplomacy. In 1935, he joined CBS radio as director of talks. In 1937 he moved to Europe to direct the network's coverage of the mounting crisis. America listened as Murrow eloquently described the continent's slide into war. His broadcasts of the London Blitz were credited with helping draw America into the fray, and his later war coverage brought the struggle alive for the home front. After the war he shifted into television; his famous attack on McCarthy played a part in the

11   JFKL PPP, box 1072. Task Force Report: USIA, 31 December 1960, p. 6.
12   JFKL PPP, box 1072. Task Force Report: USIA, 31 December 1960.
13   Interview: Frank Stanton, 28 July 2002; JFKL Salinger papers, box 132, 1961 file USIA, Robert
      Oshins (DNC) to Salinger, 21 December 1960.

Senator's demise. His more recent work included a documentary on migrant laborers: *Harvest of Shame*.[14]

Although the Kennedy camp noted "some question of how he'd handle the administrative side," he offered glamour and liberal integrity to a team dominated by cerebral conservatives such as Robert McNamara and McGeorge Bundy. Coincidentally, Murrow was also at an awkward moment in his career. Stanton had responded to the news that CBS rigged its quiz shows by publicly denouncing all the network's prerehearsed "spontaneous" programs, including Murrow's celebrity chat show *Person to Person*. Slighted, Murrow was susceptible to the right offer from outside CBS.[15]

Murrow knew that if he was to succeed as director of the USIA he needed access to the President. He accepted the directorship on the understanding that he would be given the sort of input into policy formation outlined in the Task Force report. Kennedy committed these terms to paper in a letter of 10 March 1961. The initial weeks seemed encouraging. On 1 February, before his Senate confirmation hearing, Murrow sat in on a meeting of the National Security Council, while Kennedy argued for his continued presence as necessary.[16]

Murrow's key staff at the USIA included two officials well placed with the Kennedy camp. His deputy director, Donald M. Wilson, was, as usual, a political appointee: chief of the *Life* magazine Washington bureau and a friend of Robert Kennedy. Below Wilson was Deputy Director of Policy and Plans Tom Sorensen, a young USIA officer with considerable experience in the Middle East, who happened to be the brother of the Kennedy aide and speech writer Ted Sorensen. Their connections gave the USIA important friends at Kennedy's court. These men played a vital role as Murrow's health began to fail. Many insiders saw Wilson and Sorensen as the real power at the USIA.

Murrow's personal staff choices played to his reputation as the scourge of McCarthy. Reed Harris, victim of McCarthy's purge of 1953, returned as Murrow's administrative assistant. Murrow also appointed William N. Robson to the VOA: a pioneer of radio drama at CBS who had lost his job during the red scare. Other appointments spoke of Murrow's attention to the journalistic craft – recruiting David McCullough from *Time*, and Mike Fodor from CBS – and even sensitivity to gender. Murrow made the first assignment of a woman – Barbara White – to a major PAO post (Chile). Here, it seemed, was the perfect director to nurture the values of ethical international communication. Murrow told his Senate confirmation hearing that the USIA must give a balanced account to the country: "We cannot be effective in telling America's story abroad if we tell it only in superlatives."[17]

14 For biographical studies see Alexander Kendrick, *Prime Time*; A.M. Sperber, *Murrow: His Life and Times*, London: Michael Joseph, 1986; Joseph E. Persico, *Edward R. Murrow: An American Original*, New York: McGraw-Hill, 1988.
15 Sperber, *Murrow*, p. 611; Persico, *Murrow*, p. 465.
16 Sperber, *Murrow*, pp. 614–19; JFKL NSF, Meetings and Memoranda, box 313, folder 2, NSC meeting 475, 1 February 1961.
17 Kendrick, *Prime Time*, p. 457; Interview: Donald Wilson, 2 July 1996; Arndt, *First Resort of Kings*, pp. 321–2.

Murrow's ethical stand did not last long. A press leak revealed that he had attempted to halt a screening of his CBS documentary *Harvest of Shame* on British television. The President's press secretary, Pierre Salinger, apparently feared that the export of such a film by a member of the administration could offend domestic farming interests. The BBC refused to pull the film and Murrow's attempt to censor his own journalism became a brief scandal.[18] The slip was symptomatic of the degree to which Murrow had traded in his old journalistic hat for a new role in government. For Robert B. Goldmann, who had defied McCarthy and carried the banner for balanced news at the VOA, Murrow came as a sorry disappointment. When Goldmann complained about State Department pressure to shape the news, Murrow declined to intervene. "I am now in management," he told the editor; "the day I tell an editor in the news-room what to do and what not to do I should be put out to pasture." Unsupported, Goldmann left the VOA in 1962 to run press relations for the Alliance for Progress.[19]

*

Despite the findings of the Sprague Committee, the Kennedy Administration had no time for the Operations Coordinating Board and immediately abolished it. Kennedy felt confident that the conventional policy-making apparatus of the State Department, bolstered by the expanded role of the USIA, would suffice. For the field, Kennedy emphasized the concept of the "country team." USIS officers overseas would be a full part of the team serving under the ambassador and would play a role in generating the "country plan" for that location.[20]

The USIA was ready and able to support Kennedy's major foreign policy initiatives, such as the Peace Corps, announced on 1 March. The Peace Corps, Murrow wrote to Kennedy, had Moscow "really squealing." The Soviets could not match the spectacle of American youth volunteering in the developing world. As Murrow noted, "they can not risk sending their youth abroad except under conditions of strictest control."[21] The USIA used the Peace Corps as an image of American benevolence, although – at the request of the Corps – the agency took care not to compromise the impression of distance between the cheery young volunteers of the Peace Corps and the other agencies of U.S. foreign policy.[22]

The USIA also reported excellent reactions to Kennedy's proposed mutual aid package for Latin America: the Alliance for Progress. One Colombian commentator

---

[18]   Kendrick, *Prime Time*; Sperber, *Murrow*, 629; Interview: Clifford Groce, 30 November 1995 also Frank Cummins and Bernie Kamenske; "TV: Defense for Murrow," *New York Times*, 28 March 1961.

[19]   Interview: Robert Goldmann, 26 December 1996.

[20]   Interview: Abbott Washburn, 1 December 1995; JFKL NSF, D&A OCB, General, box 284, presidential Statement, 17 February 1961. Ex-USIA director Larson did not mourn the passage of the OCB. He considered it redundant, though he acknowledged that the committee had introduced sandwiches and fruit rather than a full roast at official lunches. Larson, *Eisenhower: The President Nobody Knew*, p. 17.

[21]   JFKL POF, Depts & Agencies: USIA, box 91, Murrow to Kennedy, 21 March 1961.

[22]   LBJL Bill Moyers papers, box 44 (file: "C" correspondence, general, 1963), Moyers (PC) to Carter (USIA) 16 April 1963 and Wilson to Moyers, 15 April 1963.

hailed it as "the most significant contribution to Pan-Americanism in one hundred years." Western Europe praised the plan as a worthy successor to Marshall Aid.[23] The USIA expanded its activities in Latin America with new posts and specialist staff trained to work with students and labor leaders. The VOA also began work on what would be the world's most powerful shortwave radio transmitter in Greenville, North Carolina. At a total output of 4.8 million watts, the transmitter doubled the VOA's power and made possible a clear signal to two major target areas, South America and West Africa. Opened by Murrow in February 1963, in time the transmitter would bear his name. The VOA also expanded its Spanish language programming for Latin America, which had previously been restricted to just an hour or so each day.[24]

Other advances included the foundation of a Foreign Press Center, staffed by USIA personnel in New York, to assist the work of the 500 foreign correspondents permanently based in that city. Located at 340 East 46th street, the center was just three blocks from the United Nations. Its first director, Ernest Wiener, had been deputy public affairs officer in Vienna and was fluent in German, French, and Czech. Early guests for informal press sessions included Robert Kennedy and Ambassador J. K. Galbraith. Participants included an eager representative from Radio Moscow.[25]

The arrival of the Kennedy administration provided an opportunity to reshape the structure of U.S. exchange and information overseas. Following the suggestion of the Task Force, the Kennedy administration dramatically expanded its cultural and educational programs overseas. But Kennedy declined to rename the USIA, make the agency director an ex-officio member of the NSC, or move the cultural program under the sole control of the USIA. As in 1953, Senator Fulbright insisted that educational exchanges should remain the responsibility of State, to avoid tainting "his" scholarship program with any hint of propaganda. The USIA had no desire to "pick a losing fight" on the issue in the Senate. The agency duly conceded that these exchanges should continue to be administered by the State Department in Washington and USIS staff in the field. Beyond this, the Kennedy administration increased the clout of the State Department's cultural bureau by elevating the director of CU to the level of Assistant Secretary of State. The first to hold the post was Philip B. Coombs, an idealistic internationalist from the Ford Foundation in New York.

In the spring of 1961, a new Mutual Education and Cultural Exchange Act (known as the Fulbright–Hays Act) sailed into law. The act consolidated existing schemes, added initiatives in book translation, exhibitions, and American studies, and provided

23 JFKL POF, Depts & Agencies: USIA, box 91, Office of Research and Analysis R-11–61, 22 March 1961: Reactions to President Kennedy's Address on Latin America. The quotation came from a sympathetic Colombian provincial paper, *La Patria*, in Maizales.

24 *USIA 16th Review of Operations, 1 January–30 June 1961*, p. 9. The commercial shortwave station WRUL had previously carried the burden of U.S. broadcasting to Latin America.

25 JFKL WHCF Subject file: FG296 USIA, box 184, Executive, Salinger to Wilson, 25 August 1961 and attached White House press release, 24 August 1961; Wiener to Gildner (White House) 13 November 1961.

for new American cultural centers around the world. For the USIA the boost of new resources was matched by the perceived challenge of a reinvigorated rival in CU. Despite the friendship of Coombs and Murrow, a counterproductive bureaucratic war broke out between the two centers of power in U.S. cultural work overseas. Among Coombs's ideas that raised the hackles of the USIA was a proposal to elevate the status of the CAO on an Embassy team to rank alongside the PAO. The USIA blocked this and more. As veteran cultural diplomat Richard Arndt has noted, the battle was not merely one of turf but included a marked difference in the approach to international culture, with the USIA's unilateralism grating against Coombs's vision of mutuality at State. Worn down, Coombs lasted only until April 1962. He was succeeded by Lucius Battle, who managed at least to placate Congress and secure the budget.[26]

At the end of March, Murrow placed his budget for an expanded USIA before the appropriations subcommittee of the House of Representatives. He found the chairman, Congressman John R. Rooney, obtuse as ever, making a virtue of his geographical ignorance and firing off questions about how many homosexuals had been fired from the USIA over the past year. Rooney refused to be beguiled by the television celebrity and the agency's budget remained static, as Murrow noted, at a level somewhat below the price tag of a single nuclear missile.[27] There was worse news to come. On 12 April the U.S.S.R. launched the first human into space: Yuri Gagarin. It seemed like another piece of evidence to underpin the Soviet claim to the world that their system represented the wave of the future.[28] Meanwhile, unknown to the rest of the USIA, Murrow and Wilson nursed the knowledge of the imminent invasion of Cuba.

*

Kennedy noted Murrow's fury over being left in the dark during the planning of the Bay of Pigs invasion. He feared that Murrow would resign. In the event the director accepted the administration line and did not pass on his knowledge of the plan to his own staff. Promised State Department guidance on how to present the landings, due three days before "D-Day," never came. Henry Loomis, director of the Voice of America, learned of the invasion over the car radio on his way to work on the morning of 17 April. In an angry phone call he reminded Murrow about the need to be "in on the take offs." Within two hours he rallied the Voice to expand their Spanish language broadcasting to Latin America, from an hour of programming a day

---

26   JFKL, POF, Depts. & Agencies: USIA, box 91, Donald Wilson to President, 26 January 1961 PL 87–256; signed by Kennedy on 21 September 1961. For a succinct treatment of Fulbright–Hays and Coombs see Arndt, *First Resort of Kings*, chapter 14. See also Philip H. Coombs, *The Fourth Dimension of Foreign Policy: Educational and Cultural Affairs and Foreign Relations*, New York: Harper & Row, 1964; Randolph Wieck, *Ignorance Abroad: American Educational and Cultural Foreign Policy and the Office of Assistant Secretary of State*, Westport, CT: Praeger, 1992.
27   Persico, *Murrow*, pp. 478–9; Sperber, *Murrow*, p. 655.
28   JFKL Salinger papers, box 132, 1961 file, USIA, ORA report R-17–61, Initial World Reaction to Soviet "Man in Space," 21 April 1961.

to a marathon nineteen hours, which the VOA maintained until the final defeat of the landings on 22 April.[29]

The Voice struggled hard to establish the facts of the invasion. Loomis noted, "While there was a wild outpouring of stories and items, there was a dearth of hard items and confirmable detail...."[30] The Voice attempted balanced coverage. It reported Fidel Castro's claim that aircraft from the United States had bombed Cuba, but gave a little more weight to Adlai Stevenson's statement to the United Nations that these bombers were actually defecting pilots from Castro's own air force. Unfortunately, Stevenson had been misinformed.[31] The news analyses cleared by USIA policy officials were as compromised by rumor as any other American report. The analysis by Ronald Dunlavey carried on 17 April castigated Castro for implicating the United States in an *invasion*, as the word "implies an attack by a foreign power. The invaders in this case appear to be Cubans returning to their homeland...The United States is not intervening." The analysis recycled CIA wishful thinking and reported sympathetic revolts elsewhere in Cuba.[32] Soon the true scale of the disaster emerged. Castro's army had rounded up the exiles on the beaches. On 20 April, Kennedy addressed the nation, publicly taking the blame for the fiasco.[33] Despite the achievement of the Spanish language branch in expanding their output virtually overnight, this was not the VOA's finest hour. Loomis and his team resented the way they had been fed misleading material by the State Department and the USIA policy office.[34]

Murrow's immediate response to the debacle was to further upgrade USIA provision in Latin America. He invited Tad Szulc to serve as assistant director of the USIA for the region. After a night out with Murrow and Wilson, Szulc agreed, but in the cold light of day and after a sobering discussion with his wife and uncle, he resolved to stay with the *New York Times*.[35] Murrow also took steps to define the relationship between the USIA and the CIA. The USIA needed to know what the CIA was doing and any cooperation between the CIA and the USIA required his approval. Murrow was particularly keen to avoid his agency being used as a cover for the CIA, as this could endanger the credibility of USIA work.[36] Beyond this, Murrow and his team knew that any future crisis should be handled very differently. He strengthened the role of the IOP, Sorensen's policy office at the USIA responsible for

29   *FRUS 1961–1963*, Vol. X, doc. 231, Cuba Study Group to President, 13 June 1961, item 40; Sperber, *Murrow*, pp. 623–4; JFKL USIA director files, reel 7, Loomis to Murrow, IBS Monthly Report, 5 May 1961.
30   JFKL USIA director files, reel 7, Loomis to Murrow, IBS Monthly Report, 5 May 1961.
31   Bernie Kamenske to author, 28 November 2000; Wyden, *Bay of Pigs*, pp. 185–90.
32   JFKL VOA microfilm reel 1, News Analysis 1647, 17 April 1961, Ronald Dunlavey, "The Invasion of Cuba."
33   Murrow was profoundly impressed by this and stopped his practice of referring to Kennedy as "that boy in the White House. Hereafter it was 'the president.'" Interview: Donald Wilson, 2 July 1996.
34   Interview: Kamenske.
35   *FRUS 1961–1963*, Vol. X, doc. 205, NSC action 2422-m, 5 May 1961; Interview (telephone) Tad Szulc, 30 October 2000. Kennedy also attempted to recruit Szulc to the Alliance for Progress.
36   Sperber, *Murrow*, p. 636.

coordinating the political message of agency output.[37] These changes ensured that the Cuban missile crisis would be far more dexterously handled, but in the meantime the United States had slid back yet another notch in world opinion.[38] America needed a success.

A little light came on 5 May 1961 with the launch of Alan Shepherd, the first American in space. The Gagarin flight of 12 April had been shrouded in secrecy, but the USIA ensured that coverage of Shepherd's flight was as open as possible. The agency assembled a fat packet of scientific background pieces and photographs; the wireless file carried Shepherd's own account to ninety USIS posts in eighty-three countries, and newspapers as far apart as Venezuela, Poland, and Pakistan stopped their presses to run USIA material. The VOA presented detailed coverage of the flight in multiple languages. The television section produced a widely screened fifteen-minute documentary of the build-up to the flight, called *Shadow of Infinity*, and a matching account of the launch, flight, and splashdown, called *The Astronaut Launching*. The USIA, NASA, and the Department of Defense then rushed Shepherd's capsule to Paris for display at the International Air Show and to Rome for the International Science Fair. The spirit of openness was evident even at the White House reception of Alan Shepherd. Newsreels of the event showed Kennedy dropping Shepherd's medal and jokingly presenting it "from the ground up." This was not the Soviet style. But one space flight could not atone for the humiliation on the beaches of Cuba.[39]

During the days following the disaster in Cuba, Kennedy's foreign policy team pondered the nation's next move. Kennedy's deputy special assistant for International Affairs, Walt Rostow, called for an expansion of the Alliance for Progress.[40] By October 1961 the Alliance seemed to be paying dividends. The USIA's researchers reported a marked decline in Castro's influence in Latin America. The Alliance was winning friends and "the current U.S. policy of ignoring Castro is robbing him of his 'Yankee Imperialism' ammunition."[41] On 30 November 1961, the President approved a campaign of anti-Castro propaganda and sabotage codenamed Operation Mongoose. Murrow was not a member of the steering group but ensured the USIA's "vigorous

---

[37] JFKL NSF, Depts & Agencies: USIA, General: box 290, Murrow to staff, 22 April 1961 as transmitted to McGeorge Bundy, 27 April 1961.

[38] JFKL NSF, Cuba, General, Box 35, Schlesinger to President, Confidential, 3 May 1961: "Reactions to Cuba in Western Europe" reports the incomprehension of his contacts in British and French elite (including Isaiah Berlin, Roy Jenkins and Perigrine Worsthorne).

[39] JFKL Salinger papers, box 132, 1961 file USIA, Murrow to President, Weekly Report, 16 May 1961; USIA, 16th Review of Operations, 1 January–30 June 1961, pp. 7–9, 12, 25. The newsreel was used in the USIA's obituary film *John F. Kennedy: Years of Lightning, Day of Drums*. Other USIA offerings in the space field included *Trailblazer in Space*, a one-reel documentary about Ham the chimpanzee.

[40] JFKL NSF, Subjects: Policy Planning, box 303, Rostow to President, Top Secret, 21 April 1961, "The Problem We Face."

[41] JFKL POF, Depts. & Agencies: USIA, box 91, Wilson (acting dir.,) to President, 20 October 1961, with report "Castro's current standing in Latin America," 19 October 1961.

participation" in the project, making particular use of the testimony of Cuban refugees over the VOA.[42]

*

In the first week of June 1961, President Kennedy traveled to Vienna to meet his Soviet adversary Nikita Khrushchev face to face. The wily Ukrainian felt he had the measure of the young President and immediately demanded the demilitarization of the symbolic city of Berlin, as a prelude to its being absorbed into East Germany. Khrushchev had chosen the next Cold War battleground. Rostow compared the coming clash to Gary Cooper's lonely stand as the sheriff in the classic western *High Noon*.[43]

Rising to the challenge, the USIA prepared to confront Soviet propaganda. On 8 June 1961, Murrow and Secretary of State Dean Rusk announced an American slogan to compete with "Peaceful Coexistence," the theme around which the Soviets had based their propaganda since 1956. America's response would be the concept of "peaceful world community." Murrow instructed all USIA media to use the phrase as appropriate.[44] At the White House, Arthur Schlesinger Jr. was unimpressed by the phrase because of translation problems. He reported that the Russian adjectives for peaceful and worldwide were the same (*mirnoye*) and added that in many languages the word *community* is rendered as either *village* or *communism*. The United States needed to avoid the suggestion that it wanted "peaceful worldwide communism."[45] Murrow took the point. A luncheon meeting of the principal figures in U.S. foreign policy, including Murrow, held on 29 June, generated an alternative, "world of free choice," and commissioned the USIA to "spread this phrase and its full meaning around the world." The first major use of the phrase came in a speech to the Press Club by Secretary of State Dean Rusk on 10 July, characterizing the international situation as a choice between "the world of free choice and free cooperation" and "the world of coercion." Kennedy added his blessing to what became "National Security Action Memorandum 61" and instructed the White House to use the concepts as necessary.[46]

NSAM 61 whetted the appetite of the USIA for linguistic sensitivity. Murrow instructed his staff to drop such terms as "under-developed" and "backward

42 James W. Hilty, *Robert Kennedy: Brother Protector*, Philadelphia: Temple University Press, 1997, pp. 421–31; *FRUS 1961–1963*, Vol. X, *Cuba, 1961–1962*, doc. 347, Lansdale (chief of operations, Mongoose) to Special Group (Augmented), 14 June 1962.
43 JFKL POF, Staff Memoranda, box 65, Rostow, 17 June 1961: "The Shape of the Battle." Rostow compared the situation to the turning point of the Second World War, 1942, and noted, "To turn the tide we must win our two defensive battles: Berlin and Viet-Nam." JFKL, NSF, CO Germany, Berlin, General, Box 81, Rostow to President, Secret, "A High Noon stance on Berlin," 22 July 1961.
44 JFKL NSF, Meetings and Memoranda, box 330, NSAM 61, Rusk and Murrow to President, 8 June 1961.
45 JFKL NSF, Meetings and Memoranda, box 327, Staff memoranda, Schlesinger to McGeorge Bundy, 9 June 1961.
46 JFKL NSF, Meetings and Memoranda, box 330, NSAM 61: Minutes of lunch meeting, 29 June 1961, McGeorge Bundy; Murrow to McGeorge Bundy, 30 June 1961; McGeorge Bundy to Rusk/Murrow, 14 July 1961.

countries" from their lexicon and use positive terms such as "developing countries" or "modernizing countries" instead. He also requested suggestions for substitutes for such Eisenhower-era clichés as "East–West," "Cold War," and "pro-American."[47] From the White House, Arthur Schlesinger Jr. added that "Free World" was hardly the best way to describe Spain, Portugal, Paraguay, Haiti, or Taiwan.[48] Murrow saw the irony and ended the agency's glorification of the regime in Taiwan.[49]

A second National Security Memorandum – NSAM 63 – issued on 24 July 1961 clarified the chain of command in broadcasting. The State Department would be the source of guidance, but the director of the USIA would be the intermediary who transmitted it not only to the VOA but also to the Pentagon's outlets: Armed Forces Network radio and television and the Voice of the United Nations Command in South Korea. The policy also applied to clandestine stations operated by the CIA. The USIA director also now had the power to add unattributed material as he felt necessary, and even to "pre-empt time," taking over civilian and military transmitters alike for special programs when the national interest demanded.[50]

Meanwhile, the situation in Berlin deteriorated further. On 23 July, the East Germans implemented new restrictions on travel to West Berlin. Two days later, Kennedy broadcast his determination to defend the city and announced further arms spending. Soviet jammers attempted to drown out his description of West Berlin as an "escape hatch" and references to refugees "voting with their feet" and to America's willingness to negotiate.[51]

The USIA had expected the crisis. Since April it had been preparing a steady stream of material to support the Western position on Berlin.[52] Output included film versions of all Kennedy's major speeches and a half-hour documentary, *Journey across Berlin*, which by the end of June had reached ninety-eight countries. On the front line in Berlin, RIAS celebrated its fifteenth birthday. Three quarters of East Berliners regularly tuned in.[53] As the crisis deepened, RIAS began broadcasting round the clock on long, short, and FM wave bands and added a powerful new antenna to reach deep into East Germany. New mobile vans allowed on-the-spot radio coverage around the city. The VOA carried English, Polish, Russian, and Czech versions of a program called "West Berlin Today: A Refugee a Minute." The USIS successfully distributed a series of in-house radio programs on the crisis, including the three-part *The Manufactured Crisis* and seven-part *The Berlin Story*, on domestic radio networks as far apart as Bolivia

47   JFKL POF, Depts. & Agencies: USIA, box 290, General, Murrow to Sorensen, 19 July 1961.
48   JFKL Schlesinger papers, White House files, box WH-23, USIA. Schlesinger to Murrow, 1 August 1961; the "hand-holder" quote comes from NSF, Meetings & Memoranda, box 327, Staff Memoranda, Schlesinger, Memo to Salinger, 7 June 1961.
49   Sperber, *Murrow*, p. 659.
50   JFKL NSF, Meetings and Memoranda, box 330, NSAM 63, Policy Guidance and Pre-emption of U.S. government-controlled broadcasting, 24 July 1961; JFKL NSF, Depts. & Agencies: USIA, General, box 290, Murrow to President, Top Secret, Weekly Report, 1 August 1961.
51   JFKL POF, Depts. & Agencies: USIA, box 91, Murrow to President, 26 July 1961.
52   JFKL USIA director files, reel 5, Murrow to Rusk, 12 July 1961.
53   *USIA 16th Review of Operations, 1 January–30 June 1961*, p. 24.

and Iran.[54] At the end of August, Murrow used the authority of NSAM 63 to take time on Armed Forces networks to broadcast a one-hour USIA radio documentary and half-hour television program stating the U.S. case on the Berlin crisis.[55] A special Berlin Steering Committee, including Don Wilson for the USIA, drew up longer-term propaganda plans, including a celebration of the anniversary of the Berlin airlift in September. In the event the Soviets provided a much stronger theme: the Berlin Wall.[56]

In mid-August, Murrow visited Berlin to inspect USIA facilities. While he watched, the East Germans began to build the Berlin Wall as a solution to the daily hemorrhage of refugees.[57] The Wall proved to be an enduring gift to the USIA. The agency distributed a stream of images of East German escapees, including the famous shot of a frontier guard in midair as he leapt to freedom across barbed wire. These pictures formed the backbone of *The Wall*, a photographic exhibition devised by USIS Berlin, ten copies of which toured USIS posts worldwide. Images of the Berlin Wall hence reached as far as Kathmandu and the winter fair in Udorn, a small Thai town, only fifty miles from the Laotian border. USIA television created a related documentary called *Focus Berlin: Barbed Wire World*.[58] The agency understood that the best propaganda came from independent witnesses and helped the German government in bringing 750 foreign journalists to Berlin to view the wall for themselves, placing emphasis on journalists from the "Afro-Asian" world, where interest in the crisis had been limited. For similar reasons, a segment called "Berlin through African Eyes" reached the thirty million viewers of the USIA's monthly African film magazine, *Today*. These were the most potent images since Soviet troops crushed Hungary in 1956.[59]

The Berlin crisis spurred an adjustment in the wider U.S. propaganda strategy. On 16 August, Robert Kennedy suggested a major initiative in psychological warfare, mobilizing America's friends in "business, labor, universities, all across the world." He dismissed the State Department's attitude to propaganda and the CIA's existing efforts, and although confident that the USIA was "in good hands under Murrow," he made it clear that he now imagined a far more comprehensive effort. The first step, he argued, would be a single organization to plan an American propaganda offensive.[60]

---

54 *USIA 17th Review of Operations, 1 July–31 December 1961*, pp. 4–6; JFKL, NSF, CO Germany, Berlin, General, box 81, Murrow to President, 20 July 1961: "USIA Exploitation of Current Exodus from East Germany."

55 JFKL Salinger papers, box 132, 1961 file, USIA, Murrow to President, Top Secret, weekly report, 29 August 1961.

56 JFKL USIA director files, reel 4, Wilson to Rusk, secret, "USIA Berlin Program," 2 August 1962.

57 Sperber, *Murrow*, p. 644.

58 *USIA 17th Review of Operations, 1 July–31 December 1961*, p. 5–7.

59 *USIA 17th Review of Operations, 1 July–31 December 1961*, p. 5–7; JFKL, NSF, CO Germany, Berlin, General, box 81, Murrow to Rusk, 10 July 1961: "USIA Planning and Action on Berlin"; Salinger papers, box 132, 1961 file, USIA, Murrow to President, weekly report, 22 August 1961. The death of a refugee on the Berlin Wall was featured in the 1963 USIA film *The American Commitment* directed by Leo Seltzer and narrated by Howard K. Smith) (see NASMPB RG 306 387). The film shows the USIA sending news of the death around the globe. Memorable images include scenes of a public affairs officer in Central America driving past a wall decorated with the slogan "Castro Si, Yankis Non!"

60 JFKL NSF, CO German Berlin, General, box 82, Attorney General to President, 17 August 1961.

The Kennedy administration had, of course, destroyed exactly this sort of body when it abolished Eisenhower's OCB. On 19 September an ad hoc propaganda committee, including Murrow, met and resolved that the State Department should appoint a "Special Assistant for Special Projects" to "give full time the coordination and overall supervision of all United States resources in the propaganda–political warfare field." Rusk selected a member of his planning staff and former *New York Times* foreign correspondent, William J. Jorden, to fill the post and convene an interdepartmental committee. The resulting Psychological–Political Working Group began work in the spring of 1962. It brought a measure of coherence to administration policy in such sensitive matters as handling treatment of the emerging Sino–Soviet dispute.[61]

On 31 August 1961, the Soviet–American crisis took a further turn for the worse. The instruments of the United States Atomic Energy Commission detected the first Soviet nuclear test since 1958. Much of the world press immediately objected. The USIA produced a map showing the location of the Soviet test site and "estimated deposit of strontium 90 in millicuries per square mile from a fifty-megaton nuclear explosion." An ugly black stain stretched eastward from the testing ground in Soviet Asia in a belt of poison reaching across Japan, the Pacific, and the United States to a bulb over Britain and Northern Europe. Versions of this map made the front page of papers including London's *Daily Express*, the *Vienna Kurrier*, and seven papers in Rio de Janeiro.[62] The VOA's beamed news of world indignation back into Russia. Although the Soviet government had announced its decision to resume testing, the population did not know that the explosions had actually happened. By 6 September, the Atomic Energy Commission had recorded four blasts. Exposing this secrecy gave an additional value to VOA broadcasts on the subject.[63]

Meanwhile, the Kennedy administration pondered its response. Even before the Soviet move, the military pressed for the United States to resume its own atmospheric nuclear test program. The USIA had long stressed the importance of the U.S. commitment to disarmament. In a secret memo of 24 June, Murrow called the U.S. commitment to a nuclear test ban "a key, conceivably *the* key, to our Cold War posture in the coming year. Unless we persuade our allies and the uncommitted nations of the righteousness of our cause in this respect, we stand in grave danger of losing their support on other issues, notably Berlin." Any new American nuclear tests would take

---

[61] NA RG 59, State, CPF 1960–63, box 1046, 511.00/3-9-962, Rusk to Murrow, 8 March 1962 et seq. For Murrow's policy on the Sino-Soviet dispute see JFKL Salinger, box 132, USIA 1962, Murrow to all principal USIS posts, 20 June 1962, calling for publicity on the split, while taking care not to suggest that the United States either partial was or sought to widen it. In the autumn of 1963 the working group circulated a "Primer on Sino-Soviet Dissension" to all U.S. posts; see NA RG 59, State, CPF 1963, box 3267, INF 8 Psychological Political Working Group Minutes, 15 November 1963, item 1.

[62] *USIA 17th Review of Operations, 1 July–31 December 1961*, p. 15; JFKL POF, Depts. & Agencies: USIA, box 91, Murrow to President, 31 August 1961. The *Daily Express* version (2 September 1961) showed only the site and relative location of Western Europe, but associated articles dealt with the risk of fallout.

[63] JFKL VOA, reel 1, News Analysis, 1847, Raymond Swing, "The Soviet people are not told," 6 September 1961.

six months to prepare. Murrow proposed filling this time with a massive information effort to establish Soviet bad faith and the U.S. commitment to a test ban. Suggestions included a coordinated effort with the Macmillan government in London and even a CIA rumor campaign to suggest that any earthquakes or TNT explosions detected in the U.S.S.R. were actually illicit nuclear tests.[64]

In July 1961, Murrow argued that establishing America's commitment to the test ban was the first priority for the USIA.[65] Now that the Soviets had broken the truce on testing, Murrow argued against an immediate resumption of American tests. On 31 August he noted that a delay in resuming testing could "be used to isolate the Communist Bloc, frighten the satellites and the uncommitted, pretty well destroy the *Ban the Bomb* movement in Britain, and might even induce sanity into the SANE nuclear policy group in this country."[66] Developing his argument, on 1 September he wrote to the President,

> It is obvious that the longer we can delay our announcement, the greater the international political benefit. Our surveys of foreign press and radio indicate that the Soviet decision has been a tremendous political warfare windfall. Khrushchev has become the focus of fear. The United States is, for the time being, the repository of hope. Our posture should be a combination of restraint, reluctance, plus a determination to exhaust all possibilities before resorting to a competition, which may turn out to be uncontrollable.[67]

For the time being, at least, Kennedy followed Murrow's advice. The archival record suggests that it was his only decisive contribution to Kennedy's foreign policy-making.

The immediate audience for America's display of restraint was the conference of the twenty-four nonaligned states then meeting in Belgrade. Nehru obliged with a ringing denunciation of the Soviet tests. Murrow noted a general acceptance of the view expressed in the White House statement of 31 August that the new nuclear tests served no useful military purpose and amounted to "atomic blackmail." He referred Kennedy to Joseph Goebbels' dictum that "He who speaks the first word convinces much of the world."[68] Although the United States resumed underground tests on 15 September 1961, before the end of the month the USIA announced that the

64 JFKL USIA director file, reel 6, Murrow to Bowles, 24 June 1961, secret, "The Nuclear Test Ban Issue."
65 JFKL USIA, box 1, memoranda file 2, Murrow to heads of all agency elements/all USIS posts, "Special Program Emphasis," 24 July 1961: priorities were (1) test ban, (2) defense of West Berlin, (3) empowering the UN, (4) the West as the "world of free choice," and (4) the role of democracy in "modernization."
66 *FRUS 1961–1963*, Vol. VII, *Arms Control and Disarmament*, doc.59, Murrow to President, 31 August 1961; Considerations regarding nuclear testing. SANE (the National Committee for a Sane Nuclear policy) had been founded in 1957 by Norman Cousins and Clarence Pickett as a nonpartisan pressure group for restraint in nuclear policy. Early objectives included a nuclear test ban treaty and the U.S. disarmament administration. The organization's papers are held in the Swarthmore College Peace Collection.
67 JFKL USIA director file, reel 4, Murrow to President, Confidential, 1 September 1961.
68 JFKL POF, Depts. & Agencies: USIA, box 91, Murrow to President, 1 September 1961 and undated "reactions to nuclear tests." For text of White House statement of 31 August see *Public Papers of the Presidents: John F. Kennedy, 1961*, pp. 584–5.

United States had also established a Disarmament Administration, the world's first government agency dedicated to disarmament and peace.[69]

Tension over Berlin remained high. In the last week of October 1961, American and Soviet tanks faced each other nose-to-nose at Checkpoint Charlie. No sooner had the tanks rolled back than the Soviet tests reached a new crescendo. On 31 October, Russia detonated a fifty-megaton device. At the NSC meeting of 2 November, Secretary of Defense Robert McNamara demanded that the United States also resume immediate atmospheric testing. Murrow again insisted that Kennedy's best option would be to milk the propaganda value of the situation.[70] He noted that the United States "had a tremendous propaganda advantage" and "should make the most of it as long as possible."[71]

The VOA provided the centerpiece of the USIA's response to the nuclear tests with a one-hour documentary called *Have You Been Told?* designed to present the Soviet people with the facts of the tests and the danger of fallout getting into the food chain. The Talks and Features section of the VOA knew that the United States would soon resume its own tests and disliked the element of hypocrisy in the project. The section did its best to write a balanced script for the program, in keeping with the VOA's charter of 1960. A delegation of VOA director Henry Loomis, program manager Alex Klieforth, and the head of Talks and Features, Len Reed, took the script to Murrow's office for approval. To their dismay, Murrow pronounced their effort "dull." As Reed recalled, Wilson and Sorensen nodded in synchronous agreement: "dull." Wilson picked out a passage for particular scorn, apparently unaware that it was a direct quotation from the President. Murrow requested a revised script with increased ideological content and music to "hold an audience." Back at the VOA, Reed, Cliff Groce (from Central Program Services), and Ed Gordon hurriedly set to work on their typewriters, hammering out a revised broadcast, while Reed's secretary sustained them with martinis. They "hammed it up" and mixed in such innovations as sound effects. Now a dramatic explosion noise followed the ominous question *Have You Been Told?* and the whole piece was spiced with impassioned editorials from around the globe about the issue of poisonous fallout. Klieforth wondered whether the Voice could get away with such overt propaganda, but Murrow seemed happy.[72]

On Sunday, 5 November 1961, the VOA cancelled all of its regular programming to the U.S.S.R. and, again using the authority of NSAM 63, let rip with 4,331,000 watts of primetime propaganda over eight hours and eighty frequencies, the combined output of fifty-two transmitters in Russian, English, Ukrainian, Georgian, Armenian, Latvian, Estonian, and Lithuanian, including the 1,000,000 watt medium-wave transmitter at Munich. *Have You Been Told?* had been heavily advertised to avoid losing

---

[69] JFKL WHCF Subject file: FG296 USIA, box 184, Executive, Murrow to all posts, 27 September 1961.

[70] Richard Reeves, *President Kennedy: Profile of Power*, New York: Simon and Schuster, 1993, p. 251.

[71] Persico, *Murrow*, p. 476.

[72] Interviews: Len Reed, 12 December 1995; Cliff Groce, 30 November 1995; Alex Klieforth, 7 January 1997.

regular listeners in Eastern Europe. The VOA expected the Soviets to mobilize their 2,000 noise transmitters to jam the Voice's frequencies.[73] In the event, the jammers seemed less efficient than expected. The English language channel remained open as usual, and only the Armenian version failed to get through altogether. The VOA's director, Henry Loomis, speculated, "perhaps they [the jammers] have Sunday off too." On some frequencies the jammers switched off their noise for long enough to allow the key message to get through. In the final analysis the USIA believed that the broadcast was audible on at least half of the frequencies used, even in the most heavily jammed areas. Some listeners even reported hearing the program on car radios.[74] The program had shown the power of radio, but the role of the USIA director in shaping its content did not sit well with the staff at the VOA, especially after the field noted that Russian audiences preferred broadcasts with a less strident tone. Loomis and his team felt that their initial concern had been justified. The USIA and VOA had shifted onto a collision course.[75]

On 20 November, the test ban talks reopened in Geneva. By February the Kennedy administration had resolved to resume its own atmospheric tests, but the National Security Council saw lively debate over the best way of announcing the decision and timing the tests.[76] Kennedy handled the announcement perfectly. In a television and radio address to the nation on the evening of 2 March 1962, he presented a detailed argument to support the American intention to resume atmospheric tests unless the U.S.S.R. signed a test ban. The U.S. tests recommenced on 25 April 1962, but the image of the United States remained substantially intact. Despite the absolute supremacy of the United States in nuclear weapons, a USIA survey of global media reaction suggested that the world accepted Kennedy's decision as the act of a moderate man doing the minimum to keep pace with an aggressive opponent.[77] Other trends in world opinion caused the USIA concern. Although polls suggested growing Western European confidence in America's world leadership and "dedication to peace," the same nations also believed that the U.S.S.R. was militarily stronger than the United States and ahead in the "space race."[78] An eleven-country Gallup survey in October

[73] JFKL WHCF: Subject file, National Defense, ND21–1, box 640, Executive, USIA press release, 1 November 1962; POF, Depts. & Agencies: USIA, box 290, general, Murrow to Bundy, 30 October 1961. RFE and RL remained on the air, but broadcast special programs of their own on the same theme. The USIA asked the BBC to do the same. Later in the week versions of the same program aired in Czech, Hungarian, and other Eastern European languages.

[74] *USIA 17th Review of Operations, 1 July–31 December 1961*, pp. 16–18; JFKL VOA microfilm, reel 5, Loomis to Murrow, IBS Monthly Report, 18 December 1961. On extent of jamming see NA RG59, State CPF 1960–63; box 1064, Moscow 1455, 522.604/11–561, Thompson to USIA, 5 November 1961.

[75] Interview: Groce; JFKL VOA microfilm, reel 5, Loomis to Murrow, IBS Monthly Report, 18 December 1961.

[76] JFKL NSF, Meetings and Memoranda, box 313, folder 29, Memo to President, top secret, The National Security Council Meeting on Testing, 27 February 1962.

[77] JFKL POF, Depts. & Agencies: USIA, box 91, USIA Research and Reference Service, "Reaction to the Presidential Announcement on Nuclear Testing," R-21–62, 6 March 1962; Murrow to President, 3 August 1962; *Public Papers of the Presidents, John F. Kennedy, 1962*, pp. 186–93.

[78] JFKL POF, Depts. & Agencies: USIA, box 91, ORA report WE-1, "The Current State of Confidence in the U.S. among the West European Public," August 1961; Wilson to President, "Western European

1961 found that in nine countries a majority of respondents placed the U.S.S.R. ahead in the Cold War.[79] Such sentiments could not be changed overnight.

2) REPRESENTING AMERICA IN 1962
USIA FILM AND CIVIL RIGHTS

The year 1962 began with a celebration. On 26 February, President Kennedy visited the Voice's building to mark the VOA's twentieth birthday. In a speech relayed around the world he endorsed the station's opening pledge from 1942, "The news may be good or bad. We shall tell you the truth," and supported the role of the radio station in presenting a balanced view of America, embracing imperfection as well as ideals and diversity as well as unity.[80] Murrow echoed these themes, noting, "Voice of America stands upon this above all: the truth shall be the guide."[81] The year brought both the USIA and the VOA many opportunities to present both imperfection and uncomfortable truth.

The USIA continued to make great play on the space program. In February 1962, the Voice of America mounted a massive effort to broadcast full coverage of John Glenn's orbital flight. The USIA provided documentary support and arranged a global tour for Glenn's Friendship Seven capsule. Slowly the agency made up ground lost to the Soviet Union. What the country still lacked in execution it made up for in openness and ambition; in September Kennedy declared that ambition to be landing a man on the moon within the decade.[82]

The Exhibition Service followed up the success in Moscow in 1959 with touring exhibitions in the Eastern bloc, including Transport U.S.A. and Medicine U.S.A. In 1962 alone these attracted three million visitors.[83] *America Illustrated* remained in high demand in the U.S.S.R. The agency produced 55,000 copies of the fifth anniversary issue and noted that copies of the magazine regularly changed hands on the black market at six times the official price.[84] In Latin America, the agency filled 1,235,000 orders for its latest propaganda comic book, dealing with the experiences of children in Cuba. The year 1962 saw the inauguration of the agency's third Regional

Public Confidence in the United States," 19 October 1961: in Britain 56% answered U.S.S.R. to the question: "which country do you think is ahead in total military strength at the present time – the U.S. or the U.S.S.R.?" and 78% believed the U.S.S.R. to be ahead in space.

79   JFKL Salinger papers, box 132, 1961 file, USIA, Wilson to President, Weekly Report, 17 October 1961. The average split was 29% for Russia winning, 14% West, 22% neither, and 35% no opinion. The other countries surveyed were the United States, the United Kingdom, Ireland, Vietnam, West Germany, Holland, France, Finland, and Uruguay.

80   JFKL WHCF – subject file, box 184, FG 296 USIA, Executive, Wilson to Hatcher, 23 February 1962.

81   Tufts University, Murrow papers, reel 45, text of remarks, 26 February 1962.

82   *18th and 19th Review of Operations*; *Public Papers of the Presidents*, pp. 668–71, Address at Rice University, Houston, 12 September 1962.

83   JFKL USIA box 1, Memoranda file 3, Office of Public Information to USIA employees, 28 October 1963, "Some changes in USIA since March 1961," p. 13.

84   JFKL POF, Depts. & Agencies: USIA, box 91, Wilson to President, 18 August 1961 and 23 January 1962. The Soviet government allowed only 52,000 copies of *Amerika* to be sold. The remaining 3,000 were given away at exhibitions.

Service Center, this time located in Mexico City and dedicated to printing material for use in Latin America.[85] In Thailand, the USIA promoted the spread of community television sets into the interior; in Indonesia, it worked to establish chairs of American studies in colleges and universities.[86] At the suggestion of Robert Kennedy, global themes included a renewed attention to youth as a target audience. The Office of Policy duly acquired a Youth and Student Affairs officer.[87] But the most dramatic transformation came, as one might expect in an agency run by a television journalist, in the field of film and television propaganda.

Ed Murrow understood the degree to which film created the international image of the United States. He also believed that neither the stodgy and ideologically charged USIA film output of the 1950s nor the sensationalism of Hollywood film served the best interests of American foreign policy overseas, and took steps to change things. In November 1961, Murrow traveled to Los Angeles to cajole the leading lights of Hollywood into producing feature films that avoided mere escapism and showed the United States in a good light. "Movies," Murrow warned a gathering of film makers on 5 November, "are doing a lot of harm to America. They convey the notion that America is a country of millionaires and crooks."[88] At the same time he began the search for a dynamic head for the motion picture branch. No sooner had he begun his search than a suitable candidate presented himself. A young film producer named George Stevens Jr. (the son of the legendary director of such classics as *Shane*) approached Murrow with a proposal for a USIA documentary on Jacqueline Kennedy's imminent visit to Pakistan.[89] Murrow swiftly realized that he had found both his producer and an ideal prestige project. Stevens offered a unique combination of youth, energy, and Hollywood connections. January 1962 found Stevens taking the reins of USIA film production in Washington, DC. He pledged to "improve the quality of USIA films" and "strengthen" the agency's "relationships with the film industry." The Jackie Kennedy film became his pilot project.[90]

Jackie Kennedy's European tour of June 1961 had been one of the year's few unqualified propaganda successes. She seemed to represent the pinnacle of the American way of life. Jackie's visit to Pakistan seemed an ideal opportunity for a film to showcase America's interest in the developing world. To avoid offending India, Stevens also planned a parallel documentary on her visit to that country as well. Although obliged to assign the project to the lowest bidder – in this case Hearst

85   *FRUS 1961–1963*, Vol. X, doc. 347, Lansdale, Progress: Operation MONGOOSE, 14 June 1962.
86   *FRUS 1961–1963*, Vol. XXIII, South East Asia, doc. 289, Murrow to Rusk, 14 September 1962; doc. 414, State to Embassy Bangkok, 8 July 1961.
87   Interview: Washburn; JFKL Salinger papers, box 132, USIA 1962, Murrow to President, 28 August 1962; *20th Review of Operations, 1 January–31 June 1963*, pp. 18–21, 28–35.
88   "Murrow Furrows H'wood Brow – Criticizes 'Image' of U.S. Abroad Created by Films ...," *Variety*, 6 November 1961, and "H'wood Asks Murrow Provide Consultant to Mirror 'Image,'" *Variety*, 7 November 1961.
89   Interviews: George Stevens Jr. (10 and 14 April 1998).
90   JFKL Salinger papers, box 132, 1961 file USIA, Wilson to President, weekly report (Secret), 9 January 1961 noted that Stevens' experience included work as a producer on *The Greatest Story Ever Told* and *Diary of Anne Frank*, both directed by his father.

Metrotone – Stevens persuaded them to allow an independent, Academy Award-winning documentarist, Leo Seltzer, to direct the films. The resulting films, *Invitation to Pakistan* and *Invitation to India*, fulfilled Stevens' hopes. They mixed exquisite views of India and Pakistan with images of Jackie's tour. At the suggestion of the deputy PAO in New Delhi, VOA veteran Barry Zorthian, Seltzer played up Jackie's contact with ordinary people. In fact, through judicious cutting, the film suggested rather more contact with "ordinary" India than had been possible. The soundtrack used much local music, though an Indian linguist at the USIA recommended against the inclusion of a folk song captured at an Indian railway station; the lyrics were monumentally obscene.[91]

The South Asian newspapers showered praise on the two films, but unfortunately, the U.S. press could not see beyond the price tag of $73,000. The criticism shook Stevens. At one point he found himself sitting – head in hands – in Washington, DC's Dupont Circle, terrified that his initiative at the USIA had done more harm than good. Fortunately the White House blunted the criticism by persuading sympathetic columnists to describe the films as excellent value for money.[92] The USIA rushed to release the films in seventy-eight countries in multiple language versions. Kennedy admired the films and suggested a domestic release. By December Congress had provided the requisite permission. United Artists handled the distribution and released the film in a single thirty-minute edited version entitled *Jacqueline Kennedy's Asian Journey*. The critical response was warm enough to justify the USIA spending. Stevens had been vindicated.[93]

Stevens planned to develop the USIA's film output by recruiting the best young documentary filmmakers and developing a "school" along the lines of that which had flourished in Britain in the 1930s. He even arranged for John Grierson, the prophet of the British movement, to visit the USIA and cast a grandfatherly eye over the heirs to his tradition. To build a sense of a documentary heritage, Stevens also screened classic films from the National Film Board of Canada and the U.S. government's own films from the 1930s.[94]

It was a testament to the bipartisan spirit of the Kennedy years that Stevens united the talents of established filmmakers from across the political spectrum, including James Blue, a Paris-trained liberal, whose early work focused on life in Algeria; Charles Guggenheim, a director/producer who had worked for Adlai Stevenson; and Bruce Herschensohn, a "Goldwater conservative" from California, whose specialty had hitherto been making documentary films about missiles for the defense industry. Stevens

---

[91] Interview: Leo Seltzer, 6 April 1998. For a full treatment of this film see Nicholas J. Cull, "Projecting Jackie: Kennedy Administration Film Propaganda Overseas in Leo Seltzer's *Invitation to India, Invitation to Pakistan* and *Jacqueline Kennedy's Asian Journey* (1962)," in Bertrand Taithe and Tim Thornton (eds.), *Propaganda: Political Rhetoric and Identity, 1300–2000*, Stroud, Gloucestershire: Sutton, 1999, pp. 307–26.
[92] Interview: Stevens; Cull, "Projecting Jackie," pp. 312–14.
[93] Interview: Stevens; Cull, "Projecting Jackie," pp. 318–20.
[94] For a survey of the Stevens period at the USIA see Richard Dyer MacCann, *The People's Films: A Political History of U.S. Government Motion Pictures*, New York: Hastings House, 1973. Interviews: Stevens, Guggenheim, and Herschensohn.

also drew in Terry and Denis Sanders, who had won the best short subject Oscar for their 1954 Civil War film *A Time Out of War*. All would distinguish themselves.

Older contributors to the new initiative at the USIA included Seltzer[95] and some of the best filmmakers then working in the commercial newsreels, such the Dutch-born Walter de Hoog of Hearst. Within the agency Stevens drew on the administrative talents of his capable deputy Tony Guarco. Much USIA work happened at the home facilities of the filmmakers who accepted USIA contracts (Herschensohn worked in California and Guggenheim in St. Louis), but Stevens also developed in-house production with the USIA intern program. Early recruits included Jerry Krell and Meyer Odze, who would continue to make films into the administration of George W. Bush; Carroll Ballard, who later distinguished himself as a feature film maker specializing in working with animals; and Donald Wrye, who wrote and directed the notorious 1987 miniseries for ABC television, *Amerika*, which imagined a Soviet invasion of the United States. Such crudity had no place in Stevens' USIA.[96]

Under Stevens' guidance, these filmmakers created a genre of propaganda film dubbed by *Newsweek* the "soft policy" film. The films typically showed the human side of one of the issues then central to the USIA. Early examples included films in support of the Alliance for Progress. James Blue made *The School of Rincon Santo*, *Letter from Columbia*, and in 1963 *Evil Wind Out*, dealing with a Colombian doctor's overcoming of superstition in his practice. In the same cause Bruce Herschensohn offered *Bridges of the Barrios*, narrated by Paul Newman.[97] Seltzer added a more conventional contribution: an account of Kennedy's visit to Mexico called *Progress through Freedom*. Other regular subjects for USIA films during the era included the space program and divided Berlin. Walter de Hoog's powerful short documentary *The Wall* depicted ordinary life in the shadow of the Berlin Wall; Leo Seltzer's *The American Commitment* demonstrated USIA support for the free flow of news around the word, taking the story of the death of a refugee on the wall as its case. Meanwhile, Bruce Herschensohn's film of John Glenn's flight, *Friendship Seven*, commissioned by NASA, became a much-appreciated addition to the USIA repertoire.[98]

The policy sections of the USIA had minimal input into these films. As Charles Guggenheim recalled, they might generate a general idea for a film and brief the filmmaker before he began work on a project, but they did little else until the final stages of production. Krell suspected that he had more freedom than ninety percent of

[95] Seltzer's other USIA films included *Saturn, Space Vehicle* and *Gemini 4* (both 1964) on space; *Poland Abroad* (1964) on a touring exhibition about Polish-American culture; *Day in Malaysia* (1964) on LBJ's visit to that country; *Summit* (1964) on the Punte del Este economic assistance conference; *Sinews of Freedom* (1966) on the economy of Taiwan; and two visit films made as gifts for the leaders featured: *Crown Prince of Laos Visits America* and *A Visit of the President of Tsirinana* (Malagasy Republic) (1968). With the advent of Nixon, Seltzer redirected his talents to teaching, serving on the faculty of the College of Staten Island, Columbia University, and the Philadelphia College of Art before ending his career as Professor of Film at Brooklyn College.

[96] Interviews: Krell, Odze, Herschensohn, de Hoog.

[97] NA MPSVB, RG 306.5915, *The School of Rincon Santo*; RG 306.3321, *Letter from Columbia*; RG306.338, *Evil Wind Out*. Interviews: Stevens and Herschensohn.

[98] Interviews: Seltzer and Stevens.

filmmakers working for the U.S. networks at the time. As the film neared completion, the various USIA area directors would gather for a screening of the "interlock" print. At this stage all hell could break loose with various political criticisms from the floor. Guggenheim suspected that the regional specialists felt compelled to exhibit some sort of insight in front of their colleagues. Fortunately, Stevens became a master of defending the artistic integrity of his filmmakers' work. He knew he could count on Murrow to support his decisions.[99]

While Stevens ran the USIA films, Charles Hill oversaw television output. Hill, a producer from NBC, arrived in 1962 as part of the wave of Kennedy-era volunteerism. Hill's unit provided policy-related programs for placement around the world, producing to astonishingly tight schedules with in-house, regionally specific capacity rather than using contractors like the film branch. Success stories included a thirteen-part series for Japan on everyday life in the United States – *World Americana* – and a fifteen-minute weekly political discussion program in Spanish and Portuguese – *Panorama Panamericano* – which by 1963 could be seen in nineteen Latin American countries. The USIA also helped program makers from about the world and claimed particular credit for assisting with French and Italian programs on the civil rights issue. Hill left the USIA in the summer of 1963. NBC had begun to screen his series *Espionage* and he feared that their plans to sell the program abroad might cause a "conflict of interest" with his USIA work.[100]

USIA continued to produce newsreels, often in languages such as Lao for which a newsreel would not otherwise be commercially viable. The agency also maintained the classified project codenamed "Kingfish" through which the agency subsidized MGM's commercial newsreel, then playing in twenty-eight countries across Africa and Asia, supplying funding and footage of politically useful events. As Stevens recalled, 80 percent of this material would probably have been used anyway, but the project served as a useful channel to a massive viewing public.[101] Other covert projects included an entire unattributed newsreel produced for use in the Congo.[102] In the course of 1962 the USIA produced 36 films within the United States and a further 147 overseas and issued 197 newsreels. They had 50,000 film prints in circulation in 106 countries, reaching an estimated audience of 600 million people.[103] The agency also managed American participation in international film festivals. Stevens made good use of films that showed America facing up to its social and racial problems, such as Stanley Kramer's *The Defiant Ones* (1958), featuring the actor who personified the struggle

[99]   Interviews: Guggenheim, Stevens, Krell.
[100] JFKL USIA box 1, Memoranda file 3, Office of Public Information to USIA employees, 28 October 1963, "Some changes in USIA since March 1961," p. 16. *New York Times*, 19 June 1963, p. 75. Interview: Ashley Hawken, 17 September 2007. An early transatlantic co-production with Britain's ATV, *Espionage* ran for 24 episodes including 3 directed by the British filmmaker Michael Powell.
[101] LBJL WHCF CF, box 135, CF USIA, Wilson to President, 27 November 1963; interview: Stevens, 10 April 1998.
[102] JFKL Salinger papers, box 132, USIA 1962, Murrow to President, 18 December 1962.
[103] Seltzer papers, *Journal of the SMPTE (Society of Motion Picture and Television Engineers)*, Vol. 72, p. 374.

of the African American in that period, Sidney Poitier.[104] The USIA's own films on the subject of the civil rights struggle proved a valuable addition to the wider agency effort on the subject of American race relations.

*

The issue of race dominated the Kennedy era at the USIA. The first crisis came on 14 May 1961 when members of the Ku Klux Klan intercepted a bus in the vicinity of Anniston, Alabama carrying the Freedom Riders, blacks and whites who challenged local segregation laws by the simple act of sitting together in busses and terminals. The Klan burned the bus and savagely beat its occupants.[105] Voice of America, like every other major news carrier, reported the violence. The U.S. embassy in Moscow objected. It fell to Chester Bowles at the State Department to defend the VOA, insisting that the broadcasts had been "handled as well as a difficult story could be and in a manner designed [to] advance VOA credibility and place [the] incident in perspective for a foreign audience."[106] The wider USIA coverage of these events in Alabama followed the established pattern. As Murrow explained, "USIA policy has been to stick to hard news, playing down the violence and emphasizing federal action to protect the civil rights of Negro citizens."[107] Observers relying only on USIA sources for their picture of the African-American civil rights movement would have the impression that the hero of the civil rights era was the federal government, which came to the aid of the distressed black citizens. Although the USIA's analysts recorded a massive wave of international revulsion against the racial attacks in Alabama, the agency drew satisfaction from evidence that the world understood that Kennedy wanted to help. That help was painfully slow to materialize.[108]

Civil rights issues also had a practical impact on USIA activity. The indignities heaped on African diplomats assigned to the segregated city of Washington, DC hurt the agency's approach to Africa. In an address to the National Press Club, Murrow pointed out that at least thirty African diplomats currently lived in "unsatisfactory housing" because white landlords would not rent to them. Ominously, he quoted Shakespeare's *Merchant of Venice*: "If you wrong us shall we not revenge?" Agency and State Department guidance appealed to other sections of the American bureaucracy to be tactful when handling African visitors. They flagged trips to African-American ghettos and tales of how much one appreciated the cook when growing up as particularly counterproductive.[109]

104 Interview: George Stevens Jr., 14 April 1998.
105 Taylor Branch, *Parting the Waters: America in the King Years, 1954–63*, New York: Simon and Schuster, 1988, pp. 419–24.
106 JFKL NSF, Confidential, U.S.S.R., General, box 177, Bowles to Moscow, Confidential, 2006, 18 May 1961, as drafted by J. R. O'Brien, IBS (VOA).
107 JFKL Salinger papers, box 132, 1961 file, USIA, Murrow to President, 23 May 1961.
108 JFKL USIA director's papers, reel 6, Murrow to Adam Clayton Powell, 21 June 1961, with attached "report summary worldwide reaction to racial incidents in Alabama."
109 JFKL POF, Depts. & Agencies: USIA, box 91, address by Murrow, "Who Speaks for America?" 24 May 1961.

Murrow urged Kennedy to open the space program to black astronauts. When NASA argued that it only trained qualified test pilots, Murrow pressed Kennedy to begin training black test pilots as well.[110] While NASA dragged its feet, the USIA led the way in hiring African-Americans.[111] Between 1960 and 1963, the number of black Americans in the USIA's career service doubled. By the end of the Kennedy years, black people held one in ten of all senior and middle-grade USIA career posts.[112] The USIA used these officers extensively in African work. The presence of black staff enabled the agency to give a positive racial spin to otherwise "white" subjects such as the space program. The USIA hired two black "special lecturers" to present the space program to schools and universities around Africa. The English-language lecturer John Twitty, recruited in 1962, had previously worked as a journalist for the African-American press, including *Ebony* magazine and a spell as city editor for *Amsterdam News*. As Twitty recalled, after six months training with NASA he spent two years on the road in Africa with a selection of models, diagrams, and other visual aids, presenting a one-hour lecture on the space program. He even appeared on children's television in Nigeria. His skin color added another level to the operation, although he soon discovered that his audiences knew little of black American life. Nigerian school children regularly asked whether he was a slave and applauded when he told them that he was free. A group of Muslim pupils asked him to sing a spiritual. Twitty obliged them with an appropriate song, before beginning his usual lecture.[113]

Voice of America carried talks on the racial situation from a number of key figures in the civil rights movement, including Roy Wilkins of the NAACP and James Farmer, National Director of CORE, the Congress For Racial Equality, and the USIA distributed images and speeches detailing their activities. The USIA gave careful context to this coverage. The agency always stressed the wider background of Black American progress; agency events in 1962 included a multinational conference on this subject held in Paris for foreign opinion leaders. Second, the USIA claimed the civil rights movement as a positive expression of the American democratic spirit.[114] VOA news analyses praised Martin Luther King Jr., but presented his protest as within the framework of the American religious and political tradition, and as supportive of federal action on civil rights rather than being the cause of it. An analysis of 10 July 1963 by the veteran correspondent Larry LeSueur quoted King saying that Kennedy"s "strong, meaningful and far-reaching" civil rights program would, if implemented, "go a long way toward making the American Dream a reality."[115]

USIA concern over the civil rights issue peaked in the spring of 1963 when black protests in Birmingham, Alabama produced a backlash of white police violence. While

[110] Persico, *Murrow*, p. 483, Sperber, *Murrow*, p. 657.
[111] JFKL WHCF subject file FG 296 USIA, box 184, Executive, Wilson to Frank D. Reeves, 9 May 1961.
[112] LBJL, Panzer papers, box 469, USIA, summary memo: "United States Information Agency," 1 October 1963.
[113] Interview: John Twitty, by telephone, 15 November 2000.
[114] *19th Review of Operations, 1 July–31 December 1962*, pp. 14–17.
[115] JFKL VOA reel 4, Larry LeSueur, News Analysis 3146, "The Philosophy of Martin Luther King," 10 July 1963.

the news cameras rolled, the Birmingham police department used high-pressure fire hoses and dogs to disperse demonstrators. The world press recoiled in horror. In Paris the usually sympathetic Socialist paper *Populaire* proclaimed, "Violence in Alabama, a dishonor for the US."[116] As violence escalated with the murder of civil rights activist Medger Evers and mass jailing of protestors, Communist bloc propaganda went into overdrive. Radio Moscow devoted twenty percent of its coverage to the story and reported that "racist . . . storm troop detachments" marched through the streets and African-Americans were being "herded into concentration camps of the Buchenwald and Auschwitz pattern."[117] Chinese sources warned Asia to heighten its "vigilance against the sweet words of the United States Imperialists" and take note of "their filthy deeds."[118] The President's address on the issue on 11 June attracted more positive reporting. The *Morning Post* of Nigeria praised Kennedy as "one of the greatest champions of the rights of man that ever lived." A Singapore paper dubbed Kennedy "the most enlightened president of the United States since Lincoln."[119] The USIA found the station in Dhahran, Saudi Arabia unwilling to air the 11 June speech, fearing it might "offend" the government.[120]

The March on Washington in August 1963 fitted easily into the USIA approach to civil rights. The symbolism of the location helped associate the ideals of the march with Federal policy. The VOA built up to the event with interviews. The English language "Dateline" rebroadcast "Meet the Press" programs featuring Roy Wilkins and Martin Luther King Jr. and a "Press Conference U.S.A." featured the March's originator, A. Philip Randolph. Coverage of the march itself included on-the-spot running reports in English and Swahili, and coverage took over the entire East African service for the day. The Hindi service stressed the triumph of Gandhian nonviolence, whereas the Chinese service paid particular attention to the radical speaker James Farmer, who pointedly rejected an offer of aid from Mao Tse Tung.[121] The USIA supported this coverage with written reports and photographs. The agency immediately shipped film of both the event and follow-up discussions with participants.[122] But a 35 mm documentary film formed the centerpiece of the USIA's coverage. George Stevens assembled a team of his own interns and contracted cameramen from Hearst to film the event under the direction of James Blue. The film would not be ready until early 1964. It would become a focus for familiar controversy.

---

116   NA RG 59 State CPF 1960–63, box 3269, INF France, Embassy Paris to State Department, 8 May 1963.

117   JFKL POF, Depts. & Agencies: USIA, box 91, Sorensen to President, "Reactions to your civil rights Speech," 14 June 1963; Salinger papers, box 132, USIA 1963, Wilson to President, 14 May 1963.

118   NA RG 59 State CPF 1960–63, box 3271, INF 11 PAK, Embassy Karachi to Dept. of State, 22 June 1963.

119   JFKL POF, Depts. & Agencies: USIA, box 91, Sorensen to President, "Reactions to your civil rights Speech," 14 June 1963.

120   NA RG 59 State CPF 1960–1963, box 3267, INF8 VOA, Horner to Rusk, 18 June 1963.

121   JFKL VOA reel 11, Loomis to Murrow, 24 September 1963, IBS Monthly Report, August 1963; for news analyses of the March see reel 4.

122   JFKL Schlesinger papers, box WH 48, USIA (confidential subject file), Murrow to President, Weekly Report, 27 August 1963.

3) THE CUBAN MISSILE CRISIS

On 14 October 1962, a U-2 spy plane flying over Cuba photographed what appeared to be launch sites for Soviet nuclear missiles. The NSC anticipated that such missiles posed not only an obvious strategic threat to the United States but also, as McGeorge Bundy argued in August 1962, a substantial psychological threat to the U.S. regional and global standing.[123] On 16 October, President Kennedy assembled an executive committee of the National Security Council to ponder the U.S. response to Khrushchev's gambit. The Cuban missile crisis had begun.[124]

The ExCom did not originally include a representative from the USIA. Eventually Don Wilson represented the agency, Ed Murrow being sick with what proved to be lung cancer. The agency's first involvement came at 6 p.m. on Friday, 19 October, when Assistant Secretary of State George Ball summoned Wilson and asked him to find a way to ensure that the Cuban people could hear Kennedy's speech on the crisis. At the meeting the following day, attended by Wilson, Kennedy decided that the best date would be that coming Monday. Wilson prepared in secret. He had permission to discuss the matter with only Loomis at the VOA, Sorensen in Policy and Plans, and the assistant director for Latin America, Hewson Ryan.[125]

Wilson believed that the key to the crisis lay in ensuring that the world understood the U.S. position. There could be no room for mixed signals where nuclear missiles were involved. For this reason, Wilson decided to take the unprecedented step of taking direct control of the Voice of America. On the morning of Sunday, 21 October, Wilson called old USIA hand Burnett Anderson into his office and instructed him to "go down to the Voice of America now, and stay there until further notice . . . You are personally responsible for every word said on the air." Anderson arrived at the VOA to find Henry Loomis on the brink of resignation after finding his authority suspended. Anderson assured Loomis that he had no desire to supplant him and tactfully allowed Loomis to retain his office and secretarial support. Anderson took a desk in the "mouth" of the Voice of America: the VOA news room. From that point until the end of the crisis, nothing went on the air without his approval. He had no hesitation in killing stories that he felt likely to be counterproductive.[126] Concerns included not only misrepresenting the American position to the Soviet Union but also encouraging the Cuban people in an incautious uprising.[127]

---

[123]   JFKL NSF, Meetings and Memoranda, box 338, file on NSAM 181, Bundy to Kennedy, Top Secret and Sensitive, 31 August 1962 (reproduced in *FRUS 1961–1963*, Vol. X, document 331 m).

[124]   JFKL NSF, Meetings and Memoranda, box 339, NSAM 196, Establishment of Executive Committee of the NSC, Bundy to Miss Baldrige, 31 October 1962.

[125]   JFKL Interview: Donald Wilson, 2 September 1964; interview: Don Wilson; Persico, *Murrow*, p. 484.

[126]   Interview: Burnett Anderson, 14 December 1995; ADST Oral History, Anderson; interview: Bernie Kamenske, 6 December 1995. Anderson and Loomis worked well together during the crisis and, in later years, Loomis invited Anderson to serve as his deputy at the Corporation for Public Broadcasting.

[127]   Gary D. Rawnsley, *Radio Diplomacy and Propaganda: The BBC and VOA in International Politics, 1956–64*, London: Macmillan, 1996, p. 119.

On 22 October, the VOA carried President Kennedy's speech on the Cuban crisis to the world. He publicly revealed the existence of the missile sites and his intention of blockading Cuba.[128] Wilson's secret efforts over the weekend ensured that Cuba heard the speech live. Wilson knew that he would get an even larger audience if he used medium-wave transmitters as well as shortwave. Working with Pierre Salinger at the White House and, from Monday morning, Newton Minow of the Federal Communications Commission, he selected eight of the most powerful transmitters in cities as far apart as Key West, Cincinnati, and New Orleans, whose signals could be heard in Cuba at night. Without telling the stations, they arranged for White House telecommunications experts to secretly install landlines to the stations. At around 6 pm on Monday, 22 October, each of the station presidents received a call from Salinger asking them to clear their airwaves for a broadcast at seven. He could not give exact details but stressed the national security interest. They agreed and surrendered their airtime that night (and for as many nights as necessary) to carry a VOA Spanish language feed. For the next three weeks, the VOA broadcast in the hours of darkness on these stations and round the clock in Spanish on thirty-three shortwave frequencies.[129]

On 23 October, the USIA used the new communications satellite Telstar to transmit pictures of the President's speech to Europe. On 25 October, the VOA mounted a "Truth Barrage," using fifty-two transmitters and 4,331,000 watts of power to send Kennedy's speech of 22 October in ten Eastern bloc languages deep into the Soviet sphere. Regular VOA programming noted that the Soviet press had not told readers about nuclear missile sites on Cuba, and the Cubans had not been told that the Organization of American States had upheld Kennedy's decision to quarantine their island.[130]

The USIA's other media distributed a stream of speeches and translated statements to justify the American action. USIA motion pictures produced film versions of Kennedy's crisis speech and a daily five-minute film commentary on developments, for placement with television stations around the world.[131] At the core of the agency's effort was the portfolio of fourteen U-2 photographs showing the installations on Cuba. As Wilson recalled, the new CIA director, John McCone, wanted to conceal the full U.S. photographic capability and had refused to release the pictures. Kennedy needed persuasion from Don Wilson, Pierre Salinger, and others before he agreed to overrule McCone, but on Wednesday, 24 October, the White House passed the images to the press and television networks. The USIA distributed some 50,000 prints around the world. Salinger later spoke of the distribution of these pictures as "the best thing that ever happened. Those pictures played a major role in persuading foreign opinion that the President was justified in taking action."[132] The USIA's Research and

[128] *Public Papers of the Presidents, John F. Kennedy, 1962*, pp. 806–9.
[129] JFKL Interview: Donald Wilson, 2 September 1964; interview, Wilson; JFKL NSF, CO Cuba, Box 37, General, Wilson to Kennedy, 2 November 1962.
[130] *19th Review of Operations, 1 July–31 December 1962*, pp. 5–12.
[131] *19th Review of Operations, 1 July–31 December 1962*, pp. 6–8.
[132] Interview: Don Wilson, 2 July 1996; Robert Smith Thompson, *The Missiles of October: The Declassified Story of John F. Kennedy and the Cuban Missile Crisis*, New York: Simon and Schuster, 1992, pp. 298–9. JFKL Interview: Donald Wilson, 2 September 1964, pp. 22–3.

Reference Service noted an especially marked shift in the British press toward the administration's position.[133]

Just as the U.S. used the VOA as a channel for reaching the U.S.S.R., so the Soviets used Radio Moscow as a channel for their replies. On 27 October, Radio Moscow carried a message from Khrushchev to Kennedy containing suggested terms for a resolution of the crisis. On the morning of Sunday, 28 October, a second message from the Soviet Premier noted that he had ordered the "weapons which you describe as 'offensive' to be dismantled, packed up and returned to the Soviet Union." Responding to a simultaneous translation of Khrushchev's words, Kennedy broadcast his "welcome" for "Chairman Khrushchev's statesmanlike decision." The worst of the Cuban missile crisis had passed.[134]

Despite Khrushchev's retreat, the ExCom still needed to manage the aftermath of the crisis. To maintain a consistent picture of American foreign policy, Kennedy authorized only White House sources Pierre Salinger, McGeorge Bundy, and Ted Sorensen to speak to the domestic press. Burnett Anderson remained at his post at the VOA. At the ExCom, Don Wilson raised the issue of Cuban exiles, who wanted to buy time on domestic U.S. radio stations in order to broadcast their own views to the island. Assuming that they would attempt to foment an uprising, Kennedy authorized Wilson to take the matter to Minow at the FCC to find a discreet way of blocking any such broadcasts.[135] The VOA took extreme care with all of its programming. On 31 October, Wilson told the ExCom that the Voice was avoiding "gloating . . . in either content or tone" or any "denunciatory anti-Communist materials that might upset the Russians." The agency also killed any speculation on the future of the Castro regime. Kennedy approved and requested that the entire administration avoid attacks on Castro for the rest of the week.[136]

By mid-November, Murrow had returned from sick leave and Loomis had resumed command of the VOA. Cuba remained a major target for its broadcasts. Although the VOA released the eight commercial medium-wave channels that it had commandeered for the duration of the crisis, it shifted programming to two specially relocated fifty-kilowatt medium wave transmitters in Florida. The USIA continued to purchase airtime at commercial Florida stations, as they had previously sold airtime to Cuban exile groups and this seemed like the best way of keeping the militant anti-Castro voices off the air. Murrow also informed the President that the USIA now had access to two Defense Department DC-6 aircraft capable of transmitting television programs

[133] JFKL Salinger papers, box 29, Cuba (overseas reaction), RRS report R-126–62 (A), Overseas Reaction to the Cuban Situation, 27 October 1962.
[134] Rawnsley, *Radio Diplomacy and Propaganda*, pp. 130–36; *Public Papers of the Presidents, John F. Kennedy, 1962*, pp. 814–15; Thompson, *The Missiles of October*, pp. 341–2.
[135] JFKL NSF, Meetings and Memoranda, box 316, Executive Committee, Meetings Vol. II, ExCom meeting No. 13, 30 October 1962.
[136] JFKL NSF, Meetings and Memoranda, box 316, Executive Committee, Meetings Vol. II, ExCom meeting No. 15, 31 October 1962; JFKL NSF, Countries, box 37, Cuba, General, Wilson to Bromley Smith (executive secretary, NSC), 31 October 1962.

into Cuba or jamming Castro's own programming. As the Cubans could be expected to mount effective jamming after ten days, Murrow proposed holding the planes in reserve for an emergency.[137]

The Cuban missile crisis did nothing to enhance the relationship between the USIA and the Voice. In the aftermath of the crisis, VOA director Loomis broached his concern over the level of USIA control and State Department influence in a letter to Murrow. Despite personal respect for Burnett Anderson, and acceptance that news had been largely unaffected, Loomis regretted the degree to which VOA commentaries had been shaped by the USIA. This left little room for the VOA to discharge its charter obligation to present "responsible discussion and opinion on these policies." Murrow's compromise response was to reaffirm both the charter and the existing USIA guidance procedures. On 4 December 1962, Murrow imposed what he termed "special procedures" on the VOA, commissioning the Voice director to "devote a major part of his attention to policy matters." Although restating the VOA charter, Murrow's memorandum left no doubt that he wanted VOA commentaries and analyses to be very closely tied to policy. Loomis read this revised charter suspiciously. It contained three sentences. The first – "Official U.S. broadcasts are listened to and monitored for indicators of the intentions and policies of the government. It is vital that our broadcasts not mislead our enemies or our friends about the nature, intent, and implications of our actions and purposes" – was unobjectionable. The second – "Therefore VOA commentaries and analyses on foreign affairs should at all times, and especially on subjects involving vital U.S. interests, reflect the nuances and special emphases, as well as the main thrust, of the policies and intentions of the U.S. Government" – seemed to confirm that in the future the VOA would not be barred from the sort of discussion that had been prohibited during the missile crisis. But the third really worried Loomis: "Commentaries should give an accurate picture of U.S. public policy *as it can most persuasively be presented* up to airtime." For Loomis the emphasis on persuasion flew in the face of Murrow's pledge to his confirmation hearing that "USIA would seek to make U.S. foreign policy everywhere intelligible *and wherever possible* palatable." Murrow now wanted something other than "the U.S. – warts and all."[138] The compromise paragraph had solved nothing. The Cuban missile crisis became another milestone in the mounting dissatisfaction at the VOA. The war in Vietnam brought matters to a head.

[137] JFKL Salinger papers, box 132, USIA 1962, USIA weekly report, 13 November 1962; JFKL POF, Depts & Agencies: USIA, box 91, Murrow to President, weekly report, 20 November 1962, and "Airborne Television Capability," 3 December 1962.

[138] For documentation see NA RG 306, 89.0180, director's chronological file, 1969–1970, box 17, reel 34, Murrow, "Voice of America Policy," 4 December 1962 attached to Shakespeare, "Instructions to the Voice of America...," 9 June 1970. For Loomis' account of this see USIA Alumni Association, *"The U.S. – Warts and All" Edward R. Murrow as Director of the USIA, Presenting the U.S. to the World: A Commemorative Symposium*, Washington, DC: USIAAA/Public Diplomacy Foundation, 1992, pp. 19–22. The extra paragraph was not included in the VOA charter when it became law in 1976.

4) FROM VIETNAM TO DALLAS

At the beginning of the Kennedy years, there was nothing particularly remarkable about the USIA's effort in Vietnam. Initially the agency paid rather more attention to Laos. But the administration always considered the American commitment to South Vietnam to be symbolically linked to the global reputation of the United States. In the aftermath of the Bay of Pigs, Vietnam emerged as a logical arena for a display of American power. Rostow argued that "Viet-Nam is the place where – in the Attorney General's phrase – we must prove we are not a paper tiger."[139] President Kennedy appeared susceptible to this argument, telling James Reston of the *New York Times*, "Now we have a problem making our power credible, and Vietnam is the place."[140] Such a mission faced one major problem. Although global strategy needed a visible American victory and local necessity called for massive aid to boost the personal prestige of President Diem, this same aid undermined the nationalist credentials of the Diem government. The Diem regime seemed to speak for and through the Americans. Diem's attempt to break this self-defeating loop merely hastened the day when the United States would seek an alternative protégé in South Vietnam.

In autumn 1961, the Kennedy administration set up a central counterinsurgency task force with a major role directing work in Vietnam.[141] Ed Murrow represented the agency personally. The USIA also contributed to the task force on Vietnam, which coordinated the U.S. effort in the country. Major tasks "in country" included information support for the strategic hamlet program,[142] development of South Vietnamese radio broadcasting,[143] and presentation of the Diem regime. Murrow's concerns included the potential for a bad press if the United States acceded to Diem's request to use defoliant chemicals. Murrow feared that "food denial" attacks on "enemy" crops would alienate the United States from world opinion and insisted that any use of defoliants should be presented carefully alongside facts about the moral case against the Viet Cong and assurances of the "non-toxicity-to-humans" of substances used.[144] On 30 November 1961, President Kennedy approved limited use of defoliants. Experimental spraying to eliminate enemy cover began in January. Radios Moscow and Peking made capital of the development, but comment in the Western media seemed

139   JFKL NSF, Subjects: Policy Planning: box 303, Rostow to President, Top Secret, 21 April 1961, "The Problem We Face."
140   Stanley Karnow, *Vietnam: A History*, New York: Penguin Books, 1984, p. 248.
141   JFKL NSF, Meetings and Memoranda, box 326, Staff Memoranda, Rostow; Komer to Rostow/Bissell, Annex 1: Country Team and Washington Organization, 5 October 1961.
142   Sperber, *Murrow*, pp. 646–8; JFKL Salinger, box 132, USIA 1963, Murrow to President, 17 September 1963. On the strategic hamlet plan in general see Hilsman papers, Countries, Vietnam, box 3, Hilsman to Harriman, 2 April 1962.
143   JFKL NSF, CO Vietnam, box 194, general, Wilson to Rostow, 10 October 1961; *FRUS 1961–1963*, Vol. II, doc. 203, Trueheart to State 23 May 1962; *FRUS 1961–1963*, Vol. II, doc., 163, Bagley to Maxwell Taylor, 18 April 1962: Vietnam Task Force Meeting, items c & d.
144   JFKL POF, Depts. & Agencies: USIA, box. 91, Murrow to President, Secret, 27 November 1961; NSF, Meetings and Memoranda, NSAM 115, Defoliant Operations in Vietnam, Box 311.

sufficiently muted to permit expanded tests.[145] Whether by luck or careful framing, the story had a negligible impact on world opinion at the time.[146]

In May 1962, the U.S. embassy in Saigon acquired a dynamic new public affairs officer, the former *Time* journalist John Mecklin. His initial ideas included renaming the Viet Cong with a title that did not carry an inbuilt allusion to their nationality. He offered a $50 prize to local staff who could devise a better alternative. There is no record of the prize being won.[147] Mecklin moved USIS work into high gear. In the spring of 1963 the USIA and the South Vietnamese collaborated on a major new initiative to undermine Viet Cong morale: the *Chieu Hoi* (Open Arms) program to encourage desertion from the VC. The campaign officially began on 17 April with a grand proclamation of amnesty by Diem.[148] The United States helped get the message out, dropping leaflets and providing the South Vietnamese air force with loudspeaker aircraft.[149] Soon the Vietnamese countryside echoed with the eerie sound of live or taped testimonials from defectors. In time the words *"Chieu Hoi"* would become one of only three or four Vietnamese phrases known to every GI.[150]

USIS Saigon faced one task above all others: management of world press reporting of the conflict. The structure of the U.S. mission did not necessarily help. The USIA ran the press affairs of the U.S. embassy, but the army had press mechanisms and opinions of its own. On 21 February 1962, the State Department and the USIA issued joint guidance in "Cable No. 1006" for military and civilian public affairs officers in Vietnam: "We conclude that in the absence of rigid censorship, U.S. interests best be protected through a policy of maximum feasible cooperation, guidance and appeal to the good faith of correspondents." The path of this "guidance" was clear: steer the American press away from unhelpful criticism of the South Vietnamese and stories implying that the United States ran combat missions, and present the war as a South Vietnamese effort.[151] Unfortunately the mission used "Cable 1006" to justify an absurd level of noncooperation with the press, culminating in a refusal to acknowledge the rather obvious presence of the massive aviation transport ship U.S.S. *Core* in the Saigon River. Mistrust between the mission and the press abounded.[152]

The Diem regime added to the USIA's difficulties by mishandling the world's press, expelling journalists it disliked and alternately ignoring the rest or subjecting

[145] NSF, Meetings and Memoranda, NSAM 115, Defoliant Operations in Vietnam, Box 311, McNamara to President, 2 February 1962.
[146] *FRUS 1961–1963*, vol. III, doc. 96, State Dept Memo: Chemical Defoliation . . . in South Viet-Nam, 18 April 1963.
[147] *FRUS 1961–1963*, Vol. II, doc., 179, USIS Saigon Staff Meeting, 2 May 1962.
[148] *FRUS, 1961–1963*, vol. III, doc. 10, Nolting to State, 11 January 1963; NA RG59 State CPF 1960–1963, box 3272, INF 13 S.Viet, Manfull (Embassy) to State, 18 April 1963; box 3273, POL 26–1 S. Viet, Saigon, 973, Rusk to Embassy, 19 April 1963.
[149] NA RG59 State CPF 1960–1963, box 3272, INF 8 US–S. Viet, Saigon 105, Nolting to Sec. of State, 18 July 1963 and Saigon 67, Hilsman (Ball) to Embassy Saigon, 12 July 1963.
[150] Gloria Emerson, *Winners and Losers*, New York: Norton, 1992, p. 325.
[151] *FRUS, 1961–1963*, Vol. II, doc. 75, State/USIA to Embassy, Vietnam, 21 February 1962, drafted by Rowan.
[152] *FRUS, 1961–1963*, vol. III, doc. 39, Rusk to Nolting: 15 February 1963; doc. 46, Rusk to Nolting, 27 February 1963.

them to deranged briefings by Diem's increasingly unstable brother Nhu or Nhu's equally volatile wife.[153] Despairing, Mecklin persuaded the U.S. Military Advisory Assistance Command, Vietnam to institute daily briefings to guide Western correspondents, and when possible leak positive news of South Vietnamese successes.[154] In January 1963 Diem relaxed restrictions to allow reporters better access to the battlefield. They arrived in time to see the humiliation of the South Vietnamese army (ARVN) at Ap Bac. When accounts of the defeat hit the newsstands, the Diem regime backed away from the American media yet again.[155] When, in the early summer of 1963, Diem clamped down on Buddhist opposition, American correspondents found themselves subject to active harassment.[156]

*

Vietnam notwithstanding, 1963 brought positive news for the USIA. On 25 January, Kennedy signed a revised, classified mission statement for the agency:

> The mission of the United States Information Agency is to help achieve United States foreign policy objectives by (a) influencing public attitudes in other nations, and (b) advising the president, his representatives abroad and the various departments and agencies on the implications of foreign opinion for present and contemplated United States policies, programs and official statements.

The emphasis on the agency's advisory function had particular significance. The statement specified that this advice should be both at all levels in Washington and in the country teams overseas. The director now had the right to "take the initiative in offering counsel when he deems it advisable" and all agencies now had to consult the agency about any program "which may substantially affect or be affected by foreign opinion." The statement asserted that "Consultation with the United States Information Agency is essential when programs affecting communications media in other countries are contemplated." The USIA also now had the authority to work with the CIA to "communicate with other peoples without attribution to the United States government." This authority allowed an escalation of psychological warfare in Vietnam. The mission statement came as the final redress for Kennedy's neglect of the USIA during the Bay of Pigs. The position of Murrow and his successors within the bureaucracy had been substantially strengthened. It seemed a satisfying way for the agency to enter the tenth year of its existence.[157]

153   *FRUS, 1961–1963*, Vol. II, doc. 311, Mecklin to USIA, 5 November 1962; Mecklin, *Mission in Torment*, pp. 129–138.
154   *FRUS, 1961–1963*, Vol. II, doc. 322, Mecklin to Nolting, 27 November 1962: Press Relations.
155   William M. Hammond, *Reporting Vietnam: Media and Military at War*, Lawrence, KS: University of Kansas Press, 1998, pp. 7–8; William M. Hammond, *United States Army in Vietnam, Public Affairs: The Military and the Media, 1962–1968*, Washington, DC: US Army, 1998, pp. 29–35; *FRUS, 1961–1963*, vol. III, doc. 14, Minutes of CI, 17 January 1963; doc. 24, Harriman to Nolting, 30 January 1963; doc. 28, Moore (USIA Pacific/Far East) to Wilson, 1 February 1963; Doc 30, Nolting to State, 5 February 1963.
156   *FRUS, 1961–1963*, vol. III, doc. 225, Minutes of meeting between Manning, Mecklin and Nhu, 17 July 1963; doc. 239, Manning to JFK on Report on the Saigon Press Situation, c. 26 July 1963.
157   JFKL NSF, Depts. & Agencies: USIA, box 290, General, President to director, USIA, 25 January 1963, Confidential.

Although relations with the White House flourished, John Rooney and the House of Representatives appropriations committee remained unsympathetic. Unfavorable hearings in the House in 1962 delayed such important agency programs as Project Bamboo, a high-power shortwave transmitter facility for East Asia, to be built in the Philippines. The agency's budget also took a severe knock in the House in June 1963. Murrow defiantly vowed to try for more funds in the 1964 round. Murrow also noted the need for a rationalized and adequate headquarters for the USIA and VOA. The USIA's 3,000 Washington, DC-based staff were scattered between eleven buildings. It had clearly outgrown the old headquarters at 1776 Pennsylvania Avenue.[158]

Murrow and his colleagues drew comfort from evidence of success. A survey of world opinion showed renewed sympathy for the United States.[159] Then, in June, the U.S.S.R. suddenly stopped jamming VOA (and BBC) broadcasts. Kennedy's sustained pressure on the Soviet Union in the matter of the nuclear test ban finally bore fruit with an atmospheric test ban treaty. For a third time, Murrow used his power to preempt airtime on RFE, RL, and the Armed Forces Network to ensure that as many people in the Eastern bloc as possible heard Kennedy's radio and television address on the treaty of 26 July. The President's speech carried hope for the future, urging America to "step back from the shadows of war and seek out the way of peace." The administration's careful handling of the test ban issue the previous autumn had been justified, although editorial comment around the world noted that a comprehensive treaty would need to encompass France and China too.[160]

There was encouraging news about U.S. cultural diplomacy. The Fulbright–Hays legislation had created a new United States Advisory Commission on International Educational and Cultural Affairs and empowered it to "submit such reports to the congress as they deem appropriate." The first such report was released in April 1963 under the title *A Beacon of Hope: The Exchange-of-Persons Program*. It would be a landmark largely for its endorsement of the value of the exchange program, based on both a program of interviews with 2,696 former grantees in twenty countries and parallel inquiries at key U.S. posts. The report claimed "conclusive" evidence "that the program has proved itself an essential and valuable part of America's total information effort." Its recommendations for improving its effectiveness included a major review of the status of the cultural affairs officer within the structure of the USIA and issues of budget, interagency coordination, and links to the wider world of U.S. universities.[161]

[158] JFKL Salinger papers, box 132, USIA 1962, Murrow to President, 16 October 1962; *NYT*, 2 April 1963, p. 22; 19 June 1963, p. 33; 5 July 1963, p. 15; POF, Depts. & Agencies: USIA, box 91, Murrow to President, 3 April 1963.

[159] JFKL POF, Depts & Agencies: USIA, box 91, Wilson to President, 10 July 1963: "First effort to measure 'world opinion.'"

[160] JFKL USIA, box 1, memoranda file 2, Wilson to Salinger, 22 June 1963; *Public Papers of the Presidents, John F. Kennedy, 1963*, pp. 601–6; Salinger papers, box 132, USIA 1963 file, Murrow to President, Weekly Report, 30 July 1963; POF, Depts & Agencies: USIA, box 91, Research and Reference Service Report, R143–63 (A), Initial Media reaction to the US–UK–U.S.S.R. Test Ban Agreement, 30 July 1963.

[161] UoA CU 191–9, "A Beacon of Hope: The Exchange of Persons Program, a report from the U.S. Advisory Commission on International Educational and Cultural Affairs," April 1963. For a follow-up

That summer saw a second report from the commission. A major review of American studies by commission member and University of Chicago historian Walter Johnson was submitted in July 1963. The report called for both better funding and a better structure to support American studies and became the agenda for expansion in this field in the years ahead.[162]

*

By the summer of 1963, the Voice of America had assumed an unprecedented importance in South Vietnam. Thanks to rebroadcast over the new transmitter network, the VOA was the country's most widely available source of news. In keeping with its charter, VOA news reported not only the buoyant official estimates of the war but also the pessimistic assessments of journalists such as David Halberstam. Supporters of the American role in Vietnam objected.[163] On 20 August, the South Vietnamese government launched a series of violent raids on Buddhist pagodas in search of Communist propaganda and weapons. The VOA followed the embassy understanding of events and blamed units of the South Vietnamese army. The ARVN protested its innocence, and soon evidence mounted that the true culprits were secret police under the control of Nhu. It seemed that a nudge from the United States might encourage key generals to overthrow Diem. On 24 August, the Saigon mission sent a memo setting out these points. At the State Department the Assistant Secretary of State for Far Eastern Affairs, Roger Hilsman, drafted a response. This cable proposed a blunt ultimatum: press Diem to remove Nhu and if he refuses "face the possibility that Diem himself cannot be preserved." The cable also undertook to "have Voice of America make a statement" on the Pagoda raids.[164] Hilsman believed that the best way for the VOA to correct the story was to place a revised version with the wire services, which could then be reported by the VOA as news. He then leaked the unclassified portions of the memo dealing with the events of 20 August to the United Press.[165] The VOA reported the wire story as news, stressing both the army's innocence and U.S. readiness to cut all aid to Diem unless he sacked the officials responsible.[166] But Hilsman was disappointed. The broadcast did not kick off a coup.[167]

later in the decade see Dean B. Mahin, "The Department of State's International Visitor Program, 1948–1968," *International Educational and Cultural Exchange*, Fall 1968.

[162] "A Special Report on American Studies Abroad: Progress and Difficulties in Selected Countries," by Walter Johnson, a report to Congress, referred to the Committee on Foreign Affairs, 11 July 1963, filed at UoA CU 166–14. For discussion and implementation see UoA 165–34 and 165–35. For an abridgement as released in December 1965 see UoA CU 1–20, Brookings Research Report 46, "Cultural and Educational Aspects of Foreign Policy."

[163] Sperber, *Murrow*, p. 680–81; interview: Bernie Kamenske, 6 December 1995; Mecklin, *Mission in Torment*, p. 164.

[164] David Kaiser, *American Tragedy: Kennedy, Johnson, and Origins of the Vietnam War*, Cambridge, MA: Harvard University Press, 2000, pp. 226–31; JFKL, NSF, Meetings and Memoranda, box 316, Vietnam, Ball to Lodge, Top Secret, 24 August 1963.

[165] Roger Hilsman, *To Move a Nation*, New York: Doubleday, 1967, pp. 484–90.

[166] *FRUS, 1961–1963*, Vol. III, doc. 287, Voice of America broadcast, Saigon, 26 August 1963; JFKL Hilsman papers, box 3, Countries, Vietnam, "VOA Vietnamese Broadcasts re. U.S. aid," 26 August 1963. For a similar text see GRFL NSC Convenience file, box 6, File: Henry Cabot Lodge/Diem Coup 1, "From VOA English language broadcast, 26 August, 1963, 8.00 am."

[167] *FRUS, 1961–1963*, Vol. III, doc. 289, Minutes of Meeting at White House, 26 August 1963.

Ambassador Lodge was furious that the VOA had carried the story. "If VOA causes failure of our plan," he wrote, "the effect in Congress will certainly be unfortunate.[168] Secretary of State Rusk apologized for the broadcast, blaming the "failure of machinery here over the weekend to carry out policy instructions."[169] Hilsman also blamed the Voice, claiming that journalists had failed to check the relevant guidance cable.[170] Henry Loomis and the staff at the VOA disputed this. After all, Hilsman himself had called the Voice to direct them to cover the story in the first place. Program manager Alex Klieforth had smelled a rat even at this stage and, being unable to reach Murrow for guidance, instructed the news room to tone down the implicit attack on Nhu. The writer responsible for the VOA story was Obey Bradley, number two on the Far East News Desk. As Bernie Kamenske, who sat opposite Bradley that Sunday evening, recalled, Bradley called back Hilsman's office to confirm the UPI story. The news room realized that a pro-coup clique within the American government had manipulated the VOA. Ed Murrow accepted that the Voice had "been had" and told the journalists to take the rebuke "in the national interest."[171]

Murrow did not let the matter lie. In a secret memo he warned McGeorge Bundy that the VOA should not be used in this way:

> I also suggest that 1) VOA can be used tactically to incite only once, and therefore that this weapon be held until the right moment; 2) in the event of a change in the U.S. public position on Viet-Nam that such a change be announced publicly (e.g. by the president, the Secretary, Hilsman or Phillips) rather than backgrounded anonymously and therefore ambiguously.[172]

*

During the following weeks the Kennedy administration applied pressure on Diem to reform his regime. On 14 October, at the request of Ambassador Lodge, the VOA Vietnamese service began broadcasting "Roots of Freedom," a series of five-minute dramatized vignettes in Vietnamese and English recreating landmarks in the making of American democratic values.[173] But Diem merely lashed out at the USIS and VOA as agents of conspiracy. Acting director of the USIA Don Wilson feared

---

[168] *FRUS, 1961–1963*, Vol. III, doc. 288, Embassy to Harriman, 26 August 1963 (also at JFKL Countries: Vietnam, Box 198, CIA cables).

[169] JFKL NSF, Countries: Vietnam, box 198, State Cables, Rusk to Lodge, 26 August 1963.

[170] Hilsman, *To Move a Nation*, pp. 489–90.

[171] *New York Herald Tribune*, 27 August 1963, "In Viet, We Absolve, While We Blunder: Our Voice," pp. 1, 10; interview: Bernie Kamenske, 6 December 1995; Alex Klieforth, 7 January 1997; JFKL VOA, reel 11, Loomis to Murrow, 24 September 1963, IBS Monthly Report, August 1963; Maxwell Taylor, *Swords into Plowshares*, New York: Norton, New York, 1972, pp. 292–4. Klieforth visited Vietnam shortly after this incident and explained the VOA version of events first to Lodge (with whom he had worked in the 1950s) who accepted the VOA version and then, on the return journey, to Ambassador Edwin Reischauer in Tokyo, who had been alarmed by the story.

[172] JFKL Hilsman papers, box 3, Countries, Vietnam, Murrow to Bundy, Secret, 28 August 1963.

[173] *FRUS 1961–1963*, Vol. IV, doc. 153, Lodge to Murrow, 27 September 1963; NA RG59 CPF 1961–3, box 3273, INF 8 US, Lodge to Rusk, 9 October 1963; Rawnsley, *Radio Diplomacy and Propaganda*, pp. 150–51.

that the regime planned to close USIS field posts and even expel Mecklin.[174] On 1 November 1963, the South Vietnamese army finally moved to overthrow Diem and Nhu. Both died during the coup. The war, and the USIA's role in it, grew relentlessly from this point.

*

Inside the USIA one major cloud darkened the fall of 1963: Ed Murrow's future. In September, his lung condition returned. In October, doctors diagnosed cancer and removed one of his lungs. Even without the illness, Murrow's days at the USIA were numbered. Murrow felt uneasy about the influence of Robert Kennedy, a man who had been close to his old enemy Joe McCarthy. Once, when Murrow found a strange man rifling through his desk at the USIA, he slammed the drawer shut on the man's hand and threw him out yelling: "tell Bobby if he wants to know something, he can *ask Jack.*"[175] More than this, he increasingly despaired of the Kennedy administration's chaotic Vietnam policy-making. A White House minute of 10 September reflected Murrow's mood: "Mr. Murrow asked that he be relieved of writing press guidance until after tomorrow's meeting in view of the fact that the guidance could not be written until our policy was clear." Murrow quietly approached ABC News in search of a new job.[176]

*

There should have been nothing memorable about the early afternoon of Friday, 22 November 1963, for the USIA. Murrow convalesced at home; Herschensohn sat on a plane to New York, on the first leg of a journey to film the experience of refugees from communism around the globe. In the VOA newsroom a young writer named Philomena Jurey put the finishing touches to a story on the President's speech, scheduled to be delivered that afternoon in Dallas. Then came the news.

At 1.34 p.m. a UPI news wire announced that President Kennedy had been shot. At the VOA, Jurey – stunned – began to prepare the news bulletin on the report. The incoming wires clattered with the news – Dallas . . . three shots . . . open topped car . . . rushed to hospital – but no word on the President's condition. Suddenly, as the Latin American news editor Bernie Kamenske recalled years later, the incoming wires ceased and an eerie silence descended on the news room. They waited for further confirmation. Although the wires remained silent, the VOA studio engineers came to the rescue. By eavesdropping on the Secret Service radio channel, they gleaned key details and passed them on to the newsroom. These signals confirmed that Kennedy had, indeed, been shot, and that it looked bad. Working from this source and the news agency story, Jurey hammered out an initial report for the imminent simplified "Special English" newscast. This went onto the VOA's house wire at 1.54 p.m. Kamenske

[174] Mecklin, *Mission in Torment*, pp. 201, 235; *FRUS, 1961–1963*, Vol. IV, doc. 199, Wilson to Mecklin, 18 October 1963.
[175] Persico, *Murrow*, p. 485, Sperber, *Murrow* p. 659.
[176] Persico, *Murrow*, p. 487; Reeves, *President Kennedy: Profile of Power*, p. 597; Sperber, *Murrow*, p. 681.

prepared a piece on the law of succession. As the details dribbled in, Jurey frantically typed further bulletins; Kamenske recalled looking across at her rising out her chair "like a jockey." Some minutes later she added, quite accurately, that "Dallas, of recent months, has been the scene of extreme right-wing movements." It was the beginning of a plausible motive for the assassination: a backlash against civil rights reform. The program manager – Alex Klieforth – soon removed the sentence from bulletins, but it sparked the ire of certain senators. *New York Times* columnist Arthur Krock alleged that the phrase had inspired Radio Moscow to proclaim Kennedy's death to be the product of a right-wing conspiracy.[177]

At a little after 2 p.m., the Secret Service radio said that Kennedy was dead. Jurey prepared the necessary bulletin and took it to the newsroom chief Jerry Thiese, who in turn took the bulletin to the program manager, Klieforth, and VOA director Henry Loomis, who had positioned themselves next to the wire room, waiting for any further news. Loomis wondered whether he had the authority to pass the news on to the world and proclaim the President dead. The official status of the Voice of America added weight to any VOA broadcast of the story. No one in the government would confirm the story, and the Voice could hardly go on the air with information derived from a radio intercept. The first wire reports of the death came at 2:35. Loomis told Klieforth to decide whether or not to confirm that the President had died. The sight of Walter Cronkite announcing the death over CBS pushed Klieforth to release the story. He felt oddly as though he had somehow killed Kennedy by the action. At around 2:36, the VOA news flash sped off, accompanied by the tolling of ten bells (to stress the extraordinary significance of the story) on the wire machine before and after the transmission. A dozen machines tolled in unison.[178]

During the hours and days following the assassination, the Voice of America pulled off the greatest feat of continuous reporting in its history. English services remained on the air twenty-two and a half hours a day from the Friday of Kennedy's death until the following Tuesday. Central Program Services issued thirty News Analyses, twenty features, sixty-four correspondent's reports covering news and reactions from the U.S. and around the world, and six hours of appropriate music. The Technical Division used fifteen million feet of recording tape. The studio resources of the Voice had been strained to the breaking point, but had held. Voice coverage of the Kennedy assassination had been a triumph.[179]

[177] Philomena Jurey, *A Basement Seat to History: Tales of Covering Presidents Nixon, Ford, Carter and Reagan for the Voice of America*, Washington, DC: Linus Press, 1995, pp. 12–14; interview: Bernie Kamenske, 6 December 1995; Arthur Krock, "In the Nation," *New York Times*, 26 November 1963. Right-wingers in Dallas had recently harassed Adlai Stevenson and Lyndon Johnson. Kennedy himself had privately described the trip as "heading into nut country." On the right in Dallas see *New York Times*, 25 November 1963. For the response of acting USIA director Wilson see LBJL WHCF CF, box 135, CF USIA, Wilson to President, 27 November 1963 and WHCF Ex, box 317 Ex FG 2961–1, VOA, Wilson to President, 21 January 1964.

[178] Interview: Bernie Kamenske, 6 December 1995; Alex Klieforth, 7 January 1997 and 28 November 2000; Kamenske to author, 10 November 2000. For a chronology of other news channels see William Manchester, *The Death of a President*, pp. 243–4.

[179] JFKL VOA, reel 11, Loomis to Wilson, Monthly Report, November 1963, 19 December 1963.

For much of the world hearing it, the VOA story made the Kennedy assassination official. Broadcasters across Europe and Latin America cited the VOA bulletin as their source for the death of the President. As with so much in the Kennedy years, their end had underlined the importance of international communication. It now fell to the USIA and the VOA to somehow maintain the image of confidence during a difficult transition.

5 Maintaining Confidence

THE EARLY JOHNSON YEARS, 1963–65

> It is essential that we help maintain a high level of foreign confidence in the
> continuity of American government and policy under President Johnson and in
> our nation as the leader of the Free World.
>
> Edward R. Murrow, 20 December 1963.[1]

**At 3:38 p.m. Dallas time on Friday 22 November 1963 Lyndon Baines
Johnson** stood in the humid cabin of Air Force One and took the oath of office as
President of the United States. He faced many challenges, including a crisis in his
country's international image. Like John F. Kennedy, Lyndon Johnson understood
that image played an important part in politics at home and abroad. Unfortunately,
he clearly lacked Kennedy's natural assets as a focus for such image-making. The
existing image problems of the Cold War, Vietnam, and civil rights were suddenly and
brutally compounded by the shock of the Kennedy assassination. Johnson needed to
reassure the world that the United States would remain both a sound ally to friends
and a formidable opponent to enemies. He needed to counter the impression of
lawlessness left by the killing in Dallas. He also wanted to prove to the world that
the assassination had been the act of a lone gunman and not a conspiracy involving
either, as he feared, the Soviet Union or the homegrown extreme right. Either of these
perpetrators would present major political problems and hinder getting back to the
business of government. Johnson assigned the task of settling the questions raised by
the assassination to the Warren Commission. The task of restoring the international
image of the United States belonged to the USIA.[2]

Ed Murrow knew that the USIA could not respond to the Kennedy assassination
without additional funding. He rose from his sick bed and lobbied personally for an
extra $9 million. A few well-placed calls mobilized the necessary majority in the Senate,

---

[1] LBJL Leonard Marks papers, box 27, USIA Media Priorities, Murrow to Staff, 20 December
1963.

[2] On the establishment of the Warren Commission see LBJL Moyers papers, box 55, memos re. Death of
President Kennedy, Katzenbach (Deputy Attorney General) to Moyers (White House), 25 November
1963, recommending a commission to cut off speculation on motives and conspiracies, and because
"the public must be satisfied that Oswald was the assassin" and acted alone. On Johnson's fears of a
Soviet plot see Carl T. Rowan, *Breaking Barriers: A Memoir*, Boston: Little, Brown, 1991, p. 233.
Murrow's post-assassination priorities for the USIA were (1) The Pursuit of Peace; (2) Strength and
Reliability; (3) Free Choice; (4) Rule of Law; (5) United Nations. See LBJL Leonard Marks papers,
box 27, USIA Media Priorities, Murrow to Staff, 20 December 1965.

but the Congressional subcommittee demanded a reduced figure of only $5 million. Wheezing on his single lung, Murrow dragged himself up the steps of the House office building to confront his old adversary, Representative John B. Rooney. Faced by a dying man, the New Yorker compromised and allowed the USIA an additional $8 million to cope with the crisis.[3]

The agency proved its worth that winter. USIA coverage of the transition demonstrated exactly what a properly funded communications machine armed with a powerful message could achieve. Within weeks of the assassination, Murrow's ill health compelled him to resign. Johnson chose the African American journalist Carl Rowan to succeed him. Rowan not only projected the image of civil rights reform around the world, but also personally embodied the opportunities available within the United States. As Rowan became a regular participant in NSC meetings, the place of the USIA as a key player in U.S. foreign policy seemed secure. But being eager to develop his agency's profile, Rowan expanded the USIA's role in South Vietnam. The agency's presence in Vietnam escalated in tandem with U.S. military activity. Just as the USIA's Kennedy assassination work demonstrated what well-executed international information could achieve, so the Vietnam conflict became an object lesson in its limits.

1) ZENITH
THE USIA AND THE KENNEDY ASSASSINATION, NOVEMBER 1963–AUGUST 1965

The USIA worked hard to introduce Lyndon Johnson to the world. The agency used its authority under NSAM 63 to mount a live mass broadcast of Johnson's joint session speech on 27 November. The VOA provided simultaneous translation in Spanish and Portuguese; thirty-six other translations followed that day and night. The agency wireless file carried the text of the speech, while couriers rushed film of Johnson's performance to TV stations and newsreels around the world. Europe received highlights via the magic of communications satellite.[4]

In the eight days following Kennedy's death, the USIA's Press Service sent out an unprecedented stream of stories, photographs, briefing papers, and supporting documents: 110 posts in 103 countries received "material designed to aid understanding and reassurance." The publications section produced special inserts on Kennedy and Johnson for *America Illustrated* for Poland and Russia and *Al Hayat fi America* for the Arab world; within two weeks the USIA had shipped out 2,000 copies of a panel exhibit on Johnson's life, emphasizing his foreign policy interests.[5] The agency issued more than a million copies of an illustrated pamphlet introducing Johnson in eighteen language versions. The Spanish-language print run for Latin America approached half a million.[6] The USIA also created a short biographical piece on Johnson for newsreel

---

[3] Sperber, *Murrow*, p. 685.
[4] LBJL WHCF CF, box 135, CF USIA, Wilson to President, 27 November 1963.
[5] LBJL Lee White papers, box 6, civil rights misc., Rowan to White, 12 March 1964.
[6] LBJL Salinger papers, box 1, Agency reports for the President, Wilson to President, 4 February 1964.

and television use around the world and a longer television program about Johnson called *Let Us Continue*. By the end of 1963 this program was on its way to seventy-four countries with television and thirty-two without, in English, Spanish, Portuguese, and French versions, but the major film effort still lay ahead.[7]

USIA surveys of editorial opinion around the world revealed a surge of sympathy for the United States at the time of Kennedy's death. This could have been expected. More significantly, the agency also noted strong approval for Johnson's early statements on foreign policy.[8] In the U.S.S.R., propagandists seized on Johnson's public commitment to peace and blamed the less attractive aspects of U.S. foreign policy on his advisors. McNamara proved a favorite target. As a gesture of goodwill, Radio Moscow unexpectedly gave full coverage to the new USIA exhibition – Graphics U.S.A. – and even broadcast instructions on how to obtain tickets. Even the most hostile voice of the era, Communist China, slipped into moderation, although Radio Beijing still suggested that LBJ represented "the interests of big petroleum merchants and ranchers of the southern United States and bankers in the North."[9]

Longer-term projects included a major initiative to translate and distribute books about Johnson. On 1 February, just three weeks after an updated version of Booth Mooney's 1956 biography *The Lyndon Johnson Story* appeared in America, the USIA released French and Arabic translations priced at 25 cents each. In March an agency run of 25,000 Spanish copies of the same book hit Buenos Aires. With seventeen more translations, global sales by April 1965 topped 190,000.[10]

*

The true centerpiece of the agency's response to the assassination would be two films. Within hours of the news from Dallas, George Stevens Jr. formed a plan to commemorate Kennedy's life with a feature-length documentary film built around 35mm color footage of the funeral. Murrow agreed. Stevens hastily arranged multiple camera positions for the funeral and secured the services of Bruce Herschensohn to direct. The film, *John F. Kennedy: Years of Lightning, Day of Drums*, became the most

7   LBJL WHCF CF, box 135, CF USIA, Wilson to President, 31 December 1963. The USIA's television coverage of the funeral sparked controversy when the *New York Times* reported that scenes showing a rabbi had been deleted from material shipped to the Middle East. The agency denied the charge, with the full support of the U.S. Jewish community's National Community Relations Advisory Council. For press release see WHCF, box 316, FG 296, general, USIA press release, 18 December 1964.

8   LBJL WHCF, CF USIA, box 135, Wilson to President, 10 December 1963 notes a British Gallup poll report of 89 percent approval of Johnson's pledge to continue to seek increased East–West understanding.

9   LBJL WHCF, Ex FG1, box 9, USIA Report R-223–63, Worldwide reaction to the first month of the Johnson Administration, 24 December 1963; WHCF CF, box 135, CF USIA, Wilson to President, 10 December 1963. As a result of Radio Moscow's help, 16,000 people attended the opening on Graphics – U.S.A. on Saturday, 7 December. Another 43,000 waited for up to four hours to visit on the following day. The show attracted a total of one and one-half million visitors.

10 LBJL Salinger papers, box 1, agency reports for the President, Wilson to President, 4 February 1964; WHCF CF, box 135, CF USIA, Rowan to President, 24 March 1964; NSF Agency, USIA Vol. 2/2, doc. 92, Rowan to President, 30 June 1964; NSF Vol. 2/1, doc. 63, Rowan to President, 4 August 1964; WHCF Ex FG296, box 314, Wilson to McPherson (White House), 6 April 1965.

widely seen of any agency production. Murrow also insisted that Herschensohn make a ten-minute profile of LBJ to stress political continuity. Stevens and Herschensohn hurried to the White House to film Johnson at work at his desk. The new President wrote intently while the cameras rolled. Stevens peeked at his desk to see what he had been writing. He saw an entire page covered with his signature.[11]

Herschensohn worked swiftly to complete *The President*. Narrated by Gregory Peck, the film presented Johnson as "a man of God, freedom and peace." After reviewing Johnson's career, with emphasis on his commitment to civil rights and space exploration, the film reached a climax with Johnson's speech to the joint session of Congress. Just forty-five days after the assassination, the film was ready. The agency shipped more than a thousand prints in thirty-nine languages to over a hundred countries. United Artists and MGM both tacked the film onto their big overseas releases that winter.[12]

Herschensohn structured his epic funeral film, *Years of Lightning, Day of Drums*, in six segments – the "six faces of the New Frontier" – which each displayed an aspect of JFK's achievement: the Peace Corps; the Alliance for Progress; the space program; civil rights; the "defense of freedom" (the Cold War); and the "quest for peace," all of which he intercut with footage of the funeral. This balance fitted a global and nonaligned audience. He hoped to bring his viewers on board during the first four segments, before addressing the President's controversial engagement with the U.S.S.R.[13] He illustrated each segment with actuality footage selected for its raw visual power. He opened with an immense sunset and included numerous parades, culminating in the final drive through Dallas. Such scenes conveyed an impression of strength, power, and control. He also established Kennedy as a leader in dialogue with the people, using many shots of reactions of the people around him. Kennedy's humanity emerged from scenes in which he joked about his poor Spanish in Costa Rica or dropped the medal intended for the astronaut Alan Shepherd, but above all from the home movies used in the final sequence of the film. Footage made available by Jackie Kennedy and selected with the help of Kennedy's sister, Patricia Lawford, included Kennedy with his children: Caroline on a horse, John-John waddling toward the camera with a laundry basket on his head. These shots drew the viewer into a personal place. The transition to Dallas became all the more shocking. At the fatal moment, images of JFK in his motorcade gave way to confused shots from a shaking handheld camera and eloquent silence on the soundtrack.[14]

[11] Interview: Stevens and Herschensohn.
[12] Interview: Stevens and Herschensohn, LBJL MPSVB *The President*. LBJL Salinger papers, box 1, agency reports for the President, Wilson to President, 21 January 1964; WHCF CF, box 135, CF USIA, Rowan to President, 19 May 1964. United Artists released the film in France and the Philippines, and MGM managed Belgium, Brazil, and India. In Mexico the film played in a chain of 198 theaters (with an audience of fourteen million), on eleven television stations (with an audience of two million) and in schools, at labor meetings, and in other groups.
[13] Interview: Herschensohn. The "Six Faces" were Herschensohn's invention, but deliberately echoed FDR's Four Freedoms.
[14] Interviews: Stevens and Herschensohn; "JFK Movie made from best of near million feet of pictures," *Cincinnati Enquirer*, 10 September 1966, p. 4.

Gregory Peck delivered a spare narration. The Kennedy family requested only one change to this. Rather than state that Kennedy "failed at the Bay of Pigs" the revised script used the euphemism "set back." But the most important voice in the film was that of the dead President. Herschensohn used long extracts from key Kennedy speeches on civil rights, Berlin, and the Cuban missile crisis.[15] The film included some unexpected scenes: Images of demonstrators outside the White House gave proof of America's tolerance of dissent. Scenes of numerous rocket failures reminded audiences of American openness: being prepared to fail in public.[16] The most remarkable addition was a montage of reactions to Kennedy's assassination around the world. Cutting from continent to continent, Herschensohn showed images of memorial ceremonies in different faiths and cultures, but united by the same soundtrack: the drumbeat from the Washington funeral procession. Returning to shots of Kennedy's grave in changing seasons, the film ended with the commentary, "John F. Kennedy is now silent and invisible but so is love and faith and so is peace and freedom and so are memories and dreams."[17]

Herschensohn completed the film in October 1964. The USIA prepared premieres to mark the first anniversary of Kennedy's death. *Years of Lightning* premiered simultaneously in Washington, Rome, Beirut, and Mexico City on 16 November 1964. Worldwide showings followed.[18] Most critics praised the film. *Corriere della Sera* in Milan argued that the honest presentation of civil rights and the early failures of the space program showed "the impartiality and courage, which are the best proof of the strength of the American democracy." In South Africa, the deputy-chief editor of *The Johannesburg Star* wrote simply, "This film makes one want to be American."[19] The USIA recruited international stars to narrate the foreign language prints. Maximilian Schell performed the German version, which MGM released commercially in the holiday week of June 1965. *Die Zeit* dismissed it as "a half baked propaganda ham," but according to one USIS observer, the audience left the premiere "too moved to speak."[20] With such acclaim, pressure grew for *Years of Lightning* to be commercially released in the United States. After a tussle on the Hill over the ethics of

[15] Interviews: Stevens and Herschensohn.

[16] NA RG 59, CPF 1964–66, box 418, Culture and Information, MP7-Motion Picture Films, A-331, Sofia (Richard E. Johnson) to USIA/State, 13 March 1965 notes that the inclusion of the scenes of rocket failure baffled Communist bloc diplomats who attended the film's premiere in Sofia.

[17] Interview: Herschensohn.

[18] Twenty-five more premieres followed that week, and by the end of the year the film had played in 114 countries. Twenty-nine foreign language versions soon extended this audience. By January 1965 the USIA had 352 English prints available and a further 290 foreign language prints in distribution or on order. Full commercial distribution was under way or imminent in forty-four countries. NA RG 59, CPF 1964–66, box 418, Culture and Information, MP7-Motion Picture Films, Rusk to Moscow, 16 October 1964; NA RG 306 A1 (1066) USIA historical collection, box 157, *Years of Lightning* file, Memo to Carl Rowan, 16 November 1965, "CBS Interview" and memo for I/R, "response Newsweek inquiry," 22 January 1965.

[19] NA RG 306 A1 (1066) USIA historical collection, box 157, *Years of Lightning* file, USIS Review Report.

[20] Interview: Herschensohn; NA RG 306 A1 (1066) USIA historical collection, box 157, *Years of Lightning* file, USIS Bonn to USIA, 20 July 1965, *Die Zeit*, 9 July 1965.

propagandizing the American people at the taxpayer's expense, the film reached U.S. screens in time for the second anniversary of the assassination.[21]

But one documentary, however stunning, could not resolve the publicity issues generated by the Kennedy assassination. The murder of Oswald just two days after Kennedy's death laid the foundation for doubt.[22] As early as the spring of 1964, the USIA noted a growing global conviction that Kennedy had been the victim of a right-wing conspiracy. Writers in all regions complained about the delays of the Warren Commission, its closed hearings, and the membership of a former CIA director. The agency "furnished all U.S. missions with all the facts available on the public record," but still "found overseas observers difficult – and in some cases, impossible – to persuade." The USIA hoped that the final publication of the report might ease matters.[23]

The Warren Commission report finally appeared on 27 September 1964. The USIA created a range of supporting materials, including VOA features in thirty-seven languages. The USIA distributed printed commentaries, placed highlights on the wireless file, sent out special film and television materials, and arranged international transmission for a two-hour CBS documentary on the Commission's findings. Each USIS library received all twenty-six volumes of the report.[24] The USIA noted that the Warren Commission impressed Australia and the Philippines and reassured editors in Britain and Latin America, and to a lesser extent in India, Italy, and Germany. But French, Belgian, and Austrian editors remained unconvinced. *Le Monde* spoke for many when it declared, "A considerable fraction of the old continent's public opinion remains skeptical."[25] A succession of investigative books kept the issue alive. The third anniversary of Kennedy's death brought a "second gunman" story to the front page of the London *Times* and tales of missing witnesses in *Le Monde*, while the Italian media focused on *Life* magazine's call for a new investigation. The USIA instructed "all field officers not to engage in a debate on this issue, but to provide the media with those portions of the Warren Commission report refuting the rumors and outlining the extensive evidence which was taken."[26]

However hard USIS field officers worked, the conspiracy theories refused to die, especially with Moscow's propaganda machine on hand to stoke the embers. The deaths of Robert Kennedy and Martin Luther King Jr. came as a gift to the Soviet propagandists. On 12 June 1968, *Izvestia* reported that Robert Kennedy himself believed in a conspiracy and had pledged to find out the truth, telling New Orleans District

[21] NA RG 306 A1 (1066) USIA historical collection, box 157, *Years of Lightning* file, *Congressional Record*, HoR, 9 June 1965, p. 12156. In the Senate the ringleader of opposition was Senator Hickenlooper. The law was PL 89–274, approved on 20 October 1965. For review see Bosley Crowther, "Screen: *Years of Lightning, Day of Drums* here," *New York Times*, 4 November 1965. All proceeds from domestic screenings went to the Kennedy Center for the Performing Arts.

[22] LBJL Bill Moyers papers, box 55, Death of President Kennedy file, Wilson to President, 25 November 1963.

[23] LBJL WHCF CF, box 135, CF USIA, Rowan to Johnson, 28 April 1964.

[24] *USIA 23rd Review of Operations, 1 July–31 December 1964*, pp. 12–17, also in LBJL WHCF Ex, box 314, FG296, filed at 10/1/64–12/3/64.

[25] LBJL NSF agency, box 73, USIA Vol. 2/2, doc 125, Rowan to Johnson, 30 September 1964.

[26] LBJL WHCF CF, box 52, CF FO6–3 Publicity, Marks to President via Kintner, 29 November 1966.

Attorney Jim Garrison, "If I am elected president, I shall prosecute those who are guilty." The Soviet report concluded, "There is in America a well-financed syndicate of political murder which not only cleverly covers up traces of the crime, but misleads the public." *Trud* added, "There are influential, if not decisive, forces in America which at any moment can kill those who are considered inconvenient, regardless of whether the victim is a president, a senator or the recipient of a Nobel prize." But by 1968 conspiracy theories seemed the least of the USIA's worries.[27]

2) CARL ROWAN
CIVIL RIGHTS AND COLD WAR PROPAGANDA

Winning the extra Kennedy assassination budget became Murrow's last victory at the USIA. In December 1963, he submitted his resignation on grounds of ill health. He died of cancer in April 1965, some months after receiving the presidential Medal of Freedom. Like Kennedy's, Johnson's first choice for the post was his friend and president of CBS, Frank Stanton. Once again, Stanton declined, but agreed to serve in a supporting capacity as chairman of the President's Advisory Commission on Information.[28] In Stanton's place Johnson selected the African-American journalist and ambassador to Finland Carl T. Rowan.

Despite Rowan's diverse media experience, Johnson's choice stemmed chiefly from his eagerness to demonstrate his commitment to civil rights. As Johnson explained when selling his decision to Roy Wilkins of the NAACP, although not a cabinet post, the USIA director sat on the NSC, and Rowan would have the added kudos of succeeding Murrow.[29] Privately, LBJ conceded that the appointment was all that could be done at the time. He told one ally, "I want a nigrah in the cabinet but I haven't got a place."[30] Johnson's old Georgian friend Richard Russell immediately expressed doubts. He fretted over what would happen when the USIA "pitches in and gives the South hell" in its coverage of civil rights. Johnson assured Russell that Rowan understood the Southern way of doing things: "He's a Tennessee boy and he's got more sense than that."[31] The President also called the potentially troublesome Senator John McClellan of Arkansas, chairman of the committee on Government Operations, to warn him of his intentions. He feared that the segregationist senator might rebel against the surprise appointment of a black man and, as Johnson put it, "operate with

---

[27] LBJL WHCF CF, box 135, CF USIA, Marks to President, 19 June 1968.
[28] LBJL tape WH6401.17, PNO 4, LBJ/Murrow, 20 January 1964; WH6403.02, PNO 12, LBJ/Feldman, 3 March 1964; WH6403.04, PNO 1, LBJ/Jenkins, 6 March 1964; Interview (telephone): Louis T. Olom, 3 April 2001. Stanton combined academic and media experience. He had invented an audience research device for CBS and worked to develop the Carnegie Trust, RAND Corporation, and Institute of Behavioral Science. Also useful in the Johnson era Advisory Commission was the journalist Palmer Hoyt (1965–9). Hoyt replaced the conservative columnist Clark Mollenhoff (1962–5), who attracted Johnson's ire.
[29] LBJL tape WH6401.15, PNO 2, LBJ/Rusk and WH6401.15, PNO 4, LBJ/Wilkins, both 16 January 1964.
[30] LBJL tape WH6401.15, PNO 13, LBJ/Martin, 17 January 1964.
[31] LBJL tape WH6401.17 PNO 12 and 13, LBJ/Russell, 20 January 1964.

a knife" at the appropriations hearing, and send Rowan back from the Hill "without his Peter."[32] LBJ announced the appointment on 24 January, trusting that the world would be impressed by his promotion of a black American, and that the grateful black American would "rock-the-boat" less than a white liberal.[33]

*

Carl T. Rowan was born into poverty in Tennessee in 1924. He paid his way through Tennessee State College by scrubbing porches at the local tuberculosis hospital. His war service as one of the first African-Americans commissioned in the U.S. Navy provided unexpected educational opportunities. Through the GI bill he first attended Oberlin College in Ohio to study mathematics and then took a master's degree in journalism at the University of Minnesota. He became a journalist with the *Minneapolis Tribune*. In 1951, he made a swift reputation with a series of articles on segregation in the South: "How Far from Slavery?" A book called *South of Freedom* followed. As Rowan moved into foreign correspondence, he lectured for the USIS in India and elsewhere. In 1961, he joined the Kennedy administration as deputy Assistant Secretary of State for Public Affairs. His duties included "bear leading" Vice President Johnson on a world tour where, by his own account, he impressed the Texan by showing a willingness to "talk back." Now, Johnson asked Rowan to take on a rather more substantial task.[34]

Even as Johnson arranged Rowan's appointment, the USIA slipped back into controversy over the issue of civil rights, the occasion being James Blue's stunning documentary about the March on Washington, *The March*.[35] Although the President felt that the film had its virtues, key Southern senators raised objections. McClellan complained about the USIA "just throwing money away" on a film "showing the worst side of America." Some hinted at a further problem. When Stevens screened the film at a closed session on Capitol Hill, John Rooney asked, "did you get a security clearance on your star?" which was to say, Martin Luther King Jr.[36]

Lyndon Johnson saw the film as a trap. He told Texas Governor John Connally that if the USIA withdrew *The March*, "every nigrah's gonna get mad because it looks like its a reflection on him," and that the "son-of-a-bitch *Washington Post*" would cry censorship.[37] But positive responses from the field convinced the USIA that the film had immense value. The agency re-released the film with a prologue by Carl Rowan, which pulled the film into line with its usual approach to civil rights as "a profound example of the procedures unfettered men use to broaden the horizons of freedom

---

[32] LBJL tape WH 6401.15 PNO 6, LBJ/McClellan, 16 January 1964.
[33] LBJL WHCF Ex FG296/A USIA, box 316, Statement by President and Rowan, 24 January 1964.
[34] Carl T. Rowan, *Breaking Barriers: A Memoir*, Boston: Little, Brown, 1991.
[35] For background and analysis of the film see Cull, "Auteurs of Ideology: USIA Documentary Film Propaganda in the Kennedy Era as Seen in Bruce Herschensohn's *The Five Cities of June* (1963) and James Blue's *The March* (1964)," *Film History*, 10 (1998), 295–310.
[36] LBJL tape WH6401.17 PNO 13, LBJ/Russell, 20 January 1964; WH 6401.15 PNO 6, LBJ/McClellan, 16 January 1964; WH602.05, PNO.11, LBJ/Rusk, 4 February 1964; and WH6402.06, PNO 14, LBJ to Wilkins, 6 February 1964.
[37] LBJL tape WH6402.10, PNO.5, LBJ/Connally, 8 February 1964.

and deepen the meaning of personal liberty."[38] With this prologue the film became a staple of agency work. Rowan had weathered his first storm.[39]

The next major USIA film to address the issue of race took a safer approach than *The March*. Inspired by a *New York Times* magazine story, George Stevens Jr. commissioned Charles Guggenheim to make a film telling the story of the later lives of the nine black students who had broken the color line to attend a previously white high school in Little Rock, Arkansas in 1957, and their lives as students, teachers, journalists, and a civil rights organizer. It presented racism in America as a local issue being addressed by a benevolent federal government. The film concluded that no one knew exactly how many victories there had been for the cause of civil rights, but Little Rock had produced nine. *Nine from Little Rock* became one of the most successful USIA films, seen in ninety-seven countries and seventeen languages. In April 1965 it won the Academy Award for best documentary short.[40]

Rowan soon learned exactly why Representative Rooney had raised questions about King. At a meeting to prepare for the forthcoming budget round, Rooney warned the USIA away from making too much use of Dr. King in its propaganda. The Congressman explained that J. Edgar Hoover suspected King of Communist connections. These fears evidently centered on King's left-wing advisor Stanley Levinson, but beyond this, Rooney went on to recount how the FBI director had played him a tape of what Hoover described as "an orgy" in King's suite at Washington's Willard Hotel. Rooney had been particularly disturbed by a graphic piece of apparently homosexual banter between King and civil rights organizer Ralph Abernathy. Rowan assured the Congressman that this might just have been the sort of comradely talk typical of black men in the South, but left the meeting profoundly troubled. Clearly, world opinion was not the only thing that Johnson expected him to influence. The President had already asked Rowan to generate talking points for his meeting with the influential black magazine mogul John H. Johnson. As Rowan expected, when King began to criticize the Vietnam War, the President asked him to warn the civil rights leader away from friends and statements that made it harder for the President to help black Americans. Rowan duly delivered the warning together with news of Hoover's lurid claims. King promised to distance himself from Levinson. Although abhorring the FBI's campaign against King, Rowan personally regretted King's statements on foreign policy. King did not figure prominently in the output of Rowan's USIA.[41]

---

[38] Rowan's introduction survives on the National Archives print of the film.
[39] Interview: Stevens. For legislation introduced in 1986 to allow *The March* to be shown domestically (specifically excepted for a TV documentary on King) see HR 4985, 99th Congress, noted in Ronald Reagan Library, WHORM sf PR 011, 406127, Miller (OMB) to President, 25 July 1986.
[40] Interview: Guggenheim; LBJL WHCF Ex, box 314, Ex FG296, Rowan to President, 8 April 1965; NA MPSVB, RG 306.5160, *Nine From Little Rock*.
[41] Rowan, *Breaking the Barriers*, pp. 254–61. See also David J. Garrow, *The FBI and Martin Luther King, Jr.*, New Haven, CT: Yale University Press, 2001. The talking points for the John H. Johnson meeting are at LBJL WHCF Ex, box 2, HU2 Equality and Race, Rowan to President, 28 January 1964.

Ever the micromanager, Johnson corresponded with Rowan on the USIA's priorities. They agreed on the need to emphasize progress in civil rights.[42] It helped that in the summer of 1964, at least, the USIA had good news to report: the passage of the Civil Rights Act. Australia's *Canberra Times* observed, "In the long run the majority of the American people will always come down on the side of decency, democracy, and progress."[43] In preparation for Johnson's signing the bill on 2 July, the USIA prepared a global campaign to explain its meaning, including a thirty-minute television roundtable, featuring Roy Wilkins and other African-American leaders.[44] Using British opinion as a barometer, the USIA felt satisfied that its message had got through. Although 53 percent of people polled still believed that black Americans lived in inequality, 60 percent; felt that the U.S. government was working hard to correct matters.[45] But the publicity value of these advances remained vulnerable to the next outrage. The assassination of Malcolm X in February 1965 prompted Istanbul's *Milliyet* to remark, "America, which has reached the highest point of civilization, unfortunately seems worse than most primitive tribes on the subject of race."[46]

*

Rowan approached the U.S.S.R. with a sense that times were changing. Encouraged by the cessation of jamming in 1963, the VOA began a major "revamp" of its Russian programming. Now it would be lively current affairs programming mixed with jazz and popular music shows, with news "on the hour" with minimal repetition. Rowan told Johnson, "The tone of the content is also being modified to make it less polemical," although broadcasts remained "at the same time clear and firm in the enunciation of American policy."[47]

The thaw also took deputy director Don Wilson to the U.S.S.R. in June 1964, on a mission to increase Soviet–American cultural exchanges. In the process he spoke to numerous Soviet scholars and students and evaluated the USIA's cultural operations to date. VOA listeners, including the film director Andre Tarkovsky, underlined their appreciation of the Voice as a news medium. VOA Jazz also remained

---

[42] In March, Rowan informed Johnson that the agency's priorities could be summarized as "The U.S. pursuit of peace, our strength, and our reliability as an ally; Our belief in a world of free choice; Our commitment to the rule of law both at home and abroad; Our support for the peacekeeping machinery of the UN" (see LBJL WHCF CF, box 135, CF USIA, Rowan to President, 24 March 1964). To these Johnson added his own request that the USIA "emphasize those aspects of American life and culture which facilitate sympathetic understanding of United States policies." In early April 1964 all USIS posts received a summary of the aspects of American life to which the President attached particular importance. The list included economic strength but at the head read "Racial and Ethnic progress." The directive stressed the American "melting pot" and access of all to the fruits of American life. See LBJL Leonard Marks papers, box 27, USIA media priorities, Sorensen to all staff, 6 April 1964.
[43] LBJL WHCF Ex, box 314, Ex FG296 USIA, Rowan to President, 23 June 1964.
[44] LBJL NSF Agency, USIA, box 73, vol. 2/2, doc. 92, Rowan to President, 30 June 1964.
[45] LBJL WHCF CF, box 135, CF USIA 1965, Wilson to President, 13 July 1965.
[46] LBJL NSF Agency, USIA, box 74, Vol. 3a, doc. 40, Rowan to President, 24 February 1965.
[47] LBJL WHCF CF, box 33, CF FG296–1 VOA, Rowan to President, 2 May 1964. Radio Liberty remained subject to jamming. Most Soviet bloc countries also relaxed their jamming of the VOA and RFE at this time; see LBJL Salinger papers, box 1, agency reports, Wilson to President, 14 January 1964.

popular, although some connoisseurs mentioned that Radio Luxembourg was more up-to-date. Some complained about VOA propaganda, resenting not the presentation of communism, but the apparently inflated picture of the quality of life in the United States. The new initiative at the Russian branch eased these objections. Looking at other USIA activity, Wilson praised the Graphics – U.S.A. show and noted the importance of the Moscow embassy African expert, assigned to cultivate the ever-expanding corps of students and diplomats from newly independent African nations. Finally, Wilson observed that although many Russians believed that that Kennedy had been killed by a conspiracy, they liked Lyndon Johnson. Wilson attributed this not to Johnson's charm but to Soviet censorship. *Pravda* printed only the President's most conciliatory statements on foreign policy. The Soviet media had begun to prepare its people for what became détente.[48] Other changes followed. In mid-October 1964, a palace coup removed Khrushchev and installed hardliners Leonid Brezhnev and Alexei Kosygin at the helm of the Soviet Union in his stead. Cultural exchanges continued regardless.[49]

The USIA position in the Soviet Union had improved partly because the United States was no longer the sole object of Soviet antipathy. The Sino–Soviet quarrel had deepened. On 30 July 1964, the Soviets began to broadcast loud music on Radio Peking's Russian language channel. Radio Moscow then shifted its domestic programming onto Radio Peking's European frequencies. The Chinese tried in vain to evade the Russians by shifting their signal.[50] The Sino–Soviet split also showed up in Eastern bloc humor. Wilson reported political jokes on the subject anticipating the year 1970. One had LBJ sitting next to Khrushchev in a Chinese prison camp in 1970 and remarking, "I kept trying to tell you that Germany wasn't the *real* problem."[51] International propaganda had become a three-handed game. The USIA accordingly sought more cultural exchange with the Soviets, improved VOA signals to China, and prepared to wage ideological war in the developing world.

3) THE USIA IN THE DEVELOPING WORLD

FROM THE INDONESIAN CRISIS TO THE DOMINICAN INTERVENTION, 1964–65

Jordan Tanner had a bad feeling about the future of Indonesia. A young USIA CAO with experience of Korea (and the distinction of being one of the USIA's first Mormon officers), Tanner was no stranger to political unrest, but Indonesia was different. Since arriving in Jakarta in October 1961 to run the new USIS Cultural Center, he had noted two things. The first was rising anti-Americanism. Instigated largely by the PKI – the Communist Party – it was readily palpable on university

---

48 LBJL NSF Agency, box 73, USIA Vol.2/2, doc 128A, Wilson to Rowan, 1 June 1964.
49 *FRUS, 1964–1968*, Vol. XIV, *The Soviet Union*, doc 53, Meeting of Executive Group of NSC, 16 October 1964, pp. 124–5. For analysis see James E. Hoofnagle, "USIS libraries – lightning rods for violence," Foreign Services Institute, 11 June 1965, filed in NA RG 306 A1 (1070) USIA historical collection, reports and studies 1945–94, box 4.
50 LBJL NSF Vol. 2/1, doc. 63, Rowan to President, 4 August 1964.
51 LBJL NSF Agency, box 73, USIA Vol.2/2, doc 128A, Wilson to Rowan, 1 June 1964.

campuses and even within government departments. The second was the inability of the U.S. ambassador, Howard Jones, to sense the storm ahead. In the early morning embassy staff meetings, Jones would often comment that he and President Sukarno were "the best of friends" and even brag that he was the only ambassador with free entrée at the Merdeka Palace. At his Cultural Center, Tanner worked to meet Indonesian students. His evening jazz sessions, book reviews, and visiting exhibits gradually gained popularity, but Tanner's student contacts also passed on the campus buzz from radical circles against the "inroads the Americans were making." The PKI began to mount huge anti-American parades in the street in front of the Center, and some students worried for their safety when visiting. There were tangible warnings of what was to come. In August 1964, protesters seized the Thomas Jefferson library in Yogjakarta and forced its closure, and in September 1964, a cordon of police narrowly prevented the destruction of the American library in Surabaya (the mob destroyed the U.S. consulate instead). Nervous, Tanner asked the embassy security team to consider posting guards at the Center. The new guards appeared only at the embassy.

Just before noon on 4 December 1964 it happened. Three hundred students armed with clubs attacked the American Cultural Center. Rocks spun in through Tanner's second-floor office window, and as he dived for cover, he could hear book racks falling in the library below and the sound of the Great Seal of the United States being smashed into pieces. As the rioting students surged upstairs, Tanner assumed he was about to die. A student stopped directly in front of him and said, "We are not here to harm you, but to send a message to your government." With the damage done, the students left. But the protests continued. On 8 December, rioters razed the USIS library in Surabaya. The need to reach to young Indonesians could hardly have been greater, so a few weeks later the center in Jakarta reopened. On 12 February 1965, the protesters returned. A huge crowd surrounded the Center and began chanting anti-American slogans. They declared that the American director would not be permitted to leave the building. The local staff had already escaped over the back wall, but Tanner was a hostage. It took several hours of embassy appeals to Sukarno to raise a detachment of his palace guard to escort the center director through the screaming mob to the safety of an embassy sedan. A message was being sent indeed. Rowan reluctantly decided to end all USIA operations in Indonesia. In the spring of 1965 the agency withdrew entirely from the country, USIA staff were transferred to other posts (Jordan Tanner went back to Korea), and the agency donated its surviving stocks of books to university libraries around the country as a resource for the future.[52]

Although Indonesia was the only country to be completely abandoned by the USIA, it was certainly not the only example of such rioting. Such incidents became an occupational hazard for USIS work in the developing world, and staff joked

[52] Jordan Tanner to author, 11 April 2007; LBJL NSF Agency USIA, box 74, vol. 3a, doc 23, Rowan to President, 16 March 1965. "Indonesians Sack a 2d U.S. Library," *New York Times*, 8 December 1964, p. 1.

grimly about being typically located "just a stone's throw from the nearest university." The year 1964 alone saw three other incidents in East Asia, two in the Middle East, and nine in Latin America. From Nasser's United Arab Republic to Nkrumah's Ghana, USIS libraries burned. Rowan cursed the "fad" and mourned the refusal of the host governments to censure the rioters, but insisted that the USIA's work continue.[53]

The declared cause of several of the riots – including those in Indonesia – was U.S. "intervention" not in Vietnam but in the Congo. The Congo had concerned Rowan since his diplomatic work for Kennedy. By 1964, he feared that its ongoing troubles could escalate into a conflict with propaganda needs equivalent to those of Vietnam.[54] On 24 November 1964, American C-130 aircraft and Belgian airborne troops launched a surprise operation to rescue hostages in Stanleyville. With the airfield secure, the joint force successfully evacuated around 18,000 Americans and civilians from some twenty other countries from advancing rebels. Agency officers worked hard to explain the emergency action to the world. Rowan gave orders to "play-up evidence of rebel atrocities, callous disregard for lives of Congolese and other non-combatants" and their "defiance of worldwide condemnation." He assured LBJ in a secret memorandum that the USIA could "rely heavily on rebel brutality as a means of influencing world opinion." Accordingly the USIS post in Leopoldville became a clearinghouse for images of outrage. Rowan's deputy director for policy and plans, Tom Sorensen, believed that the atrocity line worked well to undermine the credibility of the rebels and their Chinese backers, but the Congo operation enraged many young Africans. Mobs attacked USIS libraries in Bujumbura, Burundi, Nairobi, Kenya, and Cairo, Egypt as a result.[55]

Anti-American riots notwithstanding, the USIA increased its engagement in Latin America. The agency remained a key tool of the Alliance for Progress, although it seemed that victories lay more in the realm of image than in that of hard reality. Alliance projects included a "plan to improve the public relations and image of U.S. businesses in Latin America."[56] In day-to-day work, the USIA focused on teaching English, especially at the binational centers. Enrollments in locations such as Lima and Mexico City averaged 20,000, and by 1966 the agency estimated a global enrollment in USIS language programs in excess of 300,000, excluding students following the VOA or USIA TV courses. The USIS supported teachers with seminars and a language journal, *English Teaching Forum*, launched in March 1963. In 1965, the USIA released its "Ladder Series" of books in simplified English in Latin America. Launched in Asia in late 1957, each book ran for about 30,000 words and worked with a controlled vocabulary of between one and five thousand words. The all-time best seller was an

53 LBJL WHCF CF, box 33, CF FG296 USIA, Rowan to Rusk, 31 December 1964.
54 LBJL WHCF CF, box 12, CF CO312 Vietnam (1964–5), Rowan to President, 19 June 1964.
55 LBJL NSF Memos to the President, box 2, file 7, doc. 9, Rowan to President, 21 December 1964, Sorensen, *The Word War*, pp. 259–60.
56 LBJL WHCF CF, box 135, CF USIA, Rowan to President, 28 April 1964. This plan was developed in collaboration with industrialist David Rockefeller and the steering committee of the Business Group for Latin America.

edition of Edgar Allen Poe stories developed for Japan. Evidence of their popularity abounded; a South Vietnamese priest even claimed to have built his church on designs derived from the USIA's Ladder biography of Frank Lloyd Wright.[57]

The agency noted that the spread of the English language in Latin America brought an increased demand for the USIA's political publications and swelled the audience for USIS lectures and film screenings. The entire global English language program received a major boost in June 1965 from National Security Action Memorandum 332, a statement of "U.S. Government Policy on Teaching English Language Abroad," which committed the USIA, AID, Defense, Peace Corps, and HEW to respond to the global demand for English teaching under the leadership of the Assistant Secretary of State for Education and Cultural Affairs. The document noted that the "rapidly growing interest in English" cut "across political and ideological lines." Testament to this came from the Soviet propagandists who, as the *New York Times* noted in 1966, began to use and even to teach English as the language of political communication in Chile.[58]

One great success for the USIA in Latin America came in the field of popular television: a twenty-six-part propaganda soap opera created to support the Alliance for Progress, *Nuestro Barrio* [Our Neighborhood]. Launched in Mexico in early 1965, by March this everyday story of anti-Communist folk topped the ratings in Mexico City.[59] The plot concerned the adventures of a young doctor, his struggle against an evil oligarch, and his inconvenient love for the same man's daughter. Within the story, characters learned the value of self-help.[60] The show's astonishing success in Mexico ensured distribution elsewhere in South America. By November 1965, stations in sixteen countries carried the program in a prime time slot.[61]

*

The USIA's biggest test in Latin America came on 28 April 1965, when Johnson deployed the first of some 23,000 troops from the United States and the Organization of American States to end a rebellion in the Dominican Republic. The initial wave established a "security zone," ostensibly to protect Americans. The military

[57] LBJL WHCF CF, box 52, CF FO6–3 Publicity, Marks to President via Kintner, pp. 2–3, 29 November 1966; Leonard Marks papers, box 16, Ladder Series, Fredman to Marks, 18 September 1967. In 1967, Leonard Marks suggested using the Ladder Series as a way to correct the image of the United States in textbooks around the world: WHCF CF, box 135, CF USIA 1967, Marks to President via Maguire, 20 September 1967.

[58] LBJL WHCF CF, box 52, CF FO6–3 Publicity, Marks to President via Kintner, pp. 2–3, 29 November 1966. LBJL NSF, NSAM 332, 11 June 1965 available online at http://www.lbjlib.utexas.edu/johnson/archives.hom/NSAMs/nsam332.asp.

[59] LBJL WHCF CF, box 135, CF USIA, Rowan to President, 23 March 1965.

[60] John Goshko, "A Latin Audience for USIA Drama" *Washington Post*, 4 August 1966.

[61] LBJL NSF Agency USIA, box 74, doc 116, Marks to President, 2 November 1965. By August 1966 the USIA could boast ratings of 88% for repeat screenings in Mexico and scores consistently in excess of 40% in the most competitive markets elsewhere in the region. The agency set to work making a radio spinoff and a new series – *Emilio Espina* – featuring the adventures of a crusading Latin American journalist. LBJL WHCF Ex, box 347, Ex PR16 Kintner to President, 5 August 1966; Marks to Kintner, 4 August 1966, and Goshko, "A Latin Audience for USIA Drama," *Washington Post*, 4 August 1966.

dictatorship in Santo Domingo had little to commend it. The rebels claimed to be loyal to the more attractive figure of the exiled liberal writer and former president, Juan Bosch, but Johnson feared that without U.S. intervention the Dominican Republic would turn to communism and become a second Cuba. His special envoy to the island, Ambassador John Martin, warned that any use of troops could be compared to the Soviet intervention in Hungary in 1956. Johnson risked a propaganda disaster.[62] The President maintained tight personal control over the crisis, acting, as one Senate staffer recalled, as "his own Dominican desk officer." He personally prevailed on Rowan to send a USIS team in with the second wave of U.S. troops. He also demanded psychological situation reports from the USIA, which arrived two or three times a day.[63]

The Dominican intervention presented a major challenge for the USIA. The agency needed to justify the move to the people of the Dominican Republic and to Latin American opinion in general. Both proved to be uphill tasks. Early regional editorials deplored Johnson's unilateral action and challenged his claim that the rebels were Communists. Rowan suggested that Johnson stress his humanitarian motives and enroll regional leaders to "push" the issue of anti-Communism. Johnson hammered on with the anti-Communist theme, but looked to the USIA to handle the situation on the ground. The direct role of the USIA began on 1 May with the arrival of a small USIA taskforce to organize all psychological operations, led by the associate director and former assistant director for Latin America, Hewson Ryan.[64]

The USIS team took up residence in the home of the resident USIS public affairs officer, Malcolm McLean. Initial problems included limited printing facilities, but soon the USIS had taken over a small print shop, found behind the police station in the American controlled sector, and set about producing leaflets explaining the U.S. presence. The next problem was radio. With only an estimated 60,000 shortwave listeners on the island, the mission needed access to the medium-wave band. Here McLean's young assistant information officer, Al Laun, proved his worth. A keen radio ham, Laun knew most of the Dominican broadcasters and their sites. He also knew the VOA engineer in the Task Force, Ray Aylor, from the Potomac Valley Radio Club. The two men borrowed an army truck and set out to find a suitable transmitter in the U.S.-controlled sector. They arrived at the most promising, *Onda Musical*, to find that the Dominican police had confiscated the transmitter crystal. Aylor had brought a supply of spares, but in this case, Laun called the station manager and learned that the station had an exact duplicate hidden at the bottom of a jar of nuts and bolts against

62 Abraham F. Lowenthal, *The Dominican Intervention*, Baltimore: Johns Hopkins University Press, 1995, p. 123.

63 Gaddis Smith, *The Last Years of the Monroe Doctrine, 1945–1993*, New York: Hill and Wang, 1994, p. 129.

64 LBJL NSF Agency box 74, USIA Vol.4, 4/65, #2, docs. 58, 59, and 60, all Rowan to President, 1 May 1965. ADST Oral History: Hewson Ryan. The Kennedy-era PAO in Santo Domingo, Serban Vallimarescu, went to coordinate press relations with Darrell Carter to assist and two VOA staff, Ray Aylor and Ray Millette, to supervise the relay of broadcast material. Wilson represented the agency on the crisis committee in Washington. Ryan had participated in plans for the intervention.

just such an eventuality. Laun retrieved the duplicate and shortly thereafter this station began to relay VOA Spanish transmissions.[65]

Cable and wireless communications with Santo Domingo remained uncertain throughout the crisis. The VOA correspondent Harry Caicedo covered events over a single telephone link shared with 100 other journalists. Laun's amateur radio skills came to the rescue. He and Aylor rigged a radio antenna in a tree and established contact in Morse code with the Potomac Valley Radio Club. Their club-mates set up round-the-clock monitoring on their frequency and transcribed the VOA correspondent's reports as they came through. At the Voice of America newsroom's Latin American desk, Bernie Kamenske was amazed to receive a call from the radio club but, having verified the source, he began preparing the reports for the in-house Latin America news wire and sending back questions for clarification. Kamenske and two colleagues worked in worked in rotation for thirty-three days straight, covering the story largely from Laun's transmissions. Laun's contacts brought information from all quarters, and thanks to the Potomac Valley volunteers, events in Santo Domingo could be on the VOA and hence known all over the island within hours. With the VOA's reporting as a benchmark, unfounded atrocity stories, such as those heard early in the crisis, failed to gain hold and neither side mounted reprisals.[66]

By 3 May, Ryan's team had prepared thousands of leaflets and posters to explain the U.S. action, dropped 10,000 such leaflets on key areas of the capital, and, using borrowed U.S. army resources, begun a program of loudspeaker appeals. A second medium-wave transmitter maintained by VOA engineers began to broadcast locally produced appeals featuring Dominican voices. Owing to power shortages, the rebels' only reply came over a feeble ham radio signal called Radio Constitution. The junta, in contrast, controlled Radio San Isidro and aired a diet of strident anti-rebel propaganda punctuated by "The Stars and Stripes Forever." As the United States claimed to be independent from the junta, these broadcasts were a mixed blessing.[67]

On 5 May, the USIS mission began broadcasting on a 5,000-watt medium-wave transmitter provided by the U.S. army. This station – Radio in the Security Zone, and later Voice of the Security Zone – carried VOA news and information regarding food and medical supplies and devoted ten minutes an hour to "Operation Families," a project to allow Dominicans to send and receive messages about relatives separated by the crisis. Peace Corps volunteers manned three phones to maintain contact with the public.[68] Now, leaflets fluttered daily across the island bearing extracts from Johnson's speech on the crisis or identifying "known" Communists in the rebel camp, citing the

[65] Interview (telephone): Al Laun, 18 January 2001; Sorensen, *The Word War*, pp. 265–7; LBJL WHCF CF, box 70, CF ND19/CO 62, Dominican Rep., Situation Reports, Rowan to President, 4 May 1965, notes that at night the VOA could also be heard on a medium-wave transmitter in Florida and on six Puerto Rican medium-wave stations. Estimates of their audience exceeded half a million.

[66] Interview: Bernie Kamenske, 6 December 1995. The VOA version of events proved so reliable that the USIA placed the news text on its daily wireless file for distribution to all posts worldwide

[67] LBJL WHCF CF, box 70, CF ND19/CO 62, Dominican Rep., Rowan to President, 3 May 1965; WHCF Ex, box 314, Ex FG296 USIA, Rowan to President, 3 May 1965.

[68] LBJL WHCF CF, box 70, CF ND19/CO 62, Dominican Rep., Psychological Situation Reports, Rowan to President, Confidential, 4 May 1965 and Confidential, 11 am, 6 May 1965.

country – Cuba, China, or elsewhere – in which they had been trained. Ryan attempted to sweeten the message of the roving loudspeaker vans by adding "music popular amongst Dominicans."[69] The USIA relished rebel protests against their propaganda operations, although similar objections from the OAS Commission seeking to resolve the crisis remained, for a while, politically "thorny."[70]

Ryan's operation ran into one major difficulty: what Rowan called the "cynical disbelief" on the part of the U.S. press corps on the island that the rebels were Communist-controlled. Tad Szulc of the *New York Times* and Dan Kurzman of the *Washington Post* proved particularly skeptical. The task force press officer Serban Vallimarescu hammered on with the Washington line regardless, denying that the United States was in cahoots with the junta.[71] Equally seriously, around 2 p.m. on 5 May, the rebels began broadcasting on Radio Santo Domingo. At 10,000 watts, it had the most powerful signal in the country. A simultaneous act of sabotage of the power system silenced U.S. transmitters on the island. The rebels enjoyed a brief monopoly of the airwaves. As Radio Santo Domingo lay outside the U.S.-controlled zone, the USIS team could not close down the station by force. Ryan braced for a propaganda duel.[72]

In Washington, President Johnson received a little encouragement from reports that the more conservative Latin American papers now accepted that the rebels had Communist links.[73] Meanwhile, Rowan sent a television crew to the island to record the humanitarian effort in food distribution, aid to refugees, and Peace Corps work. USIS posts achieved some success in placing material with local news media around the region.[74] Back on the island, the radio duel also extended to television. On 6 May, Radio Santo Domingo began to broadcast a television signal including images of captured U.S. Marines. The Dominican Navy replied on 7 May with a selection of USIA material. Programs included the *Panorama Panamericano* news digest and a film documenting the Cuban arms cache found in Venezuela.[75] By week two

69 LBJL WHCF CF, box 70, CF ND19/CO 62, Dominican Rep., Psychological Situation Report, Confidential, Rowan to President, 5 May 1965.
70 LBJL WHCF CF, box 70, CF ND19/CO 62, Dominican Rep., Psychological Situation Reports, Rowan to President, Confidential, 4 May 1965, Confidential, 11 am, 6 May 1965.
71 LBJL WHCF CF, box 70, CF ND19/CO 62, Dominican Rep., Psychological Situation Reports, Rowan to President, Confidential, Secret 2.30 p.m., and Top Secret, 7.00 pm, 5 May 1965, and Secret, noon, 7 May 1965.
72 LBJL WHCF CF, box 70, CF ND19/CO 62, Dominican Rep., Psychological Situation Reports, Rowan to President, Confidential, 5 May 1965; Confidential, 11 am, 6 May and Secret, noon, 7 May 1965.
73 LBJL NSF Agency box 74, USIA Vol.4, 4/65, #2, doc. 52, Daily Reaction Report, Rowan to Johnson, 5 May 1965. Johnson's advisor, Jack Valenti, suggested that the President develop the trend at a White House press conference by displaying the CIA report "The Communist Role in the Dominican Revolt," although "without actually letting them see it." Valenti hoped that the claim to posses evidence linking the rebels to Communism might be enough. LBJL WHCF Ex, box 215, ND19/CO312, Valenti/Cater to President, 12 May 1965.
74 LBJL WHCF CF, box 70, CF ND19/CO 62, Dominican Rep., Psychological Situation Reports, Rowan to Johnson, Secret, 5 pm, 11 May 1965.
75 LBJL WHCF CF, box 70, CF ND19/CO 62, Dominican Rep., Psychological Situation Reports, Rowan to Johnson, Confidential, 11 am, 6 May 1965.

of the intervention, the junta had put forward a new president, Brigadier General Antonio Imbert Barrera. The propaganda battle on the island settled into a familiar pattern of sniping between Radio Santo Domingo, the U.S.-controlled stations, and the junta's Radio San Isidro. The USIS team launched a two-page daily newspaper in Spanish called *Voice of the International Security Zone*. Although officially unattributed, its distribution at food depots and by U.S. airdrop clearly betrayed its origin.[76] Leaflet drops continued, though during the third week rebel small arms fire forced the USIA to briefly suspend all daylight airborne operations. Frustrated, the United States resorted to the unethical expedient of jamming Radio Santo Domingo. Against Ryan's expectations, by 18 May the rebel signal was reported to be weak and sporadic.[77]

By 21 May, Radio Santo Domingo had passed to the control of the Imbert government, while Caamaño's rebels struggled to maintain a signal of their own. As the United States worked to redefine the effort in Santo Domingo as a joint enterprise of the OAS, the USIS team spent a week attempting to persuade Imbert and his junta to surrender Radio Santo Domingo to OAS control. Ryan planned a "Radio of the OAS and the Inter-American Force" carrying no internal Dominican news, in order to avoid upsetting either faction. But General Imbert had no intention of giving up the station.[78] On 29 May, the USIS team converted its own broadcasting efforts into "Voice of the OAS" along the lines imagined by Ryan. The USIS team then began to offload the rest of its information work, including its newspaper, into OAS hands, albeit with the USIS providing technical support.[79]

The increased role of non-U.S. troops and the shift of the information effort away from the United States seemed to ease the situation. The year 1966 brought free elections, which returned Joaquín Balaguer to power. Like the *cause célèbre*, Juan Bosch, Balaguer had opposed the junta from exile, but his politics seemed reassuringly conservative to Washington. The crisis had passed. But events had a wider significance for the USIA. Hewson Ryan's efforts in the field had justified a leadership role of civilian information specialists in a psychological warfare situation. Ryan's tactical success in the Dominican Republic justified the emerging role of the agency in South Vietnam.[80]

76 LBJL WHCF CF, box 70, CF ND19/CO 62, Dominican Rep., Psychological Situation Reports, Rowan to Johnson, Secret, 5 pm, 11 May 1965.

77 LBJL WHCF CF, box 70, CF ND19/CO 62, Dominican Rep., Psychological Situation Reports, Rowan to Johnson, Secret, 4.30 pm, 17 May 1965, Secret, 18 May 1965. Interview: Laun. The first attempt to do was made by modifying the tuning circuit at Radio Guarachita, to move the signal from its usual position adjacent to RSD. Unfortunately, this system was not designed to transmit a single tone for a sustained period, and the station's transformer burned out after an hour. In the end a specially imported U.S. Army transmitter did the job. After the crisis, Laun delivered a replacement transformer to the station chief of Guarachita, on behalf of an apologetic United States.

78 LBJL WHCF CF, box 70, CF ND19/CO 62, Dominican Rep., Psychological Situation Reports, Rowan to Johnson, Secret, 24 May 1965.

79 LBJL WHCF CF, box 70, CF ND19/CO 62, Dominican Rep., Psychological Situation Reports, Rowan to Johnson, Secret, 29 May 1965.

80 LBJL WHCF Ex, box 317, Ex FG 296–1, VOA, Wilson to Reedy, 1 June 1965; ADST Oral History, Hewson Ryan, who following the crisis became chair of the interagency PSYOPS group.

4) **THE ROAD TO JUSPAO**
THE USIA IN VIETNAM TO JULY 1965

The story of the Johnson-era USIA effort in Vietnam is inseparable from one man – Barry Zorthian, the ebullient Armenian-American ex-Marine who as VOA program director had been co-architect of the VOA Charter. In February 1964, Zorthian left his post as deputy PAO in New Delhi to become the senior USIA officer in South Vietnam. Zorthian clashed with some correspondents but charmed others, earning the rather obvious nickname "Zorro." David Halberstam of the *New York Times* thought him "the most subtle member of the Embassy, a man whose own skepticism about the mission was considerable but who was brilliantly effective in quashing the doubts of others."[81]

The drive to increase the role of the USIA in South Vietnam came not from Zorthian but from the agency director, Carl T. Rowan. Vietnam was now the biggest cause in town and cooperation with the war effort offered a swift route to build the standing of the agency and its director in Washington, DC.[82] The USIA role in Vietnam grew alongside the rest of the American presence. Like the Army, the USIA began with advisory operations to support South Vietnamese "counterparts," the Vietnam Information Service of the Ministry of Information or the ARVN "psywar" section "S-5," but soon the United States seemed to be running its own propaganda war in South Vietnam.

To begin with, Ambassador Bunker limited Zorthian's role in Saigon, but mounting press troubles changed his mind.[83] In March 1964, the *Indianapolis News* printed a widely quoted letter from an American airman killed in action over South Vietnam in which he criticized both the U.S. effort and the failure of the government to communicate the story of the war to the American public.[84] Meanwhile, the new South Vietnamese military government proved as inept as the Diem regime in its handling of the press. Censorship included confiscating critical foreign periodicals at their point of entry into the country.[85] Rowan responded with a review of all information activities within South Vietnam. In a memo of 21 April, he informed President Johnson that "the information effort will fail, no matter what resources we pour into it, unless it has the clear direction of a single individual."

81 Interviews: Zorthian, 4 December 1995 and Halberstam, June 1991. David Halberstam, *The Best and the Brightest*, p. 352. For background pieces on Zorthian see *Newsweek*, 4 October 1965; Emile Schurmacher, "Chief Zorro," *Stag*, June 1966, pp. 28–30, 65–70; and Maynard Parker, "The Mark of Zorthian," *Life*, 12 May 1967, pp. 51–5.
82 For an example of LBJ's personal feelings, LBJL WHCF Ex, box 314, Ex FG296 USIA, President to Sec. of State et al., 6 June 1964, in which the President offers to write personally to any doubting officials to convince them of the value of taking assignments in Vietnam.
83 Interview: Zorthian; NA RG59 CPF 1964–66, box 420, PPB 9, Saigon 1285, Lodge to Murrow, 10 January 1964. On the AID psyops piaster fund see box 417, INF 8, Saigon 2138, Ball to Saigon, 30 May 1964.
84 Hammond, *Reporting Vietnam*, p. 22.
85 NA RG59 CPF 1964–66, box 444, PPV 1–2 Viet S., Saigon 1311, Lodge to State, 15 January 1964 and 1325, Lodge to State 17 January 1964.

He nominated Zorthian for such a role, and the USIA as the planning agency in Washington, DC.[86]

On 2 June 1964, with these issues still unresolved, the key architects of U.S. policy, including Rowan, met in a conference in Honolulu.[87] The conference agreed that the United States needed a single "communications tsar" in Saigon to act as principal public affairs adviser to both the ambassador and the new commander, U.S. Military Assistance Command, Vietnam: General Westmoreland. It also agreed that Zorthian was the best man for the job. His hand would be strengthened by guaranteed access to helicopter transport for the press corps. Zorthian now wore two hats in Saigon: his embassy role as "minister counselor for information" and his duties as director of USIA operations "in the country," including its developing psychological warfare activities. On 6 June, the State Department confirmed Zorthian's new role, stressing the need for him to "help newsmen cover the positive side of the news."[88]

On the way back from Honolulu, Zorthian sat next to the Saigon bureau chief of *Time* magazine, Frank McCulloch. The journalist suggested that Zorthian might introduce daily briefings at a regular time. Zorthian selected five o'clock, a time immortalized in a nickname used by both journalists and officials for these sessions: "The Five o'Clock Follies." The meetings began informally in Zorthian's own office. With the arrival of a new ambassador – General Maxwell Taylor – Zorthian reconsidered the mission's position on censorship. Like his predecessor, he too concluded that the United States could take no action that might infringe on the sovereignty of the South Vietnamese. The U.S. and other correspondents in Vietnam could, he felt, be trusted not to print sensitive stories that would endanger life or distress the family of a named serviceman. The key to Zorthian's approach to the press would be in the efforts he and his staff took to open the war experience to the press and to cajole them into positive reporting. The U.S. and South Vietnamese military agreed, subject to restrictions on the release of some military information, announcing casualty figures only on a weekly basis, and avoiding any details until it was clear that the information would have no tactical value to the enemy.[89]

Zorthian worked well with General Westmoreland, who made improved press relations a key element in his approach to command. When a directive from the State Department of 7 July called for "maximum candor and disclosure consistent with the requirements of security," Zorthian and Westmoreland were happy to oblige. The "maximum candor" policy, however, grew from an assumption that the South Vietnamese would provide positive news of sustained victories to be reported. In the

[86] *FRUS, 1964–1968, Vol. I, Vietnam 1964*, doc. 122, Rowan to President, 21 April 1964, italics in original; doc. 124, 528th meeting of NSC, 22 April 1964.
[87] NA RG59 CPF 1964–66, box 417, INF 8 US-Viet S., Ball to Saigon, 2144, 1 June 1964.
[88] *FRUS, 1964–1968, Vol. I, Vietnam 1964*, doc. 189, Meeting, Honolulu, 2 June 1964; doc. 192, McGeorge Bundy to President, 3 June 1964, doc. 197, Rowan to President, 4 June 1964; doc. 203, Rusk to Saigon, 6 June 1964. Johnson agreed to an equivalent concentration of responsibility within the United States under Robert Manning at the State Department; see doc. 219, NSAM 308, 22 June 1964.
[89] Interview: Zorthian; NA RG59 CPF 1964–66, box 417, INF 6, Saigon 4205, Zorthian to USIA/DOD, 15 June 1964; Hammond, *Reporting Vietnam*, p. 27.

short term, relations between the U.S. mission and the media improved, but the reform ensured that any downturn in the war would be as visible as the expected successes.[90]

*

In August 1964, Lyndon Johnson persuaded Congress to adopt the "Gulf of Tonkin resolution," a legislative blank check allowing him full power to escalate the war. The USIA noted mounting doubt in the world's press, but mobilized all its channels to disseminate LBJ's speech in justification. Twenty-seven transmitters with a combined power of four million watts carried Johnson's words live to the countries of Asia, with supporting material in English, Chinese, and Vietnamese. Related programs followed in thirty-nine VOA languages.[91]

In the months that followed, the USIA's staff in South Vietnam virtually doubled to fifty-four, with a further 200 military and AID personnel working on propaganda under their guidance. But major problems remained. Despite U.S. advice, the South Vietnamese government had yet to deliver sensitive handling of the press, economic development, or "military victories over the Viet-Cong."[92] Regardless of the failures of the Saigon government, Zorthian's team worked hard to win the battle for "hearts and minds" by building the image of provincial government in the countryside. In a test case in a village called Tam Ba in Phuoc Thanh province, U.S. and South Vietnamese personnel worked together to "pacify" what had become a key region of "Viet Cong" support. Initiatives included training South Vietnamese propaganda teams; dropping over a million leaflets; making and distributing special films, posters, and badges and a wall newspaper; and retraining the *Van Tac Vu* traveling theatre teams to do more than just insult the enemy. The USIS field representative organized metal signs for new schools, clinics, wells, and marketplaces, reading, "another self-help project with the help of your local government" – similar messages appeared on the wrappers of medicines distributed by the clinic and goods sold in the marketplace. U.S. funding, distributed from the specially established psyops "trust funds," seemed lavish by Vietnamese standards, but the entire Tam Ba project cost around $279.[93] Later in the war, U.S. province advisors received money from the CIA for these sorts of schemes in the so-called "Black Bag."[94] All such projects required achievements by the provincial governments upon which to build. As the war ground on these proved harder to find; moreover, U.S. military activity began to constitute a counterargument in its own right.

The enemy proved well able to respond to any psychological or military victory by the South Vietnamese and their American allies, more especially as the North Vietnamese stepped up their "infiltration" of fresh forces. American analysts detected a

[90] Zorthian to author, 1 September 2001; Hammond, *The Military and the Media*, pp. 80–85.
[91] LBJL NSF Agency, USIA Vol. 2/1, box 73, docs. 60 & 61, Rowan to President, 7 August 1964.
[92] LBJL WHCF CF, box 12, CF CO312, Wilson to Reedy (White House), 22 July 1964; WHCF CF, USIA, box 135, Rowan to President, 8 September 1964.
[93] LBJL, NSF Country – Vietnam, Rowan, 1c, Zorthian to USIA, 28 January 1965. The operation cost 20,432 ps at 73 ps to $1.
[94] Interview: Zorthian.

marked shift in the origin of enemy fighters from interviews with prisoners and captured weapons. The war now seemed increasingly international rather than internal to South Vietnam, especially as Lyndon Johnson had just extended U.S. bombing to the neighboring country of Laos. In February 1965 the State Department published a white paper entitled *Aggression from the North*, presenting evidence for North Vietnamese infiltration. The USIA publicized its findings with materials including a fifteen-minute television program, *Report from Vietnam*. A similarly named half-hour documentary film, *Report on Vietnam*, followed in 1966. The foreign nature of the fighters in South Vietnam became a major theme in Zorthian's war story.[95]

Zorthian and his colleague developed the "enemy as North Vietnamese invaders" theme at an expanded version of the daily five o'clock press briefings held in the auditorium downstairs at the U.S. embassy. One of Zorthian's staff briefed journalists on both U.S. and South Vietnamese military actions. Every Wednesday afternoon Zorthian himself offered personal and detailed weekly background briefings for the core correspondents on subjects as requested. However, the cultivation of an inner circle of correspondents left a number of more junior journalists out in the cold, and predisposed to look for stories in the field that ran counter to the mission's preferred line on the war. The most successful of these younger journalists was Peter Arnett of the Associated Press. He soon became a thorn in Zorthian's flesh.

In January 1965, Peter Arnett cabled a scoop. He had found a "Hollywood" camera crew using ARVN troops to "fake" combat sequences for a USIA propaganda documentary called *Night of the Dragon*. George Stevens Jr. had secured the services of Charles Guggenheim, who in turn had hired a young filmmaker named Richard T. Heffron to produce and direct. When the Arnett story hit the papers on 13 January, Stevens found himself vainly explaining that World War Two-era documentarists routinely restaged scenes for their cameras, and likewise, the USIA did not require its crews to place themselves in harm's way. Rowan took a different tack. He apologized to the press and pledged to destroy the "faked" sequences.[96]

Fortunately for the USIA, memories proved short. The final cut of *Night of the Dragon* included some of the "staged" scenes. Heffron's film – narrated by Charlton Heston – made a vivid case. In keeping with the new theme in U.S. propaganda, it blamed the war squarely on North Vietnam, arguing that South Vietnam's agricultural abundance had "tempted an enemy with an appetite for power to invade their land." Heffron exposed "Viet Cong" atrocities, focusing on the murder of civilians. He

[95] *FRUS, 1964–1968, Vol. I, Vietnam 1964*, doc. 450, Ball to Saigon, 19 December 1964; NA RG59 CPF, 1964–1966, box 446, circular 1698, Rusk to posts, 15 March 1965; Interview: Zorthian. For follow-up publicity see LBJL WHCF Ex ND19/CO312, box 214, Wilson to President, "USIA pamphlet on North Vietnamese arms shipment," 8 March 1965, with booklet: *The Evidence at Vung Ro Bay*. See also NA MPSVB, RG 306.5438, *Report on Vietnam*, 1966.

[96] Peter Arnett, "Filming in Vietnam: 'Battle' is staged for USIS," *Washington Star*, 13 January 1965; Interviews: Stevens and Guggenheim; Peter Arnett, *Live from the Battlefield: From Vietnam to Baghdad, 35 Years in the World's War Zones*. London: Corgi, 1995, pp. 196–8. Use included commercial screenings in the Philippines: see LBJL NSF Agency USIA, box 74, doc 116, Marks to President, 2 November 1965. LBJL WHCF Ex, ND19/CO312, box 215, Valenti/Cater to President, 12 May 1965

included horrific images of dead teachers, village elders, and their family members. He emphasized South Vietnam's own efforts and placed U.S. assistance alongside parallel aid from Japan, Germany, Australia, the Philippines, and South Korea. Heffron aimed for the heart with many sequences stressing the endurance of South Vietnamese children, including a five-year-old boy who had lost his legs in a minefield. *Night of the Dragon* circulated on the same bill as the year's hit musical *My Fair Lady*. Some PAOs considered it too strident, but the USIA successfully used the film on the Hill to justify its own budget and the Vietnam War effort in general.[97]

Although the world seemed slow to accept North Vietnamese responsibility for the war, LBJ proceeded under the assumption that a sufficiently punishing campaign against the North could turn off the war the war in South Vietnam like a magic switch. Johnson planned air strikes against North Vietnam accordingly. An ideal opportunity for this escalation came on 7 February, when the Viet Cong attacked an American barracks in Pleiku. U.S. bombers flew immediate reprisal missions under the codename Operation Flaming Dart and prepared to launch Rolling Thunder in March, but the wider question of escalation still hung in the balance.

The Pleiku attacks ushered in the last phase of debate before the wholesale Americanization of the Vietnam War. Although world opinion already reflected growing disquiet over U.S. involvement, at this crucial moment Carl Rowan used USIA research data to justify a continued commitment to the conflict. Pleiku found Rowan smarting from being excluded from the first rank of policymaking. He had gained admission to the NSC only to find that decision-making was confined to an inner circle around the President. Rowan felt compelled to participate in the debate over Pleiku and, despite being ill in bed with the flu, drove over to the emergency NSC meeting held on Sunday 7 February regardless. In a secret memo to Johnson written on Monday 8 February, Rowan presented a digest of USIA research and warned Johnson not to climb down, as this would lead to unbridled Communist influence in the Asian region, with pro-Communist regimes in Vietnam and Laos and a decline in the "Thai will to maintain an anti-Communist posture." The United States would be seen as an "imperialist paper tiger." The best evidence suggests that Johnson had already made up his mind to remain and escalate the war, but this memo retains an ironic value as an argument, couched in terms of public opinion, to hold to a policy that would undermine the international standing of the United States for years to come.[98]

---

[97] LBJL MPSVB, RG 306 05798, *Night of the Dragon*; Interviews: Guggenheim and Zorthian. Heffron went on to a career in television movies, where he recreated Vietnam with impunity for *A Rumour of War* (CBS, 1980). His great success was the Civil War miniseries *North and South* (ABC, 1985). For release with *My Fair Lady* see Robert Elder, *The Information Machine*, p. 9. For use on the Hill see LBJL WHCF Ex FG296, box 315, Marks to President, 13 January 1966.

[98] LBJL NSF Agency, USIA Vol. 3 A, file 2, box 74, docs. 83 a to n., Rowan to President, Secret, 8 February 1965, and attached documents. The covering letter bears only the drafting initials CTR and hence must be assumed to be solely Rowan's initiative. He mentions on an accompanying slip that the memo followed an informal note to the President, passed earlier that day, containing the same response. For Rowan's disgruntlement at being excluded from policy meetings see Rowan, *Breaking Barriers*, p. 267. The best analysis of Johnson's decision-making at this time is Frederik Logeval, *Choosing War*, Berkeley, CA: University of California, 2000.

USIA evidence gathered within Vietnam suggested a different response. Three weeks later Rowan sent over a USIA survey of opinion in Long An province, just thirty miles south of Saigon, which noted, "the population is largely apathetic and is primarily interested in ending the twenty years of war; they care less as to which side will win, although there appears to be a substantial degree of approval of the Viet Cong." This was not the advice that Johnson wanted to hear.[99]

While Johnson planned the escalation of the Vietnam War, Rowan found himself at war with the VOA over the issue of policy control. The Pleiku attack brought that issue to a head. President Johnson's retaliatory strike coincided with the visit of the Soviet premier Kosygin to Hanoi, and so the President insisted that the raids avoid the city and U.S. presentation of the event avoid pushing the U.S.S.R. When Rowan identified what he thought to be unnecessarily confrontational passage in a VOA commentary, he forbade its use. He insisted on "very tight control over everything said about the Viet-Nam situation except for straight, authoritative news."[100] The agency feared that VOA speculation on the imminence of negotiations over Vietnam might prevent their actually happening. But old hands at the Voice complained that the level of political control was "almost as bad as the McCarthy era" and aggravated by the fact that the Voice now claimed to be more than a crude arm of propaganda. In late February the Voice and the USIA clashed over the reporting of criticism of Vietnam policy. The USIA policy office forbade the VOA to mention two hostile editorials in *Le Monde* and the *New York Times*. Even coverage of Senate debates became moot. The USIA pushed the VOA toward heavy coverage of Senator Thomas Dodd's defense of LBJ's Vietnam policy on 23 February 1965 but restricted coverage of Frank Church's criticism until the administration had responded.[101]

Rowan noted the growing dissent and suspected that VOA director Henry Loomis had manipulated the issue in order to build the case for VOA independence. By his own account, Rowan informed Loomis that "If you can't understand that the president and I determine the editorial content of what goes out over the Voice of America, your ass is gone."[102] Within a month, Loomis found other employment as the number two at the Department of Education.[103] On the morning of 4 March 1965, Henry Loomis made a farewell address to staff of the Voice of America. His speech covered the achievements of the Voice as it rose to meet the external challenges of new nations and dramatic changes in the old ones. He spoke of Special English and of the successful concentration of the radio's administration in Washington. His review of internal problems ranged from the continued problem of limited space to the quirks

---

[99]   *FRUS, 1964–1968, Vol II, Vietnam January–June 1965,* doc. 172, Rowan to President, 27 February 1965.

[100] LBJL WHCF CF, box 33, CF FG296–1 VOA, Wilson to Moyers, 5 March 1965, notes, "All commentaries, news analyses, features, correspondents' reports, etc." were now "read in advance" at the highest level of the USIA; Rowan, *Breaking Barriers,* pp. 268–71.

[101] Mary McGrory, "Voice Chiefs Chafe at Curbs," *Washington Evening Star,* 5 March 1965.

[102] Rowan, *Breaking Barriers,* pp. 270–71. Loomis' new job is mentioned in the AP story, Lewis Gulick, "American Radio Policies Overseas Discussed," *Washington Post,* 7 March 1965.

[103] Rowan claims he fired Loomis as a result of the McGrory article, but this piece included news of Loomis' transfer.

of VOA food vending machines. He spoke of the need to maintain a commitment to broadcasting "truth" even when that truth did not flatter the United States. With deliberate irony, he cited Carl Rowan's eloquent defense of VOA coverage of the civil rights issue to support his case. Above all, Loomis defended the VOA charter of 1960:

> The charter is a statement of the principles which guide our decisions. It is not a substitute for judgment, nor is it a password or a mystical rite revealed only to members of the broadcasting fraternity. It must be the common yardstick by which you, your colleagues in USIA and your listeners make value judgments and measure the success of your endeavors. It is my hope – it is my belief – that the charter, like the Constitution is so fundamental and so represents the realities of the world and the moral principles that undergird this nation; that the charter will endure for the life of the Voice.[104]

Mary McGrory in the *Washington Evening Star* reported Loomis's words. Rowan's deputy, Wilson, rebuked Loomis for airing his grievances in public.[105]

*

In March 1965, the first regular U.S. combat forces arrived in South Vietnam. Their deployment prompted a reassessment of the U.S. mission's press policy. The official line remained "maximum candor and fullest disclosure of the facts consistent with national security interests," though this doctrine left considerable room for debate.[106] The deployment of troops strengthened the hand of the U.S. military within the Saigon bureaucracy and brought on a clash of press cultures in the field between an open USIA approach and the circumspect instincts of the Pentagon. In February the Defense Department had called for reporting restrictions to prevent the release of any information that could embarrass the military or help the enemy. Zorthian leapt to decry any rules that either forced his staff to deny the obvious or smelled of a "cover-up." He agreed to a voluntary code of practice with the leading correspondents. Following an ill-advised attempt to exclude correspondents from Da Nang airbase during the early weeks of the Rolling Thunder bombing, Zorthian also persuaded the military public affairs officers to accept this voluntary approach.[107]

Meanwhile, U.S. press coverage of the war had taken a turn for the worse. The AP's Peter Arnett had stumbled on evidence that the U.S. Army had given tear gas to the South Vietnamese. Army sources declined to comment. Arnett hammered out the story. Rather than the more usual term "tear gas," the AP Tokyo bureau substituted the more ominous "non-lethal gas." World opinion exploded. In West Berlin

104 Tufts University, Murrow Papers, reel 45, Loomis departure speech, 4 March 1965.
105 LBJL WHCF CF, box 33, CF FG296–1 VOA, Wilson to Moyers, 5 March 1965.
106 NSF Agency, USIA Vol. 4, file 2, box 74, docs. 45 a & b, Rowan to President, 12 May 1965.
107 NA RG 59 State, CPF 1964–66, box 444, including Saigon 3548, Zorthian to USIA/DOD, 27 April 1965; Interview: Zorthian; "The Image Comes First: USIA Rules Viet War News," *Washington Evening Star* 21 April 1965; Hammond, *Reporting Vietnam*, pp. 39–43. Hammond notes that by the summer some correspondents even favored censorship, pp. 52–3.

the *Spandauer Volksblatt* proclaimed, "gas warfare is one more step towards a major catastrophe . . . talk of harmless combat gasses is as nonsensical as talk of a clean atom bomb."[108] "Poison Gas War" instantly became a favorite theme in Eastern bloc propaganda about Vietnam in radio broadcasts and events, such as the anti-American photographic exhibition that opened in Sofia in July.[109] Terrified by the upsurge of opinion, the U.S. government suspended the use of gas and took great care with its use in Vietnam thereafter. Had the U.S. Army briefed correspondents about the use of tear gas before they deployed it and responded to Arnett's request for information, they would have avoided a damaging issue completely.[110]

Meanwhile, Rowan toured South Vietnam, presenting the Saigon government with a twelve point plan to revitalize their approach to their own population.[111] He returned eager to take up the challenge of Vietnam. His report to the President stressed the need for yet more direction in the propaganda effort and proposed a further consolidation of the information machinery in Vietnam under the leadership of the USIA. Rowan also noted the need for a fresh initiative to develop the propaganda activities of the South Vietnamese government in such fields as radio and television broadcasting and for training a larger pool of counterinsurgency specialists back in the United States. The NSC approved this agenda in early April 1965. In so doing, it reaffirmed the primacy of USIA in information matters in both Saigon and Washington, DC. Their decision, NSAM 330, would later be seen as the Rubicon for explicit involvement of the USIA in psychological warfare duties in Vietnam.[112]

On 1 July 1965, JUSPAO (pronounced "jus-pow"), the Joint United States Public Affairs Office in Saigon, came into being. Zorthian now commanded 153 Americans and 400 Vietnamese. JUSPAO combined press functions and a tactical psychological warfare role, absorbing activities and personnel from the U.S. military, AID, and the CIA as well as the USIA. When a European correspondent asked for a translation of the word JUSPAO, one of Zorthian's staff quipped that it was the Armenian word for chaos, but by 1966 the independent journalist I. F. Stone noted, "It is easier to get

108   Arnett, *Live from the Battlefield*, pp. 145–6; LBJL NSF Agency, USIA Vol. 3 A, file 1, box 74, doc. 17, Rowan to President, 23 March 1965; WHCF Ex ND 20–1, Atomic-Bio, box 422, Sylvester (Defense) to Reedy (White House), 12 May 1965. Also Caroline Page, *US Official Propaganda during the Vietnam War, 1965–1973*, Leicester: University of Leicester Press, 1999, pp. 116–20.
109   NA RG59 CPF 1964–66, box 412, INF 8 Bul-US, Sofia-US, Embassy to State, 24 July 1965.
110   Interview Zorthian; Zorthian to author, 1 September 2001. At the White House, Jack Valenti wrote bitterly to LBJ that the correspondent had done more damage "than a whole division of Viet Cong"; see LBJL WHCF Ex, ND19/CO312, box 215, Valenti/Cater to President, 12 May 1965.
111   *FRUS, 1964–1968, Vol II, Vietnam January–June 1965*, doc. 178, Defense to Saigon Embassy, 2 March 1965; NA RG59 CPF 1964–66, box 417, INF 8 Viet S., Saigon TOUSI 625, Rowan to USIA, 9 March 1965. The plan included a distinct South Vietnamese credo and dedicated central "psywar" ministry.
112   LBJL NSF Country, Vietnam, box 190, Rowan to President, 16 March 1965; *FRUS, 1964–1968, Vol II, Vietnam January–June 1965*, doc. 203, McGeorge Bundy to President, 17 March 1965. The plan received approval under NSAM 328 and 330; see doc. 242, 6 April 1965 and doc. 246, 9 April 1965. For the Nixon-era retrospective view see NA RG 306 87.0018, director's subject files, box 25, Ablard (General Counsel) to Loomis (deputy director), "Authority for Establishment and Operation of JUSPAO," 6 August 1971.

away from a bar girl on Nguyen Hué street than from the loving arms of the Press Chief Barry Zorthian's bureaucratic octopus for tenderizing (and ultimately digesting) the visiting correspondent."[113]

In August 1965, Zorthian returned to Washington, DC to take part in high-level consultations, including sitting in on the National Security Council. The President further strengthened his hand by promoting him to ambassador's special assistant for public affairs.[114] The USIA was now strong in Vietnam. Unfortunately, Zorthian found administrative upheavals at home as the tension between the VOA and the USIA flared. Henry Loomis' resignation from the VOA directorship merely set the scene for further conflict between the USIA and the VOA. The Dominican intervention inflamed matters. As during the Cuban missile crisis, the agency, working to State Department guidance, insisted on dictating news commentaries during the crisis. To the merriment of the VOA staff, Rowan even tried to write a commentary himself. As in 1962, Burnett Anderson of the USIA policy office took control and insisted that the Voice follow the party line. The VOA complained bitterly. Rowan's inability to handle the situation enraged LBJ, more especially when *Newsweek* ran a stinging piece describing Rowan's administration of the USIA as "ham-handed." Rowan's days at the USIA were numbered.[115]

The final blow came in July when LBJ refused to allow Rowan to travel to Thailand to conclude a VOA transmitter deal and made disparaging remarks about officials traveling because they liked to buy carpets. Rowan resigned immediately. He later claimed that LBJ apologized and begged him to stay, but the President lost no time recruiting a replacement. Rowan sent in his formal resignation on 8 July. By the time he left the agency on 31 August, he held lucrative contracts from the Publishers' Newspapers Syndicate and *Readers' Digest*. His position as America's first mainstream black newspaper columnist was secure. He died in 2000. Tributes included the naming of the newly refurbished press auditorium at the Department of State in his honor.[116]

[113] I. F. Stone, *In a Time of Torment*, London: Jonathan Cape, 1968, p. 274: "What Vietnamese Say Privately in Saigon," 16 May 1966.
[114] *FRUS, 1964–1968, Vol III, Vietnam June–December 1965*, doc. 110, 554th meeting of NSC, 5 August 1965, note 3, p. 322; "Pyswar," *Newsweek*, 4 October 1965, p. 40.
[115] LBJL WHCF Ex, box 317, Ex FG 296–1, VOA, Wilson to Reedy, 1 June 1965. Interviews: Kamenske, Anderson; "His Master's Voice," *Newsweek*, 7 June 1965; "'Voice' Policies Disturb Aides," *New York Times*, 5 June 1965; "America's Voice," *New York Times*, 11 June 1965.
[116] Rowan, *Breaking Barriers*, pp. 275–8; LBJL WHCF name, box 305, Rowan to Valenti, 19 July 1965. Johnson's telephone tapes reveal that besides creating a vacancy at the helm of the USIA, Rowan's departure also left Johnson needing another senior black appointment as soon as possible. He swiftly recruited Thurgood Marshall as Solicitor General, WH6507.03, program no. 1, LBJ to Katzenbach, 2 PM, 9 July 1965. Carl Rowan played an important part in the history of the black media in the United States. His column ran in over sixty newspapers and he hosted the television show *Inside Washington* from 1967 to 1996. Rowan played a key role in the campaign for Native American rights. He created an educational charity – Project Excellence – to encourage students to complete high school. He campaigned for gun control, which left him vulnerable to criticism when, in 1988, he wounded an intruder in his Washington home with a gun belonging to his son. Political enemies had a field day, but Rowan escaped conviction. Elaine Sciolino, "Carl Rowan, Writer and Crusader, Dies at 75," *New York Times*, 24 September 2000, p. 54; J. Y. Smith, "Columnist Carl Rowan dies at 75," and editorial, "Carl T. Rowan," *Washington Post*, 24 September 2000, pp. A1 and B9; also http://blackjournalism.com/carl.htm.

Rowan's tenure at the USIA had built on the institutional foundations of the Murrow years, but relations with the VOA seemed worse than ever, and the "starring role" that Rowan had secured for the agency in Vietnam certainly proved a mixed blessing. In later years Rowan conceded that he "erred" in his eagerness to expand propaganda in Vietnam and had "underestimated the factors of anti-colonialism, nationalism, hatred of racism," and "anger over economic exploitation for generations."[117] Rowan's successor – Leonard Marks – inherited the consequences of his error.

[117] Rowan, *Breaking Barriers*, pp. 262–3.

6 "My Radio Station"

THE JOHNSON ADMINISTRATION, 1965–69

> This nation and this government have no propaganda to peddle. We are neither
> advocates nor defenders of any dogma so fragile or a doctrine so frightened as to
> require propaganda.
>
>   Lyndon B. Johnson, 31 August 1965.[1]

In the autumn of 1965, Voice of America engineers installed a neat
wooden box with a speaker and dials in the family reception hall at the White House.
This was a "Monitron," a device to allow the listener, in this case the President of the
United States, to tap directly into multiple feeds from a radio station, in this case the
studios of the VOA. The President tuned in from time to time to hear how the VOA
covered particular stories, and from February 1967 the device carried English feeds
from Radio Moscow and Radio Beijing as well.[2] Johnson's reactions to the broadcasts
were relayed to Voice staff via the USIA director, and it boosted morale to know that
the President was listening. But LBJ didn't always like what he heard. Norm Gerin,
who broadcast the VOA's weekly press roundup, was astonished to pick up a ringing
phone in his studio after a broadcast to hear the voice of the President apoplectic with
rage over the content of his program. For LBJ the Voice was "*my* radio station" and
had a duty to keep step with his foreign policy.[3]

Although parsimonious as a senator, as President, Johnson had always understood
the importance of a sound international information effort. He supported his new
USIA director, Leonard Marks, and integrated the agency into policy as never before.
Marks possessed two characteristics essential for success: a vision of the future of
U.S. information and a personal relationship with the President that was close enough
actually get there. Marks also deployed a new weapon to build the USIA, a newly
minted term to describe its activities: "public diplomacy." He was able to make a
difference.

The later Johnson years saw many significant shifts in world affairs, including
a thaw in Soviet–American relations, changes in China, and new challenges in the

---

1   *Public Papers of the Presidents, Lyndon B. Johnson, 1965*, Vol. 2, doc. 468, remarks on the swearing in
    of Leonard Marks, 31 August 1965, pp. 955–6.
2   LBJL WHCF Ex, box 3, Ex UT-1-1, Marks to LBJ, 26 September 1965; box 317, Ex FG 296–1
    VOA, Marks to Watson, 17 February 1967.
3   Interview: Frank Cummins, 9 November 1995; LBJL John Chancellor oral history, 25 April 1969,
    p. 18.

Middle East, but the Vietnam War dominated. The war engaged the USIA at every level and justified the highest budgets in the agency's history. Within South Vietnam, JUSPAO officers fought the "psychological" war and attempted to manage the press, while around the world USIS public affairs officers struggled to justify the wars to their client governments, presses, and publics. The USIA documented the shift of world opinion. Unfortunately, from 1965 onward that shift was uniformly detrimental to the United States. President Johnson responded by no longer listening to the bad news. In the autumn of 1965 Johnson intervened to order the USIA to halt the running survey of U.S. prestige in world opinion. Agency staff presumed that LBJ was worried that the news of America's plummeting standing could become public by the time of his presumed reelection bid in 1968, a real possibility given that even without leaks, the polls became public after two years. Leonard Marks tried hard to use his personal influence to keep the President engaged. He sought, when necessary, to present the facts of world opinion to the President, but he too was to learn that some messages are too bleak even for friends to deliver.[4]

1) "PUBLIC DIPLOMACY" AND A PUBLIC DIPLOMAT
LEONARD MARKS AT THE USIA

Leonard H. Marks was a trusted member of the Johnson camp. Born into a Jewish family in Pittsburgh in 1915 and educated at the University of Pittsburgh, he was consistently at the head of his class and rose swiftly in communications law. Between 1942 and 1946 he served as assistant to the general counsel at the Federal Communications Commission. In 1946, he became a partner in the firm of Cohn and Marks. Marks had known LBJ since 1947, when he first represented Lady Bird Johnson's Texas broadcasting interests, encouraging the early entry of her station – KTBC – into television. He played a part in persuading LBJ to run for President in 1960 and managed the television aspects of the campaign. Marks had also helped draft the Smith–Mundt Act and had served on the U.S. delegation to the International Broadcasting Conference and on the board of directors of COMSAT, the corporation created by the Kennedy administration to oversee communications satellites. More than any previous USIA director, Marks arrived with a vision. He was convinced that international communications had the power to transform life on earth for the good.[5]

In March 1965, Marks wrote to Johnson noting a crisis of morale at the USIA and offering to conduct an investigation looking especially at its use of technology.[6]

---

[4]   On reform of the system for reporting world opinion see LBJL WHCF Ex, box 31, Ex FG296, Valenti to Marks, 18 September 1965. On World Opinion Survey 1965 see NSF Agency Vol. 6, 2, box 75, doc. 69, Ackers to President, 14 December 1965. By 1968 Johnson had also reduced his weekly report on USIA activities to a "Bimonthly Achievements Report"; see WHCF Ex, box 17, Ex FG1, Marks to President, 29 February 1968. Sorensen, *The Word War*, 77. For comment see Haefele, "John F. Kennedy, USIA and World Public Opinion," pp. 83–4.

[5]   LBJL Oral History: Marks Interview I, June 1970 and II, January 1976,

[6]   LBJL WHCF Ex, box 314, Ex FG296, Marks to President, 17 March 1965.

Johnson did not respond to this note until 9 July 1965, a day after Carl Rowan submitted his resignation. At 11:35 a.m. he called Marks and bluntly offered him the post of USIA director and proposed to announce the appointment immediately.[7] Although, as a concession to Marks' need to tell his wife and business partner, he actually made no formal announcement until 13 July, LBJ immediately began to speak about the appointment as a fait accompli. He asked columnist Drew Pearson to organize a lunch to introduce Marks to the key editors and columnists in town. Johnson confided in Pearson that he hoped the appointment might please American Jews, who he thought were feeling "neglected."[8]

Carl Rowan took time to help Marks find his feet at the USIA, taking him to a NSC meeting and showing him around the agency. Johnson prepared the ground on Capitol Hill by inviting the troublesome Representative Rooney to meet Marks in the Oval Office and asking him to advise on the best way to develop the USIA. Rooney suggested that Marks speak to the agency's founder and enduring champion, Dwight Eisenhower. Johnson duly arranged such a meeting. As Marks recalled, Ike stressed the significance of the USIA and wished he had given the agency even more of a voice in policy-making. Johnson duly invited Marks to both NSC and cabinet meetings. Once Marks was in post, Johnson and Marks spoke often on the telephone, with LBJ typically ringing at 7:15 in the morning to chew over the morning news or at 11:30 in the evening as the smoke of the day cleared. These conversations, which occurred at intervals varying from every day to once a month, were not taped, and as Marks recalled, generally had nothing to do with the USIA. Johnson sought Marks' advice on various political matters and, as Marks put it in later years, "I was still his lawyer." All Washington knew that Marks could call on LBJ's aid if challenged by a rival agency; hence no agency ever mounted a challenge. Marks never needed to ask a favor.[9]

7 For the conversation see LBJL WH6507.02, program no. 12, LBJ to Marks, 11.35 AM, 9 July 1965; Interview: Leonard Marks, 15 May 2003; LBJL Oral History: Marks Interview I, June 1970, pp. 20–22; *PPP LBJ 1965*, vol. II, doc. 353; ADST Oral History: Marks interview. The tape of their conversation provides a fascinating snapshot of President Johnson at work. He stressed the significance of the USIA directorship as "a job with Rusk and McNamara and with one hundred and twenty nations" that "affects the lives of every human being, the schools and the education and the peace and everything else." Johnson emphasized the centrality of the USIA to Vietnam, observing, "the Vietnam thing is the most important thing in the world." Clearly flattered by the President's offer, Marks hurriedly began to recite the highlights of educational and legal career to date. The President probed his friend's background for possible problems. Johnson: "You haven't got any liberal organizations that would give us any FBI trouble?" Marks: "Hell no, I was called a fascist at college!" Johnson: "Have you got anything FBI that would give us any trouble or problem?" Marks: "Sir I can swear to that, I can tell you without any equivocation, there are no women in my life but my wife." Johnson stunned Marks by saying that he intended to announce the appointment that day. Marks begged for a day's grace to conclude some business affairs and talk the matter over with his wife and business partner.

8 LBJL WH6507.02, program no. 12, LBJ to Marks, 11.35 AM, 9 July 1965 and WH6507.03, program no. 9, LBJ to Pearson, 2.25 PM, 13 July 1965. LBJ's exact words to Pearson were, "He is clean looking and neat dressing and he is the only top Jewish fellow we've had there in that spot and I think that's very important as they [American Jews] are beginning to feel like they are neglected." Interview: Leonard Marks, 15 May 2003; LBJL Oral History: Marks Interview I, June 1970, pp. 20–22; *PPP LBJ, 1965*, vol. II, doc. 353; ADST Oral History: Marks interview.

9 Interview: Marks, 15 May 2003; ADST Oral History: Marks.

While preparing to assume command, Marks wrote his report on the agency. He stressed the need for leadership at the USIA and budget cuts in Western Europe. He proposed a campaign to publicize Johnson's "Great Society" programs, a global network of ground stations for satellite communications, and changes to make the Voice's output "more listenable." It was a full agenda.[10]

Johnson arranged a high-profile swearing-in ceremony for Marks in the Rose Garden of the White House on 31 August 1965.[11] Marks used the ceremony to cultivate the key figures in Congress. He invited Rooney to attend. No previous USIA director had thought to do this, and unlike his predecessors, Marks had no major problems on the Hill. Rooney and the appropriations committee warmed to Marks's command of the agency's affairs: he was the sole witness at hearings; he kept within budget and he returned an unspent balance at the end of each year. In later years, when asked which element in his tenure at the USIA gave him the most pride, Marks led off with "Our Congressional relationship."[12]

The new USIA director worked well with Secretary of State Dean Rusk. At Johnson's suggestion, Rusk brought Marks into policy discussions, and he attended Rusk's daily morning meetings with his assistant secretaries. Rusk often asked Marks to interject his views. It was a relationship with a future. Marks understood that if LBJ won in 1968 he would become deputy Secretary of State.[13]

By one index Marks swiftly made an impact. In October 1965, Radio Moscow attacked Marks personally, comparing him to an ideological burglar "trying to break into other people's homes by whatever means possible." Marks proudly forwarded the quote to President Johnson.[14] In 1966, Moscow's Publishing House for Political Literature produced a detailed primer on American propaganda: *Operation "PW": The Psychological Warfare of the American Imperialists.* Moscow seemed particularly impressed by the immediacy of the VOA, the speed of the USIA's film and TV response to Kennedy's death, and the "brainwashing" powers of the New York Foreign Correspondents Center. With such praise, Marks opened a similar center for the 180 foreign journalists working in Washington, DC in June 1968.[15]

---

[10] LBJL WHCF Ex, box 314, Ex FG296 USIS, Marks to President, 18 August 1965 and 7 October 1965 for a review of progress, including $250,000 in budget cuts in West Germany, Britain, and France. These programs had been cut since 1960 to the level of 24 percent in salary/expenses, 31 percent in U.S. staff, and 43.5 percent in local staff. Nearly half of all USIA installations in Europe had closed; see Leonard Marks papers, box 27, USIA briefing papers, doc. 2b, Lincoln to Marks, 28 July 1965.

[11] *PPP LBJ 1965*, Vol. 2, doc. 468, remarks on the swearing in of Leonard Marks, 31 August 1965, pp. 955–56.

[12] Interview: Marks, 15 May 2003; Marks rated his other major contributions as support for the war in Vietnam, passage of career legislation, and raising the profile of the agency at the highest levels of policy-making. See also LBJL Oral History: Marks Interview I, June 1970.

[13] Interview: Marks, 15 May 2003; ADST Oral History: Marks. In contrast, Marks felt his relations with Defense were merely adequate.

[14] LBJL WHCF Ex, box 317, Ex FG296–1 VOA, Marks to President, 3 November 1965.

[15] LBJL Leonard Marks paper, box 15, "Anti-American diatribes in Soviet Press," memo "Operation PW," undated, circa January 1967, citing esp. pp. 68–9, 74–7, 82. Also Marks box 18, Foreign Correspondents Center, announcement 3 June 1968.

*

As Marks set out to sell the USIA around Washington, DC, he was assisted by
the new term for the agency's activities: "public diplomacy." The American people
had never been comfortable with the word propaganda, with its connotations of distortion, trickery, and downright lies. "Public diplomacy" gave the USIA a fresh turn
of phrase upon which it could build new and benign meanings; it was a perfect piece of
propaganda about propaganda. The term "public diplomacy" covered every aspect of
USIA activity and a number of the State Department's cultural and exchange functions. It gave a respectable identity to the USIA career officer, being one step removed
from the "vulgar" realm of "public relations" and, by its use of the term *diplomacy*,
enshrined the USIA alongside the State Department as a legitimate organ of American foreign relations. The term itself became an argument for the USIA against the
challenge of the Bureau of Education and Cultural Affairs at State. If public diplomacy existed as a variety of modern diplomacy – the argument ran – then surely the
United States needed a dedicated agency to conduct this work, and that agency was
best structured with a monopoly over all U.S. work in the information and cultural
field overseas.

Marks had Edmund Gullion to thank for coining the term. The dean of the
Fletcher School of Law and Diplomacy at Tufts University near Boston, Gullion had
recently retired from an illustrious career as a foreign service officer, which included
a term as staff director for the Sprague Committee and as Kennedy's ambassador to
Congo. He had a keen respect for the role of information in diplomacy in general
and for Murrow in particular. Gullion hoped that Murrow might join the faculty at
Tufts following his retirement from the USIA and help train a new generation of foreign service officers with real media competence and build links between American
diplomats and the world of journalism. Murrow had blessed Gullion's "happy idea"
in the autumn of 1964, noting, "This really vital problem is not adequately treated by
any other school." But Murrow's health precluded any further role. Undeterred by
Murrow's death in April 1965, Gullion established the Edward R. Murrow Center of
Public Diplomacy as his memorial. USIA officials would rotate through to teach, and
the center immediately engaged two foreign correspondents as lecturers and inaugurated a lecture series on public diplomacy and the social sciences. The *New York Times*
announced the project in July and Vice President Hubert H. Humphrey formally
opened the Murrow Center in December 1965.[16] An early Murrow Center brochure
provided a summary of Gullion's concept:

> Public diplomacy ... deals with the influence of public attitudes on the formation
> and execution of foreign policies. It encompasses dimensions of international
> relations beyond traditional diplomacy; the cultivation by governments of public
> opinion in other countries; the interaction of private groups and interests in one

16 LBJL Leonard Marks papers, box 14, *USIA Correspondent*, Vol. 8, No. 1, January 1966; "Law School
of Tufts Names New Center after Murrow," *New York Times*, 2 July 1965; "Edward R. Murrow
Center: News, Diplomacy Linked," *Christian Science Monitor*, 8 July 1965, p. 11.

country with another; the reporting of foreign affairs and its impact on policy; communication between those whose job is communication, as diplomats and foreign correspondents; and the process of intercultural communications.

The USIA manifestly sat at the heart of such a project.[17]

Gullion was shy of claiming the coinage of the term for himself but rather spoke of it in the first person plural, as a team effort. When Dante Fascell used the words during House hearings in 1968, Gullion noted,

> [M]ay I compliment you, Mr. Chairman, on adopting that term. It is a term which may make old time professional hack bureaucrats in foreign affairs like myself cringe a bit. We in our institution, the Murrow Center of Public Diplomacy, also tried to come up with a phrase that would connote all the things you are talking about – public and private activities in international relations. Public diplomacy was our best effort.[18]

Gullion was happy to acknowledge its roots as a euphemism: "I would have liked to call it 'propaganda,'" he wrote in 1967.

> It seemed the nearest thing in the pure interpretation of the word to what we were doing. But "propaganda" has always had a pejorative connotation in this country. To describe the whole range of communications, information and propaganda, we hit upon "public diplomacy."[19]

The term "public diplomacy" was little used outside the USIA until the 1980s. By the 1990s it had also entered common use overseas in official circles, and following the attacks of September 2001, it finally broke into American public consciousness. There is no disputing its value to the USIA.

*

The coining of "public diplomacy" coincided with two other significant developments at the USIA. In March 1965, Rowan secured a consolidated site for the USIA's offices, moving 1,400 staff to new quarters at 1750 Pennsylvania Avenue,

17 Interview: Tuch. In 1988 the concept acquired a second supporting institution, The Public Diplomacy Foundation, which included many USIA veterans. The Murrow Center quotation comes from the PDF Web site "What is Public Diplomacy" page (http://www.publicdiplomacy.org/1htm). The author is grateful to Professor Lee McKnight, director of the Murrow Center, for his account of its origins, given over the phone on 13 March 2001. The interdependence of Public Diplomacy and the USIA is suggested by the fact that following the demise of the USIA in 1999 the Center became the Murrow Center for International Information and Communications.

18 "The Future of United States Public Diplomacy," part XI of hearings on Winning the Cold War: The U.S. Ideological Offensive by the Subcommittee on International Organizations and Movements of the Committee on Foreign Affairs of the House of Representatives, pursuant to H. Res. 179, 22 July 1968, p. 36, filed in NA RG 306 A1 (1061), USIA historical collection, misc. files, 1940–1990s, box 15.

19 Robert F. Delaney and John S. Gibson (eds.), *American Public Diplomacy: The Perspective of Fifty Years*, Medford, MA: The Edward R. Murrow Center of Public Diplomacy, Fletcher School of Law and Diplomacy/Lincoln Filene Center for Citizenship and Public Affairs, 1967, p. 31, as cited in John Brown, "The Anti-Propaganda Tradition in the United States," *Bulletin Board for Peace*, 29 June 2003, posted at http://www.publicdiplomacy.org/19.htm.

NW. Now, Marks took steps to address the long-standing iniquities between agency employees and State Department Foreign Service Officers. Up to this point, USIA staff had served overseas as members of the U.S. Foreign Service Reserve. They had neither the job security nor pension rights of the State Department foreign service officers, and the separate career structure prevented the interchange of personnel or the promotion of able officers to ambassador level. In 1964, former Secretary of State Herter had issued a report proposing to transform over 900 USIA officers into full FSOs or their equivalent. Johnson signed the necessary legislation in August 1968, and by October the Senate had confirmed the first group of nearly six hundred foreign service information officers. On 24 October, the first 200 FSIOs took their oaths of office. Many, including Burnett Anderson and Hewson Ryan, went on to run embassies of their own. Information specialists were respectable diplomats at last.[20]

*

Like every incoming director, Marks needed first-rate senior colleagues. Johnson appointed a retired newspaper editor from Beaumont, Texas named Robert Wood Ackers to be Marks's deputy. Marks himself chose a media executive from San Diego, Howard Chernoff, to serve as executive assistant. Chernoff rather than Ackers acted as Marks's number two.[21] Marks also needed a new director for the VOA. He and LBJ swiftly settled on NBC's White House correspondent, John Chancellor. Johnson already had cordial relations with Chancellor, using him as a discreet point of contact with NBC news in New York. Johnson did not equivocate over the appointment. He summoned Chancellor from the pressroom into the Oval Office one Saturday and bluntly asked him to take the job. Chancellor resisted for twelve days or so but with his boss, the president of NBC Robert Kintner, eager to present him to the President "as a gift," he was caught in a pincer movement. In the finish, LBJ argued, "If I can send boys over to Vietnam it seems to me that I can send you to Independence Avenue." Chancellor had been drafted.[22]

Both Johnson and Marks promised Chancellor full autonomy as VOA director, and he felt that both men were true to their word. Chancellor had little or no direct contact with the White House, and his policy disagreements with Marks would be few

---

[20] LBJL WHCF, CF FG 296, box 33, USIA (1964–66), Rusk/Rowan to President, 28 September 1964; Leonard Marks papers, box 14, *USIA World*, Vol. 2, Nos. 4, 5 & 6, September, October & November 1968. Other distinguished USIA officers to reach the rank of ambassador included William Weathersby, John Reinhardt, John Shirley, and Michael Pistor. It should be noted that the legislation also made it easier to fire incompetent people at the point of transition to FSO status; see Leonard Marks papers, box 27, USIA briefing papers, doc. 10a, Wright to Marks, 28 July 1965. USIA staff had held principal posts before. Murrow had negotiated an informal agreement that one such post in each region should be held by a USIA person. The career structure made the career path to an embassy normal. ADST Oral History: Hewson Ryan. For a critical perspective on the USIA's ambassadors see Arndt, *First Resort of Kings*, p. 488.

[21] Sorensen, *The Word War*, p. 275.

[22] LBJL John Chancellor oral history, pp. 3–6; 12–16. LBJL telephone tapes, WH6503.16, 2 &3, Chancellor/President, 31 March 1965 and WHCF Name file, Chancellor, John; Valenti to President, 2 June 1965; Interview: Dick Krolik, 21 December 1995; Interview: Marks, 15 May 2003.

and small.[23] Chancellor immediately began a radical reform of the VOA's output. He
changed much. He dropped the old call sign, "Columbia, the Gem of the Ocean,"
in favor of the more up-beat "Yankee Doodle Dandy." He worked closely with Dick
Krolik, an old NBC colleague then working for Time Life. Together, they launched
the "New Sound" first, in November 1966, for VOA Worldwide English evening
programs, and then for other key languages, including Russian. "New Sound" meant
trading Zorthian's old structure of news, commentaries, and occasional features for
a "magazine" format based around a two-hour cycle. Like NBC's much admired
Monitor program, the VOA "New Sound" mixed music and short features with news
stories. The journalists objected, but the changes advanced regardless.[24]

Chancellor also reformed elements in the news-gathering process. He strengthened the journalistic element at the VOA by bringing together the English language
reporting and wire rewrite desks and central news desk to create a News and Current
Affairs (NCA) branch, modeled on a network newsroom. NCA provided most news
and feature material for the whole VOA. The language services soon found themselves
translating centrally written material. Chancellor also created a twenty-four hour operations center at the VOA. The staff always knew how to reach him. Hence, when fire
claimed the Apollo spacecraft and crew during launch-pad training, the Voice operations center had the news within moments and called Chancellor at a party to pass on
the news; Marks – a guest at the same party – was reportedly peeved that Chancellor
had the news first.[25]

Chancellor campaigned over the matter of the VOA's accommodation, arguing
that federal prisons required one hundred square feet of dormitory per prisoner, but
in the main VOA building staff had only fifty six feet per person.[26] In 1966 the VOA
acquired an additional chunk of the Health, Education, and Welfare building, and
in October 1967, staff moved into a 5,000-square foot refurbished newsroom in the
basement.[27] Chancellor also improved fraternal links with the BBC World Service.
The two broadcasters began a series of twice yearly meetings to share experience
and coordinate responses. The location alternated between Washington and London,
which, Voice staff joked, gave the dapper Jack Chancellor an excuse to visit his favorite
London tailor.[28] In developing these links the VOA followed an established USIA
practice. Since the Eisenhower era a "US–UK Information Working Group" had met

23 LBJL John Chancellor oral history, 25 April 1969, pp. 12–16. See also letter by John Chancellor, *The Nation*, 25 September 1967, p. 258.
24 Interviews: Groce, Kamenske, Cummins. USIS posts around the world, canvassed in early 1967, responded well to the new format. USIS Addis Ababa spoke of a "lively, boredom-proof pace." USIS Beirut noted that "The MC's thoroughly American approach provides the output with its own character and subtle credibility as well as its own identity." But others balked at the revolution. USIS Amman complained of "a continuous talking drum," whereas Geneva regretted the "shotgun" approach to the news, seeking a general audience, at a time when the USIA urged other sections "to use a rifle" and aim at specific audiences; see LBJL Leonard Marks papers, box 32, VOA New Sound, Chancellor to Marks, 22 March 1967, with attached summary of reaction.
25 Interview: Bernie Kamenske, 6 December 1995.
26 LBJL WHCF Ex, box 315, Ex FG296 USIS, Marks to Knott (GSA), 15 March 1966.
27 LBJL Leonard Marks, box 14, *USIA World*, Vol. 1 No. 6, November 1967.
28 Interviews: Groce, Kamenske, Cummins.

Fig. 1. A foundational moment: President Truman signs the Fulbright Act. Senator Fulbright (center) and Assistant Secretary of State Benton look on, August 1946 (Truman Library).

Fig. 2. Communicating with the East: scene outside the USIS library in Prague, October 1949 (National Archives).

Fig. 3. Communicating with the West: a USIA Atoms for Peace show on London's South Bank, June 1961 (National Archives).

Fig. 4. The P-factor: President Eisenhower receives a "People to People" poster from the campaign's John W. Hanes Jr. and Edward Lipscomb, May 1957 (Eisenhower Library).

Fig. 5. Communicating with the South: Maasai farmers in Kenya attend a USIS agricultural exhibit, 1957 (National Archives).

Fig. 6. Taking the message to the people: the USIS mobile library on the road near Rangoon, Burma, June 1953 (National Archives).

Fig. 7. Propaganda from space: citizens of Bogotá, Colombia strain to see USIA exhibit of astronaut John Glenn's Mercury capsule "Friendship Seven," May 1962 (National Archives).

Fig. 8. New terminology: Ambassador Edmund Gullion – originator of the term "public diplomacy" – with President Kennedy, August 1961 (Kennedy Library).

Fig. 9. "Brilliantly effective in quashing the doubts . . .," Barry Zorthian, the USIA's propaganda tsar in Vietnam, pictured in 1966 (*Time & Life* Pictures/Getty Images).

Fig. 10. Captive audience: Vietnamese people watch a USIA documentary in a field adjoining a fortified village, 1963 (*Time & Life* Pictures/Getty Images).

Fig. 11. The VOA's legend on the air: jazz broadcaster Willis Conover, pictured in 1978 (National Archives).

Fig. 12. The VOA's legend behind the scenes: news director Bernie Kamenske pictured c. 1974 (Voice of America).

Fig. 13. "America's most devastating propaganda blow of the entire Cold War": the climax of the USIA video presentation to the UN Security Council on the KAL 007 shootdown, 6 September 1983 (National Archives).

Fig. 14. Giving voice to Afghanistan: Justice Omar Babrakzai (left) and three survivors of a September 1982 chemical warfare atrocity at Padkhwab-e-Shana tell their story to USIA television cameras. French human rights lawyer Michael Barry (far right) comments, April 1983. A full Afghan Media Project followed, to train the *mujahideen* in modern media techniques (National Archives).

Fig. 15. George V. Allen, USIA Director, 1957–60, a favorite with many staff (National Archives).

Fig. 16. Edward R. Murrow, USIA Director, 1961–4, lent television glamour to the agency (National Archives).

Fig. 17. John D. Reinhardt, USIA/ICA Director, 1977–80, the only director to have risen from the ranks of the USIA staff (National Archives).

Fig. 18. Charles Z. Wick, USIA Director, 1981–9, the longest serving and arguably the most successful director (National Archives).

to pool experience, coordinate policy, and even agree to responses on key issues such as the Sino-Soviet split.[29] Some of Chancellor's innovations at the VOA also found their way onto the BBC World Service. At the urging of Bill Haratunian, Chancellor allowed VOA correspondents to broadcast their reports directly from the field over the telephone line, rather than sending them in written form to be read in the studio. The BBC swiftly also adopted the same practice.[30]

VOA service to Asia improved during the Chancellor years, with increased transmitter power in the Philippines. Vietnam was not the only target. The Voice also sought to address Communist China, where Mao Zedong had just unleashed the "Great Proletarian Cultural Revolution." The VOA pieced together a detailed picture of the successive waves of purges, denunciations, and self-criticisms from diplomatic sources, world press, and broadcasting as monitored by the Federal Broadcast Information Service. Broadcasting for seven and one-half hours each day, the Mandarin service carried an expanded discussion of the mounting crisis. Global broadcasts sought to show the developing world that it could no longer count on China as an ally.[31]

On 24 February 1967, the VOA celebrated twenty-five years on the air with a gala concert, hosted by Bing Crosby and featuring such American stars as Louis Armstrong and Frank Sinatra and international musicians such as Ravi Shankar, South African singer Miriam Makeba, and, in order to attract Chinese listeners, singer and actress Li Li-Hua. The Laotian group *Mohlam* recreated the "joyous experience of listening to VOA" in song. Other celebrations included a five-cent commemorative U.S. postage stamp. Chancellor's only regret was that, despite his requests, LBJ took no part in the festivities. He never discovered the reason.[32]

Despite Chancellor's achievement at the Voice, the old tensions between the VOA and USIA remained. Some at the Voice resented the hand of the USIA in the VOA's English and Arabic coverage of the Six Day War in June 1967, which followed the pattern of the Cuban missile crisis and Dominican intervention, with tight control on VOA commentaries. The VOA's Arabic service shifted from six to eleven hours a day

[29] For an example see JFKL Salinger, Box 133, US–UK Information Group Meeting, Washington, DC, 4–6 June 1962.

[30] Interview: Bill Haratunian, 15 December 1995.

[31] For an overview of VOA Mandarin see LBJL WHCF CF, box 96, CF UT1/Communications, Marks to Rostow, Top Secret, 30 June 1966, with attached memo by Chancellor. For a review of the first year of the Cultural Revolution by policy officer John Pauker see LBJL Leonard Marks papers, box 23, Basic USIA guidelines, John Pauker (IOP), Peking's Purges, Red Guards and Anti-Cultural Campaign, 23 November 1966. VOA coverage of the Cultural Revolution marked a watershed in more ways than one. Before 1966 all VOA broadcasts had, in deference to sentiment in Taiwan, still referred to Beijing by the old Nationalist name, "Peiping." Now, the NSC allowed the Voice to use either "Peiping" or "Peking," although the politically charged term Peoples Republic of China could still only be used as part of a quotation; see LBJL NSF agency, box 75, USIA Vol. 7, 2, docs 10 & 10a., Jenkins (NSC) to Rostow, 19 March 1968 and attached memo (State). In June 1966 the Johnson administration briefly considered launching a new surrogate station, Radio Free China. Marks noted that the VOA's official status had not hampered its coverage of the Cultural Revolution and suggested that the administration's money would be better spend upgrading VOA transmitters in the Philippines to counter jamming. The NSC evidently agreed.

[32] LBJL Leonard Marks papers, box 14, *USIA Correspondent*, Vol. 9, No. 2, February 1967; *USIA World*, Vol. 1, No. 4, September 1967; LBJL oral history: Chancellor, p. 18.

on short wave. The use of medium-wave transmitters added three more hours each day. Worldwide English news broadcasts ran around the clock, including live reports from correspondents in the field. The VOA provided live feeds of all UN Security Council debates. Above all, the VOA worked to refute Radio Cairo's "big lie" that U.S. and U.K. forces fought alongside Israel. VOA journalists were not the only bruised parties. The USIA had been neglected in the buildup to the crisis. Speaking of both the VOA and the USIA, Marks reminded LBJ on 12 June, "unless USIA representatives are kept fully informed on developments effecting (sic) our foreign and domestic policy, these facilities will be wasted." Three days later he begged Johnson to prevail on National Security Advisor McGeorge Bundy to "keep me fully informed at all times."[33]

The Six Day War coincided with a transition at the VOA. Chancellor had taken the directorship on the understanding that he would serve only two years, and his resignation came into effect on day five of the war. He returned to NBC and the coveted post of anchor for the evening news. He had done much to modernize the VOA and build a news-gathering apparatus to match the ethical promise of the VOA charter. He would be fondly remembered. Although he plainly worked well with Marks and the USIA, Chancellor became an advocate of full independence for the VOA.[34]

In Chancellor's place, Johnson appointed John Charles Daly. Although best known as host of the television game show *What's My Line?* Daly had distinguished himself in a thirty-year career as a journalist for CBS and ABC. He was also the son-in-law of chief justice Earl Warren.[35] Marks and Daly were soon on a collision course. On 6 June 1968, as the VOA struggled to cope with the news of Robert Kennedy's murder, Daly learned that a Voice editor had been transferred to other USIA work without his being consulted. He immediately threatened to resign unless Marks reversed the decision. Marks insisted that Daly back down and handle the RFK story. When Daly held his ground, Marks accepted his resignation.[36]

Veteran AP correspondent and old USIS hand Richard Cushing succeeded Daly as acting director of the VOA. Cushing held fast to the ideals of the VOA charter, which

[33] LBJL WHCF CF, box 135, CF USIA, Marks to President, 12 June 1967; Marks to President, 15 June 1967. For later VOA policy on the Arab/Israeli dispute see Leonard Marks, box 23, Basic USIA guidelines, Aftermath of Arab–Israeli War, 6 August 1968. Policy included notes to "avoid emphasizing" reference to the crisis in the 1968 presidential campaign; that "a sustained U.S. effort to warn Arab audiences against Soviet influence would not be credible to those audiences"; and that although the United States did not recognize the Israeli annexation of East Jerusalem, the United States did not believe that the issue could be treated apart from a wider settlement and had hence abstained from votes on the subject in the UN.

[34] LBJL WHCF CF, box 135, CF USIA, Marks to President, 15 June 1967; Interview: Marks, 15 May 2003. In 1975 Frank Stanton, an advocate of VOA independence, read a letter from Chancellor into the USIA budget hearings: "As a journalist I have seen the anguish of the broadcaster at Voice of America. As an executive I have seen career officers in from the field put in intolerable positions. The broadcasters and journalists are loyal to Voice of America: the officers from the field are fundamentally and understandably loyal to the Ambassadors and PAO's they have worked with before and will work with again. Asking these two groups to collaborate in professional journalism is asking too much." Hearings on S.1517, 5 May 1975, p. 221.

[35] Sorensen, *The Word War*, pp. 248–9; Interview: Dick Cushing, 7 January 1998.

[36] LBJL Oral History: Marks Interview I, June 1970, p. 42; Michael Nelson, *War of the Black Heavens*, p. 130.

he used effectively against complaints from disgruntled ambassadors. He remained in this post – without major interference from the USIA, State, or the White House – until September 1969. His only brush with government came when a senior CIA man invited him to lunch and asked the VOA to carry messages to field agents. Cushing refused, the matter dropped, but he had to pay for his own lunch.[37]

As the Johnson era drew to a close, it became clear that the VOA faced more problems than just political interference. In August 1968 the Bureau of the Budget ordered a major survey of the VOA's Worldwide English broadcasting to assess its cost effectiveness. The study noted that although the VOA claimed an audience of five million for its Breakfast Show, the program had only received 191 letters in the past four months. The best guess of the weekly audience of VOA English programs as a whole still exceeded eleven million, but USIS posts suspected that this would soon diminish as television and improved domestic media won listeners away from the short wave.[38] By the end of the Johnson years, with impending budget cuts at the VOA and awkward questions in the press over the CIA subsidy to RFE/RL, the future of U.S. international broadcasting hung in the balance.

*

While Marks and Chancellor worked to reinvigorate their corners of U.S. public diplomacy, it fell to Charles Frankel to direct the State Department's Bureau of Educational and Cultural Affairs as the new Assistant Secretary of State. His experience was eloquent both to the wider issue of public diplomacy and to the problems of the Johnson era. The bureau had experienced mixed fortunes to that date. Johnson had inherited Lucius Battle as assistant secretary and replaced him in due course with a member of his own staff, Harry McPherson, as a stopgap. The period at least brought about an Interagency Council on International Educational and Cultural Affairs in January 1964 as a meeting point for State, AID, defense, education, the Peace Corps, and the USIA. CU chaired. The budget seemed healthy – a record $53 million for financial year 1966 – yet culture remained the poor sister to information.[39]

Seeking to advance the debate, the Brookings Institution commissioned Columbia philosophy professor Charles Frankel to produce a detailed study of cultural diplomacy. The resulting book – *The Neglected Aspect of Foreign Affairs* – was a prescient survey of the entire subject of cultural diplomacy and exchange. Frankel noted the paradox of the Senate insisting on a separation of culture from advocacy work while still expecting the advocacy agency – the USIA – to provide most of the staff for CU. He also identified what he called the "tangle of purposes" in cultural diplomacy: the general promotion of goodwill, advancing of particular foreign policy goals, overseas development, and

---

[37]   Interview: Cushing.

[38]   LBJL Leonard Marks, box 17, Broadcasting: World Wide English, Special Study, 28 August 1968 and associated correspondence. In FY 1968, the VOA took up 23.5% of the USIA budget, against 19 percent for information centers; 15.7 percent press/publications, 10.3 percent for motion pictures and television, and 30.9 percent for other costs.

[39]   UoA CU 2–3, J. Manuel Espinosa, "Landmarks in the history of the Cultural Relations program of the Department of State, 1938–1976," 1978, pp. 11–12; Arndt, *First Resort of Kings*, pp. 338–41.

the extension of individual opportunity, which were frequently in conflict. He called for separate agencies with parallel missions. Frankel regretted the subjugation of cultural diplomacy to information in the U.S. and recommended boosting the Assistant Secretary of State post to under secretary level to match the rank of the director of the USIA. He even mooted a "semi-autonomous foundation for [U.S.] educational and cultural exchange" along the lines of the Smithsonian or the British Council.[40]

Frankel's book circulated widely in Washington as a draft. It caught the attention of Fulbright, who immediately recognized the value of such an agenda for his beloved exchange program and recommended Frankel to LBJ as an ideal assistant secretary. Johnson duly offered the post to Frankel.[41] With an ally in the Senate, a buoyant budget, and a sympathetic President, it seemed that Frankel would be able to accomplish much. His concerns included the so-called Brain Drain, the process by which America's international education policy was harvesting the best world talent to work in the United States. Frankel's answer was reinvigorated exchanges so that there was a circulation of "brains" outward from the wealthy to poor countries as well.[42]

Frankel's spectacular debut was to write the President's speech to mark the bicentennial of the Smithsonian Institution on 16 September 1965. Here LBJ embraced the cause of international education and proposed a wide range of initiatives "to show that this nation's dream of a great society does not stop at the water's edge." CU would be the lead agency. Marks pledged the USIA's support.[43] To implement the Smithsonian speech agenda, Johnson established a Task Force on International Education, which reported in December 1965. He followed up with a message to Congress on International Education in February 1966, proposing a great International Education Act.[44] Measures included not only a raft of new exchanges and initiatives to facilitate America learning from overseas but also, at Frankel's suggestion, the creation of a new kind of attaché in major American embassies: an educational attaché from the Department of Education. The bill passed the House in June and was signed into law by Johnson in October 1966.[45] By the end of that year the United States had joined two international agreements to promote education by exempting educational materials from tariffs: the Florence Agreement for books and instruments, and the Beirut Agreement for audiovisual materials. In 1967, CU launched an initiative called the Volunteers to America program, which recruited foreigners to work in U.S. educational projects as a

[40] Charles Frankel, *The Neglected Aspect of Foreign Affairs: American Educational and Cultural Policy Abroad*, Washington, DC: Brookings Institution, 1965, esp. pp. 28, 80–98, 140, 142.
[41] For Frankel's own account of this see Charles Frankel, *High on Foggy Bottom: An Outsider's Inside View of the Government*, New York: Harper & Row, 1968, pp. 7–15. For Johnson's and Fulbright's phone conversations with Frankel and each other see LBJL WH6507.07 program no. 11, LBJ to Fulbright, 23 July 1965; WH6507.09 program no. 6, Fulbright to Frankel, 28 July 1965; and WH6508.07 program no. 13 and 14, office conversation, c. 20 August 1965.
[42] Frankel, *High on Foggy Bottom*, p. 25. See also UoA CU 2–17, Colligan to Frankel, "The Brain Drain," 21 February 1967; Council on Educational and Cultural Affairs paper 13, 21 December 1965.
[43] Frankel, *High on Foggy Bottom*. For text see *PPP LBJ 1965*, Vol. II, doc. 519; UoA CU 18–4 Marks to Frankel, 12 October 1965.
[44] *PPP LBJ 1966*, Vol. I, doc. 45.
[45] For survey of implementation see UoA CU 18–4 State Department press release no. 17, 1 February 1967.

reverse peace corps. It would not last. All too soon the Volunteers in America program would be transferred to the Peace Corps and then have all its funding withdrawn by Congress.[46]

The legislation and Johnson's initiatives fell short of Frankel's vision. The act included no appropriation of funds. The notion of a new corps of education officers in embassies was lost and the idea of an independent agency to administer cultural and educational work overseas was nowhere to be seen. Given the obvious challenge of Frankel's ideas to the USIA's dream of monopolizing public diplomacy, the assistant secretary encountered growing opposition from that agency. The decisive blow to his fortunes, however, was the issue of Vietnam and particularly the split between the President and Fulbright. Championing international education had been an olive branch to Fulbright from LBJ, and frustrating it became the punishment Johnson inflicted on the Senator for his criticism of the war in Vietnam. In November 1967, Frankel recognized the impossibility of moving forward in such a climate and resigned, declaring that the issue of Vietnam had blinded the administration to all other considerations. By financial year 1969 appropriations for CU had fallen back to around $31.5 million. On leaving office Frankel wrote an eloquent account of his experiences in government: *High on Foggy Bottom*. He went on to play a major role in the foundation of the National Humanities Center in North Carolina. Frankel died before his time in May 1979, shot to death by burglars at his home.[47] Frankel was just one more public diplomacy resource wasted by the mounting crisis in Vietnam.

2) JUSPAO AT WORK

THE USIA IN VIETNAM, AUGUST 1965–68

On 3 August 1965, President Johnson held a dinner at the White House to discuss the information problem in Vietnam. Guests, including VOA director John Chancellor, emphasized the absence of South Vietnamese input in propaganda and the need to encourage better American coverage of the war.[48] Even as the diners chatted, coverage of the war reached a new crisis point. Viewers of the CBS evening news learnt that journalist Morley Safer had witnessed a detachment of marines burn the entire village of Cam Ne in response to a single burst of gunfire. Pictures of a marine firing a thatched roof with his Zippo lighter played two days later. They became one of the news icons of the Vietnam War.[49]

---

46 *PPP LBJ 1966*, Vol. II, doc. 519, which notes that George Allen had negotiated the Florence Agreement in 1950, but the Senate had prevented U.S. membership prior to this point. See also LBJL, Douglas Cater papers, box 44, International Education, 1966, 1, Executive Order for August 1966 and UoA CU 2–3, J. Manuel Espinosa, "Landmarks in the history of the Cultural Relations program of the Department of State, 1938–1976," 1978, p. 13.

47 For a full treatment see Frankel, *High on Foggy Bottom*. For an overview see Arndt, *First Resort of Kings*, pp. 380–97. For obituary, "Charles Frankel Resigned a Post under Johnson," *New York Times*, 11 May 1979, p. B2.

48 *FRUS, 1964–1968, Vol III, Vietnam June–December 1965*, doc. 105, dinner meeting on the information problem, 3 August 1965.

49 Hammond, *Reporting Vietnam*, pp. 59–60.

The mere announcement that CBS would be screening the Cam Ne film set the policy makers thinking about censorship once more. Deputy Assistant Secretary of State for Public Affairs James Greenfield suspected that those who favored censorship "saw it as a way to prevent . . . inconvenient stories" and argued, "No system of censorship would prevent stories like the village burning or the CBS-TV film."[50] When, just a few days later, Safer broke the voluntary reporting code and revealed what could be thought militarily sensitive information, Arthur Sylvester, who ran public affairs for the Pentagon, decided to act. Claiming that, as a Canadian, Safer was immune to appeals to patriotism, Sylvester bluntly asked CBS to assign an American. Fred Friendly, president of CBS News, no less bluntly, refused.[51] Zorthian's only solution, which he presented as a guest in an NSC meeting on 5 August, was for the administration to press editors to demand balance from their correspondents in Vietnam.[52]

Back in Vietnam, USIS Saigon was increasingly involved in tactical psychological warfare. During the spring and summer of 1965, Zorthian had extended the campaign against the North by integrating leaflet drops into the overall U.S. bombing strategy. Themes – agreed upon with the South Vietnamese – included allegations of Chinese influence on Hanoi; explanations of the U.S./South Vietnamese war aim as being to end Northern "aggression"; warnings of air raids (usually two weeks before a strike); photographic evidence of Southern prosperity; and pictures of Communist atrocities.[53] The mission aimed to drop two million leaflets per week. Similar themes featured in VOA broadcasts, and on a new addition to the North Vietnamese airwaves, "Voice of Freedom," a CIA-funded station, purporting to be an independent voice from South Vietnam.[54]

As an incoming director, Leonard Marks was eager to reform USIA operations in Vietnam. He visited the country and sampled the information effort in the field by visiting a village selected at random. It proved a microcosm of America's problem in Vietnam. Although the USIS published a newspaper there, no one read it, as no one could read; although the USIS ensured that a radio signal could be heard, no one in the village listened. Real communication took place in the energetic exchanges in the market place each morning or through the songs of the traveling players in the evening. Marks resolved to use these traditional channels too.[55]

50 *FRUS, 1964–1968, Vol III, Vietnam June–December 1965*, doc. 117, Memorandum of conversation, including Sylvester, Chancellor, and Zorthian, 3 August 1965.
51 Hammond, *Reporting Vietnam*, p. 60.
52 *FRUS, 1964–1968, Vol III, Vietnam June–December 1965*, doc. 110, 554th meeting of NSC, 5 August 1965
53 NA RG59 CPF 1964–66, box 417, INF 8 Viet N., Saigon JUSPAO FM8, Zorthian to USIA, 17 July 1965: "Evolution of Leaflet Campaign for North Vietnam and future plan." William Lloyd Stearman, who managed JUSPAO's campaign against the north, later noted that the attempt to undermine the Hanoi regime by stressing its close links to China was based on the rather dated perspective of the Vietnamese refugees who had moved south in 1956. By the mid-1960s China was providing a large part of their consumer goods and weapons. This and a decade of pro-Mao propaganda ensured that the "anti-Chinese theme was going nowhere." ADST Oral History: Stearman.
54 NA RG59 CPF 1964–6, box 417, INF 8 Viet N., Saigon 4013, Taylor to USIA, 2 June 1965; Interview: Zorthian.
55 Interview: Marks, 15 May 2003.

In secrecy, Marks dispatched a high-powered group from the President's Advisory Commission on Information to Vietnam, chaired by the former general manager of the Associated Press, Frank Starzel, and including Frank Stanton. The group submitted its findings in September. Starzel felt optimistic about the military outlook in Vietnam but troubled by the political sphere. He felt that JUSPAO needed to both promote the security of the countryside and rally confidence in the South Vietnamese government, tasks he compared to "picking up mercury from a polished surface with bare hands." JUSPAO's problems included a chronic lack of Vietnamese speakers, term limits, and exclusion of families from Vietnam, which led to a high turnover of staff. Above all, JUSPAO faced the twin nightmares of coordinating competing U.S. agencies and working through South Vietnamese "counterparts."

Starzel relayed the manifold complaints of American correspondents based in South Vietnam. Limited transport and wire facilities and the continued failure of the Saigon government to adapt to the expectations of a free press all rubbed them raw. Above all, journalists objected to "lack of candor on the part of U.S. military briefers" who, contrary to Zorthian's policy, habitually withheld stories on spurious security grounds. Starzel recommended raising the caliber of military press officers and appealing to editors for better coverage.[56]

The group also commented on JUSPAO's psychological warfare operations. Starzel noted that too little energy had been given to analyzing the impact of its aerial leaflets. He was especially skeptical of the *Chieu Hoi* program. Although the U.S. claimed to have welcomed 23,000 defectors to date, Starzel found that many were civilian refugees rather than enemy fighters. JUSPAO only knew the "whereabouts" of 700, and many others had plainly returned to enemy ranks. Even so, Starzel recommended continuing *Chieu Hoi*, with a more efficient airborne loudspeaker system. His chief recommendation for the wider information effort was close to Stanton's heart: the introduction of television into South Vietnam.[57]

Starzel provided a convenient agenda for action. By October, JUSPAO had a new Vietnamese language program for staff, record numbers of leaflet drops, and better coordination of the psychological initiative, thanks to the arrival of the new deputy chief of mission, William Porter, who instituted regular meetings of the heads of all elements in the U.S. mission to eliminate overlap. Airborne transmitters successfully beamed TV pictures of World Series baseball to U.S. troops in the interior of Vietnam, proving the method sound for future propaganda use.[58]

---

56   Specifically, Starzel felt that contact with editors might enable the United States to resume use of nonlethal gas in Vietnam. Soon after the report the AP carried a dispatch by Edwin Q. White showing how tear gas could save civilian lives in Vietnam; see LBJL WHCF Ex, box 217, Ex ND19/CO312, Marks to President, 29 September 1965. Interview: Stanton.

57   LBJL Marks Papers, box 29, Report on Vietnam, Starzel to Marks, 16 September 1965, "eyes only" and Memorandum of Observations and Suggestions on U.S. information policies and programs in Viet Nam, 16 September 1965, "confidential." The President's daily diary of 9 August shows that before the group departed for Vietnam, Marks, Zorthian, Moyers, and Stanton visited the White House to speak to Johnson. Marks later spoke of this as the Stanton Report on Vietnam. Interview: Stanton.

58   LBJL WHCF CF, box 71, CF ND19/CO312, Marks to Valenti, 27 October 1965, with personal and confidential attachment. ADST: Oral History, Zorthian.

Porter's early dispatches from Saigon include a host of new initiatives for closer cooperation with the VIS. In mid-October he reported a surge in *Chieu Hoi* returnees, citing leaflets and loudspeakers as the reason for their defection.[59] On 23 October 1965, the South Vietnamese, with U.S. help, launched a major initiative in the Mekong Delta based on a claim of "inevitable victory." Forces deployed included four million air-dropped leaflets, twenty-three loudspeaker aircraft, and loudspeakers mounted on a fleet of three-wheeled Lambretta scooters. Meanwhile, in the center of the country, JUSPAO unveiled its so-called "spirit record," a ghostly mixture of traditional Vietnamese funeral music, unnerving sound effects, and the grotesquely amplified sound of a weeping women or a child crying, "Daddy! Daddy! Come home. . . ." The breakthrough lay in effective U.S. cooperation with the South Vietnamese.[60]

JUSPAO began 1966 in style with a month-long offensive to coincide with the Tet festival. The air force dropped ten million greetings messages on North Vietnam pleading for an end to "aggression," and 7,500 gift packages containing a child's sweater, toys, buttons, needles, and thread, a new year diary, and a letter from a South Vietnamese schoolchild.[61] In addition to the usual *Chieu Hoi* appeals, U.S. and Vietnamese radio played two records specially commissioned by Zorthian to tug at the heart of a homesick guerrilla, "A Ballad Prayer for Tet" and "Tet Without You." The campaign inspired a record 1,672 defections across the month. Follow-up surveys suggested that leaflets had proved the most effective mechanism. One defector spoke of being particularly moved by reading a poem, written by a "Viet Cong" to his mother just before his death; others mentioned being given air-dropped safe-conduct passes by their families before beginning their trek south.[62]

On the defensive, the communists now attempted to collect and destroy leaflets that had fallen on villages under their control and engaged JUSPAO's arguments in their own propaganda. So many soldiers on the Ho Chi Minh trail now carried passes that political officers had begun spot checks. Sample excuses for possession of leaflets ranged from "I use them as toilet paper" to "I wanted an example of imperialist lies."[63] By the summer the "VC" regularly shot at psyop aircraft and targeted regional *Chieu Hoi* chiefs. In one region the Americans intercepted orders for villagers "to resist psyops planes by putting hands over ears and shouting to drown out loudspeakers, beating on pots and pans to set up a counter-noise." The Party redoubled its own

---

[59] NA RG59 CPF 1964–6, box 417, INF 8 US-Viet S, Saigon 1411, Porter to State, USIA etc., 23 October 1965.

[60] NA RG59 CPF 1964–6, box 417, INF 8 US-Viet. S, Saigon 1509, Lodge to State, USIA etc., 30 October 1965; Emile Schurmacher, "Chief Zorro," *Stag*, June 1966, pp. 67; "Psywar," *Newsweek*, 4 October 1965.

[61] NA RG59 CPF 1964–66, box 350, Cul 6 Viet, Saigon 2635, Porter to State, 23 January 1966; box 435, PPB 9 Viet S, Saigon 2639, Porter to State/USIA/DOD, 23 January 1966.

[62] LBJL Leonard Marks papers, box 30, Zorthian to Marks, Tet campaign summation, 6 February 1966; Emile Schurmacher, "Chief Zorro," *Stag*, June 1966, p. 66.

[63] LBJL Leonard Marks papers, box 30, Zorthian to Marks, Tet campaign summation, 6 February 1966.

indoctrination efforts and forbade troops to discuss the contents of JUSPAO leaflets with their comrades. Zorthian was delighted.[64]

On the evening of 7 February 1966, television came to South Vietnam. The entertainment needs of American troops and the propaganda needs of the South Vietnamese regime had combined to make a compelling case. JUSPAO deployed two (later three) Blue Eagles – U.S. Navy Super-Constellation aircraft, converted into flying television transmitters – to broadcast a signal in a 75-mile radius around Saigon. The U.S. had imported 1,500 televisions, and the mysterious osmosis of the black market ensured a rapid dispersal of cheap Japanese sets to further boost the audience. Within four years there were an estimated 300,000 private sets and 3,500 U.S.-funded communal sets around South Vietnam, though up to fifteen percent of these were reckoned to be under repair at any one time.[65]

The first night of programming began with a half-hour broadcast by the South Vietnamese government, followed by three hours of entertainment for the U.S. army. The Vietnamese soon had their own channel, THVN, which mixed entertainment, news, and propaganda. JUSPAO helped to make suitable material at Saigon's national film studio. They enrolled the creative energies of a succession of U.S. consultants, mainly from NBC, including Larry Gelbart, whose experiences doubtless informed his later account of an earlier Asian conflict in *M*A*S*H*. JUSPAO padded the schedules with old films of Vietnamese operas. Cynics noted that many Vietnamese viewers actually preferred the U.S. army channel, despite the language barrier. *Batman* and the World War Two drama *Combat* were special favorites. Others defended the popularity of Vietnamese programming, noting that Friday night's Vietnamese folk tales and Chinese opera had Americans tuning to the Vietnamese channel. No one contested the popularity of the new medium; crowds of up to 300 now spent their evenings transfixed. JUSPAO even logged "numerous reports of Viet Cong infiltrating into hamlets and joining the viewers in front of community sets."[66]

The enemy was initially unsure how to react to television. Raids to destroy community sets proved highly unpopular with villagers. On 12 April 1966, an attack on Saigon airport damaged both of the Blue Eagle transmitter planes. One could be

64 Harry D. Latimer, *U.S. Psychological Operations in Vietnam*, Brown University, 1973, pp. 119–21: JUSPAO field memorandum, 27 August 1966: "The Viet Cong Assess Vietnamese–US Psywar."
65 Five hundred twenty-three-inch television sets – flown in by AID – were in place by January, five hundred more arrived by sea in early February, and the United States presented a further shipment of five hundred sets to the ARVN. Small portable sets arrived for sale at PX posts but proved notoriously unreliable in the Vietnamese climate. Set distribution around Saigon initially caused some friction, as restaurants frequented by Americans clearly found it easier to acquire televisions than other establishments. One set even turned up in a jail holding an American prisoner. JUSPAO took steps to appear even-handed. LBJL NSF Agency, Vol. 6, 2, box 75, doc 65, Marks to President, 17 December 1965 (with LBJ annotation: "Excellent") and doc 36, Marks to President, 8 February 1966; ADSL Oral History, Richard McCarthy; Latimer, *U.S. Psychological Operations in Vietnam*, p. 32; Leonard Marks papers, Box 25, "Report on Vietnam" (Frank Stanton), *Television in Vietnam, 1966, a Report by Loren B. Stone*, June 1966, p. 17.
66 LBJL NSF Agency, Vol. 6, 2, box 75, doc 36, Marks to President, 8 February 1966; LBJL Panzer papers, box 548, USIA, Ackers to Panzer, 13 July 1966; ADST Oral History: Richard McCarthy; Latimer, *U.S. Psychological Operations in Vietnam*, pp. 31–2.

repaired in time to maintain the evening's schedule, but the other remained out of service for a month. JUSPAO pressed ahead with plans to build land-based transmitters in Saigon and Hue.[67] But a debate within the USIA suggested that television and the "Viet Cong" message might not necessarily be antithetical.

In the spring of 1967, William Bayer, of the agency's motion picture and television branch, paid a return visit to Vietnam. To his horror, he encountered a tidal wave of criticism of the Vietnamese television channel in the local press and from his long-term contacts in the intellectual elite. Bayer's contacts spoke of television as an American cultural imposition. Television had clearly become the focus for anti-American feeling. Critics argued that when the Vietnamese channel was not showing rock and roll, it presented grotesque examples of the emerging hybrid of east and west: the bar culture of Saigon's thriving Vietnamese draft-dodger "Cowboys." The "educational" game shows were no better. All the answers lay in knowledge of the West. Bayer summed up elite feeling that

> The presence of so many foreigners in Viet Nam has stolen from the Vietnamese people nearly all forms of self-respect; THAT ALL THE VIETNAMESE HAVE LEFT IS THE TRADITION OF THEIR ANCIENT CULTURE; that television is ERODING AND DILUTING THIS CULTURE by supplanting it with a cheap vulgar entertainment style, thus polluting the tradition and creating bad taste in the children.

The crowds watching television might not have loved the United States any more as a result; rather, Bayer concluded, they saw it as "a corrosive and therefore evil force in society."[68]

It was not the USIA's fault. South Vietnamese television reflected genuine currents in Saigon life and projected them around the country. "Cowboy" bar culture was flashing neon nightly reality. Marks responded to the criticism by seeking to develop daytime educational television in South Vietnam using the existing transmitter facilities. He traveled to Japan to personally ask the Prime Minister to provide sets and advisors for the project, to avoid the appearance of yet another American ploy. But the measure could not eliminate the mounting evidence of the corrupting nature of the American presence. The "VC infiltrators" who joined villagers in their nightly viewing sessions had ample material on which to develop their argument that they were the authentic defenders of national identity.[69]

---

[67] LBJL NSF Agency, Vol. 6, 2, box 75, doc 16, Marks to President, 13 April 1966; Leonard Marks papers, Box 25, "Report on Vietnam (Frank Stanton)," *Television in Vietnam, 1966, a Report by Loren B. Stone*, June 1966.

[68] LBJL Leonard Marks papers, box 30, "Educational TV Vietnam," Bayer to Stevens, 25 April 1967. Capitals in original. Defenders of the scheme at the USIA countered that only a fifth of the Vietnamese channel fell into the popular entertainment category, and that almost all the songs were in Vietnamese. LBJL Leonard Marks papers, box 30, "Educational TV Vietnam," Oleksiw to Marks, 8 June 1967.

[69] LBJL Leonard Marks papers, box 30, "Educational TV Vietnam," Marks to President, 21 November 1967; LBJL WHCF CF, box 14, CF ED5, Maguire to President, 25 November 1966. It became a cliché of postwar American media studies to say that Vietnam was lost on American television. Historians worked hard to establish that the loss was one of reality, rather than image. The war was lost on the ground, not in the living room. But the images on Vietnamese television helped to create those political and military realities. Perhaps the war was indeed lost on television, but not on American channels.

*

JUSPAO worked to project what President Johnson called "the *other* war in Vietnam" – the civilian development programs connected to the allied presence in the country. Zorthian organized trips to hospitals, schools, and road projects. JUSPAO also began to distribute rice that had been recaptured from the enemy, using special plastic sacks decorated with an image of an ARVN soldier on horseback symbolically trampling a North Vietnamese flag.[70] In February 1966, Marks launched a scheme to encourage foreign journalists to view Vietnam and especially the "non-military aspects of the war" for themselves. By February 1967 some 300 had made the trip, eighty-four with direct subsidies from the USIA. JUSPAO interviewed its guests before and after their visits and had no doubt that the experience changed their approach to the war. Many continued to request JUSPAO information after their return home.[71] But some correspondents encountered opposition. Jan Eeb-Henriksen of Norway's *Aftenposten* found his foreign editor initially unwilling to run his Vietnam articles because of their "American bias."[72]

In February 1966, Johnson met the South Vietnamese leaders Ky and Thieu in Hawaii and obtained their commitment to an agenda of reform that paralleled his own Great Society. As the year unfolded, the USIA in Washington and JUSPAO officials in Saigon and around the countryside bent their ingenuity to improving the image of the South Vietnamese. Visiting Saigon, Marks pressed Ky to launch an overseas information program; Ky seemed receptive, but nothing significant materialized.[73] In September 1966, Secretary of Defense Robert McNamara, called for a renewed propaganda initiative to build a viable state in South Vietnam. Zorthian readied a major "national reconciliation campaign" for the Tet season in January 1967, although he contrived to present the South Vietnamese government as the driving force. JUSPAO had begun to realize the self-defeating nature of conducting propaganda about national strength on behalf of the South Vietnamese state.[74] The problem was highlighted in November 1966 when a JUSPAO briefing officer mistakenly listed South Vietnamese casualties among "foreign nationals" killed in an ambush. A swift cable from the State Department highlighted the faux pas.[75]

[70] LBJL WHCF Ex, box 223, Ex ND19/312, President to Marks, 24 October 1966 with bag. For Johnson's first public use of the term "Other War" see *PPP LBJ 1966*, Statement by the President on Pacification and Development Programs in Vietnam, 16 June 1966, pp. 621–2. For early requests to emphasize nonmilitary operations see NA RG 59 State, CPF 1964–6, box 417, INF 8 VIET S., Saigon 951, State/USIA to JUSPAO, 5 October 1965.

[71] LBJL WHCF CF, box 135, CF USIA 1966 & 1967, Marks to President via Kintner, 8 November 1966; Marks to President via Kintner, 14 February 1967.

[72] LBJL WHCF CF, box 52, CF FO6–3 Publicity, Marks to President via Kintner, 6 December 1966.

[73] LBJL WHCF Ex, box 53, Ex FO7/Vietnam Meeting, Marks to President, 24 February 1966, with annotation: "Jack – tell Leonard, Excellent – keep it up – L."

[74] *FRUS, 1964–1968, Vol IV, Vietnam 1966*, doc. 245, McNamara to Johnson (draft), 22 September 1966. On plans for Tet 1967 see *FRUS, 1964–1968, Vol IV, Vietnam 1966*, doc. 316, Lodge to State, 27 November 1966. Other campaigns at this time included an initiative to keep down inflation: NA RG 59, State CPF, box 417, INF 8 VIET. S, Saigon 5415, embassy/JUSPAO/AID to State, Secret, 9 June 1966.

[75] NA RG59 CPF 1964–6, box 433, PPB 9–5 Viet S, Saigon 11690, Lodge to State, 26 November 1966.

As 1966 drew to a close, Leonard Marks nursed increasing doubts about the level of the USIA's commitment to Vietnam. In December he requested an internal review of the agency's role in "counterinsurgency situations":

> I am concerned about the increasing involvement of our personnel in the Far East in psychological warfare activities. We appear to be assuming responsibilities for some programs by default. Even though they are more logically and traditionally the responsibility of other agencies, we wind up doing them simply because they are unwilling or unable to get them done.[76]

Others in the Johnson administration shared Marks' doubts about the question of agency responsibility and sought to trim back the USIA's reach.

In the autumn of 1966, the work of Deputy Ambassador William Porter in coordinating the interagency pacification effort in Vietnam acquired a formal name: the Office of Civilian Operations. The idea was to focus efforts in an increasingly significant field and unify the work of JUSPAO, AID, the CIA, and the South Vietnamese. Unfortunately, the additional level of administration disrupted what Zorthian thought of as the "original purity" of the JUSPAO idea. A USIS officer working in the field as a psychological operations advisor now answered first to a regional command structure and Porter. Porter directed the pacification effort in much the same way as a theatre commander directed constituent units in World War Two. JUSPAO, AID, and the other contributing agencies provided the manpower and logistical support. The JUSPAO concept of a single information tsar had been eclipsed by the need for a single authoritative head of pacification.[77]

The propaganda war on the ground moved forward. The *Chieu Hoi* program gained a fresh twist as the U.S. military deployed former Communists in South Vietnamese irregular forces. These units included a number of armed propaganda teams devised by JUSPAO's field operations office to appropriate the Communists' own tactics. The brains behind this initiative came from the USIA side of JUSPAO: Ev Bumgardner (the director of the field office) and an energetic young officer called Frank Scotton. Both men spoke fluent Vietnamese. Scotton personally accompanied his teams of tough ARVN veterans and *Chieu Hoi* defectors on many of their missions, toting a prized Swedish K submachine gun. He had no doubt that a message delivered by a small, determined unit was more effective than the usual round of posters, leaflets, and loudspeaker broadcasts. The journalists who knew Scotton thought twice before reporting his activities in detail.[78]

The spring of 1967 brought yet another round of bureaucratic changes. Ellsworth Bunker became U.S. ambassador in Saigon and, in May, the responsibility for the pacification effort passed from Porter to a military organization known as the Office of the Assistant Chief of Staff for Civilian Operations and Revolutionary (later Rural) Development and Support, or CORDS for short. The dynamic head of CORDS,

---

[76] LBJL Leonard Marks, box 20, director's memos 1966, Marks to Ryan, 22 December 1966.
[77] Interview: Zorthian.
[78] Interview: Zorthian; Simpson, *Tiger in the Barbed Wire* pp. 204–05.

Robert W. Komer, achieved notoriety as the co-architect of the Phoenix Program, the controversial assault on the "VC" infrastructure launched in December 1967. In the shorter term he concentrated on support for the elections in South Vietnam, due to reach their climax in September 1967.[79]

At the end of June 1967, Marks traveled to Vietnam at LBJ's request to see how the USIA could help Komer. Marks also called on Prime Minister Ky and his latest minister of Information, General Tri, whose 12,000-strong ministry had not "been functioning with enthusiasm."[80] Marks' meeting with Ky and Tri seemed to have the desired effect. Saigon's Ministry of Information rose to the challenge of the elections with uncharacteristic enthusiasm. VIS teams took ground-based loudspeaker units around the country in the run up to the election with a thirty-minute selection of supportive songs and voting messages. The *Van Tac Vu* troupes toured performing election-related material in the traditional Vietnamese idiom. As with that year's Tet campaign, JUSPAO tried to keep its distance. Zorthian's staff worked under orders "not to be involved in posting or displaying the materials, or handing them to individuals." Even so, JUSPAO produced two short films about the importance of voting. One used animated puppets and songs, the other artwork, but both drew on examples from Vietnamese history. JUSPAO also helped Vietnamese television make two half-hour pro-election dramas and supervised election-day news coverage. On polling day – 2 September 1967 – JUSPAO's airborne loudspeakers urged citizens to vote.[81]

JUSPAO felt no obligation to step back the international presentation of the South Vietnamese election. It offered an ideal opportunity to show South Vietnam as a fledgling democracy worth fighting for. JUSPAO provided regular coverage of the election in multiple foreign languages for use on the VOA and created a radio feature in thirteen languages for distribution by USIS posts around the world. Zorthian found himself "back-grounding" numerous international election observers and an expanded corps of 575 American and other journalists. He felt that many in the U.S. election delegation had wholly unrealistic expectations for the election. Members of the visiting Moss Committee declared that they wanted the "purest election in history," when just having an election was an achievement and, Zorthian reminded them, after two centuries of practice, the United States still had corners such as Cook County, Illinois. Most observers considered the election to be fair, but postelection recriminations, culminating in the imprisonment of the runner-up peace candidate, Truong Dinh Dzu, diminished the effect.[82]

---

79 Interviews: Zorthian, Don Mathes, 12 December 1995; ADST: Oral History, Zorthian; LBJL WHCF Ex ND19/CO312, Bunker to _resident, 27 June 1967 et seq.; Leonard Marks, box 32, White House 1967, Marks to _resident, 28 June 1967. For a history of pacification see Richard A. Hunt, *Pacification: The American Struggle for Vietnam's Hearts and Minds*, Boulder, CO: Westview Press, 1998.

80 LBJL Leonard Marks, box 32, White House 1967, Marks to President, 28 June 1967.

81 LBJL Leonard Marks, box 31, USIA JUSPAO Election support file, including Oleksiw to Marks, 15 September 1967.

82 LBJL Leonard Marks, box 31, USIA JUSPAO Election support, Oleksiw to Marks, 15 September 1967. Interview: Zorthian; Hammond, *Reporting Vietnam*, p. 90. Marks' skepticism over specific operations focused on the vast volumes of printed material being dropped on enemy territory, after

For both Marks and Zorthian, the election marked a watershed. Zorthian became increasingly disillusioned with the levels of corruption in the Saigon government and Marks now doubted the wisdom of a sustained U.S. military commitment. In May 1967, Senator George Aiken of Vermont had proposed that Johnson just declare victory and withdraw from Vietnam. Marks noted a surge of world opinion in favor of the suggestion. He now felt that the successful display of democratic process in the South Vietnamese elections provided an opportune moment to withdraw. One morning shortly after the election, Marks found himself in Johnson's bedroom working through papers with the President and attempted to steer the conversation round to this idea. He suggested that Johnson withdraw his troops and maintain aid in the form of arms and money. Johnson glared. When Marks pressed him, Johnson angrily told the USIA director to "get out." For the next two weeks he was not invited to either NSC or cabinet meetings. Eventually the first lady built a bridge by inviting Marks to a surprise party for the President. Marks slipped back into the policy loop and things returned to normal. In later years Marks asked former President Johnson why he had been so enraged that morning. Johnson, who always had a flair for self-pity, replied quite simply, "Because in my heart I knew that you and George Aiken were right, and I couldn't do anything about it." Marks asked why. "Because," Johnson replied, "some of the Kennedy people might have moved for impeachment."[83]

*

Marks and Ambassador Bunker prepared for 1968 by reorganizing the U.S. press and psychological warfare apparatus in Vietnam yet again. Marks replaced Zorthian as director of JUSPAO with Edward J. Nickel from the Tokyo embassy. Zorthian moved to a special advisory post with the responsibility for dealing with the press.[84] For two years running, Zorthian had mounted major initiatives to coincide with the Tet festival. In 1968 the initiative was not his. On 31 January 1968, the "Viet Cong" mounted a nationwide guerrilla rising: the Tet Offensives. Despite casualties so high as to destroy the South Vietnamese guerrilla element in the Communist war effort – thereafter North Vietnamese regulars carried the burden of the war – the offensives gave the lie to American claims of imminent victory. Multiple attacks threw the entire U.S. operation in Vietnam into chaos.

In Washington, the VOA's Vietnamese branch responded gallantly to the crisis, doubling its output from six-and-a-half to over fifteen hours a day. The staff of twenty-six maintained a punishing schedule for the next six months, as the U.S. army struggled to regain control. But news of successful counterattacks made little difference. On

---

a week in which JUSPAO dropped 132 million leaflets on South Vietnam, Marks asked his staff, "I have previously asked to examine the need for this large quantity of material being dropped in hostile territory over South Viet-Nam. Is there a justification for this? Are studies made to determine the relative value of this large volume of material as compared to lesser quantity?" LBJL Leonard Marks, box 19, director's memos 1967, Marks to Oleksiw, 19 December 1967.

83   Interview: Marks, 15 June 2004; also interview: Zorthian and LBJL Oral History: Marks Interview II, January 1976, pp. 28–30.

84   LBJL WHCF CF, box 33, CF FG296, Marks to President via Maguire, 24 January 1968.

31 March, Johnson announced that he would henceforth be devoting himself to a settlement in Vietnam and was not seeking re-election to the presidency.[85]

On 7 July 1968, Barry Zorthian left Vietnam for a year at the Murrow Center at Tufts before reassignment to other duties. He returned to find an America more deeply divided by racial conflict and the issue of the war than he had imagined. He found too many echoes of the fractured nation he had just left behind on the other side of the world. Washington, DC lay under curfew as a result of riots sparked by the murder of Martin Luther King Jr., and his own teenage son had joined the anti-war movement.[86] LBJ prevailed on the State Department to offer Zorthian an embassy of his own. Rusk suggested Niger, a post guaranteed to frustrate an expert in media relations, as it lacked a daily newspaper. Zorthian declined the offer and resigned from the USIA to accept an executive position at *Time*. He never returned to the USIA, but supported the agency's work as an advocate for effective public diplomacy.[87]

For Zorthian's erstwhile colleagues in JUSPAO, the war for "Hearts and Minds" ground on with an unending round of *Chieu Hoi* campaigns and tub thumping for ever more tawdry South Vietnamese governments. The program delivered occasional victories, such as the defection of the North Vietnamese Army regimental commander Colonel Tuyuan or the day-to-day success stories, such as the simple fact that the rice road from My Tho to Saigon remained open, in part thanks to the efforts of the USIS psychological operations advisor in My Tho and his South Vietnamese counterparts in keeping the villages along the road loyal and supportive.[88]

Assessing JUSPAO in later years, Zorthian argued that the central concept of an integrated approach, connecting an active USIA role in policy-making to press management and psychological warfare in the field, had been sound but the application had been flawed. Beyond the need for consistent themes rooted in some sort of political reality, the Americans also needed self-restraint. Their impatience with the South Vietnamese had prompted JUSPAO to take over the communications role for themselves. "The effort," Zorthian argued, "was doomed to failure before it started. Americans have considerable trouble communicating with themselves, let alone with Asians in a completely alien setting." JUSPAO's attempt to correct this by guiding the South Vietnamese to conduct their own propaganda also failed, as the United States "insisted that the task be done with our tools, through our techniques, and in our

85 LBJL WHCF Ex, box 17, Ex FG1, Marks to President, 29 February 1968; Leonard Marks papers, box 19, director's memos, 1968, Marks to VOA 4 November 1968. Transmitters included a new one-megawatt medium-wave transmitter in Thailand (formerly codenamed Project Teak) available from April; see Marks, box 14, *USIA World*, Vol. 1, No. 12, May 1968. General Westmoreland gave orders to improve the presentation of American operations. The savage language "Search and Destroy" gave way to softer terms such as "reconnaissance in force." He limited the distribution of background material flagged "not for publication" and suggested that minimal help be given to journalists considered "beyond conversions." Hammond, *Reporting Vietnam*, p. 128.
86 ADST Oral History: Zorthian. Johnson presented Zorthian's reassignment as his own initiative. He reputedly informed the personnel director of the Associated Press that he had moved Zorthian because he had been in Vietnam for too long and hence AP might also consider moving his sometime antagonist, Peter Arnett. Arnett, *Live from the Battlefield*, p. 268.
87 ADST Oral History: Zorthian; Interview: Zorthian.
88 ADST Oral History: William Stearman; Interview: Don Mathes, 12 December 1995.

image." "What emerged, Zorthian concluded, "was something neither American nor Vietnamese, and it was often characterized by the worst of both.[89]

3) PROJECTING THE GREAT SOCIETY

In October 1965, just a few weeks after assuming the directorship of the USIA, Leonard Marks and his deputy director for policy, Burnett Anderson, agreed on their new priorities for the USIA's media output. The President's concept of "The Great Society" moved to the fore as the prime theme representing the domestic United States. Racial and ethnic progress followed in the second slot. The "rule of law" – a theme emphasized in the wake of the Kennedy assassination – left the priority list. In foreign affairs, Anderson recommended "the pursuit of peace," noting "for the first time, the proposition of building bridges to Eastern Europe and other changing societies."[90] It offered a sound agenda on which to build.

In March 1967, Marks set out the essence of his USIA. Its objectives fell into three key areas: building a general understanding of the United States; supporting policies in key policy areas such as disarmament or the Alliance for Progress; and advancing national development around the world, for as Marks noted, the USIS now functioned as the "information arm of AID abroad" in all but technical matters. He also stressed that the USIA must know its limitations. The agency should beware of taking on too much and never maintain projects "simply because they have been carried on for many years." Marks laid particular emphasis on audiences. "With rare exceptions," he wrote, "our primary audiences must be leaders, present and potential."[91]

Marks's emphasis on reaching the elite fitted with the emphasis on culture in the President's Smithsonian speech of September 1965. USIA initiatives included launching *Topic*, a lively monthly magazine in French and English aimed at the emerging elite in sub-Saharan Africa. Issues mixed features on American and African life, society, and culture. An Arabic version of *Topic* followed, replacing the old publication *Al Hayat*. In 1967 the U.S.S.R. launched its own equivalent, *New World*. Moscow at least felt the format worked.[92] In February 1968, the agency added an explicitly intellectual journal called *DIALOGUE*. Published quarterly, in Spanish and English, *DIALOGUE* reprinted articles from leading U.S. journals to deliver what Marks called "a stimulating presentation of the intellectual vigor and creativity of American society today." By 1970, *DIALOGUE* appeared in seven languages, across 108 countries, in

89 Dennis Duncanson, Richard Yudkin, and Barry Zorthian, *Lessons of Vietnam: Three Interpretive Essays*, Newark: Seton Hall University/American Asian Educational Exchange, 1971, p. 47.
90 LBJL Leonard Marks papers, box 27, USIA Media Priorities, Anderson to Marks, 6 October 1965. The suggested themes were as follows: for foreign affairs, (1) pursuit of peace; (2) strength and reliability; (3) free choice; (4) United Nations; for aspects of American life, (1) the Great Society, (2) racial and ethnic progress; (3) economic strength and democracy; (4) scientific and educational strength; (5) cultural development, diversity, distribution.
91 LBJL Leonard Marks papers, box 28, PAO letters, Marks to PAOs, 6 March 1967. On development see box 25, USIA National Development, Ryan to Marks, 8 June 1967 and attachments.
92 LBJL Leonard Marks papers, box 14, *USIA Correspondent*, Vol. 7 No. 11, November 1965; WHCF Ex, box 315, Ex FG 296, Marks to President, via Maguire, 27 December 1967.

a total distribution of 122,000 copies and was claimed as a major agency channel to "policy-makers, opinion makers, and potential leaders abroad."[93]

Marks improved the USIA's administration of cultural programs.[94] He created a "super cultural officer" post for Paris, London, and Tokyo because he "wanted those countries to understand the culture of the United States; that we were not just a materialistic society." He sponsored arts, music, dance, and a wide range of culture.[95] USIS cultural officers around the world made it their business to get to know artists in their client cities. Agency veteran Mike Pistor later recalled the convivial recognition he observed when the Paris Cultural Affairs Officer entered a particularly artistic café. "Hi," said one of the patrons. "Oh, hi *man*," the CAO replied. Pistor asked whether he always spoke so colloquially. "It's OK," the CAO explained, "that was Man Ray."[96]

In other cities the USIA had links to emerging politicians. A report on the USIS in South Africa spoke of "friendly and sometimes intimate relations" with key South Africans including the Progressive Party MP Helen Suzman and the editorial staff of the *Rand Daily Mail*, the *Johannesburg Star*, and the black-oriented daily *The World*. USIS Johannesburg co-sponsored courses to train black South Africans for careers in journalism and provided a space in which otherwise censored publications could be read. Three-quarters of library patrons were nonwhite. The USIS arranged scholarships and "leader grants" to allow black South Africans to visit the United States.[97]

In London the PAO did his best to seek out the future leaders of Britain and arrange visits to expose them to American ideas. In 1967 he hit the jackpot when he arranged a trip for a young Conservative woman MP, then in opposition as shadow Minister for Transport: Margaret Thatcher. She had never been to the United States before and the visit confirmed a lifelong regard. As she wrote in her memoirs,

> For six weeks I traveled the length and breadth of the United States. The excitement which I felt has never really subsided. At each stop-over I was met and accommodated by friendly, open, generous people who took me into their homes and lives and showed me their cities and townships with evident pride.

Her personal highpoint came with a visit to NASA's space center at Houston. Here, she encountered a British scientist from her own constituency. She did not blame him for seeking out an American salary, but his presence brought her face to face with the realities of the global marketplace: "There was no way Britain could hope to compete

93 LBJL Leonard Marks papers, box 14, box 28, PAO letters, Marks to PAOs, 8 March 1968; the USIA also commissioned a series of nine pamphlets on the arts under the title *Creative America* by Howard Taubman, art critic of the *New York Times*. On *DIALOGUE* see also NA RG 306, 89.0180, director's chronological file, 1969–70, box 16, reel 33, Ablard (Congressional Liaison) to Rep. Louis Stokes, 23 March 1970.

94 LBJL Leonard Marks papers, box 28, PAO letters, Marks to all posts, 12 August 1966 cited in Marks to all PAOs 6 March 1967.

95 ADST Oral History: Marks.

96 Interview: Pistor.

97 RG 59 State, CPF 1964–66, box 335, CUL 11 S. AFR, Lewis (USIA) to Strong (State), 25 February 1966.

even in modest areas of technology if we did not learn the lessons of an enterprise economy."[98]

Marks spearheaded an initiative to bring American culture into university curricula around the world. In July 1966, he informed LBJ that "During the past six months I have stressed the need for courses in 'American studies' throughout Latin American and European universities." Immediate results of renewed USIS support included a chair in American studies at the University of Zaragoza in Spain and a chair in History and Culture of North America at Leiden in the Netherlands. Appropriately, the first professor to hold the Leiden chair – J. W. Schulte-Nordholt – had been nurtured earlier in his career by a USIS-administered exchange scholarship.[99]

In some parts of the world, Marks reaped the rewards of earlier agency efforts. Indonesia seemed a particular success. In 1965, the Indonesian military crushed a Communist bid for power, tamed the dictator Sukarno, and installed a new leader, Suharto. On 1 July 1966, USIS Djakarta opened once again.[100] The country plan for 1968 (which wisely warned against "seeking to 'Americanize' Indonesia's institutions") noted with some satisfaction that the change of government reflected the potency of the educational grant, exchange, and cultural programs administered by the USIS, AID, the Ford and Rockefeller Foundations, and others over some seventeen years.[101] For years thereafter USIA officers pointed to the role of the University of California, Berkeley-trained cabinet in Indonesia as the great testament to the value of educational exchange.[102]

Despite an emphasis on opinion formers, some Marks-era initiatives still proved crowd pleasers, the most notable being the U.S. pavilion at Expo '67 in Montreal. Housed in R. Buckminster Fuller's giant geodesic dome, the exhibition took the title "Creative America." The budget had been exhausted by the dome's construction and the contents had to be borrowed from other agencies. No one noticed the scrimping. The *Montreal Star* proclaimed that the pavilion "could have been conceived only by people of wit and imagination with real love for and a knowledge of their country and

---

[98]   Margaret Thatcher, *The Path to Power*, London: HarperCollins, 1995, pp. 153–5. In contrast, in 1969 Margaret Thatcher paid a weeklong visit to the U.S.S.R. through the Anglo-Soviet parliamentary group. That visit stood in stark contrast to her U.S. experience. The USIA had let the country speak for itself, but in Russia she found unremitting, crude propaganda: "It was relentless, an endless flow of statistics proving the industrial and social superiority of the Soviet Union over the West. At least to the visitor, the sheer unimaginative humourlessness of it was an open invitation to satire."

[99]   LBJL, WHCF CF, box 135, CF USIA, 1966, Marks to President via Kintner, 5 July 1966. For recent Dutch scholarship on Schulte-Nordholt's U.S. links see J. C. C. Rupp, *Van Oude en Nieuwe Universiteit: De Verdringing van Duitse door Amerikaanse Invloeden op de Wetenschapsbeoefening en het hoger Onderwijs in Nederland, 1945–1995*, The Hague: Sdu, 1997, pp. 238–42. On the Fulbright Program in Holland see J. C. C. Rupp, "The Fulbright Program or the Surplus Value of Officially Organised Academic Exchange," *Journal of Studies in International Education*, 3, 1 (Spring 1999). I owe these references to Giles Scott-Smith.

[100] LBJL WHCF CF, box 135, CF USIA 1966, Marks to President, via Kintner, 26 July 1966. For policy see Leonard Marks papers, box 23, Basic USIA guidelines, Pauker (IOP) to IBS/IPS/ICS/IMV, 31 October 1966.

[101] LBJL Leonard Marks papers, box 3, Country Plan Program Memorandum for Indonesia, Secret, 14 May 1968.

[102] Interview: Schneider.

supreme confidence in its strength and variety." Fifty thousand people a day visited what proved the most popular exhibit at the Expo. The fair's end left Marks with a problem, as the USIA had no money to demolish the dome. In a flash of inspiration he called Jean Drapeau, the irrepressible mayor of Montreal, and over lunch persuaded him to buy the dome for $1 as an enduring symbol of the friendship between the two nations. The mayor called for the waitress to bring two sheets of paper and pens and made up a bill of sale and, though both men acknowledged that neither had the authority to close such a deal, they signed on the spot and the future of the dome was secure.[103]

*

The USIA's activities in the U.S.S.R. grew steadily with the conclusion of each biennial Cultural Exchange Agreement.[104] By July 1966, the press was reporting stories of Muscovites lining up for hours to obtain copies of *Amerika* magazine, and high school students could be seen beneath the Kremlin walls dancing to Voice of America music on their transistor radios.[105]

On 7 October 1966, Johnson spoke openly of his desire for closer relations with the Soviet Union, noting that he hoped Vietnam would not be an obstacle. Marks did his best to support the initiative with a restrained propaganda policy. One morning in March 1967 Marks received a call from Rusk in the small hours summoning him to the State Department. He had just received word that Stalin's daughter, Svetlana Alliluyeva, had defected. Marks devised a strategy on the spot. In keeping with the emerging culture of dialogue with the U.S.S.R., he scotched all thought of gloating and called for restrained news-based coverage. Accordingly the U.S. government merely announced that she was on her way to Switzerland and left the Swiss and Svetlana herself to do the rest of the talking.[106] That same month the VOA rejected the suggestion that the Voice begin Yiddish broadcasts to Soviet Jews as too politically provocative.[107] Johnson's initiative paid off. Between 23 and 25 June 1967 the President and Soviet Prime Minister Kosygin met in Glassboro, New Jersey for a "Mini-Summit," the first such meeting since Vienna in 1961. Although the two leaders clashed over much, the very fact of their meeting gave hope for the future.[108]

103 Interview: Marks, 15 May 2003; LBJL Leonard Marks papers, box 22, Expo '67, including Country Plan, 1964, which stated the USIA's chief objective in Canada as "Diminish Canadian sensitivities and frustrations at being overshadowed – culturally, economically, militarily – by the pervasive power and influence of the American presence on the North American continent." See also WHCF CF, box 135, CF USIA 1967, Marks to President, via Kintner, 2 May 1967.
104 LBJL, WHCF CF, box 135, CF USIA, 1968, Marks to President, via Maguire, 10 April 1968, noting the difficulties in negotiating the follow-up agreement in 1968.
105 LBJL, Fred Panzer papers, box 548, USIA, Ackers to Panzer (White House), 13 July 1967. The agreement lapsed briefly in 1967 but was renewed in July 1968, which added emphasis on the exchange of feature films; see Leonard Marks papers, box 14, *USIA World*, Vol. 2 No. 3, August 1968.
106 ADST Oral History, Leonard Marks; Sorensen, *The Word War*, p. 292.
107 LBJL Leonard Marks, box 15, Advisory Panel, Religious Gps, Ronalds (IBS/VOA) to Marcy (IOP), 7 March 1967, etc.
108 *FRUS, 1964–1968*, Vol. XIV, *The Soviet Union*, docs 229–38.

*

The USIA motion picture division continued to play a major role in Marks's USIA. In April 1966, *Newsweek* wrote admiringly of such films as *The Journey*, a lyrical account of the Pope's visit to the United States, which achieved a wide audience in the Philippines as an unlikely "opener" for the James Bond film *Thunderball*.[109] Once again USIA films caught the attention of the Oscars. *Cowboy*, a short film on a perennial American theme, was nominated in the Best Documentary Short category in the 1967 Academy Awards. Meanwhile, an intern named Carroll Ballard made a wonderful feature-length documentary called *Harvest*. Armed with just a camera and an old van, he followed the advancing wave of corn and fruit across the United States for a year. Completed in 1967, this film earned an Oscar nomination in 1968. Other films dealt with Vietnam, including *The Other War*, *A Distant Province*, and a film on the *Chieu Hoi* program, *Three Who Returned*.[110]

Leonard Marks worked to increase the efficiency of the motion picture branch. By merging it with the television branch to create into a single entity known as IMV, he saved over a million dollars, but the development was a profoundly uncomfortable experience for the staff.[111] Marks developed Project Kingfish, a covert subsidy to keep a special Hearst Metrotone newsreel circulating with USIA material in Africa and Asia.[112] Kingfish reached new countries. From June 1966, distribution included Burma, Iran, and Iceland.[113] Then, on 2 February 1967, Marks abruptly withdrew all agency support for Kingfish, arguing,

> It is my firm conviction that the USIA should not engage in 'covert' operations – any such functions can be handled by the CIA. The sponsorship of the newsreel, if revealed, could be used by foreign powers to disparage our information efforts and to label USIA as a covert organization.[114]

In place of Kingfish, the USIA offered *Washington Correspondent*, a lively TV current affairs program for the developing world. By December 1967, the program aired in twenty-nine countries.[115]

Marks' speedy action in February 1967 reflected his growing worry over the agency's engagement in Vietnam, but also anticipated a gathering storm. Back in May 1966 the *New York Times* had reported that RFE and RL operated with a CIA

[109] "Films from Uncle Sam," *Newsweek*, 18 April 1966, p. 109. NA, MPSVB, RG 306.2698, *The Journey*.
[110] NA MPSVB RG 306.04630 *The Other War*; RG 306.04682, *A Distant Province* (both 1967); and RG 306.03461, *Three Who Returned* (1968). Interview: Jerry Krell, 14 April 1998.
[111] LBJL Leonard Marks papers, box 25, Motion Pictures/TV merger, Marks to staff, 28 September 1965; Marks to Stevens, 1 December 1965.
[112] LBJL WHCF CF subject, box 79, PR12 Motion Pictures, Marks to LBJ, 31 March 1966. For earlier correspondence see Leonard Marks papers, box 20, Memos to Area & Media Directors, 1965, Marks to Stevens, 19 October 1965.
[113] LBJL Leonard Marks papers, box 20, director's memos to area/media directors, Marks to Stevens, 28 June 1966.
[114] LBJL WHCF CF, box 79, CF PR12 Motion Pictures, Marks to Kintner, 2 February 1967.
[115] WHCF Ex, box 315, Ex FG 296, Marks to President, via Maguire, 27 December 1967.

subsidy.[116] The story made little impact but on 14 February 1967, as the radical mag-azine *Ramparts* prepared a detailed exposé of covert CIA support to student groups, trade unions, and RFE/RL for its March issue, the *New York Times* broke the full story again. All hell followed, and the entire U.S. public diplomacy and information community became hypersensitive to the whole subject of covert funding for decades thereafter. Marks had moved in the nick of time.[117]

Meanwhile, George Stevens developed his own idea that American film art could be a tool of public diplomacy. In 1966 he launched the "American Classic Feature Film Program," a collection of classic films selected by critics for prestige screenings at American embassies around the world. The USIA acquired three 16mm English language prints of twenty-six films including *Casablanca* (1942), *Viva Zapata* (1952), and *Some Like It Hot* (1959) and two of Stevens's father's films: *A Place in the Sun* (1951) and *Shane* (1953). Some of the films had political value for their approach to controversial subjects, such as *On the Waterfront* (1951) or the racial dramas *The Defiant Ones* (1958) and *Lilies of the Field* (1963), although the USIA insisted that art alone justified their selection. The entire idea that Hollywood film was art ran against anti-American prejudice in many parts of the world. The scheme proved such a success with embassies that by 1968 the USIA decided to limit publicity for fear that a "hostile" observer might attempt to read politics into the selection of films and thereby jeopardize the operation. The only hitch came in 1970 when guests invited to a screening of the Mexican revolutionary drama *Viva Zapata* in Mauritius took offense at the depiction of peasant rebellion against evil sugar cane growers.[118]

Stevens and Marks did not work well together. Marks wanted USIA films to meet local needs in posts rather than grand themes and pressed Stevens accordingly.[119] As Stevens recalled, where Murrow had given creative freedom and Rowan had not interfered, Marks demanded major input into content. Stevens became bitterly familiar with Marks' dismissive response to an artistically sound and subtle film, "This needs more freight." "Leonard Marks was a lawyer," Stevens later recalled, "what did he know about movies?" Stevens realized that a government agency simply was not the place to develop a national sensibility for film as art. At the end of 1966 he left the USIA to found the American Film Institute.[120]

[116] The Eastern bloc media fell on the reference with glee. The Polish newspaper *Zycie Warszawy* quipped: "We have known for a long time that the Free Europe is neither 'free' nor 'European,' but thanked the *New York Times* for confirming the fact." RG 59 State, CPF 1964–66, box 444, RAD RFE, Sherer (Warsaw) to State, 9 May 1966.

[117] Stacey Cone, "Presuming a Right to Deceive: Radio Free Europe, Radio Liberty, the CIA and the News Media," *Journalism History*, 24, 4 (Winter 1998/1999), 148–55; also Michael Nelson, *War of the Black Heavens*, Syracuse, NY: Syracuse University Press, 1997, pp. 126–8.

[118] LBJL Leonard Marks papers, box 24, Classic Film program, USIA circular 3 October 1966 and associated correspondence; NA RG 306 87.0018, director's subject files, box 13, IMV films, Brewer (Port Louis, Mauritius) to USIA, 15 August 1970; Herschensohn to Halsema, 25 September 1970 Herschensohn (by this time director of Motion Pictures) defended *Viva Zapata* on artistic merit and noted that this was the first such complaint.

[119] Interview: Marks, 15 May 2003.

[120] Interviews: Stevens and Guggenheim.

As institutional pressure to support America's war in Vietnam grew, the liberal filmmakers attracted by the spirit of Kennedy's New Frontier left the agency. In 1968 James Blue completed one last film for the USIA, an Oscar-nominated multicountry view of the problem of international food shortages entitled *A Few Notes on Our Food Problem*; thereafter Blue not only left the agency but went so far as to attack the USIA in the New York-based journal *Film Comment*.[121] The conservative Herschensohn, however, believed passionately in the justice of the U.S. cause in Vietnam and stepped into the breach to serve as the new head of the agency's Motion Picture and Television Service.[122] Whereas Stevens had aspired to documentary art and drawn inspiration from the British documentary movement, Herschensohn looked elsewhere. Seeking to unlock the secrets of truly persuasive motion pictures, he screened a wide range of propaganda films for his staff including U.S. wartime films and Soviet, Chinese, and Nazi German examples. Some, he realized, could only have appealed to audiences who had never seen moving pictures before, but films such as Leni Reifenstahl's *Triumph of the Will* still held a devastating power. Herschensohn resolved to create films for America's cause of equal impact. He had not reckoned with the USIA's policy apparatus.[123]

Leonard Marks had a strong personal interest in educational television and above all the emerging technology of the communications satellite. In March 1966, Johnson appointed Marks to chair a working group on the use of satellites for international education. The group's proposals noted that the technology, for the present, remained limited by the availability of ground stations and standard ground transmission seemed adequate and cost-effective, but the "future prospects" for education via satellite seemed boundless. The working group suggested that the USIA work to demonstrate the educational potential of satellite communications and that the State Department seek live television exchanges with the Soviet Union. Marks also believed that satellites could be used to enable "high-speed data transmission to and from foreign computers"; he therefore suggested that the Executive Branch's Committee on Scientific and Technological Information (COSATI) study the expansion of "the proposed U.S. national informational-retrieval network" to include other countries.[124]

[121]   Basil Wright, *The Long View*, cited in Gerald O'Grady, "Eulogy for James Blue," *Independent*, 3, 5 (July 1980), 4–5. *Film Comment*, 17, 1 (January/February 1981), 71. Blue found his niche as a writer and teacher at UCLA, Rice, SUNY Buffalo, and the National Film School in London, where he worked as the head of the directorial department. He still made occasional documentaries. Between 1976 and 1977 he directed *Who Killed the Fourth Ward* (1976–7), a three-part television film telling the story of the decay of an African-American neighborhood Houston. The *Fourth Ward* now makes a sad companion peace to the promise documented in *The March*. James Blue died of cancer in 1980. On Blue's later work see Peter Lunenfeld, "'There Are People in the Streets Who've Never Had a Chance to Speak': James Blue and the Complex Documentary," *Journal of Film and Video*, No. 1 (Spring 1994), 21–33. For obituaries see Colin Young, "James Blue," *Sight and Sound*, 49, 4 (Autumn 1980), 248–9; Gerald O'Grady, "Eulogy for James Blue," *Independent*, 3, 5 (July 1980); *Continental Film and Video Review*, 29, 1 (November 1981); and *Film Comment*, 17, 1 (January/February 1981), 68–71.

[122]   Interview: Herschensohn; LBJL Leonard Marks papers, box 14, *USIA World*, Vol. 1, No. 7, December 1967.

[123]   Interview: Herschensohn.

[124]   124.LBJL WHCF CF, box 14, CF ED5, Cater to President, 22 November 1966 with attachments.

Johnson approved Marks' suggestions in November 1966 and promptly commissioned him to head a further task force on educational television overseas. Marks' second report in July 1967 called for the U.S. government to advise and train developing countries on their use of educational television. A pilot scheme was already under way in El Salvador, with further projects planned in Southeast Asia through a regional task force of Ministers of Education.[125]

In November 1967, Marks presented "A Blueprint for a New Schoolhouse" in a speech to the National Association of Educational Broadcasters. His vision of "a worldwide information grid" lay at its core. Educators, he argued, needed not only to "collect knowledge electronically" but also to "learn how to route it sensibly. There is just going to be so much information that we will either learn to route it, or it will surely rout us. And, we must learn to share our knowledge with our neighbors so that all may benefit." Marks imagined this *worldwide grid* linking centers of learning across the developed and developing world: "a unique method of plugging together human minds between any points on earth." He noted that MIT had already linked its computers with machines around Latin America, using shortwave radio to "converse" with a computer in Buenos Aires. "Nothing in this era," Marks concluded, "is moving faster than communications. It is literally – and figuratively – moving at the speed of light."[126] Returning to these themes in February 1968 he argued that a world information grid of linked computers would be "a fundamental step toward lasting world peace...The culture of all lands must be circulated through the houses of nations as our technology permits."[127]

Leonard Marks' vision brilliantly anticipated the World Wide Web. In ordinary circumstances he would have been ideally placed to develop the educational aspects of this vision through the USIA, but the late 1960s were not ordinary circumstances. The agency had little time for vision. The Vietnam War and domestic racial upheavals combined to bring the United States to a new low before world opinion. LBJ looked to Marks to pick up the pieces.

4) NADIR
THE USIA, WORLD OPINION, AND THE CRISIS OF THE LATE 1960s

Lyndon Johnson fought the Vietnam War in the presence of conflicting opinions. A narrow majority of Americans supported his policy with its mix of bombing and bids for negotiation. Non-Communist Asia seemed satisfied when he got tough, but Western Europe rallied only during the negotiation phases.[128] The administration

[125] LBJL Douglas Cater papers, box 15, Cater to President, 23 November 1966, and box 45, NSAM 342 & International Education, Marks to President, 26 June 1967 with attachments.

[126] LBJL Leonard Marks papers, box 21, speeches by L. Marks, address to NAEB, Denver, 8 November 1967.

[127] LBJL Leonard Marks, box 14, *USIA World*, Vol. 1, No. 10, March 1968.

[128] LBJL WHCF CF, box 33, CF FG 296 USIA, Rowan to President, 2 August 1965, noting that in July 1965 42% of Britons and 46% of Danes disapproved of U.S. military escalation in Vietnam. For a digest of U.S. opinion to 1966 see WHCF Ex, box 347, PR16, Gallup Political Index, 12 September 1966. See also *FRUS, 1964–1968, Vol. IV, Vietnam 1966*, doc. 88, Lodge to Johnson, 2 March 1966.

responded by attempting to pursue both war and peace simultaneously, and expected the USIA to reconcile any contradictions. Inevitably, policies – such as the bombing of Haiphong Harbor – designed to impress the East enraged the West.[129]

The USIA worked to engage the war's critics. In 1965, the London embassy invited American students in the United Kingdom to speak to British students on the subject of Vietnam. Recruits included Ed Feulner, then a postgraduate fellow at the London School of Economics. Feulner's travels around British campuses taught him that the U.S. government had simply failed to present a coherent message. He never forgot the experience, and later worked to promote U.S. information overseas as a member of the Advisory Commission during the Reagan years.[130] In Denmark, the PAO, Wilford Kramer, attempted to defuse student protest outside the Copenhagen embassy by organizing a "teach-in" on the theme of U.S. policy in Vietnam and inviting "hard-core" elements of the Socialist Young League to take part. On the evening of 19 January 1966, seventy-five students attended what they dubbed the meeting "in the lion's mouth." The students heard Kramer speak about Johnson's search for peace, watched the USIA documentary *Troubled Harvest*, and debated with staff. Kramer observed, "it was possible not only to keep the group in hand but also to sense that many of them were positively influenced."[131] In the Netherlands, the USIS distributed 20,000 copies of a Dutch translation of the pamphlet *Why Vietnam* in a bulk mailing to the home addresses of university professors and secondary school teachers. The scheme backfired when a pacifist MP – Slotemaker De Bruine – asked whether the country's Ministry of Education was helping the USIS. The minister denied having supplied the mailing list and declined to comment further.[132]

On some occasions USIS posts successfully corrected clear-cut examples of mis-representation of the Vietnam War. When *Montreal-Matin* cropped a UPI picture in a blatantly selective way, the USIA objected and extracted a pledge "that it wouldn't happen again." USIS complaints against the anti-American recaptioning of agency news photographs in the Pakistani daily paper *Jang* led to the suspension of the assistant editor. When Radio Belgium announced that the United States intended to use nuclear weapons in Vietnam, the USIS issued an immediate protest and ensured that the evening radio and television news carried the American position in full. USIS Canberra supplied the Australian government with proof that photographs in a *Ramparts* magazine article purporting to show the victims of U.S. bombing in Vietnam actually depicted "Viet Cong" atrocities. The Australian government then issued its own refutation of the *Ramparts* piece. But such actions could not reverse heartfelt editorial positions on the war or negate the message implicit in the stream of images of American power let loose on a luckless corner of Southeast Asia.[133]

[129] LBJL NSF Agency, box 75, USIA vol. 7, no. 2, doc. 18 & 18a, Marks to Rostow, 5 July 1966.
[130] Interview: Ed Feulner, 10 January 1996.
[131] NA RG 59 State, CPF 1964–66, box 417, INF 8 US, A-582 from Copenhagen, Kramer to State/ USIA, 26 January 1966 with *Ekstra Bladet*, 20 January 1966.
[132] NA RG59 CPF 1964–66, box 417, INF 8 US, A-498, Tyler to State, sent 3 January 1965.
[133] LBJL, WHCF CF, box 135, CF USIA, 1968, Marks to President, via Maguire, 27 March 1968.

The spring of 1966 saw a wave of Soviet bloc propaganda against U.S. involvement in Vietnam including films, broadcasts, books, exhibits, a letter-writing campaign, and suspiciously well-organized demonstrations. The USIA responded by attempting to at least explain the reasons for the U.S. escalation in Vietnam over the VOA.[134] October 1967 brought demonstrations across Western Europe.[135] The situation worsened in the aftermath of the Tet offensives. In the first two weeks of February 1968, protestors attacked USIS libraries and cultural centers in Germany, France, Spain, Austria, and the Scandinavian countries. Marks now acknowledged widespread doubting of American policy in Vietnam. Mixed messages from the United States deepened the problem. "One of the knottiest problems to handle," a USIS officer reported to Marks, "are Europeans of good will and open mind who ask about anti-Viet-Nam statements by prominent Americans, Lippmann, Fulbright, Robert Kennedy, etc., [and] U.S. television footage. We are undoubtedly our own worst enemy in Europe." Marks believed that the best counter propaganda would have been for the South Vietnamese to explain the war themselves, but, despite his appeals, the Saigon regime remained largely silent.[136]

The nerve center of the USIA's presentation of the Vietnam War was the Vietnam Working Group. This panel of regional and media experts coordinated all of the USIA's media production and policy communications about Vietnam. They had an unenviable job. In 1968, their output included *Vietnam Roundup*, a regular anthology of significant international news clippings about the war, issued three times a week around Washington and the country at large; copies reached the White House and Capitol Hill.[137] the USIA also played a leading role in the interdepartmental Vietnam Information Group, which worked to produce briefing papers to blunt the questions from Europe. Responses to the question of "Why are we fighting in Vietnam?" ranged from variations on the theme of defending South Vietnamese liberty to pointed references to the lessons of appeasement in the 1930s.[138]

In later years, Leonard Marks often told a story to sum up his experience at the USIA, recalling how LBJ had interrupted a meeting with Marks to ask, "You have $200 million appropriations and you tell me you have the finest people. Why can't you make the world understand what we are doing in Vietnam?" Marks replied, "Mr. President, they understand us. They don't agree with us. I've done everything I can." Johnson accepted the reply with a simple "I know that" and dropped the subject. Bluntly put, the USIA could inform the world of the U.S. position but it could not guarantee the world's reaction.[139]

---

[134] LBJL, WHCF CF, box 135, CF USIA, 1966, Marks to President, 22 March 1966; Marks to President, via Kintner, 5 July 1966. For response see NA RG 59, State CPF 1964–66, box 412, INF 6, State/USIA to Bucharest etc., 4 October 1966.
[135] LBJL WHCF Ex, box 229, Ex ND 19/CO132, Marks to President, via Maguire, 23 October 1967.
[136] LBJL WHCF CF, box 135, CF USIA 1967, Marks to President, via Maguire, 14 February 1968.
[137] Interview: Schneider; for copies of *Vietnam Roundup* see, LBJL WHCF Oversize Attachment box 2353.
[138] LBJL Califano papers, box 37, VIG to Califano (White House), 2 April 1968 with attached Q & A compilation including quote from USIA Talking Paper 27, 25 February 1966.
[139] ADST Oral History: Marks.

*

The Vietnam War was not the only area of weakness in America's global image. Part of the problem lay in the perceived successes of the Soviet Union, especially in the "space race." Whatever the Americans did seemed swiftly to be surpassed by the U.S.S.R. NASA's Gemini program (which reached a climax in December 1965 with the dramatic linkup of two craft, Gemini VI and VII) was trumped in February 1966 when the Soviets landed the Luna 9 probe on the moon and sent back dramatic pictures of the surface.[140] A Gallup poll in Britain that summer found that 48 percent of people questioned believed the U.S.S.R. to be "ahead in space" (against 21 percent for the United States), whereas 56 percent believed that the Soviets would be "first to land a man on the moon" (against 23 percent for the United States).[141] The United States fell back on its only strong suit: openness. An East Asian tour by Gemini astronauts Frank Borman and Wally Schirra provoked an ecstatic reaction. "I am convinced," Marks wrote to the President, "that the use of Astronauts as emissaries is a most effective way of reaching large audiences where we need greater good will."[142] But 1967 brought disaster. On 27 January 1967, a fire ripped through the space capsule during an Apollo/Saturn launch pad test. Three astronauts – Gus Grissom, Ed White, and Roger Chaffee – died horribly.[143] The fire delayed the Apollo program, which had the potential to make the U.S. reputation in space, but by the summer of 1967 Marks had problems much closer to home.

In the spring of 1967, Vice President Hubert Humphrey undertook a "fence-mending" trip to Europe. He found the continent's image of the United States dominated by "bombs...riots...crime" and "corruption."[144] It soon got worse. The world had grown used to summer riots in black neighborhoods, but the riots of 1967 displayed a new ferocity. Newark burned, and it took regular troops to restore order to Detroit. Looking back on this period, Marks recalled, "The president didn't get to sleep some nights and neither did I. We knew what was happening and there was nothing we could do other than what we were already doing. It was a great, great tragedy...."[145]

As the European media began to speak of "rebellion" and even "civil war," the USIA's Office of Policy realized that it had to present the riots to the world "in some detail in order to maintain credibility." The agency stressed that the Johnson

[140] LBJL, Fred Panzer, box 548, USIA, Ackers to Panzer, 13 July 1966 notes audiences in millions for the *Gemini VI/VII* film: Belgium 2 million; Spain 3 million; Mexico, 3.4 million. For local opinion study see LBJL Fred Panzer papers, box 218, foreign polls, USIA IRS/AN, M-98–66, Rising U.S. standing in Tehran drops sharply after Luna 9, 28 February 1966.

[141] LBJL WHCF CF, box 135, CF USIA 1966, Marks to President, via Kintner, 26 July 1966. 21 percent believed the U.S. to be ahead in the space race and 12 percent reported "Don't know," while 23 percent believed that the U.S. would be first to land on the moon and 21 percent replied with "don't know."

[142] LBJL WHCF CF, box 135, CF USIA 1966, Marks to President, 22 March 1966.

[143] Charles D. Benson and William Barnaby Faherty, *Moonport: A History of Apollo Launch Facilities and Operation*, NASA Special Publication-4204, Washington, DC: NASA, 1978, Chapter 18.

[144] LBJL WHCF CF, box 33, CF FG 296, Marks to President, via Maguire, 31 January 1968 with RCC: The American Image Abroad, draft, 11 December 1967, p. 15.

[145] Interview: Marks, 15 May 2003.

administration sought to address the underlying social causes of the discontent. Even the violence could be portrayed as a sign of progress. The policy office quoted the *New York Times* on 27 July 1967: "Nothing is so unstable as a bad situation that is beginning to improve." The policy office urged USIA media departments to "screen the Negro press in the U.S. for constructive editorial comment which will make clear that most of America's 20 million Negroes are opposed to extremism and lawbreaking"; to look everywhere for constructive statements, "which demonstrate widespread recognition of the need to do more for the underprivileged"; to "avoid such inflammatory reports as those describing the situation as 'conspiracy,' 'civil war,' 'revolution,' etc.," and remember Johnson's call to "acknowledge the tragedy... but let us not exaggerate it."[146] But the problem did not diminish. The murder of Martin Luther King Jr. in April 1968 triggered new riots. Leonard Marks warned the President, "The events of the past week have seriously shaken the confidence of America's allies and friends around the world. We have suffered a blow from which it will take a long time to recover."[147]

At the end of April 1968, Marks traveled to Western Europe to view the damage for himself. "These events," he wrote to Johnson, "have caused the average European to question the stability of the American form of government and to cast doubt on our position as the leaders of the free world." The entire postwar relationship between Europe and the United States seemed to be in flux as a result of an almost Freudian crisis: "Instead of 'anti-American' feeling, there would appear to be loss of respect in the same way that a child is shaken when he discovers that his parents are fallible." Meanwhile, European youth had fixed on the United States and the issue of Vietnam as symbols of the old order, "a convenient way to express a difference of opinion" with their elders. With a spirit of reform abroad in Poland and Czechoslovakia, suddenly Communism was "no longer an evil word." Rather, Marks noted, "many student groups regard 'capitalism' and 'free enterprise' as systems which deprive them of opportunity." Marks called for a concerted USIA effort to open discussion with student leaders, editors, and other opinion makers. The White House issued no response.[148]

In the midst of these problems, the financial implications of the U.S. commitment to Vietnam hit home. In January 1968, the staff of the USIA learned a new acronym: BALPA, an abbreviation of "Balance of Payments" used to describe a biting round of budget cuts required by the President in all areas of federal activity overseas except Vietnam to conserve currency. The USIA immediately drew up plans to reduce its staff worldwide by 10 percent Staff began leaving posts that spring.[149]

Key observers urged reform at the USIA. In early 1968, the Republican Coordinating Committee's Task Force on the Conduct of Foreign Relations published

146   LBJL Leonard Marks papers, box 23, Basic USIA guidelines, "Violence in American Cities," 28 July 1968.
147   LBJL, WHCF CF, box 135, CF USIA, 1968, Marks to President, via Maguire, 10 April 1968.
148   LBJL, WHCF CF, box 135, CF USIA, 1968, Marks to President, via Maguire, 30 April 1968. Unlike many of Marks' reports to Johnson via Maguire or Kintner, this has neither a forwarding slip nor notes in the President's hand.
149   LBJL Leonard Marks papers, box 14, *USIA World*, Vol. 1 No. 12, May 1968.

The American Image Abroad, a report berating Johnson's stewardship of the USIA. The report recalled Johnson's attack on the agency budget in 1957, noted a failure to act on the recommendations of the Sprague committee of 1960, and poured particular scorn on the cancellation of the agency's global prestige survey. Republican Congressional leaders had commissioned a substitute survey in September 1966 and found a surge in criticism of the United States. Against the USIA's figures for March 1964, anti-American feeling had risen by 33 percent in Britain, 100 percent in France, and 300 percent in Germany. The Republicans called for a bigger budget and a strengthening of agency cultural programs to fight this feeling.[150] In early 1968, the annual report of the President's Advisory Commission on Information also called for a renewed emphasis on "long-range educational and cultural programs" and better coordinatioNon with State. Together, the two reports represented formidable pressure for change.[151]

In May 1968, Edmund Gullion called a lunch meeting for members of the Advisory Commission and others interested in public diplomacy. Gullion's agenda included a host of issues, including the rapid changes in technology and "the need for reducing the high visibility of the American mission abroad" and for an increased USIA role in development. Gullion asked whether the USIA should be prepared to take up an "aggressive public affairs role" in its presentation of the American position. The crisis now seemed so extreme as to raise the issue of a potential domestic role for the USIA as a domestic Ministry of Information. He suggested that the Murrow Center might conduct an in-depth report into the future of the USIA. Frank Stanton supported the call for an inquiry. Although he insisted that he believed in "the informational role of the Agency," he proposed ending the Smith–Mundt ban on the domestic use of USIA materials: "times have changed and there is no doubt that a free press would censor any abuse of the Agency's propaganda role, and it might be well to let America know what the USIA is doing abroad."[152]

In July, Representative Dante Fascell chaired hearings on "The Future of United States Public Diplomacy." Stanton, Gullion, Bernays, Gallup, and even Edward W. Barrett all testified.[153] But even as the hearings took place, the crisis deepened still further. Multiple chasms had opened in the social fabric of the United States setting black against white; young against old; poor against rich. The summer brought the assassination of Robert Kennedy and riots outside the Democratic National Convention

[150] LBJL WHCF CF, box 33, CF FG 296, Marks to President, via Maguire, 31 January 1968 with RNC: The American Image Abroad, draft, 11 December 1967. See also UoA CU 9/21, RNC press release 2 February 1968 and final report.

[151] LBJL Leonard Marks papers, box 28, PAO letters, Marks to PAOs, 8 March 1968. The letter also notes coming technical innovations, including the invention of "Electronic Video Recording."

[152] LBJL WHCF Oversize Attachment 3615, Task Force on Communication Policy, Gullion (Murrow Center, Fletcher School) to Cater (White House), 9 May 1968, with "Outline of May 6 Advisory Commission Luncheon Discussion."

[153] "The Future of United States Public Diplomacy," part XI of hearings on "Winning the Cold War: The U.S. Ideological Offensive by the Subcommittee on International Organizations and Movements of the Committee on Foreign Affairs of the House of Representatives, pursuant to H. Res. 179," 22 July 1968, p. 36 filed in NA RG 306 A1 (1061) USIA historical collection, misc. files, 1940–1990s, box 15.

in Chicago. The USIA tried to present the widening gulfs as evidence of national vitality.[154]

*

On 21 August, the Soviet Red Army and units of Polish, Hungarian, East German, and Bulgarian troops invaded Czechoslovakia and brought a brutal end to the "Prague Spring" and the reformist rule of Alexander Dubcek. The VOA immediately expanded its services in all Eastern European languages. Moscow responded by recommencing jamming. Marks condemned the "resumption of cold-war tactics" as "a regrettable step backward."[155] The agency strove not to respond in kind. Although the USIA Office of Policy and Research called for USIA media outlets to question how Brezhnev's action could be consistent with "peaceful coexistence," all guidance stressed caution. "Do not," the Policy Office warned in October 1968, "appear to mount a 'Cold War' campaign against the U.S.S.R." Although the USIA cancelled a number of high-profile cultural exchanges with the Eastern bloc, most remained quietly operational and were reported "only to the minimal extent credibility requires." The policy of "building bridges" to the Eastern bloc remained.[156]

The restrained reaction to Czechoslovakia presented severe problems in the USIA's media branches. In Motion Pictures and Television, Bruce Herschensohn found his plans for ideologically combative films consistently blocked by Hewson Ryan's policy office. Herschensohn proposed a ninety-minute film with the title *The American Dream*. The administration refused. Herschensohn proposed eight films on "areas in which the United States might be criticized abroad." The policy office only approved one, a civil rights film focusing on Martin Luther King: *The Dream of Kings*. Frustrated, Herschensohn threatened to resign. Marks prevailed on him to stay and encouraged him to seek inspiration on a trip. Herschensohn traveled to Vietnam and Czechoslovakia, where he saw an opportunity for a powerful documentary about the fate of the Prague Spring. Knowing that such a film would be squashed at the script stage, he resolved to create a film without a script, a record of Czech suffering composed only of music and images, and allow the images to speak for themselves. Fortunately the acting head of the USIS Special Projects Office in Vienna, Len Baldyga, had unexpectedly acquired a quantity of suitable top-quality news footage of the invasion. The Czech camera crews who shot the material entrusted it to one of the American actors then in Czechoslovakia making the David L. Wopler war film *The Bridge at Remagan*, who smuggled the cans out when he was evacuated. Herschensohn, in turn, smuggled this and other footage into USIA headquarters in anonymously

154 LBJL Leonard Marks papers, box 24, basic USIA guidelines, Ryan to all posts, 30 July 1968. Other themes included "democracy at work" in the election, the search for peace in Vietnam, and the threat of overpopulation in international development.
155 LBJL WHCF CF, box 135, CF USIA 1968, Marks to President, via Maguire, 27 August 1968; Leonard Marks papers, box 31, Soviet Jamming of VOA, Martin to Cushing (VOA); "VOA Being Jammed during Czech Crisis," *Broadcasting*, 26 August 1968.
156 LBJL Leonard Marks papers, box 23, Basic USIA guidelines, News policy note, "After the Invasion of Czechoslovakia," 30 October 1968.

labeled cans, with generic entries in the expenses ledger: "film clips: $42,000." The Czechoslovakia project was a gift awaiting the arrival of the Nixon era USIA.[157]

In the run up to the presidential election of 1968, Lyndon Johnson announced that Leonard Marks would be leaving the USIA to take up new duties at chairman of the U.S. delegation to the International Telecommunications Satellites Conference. Marks submitted his letter of resignation on 4 November. "It was," Marks wrote, "a unique privilege to serve as a member of the National Security Council, to participate in your cabinet meetings and to serve on the Task Forces to which you appointed me."[158] He had achieved much – he was far and away the most successful Democrat to hold the office – and he would doubtless have achieved even more without the dead weight of Vietnam. Marks continued to shape American public diplomacy as the chairman of the Advisory Commission on International Educational and Cultural Affairs (watchdog of the State Department cultural program) and as an important private voice for better public diplomacy. He died in 2006.[159]

The final months of the Johnson administration brought some successes. The agency, as ever, presented the presidential election as a triumph for the American political system, and Johnson's announcement on 31 October of a total halt in U.S. bombing of North Vietnam as major step toward peace.[160] More than this, the first missions of Project Apollo put the United States ahead in the space race. In October, Apollo VII spent 260 hours in orbit, longer than all Soviet flights to that date put together. On Christmas Eve 1968, Apollo VIII orbited the moon, broadcasting live pictures back to earth. The astronauts read from the book of Genesis. The VOA relayed their message to a record-breaking 1,353 stations in Latin America. Even Radio Havana twice broke into its usual programming to play VOA Spanish coverage of the flight. Apollo VIII brought back the first images of the earth as seen from deep space, which the USIA then distributed around the world. The earth appeared to be a tiny blue sphere in a sea of blackness: infinitely wonderful and somehow precarious.[161] Impossible goals – the moon and peace in Vietnam – seemed suddenly within reach. President-elect Richard M. Nixon stood ready to reap the reward.

[157] Interview: Bruce Herschensohn; Paul Grimes, "Conservatives Surround USIA Boss," Philadelphia *Sunday Bulletin*, 12 October 1969; Len Baldyga to author, 11 August 2005.
[158] LBJL WHCF Ex, box 316, Ex FG 296/A, Marks to President, 4 November 1968, and President to Marks, 6 December 1968.
[159] Interview: Marks, 15 May 2003.
[160] LBJL Leonard Marks papers, box 23, Basic USIA guidelines, USIA Potomac Cable: The Bombing Halt, 1 November 1968.
[161] USIA *31st Review of Operations, July–December 1968*, pp. 20–22; Courtney G. Brooks, James M. Grimwood, and Loyd S. Swenson, *Chariots for Apollo. A History of Manned Lunar Spacecraft*, NASA Special Publication 4205, Washington, DC, NASA, 1979, Chapter 11.

7 Surviving *Détente*

THE NIXON YEARS, 1969–74

> This whole Cold War . . . is essentially a clash of ideas. If we are not prepared to at
> least portray and advocate the ideas we believe in, we won't survive.
>
> Frank Shakespeare, 1 May 1972.[1]

Richard M. Nixon launched his administration with a flourish. On the
evening of 11 December 1968, the President-elect mounted an hour-long all-network
television program to introduce his cabinet to the American people. The twelve cabinet
officers and their wives sat in a row below the President's dais. Speaking without notes,
Nixon moved along the line describing their careers and values. As the program's
producer, Frank Shakespeare, had hoped, Nixon appeared statesmanlike, authoritative,
and connected to his team. Even Democrats seemed impressed.[2] But Nixon already
had good reason to thank Shakespeare. A former president of television services at CBS,
Shakespeare had also managed the television aspects of Nixon's presidential campaign.
He used advertisements and a series of carefully managed television debates to show
Nixon at his best and insulate him from the press. Shakespeare's strategy worked.
Nixon won. Now Nixon chose Shakespeare to direct the USIA.[3]

Soon after accepting the USIA job, Shakespeare received an unexpected invitation
to call on former President Eisenhower in Walter Reed hospital. He found the old man
propped up in a bed in a hospital gown. To Shakespeare's astonishment, Eisenhower's
attendant left and the ex-President began a two-hour briefing on the history of the
USIA and role of the director as "one of the most important jobs in the entire United
States Government." As Eisenhower drew to a close, he stressed the need for Shakespeare to attend NSC meetings. Shakespeare explained that the new NSC director
intended to restrict membership to five people and that the USIA director would attend
only by invitation. Incredulous, Eisenhower asked who the new NSC director would

---

1   *U.S. News and World Report*, 1 May 1972, quoted in To-Thi Nguyen, "A Content Analysis of Voice
    of America Broadcasts to Vietnam," Ph.D. dissertation, Ohio State University, 1977, p. 8.
2   Interview: Frank Shakespeare, 11 January 1997; for coverage of the cabinet broadcast see Robert
    B. Semple Jr., "Nixon Presents the New Cabinet," *New York Times*, 12 December 1968,
    p. 1.
3   Interview: Shakespeare; Joe McGinniss, *The Selling of the President, 1968*, New York: Trident Press,
    1969, esp. pp. 9–24, 49–50, 168. For Nixon's appreciation, see his birthday greeting: RNPM, WHCF,
    FG230 (USIA) box 1, Exec., President to Shakespeare, 9 April 1969.

293

be. "Henry Kissinger," Shakespeare replied, "it will be announced in a few days." The former President's incredulity deepened: "But Kissinger is a professor . . . you ask professors to study things, but you never put them in charge of anything . . . I'm going to call Dick about that." Two months later, Eisenhower was dead and Shakespeare found himself directing the USIA with less access to the decision-making process than any of his predecessors.[4]

Henry Kissinger radically reoriented USIA. By excluding the agency from the NSC, he ended its hard-won policymaking and advisory role. He also reduced the tactical use of the agency. The Nixon White House looked to the USIA as a general might to a faithful artillery unit, to deliver a consistent barrage in support of the broad objectives of U.S. foreign policy, while Kissinger and Nixon swept around the battlefield like plumed hussars.[5]

The ideological flexibility displayed by Nixon and Kissinger in their virtuoso diplomacy toward the Communist world presented personal problems for Shakespeare. His loyalty to the President clashed with his personal convictions, as he recalled in 1997:

> I didn't agree in my deepest private self with some of the things that were being undertaken. The root of it was this. I have always believed that communism as it existed as an idea linked to states and power was evil, I thought it represented a mortal threat, that coexistence or convergence was nonsense. You don't converge or coexist with evil.[6]

Shakespeare directed the USIA according to his convictions, which did not make for happy relations with the rest of the foreign policy machine, or an easy ride for the agency.

1) THE TRUE BELIEVER
FRANK SHAKESPEARE AND THE USIA, 1969–70

By the summer of 1967, Frank Shakespeare feared for the future of America. As cities burned in yet another round of riots, he resolved to act. Born in 1925 in New York City and educated at Holy Cross College, he had risen swiftly in the still-young television industry. A passionate conservative and Catholic, he scanned the list of Republican contenders for the White House in 1968 in search of a candidate to whom he could offer his support. Richard Nixon stood out and he made an appointment to meet the contender at his law practice in New York City. Shakespeare immediately recognized Nixon as a man he could work with and began coaching him in television

---

[4] Interview: Shakespeare, and Tuch and Schmidt (eds.), *Ike and USIA*, pp. 55–6.

[5] Nixon's first order to the USIA was to prepare a digest for the U.S. press of favorable world reaction to his inaugural address. He pressed the matter, noting to Ehrlichman, "the purpose of following up on this suggestion is that this will indicate a pattern I would like to see followed in the future." RNPM, WHCF, FG230 (USIA) box 1, Exec., President to Ehrlichman, 4 February 1969; Haldeman to Klein, 5 February 1969.

[6] Interview: Shakespeare.

technique on the weekends. When the campaign began in earnest in 1968, Shakespeare took leave from CBS and devoted himself full time to the Nixon cause. His efforts paid dividends. The medium that had been Nixon's undoing in 1960 was a particular strength in 1968. A grateful Nixon duly offered Shakespeare a job in his administration. Shakespeare asked to be Assistant Secretary of State for Latin America and Nixon made it clear that the post was his if he wanted it, but invited him to consider the directorship of the USIA instead. Shakespeare agreed to serve at the USIA for the first term.[7]

Shakespeare knew that his effectiveness as an agency director would hinge on his relationship with the White House. Nixon assured him, "Since everybody knows that you and I are close, you can do – within reason and within prudence – what you think ought to be done . . . and nobody will mess with you." Shakespeare avoided troubling the President or his intermediary – White House chief of staff H. R. Haldeman – with day-to-day USIA business, and little correspondence between the two men survives, but this is misleading. Frank Stanton, who knew the agency and its directors well, had no doubt that Shakespeare had much the closest relationship to his President.[8] Shakespeare's connection to Nixon proved a mixed blessing. The USIA became a target of opportunity for the President's enemies, including the chairman of the Senate Foreign Relations committee, William Fulbright.

Nixon's friendship with Shakespeare did not draw forth a place for the USIA in the new NSC. The President's Advisory Commission on Information questioned this. Its chairman, Frank Stanton, wrote to Nixon and Kissinger, citing the Commission's recent call for the USIA to be "assigned a role as an influence on foreign policy as well as an instrument of it." Nixon replied that "Frank Shakespeare will be invited to all meetings in which matters of particular concern to USIA are discussed."[9] The Eisenhower-era deputy director of the USIA, Abbott Washburn, urged Shakespeare to fight. Shakespeare declined, feeling sure that he would be able to reach the President whenever he needed to. For Washburn, this missed the point. "We have to be there to keep reminding them . . . we have to crank that world opinion factor in," he warned, "otherwise it will be neglected."[10] Kissinger initially went through the motions of consulting the USIA. He invited the agency to serve on one of the two subcommittees of the NSC, the NSC Review Group. But unlike the CIA or the Defense Department, Shakespeare did not receive committee papers in advance. The USIA could not be proactive or take a meaningful role in the planning process. Kissinger saw Shakespeare

7   Interview: Shakespeare; RNPM, WHCF, FG 230, (USIA) box 1, President to Shakespeare, 9 April 1969: Nixon notes: "Your professional skill, combined with your good sense, made a major contribution to the [election] victory in November."
8   Interviews: Shakespeare; Stanton. For announcement see "A New Spokesman for the U.S.," *New York Times*, 14 January 1969, pp. 1, 26;
9   RNPM, WHCF, FG6–6 (NSC) box 1, Exec., Stanton to Kissinger, 10 January 1969; FG230 (USIA) box 1, Exec., Advisory Commission to President, 3 February 1969; President to Stanton, 20 February 1969.
10   Interviews: Shakespeare and Washburn. In later years Shakespeare recalled that he never felt access to be a problem.

as a "loose cannonball on the deck," afflicted with anti-Soviet tunnel vision, and sought to manage rather than to consult him. After about a year the NSC Review Group ceased to meet. The USIA had been left in the cold.[11]

*

Shakespeare chose his senior staff well. Seeking to focus on "the critical intangible" of ideological leadership, he resolved to delegate the burden of agency bureaucratic duties to his deputy and therefore selected someone who already knew the agency well. He recruited Henry Loomis, who as VOA director had introduced the charter and then resigned in its defense. As before, Loomis shone.[12] For his director of the VOA, Shakespeare chose Kenneth R. Giddens of Mobile, Alabama. Born into a decayed planter family in 1908, Giddens had lived the American dream. He moved from a boyhood laboring on a building site to a successful architecture practice. He made one fortune in real estate and a second in broadcasting. As founder and president of CBS affiliate WKRG, Giddens had run radio and television stations and served a term as director of the National Association of Broadcasters. An old friend of Shakespeare's, he was eager to work for the public good. He told one journalist, "I think it is a calling almost as high as that of the priesthood. I see it almost as a religious opportunity. I think it is the greatest challenge of my life." He would be the longest-serving director of the Voice, holding the post from 1969 to 1977.[13] The third key post in Shakespeare's agency was the officer he saw as the visual equivalent of the VOA director, the assistant director for motion pictures and television. Here Shakespeare considered himself "blessed." He found an ideological soul mate already in post: Bruce Herschensohn.[14]

With core agency operations in safe hands, Shakespeare set out to run the ideological aspects of the USIA himself. He began with a year of intense travel to get to know his posts and their host governments. He sought out the less-visited destinations such as Romania and Saudi Arabia and was, for a while, the most senior American official ever to have visited South Africa. He traveled to learn, but at home or away he could be counted on to expound his ideas with almost uncanny flow and relentless ideological consistency. Shakespeare returned with a new sense of priorities. He worked to disengage the USIA from counterinsurgency work in Vietnam and to end the Johnson-era attempt to connect the agency to international development. He reinvigorated the agency's work in the Eastern bloc, insisting that the best staff be posted to the region, and rotating groups of senior officers through Eastern bloc posts so that everyone would be working from a direct experience of Communism. Finally,

11 ADST Oral History: Monsen.
12 Interviews: Shakespeare; Herschensohn; ADST Oral History: Loomis; "Voice of Truth?" *New York Times*, 10 April 1969, p. 46. Shakespeare recalled that he had carte blanche from Nixon to nominate his own political appointees "without one scintilla of political pressure."
13 USIA HB: Giddens biographical notes, September 1969; Helen Dudar, "New Voice," *New York Post*, 25 August 1969; Paul Grimes, "Nixon's USIA Team Shows Naiveté and a Holier-Than-Thou View," *Evening Bulletin* (Philadelphia), 8 October 1969.
14 Interviews: Shakespeare.

unlike most of his Nixon-era colleagues, he showed a prescient interest in the Persian Gulf.[15]

Shakespeare's media directors enjoyed unprecedented creative freedom. He allowed Giddens to handle broadcasting and Herschensohn to develop film and television free from the veto powers of the area directors.[16] But their freedom was bought at the cost of a marked loss of power for the area directors and FSOs in the Office of Policy, who were not used to a director with such active policy ideas. For them Shakespeare was as welcome as the plague. Hewson Ryan, who served as acting director during the three months of transition from Marks to Shakespeare, considered Shakespeare to be "a total zealot . . . convinced that the previous administration had been a tool of Soviet foreign policy." To Ryan's horror, soon after arriving at the agency Shakespeare asked about scenarios for the overthrow of Castro. Ryan was much relieved when he escaped to become ambassador to Honduras.[17]

*

Shakespeare entered the USIA eager to improve knowledge about the agency in the circles of power.[18] He swiftly set about reinvigorating the USIA's venerable watchdog-cum-helpmeet, the President's Advisory Commission on Information. Nixon allowed Shakespeare free rein in making appointments, including retaining Democrat Frank Stanton (who featured on the White House enemies list) as chair.[19] Other members of the upgraded board included the conservative journalist and editor William F. Buckley Jr.;[20] Hobart Lewis, Republican and president of *Reader's Digest* (who chaired from 1973); oilman John M. Shaheen; and novelist (and Democrat) James Michener. When Buckley left in 1972, Shakespeare recruited the polling

15 Interviews: Shakespeare; Herschensohn; ADST Oral History: Winkler, Monsen, Schmidt, Shirley, Mauice Lee, Loomis. Shakespeare's talents included a gift for mimicry. His Nixon and Kissinger were both uncanny.

16 Interviews: Shakespeare, Herschensohn; ADST Oral History: Amerson.

17 ADST Oral History: Ryan, Hemsing, Loomis.

18 Early in his tenure, Shakespeare ordered field staff to make better use of members of Congress traveling overseas, hoping "not only to communicate through them with our local audience, but also to enhance their understanding in agency programs." NA RG 306, 89.0180, director's chronological file, 1969–70, box 16, reel 33, Shakespeare, Memo for all area directors and PAOs, 23 March 1970.

19 Interview: Shakespeare. Nixon wavered on keeping Stanton as chairman; see RNPM WHSF WHCF CF, box 25, FG227 (Advisory Commission on Information), CF, Flanigan (White House) to President, 26 December 1969. In March 1969, the *New York Times* reported that Stanton had tendered his resignation because Nixon and Kissinger had ignored requests to meet. Stanton explained that he had offered to resign only because he thought Nixon might feel he had "too much CBS image" with both him and Shakespeare involved with the same agency. Benjamin Welles, "Nixon Keeps Unit on USIA Waiting," *New York Times*, 20 March 1969, p. 19, and Benjamin Welles, "Kissinger to Add USIA Staff Aide, but Won't Get Seat on Full Security Council," *New York Times*, 21 March 1969, p. 23.

20 Interview: Shakespeare; RNPM WHCF FG230 (USIA), box 1, Exec., Shakespeare to President, "Some encouraging developments," 12 November 1970. Buckley and Stanton became good friends and Shakespeare even speculated in a letter to Nixon that CBS had become more balanced in its political coverage as a result: "Bill's intellectual strength and character has exposed Stanton at close range and over a continuous period to an expert philosophical rationale of Conservatism. The effect is heart warming." Shakespeare also noted that CBS had replaced the liberal general manager of WCBS-TV New York.

pioneer George Gallup.[21] Stanton expected his fellow commissionaires to gather every month in Washington and devote a day to their duties. Members seldom skipped meetings, which included a dinner the night before at which the five commissioners could meet someone who mattered in Washington and explain the agency's work. When a hearing rolled around, Shakespeare used Stanton and Michener as his point men on a Democratic-dominated Capitol Hill. The formula worked wonderfully.[22]

The wider issue of "public diplomacy" remained moot. In 1968, both the Republican Party and the Advisory Commission had called for a major review of the USIA. No such review took place. In 1969, the House Foreign Affairs subcommittee, chaired by Congressman Dante B. Fascell (D-FL), produced a report, "The Future of United States Public Diplomacy," calling for a presidential commission to review the entire subject. The cause also attracted its own pressure group, "The Emergency Committee for a Reappraisal of United States Information Policies and Programs," chaired by Edward L. Bernays. In October 1969, Bernays organized a one-day conference for diplomats, communications professionals, and academics to discuss the present and future of the USIA, but the idea of a full-blown commission had to wait.[23]

*

In early 1969, the agency noted a surge of Soviet attacks on the VOA and *Amerika* magazine in the Soviet press. The USIA took this as evidence that their media were finding their mark among the youth and intellectuals of the U.S.S.R.[24] Shakespeare responded by sharpening the Voice of America's broadcasting to the U.S.S.R. In autumn 1969, the VOA began broadcasting from Munich over a powerful longwave transmitter exactly on Radio Moscow's frequency. Shakespeare intended the

---

21 Interview: Shakespeare and (telephone) Louis T. Olom, 3 April 2001; ADST Oral History: Olom. Shaheen figures in the early stages of the arms to Iran story; see Bob Woodward, *Veil: The Secret Wars of the CIA, 1981–1987*, New York: Simon and Schuster, 1987, pp. 152–3, 412, 418; Theodore Draper, *A Very Thin Line: Iran Contra Affairs*, New York: Simon and Schuster, 1991, pp. 134–5, 440. Stanton served till 1973 when Lewis became Chairman. Lewis, Gallup, Michener, and Shaheen remained until 1978, when, as Olom recalled, Jimmy Carter appointed "people who were for the birds" and the commission lost its way.

22 Interviews: Shakespeare & Olom. As the commission became better known around Washington, Shakespeare encountered an unexpected problem. Supporters of Nixon began to press the President for a seat on the commission, attracted by the possibility of exotic inspection trips and high-powered dinners. On more than one occasion the President ribbed Shakespeare about this. Years later Frank Shakespeare recreated the typical gruff presidential rebuke: "You're a bastard Frank. No one ever thought about that God-dam Advisory Commission, now I get more pressure to be on that fucking Advisory Commission than anything else." Switching to self-pity mode, the President would continue, "I say no now to people I need to give something to all because of that fucking Commission."

23 RNPM WHCF FG230 (USIA), box 1, Exec., Invitation from Bernays, 1 October 1969.

24 NA RG 306 87.0018, director's subject files, box 4, CSM 10–2, Press and Publications, Jenkins (IAS) to Shakespeare, 4 April 1969. For further Soviet reaction to the USIA see Box 4, CSM Soviet Media Distortions, "Current developments in Communist Propaganda," no. 5, 21 August 1969; also box 2, PB8 – Effectiveness, Shakespeare to Brumberg, 23 September 1969 with translation of Kondratov, "Ink Opium: UISA Magazine Prints Foul-Smelling Lies," *Isvestiya*, 16 August 1969, an attack on *The Problems of Communism*, which includes the line, "Without exaggeration one can say, in the words of the poet, that those connected with this press organ 'make opium ink with a rabid dog's saliva.'"

gambit to push the Soviets to lift the jamming that they had begun in 1968. Moscow increased its jamming and declined to negotiate. In November, the VOA increased the power of its own transmissions to compensate. The Soviets had chosen an expensive course. As Shakespeare pointed out the following year, it cost them an estimated $150 million to jam the VOA.[25]

Shakespeare urged the VOA to deliver "continuous coverage of both the existence and content of the '*samizdat*' underground press."[26] The agency as a whole stressed the cause of dissidents, though official guidance warned against "pontificating and shrillness." Shakespeare reminded the VOA that the most effective "denunciations of Soviet thought suppression in Communist states" came from "opinion leaders of leftist or liberal persuasion in other countries" and urged the Voice to emphasize all such statements.[27]

Shakespeare's VOA took a number of steps to play to the centrifugal forces within the U.S.S.R, including a step explicitly forbidden by the Policy Office in the Johnson era: special broadcasts for Soviet Jews.[28] In a similar vein, in March 1972, he ordered that "the people of the major nations within the Soviet Union should be referred to by their nationality i.e. Ukrainians, Georgians, Latvians, Russians, Uzbeks, Armenians etc." Following this policy, the VOA's coverage of the Munich Olympics in the autumn of 1972 spoke of Chechen, Kazak, and Lithuanian achievements as well as Russian.[29] Shakespeare was encouraged by the deepening social ferment in the U.S.S.R. and Eastern bloc. December 1970 brought riots in Poland. Shakespeare

25 NA RG 306, 89.0180, director's chronological file, 1969–70, box 17, reel 30, Hewson Ryan to Richardson (USoS), 22 August 1969; "VOA Director in Response to Guest Article on US–USSR Broadcast War," *Variety*, 27 January 1971, p. 38; Robert H. Phelps, "Soviet Jamming at Peak," *New York Times*, 9 July 1969, p. 87; "US Triples Power of Broadcasts to Soviet," *New York Times*, 8 November 1969, p. 21; Robert M. Smith, "USIA Chief Sees a Soviet Ferment," *New York Times*, 14 November 1970, p. 6.

26 NA RG 306, 89.0180, director's chronological file, 1969–70, box 17, reel 34, Shakespeare to Giddens, 19 June 1970.

27 NA RG 306 87.0018, director's subject files, box 24, 3 REA foreign audience characteristics, Hoffman to Shakespeare, "Guidance on Dissent in the Soviet Union," 11 March 1971 with attachment.

28 The broadcasts used Russian rather than Yiddish on the ground that the Jewish population was too dispersed for a single broadcast and too small to justify Yiddish programs on all VOA channels. Representative Ben Rosenthal (D-NY) of the Congressional Jewish caucus lobbied for Hebrew broadcasts, but the VOA managed to avoid the extra broadcasts by consulting with the Israel Broadcasting Authority. A VOA engineer spent three days showing the Israelis how to overcome Soviet jamming and in return gained Israeli support for the existing VOA programs. *Kol Israel* had no desire to compete with an American Hebrew service. The VOA's "Jewish hour" attracted a mixed response. In 1980 Solzhenitsyn alleged that it accidentally encouraged anti-Semitism. Laurien Alexandre, *The Voice of America: From Détente to the Reagan Doctrine*, Norwood, NJ: Ablex Publishing Corp., 1988, p. 26; ADST Oral History: Kempton B. Jenkins; Aleksandr Solzhenitsyn, "Misconceptions about Russia and a Threat to America," *Foreign Affairs*, No. 4 (Spring 1980), 823, which notes, "Hardly more felicitous is the policy of broadcasting accounts by recent Jewish immigrants to the United States, who tell in great detail about their life, their new jobs, and how happy they are here. Since it is common knowledge in the U.S.S.R. that only Jews have the right to emigrate, these programs serve no purpose except to further the growth of anti-Semitism."

29 Interview: Shakespeare; NA RG 306, 87.0018, director's subject files, box 28, file: 1972 DRO-Issuances, Shakepeare to Towery (IOP), 17 March 1972, in which Shakespeare notes, "The Union of Soviet Socialist Republics is a state; it encompasses *many* nations, and this is a multi-national state. But it is not a nation. To call it so, apart from being grammatically incorrect, is to foster the illusion

ordered a tripling of VOA broadcasts to Poland and a major increase for Czech and Hungarian programming also. On 20 December, the Polish Communist leader Wladyslaw Gomulka fell from power. His replacement, Edward Gierek, hastily promised reform. Frank Shakespeare saw no reason to be soft with the Communist bloc.[30]

*

Shakespeare worked to maintain the level of VOA services around the world despite pressure on the budget. He was skeptical of internal recommendations from PAOs in January 1970 to cut services in Turkish, Swahili, and a swath of Indian languages including Hindi. Rather, he was persuaded by Giddens that successful international broadcasting relied on a relationship with the audience that required long-term continuity. Particular services could not just be turned on and off like a tap. Giddens pledged to freeze VOA personnel levels and live within budget, and only VOA Tamil went off the air in 1970.[31]

Shakespeare respected the VOA charter. On 9 June 1970 he issued a policy memorandum reaffirming the ground rules for the USIA's relationship with the VOA. The agency's Office of Policy and Plans would serve as the sole source of policy guidance (with agency area directors and field posts feeding views into the general discussion), but the VOA had sole responsibility for determining the content of all news, background analysis, and commentary. Jack O'Brien, the co-author of the VOA charter, approvingly circulated Shakespeare's instructions alongside the restrictive directive that had been issued by Murrow in the aftermath of the Cuban missile crisis.[32] Shakespeare believed that both morality and credibility precluded the VOA from lying. He expected that reporters would use self restraint in matters of security (noting that a state-run broadcaster could not speculate in the same way as the *Washington Post*), but he did not expect the Voice to duck stories. He briefed Giddens, "I'm not going to tell you that the embassy and the Pentagon doesn't matter – but you don't work for any of those . . . you work for the President." Shakespeare was quite prepared to "take the heat." In later years he could "not recall a single instance in which VOA was wrong." But plenty of ambassadors, the Secretary of State, and Henry Kissinger begged to differ.[33]

Sometimes the VOA's coverage of a sensitive story could be justified in both news and policy terms. The Chilean presidential election of 3 September 1970 was such a

---

of one happy family rather than the imperialist state increasingly beset by nationalist problems, which is what it is." See also Alexandre, *The Voice of America*, p. 26.

[30] Robert M. Smith, "USIA Chief Sees Soviet Ferment," *New York Times*, 14 November 1970, p. 6; "East Germany Accuses Radio Free Europe of Fermenting Discontent in Poland," 19 December 1970, p. 10.

[31] NA RG 306, 87.0018, director's subject files, box 11, file: broadcasting service – general. Giddens to Shakespeare, "The Voice of America's Future," 2 January 1970; Cushing to Ronalds (IBS/P) et al., "Agency decision on VOA languages," 13 January 1970.

[32] NA RG 306, 89.0180, director's chronological file, 1969–70, box 17, reel 34, Shakespeare, Instructions to Voice of America, IOP, Area Directors, 9 June 1970; O'Brien to Giddens, 16 June 1970.

[33] Interview: Shakespeare; Tad Szulc, "Tough USIA Line Drew Complaint from Rogers." *New York Times*, 25 October 1970, p. 3.

story. By the summer of 1970 the socialist candidate, Salvador Allende, seemed bound
for victory. The USIA's policy guidance stressed that his victory would undermine the
American commercial and strategic interests in the region, but called on all agency
media to avoid presenting the election as anything other than a Chilean affair, as "any
allegation of U.S. involvement can only rebound to the benefit of leftist candidates."
Shakespeare required this restraint up and including the Chilean presidential inauguration.[34] The logic of the USIA's policy eluded Kissinger and CIA director Richard
Helms, whose agency had spent many years intriguing to prevent Allende's accession
to power. A White House task force meeting on 22 September noted, "USIA and
VOA have been putting out material which could be considered pro-Allende and this
should be watched."[35] But Egypt brought matters to a head.

In September 1970, peace in the Middle East hung by a slender thread. Egypt
and Israel faced each other nervously across the Sinai ceasefire line agreed upon a
month earlier. But it soon became apparent that Egypt had flouted the agreement
by introducing Soviet-made anti-aircraft missiles. The VOA reported the story in the
starkest terms. On 11 September, a news analysis by John Albert compared the Soviet
missiles on the Egyptian side of the truce line to Khrushchev's missiles in Cuba in 1962
and noted "once again . . . the Soviets are attempting deception." On 12 September, a
second piece spoke of "Soviet duplicity" in the Middle East. Secretary of State William
Rogers considered these comments to be counterproductive and wrote a stiff letter to
Shakespeare, arguing that legally the USIA must seek guidance on its output from the
State Department. Shakespeare replied that he reported directly to the President. He
had unilaterally ended the old requirement for every item of VOA news to be cleared
by the State Department, and believed that broad guidance would suffice. Shakespeare
argued that "an informational and communications program is something different
and newer than formal and traditional diplomacy." He simply could not afford to hold
the news until the State Department had caught up, which in this instance happened
on 9 October, when the State Department charged the U.S.S.R. with "duplicity" over
the missiles in Sinai. Tad Szulc broke the story of the quarrel in the *New York Times*
later that month.[36]

*

Shakespeare also courted controversy in his approach to U.S. popular culture.
In October 1970, he attended the Sorrento Film Festival. He was so depressed by the

[34] NARA Chile declassification project, Tranche II (1968–72), USIA INFOGUIDE No. 70–44, "Chilean Elections," Shakespeare, 31 August 1970.

[35] CIA Chile declassification project, Tranche III (1979–91), Memo for the record by Thomas H. Karamessines, 22 September 1970. For a response from the U.S. embassy in Chile see NARA Chile declassification project, Tranche III (1979–99), Korry to Kissinger/Alexis Johnson, Secret, 26 September 1970.

[36] Interviews: Kamenske; Henry Butterfield Ryan; Tad Szulc, "Tough USIA Line Drew a Complaint from Rogers," *New York Times*, 25 October 1970, p. 3. It should be noted that VOA Arabic had a relatively small audience share in the Middle East. Analysis among target groups in Lebanon in 1969 estimated market share as 7/3/1 between the BBC, Radio Cairo, and the VOA. NA RG 306 87.0018, director's subject files, box 4, evidence of effectiveness, Nalle (IAN) to Shakespeare, 27 March 1969.

vision of America presented by the films on offer that he launched into an extemporaneous attack on Hollywood, televised around Europe via a "Eurovision" hook-up:

> Most of the [Hollywood] films deal with social aberration in American society and tend to create the illusion that such activities are commonplace in our country . . . that we are a purposeless society dedicated to violence and to vice . . . Motion picture producers in our country as in yours are free to produce what they choose. That is as it should be. But some of these films may leave you with a distorted view of the U.S. I hope many of you in the audience at home will have the opportunity of visiting the real United States so as to see for yourselves real life in our country.

President Nixon wrote to congratulate Shakespeare on his "courageous stand." Shakespeare replied that he "felt like Adolf Hitler at an ADA convention" but had been heartened by private messages of support from some of the American stars present.[37] One filmmaker had Shakespeare's complete trust, his own: Bruce Herschensohn.

Bruce Herschensohn's first priority in the Motion Picture and Television Branch was the completion of the Czechoslovakia film. Working with Denis Sanders and Robert M. Fresco and editor Marvin Walowitz, Herschensohn developed *Czechoslovakia, 1968*, a short film assembled from photographs and newsreel images of Czechoslovakia throughout the twentieth century.[38] In early 1969 he screened the rough cut of the film to the policy officers. "Almost to a man," Herschensohn recalled, "they hated it." He immediately took the issue to Shakespeare, who insisted that the agency release the film. The incident deepened Shakespeare's conviction that the media director had to be in the driving seat of the agency. In the future Herschensohn sought the advice of the policy staff but not their permission. The agency distributed the film in August 1969 for use as individual PAOs thought best. It was very widely placed for both television and theatrical showings, with excellent reactions. In April 1970, it won an Oscar for the best documentary short.[39]

The nominees for the Academy Award in 1970 included a second USIA film: *An Impression of John Steinbeck: Writer*, directed by Donald Wrye and narrated by Henry Fonda. Other agency offerings of the era included a moving obituary film for Eisenhower and a spectacular account of Apollo XI, directed by Walter de Hoog, called *The Infinite Journey*.[40] Controversially, Herschensohn also sank some $80,000

37 RNPM WHCF FG230 (USIA), box 1, Exec., President to Shakespeare, 23 October 1970, Shakespeare to President, with text of remarks, 29 October 1970. Emphasis in original. Films endorsed by Shakespeare included *Tora! Tora! Tora!* (1970). The ADA – Americans for Democratic Action – was a major radical pressure group of the era. For wider administration concern over the U.S. image problem in Western European media see NA RG 306, 87.0018, director's subject files, box 31, 1972 OGA-State, John N. Irwin, II, (DSoS) to Shakespeare, 14 December 1972.

38 NA MPSVB, RG 306.4019, *Czechoslovakia 1968*; NA RG 306 87.0018, director's subject files, box 3, MVP-8, Effectiveness, Evaluation, Assessment, Rosenfeld (I/R) to Shakespeare, 3 October 1969.

39 Interview: Herschensohn; NA RG 306.01.1, USIA Historical branch, item 15, box 30, file: Motion Pictures, Aggrey (IMV/M) to Herschensohn, 4 September 1969; On problems distributing in Germany see NA RG 306 87.0018, director's subject files, box 13, IMV films, Ewing (PAO Bonn) to Herschensohn, 14 December 1970.

40 NA MPSVB, RG 306.5329, *Infinite Journey*; Interview: De Hoog. Field reactions to *Infinite Journey* were mixed. In London, Britain's government film division, which often distributed USIS films

into a fifteen-minute profile of Vice President Spiro Agnew. Narrated by John Wayne, *Agnew* emphasized such positive angles as the Vice President's civil rights record and immigrant father, but also included scenes of the Vice President berating the liberal press as "an effete corps of impudent snobs." The *New York Times* quipped that the volatile Vice President represented an excellent choice for a USIA film, as "the United States has few public relations problems of greater magnitude."[41]

Libraries and exhibitions remained a key element in the agency's program. The era's successes included an impressive U.S. pavilion at Expo 1970 in Osaka, Japan, "Educational Technology – U.S.A.," which toured Eastern Europe from 1971, and an innovative exhibition for Berlin in 1972 called "Garbage is Beautiful," which displayed works of art created from refuse as an argument for recycling.[42] Shakespeare's administration of the libraries attracted press criticism. In April 1970, the *New York Times* reported that Shakespeare had sent out a list of forty-one conservative books, including Bill Buckley's *Up From Liberalism*, which could be purchased to correct any liberal bias in library holdings. But the circular highlighted the objective of balance. If library staff detected a conservative bias, they had to order liberal books. Despite press alarm, the policy opened the way for freer purchasing and marked the end of the McCarthy-era library book black list.[43]

The most dramatic change in USIA libraries was seen in Japan, where Alan Carter took up the post of PAO in 1970. Carter saw the need to get into "a serious dialogue" with the Japanese and recruited a young USIA officer with a doctoral degree in communications, named Barry Fulton, to assist. Carter began by restructuring the rather unfocused library program. He knew that the USIA could not and should not compete with Japan's well-funded university libraries. Carter's alternative was a system that he dubbed INFOMAT (a term coined to appeal to Japanese taste for innovation). An INFOMAT collection was limited to 400 books, selected to support the five key themes of the USIS program in Japan, buttressed by periodicals, reference works, and audiovisual materials. All were color coded, attractively displayed, and managed electronically. The 400 books were always the best new works in their field and not necessarily those supporting the U.S. government line, shipped within ten days of a favorable review. USIS staff culled older books to keep the collection

---

through its film library, thought the film "too pretentious and too long by half." A Twentieth Century Fox equivalent had arrived some months earlier. UoA CU box 15, file 27, UK Country Program Memo FY 1972, 29 June 1971.

41   NA MPSVB, RG 306.5814, *Agnew*; Interview: Herschensohn; Robert B. Smith, "Information Agency Film on Agnew Presents Him as Forthright and Foe of Racial Discrimination," *New York Times*, 7 July 1970, p. 23 and editorial, 8 July 1970, p. 4; NA RG 306 87.0018, director's subject files, box 13, IMV films, Rosenfeld (I/R) to Loomis, "Media reaction to 'Agnew' film." 20 July 1970. For cartoon see Oliphant in *Denver Post*, 12 July 1970.

42   RNPM WHCF FG6–6 (NSC), box 1, Exec., Kissinger to President, 14 July 1970; GRFL WHCF subject, TA16, box 30, eleventh annual report of special international exhibitions, pp. 9, 13.

43   NA RG 306 87.0018, director's subject files, box 13, Director's Office Circulars, 1970, Hemsing (Ast dir. Europe) to PAOs, letter 7, 2 April 1970; NA RG 306 75–0016, Cultural Subject files, box 1, BKS 1 – Task Force on Book Policy, White (IOP) to Bunce (IOP) 1 July 1970 with attachments, ADST Oral History: Hemsing; Tad Szulc, "USIA Issues Conservative Book List," *New York Times*, 26 April 1970; also 8 December 1969, pp. 2, 4.

at the 400-volume limit. A USIS officer named Ray Komai (who in a former career had helped to design the famous CBS eye) created an impressive logo for INFOMAT. Fulton designed an electronic audience record system to enable the post to inform clients of the arrival of a new book in their field. Posts displayed the newest books at events that also served the five key themes. Although the audience record system made Carter's flops as visible as his triumphs, the success of INFOMAT was soon clear. Carter built on this with panel discussions that engaged Japanese participants on key issues and developed a culture of dialogue. He was rewarded by new sections of the Japanese political spectrum joining the discussion, including the Socialists. At one point even the Communist Party asked to be included, but the embassy refused. INFOMAT worked so well in Japan that other PAOs began to consider the idea. Jay Gildner, then PAO in Bonn, visited Tokyo for several days to survey the program and wrote a laudatory piece for the agency's in-house journal praising its approach. Ironically, rather than opening the way to INFOMAT elsewhere, this sparked opposition. Gildner failed to remodel USIS West Germany on similar lines. INFOMAT inspired PAO Bill Nichols to create a focused collection in Singapore, which he dubbed a "resource center." This softer model was widely adopted.[44]

*

Shakespeare's administration saw renewed attention to coordination with allies, most importantly the United Kingdom and West Germany. In March 1969 Shakespeare hosted a round of Anglo-American Information Talks. The agenda included sharing ideas on themes and audience and coordination of key activities such as English language teaching.[45] Shakespeare and the U.S. ambassador in London, Walter Annenberg, kept a weather eye on the British government's funding of the BBC World Service and prepared to lobby against any major cuts. The BBC Director General, Charles Curran, believed that Shakespeare's warning to the Foreign Office helped but requested in November 1970 – via Giddens – that he also prevail on Nixon to raise the matter with Prime Minister Harold Wilson on their next meeting. The crisis passed and the BBC World Service lived to fight another day.[46]

[44] Alan Carter to author, 30 June and 1 July 2004; ADST oral history: David Hitchcock, Bill Nichols, and for criticism see James Morad, Cliff Foster (on drawbacks of electronic audience management and reforming INFOMAT as the Carter-era PAO in Tokyo). As Alan Carter recalled, the usual critique of INFOMAT focused on the 400-book limit and "one size fits all" approach. This was based on a misunderstanding. Carter imagined each collection being tailored to its host nation. However, he maintained that "the idea of a current and idea-ridden library, articulated with the overall USIS program could apply to every USIS program."

[45] NA RG 306, 87.0018, director's subject files, box 4, file Pol: political affairs and relations, Weld (IAE) to Shakespeare, 20 March 1969 and attachments. On semiannual talks with West Germany see NA RG 306, 89.0180, director's chronological file, 1969–70, box 16, reel 27, release "USIA meets with German Information Officials," 9 May 1969; on both in 1973 see NA RG 306, 87.0018, director's subject files, box 33, file: FPD-IWE, Gildner to Shakespeare, "Information Talks with Germans and British." 14 December 1973.

[46] NA RG 306, 87.0018, director's subject files, box 10, file: broadcast private. Shakespeare to Annenberg, 5 August 1970 etc; NA RG 306 87.0018, director's subject files, box 11, Broadcasting Service – General, 1970, Curran (DG of BBC) to Giddens, (VOA), 27 November 1970 etc. In

*

The undoubted high point of USIA activity in the Nixon years came in July 1969 with coverage of Apollo XI's landing on the moon. Activities ranged from local relays of VOA coverage (live in four languages) to an audience estimated at 800 million to assistance for the foreign journalists covering the launch from Florida; help for the European press through a European Apollo News Center (operated with NASA) in Paris; a mountain of printed materials; and exhibits at 125 posts around the world. USIS New Delhi constructed a full-scale replica of the Lunar Excursion Module in its back yard and attracted over a million visitors, including the Soviet ambassador. USIS posts around the world opened their doors to crowds to view the actual landing live on television. Viewers in the U.S. Cultural Center in West Berlin were so rapt by the images of Neil Armstrong's "giant leap" that they failed to notice a thief make off with the post's eight-foot-diameter model of the moon.[47]

The agency had no doubt that Apollo XI boosted the global standing of the United States. The USIA told the White House that the "period of doubt occasioned by Sputnik" had ended. The United States had won the space race. World opinion accepted the moon landing as an achievement by all humanity, which many commentators hoped would bring the peoples of the world closer together.[48] More detailed analysis revealed a rather less dramatic story. In October the USIA presented findings of detailed surveys across Britain, France, Japan, Venezuela, India, and the Philippines of the impact of the landings. Although all seemed impressed, between forty-four and sixty percent in each country suggested that the United States should now devote more time and money to troubles on earth.[49]

USIA coverage of space continued, although by the second moon landing world attention was drifting. In April 1970 attention suddenly snapped back as Apollo XIII hung on the brink of disaster. The Apollo XIII story received "straightforward and comprehensive" coverage from the USIA. The agency assisted foreign coverage. The IPS distributed supporting material, while the VOA revised all its schedules to carry

1981 the information agency director Charles Z. Wick also worked within the Reagan administration to lobby against British Prime Minister Margaret Thatcher's cuts of the BBC language services; see RRL NSA, agency file, USIA, vol. 1, box 91,377, Wick to Allen et al., 23 July 1981.

47 NA RG 306, 89.0180, director's chronological file, 1969–70, box 16, reel 27, Loomis to Rogers, 30 June 1969; RG 306 87.0018, director's subject files, box 4, SP – Space and Astronauts, IOP to Loomis, 6 August 1969. For a policy office think-piece preparing for the contingency of the failure of Apollo XI, Wechsler to Bardos, 11 June 1969. The Berlin story is in "Down to Earth," *Washington Daily News*, 22 July 1969. On New Delhi see ADST Oral History, William D. Miller. NASA had been unable to provide precise dimensions for the LEM to USIS New Delhi, so the staff had improvised by multiplying up from their official 5", 1/49-scale model.

48 On 21 July, Daniel Schorr of CBS reported skepticism in Europe toward the U.S. space program. Shakespeare forwarded a transcript to Kissinger: RNPM WHCF FG230 (USIA), box 1,Exec., see Kissinger to Shakespeare, 6 August 1969. For digest of impact on domestic and foreign opinion see "Special USIA brief," A. P. Toner, White House, 22 August 1969. Also NA RG 306, 89.0180, director's chronological file, 1969–70, box 16, reel 27, Shakespeare to President, 22 July 1969. The Soviet Union continued to jam VOA Russian during the Apollo landings, but VOA English remained unjammed.

49 NA RG 306, 89.0180, director's chronological file, 1969–70, box 16, reel 31, memo to Richardson (USoS), "Office of Research and Assessment," 17 October 1969.

up-to-the-minute reports on the accident and the progress of the recovery plan. The world joined America in holding its breath until the astronauts were safe. The story showed that failures as well as successes could bring the United States closer to people overseas.[50]

The U.S. government extended the publicity value of Project Apollo by sending the crews on "goodwill" tours. Kissinger himself oversaw the ecstatic thirty-eight-day, twenty-four-country tour of the Apollo XI astronauts.[51] Further visits followed. Even the ill-starred crew of Apollo XIII drew massive crowds in Greece and Malta. In their guidance to the astronauts, the USIA encouraged them to emphasize the "international aspects of the space program" and its "spin-off" benefits for humanity as a whole.[52] In Pakistan the religious fringe opposed the visit of the Apollo XI crew, claiming that Buzz Aldrin was "a member of the Zionist movement." The USIA took the complaint as a testament to the iconic power of the American "moon men" whose mere presence could, according to the protestors, "erase anti-American feelings."[53] But neither the images of the astronauts bouncing in the dust of another world nor visits from the crop-headed heroes could obscure the problem at the heart of U.S. foreign policy: the ongoing war in Vietnam.

2) NIXON'S VIETNAM, 1969–74

Richard Nixon won the election of 1968 with bold talk of a "secret plan to end the Vietnam War." His strategy focused on two fronts: a diplomatic offensive to split the North Vietnamese away from their Communist allies, and a military offensive to either force the North into peace, or at least even the odds sufficiently to allow South Vietnam to assume full responsibility for its own defense.[54] The USIA was marginal in both approaches. The agency found itself alternately projecting news of successive "peace" initiatives and picking up the pieces as Nixon's latest military gambit spilled over into what world opinion considered unpardonable excess. Some claimed that Nixon's wild vacillation between peace and war was in part intended to terrify Hanoi into talking.[55] But a strategy hatched to impress Hanoi seemed guaranteed to alienate the rest of the planet.

---

[50]   NA RG 306, 89.0180, director's chronological file, 1969–70, box 16, reel 33, Shakespeare to Elliot Richardson (USoS), "USIA treatment of Apollo 13," 27 April 1972. The VOA provided feeds in Spanish, Portuguese, Arabic, Chinese, Vietnamese, and Russian. In Latin America some 1,460 stations with a total audience of 106 million listeners carried VOA coverage.

[51]   NA RG 306 87.0018, director's subject files, box 4, SP-Space and Astronauts, Weathersby to Loomis, World Astronaut Tour – a critique, 15 December 1969.

[52]   RNPM WHCF FG230 (USIA), box 1, Exec., "Apollo XIII. . . . " Memo for Shakespeare and Loomis, 5 November 1970.

[53]   NA RG 306 87.0018, director's subject files, box 4, SP-Space and Astronauts, IOP/P, to Shakespeare, Astronaut's tour, 24 October 1969.

[54]   Jeffrey Kimball, *Nixon's Vietnam War*, Lawence, KS: University of Kansas Press, 1998.

[55]   H. R. Haldeman later recalled Nixon's "Madman Theory" hatched during the campaign. Nixon explained: "I want the North Vietnamese to believe I've reached the point where I might do *anything* to stop the war. We'll just slip the word to them that. 'for God's sake, you know Nixon is obsessed about communism. We can't restrain him when he's angry – and he has his hand on the nuclear

Initially, European opinion warmed to the elements of conciliation in Nixon's approach to Vietnam. The USIA reported that his visit to Paris in February 1969 and subsequent initiatives went much of the way to restore the respect eroded during the later Johnson years.[56] But in March the administration began its secret bombing of Cambodia. Seeking to conceal the action from world opinion, briefing officers worked under orders to confirm that raids took place near the border and, if journalists pressed questions, to claim that any violation of the border would be investigated. The full story soon leaked out, opening serious questions of the legality of U.S. actions.[57] Nixon attempted to regain the initiative. In June 1969, he announced his intention to withdraw 25,000 troops from Vietnam. European and Asian opinion reacted well to the gambit.[58] He followed up in July by announcing a strategy of "Vietnamization." The United States would work toward complete withdrawal and the South Vietnamese would take over the war effort. Now the diplomatic wheels began to turn. Kissinger opened secret talks with the North Vietnamese in Paris, and the death of Ho Chi Minh opened further opportunities. In this climate Nixon turned to the USIA for tactical support.

On 1 October 1969, Nixon wrote to Kissinger proposing "a propaganda offensive . . . constantly repeating what the United States has done in offering peace in Vietnam in preparation for what we may have to do later . . . Frank Shakespeare should be running this very, very strongly at USIA and, of course, we should continue to try to get it across in the columns to the extent that we have any influence in that direction."[59] Nixon provided the core text of this offensive when, on 3 November, he addressed the nation on the subject of the war in Vietnam. He defended the American effort to date, citing Communist atrocities in North and South Vietnam. He set out his plans for negotiation, U.S. troop withdrawals, and "Vietnamization," and he asked the "Silent Majority" of Americans to support him in the months ahead.[60]

As Nixon hoped, the USIA gave the "Silent Majority" speech maximum publicity. The VOA carried the broadcast live, with simultaneous translation in French, Spanish, and Mandarin. All posts serving television stations received kinescopes of the speech. Tokyo received the speech via communications satellite. The wireless file carried interpretive and supporting articles. Loomis hoped that the surge of favorable reaction to the speech at home and abroad could be fed back into the agency's publicity as a story in its own right. "Excellent job," Nixon scrawled across Kissinger's

button.' – and Ho Chi Minh himself will be in Paris in two days begging for peace." H. R. Haldeman, *The Ends of Power*, New York: Times Books, 1978, pp. 82–3.

56   Positive European reactions are reported in NA RG 306 87.0018, director's subject files, box 29, "Fulbright file," Strasburg to Shakespeare, "Eyes Only," 30 April 1970; see also Page, *U.S. Official Propaganda during the Vietnam War, 1965–1973*, p. 262.

57   Hammond, *Reporting Vietnam*, p. 148.

58   Page, *U.S. Official Propaganda during the Vietnam War, 1965–1973*, p. 254; NA RG 306 87.0018, director's subject files, box 29, "Fulbright file," Strasburg to Shakespeare, "Eyes Only," 30 April 1970.

59   RNPM WHCF FG230 (USIA), box 1, Exec., President to Kissinger, 1 October 1969.

60   *PPP RN 1969*, doc. 425, pp. 901–7.

memo on the subject. Within two weeks the USIA had created eighteen different language versions of a fifteen-minute documentary called *Silent Majority*, which contextualized Nixon's speech with contrasting images of political protest on one side and ordinary "decent" Americans on the other. A correspondent from the target country hosted each version. Scenes included George Gallup detailing poll evidence of public support for Nixon. Delighted, the President requested a print to show the next time his daughter Julie visited. Many USIA posts deemed the film just too political to screen.[61]

In the midst of the USIA's "Silent Majority" campaign, news broke of the My Lai massacre. On 13 November, papers reported that a certain Lt. William Calley had been charged by the army with the murder of at least 109 Vietnamese civilians in March 1968.[62] For the VOA, covering the My Lai story became a badge of credibility. On 15 December 1969, the Voice issued a press release listing its coverage. The unfolding story featured in straight news, correspondents' reports, coverage of world reaction, and news commentaries. The weekly Worldwide English panel program "In the News" discussed the story. The VOA carried press conferences and statements from the White House, the Pentagon, and both hawks and doves on Capitol Hill. The VOA opened its files on the story to the domestic media. Sam Donaldson of ABC News spent two days reviewing the output and concluded, on the air, that the VOA had done well with difficult material.[63] Some felt the VOA's coverage of My Lai went too far. The USIA's deputy general counsel and congressional liaison, Gene Kopp, objected not to its treatment of Calley's initial trial but to its in-depth coverage of his subsequent appeals. The VOA was undeterred.[64]

My Lai was not the only "difficult story" to emerge from Vietnam that winter. Each month brought new reports of the decline of the U.S. military into drug abuse, interracial violence, and flirtation with mutiny. Then, on 30 April 1970, Nixon announced that the United States and South Vietnam had invaded Cambodia. This action, Nixon

[61]   RNPM WHSF WHCF CF, box 53, CF PR 11 (Motion Pictures), Kissinger to President, 28 November 1969. The meeting took place on 22 December, Kissinger to President, 20 December 1969. For images see NA MPSVB RG 306.3044, *Silent Majority*, and for script and press cuttings see NA RG 306 01.1, USIA historical branch, item 15, box 29, mopix file 2, 1969. See also Richard Halloran, "Silent Majority USIA Film Fails to Stir Foreigners," *New York Times*, 10 January 1970. Shakespeare's tenure saw an increased use of satellites to distribute key presidential messages. "The Silent Majority" speech was one of eight such occasions in Nixon's first year, including his State of the Union in 1970, the visit of the Shah of Iran, and the Apollo XI moon landing. Plans for expansion ran into issues of cost and the absence of regional TV networks in such key target areas as Africa, the Middle East, and Latin America. The USIA did most of its television work via airmail, but knew that the future would be different; see NA RG 306, 89.0180, director's chronological file, 1969–70, box 16, reel 33, Shakespeare, statement to subcommittee on National Security Policy and Scientific Developments of the Committee on Foreign Affairs, House of Representatives, 30 April 1970.
[62]   Seymour Hersh, *My Lai 4: A Report on the Massacre and its Aftermath*, New York: Random House, 1970, pp. 134–8. On 17 April 1968 Radio Hanoi announced that the 82nd Airborne had recently killed 500 civilians at My Lai. MACV dismissed the story by pointing out that the 82nd had been nowhere near. See Hammond, *Reporting Vietnam*, p. 189.
[63]   RNPM WHCF FG 230 (USIA), box 2, Exec. "VOA coverage of the My Lai story," 15 December 1969.
[64]   ADST Oral History: Gene Kopp.

argued, would "sustain America's credibility in the world." The USIA detected the opposite effect: "a traumatic reaction in the world at large" and a corresponding blow to American prestige.[65] America's campuses erupted, while some fifty young FSOs in the State Department signed a petition protesting U.S. policy. The petition found its way to the USIA; however, as the wording referred specifically to the State Department, agency officers could not simply add their names. Rather than attempt to redraft the document, they let it go forward without USIA input.[66]

In June 1970, U.S. and Vietnamese forces withdrew from Cambodia and Nixon resumed his emphasis on peace. On 7 October, he called for a "ceasefire in place" and a summit to discuss all of Indochina. World opinion rallied, more especially when the North Vietnamese refused to compromise. But Hanoi now scented victory.[67]

*

While Nixon plotted the grand strategy, it fell to the USIA to produce supportive publicity material for use in the field. Effective communication on the issue of Vietnam became a consuming passion for the Deputy Director for Motion Pictures and Television, Bruce Herschensohn. Herschensohn hired his boyhood idol, director John Ford, to produce a documentary telling the story of the U.S. presence in Vietnam and presenting America's case to the world. Working with director Sherman Beck, Ford began the project in 1968.[68] Ford himself visited Vietnam to oversee some of the making, but it was Herschensohn who managed the editing and successive versions of the hard-hitting script. By 1971, after three years and $250,000, the film – *Vietnam! Vietnam!* – was ready, but the agency now doubted the wisdom of releasing it. Test screenings to a cross section of PAOs reported that Vietnam was "no longer a major attitudinal factor and that a production dealing with earlier events in the war was not presently useful." Shakespeare allowed all PAOs to decide for themselves and sent the film to the field in September 1971. Only twenty-nine posts screened the film.[69]

The debate around the screening of *Vietnam! Vietnam!* revealed a divergence in approach between the field and USIA headquarters. European PAOs had long

65 William Shawcross, *Sideshow: Kissinger, Nixon and the Destruction of Cambodia*, New York: Simon & Schuster, 1979, p. 173; Page, *U.S. Official Propaganda during the Vietnam War, 1965–1973*, p. 283. See also NA RG 306, 89.0180, director's chronological file, 1969–70, box 16, reel 33, Loomis to Richardson, USoS, 2 April 1970 (for buildup to the invasion) and on reaction see "Foreign Media Reaction to the Cambodian Situation, an assessment," 12 May 1970.
66 ADST Oral History: Thomas D. Boyatt; George F. Jones; Nicholas A. Veliotes. Interview: Henry Butterfield Ryan, 27 November 1995.
67 For a digest of world reaction including the London *Sun*: "Nixon: My Plan to Stop Killing," see RNPM WHCF SP3–102 (Speeches) box 124, file 1, Exec., Loomis to Kissinger, 8 October 1970.
68 Interview: Herschensohn, NA MPSVB, RG 306.06279, *Vietnam! Vietnam!* For the full text of Nixon's speech see *PPP RN, 1969*, doc. 365, Address before the 24th session of the General Assembly of the United Nations, 18 September 1969, pp. 724–31.
69 NA RG 306 87.0018, director's subject files, box 26, 4. MTV – Films, 1971, Shakespeare to all PAOs, 29 August 1971; on unsuitability for Chile see Halsema to Herschensohn, 9 September 1971. On the budget see Tad Szulc, "$250,000 USIA Movie on Vietnam, 3 Years in the Making, Being Shelved," *New York Times*, 10 June 1971; "Failures in USIA's Film Program Hit," *Motion Picture Daily*, 7 January 1972, pp. 1–2; the release figure is in McBride, "Drums along the Mekong," p. 213.

since stopped attempting to distribute films about Vietnam, on the ground that such material merely embarrassed their client nations. At a regional conference of PAOs with Herschensohn and the European Area Director, Marshall Plan veteran Albert E. Hemsing, held in Brussels in 1971, field officers it made clear that they preferred to limit their Vietnam work to wireless file output and occasional press backgrounders. They refused to "make ourselves sitting ducks by programming speakers for open-to-all audiences so that the local bully-boys can have their fun." Hemsing accepted their position, but Herschensohn did not. He urged the PAOs to pledge themselves "to do something every day to win in Vietnam!" Hemsing dismissed this as the "arrogance of impotence." Shortly thereafter Hemsing moved to less politically sensitive duties as the chief of the agency's inspection corps. The same story reappeared in Africa and Asia. Herschensohn found the USIA's Vietnam films "shelved," while the field officers grew increasingly resentful of the leverage applied to encourage them to change their minds.[70]

*

While Nixon and Kissinger maneuvered at an international level to extricate the United States "honorably" from South Vietnam, the U.S. military fought on in Vietnam itself. The USIA remained a major part in the local psychological war effort, though the new director of JUSPAO, Edward Nickel, did not wield the same clout as Zorthian had either in Vietnam or in Washington. Nickel found himself bypassed in matters of policy. He had no part in planning the Cambodian incursion of 1970.[71]

Like other areas of U.S. activity in Vietnam, JUSPAO underwent a process of "Vietnamization," handing ever more of its functions to the South Vietnamese government. In mid-1971, Robert A. Lincoln assumed charge of JUSPAO with "flat-out instructions from Frank Shakespeare, first, to find a way of getting rid of the Joint U.S. Public Affairs Office; second, to get all of the military out from under USIS control ... and to change JUSPAO back to a normal USIS and to cut that back in terms of personnel and budget." The founding idea of JUSPAO had been that civilians should direct military information programs; however, the reverse was now true. Lincoln found 102 American military positions in JUSPAO, which he proceeded to

---

[70] ADST Oral History: Hemsing; also John Hutchinson (PAO, New Zealand) and Stephen Belcher (USIS, Tanzania). Hutchinson rejected a similarly combative film, *The Silent Majority*. When Herschensohn asked the PAO Conference in Manila how USIS New Zealand had used the film, Hutchinson, the PAO, replied "I took a spade and buried it in the alley." Shortly thereafter, he received a stiff "shape up" letter from Henry Loomis. Belcher, who declined to use the films in Tanzania, bitterly resented Herschensohn asking about his personal feelings about the Vietnam War, and considers that his "run in" on the matter damaged his career. An agency evaluation of films in 1972 found that posts considered space, U.S. life, and "problems and solutions" to be the most valuable themes and ideology, Vietnam, and science to be the least. NA RG 306 87.0018, director's subject files, box 34, MTV-films, Janicki (IOR/RM) to Hall (IOR/R), "Comments on the ISS analysis of worldwide survey of agency films ...," 3 May 1972.

[71] Latimer, *U.S. Psychological Operations in Vietnam*, p. 10; also A. J. Langguth, "Our Policy-Making Men in Saigon," *New York Times* (magazine), 28 April 1968, p. 22.

eliminate by the simple expedient of neglecting to replace the staff whose tour of duty ended. Lincoln also drastically reduced JUSPAO's use of local employees. By the end of 1972, USIS Saigon resembled any other USIS post.[72]

The USIA's global press responsibilities for the Vietnam War remained undiminished. In February 1971, the agency was well primed in advance to provide media support for the South Vietnamese invasion of Laos, but left a "decent interval" following Thieu's announcement of the invasion before covering the story on the VOA and in agency print media. The Policy Office believed that timely action on the story had headed off much criticism around the world and won a better press than the previous year's invasion of Cambodia.[73]

Meanwhile, domestic criticism of the USIA's role in Vietnam grew. In the course of 1971, Senator Frank Church (D-ID) introduced a bill to prevent the USIA from conducting propaganda on behalf of foreign governments, pouring particular scorn on the agency's attempts to sell the Thieu–Ky regime in South Vietnam like "a bar of soap." In July a House subcommittee examined allegations that USIA polling data taken in South Vietnam had been passed to Thieu while being withheld from his opposition in the forthcoming election. Chastened, JUSPAO withheld the entire August issue of its magazine for rural audiences, out of concern that a photograph of Thieu inside would spark further allegations of bias.[74]

The USIA continued to contribute to the propaganda war against North Vietnam, as a member of the NSC's ad hoc PSYOP committee. Initiatives in 1971 included a renewed *Chieu Hoi* campaign and leaflets pressing Hanoi for a large-scale POW exchange.[75] Yet prudence required limits. In May 1972 VOA director Giddens flatly refused to allow VOA transmitters to be used for broadcasting of "grey" propaganda to North Vietnam. "Disclosure, which would be unavoidable, would," he argued, "open us to the charge, at home and abroad that VOA was put temporarily to a covert 'Cold War' use."[76]

While the USIA scaled back at the top in Vietnam, the army and CIA maintained the momentum of the pacification effort. As a result of the restructuring of 1967, this push drew on USIS personnel at the province level and below. The election of 1968

72   ADST Oral History: Lincoln. On the earlier "Vietnamization of JUSPAO" see NA RG 306 87.0018, director's subject files, box 3, psychological operations, Green (IAF) to Shakespeare, 11 December 1969. For correspondence on the dissolution of JUSPAO see NA RG 306 87.0018, director's subject files, box 25, 10. FPD-Viet-Nam, 1971, 1971. For press comment see Iver Peterson, "US Agencies Trim Staffs in Vietnam," *New York Times*, 5 August 1971, p. 1; Malcolm W. Browne, "US Trims Psychological Warfare Effort in Vietnam," *New York Times*, 12 June 1972.

73   NA RG 306 87.0018, director's subject files, box 24, file 3, REA-Foreign Audience Characteristics, White (IOP) to Shakespeare, "Agency treatment of the Laos operation." 25 February 1971.

74   "Church Seeks Muzzle on USIA Propaganda," *Washington Evening Star*, 29 April 1971; Tim O'Brien, "USIA Accused of Aiding Thieu," AP, *Washington Post*, 22 July 1971; "US Officials Keep Magazine from Viets," *Washington Post*, 3 August 1971; see also Gloria Emerson, "Thieu Using USIA. Surveys in Vote Campaign," *New York Times*, 2 February 1971.

75   NA RG 306 87.0018, director's subject files, box 22, file 7. OGA-NSC, 1971, White (IOP) to Shakespeare/Loomis, "Report of NSC ad hoc PSYOP Committee activities, April–May 1971," 15 June 1971.

76   NA CIA-RDP80B01673R000020013008–0, Giddens to Crane (IEA), "Use of VOA transmitters for 'Grey' broadcasting," 22 May 1972.

coincided with a massive offensive against the enemy positions in the countryside. The "accelerated pacification campaign" or APC brought results. Even the most pessimistic voices in the U.S. mission seemed encouraged.[77] The architects of pacification now looked to consolidate the achievement. The centerpiece of their wider pacification effort was the Phoenix Program, which sought to use the combined forces of the Vietnamese military, police, and provincial reconnaissance units to destroy the "Viet Cong infrastructure" throughout South Vietnam. The program called for a pooling of intelligence and concerted action. The United States provided an "energizing and advisory role" under the aegis of CORDS. USIA personnel at JUSPAO provided support by publicizing the names of prominent Viet Cong.[78]

The Phoenix Program started slowly. In 1969, the United States gave the South Vietnamese the goal of "neutralizing" 20,000 Viet Cong agents. At the end of the year the Saigon government reported a suspiciously efficient total of 19,534 agents neutralized. For some this meant a few days under arrest without trial but, as the *New York Times* reported, for one in three suspects "neutralization" meant death.[79] Many observers within the U.S. mission doubted the effectiveness of Phoenix and blamed the South Vietnamese for corrupting the original concept.[80] In terms of the USIA's struggle for world opinion the Phoenix program was a disaster. Congressional hearings in 1970 and 1971 heard eyewitness accounts of torture and murder. CORDS director William Colby later conceded "the word name Phoenix a shorthand for all the negative aspects of the war."[81] Yet by its very persistence Phoenix had an impact on the enemy. The next phase of North Vietnam's war looked very different.

On Good Friday, March 1972, the North launched a massive conventional assault by vast columns of tanks and regular soldiers. It failed. This Easter Invasion provided one last success for the USIA mission in Saigon. All elements of the USIS mission responded within hours and for once they had a positive story to tell: a North Vietnamese defeat. The Cultural Affairs Officer used his library distribution points to post the latest bulletins, while the Research Officer tracked responses and misinformation emanating from Hanoi. The VOA Vietnamese service expanded rapidly, reaching eighteen hours a day by July 1972, to report on the fighting. Thanks to an earlier program

---

[77] Hunt, *Pacification*, pp. 172–92; Francis Fitzgerald, *Fire in the Lake: The Vietnamese and the Americans in Vietnam*, Boston: Atlantic–Little Brown, 1972, p. 406.

[78] Devised during 1967, the Americans planned the program with the less memorable title of "infrastructure coordination and exploitation" or ICEX; the Saigon regime preferred the name *Phung Hoang*, a mythical all-seeing bird, and Phoenix seemed the best English equivalent. Hunt, *Pacification*, pp. 113–6; NA RG 306 87.0018, director's subject files, box 22, file 7. OGA-NSC, 1971, White (IOP) to Shakespeare/Loomis, "Report of NSC ad hoc PSYOP Committee activities, April–May 1971," 15 June 1971 notes that the GVN gave priority to five programs: (1) *Phung Hoang*, (2) the role of the Popular Self-Defence Force, (3) the Land-to-the-Tiller land reform program, (4) *Chieu Hoi*, and (5) aid to veterans and war widows.

[79] Fitzgerald, *Fire in the Lake*, pp. 411–12. The U.S. Army claimed that such deaths generally occurred in firefights during arrest. The legislative authority for Phoenix forbade execution. Hunt, *Pacification*, pp. 240–42.

[80] Latimer, *U.S. Psychological Operations in Vietnam*, pp. 44–5; Fitzgerald, *Fire in the Lake*, pp. 411–12.

[81] William Colby and Peter Forbath, *Honorable Men: My Life in the CIA*, New York: Simon and Schuster, 1978, p. 272; Hunt, *Pacification*, pp. 234–51.

of dropping tiny Korean-made radios pretuned to the VOA over North Vietnam, JUS-PAO believed its version of events would be heard on an estimated 75,000 receivers in the North. The Vietnamese Service read lengthening lists of northern POWs and played sentimental music to stir thoughts of home. The Japanese government queried the use of the VOA's transmitters on Okinawa to relay propaganda, while the *Christian Science Monitor* asked how such broadcasts could be reconciled with its charter.[82]

The failure of the Easter Invasion brought the North Vietnamese back to the negotiating table in Paris. In October 1972, Kissinger and Hanoi's Le Duc Tho struck a preliminary peace agreement over the objections of President Thieu in Saigon. In January 1973, in the wake of the "Christmas Bombings" of the north, Hanoi accepted a compromise peace. America's troops began to return home. South Vietnam would face the next North Vietnamese offensive alone.

3) FIGHTING FOR CONTROL
SHAKESPEARE'S STRUGGLE FOR AUTONOMY, 1971–72

Nixon's high-risk strategy in Vietnam had serious implications on Capitol Hill, sparking four years of trench warfare between the White House and the foreign policy committees. The USIA soon became a part of this battle. The VOA was a favorite topic for congressional ire, and any slip by the Voice could land the director in a hearing, as in 1971 over the issue of Greece. In July, Representative Wayne L. Hays of Ohio had successfully introduced an amendment to cut off U.S. aid to the military dictatorship in Athens. The VOA prepared digests of American editorials on the issue but did not broadcast them. The omission caught the attention of columnists Rowland Evans and Robert Novak, who alleged that the VOA had appeased the Greek colonels to retain its Aegean transmitter. Shakespeare defended the VOA's Greek coverage at Senate hearings in September. He conceded that he personally would have broadcast the critical editorials but informed the committee that "VOA management felt a sufficient amount had been broadcast to provide adequate coverage." The matter dropped, but Senator Fulbright had smelled blood.[83]

Shakespeare next clashed with the Senate over the USIA's promotion procedures. He saw an issue of principle and, as ever, declined to shrink from confrontation. On assuming the directorship of the USIA, Shakespeare had been astonished to learn that, although he was free to assign and reassign his staff, to delegate, and to place praise and criticism on file, he could not choose which officers moved between the all-important career classes. In 1971 he refused to accept the verdict of the promotions board and, with White House support, demanded to make his own selection within

82 ADST Oral History: Lincoln; NA CIA-RDP80B01673R000200130011–6, Crane (Ast. Dir. East Asia) to Holdridge (NSC), "USIA activities targeted against NVN," 18 May 1972; NA CIA-RDP80B01673R000200130002–6, Vallimarescu (IBS/P) to Crane, "Vietnamese Programing," 12 July 1972; Bernard Zubres, "Voice Covertly Broadcasting Propaganda to Vietnamese," *Christian Science Monitor*, 11 October 1972, p. 14.
83 Evans/Novak Eye, *Washington Post*, 11 August 1971; "USIA Coverage on Aid Defended but Chief Would Have Used Editorials on Greece," *New York Times*, 14 September 1971.

the list of qualified candidates. On the Hill, Claiborne Pell (D-FL) refused point blank to accept Shakespeare's nominations, and for a year no one received promotion at the USIA. Shakespeare's standing among his own foreign service officers suffered accordingly. As the American Foreign Service Association prepared a court injunction, and the Secretary of State begged Shakespeare to stop "making waves," Shakespeare conceded defeat. The promotions procedure remained unchanged. The USIA director had other battles to fight.[84]

By 1972, Senator Fulbright had declared war on the structure of U.S. propaganda. He fought tooth and nail against attempts to continue funding Radio Free Europe and Radio Liberty, demanding in February 1972 that "these Radios should be given an opportunity to take their rightful place in the graveyard of Cold War relics." Although RFE had been something of a headache for Shakespeare, with its fundraising publicity tending to belittle the VOA, he and Stanton rallied to the station's defense. Fifty Senators petitioned Fulbright to lift his opposition. Shakespeare persuaded Nixon to intervene with a statement of support. The solution came from the Assistant Secretary of State for Congressional Relations, David M. Abshire, who hit on the idea of creating a Board for International Broadcasting as the parent body to maintain RFE and RL under a congressional grant. He persuaded Senator Mansfield to support the plan and the surrogate radios were saved. Unfortunately for Shakespeare, with the RFE/RL question solved, Fulbright turned his attention to the USIA.[85]

On 20 March 1972, Fulbright launched hearings on the USIA budget. Shakespeare suspected that the senator planned a symbolic tussle to establish his own authority over the agency, and approached the hearings defiantly. When Fulbright demanded copies of the agency's Country Plans, Shakespeare refused to comply. Fulbright hit back first with evidence that the USIA had distributed unattributed pamphlets in Latin America supporting U.S. oil interests and then by producing an agency memo "barring the use of the term Soviet" in broadcasts to the U.S.S.R., as a way to play on that country's internal tensions. The gloves were off.[86]

84   Interview: Shakespeare; "USIA Told to Halt Job Switches," *Washington Post*, 14 August 1971, p. A 15; Benjamin Welles, "USIA Chief's Bid on Jobs Assailed – Diplomats Resist Change in Promotion Policy," *New York Times*, 26 November 1971, p. 9. The four-man promotion board met annually, to number officers according to fitness reports. Two came from the "up-class" of the agency (the band into which the officers were being promoted). One came from the equivalent State Department rank to ensure parity. The fourth was the director's nominee.

85   Interview: David M. Abshire, 23 October 2006; Michael Nelson, *War of the Black Heavens*, p. 142–8. The Board was mandated in 1973 and in operation from 1974, with Abshire as its first chairman. For its first report see GRFL WHCF subject file FG 352, box 52, Abshire (chr. BIB) to President, 30 October 1974. For Fulbright's earlier opposition see Benjamin Welles, "Senate Panel Rebuffs Nixon on Radio Free Europe," *New York Times*, 22 July 1971, p. 3. UoC Benton papers, box 198/8, Benton to Stanton 18 April 1972 and editorial in defense of RFE/RL: KCBS San Francisco (7 March 1972). For associated correspondence see NA RG 306, 87.0018, director's subject files, box 34, file: RAD-private, Shakespeare to Colson (White House), 7 March 1972. RFE typically represented the VOA as broadcasting "our government's views world wide" and sending only seventy hours a week to Eastern Europe. For Loomis' earlier complaints about RFE's willingness to change see NA RG 306 87.0018, director's subject files, box 8, RPI – general policy and plans, Loomis to Stanton, 2 April 1969, and box 11, broadcasting service – general, Durkee (RFE) to Loomis, 7 August 1970.

86   Interview: Shakespeare; Woods, *Fulbright*, pp. 617–18; "Fulbright in Threat on USIA Funding," *New York Times*, 21 March 1972, p. 17; John W. Finney, "USIA Confirms Role in Unattributed Pamphlets,

In order to support the USIA, Senator James Buckley (R-NY) prepared a feature on the agency for his monthly statewide television program. He included a screening of *Czechoslovakia 1968*. It was not the film that sparked controversy, but a supporting interview in which Bruce Herschensohn lost his temper and called Fulbright's attack on the agency "naïve and stupid." The press previewed the program on 27 March. The comments were clearly inappropriate from a public servant and Herschensohn submitted his resignation. Shakespeare accepted it, but also presented the filmmaker with the agency's distinguished service award. Herschensohn soon found a new home at the Nixon White House.[87]

Fulbright struck back. He claimed that by passing *Czechoslovakia, 1968* to Buckley, the USIA had violated Smith–Mundt, and attempted to block the screening. On 1 April, Acting Attorney General Richard Klendienst ruled that a loophole in Smith–Mundt allowed the press and members of Congress to "make available" the agency's output. Buckley could – and did – show the film with impunity.[88] Furious, Fulbright now proposed slashing the agency's budget by one-fourth. On 17 April the Senate Foreign Relations Committee accepted Fulbright's motion by nine votes to four. Shakespeare knew that such cuts meant the loss of hundreds of experienced people. He resolved to act.[89] He obtained White House permission to fight Fulbright's budget cut on the floor of the Senate. He then made contact with Senator Gale McGee of Wyoming, the only Democrat who had voted for the USIA of late, and asked him to lead the fight in a floor vote. McGee agreed, with the proviso that Shakespeare decline any compromise deal: "The real issue here," McGee insisted, "is whether that son-of-a-bitch Fulbright is going to control the ideas." The Advisory Commission felt skittish about the plan, and Senator Javits warned that no one could take on a senior committee on the floor of the Senate and expect to win. Shakespeare planned to resign if the vote went against him. But McGee came through. On 1 May 1972, he won the vote by 56 to 15. No one could remember an overturn like it. Senator Henry Jackson arranged a screening of *Czechoslovakia, 1968* to celebrate. In a follow-up vote on 25 May the Senate also rejected Fulbright's bid to prevent the agency's circulating unattributed propaganda overseas by 42 to

New York Times," 22 March 1972, p. 16. A second leaflet produced by Fulbright, which circulated in Bolivia, took the form of a cartoon book about urban terrorism; *Washington Post*, 24 March 1972, p. A6. NA RG 306, 87.0018, director's subject files, box 29, file: Fulbright, including Shakespeare to *Herald Traveler*, Boston, 19 April 1972 explaining the "Soviet Union" policy. For Nixon's support on the Country Plan issue see Box 30, file 1972- OGA-NSC, Nixon to SoS/Dir. USIA, 15 March 1972.

87 Interviews: Herschensohn; Shakespeare; Richard L. Madden, "Fulbright Urges Ban on USIA Film," *New York Times*, 30 March 1972, p. 5; RNPM WHCF FG 230 (USIA), box 1, Exec., Herschensohn to Shakespeare, 31 March 1972 and reply 3 April 1972. Also UoA Fulbright papers, box 33 esp. Loomis to Fulbright, 3 April 1972 and Shakespeare to Fulbright, 29 March 1972.

88 John W. Finney, "Fulbright Not Impressed by Arguments, USIA," *New York Times*, 2 April 1972, p. E.4; John W. Finney, "USIA Aide, Critic of Fulbright, Quits, *New York Times*," 4 April 1972, pp. 14 and 45 (editorial) arguing that Buckley and Klendienst showed "poor judgment." Also UoA Fulbright papers, box 33 esp. Fulbright to Kleindienst, 28 March 1972.

89 Interview: Shakespeare; Woods, *Fulbright*, pp. 617–18; John W. Finney, "Senate Unit Backs War-Fund Cut Off," *New York Times*, 18 April 1972, p. 1.

17. Rumors began to circulate that Fulbright now planned to retire. Shakespeare had won.[90]

*

The operational challenges of Shakespeare's later years included efforts to publicize Nixon's globetrotting diplomacy. Though good copy, the logistics of Nixon's trips proved a mixed blessing. USIS posts in cities visited by the President typically picked up a bill for as much as $50,000 for installing facilities to accommodate the pack of eighty or so journalists who traveled in his wake.[91] Others worked hard to ensure that representatives of the USIA and VOA had a place in that pack. In February 1972, Stanton lobbied Kissinger for USIA places in the press party on the trips to Peking and Moscow. The VOA's White House correspondent, William Sprague, traveled to China. Shakespeare hoped that Giddens himself might travel with Nixon to Moscow as a gesture of the administration's support for international broadcasting, but the White House declined. Even so, the press plane for the Moscow trip included a three-person contingent from the USIA.[92]

The agency presented Nixon's trips to China and Russia as work for "a generation of peace." The USIA's guidance telegram on the China visit stressed that "While journey will not, rpt not result in instant solutions to U.S. differences with China, opening dialogue at highest level will serve cause world peace."[93] The overture impacted the USIA's output. Before the visit the agency quietly shelved a film on the life of the Dalai Lama.[94] In the wake of the visit the NSC began to study the possibilities of cultural exchanges with China, but inadvertently left the USIA off the circulation list of the relevant policy document, NSSM 148.[95]

The dawn of détente required a formal review of the USIA's output regarding the Soviet Union. In conducting this review, the agency examined Soviet propaganda, identifying a "general toning down of critical comment about the United

90 Interview: Shakespeare. For Fulbright's papers on this vote see UoA Fulbright box 33; Woods, *Fulbright*, pp. 617–18; John W. Finney, "Senate Votes 57–15 to Restore $45 Million to USIA Budget," *New York Times*, 2 May 1972, p. 2; John W. Finney, "Vote in Senate Gives Fulbright Another in a Series of Rebuffs," *New York Times*, 26 May 1972, p. 8. Fulbright actually left the Senate in 1974, having failed to gain renomination for his seat.
91 RNPM WHCF FG230 (USIA), box 1, Exec., Towery (IOP, USIA) to Ziegler (White House Press Sec.), 28 February 1972.
92 RNPM WHCF TR 38–4 (Travel: U.S.S.R.), box 81, Exec., Kissinger to Stanton, 9 February 1972; Shakespeare to President, 14 April 1972; Loomis to Ziegler, 4 May 1972. The agency party for the Moscow trip included Sprague; the USIA's White House correspondent, Alexander Sullivan; an agency photographer; and Eugene Nikiforov of the VOA Russian Service. In Moscow they met up with the Voice's Eastern European correspondent, Mark Hopkins.
93 NA RG 306, 87.0018, director's subject files, box 31, On the policy aspects of the Moscow visit see 1972 OGA-President's Moscow Trip, esp. Jenkins (IEE) to Kissinger, 6 January 1972 on the Beijing Trip see 192 OGA-President's China Trip, esp. Infoguide No. 72–3, 14 February 1972. For previous agency policy on détente see NA RG 306, 89.0180, director's chronological file, 1969–70, box 16, reel 33, Shakespeare to Elliot Richardson, USoS, "Public Posture on SALT," 8 April 1970.
94 "Failures in USIA's Film Program Hit," *Motion Picture Daily*, 7 January 1972, pp. 1–2.
95 NA RG 306, 87.0018, director's subject files, box 30, 1972 – OGA-NSC, Crane (IEA) to Shakespeare/Loomis, 14 March 1972, etc.

States" and increased coverage of examples of US/Soviet cooperation. The USIA now walked a delicate line. The agency clearly wanted to indicate U.S. satisfaction at the key agreements, but the VOA would still report negative news about the Soviet system when that news was there to be reported.[96] In August 1972, the VOA demonstrated its willingness to cover Soviet dissent by devoting considerable energy to publicizing Solzhenitsyn's witheringly critical Nobel Prize acceptance speech.[97]

*

The agency's review of requests made by key USIS posts for guidance in the first part of 1971 identified a broad range of requirements. Field posts noted the need for more material to explain such foreign policy themes but, by a ratio of three to two, they requested material to help portray American society. Major areas of interest included youth, labor, environmental and urban renewal issues, and above all race and minority affairs.[98]

Depicting the peaceful protests of Martin Luther King a decade earlier had been relatively uncomplicated when compared to the problems of talking about the Black Power movement. The USIA version of the Black Power era stressed the moderation of the majority of black Americans, the context of black American economic progress, and "the quiet revolution" of growing black political influence in the mainstream.[99] In the spring of 1971 the Office of Policy circulated major posts with an anthology of articles and guidance pieces on black American politics, including a piece from *The New Yorker* by Edward Jay Epstein contesting allegations of police misconduct in the deaths of some twenty-eight members of the Black Panther party. Recent USIA films provided further support. Relevant titles included *I Am a Man* (1970), a profile of three black leaders, including Jesse Jackson.[100]

96 Loomis told Kissinger, "When internal developments in the U.S.S.R. (intellectuals' dissent, the treatment of religious and national minorities) receive significant news and editorial attention outside the Soviet Union, the Voice of America will continue to report this back to its audiences in the U.S.S.R. VOA's policy is to eschew polemics, not to seek quarrels with the Soviet Union, not to attempt to magnify small incidents." NA RG 306, 87.0018, director's subject files, box 31, Loomis (acting dir.) to Kissinger, "USIA output after the Moscow Summit," 16 June 1972; and agreement Haig (White House) to Loomis, 29 June 1972.
97 NA RG 306, 87.0018, director's subject files, box 34, RAD-General, Giddens to Shakespeare, "VOA handling of Solzhenitsyn's Nobel Address," 31 August 1972.
98 NA RG 306, 75.0016, cultural subject files, box 2, file: Themes IWE, White (IOP) to Area and Media Assistant Directors, 19 July 1971.
99 NA RG 306, 75.0016, cultural subject files, box 2, file: Themes IWE, APM – Western Europe (IWE), Annex by Feiler, 1 September 1971, lists the number one priority theme for the USIA in Western Europe as solving America's social problems, and within this theme (A) "The progress of minorities: concentrate on the achievements of the black population in gaining political power," to be illustrated with voter registration statistics, black officer holding in cities such as Washington, DC, "Black politicians in action: speaking, ribbon-cutting etc.," and the Black Caucus in Congress.
100 NA RG 306 87.0018, director's subject files, box 24, 3. REA Foreign Audience Characteristics, White to Shakespeare/Loomis, 19 March 1971 with attachments. Other relevant USIA films were "a hard-hitting TV panel discussion" called *U.S.A. in Black and White* (no date), *Carl Stokes Interviewed on the*

The challenge deepened as the USIA moved to manage news of two major trials involving radical African-Americans. The first concerned the so-called Soledad Brothers, black activists who had allegedly killed a white guard at Soledad prison in 1970. A book by one of the defendants became a staple of Soviet propaganda in Africa. The second case was the trial of Angela Davis, a young African-American Civil Rights activist, who had first come to prominence in 1969 when dismissed from her job at the University of California because of her membership of the Communist Party. In August 1970, Davis allegedly provided the gun used in a shoot-out in a California courtroom in which four people, including the judge, died. Following her arrest, she too became a cause celebre for Soviet propaganda in the Third World. A USIA circular letter to all PAOs recognized that "while on the surface the Davis case seems made-to-order for hostile propaganda, the facts are pretty disarming and offer plenty of ammunition to counter Communist propaganda." The USIA used the Davis case to demonstrate the U.S. legal system in action, contrasting the rights extended to Davis with those denied in the U.S.S.R. Acting director Loomis authorized the agency to "discreetly note President Nixon's acknowledgement that his early comments on the charges against Davis should not have been made." In the United States the accused was innocent until proved guilty.[101]

The USIA sent two lawyers to Africa to lecture solely on the Davis case. The Anglophone lecturer was USIA Assistant General Counsel Frank Ruddy, who had drafted the agency's guidance on the case. Ruddy knew how to handle a hostile audience. While a law student at Cambridge, he had toured British campuses defending U.S. foreign policy for USIS. The intensity of Soviet bloc propaganda on the case amazed him. Ruddy worked to filter out the political and racial dimension. The USIA also arranged for a panel of African jurists to observe the Davis trial. The verdicts helped. All-white juries acquitted both Davis and the Soledad brothers. A string of major cases against Black Panthers also ended in acquittals, dismissals, and dropped charges. Moscow had predicted legal lynchings.[102]

Soviet interest in the Davis case was much in evidence during the Soviet tour of the latest USIA exhibit: "Research and Development – U.S.A." In Tbilisi, Georgia in January and February 1972, Georgians were eager to learn whether the Davis case was evidence of "racial prejudice and anti-Communist activity in America?" Other frequently asked questions included "who was the leader of the hippies?" The guides noted how Georgians projected their own national concerns onto the fair's one

David Frost Show (1970), *The New Job* (1969), dealing with "on-the-job training for the black disadvantaged worker," *A Voice in the City* (1968), which followed the work of an African-American trade union organizer in New York City, and *One Man: Leon Sullivan* (1969), a portrait of a Philadelphia civil rights leader.

[101] NA RG 306 87.0018, director's subject files, box 24, 3 REA – foreign audience characteristics, Jenkins to all IAS PAOs, 4 February 1971 Loomis, "Infoguide No. 71–3: The Angela Davis Trial," 21 January 1971 with attachment by Ruddy, 13 January 1971.

[102] ADST Oral History: Ruddy. For USIA coverage of the acquittal see NA RG 306 87.0018, director's subject files, box 31, 1972, PPL-Policy/Media Guidance, Office of Policy and Plans, Talking Paper No. 54, 13 June 1972 with attachment by Ruddy.

African-American guide, asking whether she was allowed to learn the "Negro language" at school.[103]

*

As the 1970s progressed, the preeminence of racial strife in the lineup of
American ills was challenged by the growing issue of illegal drugs. In June 1971 Nixon
called drug abuse "a national emergency" and in March 1972 he named it the nation's
most pressing domestic problem. Given the fact that the principal scourge of the era,
heroin, originated overseas, the White House looked to the USIA to play a role in
its anti-drug campaign. Although certain area directors – specifically Assistant Director for Western Europe Jay W. Gildner – called for a USIA film to support the U.S.
anti-drug policy, Herschensohn had flatly refused to deliver such a film, as the subject
would require depiction of the sordid underbelly of American urban life.[104] USIA
guidance on the issue reflected similar concerns. The agency asked PAOs to stress
the universality of the drug problem around the world, to show Nixon's leadership,
and to "emphasize the harmful effects of drugs on the health and motivation of the
users, the loss to society, and the rise in crime that drug addiction brings." PAOs were
warned to target their efforts at "selected decision makers who can affect their governments' policies on narcotics issues" and to encourage these governments to create their
own anti-drug campaigns. The United States did not wish to be overidentified with
this problem.[105]

Agency participation in the drugs issue gathered pace in early 1972. The USIA
took part in an interagency task force, chaired by the State Department. The International Press Service designated an "in-house" drug expert who liaised with other
agencies and generated a steady flow of material on the issue for the wireless file and
mailings. The VOA covered drug seizures and international summits on the problem
as priority news and created numerous special programs, including a half-hour documentary in English called *The Crutch That Cripples*. The USIA's audiovisual branch
acquired the rights to existing documentaries on the problem and finally began to
shoot its own treatment in cooperation with the U.S. government's Bureau of Narcotics. The agency also noted that the drug issue had developed a major following on
Capitol Hill. In early 1972, Congressman Seymour Halpern (R-NY) introduced a bill
calling for the USIA to publicize the effects of heroin addiction in producer countries.
The agency now anticipated that its drug work would be a help in its appropriation
hearings. The USIA was moving into a new world.[106]

---

103 RNPM WHCF TR 38–4 (Travel: U.S.S.R.), box 81, Exec., Shakespeare to Kissinger, 31 March 1972,
     with attached report by John Parker, 9 March 1972. The pavilion staff reported local mistreatment of
     African exchange students.
104 NA RG 306, 87.0018, director's subject files, box 34, MTV-films, esp Herschensohn to Gildner, 6
     December 1971.
105 NA RG 306, 87.0018, director's subject files, box 34, MTV-films, Infoguide 71–39, "USIA's role in
     supporting President Nixon's anti-narcotic program," 13 October 1971.
106 NA RG 306, 87.0018, director's subject files, box 31, file: 1972, PPL-Policy Media Guidance, Crane
     (IEA) to Shakespeare, "USIA anti-drug programming," 27 April 1972.

*

On the audiovisual front the agency developed a monthly half-hour television magazine program entitled *Visions U.S.A.* Launched in the autumn of 1972, early editions included stories on Louis Armstrong, blue jeans, recycling, birch bark canoes, and Don McLean's song "American Pie."[107] Worldwide documentary projects in the pipeline for 1973 included films on youth leaders and life in the new south. In deference to "Women's Lib" the agency renamed its "One Man" series "Profile," starting with *Profile: Joan Ganz Cooney*, a documentary about the children's television pioneer behind *Sesame Street*. Such productions seemed distinctly apolitical when compared to the output under Herschensohn, but this was material that the field posts were willing to use.[108]

*

At the end of September 1972, Henry Loomis left the USIA for the prestigious post of president of the Corporation for Public Broadcasting.[109] Frank Shakespeare served out his term and then returned to private life, running first Westinghouse Electric and then RKO. He remained active in conservative politics, becoming a trustee of the Heritage Foundation in 1979 and chairing its board from 1981 to 1985. He channeled his enthusiasm for public diplomacy into RFE/RL, chairing the Board for International Broadcasting from 1976 to 1985. He served as U.S. ambassador to Portugal and then to the Vatican. The *New York Times* did not mourn his departure from the USIA, noting that "During four years as director of United States Information Agency, Frank J. Shakespeare Jr. has irritated foreigners, demoralized old agency hands and embarrassed American diplomacy with his stridently propagandistic hardline approach to the presentation of American policy abroad."[110] Many USIA FSOs were not sorry to see him go. For old agency hand G. Lewis Schmidt, by the end of Shakespeare's tenure the USIA was "rapidly shifting into mediocrity, and in many places, ridicule." Even the Advisory Commission spoke of the agency "sliding down hill" and criticized Shakespeare's failure to reflect détente. Yet Shakespeare had also won a measure of independence from both the State Department and the Senate, and passed that independence on to the Voice of America. For the VOA the conservative Shakespeare had been an easier master than the sainted Ed Murrow. Granted, telling the truth about the Soviet Union produced stories that followed Shakespeare's political preference, but in circumstances where the news ran against his preference he still argued for balanced coverage. He did so not only to retain credibility but above all because he believed it to be right.[111]

107   NA MPSVB, RG 306.V.1 to V.5. The series premiered in the autumn of 1972.
108   NA RG 306, 87.0018, director's subject files, box 34. MTV-general, Woodward to Shakespeare, 7 July 1972, etc; MTV-Films, Woodward to Shakespeare, 25 September 1972.
109   RNPM WHCF FG230 (USIA), box 2, Exec., Loomis to President, 21 September 1972.
110   Editorial, "America's New Voice," *The New York Times*, 16 December 1972, p. 30.
111   Dusko Doder, "Report Urges USIA to Reflect Détente," *Washington Post*, 5 March 1973, p. A1; Interview: Shakespeare; ADST Oral History: Schmidt, Kopp.

4) WATERGATE AND JAMES KEOGH
JANUARY 1973–AUGUST 1974

Richard Nixon began his second term with a major success. In January 1973, Hanoi signed the Paris peace agreement. The USIA soon noticed a "peace dividend" in European public opinion. In July 1973, the Western European PAOs convened a panel to consider the question, "What are the deep anti-American issues that we face in Western Europe?" To the astonishment of Washington, the group concluded, "There are none." But even as the Vietnam War ended, a crisis broke much closer to home: Watergate.[112] On 8 January 1973, the trial began of seven men arrested in connection with a break-in at the Democrat National Committee offices in Washington's Watergate Hotel the previous June. Watergate presented unprecedented challenges to the USIA. Nixon needed an agency director on whom he could rely. He chose journalist James Keogh.

Born in Nebraska in 1916, James Keogh built his career as a journalist first at the *Omaha World Herald* and then at *Time* magazine. By 1956, he had risen to become *Time*'s senior editor covering the political scene. In 1956, he published an admiring study of the Vice President called *This Is Nixon*. In 1959, an appreciative Nixon invited Keogh to join his presidential campaign, but financial pressures prevailed and Keogh declined. By 1968, things had changed. Having reached the plateau of Executive Editor of *Time*, Keogh took leave to work as the chief of research and writing on Nixon's presidential campaign.[113]

In the wake of victory, Nixon offered Keogh a job. Keogh asked specifically about the USIA directorship and was disappointed to learn that the post was taken. The President prevailed on him to join the White House as a special assistant. Keogh worked on Nixon's speeches until December 1970, but found his access to the President limited. Frustrated, he returned to private life and wrote a book arguing that Nixon received a raw deal from the media, called *Nixon and the Press*.[114] In December 1972, Keogh was delighted to receive a call from Haldeman inviting him to serve as the USIA director. He accepted on the spot. He and Shakespeare went to the Oval Office for a briefing from the President. The meeting troubled Keogh. He found Nixon strangely angry, aggressive, and fixating on domestic enemies, pounding the desk and yelling "we're gonna get those bastards." He suddenly wished that he had not already committed to take the post.[115]

Keogh approached the directorship of the USIA with the model of *Time* magazine in his mind. He saw the two structures as parallel. One had correspondents, bureaus, and bureau chiefs, whereas the other had FSOs, PAOs, and USIS posts. Both had

112   RNPM WHCF FG230 (USIA), box 2, Exec., Keogh to Nixon, 20 July 1973.
113   Interview: James Keogh, 6 November 2001.
114   Interview: Keogh, 6 November 200; RNPM WHCF FG230 (USIA), box 2, Exec., White House Press Release, 13 December 1972; 16 December 1972, p. 30.
115   Interview: Keogh, 6 November 200; Linda Charlton, "Keogh, Former Aide to Nixon Is Chosen as Head of USIA," *New York Times*, 14 December 1972, pp. 1, 6; editorial, "America's New Voice," *The New York Times*, 16 December 1972, p. 30.

substantial bureaucracies at home in the United States and hence both were vulnerable to tensions between the field and the HQ. Keogh swiftly recognized that the USIA's field posts and the area directors had been sidelined by Shakespeare and sought to restore the voice of the area directors in policy making. The agency could only flourish with a steady flow of ideas from the field.

Keogh's key assistant was his deputy director, Gene Kopp. Keogh selected Kopp in the face of White House nominations as the best man for the job. Kopp had joined the agency in 1969 as deputy general counsel and congressional liaison. Since July 1972 he had served as assistant director for administration. The two men worked well together. In later years their Area Director for Europe, Jock Shirley, waxed lyrical on their combined intelligence, managerial skill, gentlemanly demeanor, decisiveness, and affection for the Foreign Service. For Shirley, the team of Keogh and Kopp understood the role of the USIA and "neither overvalued nor undervalued" that role. They never believed themselves to be "mini-secretaries of state." Keogh's USIA would be much more in tune with the mood of détente.[116]

Nixon appointed Keogh with the traditional promise that he would be fully integrated into policy making. Nixon immediately brought him in on key discussions at the White House and NSC in early 1973. It seemed as though the distance that had characterized the relationship between the NSC and Frank Shakespeare's USIA was coming to an end. Keogh had a cordial personal relationship with Henry Kissinger – the National Security Advisor's habitual greeting being, "Vell Keogh, vat the hell did you put on the Voice of America today?" Keogh and Kopp looked forward to what Kopp called "a much more relevant and influential relationship with the White House and the NSC." But Watergate changed this. When the full story broke, as Keogh put it, "the shutters came down." The White House became preoccupied with the crisis and the USIA was outside the stockade. Watergate thus crushed an opportunity for the USIA to return to the sort of policy relationship last seen in the closing years of the Eisenhower administration. Keogh's contact with the foreign policy apparatus came through attendance at the weekly State Department meeting held by Under Secretary of State Kenneth Rush. Keogh ran the USIA without "nagging" from the White House, but conversely had minimal support in his dealings with Capitol Hill.[117]

One link with the White House caused Keogh concern. In the closing days of Shakespeare's tenure, Bob Haldeman had presented the USIA with a new general counsel and congressional liaison fresh from White House service, named Gordon Strachan (which he pronounced in the true WASP manner as "Strawn"). Strachan arrived just before Keogh in January 1973. He was far more of a Nixon insider than Keogh. As one colleague recalled, Strachan strode into the USIA like a Waffen SS officer onto a World War Two battlefield and clearly expected to give orders to the kindly *Wehrmacht* general Keogh. Why the White House wanted Strachan at the USIA remains obscure. When Strachan suggested accompanying the USIA director on all his

[116] Interview: Keogh, 6 November 2001; ADST Oral History: Robert Chatten; Henry Dunlap; Jock Shirley.

[117] Interview: Keogh, 6 November 2001; ADST Oral History: Eugene Kopp.

travels, Keogh suspected that Strachan might have a brief to keep an eye on him, and swiftly squashed the idea as a poor use of agency resources. As the general counsel's duties included creating USIA material on congressional legal matters for distribution via the wireless file to the newspapers of the world, it is possible that someone at the White House imagined the post – or sold it to Strachan – as a way to influence the global representation of Watergate. Keogh and Kopp recognized the obvious potential for a conflict of interest and swiftly recalled the former Assistant General Counsel Frank Ruddy from a White House assignment to write the USIA's wireless file pieces on the affair. Ruddy ensured that the world's print media had access to the full story as Watergate unfolded.[118]

It is most likely that Strachan's assignment came from Haldeman's wish to move the man out of the White House quickly, for just as Strachan joined the USIA, his name began to appear in press reports around Watergate. As aide to Haldeman, he had served as White House liaison (or "bag man") to the Committee for the Re-election of the President. He knew about stashes of hush money and much else in the Nixon White House. Keogh obtained Strachan's resignation on 31 April 1973, the same day on which Haldeman and Ehrlichman quit the White House, and the agency thereby avoided direct connection to burgeoning scandal. On 12 July 1973, Strachan delivered astonishing testimony to the Watergate grand jury. He revealed that he and Haldeman had known about the wiretaps before the break-in and had destroyed documents afterward. Eight months later the grand jury indicted Gordon Strachan and six others for conspiracy to obstruct justice.[119]

*

While Watergate raged, Keogh worked to keep the USIA on an even keel. Key problems included a round of difficult hearings on the Hill, more especially as Keogh sought a $17.6 million increase on the $224.4 million allocated for the coming year. Keogh worried that he would be asked about links between the USIA and the CIA. He visited CIA director John Schlesinger at Langley to ask whether the CIA used USIS posts or personnel as cover to ensure that he did not perjure himself in hearings. Schlesinger reassured him, through wreaths of Alan Dulles-esque pipe smoke, that he could deny abuse of the USIA with confidence. Accordingly Keogh testified that there were "no concurrent operations of any kind" between the USIA and the CIA. He also made it clear that he had received no high-level instruction on the handling of Watergate.

But Keogh's real problems were in the House.[120] Keogh faced a new arch-enemy: Ohio Democrat Representative Wayne Hays, whose empire now included

118   Interview: Keogh, 6 November 2001; ADST Oral History, Ruddy.
119   Carl Bernstein and Bob Woodward, *All the President's Men*, New York: Simon & Schuster, 1974, pp. 125, 196, 334; Fred Emery, *Watergate*, New York: Times Books, 1994, pp. 347, 427; ADST Oral History: Kopp; Ruddy. On resignations see *New York Times* and *Washington Post*, 1 May 1973, p. 1. For testimony and profile of Strachan see *New York Times*, 21 July 1973, pp. 1, 12.
120   Interview: Keogh, 6 November 2001; "USIA Chief Cites Lag in Information," *Washington Post*, 8 May 1973, p. C6.

the chairmanship of both the House Administration Committee and the Democratic Congressional Campaign Committee. Hays had taken against the USIA over the matter of the VOA's Greek coverage; now, in early 1973, he approached Keogh to find a political job for a recently unseated colleague. When Keogh refused, arguing that the man was unqualified, Hays attacked the agency. His committee amended the USIA's appropriations authorization for 1974 to require the USIA to surrender any confidential documentation that the committee might request within thirty-five days or lose funding. The move promised embarrassing revelations. The House passed this amendment 240 votes to 178 and the Senate approved 62 votes to 29. Only communications with the President were exempt. On 12 October, Kopp wrote to the White House requesting a presidential veto. In his only major intervention on behalf of Keogh's USIA, Nixon agreed and duly vetoed the legislation on 23 October 1973, citing clear constitutional grounds. The legislation passed without the problematic disclosure requirement, but Hays would fight another day.[121]

Keogh's initiatives in the USIA's programming included a scheme to rebuild lately neglected links between the USIA and the private sector, hoping to both increase domestic awareness of the agency and supplement its limited resources.[122] In 1973, the USIA initiated a number of new schemes to promote U.S. exports and encourage tourism. Working with the Department of Commerce's New Product Information Service (NPIS) and its creator, an energetic FSO named Harry Cahill, the USIA launched both a series of newspaper columns and a weekly VOA spot called "New Products USA." By 1975 thirty-one editions of the column had been sent to the field and had been prominently placed in the press of Korea, Yugoslavia, Greece, Taiwan, and Spain, and the radio show in its English version (scripted and voiced by the versatile Cahill) and foreign twenty-six language versions reputedly achieved better ratings than any VOA program other than the Breakfast Show.[123]

Keogh also reached out to the captains of American industry. In early 1974 he organized a conference at USIA HQ with a lunch at Blair House at which fifty executives from top U.S. corporations including Ford Motors, GE, and Coca-Cola could meet senior PAOs and "explore ways and means of more effective cooperation between USIA and U.S. multi-national corporations doing business abroad." The group gathered on 7 March 1974. The PAOs briefed in the morning and Vice President Ford provided a rousing speech of encouragement. In the afternoon the executives discussed future development. The seminar agreed that the United States had fallen behind competitors like Britain, France, Germany, and Japan where business and government spoke "with one voice and work together hand in glove." Ideas focused on

121 Interview: Keogh, 6 November 2001; RNPM WHCF FG230 (USIA), box 2, Exec., Kopp to Brent Scowcroft (Dept. National Security Advisor), 12 October 1973; presidential veto message, 23 October 1973; ADST Oral History, Kopp.
122 Interview: Keogh.
123 Interview: Harry Cahill, 10 May 2006; NA RG 306 USIA historical collection, reports and studies, A1 (1070) box 7, James Moceri (IOR) to Keogh, "USIA Accomplishments 1974–1975," 15 April 1975.

the future use of USIA channels to serve U.S. business. Keogh was sketching a vision of the USIA for a post–Cold War world.[124]

Keogh also invested in the USIA's exhibitions service. He personally attended the opening of the "Recreation – U.S.A." show in Irkutsk, Siberia in 1973 and was much taken by the eagerness of the Soviet crowd for knowledge of the United States. This exhibition gave the Soviet visitor a guided tour of the world of American leisure, with displays of golfing and other sports equipment and the usual multilingual interpretation from guides. The star of the show was a fully equipped Winnebago camping van whose dimensions and furnishings exceeded those of many Soviet homes. The vehicle became such an attraction that guides had to limit the time visitors spent inspecting it. A steady stream of Siberians leaving the exhibition returned immediately to the entrance to line up for another glimpse of the American dream.[125]

On the administrative front, Keogh established an Office of Equal Opportunity under an African-American lawyer from Kansas named George Haley (brother of the novelist Alex Haley), who went on to serve as the agency's general counsel.[126]

*

Keogh's leadership of the USIA diverged sharply from that of Shakespeare. He paid more attention to views from the field, he held the Advisory Commission at arm's length, and he kept a tighter rein on the USIA's media outlets. Keogh's Assistant Director for Motion Pictures and Television, Robert S. Scott, enjoyed none of the autonomy granted to Herschensohn by Shakespeare. Now, the "front office" scrupulously viewed rough cuts of major projects to ensure a solid "party line." When Keogh applied the same approach to the VOA, the Voice objected in the strongest terms.[127]

Keogh felt that the VOA could not expect to behave like a commercial news organization and needed to deliver value to the American taxpayer. He surmised that the audience listened to the VOA because of its American government credentials, not despite them. Ken Giddens, a presidential appointment in his own right, remained VOA director and resisted Keogh's pressure to play down both Watergate and dissent in the Soviet Union. No one quite recalls exactly how Keogh and Giddens came to be at

124 RNPM WHCF FG230 (USIA), box 2, Exec., Pike to Fluor (Fluor Corporation internal minute) 13 March 1974, and associated correspondence. See also Gerald R. Ford Library (GRFL), Ford Vice-Pres., box 76, Office of Legal Counsel, Depts & Agencies: USIA.

125 Interview: Keogh, 6 November 2001. During this visit to Russia, Keogh also negotiated without success to liberalize the travel restrictions on journalists working in the U.S.S.R. "USIA Head Presses Soviet on Newsmen," *The New York Times*, 20 September 1973, p. 8; UPI, "USIA Chief Fails to Ease Soviet Curbs on Newsmen," *New York Times*, 26 September 1973, p. 8.

126 Interview: Keogh, 6 November 2001; ADST Oral History: Monsen, Kopp, Marcy. The creation of the office was not without cost. Keogh abolished the Policy Office Women's Issues specialist position and transferred incumbent Mildred Marcy into Equal Opportunities.

127 Interview: Keogh, 6 November 2001; ADST Oral History: Monsen, Kopp. On Scott's appointment see "Then a Star, Now a Director," *Washington Post*, 13 April 1973, p. B3, noting that his career had taken him from a youth on Broadway to filmmaking for the Air Force missile program and Atomic Energy Commission.

war. One Rubicon was a lunch meeting attended by Giddens and his deputy Bill Miller, Keogh, and Kopp. By Miller's account, as the four men talked, Keogh proposed "a new approach to programming" for the VOA. Keogh explained that the one magazine popular everywhere is the world was the *Reader's Digest*, and that people warmed to its peppy, upbeat material. He wondered whether the VOA might be reconceptualized as "the *Reader's Digest* of the air." Giddens and Miller recoiled in horror, surmising that Keogh doubted whether the VOA had any business covering news. The phrase "*Reader's Digest* of the air" became chiseled on Giddens' conscience like a medieval vision of damnation. He repeated the phrase to all who sought to understand his differences with the USIA. In later years Keogh could not recall using the phrase but admitted briefly considering and then dismissing the broad idea of a feature-based VOA. Regardless of Keogh's intent or exact words, the story spread swiftly through the Voice, confirming the VOA's worst fears.[128]

For Keogh, the VOA had become unacceptably independent. Giddens now lobbied on Capitol Hill with no reference to the USIA. Giddens' staff leaked stories to the press whenever they needed support against an agency decision. His journalists traveled and reported without reference to U.S. missions in particular countries. The VOA, for its part, noted that Keogh seldom visited the Voice. He and his staff preferred to issue orders and expect the VOA to jump. Even the resident USIA policy officer at the VOA at the time – Jack Shellenberger – came to resent his imperious morning phone call from the USIA's "uptown" policy office: "All right, this is what you're going to treat today, this is what you're not going to treat today. And we didn't like what one of the VOA commentators said yesterday so don't let that happen again."[129] Giddens dubbed Keogh's tenure "an age of darkness" and commented "he would have forced me to quit it he'd had the guts."[130]

Watergate became the chief battleground in the struggle between Keogh and Giddens. In Giddens' account, he argued for long-term credibility, while Keogh pushed for short-term damage reduction. Giddens defended the VOA's coverage of Watergate by arguing, "We are trying diligently to convey the idea that what the world is seeing is the genius of our checks and balances at work."[131] Keogh acknowledged the need for the VOA to report the facts of Watergate, and remarked that the "unhysterical explanations of the free and open workings of this society strikes a remarkably positive and calming reaction among the sophisticated of some lands where such openness in unknown."[132] But the exact boundary between news and speculation remained moot. Giddens had no doubt that Keogh's management crossed the line. Ten years after Watergate, Giddens bluntly told the historian Laurien Alexandre, "Keogh was a son of a bitch . . . he tried to get me to cover up Watergate. He ordered me to do it. I told

128 Interview: Groce; ADST Oral History: Miller; Vallimarescu. Interview: Keogh, 6 November 2001.
129 Interview: Keogh & Groce; ADST Oral History: Vallimarescu, Shellenberger.
130 Quoted in UoA CU 28/13, Stratmon to Roth, "Fascell subcommittee hearings." 23 June 1977.
131 *Wall Street Journal*, 16 May 1974. p. 1
132 *27th Report of the President's Advisory Commission on Information*, July 1974, appendix A, cited in Alexandre, *Voice of America*, p. 54.

him I wouldn't unless he put it in writing. He wouldn't do that. I told him it would destroy the agency and would hurt the very man he was trying to protect."[133]

*

The VOA began its Watergate coverage gently by reporting the bare bones of the burglary and trial. The News Division under USIA officer Phil Carroll shied away from commenting on its political aspects, although some correspondents' summaries of the story suggested that there was more to be told about the case. Chris Kern of Current Affairs wrote occasional features on the story. His time would come.[134] On Friday 23 March 1973, the VOA's Watergate coverage really took off. That day the world expected to hear the burglars' sentences. In the event it learned much more. Judge John Sirica unexpectedly revealed a letter from defendant James McCord claiming that he and his co-defendants had come under "political pressure" to plead guilty. McCord spoke of perjury and alleged that senior figures in the administration had prior knowledge of the Watergate break-in. In the VOA newsroom Kern elbowed his way past his astonished editors to read the letter on the AP wire. Realizing the explosive implications of the story, Kern ran to the courthouse on 4th Street to cover the rest of the day's proceedings in person. He arrived at the end of recess. Lacking a seat, he spent the second session crouching, as Sirica refused to allow standing in his court. With aching muscles Kern then dashed back to the VOA to file his report: "Watergate Defendant Offers Disclosures." Although stating that "there is no evidence of any complicity by President Nixon," Kern concluded, "the Watergate case is far from over, and there are continuing hints of new answers to the question of ultimate responsibility for the politically-charged affair." Kern then developed his points in a News Analysis piece (the equivalent of an editorial in that era): "Watergate: It Just Won't Go Away," in which he praised Sirica and the journalists who had kept the case in the public eye: "even if all the answers are never known, the fault will not lie with an insistent free press or a politically independent judiciary."[135]

Kern's boss, Kamenske, took pains to ensure that the story received the attention it deserved. He placed it first in Current Affairs' output. Overseas posts and the BBC Monitoring Service received copies. When, after the weekend, Kamenske learned that many of the language services had not used the News Analysis, he re-issued it to ensure that there would be "no escape" from the story. At this point, as Kern recalled, "all hell broke loose," with the USIA complaining about the VOA's drawing attention to a "minor political incident" and its "taking the side" of Nixon's accusers. The policy officer warned Kamenske away from any further News Analyses on the subject, but Current Affairs filled any void with features and background pieces.[136] The acting

133 Alexandre, *Voice of America*, p. 57, interview, 12 October 1983.
134 Interviews: Kern, Kamenske.
135 Interview: Kern; Kern, "Watergate: It Just Won't Go Away," 23 March 1973, in author's possession.
136 Interviews: Kamenske, Kern; Kamenske to author, 20 March 1996; Kern, "Watergate Defendant offers disclosures," 23 March 1973, in author's possession. For criticism see RNPM WHCF Herschensohn papers, Herschensohn (White House) to Keogh, 7 June 1973.

News Division chief Philomena Jurey came under pressure from the program manager to drop the word "scandal" when describing Watergate. Jurey agreed but trusted that Watergate was now synonymous with scandal whatever word the VOA used.[137]

On the morning of 3 June 1973, Watergate suddenly broke even wider open. On that day both the *New York Times* and the *Washington Post* carried an unattributed report that White House staffer John Dean was prepared to testify to Nixon's complicity in a cover-up. The White House denied the story and the Voice of America prepared an appropriate news report. At this point USIA director Keogh moved to restrain the VOA's Watergate coverage with an unwritten directive to the Voice forbidding the broadcast of "accounts based on rumor, innuendo, gossip, or unidentified sources," which killed the Dean story. The News Room rewrote the story to lead with the White House denial and then reported the allegations made by the newspapers, clearly citing their provenance. Keogh accepted the compromise, but he was in no mood to facilitate the Watergate coverage of others. The USIA denied a request from BBC television for facilities to relay a live program about Watergate on the grounds that aiding Watergate coverage "may," a USIA ruling held, "be detrimental of United States interests."[138]

The VOA's Watergate coverage developed along the lines of the "Dean compromise." As the VOA's White House correspondent Philomena Jurey recalled, the typical report opened, "The White House had declined to comment on a published report that. . . . " The Voice kept an eye on balance. Any statement from the House Judiciary Committee had to be matched with a comment from the White House. As the crisis deepened, positive statements from the Nixon camp became increasingly hard to find. One broadcast in the spring of 1974 aired with just a bland comment from Vice President Ford on Nixon's good health as its pro-Nixon item.[139] But the bad news kept coming. In spring 1974, Kamenske (now News Division chief) and the Program Manager Nate Kingsley created a dedicated VOA Watergate unit to cover proceedings at the House Judiciary Committee. The unit included two correspondents, two writers, and tape editors.[140]

The domestic media kept a close eye on the VOA's Watergate coverage for signs of political manipulation or spin. A front page story in the *Wall Street Journal* on 16 May 1974 praised both the breadth and depth of VOA coverage, quoting Kamenske: "It's a complicated story, so it takes space to tell it." The *Journal* noted that Radio Moscow had ignored Watergate, being presumably eager to retain a President with whom its leaders could work.[141] Behind the scenes, Kamenske and the journalists who regularly

---

137   Jurey, *A Basement Seat to History*, p. 60.
138   Jurey, *A Basement Seat to History*, p. 60; ADST Oral History, Shellenberger; Interview: Keogh, 6 November 2001. For a report of the directive see Associated Press, "Voice of America Sets Watergate News Curb," *Washington Post*, 8 June 1973, p. 17, and "Lowering the Voice," *Newsweek*, 9 July 1973.
139   *Wall Street Journal*, 16 May 1974. p. 1; Interview: Kern; Jurey, *A Basement Seat to History*, p. 61.
140   *Wall Street Journal*, 16 May 1974. p. 1; Alexandre, *Voice of America*, p. 56.
141   ADST Oral History, Bill Miller. See Dusko Doder, "VOA Coverage of Watergate: Tell It like It Is," *Washington Post*, 6 May 1973, p. 16. For example Arlen J. Lange, "At Voice of America, There's No Cover-Up on Watergate News; While Radio Moscow Ignores Story, VOA Is Telling All. A Major

wrote about Watergate knew that the coverage required continual struggle within the Voice as well as between the VOA and USIA. On 6 June 1974, America learned from the *Los Angeles Times* that four months earlier the Federal Grand Jury had agreed to name Nixon as "an un-indicted co-conspirator" in Watergate. Kern's account of the revelation returned from the VOA policy office so mangled as to be unrecognizable. The "front office" version spoke of ignorance and partisan antagonisms toward the President. As Kern recalled, Bernie Kamenske called Program Manager Kingsley and asked him to either withdraw his changes or have the script broadcast under Kingsley's by-line. On this occasion Kingsley relented.[142]

The VOA's Watergate coverage fell short of that seen in the *Washington Post* or *New York* or *Los Angeles Times*, and one VOA reporter – Ron Grunberg – complained that he had been prevented from conducting any investigative reports. But the VOA was not the *Washington Post*. The VOA's Watergate coverage compared honorably with that of most domestic channels and despite limited resources it surpassed many. But this had required continual struggle. Kamenske and his colleagues had no doubt that the VOA charter alone could not protect the news from political influence. The charter needed an additional protection: law.[143]

*

While Watergate ground on, Keogh worked to support the ongoing process of détente between East and West. In September 1973, with diplomacy increasingly invoking the free flow of ideas across international boundaries, the U.S.S.R. suddenly ceased jamming the VOA.[144] Radio Liberty researchers had recently begun a major program to interview Soviet travelers and – through the wizardry of a computer program designed by MIT – extrapolate data for broadcasting audiences across the Soviet Union. The first results in 1972 estimated that the VOA reached twenty-three percent of Soviet citizens each week, with RL and the BBC as runners up with eleven and five percent respectively. The end of jamming promised a still wider audience for the VOA in the Soviet Union, but it also gave the USIA a vested interest in keeping the Soviet regime happy with the VOA's content.[145] Dissidents alleged that the Voice began to pull its punches. The debate over content flared up that winter. On 29 December 1973, the *New York Times* began to serialize an astonishing novel of protest against the Soviet Regime: *The Gulag Archipelago*. On 13 February 1974, the Soviet Union expelled its author, the Nobel laureate Aleksandr Solzhenitsyn. The arrival of so provocative a text and so prominent a dissident in the west presented an immediate

Goal: Balance," *Wall Street Journal*, 16 May 1974. p. 1. The piece gave an estimated weekly audience for the VOA of 50 million.

142 Interviews: Kern; Kamenske; Jurey, *A Basement Seat to History*, p. 69. For the background to the *LA Times* story see Fred Emery, *Watergate*, New York: Times Books, 1994, pp. 226–8, 433.

143 Interview: Kamenske. Grunberg's complaint about the VOA's Watergate coverage appeared in the *Washington Star* in 1977.

144 Alan Heil and Barbara Schiele, "The Voice Past: VOA, the U.S.S.R. and Communist Europe," in K. R. M. Short (ed.), *Western Broadcasting over the Iron Curtain*, London: Croom Helm, 1986, p. 104; *New York Times*, 25 December 1973, p. 42.

145 Interview: Keogh; Parta, *Discovering the Hidden Listener*, Section 2.1.

challenge to the USIA. Keogh faced the choice of playing the role of ideological how-itzer and beaming Solzhenitsyn and his writing back to the U.S.S.R. or supporting détente and leaving the dissident broadcasts to Radio Liberty and Radio Free Europe. When initial VOA coverage attracted criticism from Soviet television, Keogh chose a middle course.[146]

Although the VOA gave heavy news coverage to the Solzhenitsyn story – the Russian branch broadcast some 387 items on *The Gulag Archipelago* between 29 December 1973 and the first week of March 1974 – the Voice kept to its usual sched-ule and did not read actual extracts from the book, lest this reinforce Soviet charges of the VOA intervening in Russian domestic politics. Extracts could be heard on RFE and RL.[147] USIA policy on this novel convinced few at the Voice, as it denied the audience the chance to judge Solzhenitsyn's work.[148] Solzhenitsyn soon learned of the tussle between the USIA and VOA. On leaving the U.S.S.R., he agreed to be interviewed in Munich by a VOA Russian Service correspondent, Eugene Nikiforov. The agency forbade the interview. The Russian Service also obtained Solzhenitsyn's permission to broadcast extracts from his novel. The policy office again intervened to forbid the broadcast. Once the dissident writer had moved to the United States, the Russian Service chief, Victor Franzusoff, requested an interview, but Solzhenit-syn declined to "speak to an organization that's afraid of offending the Kremlin." Franzusoff's own breakthrough came in 1974 when, following a press conference, he intercepted Solzhenitsyn and the newly defected cellist Mstislav Rostropovich at the Lincoln Memorial and ingratiated himself by acting as their translator. Thereafter Solzhenitsyn kept Franzusoff up to date with his activities, and Rostopovich became a regular guest on the Russian Service. But the issue of the VOA and Solzhenitsyn remained raw for the rest of the decade.[149] Soviet audiences continued to prefer the VOA to other Western broadcasters, with estimated weekly audiences in the region of nineteen percent of the total population.[150]

*

In the midst of Watergate, the VOA slipped into a private crisis, focused on alleged deficiencies in the management structure. For a season the VOA bris-tled with rumors and counter-rumors. Ken Giddens's administration at the VOA had

---

[146] *New York Times*, 29 December 1973, p. 1; 10 January 1974, p. 5.

[147] Heil and Schiele, "The Voice Past," p. 105; also *New York Times*, 2 March 1974, p. 30 and 17 March 1974, p. 14 (for a letter of complaint and reply from Assistant Dir. Margita White). Keogh defended his decision to the press by arguing that his job as USIA director was to support U.S. foreign policy and "The principal goal of American foreign policy is to affect the foreign policies of other nations toward negotiations not to transform the domestic structures of these societies." Rowland Evans and Robert Novak in the *Washington Post* howled in objection. See Rowland Evans and Robert Novak, "Voice of America Speechless on 'Gulag Archipelago,'" *Washington Post*, 7 March 1974, p. A31.

[148] Heil and Schiele, "The Voice Past," p. 105. For objections to this policy within the Nixon White House see RNPM WHCF Bruce Herschensohn papers, box 1, Herschensohn to Alexander Haig, 11 March 1974.

[149] Victor Franzusoff, *Talking to the Russians: Glimpses by a Voice of America Pioneer*, Santa Barbara, CA: Fithian Press, 1998, pp. 180–87.

[150] Parta, *Discovering the Hidden Audience*, Section 2.1, figure 1. The small decline from the 1972 estimate is as likely to be due to a refinement of the technique as to be an adverse reaction to content.

come to rely heavily on a knot of senior members of staff, who famously enjoyed long martini-fueled lunches. Giddens leaned on three men in particular, his special assistant, a veteran of the advertising industry named Grant Worrell, his head of News and Current Affairs, Clyde Hess, and Nate Kingsley, formerly of RFE, who began as Hess' deputy and soon became Program Manager. Kingsley irritated the newsroom with his meteoric rise and unflattering comparisons of the VOA to RFE, but he also soon became the focus for this language service discontent. The languages believed that Kingsley had sidelined Giddens like some aging Roman Emperor, and that the real power at VOA now lay with a so-called "coterie," headed by the Program Manager. The corridors buzzed with stories of Kingsley's plans. He reportedly intended to bring more RFE people into the VOA, turn "Music U.S.A." into a talk show, and even pull the VOA out of the USIA.[151]

In October 1973, old VOA hand Cliff Groce and a deputation from the language services began a countercoup. Groce and his colleagues persuaded Kingsley's predecessor, Serban Vallimarescu, to take the matter to Keogh. Keogh saw his opportunity to pull the Voice into line, and in the spring of 1974 Keogh sent a "management study group" to report on the Voice. He chose three retired USIA officers, G. Lewis Schmidt, Ed Schechter, and Jack O'Brien, and Brian Battey of the FBIS. Battey soon quit, reportedly when he surmised ulterior motives behind the study. The three interviewed some 200 members of staff at the Voice and after two months produced a highly critical report. Their charges ranged from administrative incompetence to the "aggressive coverage of news stories with no relevance to an international audience," such as the woes of the New York subway system. They concluded that something needed to be done. A massive reshuffle of staff followed. Worrell moved to television; Hess went back into the field and Kingsley was transferred into the State Department's Bureau of Educational and Cultural Affairs.[152] The management report had the potential to sink Giddens; however, he defended himself admirably before the inevitable Senate hearings. Keogh preferred to bury the report rather than see Giddens defend its details in public. The two men were stuck with each other. Peace had broken out.[153]

151 Interviews: Kamenske, Groce, Kern; ADST Oral History: Shellenberger, Vallimarescu; Alexandre, *The Voice of America*, p. 43.
152 Interview: Groce; ADST oral history: Groce. Groce resented Kingsley's overruling him on a choice of guest for the interview program *Press Conference U.S.A.* Groce wanted then Speaker of the House Gerald Ford, but Kingsley, preferring a story with ideological punch, substituted a Congressman who had just returned from a trip to the U.S.S.R. In the run-up to the program, Vice President Spiro Agnew resigned and Ford took his place. The VOA had traded a newsworthy contributor for cheap Cold War point scoring. This deputation included the Division Chief for Latin America, Carl Davis, and the Division Chief for Europe, Robert Warner. Interview: Kamenske; ADST Oral History: Shellenberger, Vallimarescu; Alexandre, *The Voice of America*, p. 43, and NA RG 306 USIA historical collection, reports and studies, A1 (1070) box 1, Management Report on VOA, 22 April 1974.
153 Interview: Kamenske, Groce; *New York Times*, 14 September 1974, p. 1; 19 September 1974, p. 22. On 14 September 1974, the *New York Times* carried a front-page story claiming that Keogh had sacked Kingsley because of Watergate coverage and that he, in turn, would soon be sacked by President Ford. Keogh insisted that Watergate had nothing to do with it. Keogh's version of the "coterie" was that it had "tried to decide operations policy without consulting other departmental heads" and thereby "caused demoralization."

Meanwhile, Watergate ground into its final act. On the morning of 8 August 1974, the new VOA Program Manager, Jack Shellenberger, requested that two commentaries be written, one for use if Nixon resigned, and another to cover his fighting on. He sat with the two documents secure in his desk drawer waiting for the President's statement. Only when he heard the words from Nixon's mouth would one air and the other be destroyed. The VOA carried Nixon's sixteen-minute resignation address to the American people live, with an explanatory report from Philomena Jurey. The Voice arranged for forty-six shortwave and four medium-wave transmitters to carry coverage in what a USIA review termed the largest line-up of transmitter power in its history.[154] On the evening of 8 August 1974, the VOA told the world that Richard M. Nixon had resigned from the office of President of the United States.

[154]   ADST Oral History: Shellenberger; Jurey, *A Basement Seat to History*, p. 67; NA RG 306 USIA historical collection, reports and studies, A1 (1070) box 7, James Moceri (IOR) to Keogh, "USIA accomplishments 1974–1975," 15 April 1975.

8 A New Beginning

THE FORD ADMINISTRATION, 1974–77

> Public diplomacy is a central part of American foreign policy simply because the freedom to know is such an important part of America.
>
> Frank Stanton, March 1975.[1]

At noon on 9 August 1974, Gerald R. Ford – a man virtually unknown overseas, whose highest elected office was that of congressman – took the oath of office as President of the United States. According to the USIA's digest of foreign media reaction, his assets included an encouraging wealth of good will around the world. The West welcomed Ford's retention of Henry Kissinger (initially as both Secretary of State and National Security Advisor) and was eager for American leadership in the world economic crisis. The East seemed anxious to avoid any disruption of détente. Moscow made optimistic noises while Beijing remained tactfully circumspect. Only North Vietnam, North Korea, and Cuba attempted to score political points.[2] Even so, the USIA had much work to do.

The USIA's core objective in covering the transition from Nixon to Ford was to stress the "continuity of U.S. foreign policy" and develop the wider story of Nixon's resignation as evidence of the "strength of the American democratic system." The USIA threw the bulk of its effort into support for foreign media correspondents covering the story in Washington, DC and supplying material to news organizations around the world. An internal review had no doubt that the "strength of the U.S. system *did* come across."[3]

Although the advent of the Ford administration saw dramatic changes of personnel engineered by the tough new White House Chief of Staff (and soon to be Secretary of Defense) Donald Rumsfeld, Jim Keogh remained USIA director. He became one of the few Nixon "holdovers" to complete Ford's term of office. This was not a testament to the prominence of the USIA but suggested rather that no one paid

---

[1] GRFL OA 2271, International Information, Education, and Cultural Relations, Recommendations for the Future (hereafter "Stanton Report"), chairman's preface, p. iv.

[2] GRFL WHCF FO 5–3, box 31, Falkiewicz to Jerry Ter Horst, 12 August 1974: USIA, "President Ford's inauguration and the tasks ahead, summary of foreign media reaction as of August 11 1974." Also James B. Shuman papers, box 93, file: Communist Propaganda, FBIS report: Trends in Communist Propaganda, Vol. XXV, no. 33, 14 August 1974.

[3] NA RG 306 USIA historical collection, reports and studies, A1 (1070) box 7, James Moceri (IOR) to Keogh, "USIA accomplishments 1974–1975," 15 April 1975, emphasis in original.

much attention to the agency. Keogh had virtually no direct contact with the President. He received no support in his dealings with the Hill. The White House turned down almost all the USIA's requests for interviews with foreign media organizations and refused to help the agency create a film profile of President Ford, a basic tool for introducing the new President in the field.[4]

Beyond managing the transition to a Ford presidency, the USIA had also to negotiate America's passage into the uncertain international waters of the mid-1970s. As the smoke of Watergate and Vietnam cleared, it became readily apparent that the USIA faced a new world. The chief threat to the American way of life seemed to come from the American economy: inflation soared and the Dow Jones index plunged. But the explosion of global communications had created a vast market for American information, and with the relative power of the United States so obviously diminished, the country needed to persuade friends and enemies as never before. The success of détente opened new vistas to American information and exchange, while the widening of the international North–South divide reinforced the importance of the agency's work in what was now called the Third World. This new era underlined the need for a major reconsideration of U.S. information. A series of major inquiries followed, the most significant being the Stanton inquiry, which convened in 1975. Through the Stanton panel and other initiatives to review U.S. public diplomacy, the end of Nixon became a new beginning.

1) NAVIGATING THE RAPIDS, 1974–75

Early on the morning of Saturday, 14 September 1974, Jim Keogh was woken by a telephone call from the agency's operations center alerting him to the front page of the *New York Times*. Keogh had been braced for the story but the headline still stung: "OUSTER EXPECTED FOR USIA HEAD: FORD REPORTED PLANNING TO DISMISS KEOGH." The story claimed that certain Democrats in Congress believed that Keogh had "penalized USIA employees he deemed unfriendly to Mr. Nixon" and now a "political associate" of the President claimed that the White House was about to act. The first thing on Monday morning, Keogh contacted the White House requesting an interview with the President to "clarify the

---

[4] Interview: Keogh, 6 November 2001. In February 1975, Keogh wrote to the President to ask if a USIA crew might film him for a day. Weeks later the White House press secretary Ron Nessen replied with the rather unhelpful suggestion that the USIA use existing footage taken by a naval cameraman. The footage was on 16mm film and without special lighting and merely showed the President posing for official photographs. It was not what the agency had in mind. When the USIA pressed the point, Nessen changed tack: "I am concerned that in the present climate the benefits of this filming could be off-set by any public furor over using taxpayers' money for any build-up of the president's image overseas." Ford himself was tired of being tailed by commercial camera crews and shut down all further discussion. The USIA had to complete its film from stock sources; see GRFL WHCF Subject file FG230, box 178, Keogh to President, 7 February 1975, Nessen to Keogh, 28 April 1975, and associated correspondence. The film is noted in NA RG 306 USIA historical collection, reports and studies, A1 (1070) box 7, James Moceri (IOR) to Keogh, "USIA accomplishments 1974–1975," 15 April 1975.

situation." Ford called back to set Keogh's mind to rest. He dismissed the story and pointed the USIA director toward the source of the report: Representative Wayne Hays (D-OH).[5]

Hays was already on Keogh's mind, as the representative had just refused to approve the USIA budget for the coming year. Ford had raised this subject with the Congressman at a meeting during the previous week, whereupon Hays declared that he would do no favors for Keogh because Keogh would not hire his friend. Now, with some embarrassment, Ford asked Keogh whether there was any way that the agency could dodge trouble on the Hill by hiring Hays' nominee. Keogh yielded to the President's wishes and offered the individual concerned the post of an information officer within USIS Tehran. Part of the leverage applied by Hays had been a sad story about this man's sick wife. Keogh was hence surprised when the man concerned turned up to his first meeting at USIA with his girlfriend. In the event he did not hold the post for long, but Keogh's change of heart was sufficient to open the road to budget approval and ensure him an unctuous greeting of "Mister Director!" whenever he ran into Hays on the Hill. Two years later Hays's creative approach to employment practices finally caught up with him. The press revealed that Hays had employed his own mistress as a secretary at congressional expense, despite her inability to type. Hays resigned in disgrace. Keogh heard the news over his car radio and, as he recalled years later, pulled up at a stop sign and enjoyed a good long laugh.[6]

Although Keogh's early tenure had been dominated by the short-term problems of Watergate, he also engaged big questions of the USIA's purpose and future. In 1973 Keogh received a thoughtful analysis entitled "US government overseas communication programs: Needs and opportunities in the 1970s," written by agency veteran Barbara White. The State Department and the USIA increasingly saw a confluence of their respective cultural and informational activities, and it was symptomatic of this new era that White's brief encompassed the future of both the USIA and the State Department's Bureau of Educational and Cultural Affairs. Her recommendations remain an excellent foundation for public diplomacy:

In the Seventies, the programs should

recognize communication as *essentially a long-range process* whose results are cumulative;
concentrate more on *facilitating communication* and less on direct output;
prefer *dialogue and mutuality* to one-way communication; stress *parallelism of common interests*; work where possible through *local institutions*;

5 Interview: Keogh, 6 November 2001; David Binder, "Ouster Expected for USIA Head," *New York Times*, 14 September 1974, p. 1; David Binder, "USIA Chief Denies He Faces Ouster," *New York Times*, 19 September 1974, p. 22, which gives further details of the management crisis at VOA and notes that on 18 September Hays declared his intention to hold hearings to investigate Keogh's administration of the USIA. For administration documents on this see GRFL WHCF subject file FG230, box 178, including Timmons to President, "Rep. Wayne Hays," 14 September 1974, and Keogh to Rustand (White House), 16 September 1974.
6 Interview: Keogh, 6 November 2001.

emphasize information in *depth*, *selectivity*, and *quality*;

maximize *personal communication*, which much evidence suggests is the most effective;

apply *professional knowledge and research* more consistently and systematically, both in advising on foreign opinion factors in policy and in communicating with audiences abroad;

give the programs *a more flexible and responsive operating structure*.[7]

These ideas became an important part of the USIA mix, though not necessarily for the reasons that White might have hoped. Her recommendation about placing less emphasis on direct output certainly fitted the needs of the budget. Particular casualties included the USIA's output of magazines, which diminished from fifty-six titles at the time of Keogh's appointment to fifteen within two years.[8]

In October 1973, Keogh clarified the mission of the USIA. Keogh defined the mission of the agency as

1) Conveying an understanding of what the United States stands for as a nation and as a people and presenting a true picture of the society, institutions, and culture in which our policies evolve;

2) Explaining U.S. policies and the reasons for them; and

3) Advising the U.S. government on the implications of foreign opinion for the formulation and execution of U.S. foreign policy.[9]

This broad description of the USIA's mission was by no means accepted. A report by the General Accounting Office, released on 23 March 1975, reported "substantial disagreement" between the executive branch and Congress over the role of the USIA. Congress looked for policy advocacy, whereas USIA staff favored a cultural diplomacy role. Keogh did his best to steer a middle course.[10]

The environment in which the USIA operated had changed considerably in recent years. Keogh noted that while USIA budgets had peaked in the mid-1960s with the extra expenditure associated with Vietnam, the information budgets of other nations had continued to grow. Apart from the efforts of the Communist bloc, France had more than doubled its spending on overseas information and culture over the decade

---

7 NA RG 306 A1 (1070), box 28. USIA historical collection, reports and studies, 1945–94, Barbara M. White, "US government overseas communication programs: needs and opportunities in the 1970s," July 1973, p. 7.

8 The magazine figure is cited in *USIA World*, 12, 4 (1993), 11.

9 Keogh continued: "To do this we use all available means of communication, the most important of which is, of course, the personal contact between our officers in 109 countries around the world and local opinion leaders . . . Such activities are frequently called 'public diplomacy.' It might be more accurate to say that with the explosive growth of communications and the rising surge of nationalism, informational and cultural activities have become indispensable tools of modern diplomacy." Statement of James Keogh to Murphy Commission, 16 October 1973, appended to GRFL Marsh files, box 39, "transition reports 1977, USIA," USIA transition briefing book, December 1976, pp. 166–76.

10 General Accounting Office, *Telling America's Story to the World: Problems and Issues*, Report to Congress, 23 March 1975, as cited in GRFL Marsh files, box 39, "transition reports 1977, USIA," USIA transition briefing book, December 1976, pp. 37–8.

of the 1960s, reaching $430 million by 1971. West Germany and Britain had also maintained high levels of investment in the field, with Bonn's expenditure passing the $300 million mark in 1972. The world of the 1970s offered new media. Television was now ubiquitous and easier to serve through the rapid spread of the communications satellite and videotape systems. Transistor technology had brought cheap shortwave radios within reach of a whole new audience. Radio had a new lease of life as the medium of choice for reaching the developing world. Jet travel had made international business, tourism, and professional exchange commonplace. Keogh argued that these changes provided new opportunities for the USIA but also increased the need for its work.[11]

In autumn 1974, Keogh and his policy team drew up worldwide precepts for agency activity in the coming year, emphasizing "those issues on which USIA can most effectively concentrate its resources," and suggesting that PAOs integrate these into their country plans. These fell into five categories: political/security; economics; U.S. political and social processes; arts/humanities; and science and technology. The political program emphasized the "leadership role of the United States in adapting international institutions and processes to the new age of interdependence." This meant an emphasis on the nation's initiatives first on global issues such as the environment, narcotics, and terrorism, second in reducing political and military tension around the world (the SALT process and the nuclear nonproliferation treaty and détente), and finally emphasizing the U.S. commitment to old alliances and friendships. Economic precepts included stressing the strength of the U.S. economy, and U.S. policies to expand trade, enact monetary reform, and address global resource problems. In projecting American domestic life, PAOs were urged "without harking back to Watergate events" to focus on "the long-term ability of our society to identify and resolve national problems." But a decade on from the Civil Rights Act, the USIA took a cautious approach to the question of race and preferred emphases on "the shared purposes and activities of Americans." In science and technology the agency planned to play up the U.S. commitment to disseminate its technology and its contributions in the field of energy and food technologies. In arts and humanities the agency planned to emphasize American vigor and creativity and lay the foundation for the bicentennial festivities in 1976.[12]

USIA activity reflected the new opportunities of détente. In September 1973 the Soviet Union had ceased jamming the VOA. Even Albania followed suit, until by June 1975 only China blocked VOA transmissions. The airwaves were open.[13] Cultural exchanges continued to flourish under the 1974–6 cultural agreement. When, in early 1975, an attempt to introduce "soft rock" music into Russia foundered, the USIA fell

---

11   Keogh to Murphy Commission, 16 October 1973, appended to GRFL Marsh files, box 39, "transition reports 1977, USIA," USIA transition briefing book, December 1976, pp. 166–7. For a digest of other major cultural propaganda programs see UoA CU 27/13, "External cultural and information programs of selected countries in 1974," 14 April 1975.

12   UoA CU box 10 file 7, "The 1975 Program Precepts," attached to Keogh to PAOs, 23 December 1974.

13   "China Alone Jams VOA, USIA Says," *Washington Post*, 20 June 1975, p. A15.

back on a sure-fire crowd pleaser: jazz. The summer of 1975 saw a sell-out five-city tour by the sixteen-strong New York Jazz Repertory playing a program dedicated to the music and memory of Louis Armstrong on the seventy-fifth anniversary of his birth. Venues included the Lenin Sports Palace in Moscow. "Wildly enthusiastic" crowds regularly topped 10,000.[14] The USIA also provided its customary press support for the joint Soviet–American Apollo–Soyuz space mission of July 1975, noting in guidance, "While the fact of US–USSR cooperation in space is important, it should not override the theme that space experiments of this type have important technical implications for the solution of problems on earth."[15]

In 1976, the agency attempted to rewrite the rules for the funding of international exhibitions. Since 1954 the USIA had operated a Special International Exhibitions (SIE) program funded from a separate appropriation. Since 1966, with the agreement of the OMB, most funds had gone to finance the program in the Communist bloc. In 1976 the agency attempted to gain more freedom in expenditure so that funds could be redirected especially toward the developing world. The OMB responded by cutting the budget from $5,511,000 to $3,905,000, and although the USIA eventually won a compromise budget of $4,263,000, the OMB insisted that only $250,000 could be spent outside of the Soviet bloc.[16]

In the Middle East, American mediation following the Arab–Israeli War of 1973 had increased U.S. prestige. Previously hostile regimes now seemed open to American information. With an eye to developing the U.S. position on key issues, including oil policy, the USIS planned a major monthly magazine for the region, *al-Majal*, to be produced at its Beirut Regional Service Center. As Lebanon slipped into civil war, this facility became increasingly nonviable. Then, on 22 October 1975, Islamic guerrillas seized the center's director, Charles Gallagher, and his production manager, William Dykes. While the two men were released unharmed on 25 February 1976, the USIA swiftly closed the RSC. The center in Manila took up the slack and *al-Majal* relocated to Tunis.[17]

In Latin America the agency faced the problem of U.S. identification with increasingly unsavory dictatorships. This reached a peak in September 1973 with the CIA-blessed coup against Allende in Chile and subsequent support for the rule of General Augusto Pinochet. The USIA became an obvious target for popular reprisals, and here, too, USIS personnel became targets for kidnapping. In April 1974, a group of Argentinean guerrillas briefly held Al Laun; in the Dominican Republic guerillas took

[14] UoA CU 74/8, including Shirley (IIE) to Keogh, 11 July 1975. Armstrong had cancelled his State Department tour of the U.S.S.R. in the 1960s for political reasons.

[15] UoA CU box 10 file 7, "The 1975 Program Precepts," attached to Keogh to PAOs, 23 December 1974.

[16] GRFL Marsh files, box 39, "transition reports 1977, USIA," USIA transition briefing book, December 1976, p. 135.

[17] GRFL Marsh files, box 39, "transition reports 1977, USIA," USIA transition briefing book, December 1976, pp. 120–23, 147; Paul Martin, "Americans Kidnapped by Gunmen in Beirut," *The Times*, (London) 23 October 1975, p. 6 and "Two Kidnapped Americas Freed in Beirut," *The Times*, (London) 26 February 1976, p. 5.

the USIA's Barbara Hutchinson and seven other Americans hostage and held them for thirteen days that autumn.[18]

Despite their share of the "ugly American" reputation, the USIA could have a beneficial effect on their host country. In February 1973, an earthquake hit Managua, the capital of Nicaragua. The USIS team in the city set up a communications center for the foreign press. One officer, John Barton, conducted tours through the rubble, exposing foreign journalists to evidence of the devastation and the need for relief. Aid flowed as a result.[19] In Brazil, now ruled by a right-wing dictatorship, the USIA maintained its usual links with the academic world. In São Paulo, Joe O'Connell came to know an economics professor named Paul Singer, working with a grant from the Ford Foundation. When the government arrested Singer, O'Connell alerted his colleagues at the São Paulo consulate, who caused such a stir by investigating his disappearance that they prompted his release. Once free, Singer visited O'Connell to say thank you. He went on to become an internationally known economist as an exponent of dependency theory.[20]

In Africa, the USIA faced an uphill struggle to regain the standing it held at the time of the great wave of African independence in the early 1960s. The United States had been too friendly toward South Africa and too supportive of the Portuguese in Angola, and lost immense credibility when, in 1971, Congress voted to flout sanctions and import key minerals from Rhodesia. In Ethiopia, the revolutionary government imprisoned a VOA journalist. USIA colleagues hid locally engaged Voice staff to escape the government backlash. The intimidation did not prevent VOA coverage of the crisis in that country.[21] New initiatives in the region included the opening of a reading room in Soweto in November 1974 reaching out to the immense and information-hungry population of that black township, but as advocates of the International Visitor Program argued in later years, the biggest return in South Africa probably came from a program with an immediate audience of one. In summer 1976, a young member of parliament named Frederik Willem de Klerk toured the United States as a part of the International Visitor program. He asked for particular exposure to American "diversity," which he was shown in abundance in cities including New York, Phoenix, and New Orleans. De Klerk later spoke of the importance of this trip in broadening his perspective. Fifteen years later he led South Africa beyond white minority rule.[22]

18 *New York Times*, 13 April 1974, p. 2; 14 April 1974, p. 13; 28 September 1974, p. 1.

19 RNPM WHCF FG230 (USIA), box 2, Exec., President to Barton, 28 February 1973.

20 Interview: Joe O'Connell, 9 November 1995.

21 GRFL Marsh files, box 39, "transition reports 1977, USIA," USIA transition briefing book, December 1976, pp. 100

22 Interview: Carmen Marrero, December 1995; Visitor Program Service (Meridian House International) itinerary for de Klerk, June/July 1976 (stops included presidential campaign HQs, AFL-CIO, and meeting with Senator Percy, and visits in and around Washington, Philadelphia, New York, Los Angeles, Las Vegas, Phoenix, New Orleans, and Miami (document provided by USIA). De Klerk's acknowledgement of the trip's impact is noted in Neil A. Lewis, "Frederik Willem de Klerk," *New York Times*, 12 February 1990, p. A16. The Soweto opening is noted in *USIA World*, Vol. 12, No. 4, 1993, p. 11.

On 1 August 1975, President Ford, Leonid Brezhnev, and "high representatives" of thirty-three other states from East and West met in Helsinki, Finland and
signed the Final Act of the Conference on Security and Cooperation in Europe. The
Helsinki Final Act was the pinnacle of détente and the fruit of two years' negotiation. The accords set out agreed principles for the security of Europe, cooperation in trade and science, and in a so-called "Third Basket," principles dealing with
increased contact in the personal (including tourism and freedom of travel), informational, educational, and cultural fields. The document stressed mutual exchange. It
clearly represented a unique opportunity for the USIA to bring American culture and
ideas into the Soviet orbit. Moreover, as part of the "First Basket," the signatories
had pledged to "respect human rights and fundamental freedoms," an undertaking
that promised to provide ample ammunition for American propaganda as and when
the Soviets ignored their obligations.[23] Yet at the time of signing it was uncertain
exactly how the U.S. cultural and informational work would be organized. An independent commission, chaired by Frank Stanton, had presented its findings and the
future shape of the entire U.S. information effort was under consideration in a way not
seen since 1953.

2) THE STANTON COMMISSION, 1974–75

The Stanton Commission had been a long time coming. In 1968 Stanton's own
Advisory Commission on Information called for a major external "in-depth critique"
of U.S. overseas information. In May 1973, the Senate Foreign Relations committee endorsed this idea and proposed opening the sensitive question of the division of
labor between the USIA and the State Department Bureau of Educational and Cultural Affairs. In July 1973, the State Department's cultural advisory body, the U.S.
Advisory Commission on International Educational and Cultural Affairs, now chaired
by ex-USIA director Leonard Marks, also proposed a major review. The two commissions resolved on a joint inquiry and, thanks to David M. Abshire, secured Georgetown
University's Center for Strategic and International Studies as a home. The project budget came from a clutch of foundation grants. There was only one choice for chairman:
the newly retired chair of the Advisory Commission on Information, Frank Stanton,
who accepted the chairmanship on condition that the former associate director of the
USIA – Walter R. Roberts – act as his project director. The Austrian-born Roberts
had personal experience of U.S. public diplomacy dating back to the foundation of
the VOA in 1942. He provided the core vision for the inquiry. Roberts was an admirer
of the British model of public diplomacy and saw great advantages in the three-way
separation of the BBC World Service, British Council, and British Information Service

23 For full text see http://www.osce.org/docs/english/1990–1999/summits/helfa75e.htm#Anchor-
41656. For discussion see Adam B. Ulam, *Dangerous Relations: The Soviet Union in World Politics,
1970–1982*, Oxford: Oxford University Press, 1983, pp. 141–3.

at the Foreign Office. The story of the Stanton panel was – in essence – the story of its conversion to this approach.[24]

The Stanton Panel's members came principally from the two advisory commissions. Additionally, Stanton recruited Peter Krogh (Dean of the Walsh School of Foreign Service at Georgetown), who acted as the vice chairman; W. Philips Davison (professor of journalism and sociology from Columbia University); Andrew Berding (star of the Marshall Plan in Italy and the USIA's deputy director for policy and plans in the first Eisenhower administration); Kenneth Thompson of the International Council for Educational Development; and ex-diplomat and guru of public diplomacy Edmund Gullion of Tufts. Such a team could not lightly be ignored. The panel convened in April 1974.[25]

The panel began with an extensive range of interviews. Streibert, Washburn, Loomis, and Zorthian all spoke, as did the former assistant secretaries of state for educational and cultural affairs. Walter Roberts was particularly impressed by the testimony given by Kissinger and former Secretary of State Rusk, although the most influential witnesses were the PAOs and CAOs, who knew life in the field. There was one non-American witness: G. F. N. Reddaway, deputy undersecretary at the British Foreign Office. The panel also had its disappointments. Gullion seldom attended.[26]

In the early autumn, a rumor spread that Stanton planned to call for the independence of the Voice of America. As the USIA prepared its counterargument, one prominent panel member dissented. On 5 October, Leonard Marks announced his opposition to VOA independence. He argued that it would "emasculate USIA or its successor organization by removing one the most important resources in the information-cultural effort." He also claimed that the outlay of resources to create a bureaucracy for the independent VOA would be wasteful. Stanton was unconvinced.[27] By January 1975 the commission had concluded its business. On Monday, 20 January, the full panel met and Stanton presented the provisional recommendations. The next

24 Interview: Walter Roberts, 10 November 2001, Frank Stanton, 28 July 2002, Leonard Marks, 15 May 2003, and ADST oral history: Olom. A subsequent investigation of Stanton's conclusions by the Government Accounting Office, *Public Diplomacy in the Years Ahead – An Assessment of Proposals for Reorganization*, 5 May 1977, observed that the panel actively considered recommending a British Council model for U.S. cultural work "and was dissuaded from it only by the judgement that it might not be approved by the Congress," p. 21.

25 Stanton Report, chairman's preface, pp. iii–xi. The panel's executive committee comprised Frank Stanton, Peter Krogh, Walter Roberts, Andrew Berding, W. Phillips Davison; Hobart Lewis, James Michener and John Shaheen from the Information Commission; and Leonard Marks and Leo Cherne (executive director of the Research Institute of America) from the U.S. Advisory Commission on International Educational and Cultural Affairs. The full panel added Thomas B. Curtis, David Derge, Harry S Flemming, Lawrence Y. Goldberg, Rita A. Hauser, J. Leonard Reisch, and William C. Turner from the U.S. Advisory Commission on International Educational and Cultural Affairs, George Gallup from the U.S. Advisory Commission on Information, Kenneth W. Thompson, director, Higher Education for Development at the International Council for Educational Development, and Edmund A. Gullion from the Fletcher School at Tufts.

26 Interview: Roberts; Stanton Report, annex III.

27 Interview: Roberts; UoA CU box 32 file 13, memo by Marks, 7 November 1974. For views on CU–USIA merger see memo by Marks 5 November 1974.

day he briefed Keogh, telling him he wanted the USIA to return to the State Department's control. On Friday the story broke in the *Washington Post* and *Los Angeles Times*. One detail caused particular alarm. According to the press, the board created to manage RFE and RL would also run the VOA, and hence all U.S. broadcasting would be emanating from the same stable.[28] At the VOA, staff immediately recognized a threat to the Voice's credibility in any cohabitation with RFE/RL. The VOA also raised questions about whether the State Department would be able to produce policy commentaries within the time frame required by an international news broadcaster. Stanton conceded the point and all mention of a joint board with the VOA evaporated at this stage.[29]

While Stanton's team finalized the written version of the report, the USIA prepared to fight for its life and to retain control over the Voice of America. The USIA's allies in this fight included panel members Marks and Gullion. On 7 March, Gullion wrote a sustained attack of the panel in the form of an open letter to Stanton, which Senator Ed Brooke (R-MA) read into the *Congressional Record* later that month. Gullion argued that the differences between information work and regular diplomacy would be blurred by the return of the USIA to State. He predicted that the political imperative within State would soon color all information work, while information specialists would become third class citizens, behind the political and economic specialists. He saw dangers in the splitting of information, cultural, and education work and finally felt that an independent VOA would lose its utility to U.S. foreign policy.[30]

On 11 March, Stanton and Roberts personally presented the written version of the report to President Ford. The report opened with an observation of the extent to which the world had changed since the 1950s. Recent months had shown "a remarkable acceleration in the tangible interdependence of all nations." The crises in food, finance, and energy proved as much. The report noted that such pressures and the revolution in communications had collapsed the old distance between the foreign and domestic spheres. Electorates around the world were now engaged in foreign policy as never before. U.S. information had a critical role to perform. This new world needed a new public diplomacy.[31]

Stanton recognized two divergent tasks within U.S. international information: a policy information role and a cultural diplomacy role. These two areas of activity

28   Richard M. Weintraub, "Dismantling of USIA Urged," *Washington Post*, 24 January 1975, pp. A 1 & 4; Richard Reston, "Shift Urged to Return USIA to State Department Control," *Los Angeles Times*, 24 January 1975, p. 1.

29   Author's collection: Alan Heil (IBS/PC) to Vallimarescu (IBS), "The Stanton Panel Deliberations," 28 January 1975. See also Bob Wilson (D-CA) to Ford, filed at GRFL WHCF subject file FG230, box 178, Wilson to President, 8 February 1975. During the USIA budget hearings on 5 May 1975, Stanton discussed the RFE/VOA plan: "At one point in our deliberations we considered suggesting that the Voice of America be placed under a reconstituted Board for International Broadcasting. We backed off from that and decided to go the route of the independent board to keep VOA separate from RFE and RL." Hearings on S.1517, p. 215.

30   Gullion to Stanton, 7 March 1975, as read into *Congressional Record* (Senate), 54613, 20 March 1975.

31   GRFL OA 2271, Stanton Report, p. 15

operated very differently. Policy advocacy took place in the short term, whereas cultural work required the long term. Policy information needed a very close relationship with the State Department to maximize its tactical value, whereas cultural work needed to be far enough from the great diplomatic machine to maintain integrity and avoid counterproductive politicization, but still close enough to retain relevance to the broadest goals of foreign policy. Congress and the taxpayers would expect as much. Stanton saw the ideal solution to be a radical reform of the USIA. He recommended moving its advocacy work back into a State Department Office of Policy Information, subject to an Under Secretary of State for Policy Information. Domestic and overseas projection of U.S. foreign policy would now come under one roof. The longer range agency programs would join the cultural programs of the State Department in a new Information and Cultural Affairs agency (ICA) constituted along the lines of the existing Agency for International Development (AID), with its own director and budget, but subject to the authority of the Under Secretary. Stanton saw economies of scale in his proposed structure, and also suggested that the time had come for certain agency media operations – such as much film and TV work – to be replaced by material from the commercial sphere. Stanton's approach to the Voice of America acknowledged the anomalous position of the Voice with its mix of news, advocacy, and cultural functions. He saw the VOA's independence as an important starting point for credibility, but recommended that the Voice carry editorials written within the State Department and keep ex officio seats on its board for the Under Secretary and the director of the ICA. It was the most radical rethinking of U.S. information overseas since the Jackson Committee of 1953.

On the day Stanton released his report, Keogh published his counterproposal, arguing against the breakup of the USIA. "If there is to be a change," he wrote, "it would be better to consolidate all U.S. overseas information and cultural efforts in one independent agency." As the Murphy Commission on the future shape of U.S. foreign relations bureaucracy had yet to present its findings, Keogh still had everything to play for.[32] The White House took care not to commit the administration to anything prematurely.[33]

That year's appropriation hearings became the chief arena for Keogh's battle with Stanton. On 5 May, Stanton and other members of the panel presented their ideas to the Senate. Stanton bolstered his cause by reading a statement from the godfather of American foreign policy study, George F. Kennan, supporting the separation of political and cultural information activity.[34] Keogh responded by challenging the logic

32 GRFL WHCF subject files, FG230, box 178, Keogh to Scowcroft, 11 March 1975 with press release. For a fuller version see WHCF subject files, FO5, box 30, file: information exchanges, Keogh to Scowcroft, 14 April 1975 with "a critique of the Stanton Report on Information, Education and Cultural Relations." Scowcroft replied on 5 May. See also UoA CU 32/13, Keogh "A critique of the Stanton Report . . . ," 8 April 1975.
33 GRFL WHCF subject files, FG230, box 178, Scowcroft to President, Meeting with Frank Stanton, 10 March 1975.
34 USIA authorization for FY 1976, hearings before subcommittee of international operations of committee of international relations House of Representatives, 94th Congress, 1st session, hearing 15 May 1975. Kennan quote on p. 8.

of dividing cultural and political work: "How much would mutual understanding be worth if the current problems and day-to-day issues which form much of the substance of relations between countries are intentionally avoided?" Like Gullion, he questioned subsuming the USIA's information work into the State Department, where there was a danger that the foreign audience would slip as a priority. He also doubted the operational effectiveness in the field of deploying two sets of staff each responsible to their own agency, calling this "export the artificial division that now exists in Washington." Keogh questioned the ability of the private sector to replace much of the USIA's media production. He noted that much commercial film and television was unsuitable, as, "By their very nature, private sector media emphasize the special, the extreme, the controversial, the negative." As evidence, Keogh pointed to the winner of that year's Oscar for best documentary – Peter Davis' film about the Vietnam War, *Hearts and Minds* – "a stunning piece of anti-American propaganda." The USIA only produced films to plug the gaps left by the commercial world.[35]

With regard to the Voice of America, Keogh cited a rebuttal of Stanton's proposal by former VOA director Henry Loomis: "What the Voice needs is strong support in resisting undue and unwarranted pressure and yet recognizing and being responsive to constructive suggestions." Keogh predicted that the extra funding required to set up an administrative bureaucracy for an independent VOA would require a cut in services. In his conclusion Keogh presented his alternative proposal of an enhanced USIA, arguing, "One strong agency would ensure that our efforts are coordinated in support of the national interest and that the United States would have the effective public diplomacy that the times require." He rested his case with a roll call of other dissenting voices, including former Secretary of State Rusk; ex-USIA directors Marks and Rowan; Elmer Staats, Comptroller General of the United States; and senior figures in the Foreign Service Association.[36]

Initially, Stanton retained the upper hand. Senators Charles Percy (R-IL), Clifford Case (R-NJ), Dick Clark (D-IA), Stuart Symington (D-MO), and Claiborne

---

[35] GRFL WHCF subject files, FG230, box 178, Opening statement of James Keogh, director USIA, before the committee on Foreign Relations of the U.S. Senate, 5 May 1975. Examples of USIA's "gap filling" ranged from series such as USIA's *Science Report* to a touching half-hour documentary following the journey of a truck driver named Barney Barnetzke and his encounters with working men along the way: *Stout Hearts, Strong Hands*. Hollywood did not document either American technical innovation or hardworking blue-collar lives. Keogh noted that *Science Report* played on television in 79 countries. Together with *Visions*, it accounted for two-thirds of agency film output. Major commercial film purchases used by the USIA at this time included the BBC TV/Time Life series *America* by Alistair Cooke. See "*America* around the World," *Dallas Morning News*, 23 February 1975. For a note on its effectiveness see Allen C. Hansen, *USIA: Public Diplomacy in the Computer Age*, 2nd edition, New York: Praeger, 1989, p. 108. *Stout Hearts, Strong Hands* was produced and directed by Ashley Hawken; for comment see Robert Sibley, "Study of a Man Going Nowhere," *Federal Times*, 16 April 1975.

[36] GRFL WHCF subject files, FG230, box 178, Keogh opening statement to Senate FRC, 5 May 1975. He also mentioned that George Meany, President of the AFL – CIO, and Leonard Reinsch, chairman of Cox Cable Communications and a member of the Stanton panel and the Advisory Commission, dissented. See also UA CU 30/13, Loomis to Keogh, 24 February 1975, with text of Loomis letter to the *New York Times*.

Pell (D-FL) all voiced support for the panel's ideas.[37] But the White House had the power to tip the issue one way or the other and it remained detached, watching the debate from the sidelines, deferring all comment pending the results of the Murphy Commission, expected in July. In the House, Wayne Hays tried to strongarm Ford into taking a clear stand by threatening to block the USIA's budget, but the NSC maintained its neutrality. In public, at least, the State Department was similarly noncommittal. It established a task force to study Stanton's findings under Deputy Secretary of State Robert Ingersoll and declined to testify to the Murphy Commission's hearings on Stanton in April 1975, pending Ingersoll's report.[38]

The Murphy Commission reported on 27 June 1975, earlier than expected. Its key recommendations included an increased emphasis on economic issues in the NSC, with a seat for the Secretary of the Treasury. With regard to the USIA and VOA, the commission simply endorsed and incorporated Stanton's key ideas into its own recommendations. This did not settle the matter. Commission members including Senator Mike Mansfield (D-MT) and Vice President Nelson Rockefeller dissented. The NSC immediately commissioned an interagency review, to study the Murphy and Stanton recommendations.[39]

The State Department proved slow to respond to the reports. In January 1976, it belatedly supported Keogh's opposition to the Stanton plan and indicated willingness to consolidate its own cultural bureau and the USIA in the name of "policy coherence." It only remained to be seen whether Congress would make the reorganization of the USIA a condition of its budget. In any event, Congress passed over the matter in the round of hearings in May 1976, and in July the NSC closed out its file on the Stanton Commission. On 9 August, the Government Accounting Office announced its own in-depth inquiry into "the pros and cons of the Stanton Panel recommendations." The future of the USIA would now be a matter for whoever was elected to the White House in November.[40] But in one regard, at least, events overtook the merry round of reports and studies. The issue was the status of the VOA, which was thrown dramatically to the fore by events in Vietnam in April 1975.

[37] Richard M. Weintraub, "Percy Says VOA Violated Charter," *Washington Post*, 6 May 1975, p. A10.
[38] GRFL WHCF subject files, FO5, box 30, file: information exchanges, Janka (NSC) to Scowcroft, "Jim Keogh comments on Stanton Commission Report," 28 April 1975; WHCF subject files, FG230, box 178, Janka (NSC) to Kissinger, "Stanton panel on USIA," 6 May 1975; Kissinger to President Ford, "USIA and the Stanton panel," 8 May 1975.
[39] On the Murphy Commission see GRFL WHCF subject file FG354, CF, box 192, Cannon/Scowcroft to President, 26 June 1975; GRFL Council of Economic Advisors records, Paul W. MacAvoy files, box 92, file: Murphy Commission, Davis (NSC) to agency directors, 11 July 1975. For USIA/VOA see recommendations 84, 85, and 86. For dissenting views on Murphy see GRFL Richard Cheney papers, box 2, file: Commission on Organization of Govt., Rockefeller to President, 25 June 1975
[40] GRFL WHCF subject file, FG 230 box 178, Curtis to Rumsfeld, 8 September 1975; Rumsfeld to Scowcroft, 20 October 1975; Springsteen (State) to Scowcroft, 5 November 1975; Scowcroft to Cheney, 22 December 1975; for interim comments see Max L. Friedersdorf to Kopp (USIA), 24 January 1975, and on the file closure see de Sibour (NSC) to Mcfarlane (NSC), 27 July 1976. On the Stanton debate and the GAO report see also Government Accounting Office, *Public Diplomacy in the Years Ahead – An Assessment of Proposals for Reorganization*, 5 May 1977.

3) THE END IN VIETNAM AND THE VOA CHARTER, 1975–76

The Stanton debate coincided with a major crisis in relations between the Voice and the USIA. In late 1974, *Time* magazine reported how the USIA had rejected a proposal from the VOA's Munich bureau for a series on young workers in the Soviet bloc on the grounds that "it would have been offensive to the governments involved. . . ." A VOA news report speculating on the imminent resumption of U.S. arms shipments to Yugoslavia had been killed by the embassy in Belgrade as inappropriate for an "official network." At the same time, the Area Director for Eastern Europe, Jock Shirley, reinforced a rule from 1967 requiring VOA correspondents to consult the relevant U.S. embassy before undertaking a particular story. Correspondents complained of censorship, but news from South Vietnam triggered a full-blown crisis.[41]

In the course of 1974, the Communists had made significant gains across South Vietnam. Ambassador Graham Martin ordered USIS Saigon to downplay stories of their penetrating the Mekong Delta and the failure of the ARVN to retake territory, lest this deter aid to Saigon. The new Minister Counselor for Public Affairs, Alan Carter, reluctantly complied. Skirmishes on the border, activity on the Ho Chi Minh trail, and the forward deployment of the North Vietnamese air force all augured ill. As the year ended, the post prepared to appeal for major aid to Saigon.[42] In January 1975, the North Vietnamese launched a major offensive. As the ARVN fell back, the embassy searched desperately for emotive news of a successful defensive action by the South Vietnamese or evidence of Communist atrocities. The embassy continued to talk up the South Vietnamese government. It is unclear how many people abroad believed the reassurance, but some in the mission certainly got caught up in their own story. As late as 1 April the embassy refused to begin significant steps to evacuate Americans and their South Vietnamese colleagues. Ambassador Martin worried that planning an evacuation could precipitate it. When he belatedly began to plan, Martin did not share his thoughts with such outlying elements of the mission as the USIS.[43]

On 10 April, President Ford appealed to Congress to send massive aid to South Vietnam. Their vote was scheduled for 19 April. In the streets of Saigon, people latched onto the impending vote as the likely trigger for a U.S. evacuation. Vietnamese began to form lines at American offices to lay claim to passage out of the country. In an effort to restore calm, Martin and Carter prepared a broadcast, which aired on the night of 17 April, in the form of a staged interview. Speaking though an interpreter, Carter answered questions about American intentions with lawyer-like precision. The wording of the interviewer's questions enabled Carter to deny linkage between the Congressional vote and the evacuation, while sounding as though he was completely

41 "The Press: Muted Voice of America," *Time*, 16 December 1974.
42 Interview: Carter, 29 June 2004.
43 Alan Dawson, *55 Days: The Fall of South Vietnam*, Englewood Cliffs, NJ: Prentice-Hall, 1977, pp. 156, 204, 229–31; Frank Snepp, *Decent Interval*, New York: Random House, 1977, pp. 85, 300, 305, 329–30. The chief defect of Dawson's account is that it overestimates the influence of the USIS within the embassy. The ambassador took the lead in the post's representation of events in South Vietnam.

denying that any evacuation was planned. "There is absolutely no truth at all, not a shred of truth to this rumor," Carter declared. Vietnamese television repeated the interview on two subsequent nights. Martin conceded to Kissinger that the broadcast was "thin gruel at best," but might be "enough to soften the blow" if Congress rejected the President's call for emergency aid.[44]

The Voice of America did its best to cover the mounting crisis with an expanded corps in Vietnam. Its coverage was rather too complete for some listeners. On 4 April, President Thieu had attacked the VOA (and the BBC) for spreading Communist-inspired stories of South Vietnamese defeats.[45] On 5 April, Ambassador Martin demanded that the VOA rein in its coverage. Shortly thereafter, VOA journalists received an oral order from the USIA front office not to discuss the question of a possible evacuation of Americans from Vietnam, or quote anyone talking about the subject. The VOA's White House correspondent, Philomena Jurey, was asked to delete references to a possible evacuation from her reports on a television interview by Senator Jackson and a speech by President Ford. On 14 April, the interagency task force on Vietnam explicitly limited VOA coverage of the evacuation issue to "official statements of the White House and Departments of State and Defense, and congressional action (e.g. a vote) until further notice."[46] For the respective heads of news and current affairs at the VOA, Bernie Kamenske and Alan Heil, this ruling was a betrayal of both the Voice charter and America's Vietnamese allies. The task force did not lift the gag on the VOA until 26 April. In the interim Kamenske insisted on posting a note about the ban on the newsroom's "slot board" so that the control would be explicit. He and his colleagues were now convinced that the VOA charter needed the protection of law.[47]

Unlike Ambassador Martin, the Voice of America moved early to evacuate its Vietnamese staff and their families. They flew out on Saturday 26 and Sunday 27 April. American correspondents Wayne Corey and Steve Thompson remained to

44 GRFL NSC Convenience files, box 7, file: Martin testimony support 3, Martin to Kissinger, 17 April 1975; the archive documentation is at minor variance with Dawson, *55 Days*, p. 277–9. Carter eventually saw Martin's memo at the Ford library and was shocked by the cynicism in the embassy approach.
45 Dawson, *55 Days*, p. 220.
46 Hearings before the Committee on Foreign Relations, United States Senate, 94th Congress, 1st session on S 1517, 5 May 1975, pp. 245–8. Martin's cable is noted in Heil, *Voice of America*, p. 168. For Jurey's own account of the censorship see Jurey, *A Basement Seat to History*, pp. 88–91.
47 GRFL Ron Nessen papers, general subject files, box 13, file: Indo-China/Saigon Evacuations, "VOA crackdown on U.S. evacuation stories," script by JWR, 15 April 1975; Interviews: Heil, 29 November 1995, and Kamenske, 6 December 1995; also Heil, *Voice of America*, 168–9. Richard M. Weintraub, "Percy Says VOA Violated Charter," *Washington Post*, 6 May 1975, p. A10. VOA staff informed Senator Percy that a remark by President Ford in a speech at Tulane University on 23 April that the "the Vietnam War is finished as far as America is concerned" was suppressed under the policy. Keogh produced multiple VOA scripts in which Ford's quotation was used and it emerged that the omission was made in one report only while waiting for the President to actually use the stunning remark that staff had noticed in the advanced text. For Keogh's rebuttal see GRFL Nessen papers, box 13, file: Indo-China/Saigon Evacuations, Keogh to Percy, 6 May 1975 and Hearings before the Committee on Foreign Relations, United States Senate, 94th Congress, 1st session on S 1517, 5 May 1975, pp. 248–53.

cover events as they unfolded.[48] On 28 April, Alan Carter also resolved to evacuate the 185 Vietnamese from the USIS, the Ministry of Information, the Saigon
embassy, and their families. He found the airport under attack and closed.[49] In the
small hours of 29 April, Martin finally agreed to a full evacuation, and Carter and the
four American USIS staffers were ordered to the main compound to leave by helicopter. Carter initially refused to go and remained on the phone well into the night
of 30 April, trying to secure escape for his staff. He failed. They were again turned
back at the airport. In the final count only one-third were evacuated by the United
States.[50]

Carter left Vietnam on the next to last helicopter to take off from the roof of the
U.S. embassy in the small hours of 30 April. Ambassador Martin left shortly thereafter.
The evacuation ended two and one-half decades of American involvement in Vietnam.
Much of America's activity in Vietnam had been motivated by thoughts of maintaining
U.S. international credibility. Now, that credibility lay in ruins. The United States had
poured vast sums into psychological operations in South Vietnam. The agency's best
men had sweated in the cause, and counted victories along the way, but to no avail.
As Carter's helicopter beat its way into the sky, he looked down on surging crowds lit
by burning buildings. Gun flashes and explosions spangled the city like the twinkling
of some perverse carnival. "There," he declared aloud, "are all the hearts and minds
we said we'd won."[51]

*

The official manipulation of the VOA's coverage of the last days of Saigon
appalled Senator Charles Percy (R-IL). In May he wrote to Keogh suggesting that
the VOA charter be incorporated into law.[52] Parallel attempts by the U.S. embassy in
Phnom Penh to force the VOA to downplay student demonstrations back in March

48   Heil, *Voice of America*, p. 319; Heil to author, 25 June 2004. The VOA's Vietnamese staff arrived
     in Washington via the Philippines and Guam on 3 May. Bernie Kamenske and his assistant Janie
     Fritzman organized the staff of News and Current Affairs to provide food and shelter in their own
     homes. Fritzman and a team from the newsroom worked to fix up an empty house owned by a local
     church as a further stopgap until proper accommodation could be arranged.
49   Interview: Carter, Dawson, *55 Days*, pp. 317–18.
50   Interview: Carter, Snepp, *Decent Interval*, pp. 523, 544; *55 Days*, pp. 344–5; GRFL WHCF subject
     file FG 230, box 178, President to Keogh, 10 February 1976. Accounts of what happened to the
     remaining USIS staff are fragmentary. One eight-year veteran of the USIS told journalists that a bus
     had come for them at their compound around noon, but had been turned back by guards at the airport
     and blocked from nearing the embassy by crowds. Now her relatives had asked her to stay away from
     their home because of her connection to the departing ally. Carter's own investigations suggested that
     around a third of USIS staff (and a similar proportion of other Vietnamese employed by the embassy)
     had been evacuated by the U.S. government, a further third had gotten out on their own by sea, but a
     final third had either failed or declined to escape. Carter knew that some of his staff felt betrayed and
     worked to offset his own sense of having failed them by taking duty with the White House Task Force
     on Vietnamese Refugees. He spent much of the next year administering a refugee center at Indian
     Town Gap in Pennsylvania. He and another USIS officer named Elinor Green received Presidential
     Certificates of Appreciation for their service.
51   Interview: Carter; Snepp, *Decent Interval*, pp. 523, 545.
52   Keogh's positive reply to this is reproduced in GRFL Marsh files, box 39, "transition reports 1977,
     USIA," USIA transition briefing book, December 1976, pp. 178–81.

had enraged Representative Bella Abzug (D-NY), who had been in Cambodia at that time and noticed the distortion. Both Percy and Abzug were now determined to rescue the VOA charter. Abzug's interest in the VOA would prove significant. A champion of radical and feminist causes, she was not afraid of a fight. She began by investigating VOA coverage of Watergate. She summoned Kamenske to her office and "sliced and diced" him for not doing more to cover Watergate. Even so, Abzug recognized the potential of VOA news, if only it could be freed from the policy makers.[53]

While Abzug and Percy laid their plans, VOA journalists were working on a story that underlined the station's value. Wayne Corey, one of the VOA correspondents lately plucked from Saigon, remained in the region to cover the collapse of Cambodia. Piecing together snippets of information gleaned from traumatized escapees, Corey slowly built up an appalling picture of mass murder, deportation, and starvation at the hands of the Khmer Rouge regime. The Cambodia story became a regular subject of VOA news. In September 1975, Corey reported that over one million Cambodians were dead or missing. Kamenske backed the story over the objections of the USIA's East Asian experts and colleague Cliff Groce who doubted Corey's sources. Kamenske knew that the wartime VOA had done little to cover the Holocaust and was determined that Cambodia would be different. "VOA," he said, had "a duty to be the alarm bell of civilization."[54]

Abzug and Percy resolved to turn the VOA charter into law by amending the USIA's appropriation for financial year 1977. Their bipartisan partnership helped their cause. The text of the VOA charter written into the bill differed slightly from the 1960 version, dropping, at Bernie Kamenske's suggestion, the description of the Voice as an "official radio," in order to remove a major justification for the intrusion of officialdom into news. Although there were no obvious penalties for flouting the charter law, it added great moral weight, and Kamenske theorized that anyone who actively planned to break it could be prosecuted for conspiracy.[55] On 12 July 1976, President Ford signed the Foreign Relations Authorization Act, Public Law 94–350, and the VOA charter became law. Staff soon noted a dramatic tailing off in attempts by posts to interfere with its coverage. But others in the bureaucracy still disputed the right of the VOA to cover the news objectively. More trouble lay ahead.[56]

In August 1975, Kamenske approached the White House to request an impromptu interview between Philomena Jurey and the President in Vail, Colorado. Margita White

53 Interview: Kamenske, 6 December 1995; Heil, *Voice of America*, p. 175. For a profile of Abzug see Laura Mansnerus, "Bella Abzug, 77, Congresswoman and Founding Feminist is Dead," *New York Times*, 1 April 1998, p. 1.
54 Interview: Kamenske, 6 December 1995; Heil, *Voice of America*, pp. 172–3. For a short anthology of early U.S. press reports of Khmer Rouge atrocities in Cambodia see GRFL Nessen papers, general subject files, box 14, file: IndoChina/Cambodia, "The Khmer Communists systematic use of execution and terror: Why Cambodians flee from the Khmer Rouge," c. March 1975. In fact Corey had underestimated the death toll in Cambodia (which approximated 1.6 million).
55 Interview: Kamenske, 6 December 1995; Heil, 29 November 1995; Heil, *Voice of America*, pp. 174–6.
56 Richard M. Weintraub, "Voice of America – Its Own," *Washington Post*, 1 August 1976, pp. A1 & A14; Interview: Alan Heil, 29 November 1995.

in the USIA policy office warned the White House to decline on the grounds that "Philomena Jurey would be asking some tough questions."[57] White House press secretary Ron Nessen protested the request and deputy director Gene Kopp called the VOA, objecting to Kamenske's failure to clear his request with the agency. Kopp threatened the news director with dismissal, at which point Kamenske threatened to go public. When the senior USIA officer at the Voice warned Kopp that the entire newsroom would strike if Kamenske left, Kopp backed down, but USIA pressure on the VOA continued.[58] In September, the USIA forbade the VOA to broadcast commentaries on the death of Mao Tse Tung, restricted reports of unrest in Poland, and ordered the toning down of programs marking the twentieth anniversary of the Hungarian uprising. The State Department's bureau of African affairs barred VOA journalists from traveling to Transkei, Namibia, or Rhodesia. Giddens declared, "We have even less freedom to deal with hard news today than we did four years ago."[59]

The most sustained challenge to the charter came around VOA coverage of the Middle East. Three incidents broke that autumn. First the State Department insisted that the VOA withdraw its Lebanon correspondent, Doug Roberts, because he had entered a combat zone closed to "US officials." Then the U.S. ambassador to Cairo blocked the establishment of a VOA bureau in that city.[60] But the real trouble came when the Voice correspondent in Jerusalem, Charles Weiss, telephoned the PLO to verify an alleged Israeli patrol boat attack on a vessel carrying the Lebanese leftist politician Kamal Jumblatt and the hijacking of a Dutch airliner.[61] The U.S. ambassador to Israel, Malcolm Toon, complained that Weiss had violated the ban on contact between the U.S. government and the PLO. His PAO, Stan Moss, informed Weiss that he must now either file all his reports via the embassy or relocate to Athens. Keogh issued a directive insisting that the embassy's ban on contact with the PLO applied to the VOA. In Washington, Bernie Kamenske was incandescent. He saw an obvious threat to the credibility of the Voice. He had no hesitation in running Weiss' piece and thereby became the new focus of official rage. As anger on both sides mounted, the full story leaked to the *Washington Post*. Keogh blamed Kamenske for the

57 Interview: Kamenske, 6 December 1995; GRFL WHCF subject file TR 42–1, box 61; Kamenske to Nessen, 5 August 1975; FG230–1, box 178, White to Nessen, 6 August 1975.
58 Interviews: Kamenske, 6 December 1995 and 10 April 1998. Kamenske intended that Jurey ask Ford about his visit to Poland and certain ambiguous remarks he had made on his return. Given the later difficulties of the President in answering debate questions on Poland, Kamenske mused that the President would have done much better if he had had practice on that question months earlier from the VOA.
59 Graham Hovey, "New Effort under Way to Dismantle U.S. Information Agency, Giving Voice of America Independence," *New York Times*, 16 January 1977, p. 13; Alan Heil, *Voice of America*, p. 185. Also author's collection: Heil to Giddens, eyes only: Censorship of VOA reporting and output, 18 November 1976. The attempted manipulation of the Poland story is discussed in *Voice of America at the Crossroads: A Panel Discussion on the Appropriate Role of the VOA*, The Media Institute: Washington, D.C., 1982, pp. 37–8. The incident led to the removal of Serban Vallimarescu as deputy director of the VOA.
60 Richard M. Weintraub, "US Officials Back Ambassador on VOA Reporting Curb," *Washington Post*, 27 October 1976, p. A5.
61 Charles Weiss to author, 22 April 2004; for press account see "Palestinian Hijackers Free 80 Hostages in Cyprus Surrender," *Times* (London), 6 September 1976, p. 1.

leak and wanted him fired, but the new deputy director of the VOA, Hans N. Tuch, demurred, fearing a newsroom strike. On 13 October, Keogh cabled Ambassador Toon, repudiating Kameske's views and assuring him that he had ruled that all VOA correspondents "must conform to U.S. government policies" and the local authority of the ambassador. When news of this cable reached Senator Percy, he immediately announced plans to legislate for full VOA independence.[62]

4) REHUMANIZING AMERICA
THE BICENTENNIAL, 1976

In the midst of the debate over the future, one important thing went right: the international celebration of the two hundredth anniversary of the Declaration of Independence. It did not happen overnight. The USIA began preparing for the bicentennial in March 1966.[63] In July 1966, Congress established an American Revolution Bicentennial Commission (ARBC). The commission convened in earnest only in 1969, drawing together legislators, business leaders, academics, and ex officio members such as the Secretaries of Defense and State and the Librarian of Congress. Leonard Marks declined a seat for the USIA. Harold F. Schneidman, director of the USIA's Information Center Service (ICS), acted as the agency's liaison and also served on the Federal Agency Bicentennial Task Force. Mildred Marcy, from the office of policy, served as the USIA's bicentennial planning officer.[64]

On 4 July 1970, the ARBC unveiled its proposal for a "Festival of Freedom" for the entire period up to and including 1976. The festival would have three parts: "Heritage '76" ("a nationwide summons to recall our heritage"); "Open House U.S.A." (eventually retitled "Festival U.S.A.," a plan to encourage travel within and to the United States); and "Horizons '76" (looking toward a better future). Overseas considerations were peripheral, but the commission noted that as part of "Heritage '76," the USIA proposed to work with foreign governments "preparing exhibits displaying historical relationships between the United States and other nations." The agency would also have a role in the international dimension of "Open House U.S.A." The ARBC imagined a special effort in the international visitor program. Finally, "Horizons '76" included a national and international effort to promote the "free exchange of ideas," dubbed "Communications '76."[65]

---

62 Interview: Kamenske, 6 December 1995; ADST oral history, Tuch; Richard M. Weintraub, "US Officials Back Ambassador on VOA Reporting Curb," *Washington Post*, 27 October 1976, p. A5; also GRFL WHCF subject file FG 230–1 (VOA), box 178, John Salisbury (RTNDA) to President, 22 October 1976. Also Senator Charles Percy, news release, 30 November 1976, document made available by Kamenske.

63 Dizard, *Inventing Public Diplomacy*, p. 114: The USIA bicentennial committee recommended framing the anniversary around the relevance of American democracy to the rest of the world.

64 For a summary of the USIA's input see NA RG306 A1 (1066,) USIA historical collection subject files, box 142, file: Bicentennial Planning 1973, Towery to Keogh/Kopp, 2 March 1973. For correspondence re the Task Force see GRFL WHCF subject file, FG 230 box 178, Marsh (White House) to Keogh, 28 July 1975.

65 NA RG306 A1 (1066) USIA historical collection subject files, box 142, file: Bicentennial Report, 1970, American Revolution Bicentennial Commission, Report to the President, 4 July 1970.

The agency's plan began in rather pedestrian fashion with talk of the USIA advising the ARBC on foreign opinion in relation to bicentennial events, brokering exhibit loans from overseas for domestic bicentennial displays, and presenting the key domestic events and media productions to overseas audiences. The plan only came alive in the passages in which the USIA projected a range of programs of its own. The agency spoke of creating films, magazines, VOA broadcasts, and touring exhibits and even bicentennial materials for English language teaching, but above all the agency planned to boost the discipline of American studies by building library research collections around the world.[66] The agency found it difficult to isolate the likely costs of these bicentennial plans, as much relied on adjusting existing operations. Early projections estimated $15 million.[67]

During the course of 1971, the agency received its big bicentennial commission from the ARBC: to design, build, and operate an international exhibit on the "Age of Jefferson." The agency planned to open this show in Paris in the autumn of 1974 and then take versions on the road. The USIA contracted designers Charles and Ray Eames (veterans of the Moscow exhibit of 1959) for the project. Charles Eames' reluctance to allow the USIA oversight of the design process came close to sinking the project, but he successfully persuaded the agency to broaden his canvas to incorporate Benjamin Franklin and a broader sweep of eighteenth-century life. The project became "The World of Franklin and Jefferson."[68]

The process of bicentennial planning at the USIA saw a flirtation with some radical ideas. In 1972 the USIA commissioned a professor of history at Yale, Robin W. Winks, to consider the agency's training needs in the run-up to festivities. Winks had a long-standing relationship with the cultural program. Between 1969 and 1971 he had served as cultural affairs officer in London. In September 1972 he outlined a Bicentennial Preparation Program of seminars to direct staff away from the now outmoded notion that "the American Experience is a unique one."[69] Winks also served as chairman of the USIA/CU Ad Hoc Bicentennial Planning Committee. The first meeting in September 1972 recommended that the bicentennial program seek to promote dialogue with other nations and that USIS staff be retrained in a "comparative approach" to American experience.[70]

[66] NA RG306 A1 (1066) USIA historical collection subject files, box 142, file: Bicentennial Planning, 1970–72, "Plan for USIA's role in the American Revolution Bicentennial Celebration," 30 March 1970.

[67] NA RG306 A1 (1066) USIA historical collection subject files, box 142, file: Bicentennial Planning 1973, Towery to Keogh/Kopp, 2 March 1973.

[68] NA RG306 A1 (1066) USIA historical collection subject files, box 142, file: Bicentennial Planning 1973, Towery to Keogh/Kopp, 2 March 1973 and file: Exhibits – American Bicentennial, 1976, Paul (ICS/ED) to Schneidman (ICS), 26 February 1973. Mike Schneider to author, 19 May 2004.

[69] UoA CU box 165 file 40, Winks to Marcy and Snyder (USIA), Bi-Centennial Preparation Program, September 1972. For an obituary of Winks see http://www.yale.edu/opa/newsr/03–04–08–04.all.html.

[70] NA RG306 A1 (1066) USIA historical collection subject files, box 142, file: Bicentennial Planning, 1970–72, Winks to Richardson (ASoS, CU) and Loomis (D.Dir., USIA), "Summary and Recommendations of initial meeting of the USIA/CU Ad Hoc Bicentennial Planning Committee," 11 September

Although not reshaping its training on the lines suggested by Winks, the USIA did at least upgrade its approach to American studies. A six- to eight-week "American Experience" course became a requirement for all agency foreign service officers before assignment abroad. The agency also resolved that all of its university training assignments until 1976 should be in American studies "to fill the agency's needs during the bicentennial period (and thereafter) for officers genuinely well-informed on America's past and present." It therefore fell to the thirty-five or so officers to bring the entire agency's approach to American studies up to date in time for the anniversary year.[71] Although agency staff worked tone down the flag-waving in some White House statements around the bicentennial,[72] a certain triumphalism remained in the USIA's plans. A policy office paper from November 1972 called for the United States to show "our strength and dynamism" and say "Folks, you ain't seen nothin' yet!"[73]

In the spring of 1973, the Information Center Service presented its detailed plans for marking the bicentennial at the USIA's 190 libraries. The ICS planner, Michael Schneider, insisted that the USIA's bicentennial work had to be relevant to the concerns of its audience. His strategy included an analysis of priority countries. Western Europe figured especially prominently because of ethnic ties. Other key audiences included Japan, Israel, and India, where the American Revolution was seen as a key moment in the emergence of democracy. The ICS planned to take the opening of the Franklin and Jefferson exhibit in Paris at the end of 1974 as its starting gun. Plans now also included a round of conferences to promote American studies and rebuild links between U.S. academics and overseas colleagues.[74]

1972. Other recommendations included dedicated bicentennial officers for Paris and London to serve from 1973 to 1976.

71 NA RG306 A1 (1066) USIA historical collection subject files, box 142, file: Bicentennial Planning 1973, Towery to Keogh/Kopp, 2 March 1973.

72 The draft for President Nixon's "Invitation to the World" speech urging visitors from overseas to come and participate in the bicentennial, delivered on 4 July 1972, required substantial reworking by the USIA. Reviewing a draft, the USIA's bicentennial officer Mildred Marcy warned, "Many of the words chosen to convey the invitation smack of overwriting and self-glorification, which is fine for an American audience but chauvinistic and boastful to non-Americans – 'jubilee,' 'countdown,' 'throw a party' (when the ARBC has been trying to avoid the birthday party syndrome), 'miraculously successful experiment in human freedom' (this is not always self-evident to foreign audiences, nor even to some Americans), 'respect for one another as brother *men*' (why not 'fellow human beings'), use commemoration rather than 'celebration' when possible." Marcy also steered the White House away from the sentence "African energy helped to build the Old South," which she considered "will certainly alienate many American blacks, and remind Africans of the American heritage of slavery." NA RG306 A1 (1066) USIA historical collection subject files, box 142, file: Bicentennial Planning, 1970–72, Monsen (drafted by Marcy) to John K. Andrews (White House), 29 June 1972.

73 NA RG306 A1 (1066) USIA historical collection subject files, box 142, file: Bicentennial Planning, 1970–72, Drucker (IOP/C) to Hoffman (IOP), "Bicentennial Planning Paper." 13 November 1972. This triumphalism was noted by Richard Arndt, the CAO in Rome, who would have preferred Winks' approach had it been offered. Arndt experienced USIA's bicentennial as "a piece of unidirectional show-biz, aimed at reminding the world how remarkable the U.S. was." In Rome, the bicentennial would be celebrated by two major gifts, both from the State Department's CU: a show of U.S. paintings and a visit by the Los Angeles Symphony. A microfiche collection of American studies materials was promised to Italy by USIA but was later withdrawn. Arndt to author, 15 May 2006.

74 NA RG306 A1 (1066) USIA historical collection subject files, box 142, file: Bicentennial Planning, 1973. Schneider (ICS) to Schneidman (ICS), "An Outline for ICS Bicentennial Programming," 12 July 1973.

*

In 1974, the Bicentennial Commission became the American Revolution Bicentennial Administration. There was now much in its program that served the cause of international communication, including numerous initiatives to bring foreign performers to the United States.[75] The initiative in the field of American studies had now passed to the State Department's Bureau of Educational and Cultural Affairs, which launched an American Studies Bicentennial Project. Based at Yale, this project eventually became known as the Bicentennial Committee on International Conferences of Americanists (or BCICA, which they pronounced *bi-seeka*). Robin Winks directed proceedings, along with a former Fulbright lecturer in Poland and ex-chairman of American studies at San Diego State College, Robert Forrey. The project moved from a survey of American studies around the world to a series of five regional seminars, held in early 1975 in Salzburg, Austria; Fujinomiya, Japan; Shiraz, Iran; Abidjan, Ivory Coast; and San Antonio, Texas. Five hundred scholars from 100 countries participated. The African meeting was the first conference on American studies to have been held on that continent. BCICA planned a five-day international conference to be held in Washington in June 1976, which like the seminars would cover the Revolution, approaches to American studies, and the cross-cultural impact of the United States. Single-country workshops on American studies planned for 1976 and 1977 would disseminate the ideas from the previous conferences. Finally, there would be a program of "supplementary activities" including the creation of inventories of American-related manuscripts and historical sites located overseas.[76]

BCICA walked a difficult path. Some scholars of American studies in the United States saw it as a cynical attempt to hijack international American studies for a government agenda, but plenty got on board for the ride. Forrey noted the trepidation of the European scholars who attended the opening conference in Salzberg in April 1975. "Some," he recalled, "acted like virgins in a house of ill-repute." The conference's first session was marked by a public protest from a British writer, Andrew Sinclair, against American foreign policy, while American studies guru Leo Marx of MIT denounced American exceptionalism. Forrey himself tried to steer the "future of American studies" session toward a discussion of the significance of U.S. government funding but found this path blocked by established European scholars. Disillusioned by the willingness of colleagues to trade their integrity for a conference trip, Forrey quit BCICA. Winks completed the conference cycle and felt certain that BCICA had both fostered new links between Americanists around the world and opened the domestic American studies community to the work of their international colleagues.[77]

---

[75] NA RG306 A1 (1066) USIA historical collection subject files, box 142, file: Bicentennial Legislation, 1973–6. State Dept. to all posts, A-5052, 20 June 1974.

[76] UoA CU box 165 file 30, American Studies Bicentennial Project, (CU) April 1974; also GRFL John Marsh files 1974–7, box 71, file: USIA report, *USIA and the Bicentennial*, report ca. 7 April 1976.

[77] Forrey to author, 4 May 2004; for accounts of Salzburg see Alan F. Davis, "The Politics of American Studies," *American Quarterly* (John Hopkins University Press), 42, 3 (1989), 353–74 and Dennis Donoghue, "Thoughts After Salzburg," *Times Literary Supplement*, 13 June 1975, p. 658. A combined

The USIA responded to the bicentennial initiative in American studies by creating guidelines for its field staff to use when promoting the subject. The core rationale was "to help lay the foundation for objective awareness of the development and diversity of American culture." The agency warned staff to be realistic, to prioritize, to "avoid competition with on going academic programs," and to invest in library resources and maintaining academic credibility. The agency saw its work as pump priming. Posts were urged to "work toward the day when they will no longer have to promote or support American Studies" but the discipline would flourish of its own accord. Finally, the agency established an "American Studies Support Staff" within the Information Center Service to advise on curriculum, liaise with the academic world, and provide support for American Fulbright scholars teaching American subjects overseas. All posts received details of this initiative in early 1975.[78]

On 10 January 1975 – a little later than originally planned – the World of Franklin and Jefferson opened at the Grand Palais in Paris. The show covered the 120 years of American history from Franklin's birth in 1706 to Jefferson's death in 1826. It occupied an impressive 7,500 square feet. After setting the scene with contemporaneous paintings, it laid out the events leading up to the revolution and beyond in a great timeline. Visitors walked into a large hall where monumental pillars presented the great contemporaries of Franklin and Jefferson in words and pictures; they moved on between Washington, Adams, and Paine and Europeans such as Burke, Lafayette, and Kosciusko. Artifacts included an exquisite orrery of the solar system to illustrate the order that the founders of the Republic wished to bring to the realm of government, Franklin's glass harmonica, and a plow blade handcrafted by Jefferson. An inner chamber presented the role of Franklin and Jefferson in three key documents: the Declaration of Independence, the Constitution, and the Bill of Rights. A final room dealt with "Jefferson and the West," looking at Lewis and Clarke and the Louisiana Purchase.[79] After rave reviews in Paris, [80] the show moved to the National Museum in Warsaw and then to an acclaimed season at the British Museum in London before touring New York, Chicago, and San Francisco in 1976. After a spirited campaign led by the Deputy Assistant Secretary of State for Inter-American Affairs, Bill Luers, the show also visited Mexico City.[81]

volume of proceedings appeared as Robin W. Winks (ed.), *Other Voices, Other Views: An International Collection of Essays from the Bicentennial*, Westport, CT: Greenwood, 1978, esp. 3–15.

78 UoA CU box 165 file 41, Keogh to PAO, 21 February 1975 with guidelines attached. The guidelines drew a distinction between American studies (with a lower case "s"), which could mean both single-discipline and interdisciplinary study of the United States), and American Culture Studies, which the agency used internally to designate interdisciplinary work. The USIA made no attempt to promote this distinction among the academic community.

79 NA RG306 A1 (1066) USIA historical collection subject files, box 142, file: Exhibits – American Bicentennial, 1976, Press Pack for The World of Franklin and Jefferson.

80 Mary Russell, "America's Bicentenary," *Vogue* (London), 1 September 1975. A press cuttings file may be found in NA RG306 A1 (1066) USIA historical collection subject files, box 142, file: USIA policy: Bicentennial 1976.

81 The London post sharpened the show a little by cutting back the Jefferson and West material, which they saw as extraneous to the main purpose of the show. Interview: Mike Pistor. Mike Schneider to author, 19 May 2004.

USIA initiatives in the bicentennial year itself included the distribution of a display called "Life, Liberty and the Pursuit of Happiness." Produced in seven languages and in an edition of 1,700, this show told the story of the young republic and introduced the core concepts of the American way. In Germany it opened in 400 venues. Larger exhibits included a photographic show entitled "Reflections: Images of America," which visited twenty posts around the world. The agency also presented a series of other bicentennial projects with speakers, publications, videotape, and exhibit components. The indefatigable Robin Winks coordinated an exhibit called "America in Retrospect and Prospect" for fifteen European posts.[82] A Bicentennial Partnerships program enabled the agency to provide matching funds for worthy initiatives around the world. Grants under this scheme advanced American studies in Morocco, Poland, and elsewhere and contributed $30,000 to the Bodleian Library in Oxford to purchase a Bicentennial Collection, which the London *Times* reported would "contain travelers' diaries and journals and writings on British and American culture" and books on "the development of the English language in both countries." Michael Schneider of the ICS thought the scheme especially valuable because it built institutional cooperation on the basis of shared interests and reciprocity and was not "just another example of American largesse."[83]

The Motion Picture and Television Service (IMV) produced material to support the bicentennial touring exhibits and trawled through the output of state film commissions and commercial producers to identify existing bicentennial films suitable for export. IMV also launched projects of its own. A series of half-hour programs called *Century III* explored areas of the future, while a series of one-hour profiles called *Reflections* invited distinguished Americans such as Margaret Meade to look back over their life and work. The agency commissioned a series of student films on bicentennial themes. The USIA also obtained special legislation to allow for the domestic release of some of the USIA's back catalog, including *The Numbers Start with the River*, a treatment of a small Iowa town, *Echoes*, which dramatized themes from U.S. history through the monuments in Washington, DC, and two student films: *Rendezvous*, recreating the life of pioneer fur trappers in Wyoming, and *200*, a psychedelic three-minute animated tour through the symbols of American culture. The climax of the Motion Picture Service's effort was *Salute by Satellite*, a program of live feeds and pre-recorded spots covering the bicentennial festivities around the United States on 4 and 5 July, including the magnificent fireworks display over the Mall in Washington.[84]

---

[82] GRFL John Marsh files 1974–77, box 71, file: USIA report, *USIA and the Bicentennial*, report ca. 7 April 1976; Interview: Mike Schneider. Smaller multimedia projects included "Performing Arts in America: A Retrospective," "American Literature," and "Blacks in American Society," which drew on a National Portrait Gallery exhibit called "The Black Presence in the Era of the American Revolution" and was made available to all African posts.

[83] Mike Schneider to author, 19 May 2004; "$30,000 U.S. Grant for Bodleian Book Collection," London *Times*, 12 March 1977, p. 3.

[84] GRFL John Marsh files 1974–77, box 71, file: USIA report, *USIA and the Bicentennial*, report ca. 7 April 1976; Jerry Scott, "The Bicentennial on Film and VTR: A Report from IMV," *USIA World*, 9,

VOA coverage of the Bicentennial began on 1 June 1974 with "Bicentennial Diary," a daily two-minute "on this day" spot covering events from 1 June 1774 to 4 July 1776. The Voice also ran "Bicentennial Profile" and "Bicentennial Post-card," short pieces introducing historical characters and sites, and profiles of every state and major immigrant groups. Longer programs included "Two Hundred Years Ago Tonight," a cycle of plays telling the story of the Revolution. More reflective programs included "American Perspectives," in which prominent Americans – culled from the VOA archives – discussed the past, present, and future of their country, and "American Issues Forum," a monthly discussion program funded by the Bicentennial Administration and the National Endowment for the Humanities. [85]

Individual posts hosted numerous local events. Latin American posts reported over 400 events across their region.[86] In London, the USIA helped the National Maritime Museum, Greenwich, to mount a major exhibit on the British side of the American Revolution. Eager schoolboys happily carried away free agency leaflets introducing American History.[87] In West Germany, the USIA mounted a conference on 200 years of German–American Relations, and an exhibition, "Two Hundred Years of American Painting," assembled by the Baltimore Museum of Art, opened in Bonn in July to much critical acclaim.[88] In the Eastern bloc, historians toured Russia lecturing on "the significance of the American Revolution." Other exhibitions included "American Industry: A Bicentennial Survey" at the Leipzig spring fair in March 1976, and "America – The land, the people, and the idea," which ran in Moscow from 12 November to 24 December in exchange for a reciprocal Soviet exhibition in Los Angeles to mark the sixtieth anniversary of the Russian revolution. The exhibit in Moscow drew an astonishing 10,000 visitors a day, each of whom left clutching a goody bag containing a bicentennial badge, translations of the Declaration of Independence and Constitution, a short history of the United States, and a record of some American music. Jim Keogh recalled with regret that the American public had no idea about this or any other element of the USIA's bicentennial work, though a bomb threat against the Moscow exhibition provided a small window of coverage as 1976 drew to a close.[89]

1 (July 1975), filed in NA RG306 – 01- 1 (USIA historical branch), items 15, box 29 (movies); GRFL Kuropas papers, box 11, file: USIA, Hidalgo (IGC) to Scott (IMV), 16 December 1975); "Congress Authorizes Domestic Use of Seven USIA Films," *USIA World*, 10, 4 (October 1976), filed in NA RG306 – A1 (1066) USIA historical branch box 154 (motion pictures).

85   GRFL John Marsh files 1974–7, box 71, file: USIA report, *USIA and the Bicentennial*, report ca. 7 April 1976.

86   GRFL John Marsh files 1974–7, box 71, file: USIA report, *USIA and the Bicentennial*, report ca. 7 April 1976.

87   Interview: Pistor; author's own recollection.

88   NA RG306 A1 (1066) USIA historical collection subject files, box 142, file: Exhibits,/Fairs, 200 Years of American Painting, Klieforth (USIA Bonn) to USIA Washington, "200 Years of American Painting," 18 August 1976.

89   Interview: James Keogh, 6 November 2001. For correspondence re presidential messages for Leipzig and Moscow brochures see GRFL WHCF subject file FG230, box 178, Davis (White House) to Kopp, 27 January and Davis to Keogh, 19 April 1976; Dizard, *Inventing Public Diplomacy*, p. 116.

By the end of 1976, it was clear that the bicentennial had succeeded beyond anyone's expectations. Conferences had energized American studies. Universities from Helsinki to Tehran had established chairs in the subject in honor of the bicentennial, and the subject had taken off in Indonesia. The celebration had reintroduced the world – and especially Western Europe – to the America of its best imaginings. With the USIA's help, Europe remembered the idealistic land of Franklin and Jefferson: the land of Kennedy rather than the land of Nixon. With Watergate and Vietnam now closed books, Western Europe seemed ready to take a second look at America. Looking back on the period, Mike Schneider of ICS put the agency's achievement simply: "The bicentennial rehumanized the image of America."[90]

*

The summer and autumn of 1976 saw the spectacle of a presidential election. The agency assisted coverage of the conventions for more than a dozen foreign correspondents, including a team from Hungary, and created six special *Election 1976* videotapes of events and expert discussion for use in posts. They also made good use of a PBS program, *The Bill Moyers Interview with Candidate Jimmy Carter*. But the highlights of 1976 campaign were the four televised debates, held for the first time since 1960. The USIA shipped recordings of the debates, which posts screened in their auditoriums or made available to local television. Haitian television received such a lively response to their showing of the first debate in French that they scheduled a repeat.[91]

The election fell on 2 November. Early on 3 November, Jimmy Carter claimed victory. That same day, Jim Keogh resigned from the USIA directorship, effective from 30 November. Keogh went on to work as executive director of the Business Roundtable, representing the leading chief executive officers of U.S. corporations. He died in 2006.[92] His antagonist, the VOA's Ken Giddens, broke precedent and remained director into the Carter years.

Although the intense discussion over the future of public diplomacy seen during the Ford years had achieved surprisingly little of substance, it had placed reform on the agenda. At the same time, the advance of détente had dramatically widened the scope for Western cultural outreach to the Eastern bloc. The Helsinki Final Act of August

---

[90] NA RG 306 USIA historical collection, reports and studies, A1 (1070) box 7, James Moceri (IOR) to Keogh, "USIA accomplishments 1974–1975," 15 April 1975; GRFL John Marsh files 1974–77, box 71, file: USIA report, *USIA and the Bicentennial*, report ca. 7 April 1976; interview: Mike Schneider, 14 November 1995.

[91] NA RG 306 USIA historical collection, motion pictures, box 154, "IMV's Election Year Activities," *USIA World*, 10, 4 (October 1976); "IMV Sends Presidential Candidate Debates around the World," *USIA World*, 10, 5 (November 1976). The wireless file carried the debate texts in full and 110 agency posts received 250 film and video versions including, for the first two debates, video versions in French and Spanish. These traveled to the field by pouch or airmail, but in many cases volunteers carried tapes on behalf of the USIA. The U.S. ambassador to Poland personally transported the tape of the first debate back to Warsaw.

[92] Interview: Keogh, 6 September 2001; GRFL WHCF subject files FG230/A, box 178, Keogh to President, 3 November 1976; President to Keogh, 10 December 1976; "Keogh Is Said to Resign as Head of USIA," *Washington Post*, 5 November 1976, p. A2.

1975 had cleared the way for cultural exchanges and the free flow of information on an unprecedented scale. The cycle of reforms initiated by the Stanton panel would ensure that a leaner and fitter U.S. information apparatus would be on hand to exploit this new opportunity. The payoff for the work of the Stanton panel would come in the 1980s.[93]

93 Interviews: Walter Roberts, 10 November 2001; Leonard Marks, 15 May 2003.

9 From the "Two-Way" Mandate to the Second Cold War

THE CARTER ADMINISTRATION, 1977–81

> The new Agency for International Communication will play a central role in building these two-way bridges of understanding between our people and the other peoples of the world. Only by knowing and understanding each other's experiences can we find common ground on which we can examine and resolve our differences.
>
> Jimmy Carter, 11 October 1977.[1]

He had warned the Secret Service, but it came as a surprise to the crowd. Just a short way into his inauguration parade, Jimmy Carter ordered his armored limousine to stop. The crowd fell suddenly silent, suspecting that something was wrong. The President and his family got out and walked the rest of the way along Pennsylvania Avenue to the White House. Carter's walk was symbolic of his intent to be a President for and of the people, with a new vision of America's place as a good citizen in the global community.[2] He had run against détente, Watergate, and cynicism in government. In his inaugural address he called for the country to return to its best principles and pledged to promote human rights around the world. "Because we are free," he declared, "we can never be indifferent to the fate of freedom elsewhere."[3]

The USIA pulled out all the stops to introduce Jimmy Carter abroad. The agency created a set of satellite television programs on the event for Egypt, Poland, Greece, Korea, Indonesia, Zaire, and Columbia, each fronted by a well-known journalist from that country, and a widely used four-part video series in English, Spanish, and French, called *Transition '77*, to introduce the administration.[4] Carter helped by recording a five-minute inaugural message for the world, distributed by the USIA. He ended with an appeal to join "in a common effort based on mutual trust and mutual respect."[5] Carter's interest in world opinion endured. The USIA found him far more accessible

---

[1] Speech transmitting plan to reorganize USIA to Congress, 11 October 1977, *Public Papers of the Presidents, Jimmy Carter 1977*, Vol. II, pp. 1765–72.

[2] For Carter's own account of this see Jimmy Carter, *Keeping Faith: Memoirs of a President*, New York: Bantam, 1982, pp. 17–18.

[3] For text see *PPP JC 1977*, Vol. 1, pp. 1–4.

[4] RG306 – A1 (1066) USIA historical branch box 154 (motion pictures), "USIA Tells the World about Carter Inauguration," *USIA World*, 10, 8 (February 1977); "IMV Sends More 'Transition '77' Interviews to Posts," *USIA World*, 10, 10 (April 1977).

[5] For text see *PPP JC 1977*, Vol. 1, pp. 4–5. For coverage see "Satellite Beams Carter Pledge to All Nations," *Philadelphia Inquirer*, 21 January 1977.

to the global media than Nixon in his later years or Ford at any time.[6] In the early days, at least, Jimmy Carter impressed the world. At the end of May 1977, Gallup found that 66 percent of Britons polled endorsed Carter as a "good president" and only 7 percent disapproved. A concurrent poll in France found 63 percent positive (against 10 percent negative), whereas 70 percent regarded Carter as "dynamic."[7]

Carter inherited an information agency that was already projecting many of the ideas that he would emphasize, including human rights. Unfortunately, that agency was also in the midst of reorganization. A year of administrative upheaval followed. In April 1978, a new agency arose from the merger of USIA and the State Department's Bureau of Cultural and Educational Affairs (CU): the United States International Communication Agency, abbreviated as ICA or sometimes as USICA (pronounced you-seekuh). President Carter had a particular interest in one area of public diplomacy: international exchanges. In 1972, as governor of Georgia, he traveled to Latin America with the State Department's "Partners of the Americas" program. The experience had been a personal summons to action.[8] In office, Carter strengthened international exchange provisions. He ensured that ICA's mission statement stressed "mutuality," as he intended that the United States as well as the foreign partner would be enriched by these exchanges. This emphasis on reaching the home audience became known within the agency as the "second," "reverse," or "two-way mandate." It seemed for a season that the whole shape of American public diplomacy would be transformed. Unfortunately, the second mandate, like so much else in the Carter years, had the bad luck to be born into troubled times. By 1980, the new International Communication Agency faced the challenge of a revolution in Iran and a renewed Cold War with the U.S.S.R.

1) BEYOND STANTON
TAMING THE VOA AND CREATING THE ICA, 1977–78

President-elect Jimmy Carter did not have to wait long to experience the ferment around the Stanton proposals. On 6 November, 148 USIA employees petitioned him to consolidate all U.S. overseas information and cultural work, including the Voice of America, into a single agency. Two weeks later, about two-thirds of the VOA staff signed a counterpetition calling for VOA independence.[9] Although Carter was publicly neutral on the Stanton Report, his commitment to bureaucratic reform was well known. His foreign policy staff evidently wished to build a closer working relationship between the USIA and the State Department and chose their USIA director

---

6 Examples of Carter's availability may be found at JCL WHCF sf exec., Box PR 77, file: PR 16, Press release of interview with the President by Fred Emery, *Times* (London), 25 April 1977.

7 JCL WHCF sf exec., box FG 210, file FG266, Engle (USIA Research) to Schecter (NSC press), 3 June 1977; Reinhardt to Jody Powell, 17 June 1977.

8 JCL WHCF executive, box FO 35, file FO 5, Vance to President, 10 February 1977.

9 David Binder, "USIA Workers Ask Carter to Keep Unit Independent," *New York Times*, 7 November 1976, p. 26; "The Future of the Voice of America," 19 November 1976 (author's collection), and Heil, *Voice of America*, p. 182.

accordingly. For the first time the agency would be run by a USIA career officer, and one who also knew the State Department well: John Reinhardt.[10]

John Edward Reinhardt was born in Glade Spring, Virginia, in 1920, the son of a postal worker. As an African-American, his appointment, like that of Andrew Young to the United Nations ambassadorship, emphasized the new administration's commitment to civil rights. Raised in Tennessee and educated at Knoxville College, after military service Reinhardt studied American literature at the University of Wisconsin, completing a Ph.D. on *James Russell Lowell's Appraisal of American Life and Thought* in 1950. Reinhardt taught at Virginia State College in Petersburg, but early in 1956 he sat in on a Foreign Service recruitment session aimed at his students and decided to try a change of career himself. He was accepted into the USIA, took leave from his college job, and after the usual three months of training was serving overseas. Reinhardt served in cultural posts in Manila and Kyoto and as cultural attaché in Tehran before duty in Washington as deputy assistant director for East Asia and the Pacific. As assistant director for Africa between 1968 and 1970, he famously stood up to Frank Shakespeare's wish to indulge South Africa in the name of Cold War strategy. Reinhardt was ambassador to Nigeria between 1971 and 1975 and then directed the State Department's domestic public relations as Assistant Secretary of State for Public Affairs.[11] No director since George V. Allen had such a sound standing with the State Department. This connection was reinforced by Reinhardt's own choice of deputy: a foreign service officer (who had been Reinhardt's Deputy Assistant Secretary) named Charles W. Bray III. One or the other attended the big weekly meeting with the Secretary of State for senior staff.[12]

Although Reinhardt fitted in well with the State Department, he made little impression elsewhere. He had little direct contact with President Carter. He visited the White House only twice.[13] Carter telephoned occasionally, but more often word came from the National Security Advisor, Zbigniew Brzezinski. Brzezinski showed much more interest in public diplomacy than any senior White House advisor since C. D. Jackson. His core objectives were "to increase America's ideological impact on the world" by emphasizing human rights; to "improve America's strategic position" by tempering Soviet power and improving U.S. relations with China; and "to restore America's political appeal to the Third World."[14] Each of these tasks had a clear public diplomacy dimension. Brzezinski requested a weekly foreign media reaction report from the agency (reviving a practice last seen in the early Johnson years) and instituted a weekly meeting with agency staff. Although he did not see the necessity of the USIA director sitting on the NSC, Brzezinski brought Reinhardt into his

[10] "Reinhardt Is Selected to Be USIA Chief," *New York Times*, 4 January 1977, p. 3.
[11] Interview: Reinhardt, 10 November 2001. David Binder, "The Intercultural Communicator: John Edward Reinhardt," *New York Times*, Saturday, 1 April 1978, p. 46.
[12] Interview: Reinhardt. For biographical note on Bray see *PPP JC 1977* Vol.1, pp. 732–3. Reinhardt recalled that the big weekly meetings at State were unwieldy and not terribly productive.
[13] On 25 March 1977 for his swearing in and on 7 March 1980 to introduce a new VOA director.
[14] Zbigniew Brzezinski, *Power and Principle: Memoirs of the National Security Adviser, 1977–1981*, New York: Farrar, Straus, Giroux, 1983, p. 3.

interdepartmental Special Coordinating Committee (SCC) and other subcommittees as needed. Brzezinski's interest in public diplomacy was, however, skewed toward broadcasting. Reinhardt soon came under pressure to tweak the VOA's output.[15]

Reinhardt's agency background generated its share of problems for the director. Although technically a political appointee, he did not enjoy the special relationship with the President of a true political associate. He could never be a Leonard Marks to Carter's LBJ. He had no special links on Capitol Hill and brought in no store of external professional experience, as Murrow had from CBS. He even lacked an obvious constituency within the agency, where some of his old colleagues felt that he was now too close to State. Others lamented that he did not fight more to shape foreign policy. Although he managed the merger with CU with aplomb, many felt that the agency lost momentum under Reinhardt.[16]

Reinhardt's personal approach to U.S. "public diplomacy" was dominated by his experience in the field and, accordingly, he resolved to "let the field be the field" during his tenure. He felt that if the USIA had 100 posts there should be 100 different programs. The embassy country teams should determine their own needs and as far as possible the USIA bureaucracy in Washington should serve these needs. As Reinhardt recalled in later years, the concept did not please his area directors, who felt sidelined and resented their sometimes rough treatment at the hands of Bray. Reinhardt also became aware that some of the PAOs in the field felt too much pressure to originate programs.[17]

Reinhardt knew he would have to preside over a major bureaucratic upheaval at the USIA. The Senate Foreign Relations Committee cross-examined him at length to discern his views on the Stanton panel during his confirmation hearings, but he refused to be drawn in. Privately he was still "in two minds" about merging the USIA and the State Department's cultural program, but conceded that it made no sense to split the direction and implementation of the exchange program between two agencies. Reinhardt became a prime target for anyone with an agenda for the future of U.S. information. He saw "rather too much" of former Senator Fulbright, who tried desperately to head off the merger of exchanges into the general pot. In one meeting Fulbright told Reinhardt dramatically, "Deep down you know you shouldn't win. I trust *you* but I don't know who the next guy will be, and Cultural Relations is too important to be left to personalities." But the wheels ground on regardless.[18]

15 Interview: Reinhardt, 10 November 2001; for the weekly reaction report system see JCL NSC BM sf, box 1–9, file: ICA, Reinhardt to Brzezinski, 18 February 1977; for text of President's remarks at Reinhardt's swearing in see *PPP JC 1977*, Vol.1, pp. 511–12. For a press story on Reinhardt's commitment to VOA objectivity see "USIA Chief Pledges Straight US News," *The Washington Post*, 17 July 1977, p. 20. Brzezinski was also much interested in the journal *Problems of Communism*. See JCL NSA SM Henze papers, box 2, Brzezinski to Reinhardt, 31 July 1978, and Henze to Brzezinski, 8 August 1978.

16 For critical assessments of Reinhardt, Bray, see ADST oral history: Charles R. Beecham, Stanton Burnett, Robert Chatten, Robert Nichols.

17 Interview: Reinhardt, 10 November 2001.

18 JCL NSA SM Henze papers, box 1, Henze to Brzezinski, BIB VOA & related issues, 18 March 1977. Interview: Reinhardt, 10 November 2001.

Reinhardt's approach to public diplomacy was based on international dialogue rather than one-way lecturing. He saw dialogue as a process at the heart of American culture: "We have been so greatly enriched by the gathering in of others . . . that we are in fact ourselves a dialogue. We know it works. We know the power of listening. We should extend its realm."[19] This impetus to dialogue was reinforced by the second key character in early Carter-era public diplomacy: Assistant Secretary of State for Cultural Affairs Joseph D. Duffey. A liberal academic with a background in theology and politics, Duffey had worked for the Carter campaign team.[20] Although he accepted the CU job knowing that his bureau was slated to be merged into the USIA, he was willing to fight a rearguard action in defense of the immense value he saw in the presence of the CU within the State Department as an "island of cultural perspective." Duffey's personal belief in international dialogue matched the long-term commitment of the CU bureau itself. While Assistant Secretary, he spoke about the importance of "mutuality" and moving beyond the "one-way process" in cultural diplomacy. He worked to ensure that the CU's "mutual" approach would not be lost when its 236 souls joined the 8,500-strong USIA in a new agency.[21]

*

Jimmy Carter came into office with a commitment to improve U.S. international broadcasting. In a position paper prepared during the election for correspondence (but never used in a speech), Carter stressed that "If détente with the Soviet Union and the countries of Eastern Europe is to have real meaning, we must work toward a freer flow of information and ideas. The most valuable instruments that this country has for this purpose are our international radio stations: Voice of America . . . Radio Free Europe and Radio Liberty." The document noted that the Voice was hampered by "a web of political restrictions imposed by the Department of State," whereas RFE and RL still lacked the new transmitter facilities called for by a review of the radios back in 1973. Carter saw these problems as symptomatic of the Nixon/Ford "inability . . . to appreciate the importance of a free flow of information and ideas through mass communication" and their preference for private deals with the Soviets.[22] Once in office, Carter did not have to wait long to put these views into action.

---

19 JCL WHCF subject file exec., box FG 210, file FG266, news release and speech 28 May 1977 as forwarded to Brzezinski by Bray. Brzezinski's acknowledgement of 3 June 1977 called this an "extraordinarily thoughtful discussion. . . . "

20 Interview: Joseph D. Duffey, 2 April 2004. Carter initially offered him the post of Secretary of Education or director of the National Endowment for the Humanities, but being weary of academic politics, he declined.

21 Interview: Joseph D. Duffey, 2 April 2004. Duffey papers: Remarks at luncheon for the American Association of University Presidents, Williamsburg, VA, 25 April 1977; "United States International Cultural Policy: Perspective of a new administration," remarks to meeting of cultural officers and attaches of Washington embassies, 10 May 1977, published in *Exchange*, summer 1977, pp. 7–9; Remarks at East-West Center, Hawaii, 27 June 1977.

22 NA RG 306 A1 (1055) box 112, USIA historical collection sfs, VOA history 1977, "USIA broadcasting serv. 1976." This policy document is mentioned in JCL WHCF sf executive, box IT2, IT 11, Thomas F. Barthelemy to Brzezinski, 24 February 1977 as being prepared by Barthelemy and Maurey Lisann, submitted via John Kotch, and approved by Brzezinski in June 1976.

On 31 January, Brzezinski pointed out that, under a clause inserted into the Foreign Relations Authorization Act for FY 1977, the White House was required to submit a report to Congress by that very day on the state of the U.S. international broadcasting program.[23] The White House obtained an extension, and on 22 March, Carter submitted a report to Congress. The report called for a major investment in transmitters for the VOA and RFE/RL, requesting not only sixteen new 250-kW transmitters for broadcasting to the Soviet Bloc but also twelve more for VOA broadcasts to Africa and Asia. Moreover, by rejecting any expansion of the RFE/RL model of surrogate broadcasting as "highly impractical," the report strengthened the position of the VOA.[24] In fact, the seventeen new transmitters purchased for the VOA under this initiative did not help much. Only two were actually installed overseas, and by the time that the remainder found their way to sites in the United States, many had developed faults and were past their warranties. VOA modernization became a Reagan campaign issue in 1980.[25]

Even as the Carter administration prepared its radio policy, it experienced its first major taste of just how controversial international radio could be. Senators Percy and McGovern lobbied hard to see Frank Stanton appointed to chair the Board for International Broadcasting (which ran RFE/RL) over Brzezinki's candidate.[26] Though the post was unrelated to the issue of the Stanton report, it became a tussle over the validity of Stanton's ideas for the VOA. Brzezinski appealed to the President with a negative account of the Stanton panel, arguing that "the total effect" of Stanton's recommendations "would be to make U.S. information programs harder for the Government to manage and less amenable to White House influence."[27] Brzezinski's own views were reinforced by his point man on international radio at NSC, a veteran of RFE and CIA covert broadcasting and former CIA station chief in Turkey named Paul B. Henze. Henze took a hard line on VOA independence, warning Brzezinski, "The U.S.

23 The Ford administration had commissioned an investigation (NSSM 245), which identified the need to build sixteen new 250-kW transmitters for the VOA, RFE, and RL, but this had foundered when the OMB demanded a limit of only six. JCL National Security Affairs, Brzezinski Material (hereafter NSA BM) sf, box 1–9, file: Board for International Broadcasting, Brzezinski to President, "Report to Congress on the US international broadcasting program," 31 January 1977. For discussion see WHCF executive sf box IT-2, IT 11, Barthelemy to Brzezinski, 24 February 1977.

24 For text see *PPP JC 1977*, Vol.1, p. 478. "US international broadcasting," message to Congress transmitting a report, 22 March 1977. For press discussion see Michael Geiler, "US Broadcasts Reach Soviet Jails," *Washington Post*, 7 April 1977, p. A9. Carter's tough line against the Soviet Union did not play well in Germany, where Chancellor Helmut Schmidt had his own notions of East–West reconciliation. Schmidt took particular exception to the administration's decision to upgrade RFE's Munich transmitters without consulting his government and caused a brief diplomatic row on this subject in late June 1977. For documents on the Schmidt affair see correspondence filed at JCL NSA sf, box 9, file: BIB (RFE/RL/VOA); also Brzezinski, *Power and Principle*, p. 293.

25 For a summary of the fate of this investment see Alvin A. Snyder, *Warriors of Disinformation: American Propaganda, Soviet Lies, and the Winning of the Cold War*, New York: Arcade Publishing, 1995, pp. 35–6.

26 JCL National Security Affairs Staff Material Horn/Special (Henze papers), hereafter NSA SM Henze papers, box 1, Henze to Brzezinski, 2 March 1977, Brzezinski to President, ND; David Binder, "Radio Board Choice Stirs Controversy," *New York Times*, 12 March 1977, p. 6; Richard M. Weintraub, "2 Senators Oppose Proposed Broadcasting Unit Nominee," *Washington Post*, 13 March 1977, p. B3; JCL NSA sf, box 9, file: BIB, Henze to Brzezinski, 14 March 1977; Brzezinski to President, c. 14 March 1977; Jordan to President, 14 March 1977.

27 JCL NSA sf, box 9, file: BIB, Brzezinski to President, 18 March 1977.

government needs a voice in the world and VOA should play this role. There is very little justification for the money spent on it if it doesn't."[28] An anti-Stanton position took root at the NSC. On 18 March, Carter approved the appointment of Brzezinski's candidate (former ambassador John A. Gronouski) over Stanton. The argument was merely a foretaste of the struggle over the future of the VOA.[29]

In mid-March 1977, all of the surviving USIA directors spent an evening with John Reinhardt discussing the Stanton report. Leonard Marks, who was bent on sinking Stanton's plans, reported, "Advice was unanimous that VOA should remain in USIA and CU should be amalgamated with USIA which should oversee all cultural and information programs."[30] Meanwhile, the Subcommittee on International Operation of the Senate Committee on Foreign Relations, chaired by Senator George McGovern, probed the future of the VOA. Senator Charles Percy had presented an amendment to grant the VOA full independence. For the journalists at the VOA, the Holy Grail was at last within their grasp. Reinhardt allowed the VOA staff immunity to testify as their consciences dictated at the hearings. The hearings began on 29 April. Star witnesses included the VOA's news chief, Bernie Kamenske, and head of current affairs, Alan Heil. With the case for independence made, the subcommittee adjourned.[31]

On 4 May, the committee reassembled to "mark-up" the bill. A shadow flitted across the hope for VOA independence when McGovern mentioned that Deputy Secretary of State Warren Christopher had "reservations" over the move. The next day Senator Percy revealed that Christopher explicitly opposed the bill on the grounds that it limited the administration's options in restructuring the USIA. Nevertheless the four senators present voted unanimously to approve the amendment, but referred the measure to the full committee, due to convene on 10 May.[32] Then it happened. On 5 May, the General Accounting Office published its report on the future of the USIA and VOA: *Public Diplomacy in the Years Ahead – An Assessment of Proposals*

[28] JCL WHCF sf, exec., box FG 210, file FG266–1, Henze to Brzezinski, BIB, 8 February 1977.
[29] JCL NSA SM Henze papers, box 1, Henze to Brzezinski, BIB VOA & related issues, 18 March 1977; JCL NSA SM, box 1, file 21, Henze to Clift, 24 March 1977. Henze's earlier in CIA clandestine broadcasting from Munich and Ethiopia is noted in David Binder, "US Wary of Islamic Upheaval to Increase Broadcasts to Muslims," *New York Times*, 17 December 1979.
[30] JCL NSA SM, box 1, file 3/77, Henze to Brzezinski, "Leonard Marks on Cultural Exchange...," 24 March 1977; At the same time Marks pressed for an expansion of exchange activities in his capacity as chairman of the advisory commission on educational and cultural exchange (JCL WHCF sf – exec, box FO 35, FO 5, Marks to President, 21 March 1977). Marks also lobbied energetically for his own reappointment to the chairmanship of the U.S. advisory commission on International Educational and Cultural Affairs, duly made in April. He was, however, denied the chairmanship of the combined advisory board created by the merger of the USIA and CU, but was appointed to a UNESCO ambassadorship; see JCL NSA agency files, box 9, ICA file: 2–7/77, Henze to Brzezinski, 13 April 1977; Brzezinski to President, 16 April 1977; NSA SM Henze, box 1, Fascell to President, 22 December 1977 etc.; and NSA Staff Materials, box 1, file 01/78, Henze to Brzezinski, 31 January 1978.
[31] Interviews: Kamenske and Heil; "Voice of America Falters, Ex-head Warns Hill Panel," *Washington Post*, 30 April 1977, p. A3; see also Linda Charlton, "Autonomy Unlikely at Voice of America," *New York Times*, 29 May 1977, p. 5.
[32] Alan Heil, *Voice of America*, p. 187.

for Reorganization. endorsing the consolidation of all U.S. cultural and information programs into a single agency, the report roundly rejected any idea of VOA independence. It was a major blow.[33]

Over the following weekend two further documents became public. The first was a memorandum by Reinhardt in which he called for the promotion of the VOA director to "associate director" status within the USIA and set out his guidelines for implementing the VOA charter. In words chosen to reassure VOA journalists, Reinhardt declared, "VOA will be solely responsible for the content of news broadcasts. I expect VOA to continue to apply its double-source rule." He then noted that the USIA's Policy Office (IOP) would alone be responsible for overseeing the station's charter obligation to "present the policies of the United States clearly and effectively," but would do so through mutual consultation when time permitted. "There will be no prior script clearances of VOA commentaries or analyses." The IOP staff would operate by reading material after it had been broadcast and providing constructive feedback.[34] The second and final document dropped into the mix was the 28th annual report of the United States Advisory Commission on Information, which argued, "The Voice of America must remain a vital participant in the U.S. Information Agency."[35] Three of the Stanton panelists – Hobart Lewis, George Gallup, and John M. Shaheen – co-wrote the report. They had changed their minds about VOA independence, and indeed the *Washington Post* revealed that the report had been rushed into print specifically to influence the Senate vote.[36]

On Tuesday, 10 May, the Senate Foreign Relations Committee met to consider VOA independence. The three documents and Leonard Marks' "lobbying blitz" had turned key senators against the bill. The committee rejected the amendment. The final blow came in a mark-up session on 28 May. "We set up VOA for a purpose," Senator Humphrey remarked, "and that purpose was as official government information or propaganda agency, call it what you will." Senator Church concurred: "If Voice of America is not going to be the expression of the American government in its foreign policy and its objectives abroad, why do we maintain it?" It was the coup de grâce. The VOA would remain within the USIA.[37]

33 Government Accounting Office, *Public Diplomacy in the Years Ahead – An Assessment of Proposals for Reorganization*, 5 May 1977, p. iv. (for file copy see UoA CU 28/2).
34 RG306 – A1 (1066) USIA historical collection, sfs box 112, file: VOA history 1977, Reinhardt to acting director VOA, 4 May 1977. He suggested that comments from embassies and USIS posts should be "welcomed" by the VOA and that any policy issues raised therein "be considered jointly by IOP and VOA." Interview: Reinhardt, 10 November 2001; David Binder, "US Has Lost an Agency But Gained a New Voice . . .," *New York Times*, 2 April 1978, p. E4.
35 JCL WHCF sf exec., box FG 208, file FG262, Advisory Commission press release, 10 May 1977 and 28th report, United States Advisory Commission on Information. The report held that the clashes between journalists and diplomats at the Voice were "healthy" and had enhanced both VOA journalism and U.S. diplomacy.
36 Lee Lescaze and Richard Weintraub, "3 Drop Recommendation to Break Up the USIA," *Washington Post*, 10 May 1977.
37 Interviews: Kamenske & Heil; for press criticism of Percy's plan see the editorial "International Broadcasting," *Washington Post*, 9 May 1977, p. A22; Linda Charlton, "Autonomy Unlikely at Voice of America," *New York Times*, 29 May 1977, p. 5.

Reinhardt wasted no time in going to bat for the Voice. On 1 June he had submitted a detailed memorandum to Brzezinski calling for investment in the information program. "VOA," Reinhardt noted, "must be the only serious radio in the United States which is still dependent on the vacuum tube... the Voice must literally go to junk sales to find replacement tubes since they are no longer being manufactured." Brzezinski took the point and suggested that the USIA plan for "full modernization of VOA" and also "for expansion of exchange and leader programs, for exhibits in communist countries and elsewhere," and build the plans into the budget for FY 1979.[38]

*

With the issue of the VOA resolved, debate progressed to the wider question of the future of the USIA. Between 8 and 24 June, the House Subcommittee on International Operation, chaired by Dante Fascell, heard evidence from witnesses including the Stanton panelists and a procession of ex-USIA directors and veterans.[39] The Senate built a time limit into the debate by inserting a requirement for the White House to submit a report on the reorganization by October 1977 into the agency's budget authorization. On 3 August, Fascell presented his conclusions to the President. He opened by observing that the reorganization was a small problem compared to the greater need to understand and use "our public diplomacy resources... to further policy objectives." His list of proposed reforms included the familiar cry that the director of the USIA be included in both NSC and cabinet meetings, and that the USIA be both independent and augmented by the cultural apparatus of the State Department.[40]

During the hearings, Brzezinski did his best to brief the President with the various policy options. On 15 June, he reported to Carter that Cyrus Vance favored "putting all 'public diplomacy' operations under USIA, and, in turn, putting USIA under State in the same kind of relationship as currently exists with AID." John Reinhardt, in contrast, favored consolidation but into a more independent agency subject only to loose guidance from State, on the lines of the Arms Control and Disarmament Agency.[41] Assistant Secretary of State for Educational and Cultural Affairs Joseph Duffey also contributed to the debate. Although Duffey now accepted the impending merger of CU into USIA, he argued that the creation of a new structure presented a major

[38] JCL WHCF sf exec., box FI-19, file FI4-FG266, Reinhardt to Brzezinski, 1 June 1977; Brzezinski to Reinhardt, 7 June 1977. Reinhardt also noted that the agency could only afford one major exhibit in the Soviet Union each year and a humble 5,000 inward and outward exchange places for the entire globe.
[39] For copies of testimony see UoA CU 28/13 and JCL WHCF sf exec., box FG 151, file FG 33–11, esp. Clift to Aaron 9 June 1977 for testimony by pres. of American Foreign Service Assoc. favoring integration of the USIA into State. Also UoA CU 28/12, Fulbright to President, 12 July 1977.
[40] UoA CU 28/13, Fascell and committee to President, 3 August 1977 with report, also filed at JCL WHCF executive, box FO 35, file FO 5.
[41] JCL, WHCF CF FG 266, Brzezinski to President, "Reorganization of USIA," 15 June 1977. Brzezinski, for his part, worried that State might easily encumber the new agency with the "many working-level pressures for conformity and blandness." For a view of positions by State see UoA CU 28/1, Warren Christopher to Vance, "State USIA reorganization," 9 June 1977.

opportunity to rethink the fundamentals of American public diplomacy for a new world of multiple interconnections. "In simplest terms," Duffey explained in a memo to Cyrus Vance, "the current mission of USIA is oriented largely toward the dissemination of information about the United States, while CU's is the promotion of higher levels of mutual understanding through programs of *two-way* cultural exchanges." His conclusion was simple: "Approaching the issue of reorganization with concern for a clear definition of mission suggests an organization different from either the present USIA or CU. This could be a new beginning for our informational, cultural and educational programs which requires a new agency with a new name." At this point Duffey left State to become chairman of the National Endowment for the Humanities. Sixteen years later he became Bill Clinton's director of the USIA.[42]

As Carter's policy crystallized, Stanton lobbied to put his case directly to the President. On 15 August, he and the former Assistant Secretary, Charles Frankel, sent a telegram requesting an appointment to present their views. The President's special assistant for media and public affairs, Barry Jagoda, saw no need to hear Stanton's views again, and declined such a meeting. Stanton had finally run into a wall.[43] On 26 August, Bert Lance, director of the Office of Management and Budget, presented President Carter with a set of policy options for the future of the USIA and VOA. The key recommendation was to "Consolidate the educational and cultural exchange activities of State and the information and cultural activities of USIA to produce a new organizational entity." The document took account of Duffey's pleas to preserve the integrity and unique outlook of the exchange program: "A presidential statement defining the mission of the new entity and assuring the continued integrity of educational and cultural exchange organization, activities and budget should accompany the consolidation." No one on Carter's staff backed VOA independence, but all recommended a "presidential guarantee of independence of its news gathering and reporting." The President made his decision that same day. He formally endorsed both these policies and selected Reinhardt's favored model of the Arms Control Agency as the pattern for the relationship between the new agency and State. State would give "guidance" but the new agency would be master of its own destiny.[44]

With the decision made, the Carter White House prepared what came to be known as Reorganization Plan No. 2 for presentation to Congress on 11 October 1977.[45]

42 UoA CU 28/1, Duffey to Vance, "Organization of International Information, Education and Cultural Relations," 8 June 1977. Emphasis in original.
43 JCL WHCF sf exec., box FG 210, file FG266, Stanton/Frankel to President, 15 August, with minute by Jagoda.
44 JCL WHCF executive, box FO 35, file FO 5, Lance to President, 26 August 1977. Lance reported that he had discussed the plans with Brzezinski and his deputy David Aaron at NSC, Jagoda in the White House, Reinhardt at USIA, Duffey at CU, and Under Secretary of State Christopher. President to Fascell, 14 September 1977; for press coverage see Linda Charlton, "Autonomy Planned for US Radio Unit: Carter Intends to Give Independence to Voice of America, Merge USIA and Culture Agency," *New York Times*, 1 September 1977, p. 9.
45 The eventual text of Carter's plan blurred some of the policy decision made in August. Brzezinski was concerned to note that the director of the new agency would be "under the direction" of the Secretary of State rather than subject to his guidance. But Carter's text also promised a stronger policy role for the

The commitment to dialogue was much in evidence as the President unveiled what the new agency would call its "reverse" or "second mandate":

> The new agency will have two distinct but related goals:
>   To tell the world about our society and policies in particular our commitment to cultural diversity and individual liberty.
>   To tell ourselves about the world, so as to enrich our own culture as well as give us the understanding to deal effectively with problems among nations.[46]

Carter's speech also reflected the emphasis that Reinhardt placed on integrity in the output of the VOA and the new agency: "The new agency's activities must be straight-forward, open, candid, balanced, and representative." He declared, "They will not be given over to the views of any one group, any one party or any one administration. The agency must not operate in a covert, manipulative or propagandistic way." This proved easier to promise than to deliver.[47]

                                    *

With the merger between the USIA and CU now impending, work began on choosing a new name for the agency. Reinhardt commissioned a small task force to study the issue and they soon generated a computerized list of 150 alternatives. They felt that the word "information" was too narrow for the new agency and suggested that the title should include the broader concept of "communication." No one considered hiring a public relations firm to research responses overseas; rather staff circulated alternatives and their translations and pondered connotations themselves. Leading candidates included "Agency for International Communication and Exchange" and "Agency for International Understanding." But French speakers considered that *agence pour la comprehension internationale* sounded vague and Spanish speakers thought that *agencia para la comprensión internacional* sounded trivial, whereas *agencia para la communicación et l'intercambio* had connotations of "telephones."[48]

Drafts of President Carter's message to Congress used the name "International Communications and Exchanges Agency," but the NSC staff countered with the "higher sounding and less political" title of "United States Information and Cultural Agency." The eventual speech employed the title "Agency for International

---

agency director as "The principal advisor on international information and exchange activities to the President and the National Security Council and the Secretary of State." For file on the development of the 11 October speech see JCL WHCF sf, exec., box SP-7, file SP2-3-50, esp. Schecter (NSC) to Hirschhorn (OMB), 3 October 1977; also JCL WHCF sf, exec., box FG 236, FG 999–7, Brzezinski to President, "Reorganization plan no. 2 – Public Diplomacy," 7 October 1977.

[46] Carter speech to Congress, 11 October 1977; *PPP JC 1977*, Vol. II, pp. 1765–72.
[47] Carter speech to Congress, 11 October 1977; *PPP JC 1977*, Vol. II, pp. 1765–72.
[48] Task force members included Alan Carter, Barry Fulton, and Mike Schneider, who had a hankering for "Public Affairs Cultural Exchange Agency" and the dynamic acronym PACE. For discussion of possible names see UoA CU 27/14, Perez to Lejins, 9 September 1977.

Communication" generated at USIA.[49] During the joint committee hearings on Capitol Hill, legislators complained that AIC was CIA backward, and OMB responded by proposing "Agency for International Understanding." Vance and Brzezinski both objected and proposed either "Agency for Cultural Cooperation and Information" or "Agency for International Information and Cultural Cooperation."[50] As the deadline neared, President Carter himself called Reinhardt to ask where the name question stood. Reinhardt mentioned that they had most recently been considering "International Communication Agency" but had "some problems with it." Carter cut in: "You know what? You've got yourselves a name." The House approved the plan (with the ICA name) by 357 votes to 34 on 29 November. The full Senate did not vote, so sixty days after Carter's original submission, Reorganization Plan No. 2 became law.[51]

The new name was unloved. Agency veteran Henry Butterfield Ryan thought it "made the agency sound as if they made the bearings for satellites." On 15 June 1978, the front page of the *Washington Post* reported that people around the world were indeed confusing ICA with CIA, the very worst case of mistaken identity possible for the new agency's credibility. In the Senate, McGovern moved to compel a further change, but this came to nothing. The Reagan administration soon changed it back.[52]

*

The OMB oversaw the transition to the International Communication Agency.
The agency was divided into four associate directorates, Broadcasting (Voice of America), Programs and Plans (P Bureau), Management (M bureau), and Education, Culture, and Exchange (ECA or the E Bureau), and five areas directorates, African, European, East Asian and Pacific, American republics, and the catch-all "North African, Near Eastern and South Asian affairs." The planners took care that the East–West Center and the Fulbright and other foreign exchanges would be insulated from politics. The two advisory commissions that had served CU and the USIA were combined into a single Advisory Commission on Public Diplomacy.[53] At the State Department,

---

49   JCL NSA BM sf box 1–9, file: ICA, Schecter (NSC) to Hirschhorn (OMB) 3 October 1977; Henze to Schecter, 3 October 1977. Brzezinski himself requested that any title include the words United States.

50   JCL WHCF sf, exec., box FG 236, file: FG 999–7, James Mcintyre (OMB/President's Reorganization Project) to President, 31 October 1977; Henze to Brzezinski, 1 November 1977.

51   Interview: Reinhardt, 10 November 2001; UoA CU 27/14, Reinhardt to all agency personnel, 13 December 1977; for press coverage of the vote see "House Approves 2nd Presidential Reorganization Plan," *Washington Post*, 30 November 1977.

52   Interviews: Reinhardt, 10 November 2001 and Henry Butterfield Ryan, 27 November 1995; "2nd New Name for Old USIA," *Washington Post*, 10 May 1978, p. A13 – McGovern's bill required the name to be "Agency for Information and Cultural Exchange." Ward Sinclair, "What's in an Acronym? Foreigners Mistake US Drumbeaters for Spies," *Washington Post*, 15 June 1977, p. A1; "ICA Who? USIA on the Way to Getting Old Name Back," *Washington Post*, 22 September 1981, p. A19.

53   UoA CU 31/1, Ben Read (D USoS) and R. T. Curran (Acting Assoc. Dir.) to member of Working Groups on Implementation of Reorganization, 10 November 1977. For a report on the early operation of the ICA exchange program see NA RG 306- A1 (1070) box 26, USIA historical collection, reports and studies, 1945–94, "An Assessment of the International Visitor's Program," June 1979. ADST oral history: Mildred Marcy. For John Reinhardt's description of the new structure see UoA CU 3.3, remarks by USIA director ... 6 February 1978; also statement by John E. Reinhardt ... before

Warren Christopher devised a new set of procedures to cover policy guidance for the ICA. All policy advice would be channeled through the department's Bureau of Public Affairs, with a duty officer available outside normal working hours to advise on breaking news. Christopher asked for ICA staff to be included in regular staff meetings in the Department's bureaus and independent offices, and for these divisions to keep the ICA briefed on their plans, making formal links that had existed informally in the past.[54]

Reinhardt and Bray used the reorganization to advance their notion of empowering the field. They intended the new Bureau of Programs and Plans at the ICA to be the "intellectual nerve center of the agency" and to furnish the material that the field requested. At the helm of the "P bureau" was Associate Director for Programs Hal Schneidman, with Alan Carter as his deputy. Schneidman and Carter were particularly committed to reaching out to what they saw as the increasingly interconnected community of thinkers and opinion formers in the "Global Village," and sought to steer the agency away from what they saw as crude and ineffective local appeals aimed at a mass audience. With this in mind, Reinhardt and Bray created a complex system of resource allocation by which PAOs submitted country plans outlining their activities for a coming year and agency computers processed the data to arrange the optimum allocation of resources. Although logical on paper, the system lacked flexibility in practice. A PAO could be tripped up by the unexpected, as when USIS Hong Kong ran into the exodus of Vietnamese boat people without anything in their plan for refugees. Some field officers complained bitterly. Relations between the P bureau and the agency's research office were especially poor. Alan Carter suspected that posts were actually fighting the very idea of centralized "directed and focused planning."[55]

In December, Reinhardt suggested building a new home for the agency, consolidating its twelve locations around Washington to just one site, and even incorporating the NEH and NEA. He proposed a convenient location between the State Department and the Kennedy Center. Unfortunately, budgetary concerns intervened. ICA headquarters remained at 1776 Pennsylvania Avenue. There was some solace in the dedication of a small triangle of grass opposite the building as "Edward R. Murrow Park".[56]

Subcommittee on International Operations, House of Representatives, 21 February 1978. A diagram of the new structure may be found in the *US Government Manuel*, 1980, p. 598; also in RRL Lord papers, box 90051, file: ICA Feb-March 1981 (3). The first Associate Director of the E bureau was Alice Ilehman.

54 Author's collection: Christopher to All Assistant Secretaries. 14 April 1978. The Policy Planning Staff (S/P) and bureaus had the responsibility for preparing briefing and background material on "issues and events of consequence." The whole process of coordinating the State–ICA relationship was the responsibility of the Office of Management and Operations (M/MO).

55 For an anonymous critique of this resource system as passed to NSC see JCL NSA BM sf, box 10, file: ICA, Thornton to Henze, 13 December 1979 with memo "The State of USIA – What needs to be done." See also ADST oral history: Stanton Burnett, James L. Morad, Gordon Winkler. In 1979 Carter moved to be PAO area director for the Far East and was replaced by Gordon Winkler. In September 1980 Jock Shirley replaced Hal Schneidman. Carter to author, 22 July 2004.

56 JCL WHCF sf, exec., box FG 236, file: FG 999–7, Reinhardt to Brzezinski, 15 December 1977.

On 3 February, as expected, the White House announced the nomination of Reinhardt as director of the ICA.[57] On 8 March, Reinhardt forwarded the draft text for a new presidential mission statement for the agency. The White House accepted the text with minor editorial changes and issued it to the press on 13 March.[58] The statement declared the first objective of the ICA to be "To encourage, aid and sponsor the broadest possible exchange of people and ideas between our country and other nations."[59] The prominence of the "second mandate" posed an obvious problem for the old USIA staff used to thinking in terms of one-way transmission. There were no extra funds attached to the wider brief, and the new agency was still subject to the strictures of the Smith–Mundt Act prohibiting the domestic dissemination of its materials. An ICA discussion document concluded that the agency need not apply the new mandate to every single program component. Hence, the wireless file could continue to operate in one direction only, but the mandate had to be present in the wider program. The agency interpreted the second mandate as a duty to facilitate exchange, to strengthen existing two-way processes, and to help "indigenous institutions" connect with "counterpart American institutions," including connections to the domestic media.[60] The most visible manifestation of the new mandate was the so-called "American Learning" program, a system of competitive grants to enable U.S.-based institutions to build contacts with and gather expertise from peers overseas. The resources were never available for a large-scale initiative.[61]

---

[57] JCL WHCF sf, exec., box FG 218, file: FG 298, Gammill (White House) to President, 2 February 1978.

[58] JCL WHCF sf, exec., box FG 217, file: FG 298, Reinhardt to President, 8 March 1977; President to Reinhardt, 13 March 1978, etc.

[59] The mission statement identified five main tasks: "1) *To encourage...exchange* of people and ideas between our country and other nations." This task had three elements: continuing and improving the existing exchange program; encouraging private exchange and providing "counsel and information"; and maintaining broad participation in the exchange programs conducted throughout the US government. "2) To give foreign peoples the best possible *understanding of our policies* and our intentions, and sufficient information about American society and culture to comprehend why we have chosen certain policies over others...." The statement suggested using multiple communications media, and presenting American art and culture and English language teaching "where necessary and appropriate." "3) To help ensure that our government adequately *understands foreign public opinion and culture for policy making purpose*s, and to assist individual Americans and institutions in learning about other nations and their cultures." "4) To assist in the development and execution of a comprehensive national policy on international communications, designed to allow and *encourage the maximum flow of information* and ideas among the peoples of the world. Such a policy must take into consideration the needs and sensitivities of others, as well as our own needs." "5) To prepare for and *conduct negotiations on cultural exchanges* with other governments, aware always that the most effective sharing of culture, ideas and information comes through individual people rather than through formal acts of government." Italics added. Reinhardt sent the mission statement to all staff at home and abroad on the ICA's first day of business, as its first outgoing cable; see UoA CU 29/5, Reinhardt to colleagues, 3 April 1978; JCL WHCF sf, exec., box FG 217, file: FG 298, Reinhardt to president, 3 April 1978.

[60] UoA CU30/10, ICA's two-way communication mandate, n/d, circa April 1978. As this document put it: "Taken *as a whole*, however, the *intent* of the program activities of any agency element or post must be designed to stimulate exchange, rather than simply to inform or to address."

[61] JCL Plains file, box 16, file: Accomplishments...ICA, Reinhardt to President, "Major Accomplishments of USICA during your administration," 16 December 1980. On the "American Learning" concept at CU see UoA CU 30/10. For further comment on the Second Mandate see Allen C. Hansen, *USIA: Public Diplomacy in the Computer Age*, 2nd edition, New York: Praeger, 1989, p. 30.

On 27 March 1978, President Carter signed Executive Order 12048, establishing the International Communication Agency as of 3 April. The text addressed one issue missing from the mission statement – it made the ICA director "the principal adviser to the president, the National Security Council and the Secretary of State on international information, education and cultural matters."[62] This was not followed up in practice. John Reinhardt was seldom drawn into foreign policy-making and never sat on the NSC.[63]

On Saturday, 1 April, the United States Information Agency closed its doors. Workmen removed the sign with its "Telling America's Story to the World" motto from 1776 Pennsylvania Avenue. The International Communications Agency – with a budget of $413 million, a staff of 9,000, and 145 posts in 125 countries – opened for business on the morning of Monday, 3 April 1978.[64]

2) JOHN REINHARDT'S GOOD FIGHT
CARTER'S FOREIGN POLICY TO DECEMBER 1978

Throughout the process of reorganization, the USIA and then the ICA provided sustained support for Carter's foreign policy.[65] Early priorities included developing proposals in the field of human rights.[66] Human rights sat the core of Carter's foreign policy. Even before the President took office, the agency knew that his convictions on this subject would have major significance, especially in Latin America.[67] Carter's special inauguration day message to the world, his speech to the United Nations on 17 March, and his speech to the Organization of American States on 14 April all emphasized human rights. In May 1977, the Advisory Commission on Information applauded "the successful efforts of President Carter and the Congress to recapture the initiative in the ideological arena and in the struggle over issues before the court of world opinion" through the "cause of human rights."[68]

---

62   EO 12048, 27 March 1978, *PPP JC 1978*, vol. 1, pp. 606–7. The order continued: "As such the director shall provide advice within policy formulation activities of the NSC when such matters are considered . . . The scope of the director's advice shall include assessments of the impact of actual and proposed U.S. foreign policy decisions on public opinion abroad."

63   Interview: Reinhardt.

64   "New Bureaucracy Absorbs USIA and Voice of America," *Washington Post*, 3 April 1978, p. A9; David Binder, "The Intercultural Communicator: John Edward Reinhardt," *New York Times*, Saturday, 1 April 1978, p. 46. For an anthology of editorial reaction see UoA CU 33/14, Pistor to heads of elements and services, 20 April 1978.

65   Reinhardt and his key staff had daily contact with the State Department. From May 1977, the deputy director and head of policy at the USIA also attended a weekly meeting with NSC staff; see JCL WHCF sf exec., box FG 210, file FG266, Henze & Schecter to Brzezinski, 18 May 1977. Issues in May included long range guidance and planning, with the USIA stressing the need to have presidential speeches as far in advance as possible, and requesting an interview with Rosalind Carter to explain her forthcoming Latin American tour.

66   JCL WHCF sf exec., box FG 210, file FG266, Schecter to Brzezinski, 7 June 1977.

67   GRFL Marsh files, box 39, "transition reports 1977, USIA," USIA transition briefing book, December 1976, pp. 116–17.

68   JCL WHCF sf exec., box FG 208, file FG262, 28th report, United States Advisory Commission on Information. The US and OAS speeches may be found at *PPP JC, 1977*, Vol. 1, pp. 444–51 and 611–16.

The NSC codified the administration's plan for human rights in a document called Presidential Review Memorandum 28 of July 1977. PRM 28 praised the USIA and VOA for their coverage of the early months of Carter's human rights initiative. It went on to recommend that

> Coordinated, balanced and consistent future programming should develop the theme that human rights is a universal human aspiration, not an American idiosyncrasy, and should cover positive human rights developments, particularly outside the U.S. as well as the record of continuing violations of human rights.

The document noted a need for tact in closed societies where the United States had to beware of crossing the line into raising false hopes or sparking rebellion. In the coming months the VOA planned a series of twenty-minute "VOA Forum" shows dealing in depth with human rights issues. The USIA's film and television branch, IMV, had plans to increase the purchase and production of human rights–related films and to introduce relevant material into its existing range of widely placed television series.[69] Regional achievements of the USIA in the field of human rights included an intensive program across Africa and the launch in Argentina of a series of programs called "Return to the Rule of Law," which brought together jurists from the U.S. and Argentina to discuss legal reform. Later in the Carter period, the ICA played midwife to the creation of the South Asian Committee on Human Rights and Development (SACOHRD), a five-nation nongovernmental forum to promote these issues.[70] Carter's human rights message won friends in the developing world, but it placed Moscow on the defensive.[71] The Soviet government denounced Carter's criticism of their treatment of dissidents as an "inadmissible intervention in domestic affairs" and retaliated by giving global play to alleged human and civil rights violations by the FBI and CIA, hinting that one or both agencies had a hand in the Kennedy and King assassinations. It was propaganda hardball.[72]

In one aspect of human rights – equal opportunity in the workplace – the USIA/ICA landed on the wrong side of the story in the Carter years. In March 1977, a former agency employee named Luba Medina filed an individual suit under the Equal Employment Opportunity Act, alleging that the agency had failed to rehire her on grounds of her gender. On 25 November 1977 a second woman – Carolee Hartman – broadened the case by filing a civil class action on behalf of all women "who have made applications to work for and/or are currently employed by the United States Information Agency . . . and who have been and continue to be adversely affected by

69 PRM 28, 7 July 1977, pp. 60–62, http://jimmycarterlibrary.org/documents/prmemorandums/prm28.pdf.
70 JCL Plains file, box 16, file: Accomplishments . . . ICA, Reinhardt to President, "Major Accomplishments of USICA during your administration," 16 December 1980. Some USICA staff question the achievement of Carter's human rights policy in Latin America, and consider that it set matters back. Interview: Don Mathes, 12 December 1995.
71 JCL WHCF sf exec., box FO-39, file: FO 6, Reinhardt to Brzezinski, 30 September 1977.
72 JCL NSA BM sf box 1–9, file: ICA, Reinhardt to Brzezinski, 6 April 1977, with "Recent Soviet media treatment of US domestic affairs."

the [Agency's sexually discriminatory] employment practices." Hartman's case arose from an application for the job of writer/editor on the USIA magazine *Horizon*, during which the male interviewer had stated that he was looking to hire a man for the job. In 1978 the court provisionally accepted the Hartman case as a class action. More plaintiffs joined the cause, including Luba Medina, Toura Kem, Josefina Martinez, and Rose Kobylinski. Evidence suggested that gender bias was especially entrenched at the Voice of America, where certain language services seemed shamelessly sexist. One applicant was rebuked for attempting to "take a job away from a man." The plaintiffs soon included veteran broadcasters from other countries, including the BBC World Service and a Bangladeshi novelist, all turned away by the VOA in preference for less qualified men. The USIA's attorneys fought the case every step of the way, arguing back and forth across statistical evidence. The case nearly collapsed in 1979 when, following an adverse ruling, Hartman's firm of lawyers felt unwilling to appeal. Her young attorney, Bruce Fredrickson, agreed to handle the case in his spare time. The Hartman case became the agency's equivalent of Jarndyce v. Jarndyce in Charles Dickens' *Bleak House*. Successive USIA directors inherited and lived around the case like an ugly piece of furniture, while certain discriminatory practices continued, creating a legal time bomb for a future director.[73]

*

In the summer of 1978, the Carter administration finally announced its choice for VOA director: Peter Straus. R. Peter Straus was born in 1923 into a wealthy New York Jewish family with a tradition of public service. After graduating from Yale in 1943, he commanded a bomber in World War Two, served in OMGUS in post-war Germany, and worked for public relations pioneer Edward L. Bernays. He then became director of special features at the New York radio station WMCA, owned by his father. With his father, he was involved in the first publication of *The Diaries of Anne Frank*, and later he wrote a biography of Anne's father, Otto Frank. From 1950 to 1958 Straus worked for the International Labor Organization in Geneva, and then he returned to the Straus Broadcasting Group to serve as its President. Under his leadership, WMCA became an essential part of the 1960s in New York, playing all the best new music first and then, as the decade ended, converting to an all-talk format. Straus was a staunch Democrat. In 1964 he chaired Robert Kennedy's successful campaign for the Senate in New York. In 1966 he consulted for the USIA on Latin America. From 1967 to

[73] Twenty-three years later the case ended in massive compensation for the plaintiffs and a trial lawyer of the year award for Fredrickson. Documentation on the case may be found online at http://caselaw.lp.findlaw.com/cgi-bin/getcase.pl?court=dc&navby=case&no=955030a and http://www.usdoj.gov/osg/briefs/1996/w961522w.txt. Fredrickson's story is told in his award citation from Trial Lawyers for Public Justice at http://www.tlpj.org/pr/tloy_winner_080200.htm. For press coverage see Sharon Walsh, "Huge Sex Bias Case Enters Last Phase," *Washington Post*, 19 December 1996, p. A1. For thumbnail sketches of plaintiffs see Webster, Fredrickson & Brackshaw press release, 22 March 2000, on line at http://www.contilaw.com/articles/usiasettlementpr.htm and the film's own account of the case at http://www.wfb-law.com/hartman.php.

1969 he served as Assistant Administrator for Africa in the Agency for International Development. Although Straus joked that he was appointed director of the VOA because he was the only Democrat who owned a radio station, his mix of experience equipped him admirably.[74]

Straus saw his core mission at the VOA as moving the Voice beyond its old Cold War focus to reach out to the wider world. On Capitol Hill, however, he found it rather easier to sell the idea of building transmitters in the United States than broadcasting to particular language groups. Legislators seemed particularly uninterested in Africa and Latin America. Straus felt that he never really had a good answer for the perennial question "how do you know that people are listening?" The return of Cold War pressure set some of these concerns to rest.[75] Within the Voice, Straus sought to establish a tighter rein on the language services and to ensure that all thirty-six languages said essentially the same thing. He soon realized that it was actually quite difficult to determine exactly what was being broadcast. To maintain discipline around the message, he introduced a system of surprise back-translation exercises. Each day, output in a different language would be put under the microscope. The exercise laid bare the multiple linguistic problems in communicating the news and obvious parallel problems in getting the foreign staff to understand the VOA's mission.[76]

Significant VOA broadcasts early in Straus' tenure included, in September 1977, the transmission into the U.S.S.R. of an "Appeal to the Parliaments of All Countries Signatory to the Final Act of the Helsinki Conference," as submitted to the *New York Times* by the dissident Andrei Sakharov.[77] The Voice prioritized one international story in particular: Cuban and Soviet activities in Angola and the Horn of Africa. In December 1977, the USIA began a regular series of reports for the NSC, sent every eighteen days, surveying the VOA's output on this subject. Early indications of effectiveness included complaints about the VOA's African coverage on Radio Moscow, though, writing in May, Brzezinski asked the VOA to pay particular attention to getting news of the world's concern over African interventions to the people of Cuba and the U.S.S.R.[78] Subsequent themes for the VOA

[74] Interview: Peter Straus, 3 April 2004; Don Oberdorfer, "Straus Seen VOA Director," *Washington Post*, 12 June 1977, p. A20. The youngest of three brothers, Straus was initially named Rachel, as his mother had been promised a girl. He used his middle name until he joined the Army Air Force, when it was "politic" to exchange the Rachel for Ronald.

[75] Interview: Straus and Reinhardt. Reinhardt experienced the same on Capitol Hill. He recalled a senator explaining that although he was personally interested he had to think about his constituency and "the people of Minnesota don't much care about international information."

[76] Interview: Straus, 3 April 2004.

[77] "A Letter from Andrei D. Sakharov," *New York Times*, 4 February 1978, p. 19 complains that the text printed in the newspaper and hence broadcast by the VOA included certain changes not cleared in advance with him.

[78] Broadcasts included digests of American editorial reaction and press reporting, coverage from the UN, and reports from National Public Radio when there were gaps in the VOA's own field reporting. Between 1 and 17 February 1978 the VOA carried fifty news items, excluding summaries and headline recaps. Then, from 18 February to 7 March, the VOA broadcast sixty-seven daily news reports, thirty-nine correspondent reports, and a major radio documentary entitled "Close-up: The Horn of Africa,"

suggested by Brzezinski included emphasis on the cost of Soviet/Cuban adventurism at home.[79]

Straus still had his problems. While the charter had established the right and duty of the VOA to speak freely on the air, the autumn of 1976 had shown that the Voice still needed to resolve the relationship between its journalists overseas and U.S. embassies. The hybrid status of a VOA reporter as both journalist and U.S. government official was at the root of many problems. It boiled down to this question: Was the ambassador's word law? Yet the VOA would lose a lot if it severed its link with U.S. embassies. The VOA's fifteen foreign bureaus rode piggyback on the embassies and cultural centers in which they were located, enjoying free accommodation and access to communications technology. This problem reached a critical point in November 1977 when the State Department blocked the VOA's Doug Roberts from talking to the Polisario guerrilla army in the western Sahara. Straus and Reinhardt agreed that the issue of a correspondent's role had to be settled once and for all.[80]

On 21 December 1977, Straus announced that a panel of experts under the chairmanship of the recently retired *Washington Post* diplomatic correspondent Chalmers Roberts would review the whole matter of the VOA's foreign newsgathering and develop "guidelines and procedures."[81] The panel worked swiftly and presented its report on 9 March 1978. The report declared that the VOA "must have the right, free of diplomatic restrictions to gather and send news to Washington headquarters" and that the status of VOA correspondents should be "as close as possible to that of correspondents of commercial American press and broadcasting organizations." This meant that VOA correspondents should no longer have diplomatic passports or special visa privileges, or work from embassies. The panel also called for a redeployment of VOA correspondents away from Europe, which was then well served by U.S. commercial journalism, to focus on the Eastern bloc and the "Third World," where they could usefully generate "background and explanatory material . . . to give depth to the news." There was a small sting in the tail. Roberts also expressed a measure of criticism of VOA personnel, noting, "If VOA news persons are to be considered bona

as well as original programming in English and Portuguese to Africa services. See JCL NSA SM Henze, box 1, Reinhardt to Brzezinski, 1 December 1977; JCL WHCF sf, exec., box FG 210, file: FG 266–1, Reinhardt to Brzezinski, 25 January 1978 and 10 February 1978; JCL WHCF OA: 5561 (1), Reinhardt to Brzezinski, 2 March 1978; JCL WHCF sf, exec., box FG 39, file: FO 5–3, Reinhardt to Brzezinski, 9 March 1978; JCL NSC BM sf, box 1–9, Brzezinski to Reinhardt, 30 May 1978. For report from May 1978 see WHCF OA: 4852.

79 JCL NSA agency files, box 10, file: ICA, 9–12/79, Brzezinski to director ICA, "broadcasts to USSR and Eastern Europe," 1 October 1979, drafted by Michael Brement: "Moscow provides petroleum to Havana at a substantial discount and pays the Cubans five times the world price for sugar. The net effect is a direct lowering of the standard of living of Soviet citizens."

80 Interviews: Kamenske, 6 December 1995, Heil, 29 November 1995; Straus, 3 April 2004; Richard M. Weintraub, "VOA, State Dept. in Conflict over a Correspondent's Role," *Washington Post*, 22 November 1977, p. A15. The fifteen bureaus were in London, Paris, Munich, Vienna, Jerusalem, Cairo, Abidjan (Ivory Coast), Nairobi, Johannesburg, New Delhi, Bangkok, Hong Kong, Tokyo, Mexico City, and Rio de Janeiro.

81 The other members of the panel were E. W. Kenworthy, formerly of the *New York Times*; Pauline Frederick, international affairs analyst for National Public Radio; William Scott, vice president for radio news at Westinghouse Broadcasting; and the former U.S. ambassador to Ghana, Franklin H. Williams.

fide journalists by their own government, or anyone else, they should be the best and most professional that VOA can attract. This is not now the case."[82]

Straus and Reinhardt agreed on a new set of guidelines for VOA correspondents along the lines suggested by Chalmers Roberts. VOA correspondents now lost their special PX privileges at U.S. government facilities overseas. They would be treated in just the same way as any other American journalists. Correspondents were no longer required to ask an ambassador's permission to enter a country or conduct a controversial interview. Permission came from the chief of news in Washington. They were, however, expected to inform the embassy of such plans in advance to allow the embassy an opportunity to raise the matter in Washington if they thought it necessary. Reinhardt noted that the new procedures in some ways would benefit the embassy, as they "relieve the ambassador and his mission colleagues from even the appearance of responsibility for the content of VOA news broadcasts." Finally, the VOA followed Roberts' suggestion and scaled back its European operations in order to invest in Africa, Asia, and Latin America.[83] The system worked well. Chalmers Roberts himself heralded a new era in VOA journalism. The VOA had even been able to broadcast a documentary about the Middle East featuring a statement from a PLO spokesman in his own voice. When the U.S. embassy in South Korea objected to an interview with opposition leader Kim Young Sam, it went ahead regardless.[84]

Although the new correspondent guidelines placed an increased distance between the VOA and the foreign policy bureaucracy in the matter of news, there was a tradeoff elsewhere in the Voice output. In the second major change of 1978, Straus oversaw a major revision of the old system of commentaries to become what amounted to editorials expressing U.S. foreign policy. For Straus the introduction of formal daily editorials that would be carried in all VOA languages was logical and necessary, as it had been for his father when he introduced editorials at WMCA New York. At the ICA, Reinhardt agreed and saw policy commentaries as means to fulfill the VOA's charter obligation to "present the policies of the United States clearly and effectively." In August 1978, Reinhardt suggested a set of procedures for the commentaries. Although the regular staff of the VOA's current affairs unit would write the commentaries, they would be separated from regular programming for broadcast. They would be clearly labeled as a commentary, and in most language services the announcer reading the commentary

82 Interviews: Kamenske, 6 December 1995 and Heil, 29 November 1995; "Ex-reporter Heads Study on VOA News Role," *Washington Post*, 21 December 1977, p. A8; Chalmers Roberts, "Report of the Panel to Study the Role of Foreign Correspondents at Voice of America," 9 March 1978; Richard Weintraub, "Sweeping Changes Urged for VOA Correspondents," *Washington Post*, 12 March 1978, p. A32.

83 JCL WHCF sf, exec., box FG 218, file: FG 298–1, Reinhardt to Brzezinski (cc. Vance), "New guidelines for VOA correspondents," 1 June 1978 with draft guidelines (Brzezinski reacted to this with a handwritten note asking "whether this doesn't go too far. State should *control* more"); Christopher to Reinhardt, 16 June 1978 (with suggested revisions). The final version was issued on 30 June 1978. For press coverage see Richard M. Weintraub, "VOA Limits Embassy Ties to Its Staff," *Washington Post*, 6 July 1978.Interviews: Kamenske, 6 December 1995 and Heil, 29 November 1995.

84 Chalmers M. Roberts, "New Image for Voice of America," *New York Times*, 13 April 1980, Sunday Magazine, pp. 27 et seq.

would not be heard elsewhere in programming. Reinhardt imagined at least three commentaries each week. The writers were expected to seek guidance on themes and content from ICA policy staff (specifically an Office of Fast Policy Guidance, then headed by Paul Blackburn) and through them State and NSC. But script clearance, although sometimes recommended, was not compulsory. As promised in Reinhardt's memo of the previous spring, content would be reviewed after broadcast. As Straus recalled, Brzezinski requested approval of all commentaries in advance, but following a ruling from the President himself was obliged to accept sight of the scripts after the fact. The editorials began in October 1978. Staff hated them, but they made the VOA's value clear on Capitol Hill.[85]

*

Shortly after the creation in April 1978, the ICA launched two major public diplomacy initiatives. The first was a package of measures to reach out to the so-called "successor generation" in Western Europe for whom, Reinhardt noted, 'the U.S. is often viewed through the prism of Vietnam, Watergate, and anti-capitalist sentiment." The agency redirected resources accordingly and was glad to see this theme taken up in a "successor generation" working group in the Atlantic Council and a special resolution at the North Atlantic Assembly.[86] The theme would remain a major element in the USIA's output for many years. The second major theme was disarmament.

In June 1978, Brzezinski created an Interagency Committee on Public Diplomacy and Disarmament. Arms had emerged as a controversial issue in the summer of 1977 when the *Washington Post* revealed that the Carter administration planned to deploy neutron bombs in Europe. Western Europeans disliked the implied willingness of the United States to fight a limited nuclear war on their soil, and the Soviet Union made swift capital.[87] Brzezinski did not intend to be caught out twice and hence launched a year-long interagency initiative to stimulate international discussion on disarmament. The ICA acted as the lead agency, with deputy director Charles W. Bray as its chair. Brzezinski's objectives included drawing new foreign groups and individuals into the debate around arms, to broaden support for American policies in the field, and "to diminish the ability of the Soviet Union and other to command public attention in foreign countries on the basis of emotional rhetoric." Proposed methods included regional seminars on arms control and disarmament issues; bringing foreign journalists and scholars to the U.S. to discuss the subject with their American counterparts and

---

85   Interviews: Straus and Haratunian (15 December 1995); Haratunian papers, Reinhardt to Straus, "VOA commentaries," 14 August 1978; Bray to Christopher, 23 October 1978. Internal guidelines on commentaries issued by the VOA on 24 January 1980 (Haratunian papers, memo by Robert E. Kays, "In house handling of commentaries and news analyses") permitted commentaries to advocate policy, set up "straw men" in argument, and assigned responsibility for ensuring that the commentaries complied with policy to the VOA Policy Application Staff.

86   JCL NSC BM sf, box 1–9, file: ICA, Reinhardt to Aaron, "Proposed presidential initiative: The "successor generation" and the NATO summit," 19 May 1978; JCL Plains file, box 16, file: Accomplishments...ICA, Reinhardt to the President, "Major Accomplishments of USICA during your administration," 16 December 1980.

87   For Brzezinski's account of this affair, see Brzezinksi, *Power and Principle*, pp. 301–15.

disseminating their conclusions back to their home countries; and research to inform American policy makers about foreign opinion on the subject. The approach worked well.[88]

While Reinhardt was generally encouraged by the progress of the ICA, he noted the problem of underfunding in international exchange. Although, as of 1978, thirty-eight sitting heads of government had participated in U.S. exchanges, including Anwar Sadat in Egypt, Valéry Giscard d'Estaing in France, Malcolm Fraser in Australia, Mario Soares in Portugal, Julius Nyerere in Tanzania, and Helmut Schmidt in West Germany, the total U.S. exchange budget had shrunk by fifty-seven percent in inflation-adjusted dollars since the peak in the Johnson years. Reinhardt had asked for $13 million to help correct this at the end of 1977, but to no avail. Brzezinski noted that military spending had long since outstripped "expenditures on the competition for ideas." "We have," he wrote, "a serious lag to make good."[89] Reinhardt created a detailed proposal to rectify any neglect of the exchange program with an initial expenditure of $6.25 million in the first year. The President found no funds for this in the 1980 budget but urged Reinhardt to keep the proposal alive for future consideration.[90] In his State of the Union address on 25 January 1979, President Carter pledged to "strengthen the programs of the ICA which present a diversity of American culture to the world and deepen our appreciation of other cultures."[91] For the time being there was at least one element of expansion: the Hubert Humphrey program.

In March 1978, Jimmy Carter toured Latin America. It was a public relations triumph. At a state dinner in Caracas he unveiled a new exchange initiative in memory of the late Senator Humphrey to "bring poor but outstanding students from Latin America and throughout the world to study in the colleges of the United States." The idea began with President Omar Herrera Torrijos of Panama. During interdepartmental discussions to develop the plan, Charles Bray of the ICA suggested giving the scholarships an emphasis on public administration and development, which influenced the shape of the program: bringing midcareer professionals from the developing world for a year of graduate study in the United States. Carter persuaded Congress set up a $1 million trust fund to prime the scholarships and signed the necessary legislation on 30 May. He unveiled the Hubert H. Humphrey North–South scholarship program on 5 December 1978. The ICA administered the program with the Institute of International Education. The first fellows arrived in September 1979.[92]

88 The committee focused its work on SALT (the priority in Europe), nonproliferation, and the push for a comprehensive test ban and the parallel debate around conventional arms transfers and regional arms control agreements (all of which were emphasized elsewhere in the world); see JCL NSC BM sf, box 1–9, file: ICA, Brzezinski to Secretary of State et al. "Interagency Committee on Public Diplomacy and Disarmament," 8 June 1978; Bray to Brzezinski, 5 September 1978, and Brzezinski to Dir. ICA et al., 16 October 1978, ordering continued interdepartmental cooperation to execute this plan.

89 JCL NSC BM sf, box 1–9, file: ICA, Reinhardt to President, 5 October 1978; Brzezinski to President, 24 October 1978. Also JCL NSA SM Henze paper, box 3, McIntyre to President, 1 December 1978 etc. On Reinhardt's 1977 bid see JCL NSA SM Henze, box 1, Henze to Aaron, 5 December 1977.

90 JCL WHCF executive, box FO 35, file FO 5, Brzezinksi to Reinhardt, 15 December 1978 etc.

91 For text see *PPP JC 1979* Vol.1, p. 142.

92 For NSC documentation see JCL WHCF sf exec., box FO-35, file: FO 5–1, Brzezinski to Vice President et al., 17 April 1978; Bray to Brzezinski, 22 April 1978; Dodson to Vice President et al.,

In his report to the President on the first six months of ICA activity, Reinhardt could boast of support for U.S. policy. He reported Soviet research revealing up to seventy-five percent audience penetration for the VOA among the urban intelligentsia of the U.S.S.R. He took pride in a well-oiled ICA press service that had transmitted the full text of the Camp David accords to the world overnight. The ICA had accomplished this with less per capita expenditure on public diplomacy than France, West Germany, Japan, or the United Kingdom, and twenty-nine percent fewer staff than in 1966. As the ultimate proof of the ICA's effectiveness, Reinhardt cited the mounting attacks on the ICA from the U.S.S.R. Russia, he surmised, understood the power of Carter's human rights message. The United States had regained the initiative in the war of ideas. On reading the report, President Carter wrote just one word: "good."[93]

3) PROGRESS AND PERIL: THE ICA IN 1979

The Carter era brought closer cultural relations with the People's Republic of China. Although initial feelers from Beijing in 1978 looked for exchanges based on technology, Reinhardt's staff worked successfully to inject a cultural dimension into the discussion. Small-scale academic exchanges began as the year ended.[94] January 1979 brought a breakthrough. On 31 January 1979, during Vice Premier Deng Xiaoping's visit to Washington, the United States and China concluded a full cultural exchange agreement. The United States moved swiftly to build on this opportunity, encouraged by the fact that the Minister of Culture was the former head of the PRC's liaison office (effectively ambassador) in Washington, Huang Chen. Reinhardt impressed the NSC with his enthusiasm to develop student and cultural exchanges. On 14 March, the NSC asked the ICA to develop a detailed plan by 1 April 1979 to include the National Endowments for the Arts and Humanities, Office of Education, and Library of Congress. Early ICA offerings in China included an exhibit at the American embassy in Beijing called "US advances in control of crop insect pests."[95] On 28 August 1979, Vice President Mondale and Vice Premiere Deng Xiaoping signed an "implementing accord" for cultural exchanges in Beijing. The countries exchanged art exhibits and ten foreign language educators to enhance the teaching of the other's language and began mutual projects in translation and publication. The VOA and Radio Beijing agreed

17 May 1978; "Humphrey Scholarships Approved," *New York Times*, 31 May 1978, p. A11; Arthur O. Sultzberger Jr., "Humphrey Scholarships Initiated," *New York Times*, 6 December 1978. For President Carter's speeches launching this program see *PPP JC 1978*, Vol. I, 28 March 1978, pp. 617–19; Vol. II, 15 November 1978 (p. 2038) and 5 December 1978 (pp. 2158–60).

93   JCL NSC BM sf, box 1–9, file: ICA, Reinhardt to President, 5 October 1978.
94   JCL Plains file, box 16, file: Accomplishments . . . ICA, Reinhardt to the President, "Major Accomplishments of USICA during your administration," 16 December 1980.
95   For text see *PPP JC 1979* Vol. 1, pp. 207–10; JCL NSA agency file, box 9, file: ICA, 1–5/79, Oksenberg (NSC) to Brzezinski, 8 March 1979; Aaron to Reinhardt. 14 March 1979; JCL WHCF sf, exec., box PR 44, file: PR 8, Cohen (ICA) to Dodson (NSC) 25 June 1979.

to exchange staff for study tours, and an academic advisor joined the U.S. embassy in Beijing. It was an exciting beginning.[96]

The agency developed its exchange work in Eastern Europe. In 1977, the USIA had concluded new cultural agreements with Hungary and Bulgaria. The ICA renewed these agreements in 1979 and 1980, respectively. Its flagship exhibition in the region was a major art show housed in a geodesic dome, entitled "America Now – a Look at Arts in the 1970s." The wife of Vice President Mondale opened the show in Belgrade in June 1979. Its tour included stops in Budapest, Hungary and Bucharest, Romania, where it attracted 130,000 visitors. Exhibits in 1980 included "Laser World U.S.A." at the Leipzig spring fair. ICA increased its representation in Yugoslavia, opening an information center in Titograd in 1980, which meant that every Yugoslav republic now had a USIS post.[97]

The Carter years had seen increased U.S. public diplomacy in the Middle East to advance Carter's peace agenda and ease relations with the oil producers. In August 1977, the VOA upgraded its Arabic service, relaying programming by its first ever satellite circuit from Washington to the relay station on Rhodes. That same month USIA launched its wireless file in Arabic.[98] In 1979, the ICA mobilized in support of the Middle East peace process. Initiatives included a specially funded group of "cultural normalization" international visitor grants created to bring together Israelis, Egyptians, and other Arabs and the creation and distribution by satellite of video documentaries outlining the Camp David accords and other developments. The ICA also supplied feedback on the state of world opinion.[99]

The agency also showed its mettle with skilled media work around the deployment of theater nuclear forces (TNF) in Western Europe in 1979. The ICA avoided a repeat of the sort of alarm caused in 1977 by discussion of the neutron bomb. Extensive contact between ICA officers and European opinion leaders paved the way, with supporting work in the form of speakers, briefings, press materials, and video. Although a level of opposition persisted, most especially in the Low Countries, the agency claimed that by the end of the Carter years "public diplomacy" had "in large measure defused European anxieties and neutralized the Soviet Union's vigorous anti-TNF campaign."[100]

---

[96] UoA CU 34/8, "Implementing Accord on Cultural Exchanges Signed in Beijing," *USICA World*, Vol. 1, no. 5, October–November 1979, p. 1.

[97] UoA CU 34/8, *USICA World*, Vol. 1, no. 4, August–September 1979; JCL WHCF CF, box PR 44, box PR8, Dodson to dir. ICA, 27 December 1979; Dodson to Cohen (ICA), 23 November 1979; JCL Plains file, box 16, Reinhardt to the President, "Major Accomplishments of USICA during your administration." 16 December 1980.

[98] *USIA World*, Vol. 12, no. 4, p. 12. Other agency activities included a trip to Washington for nine Arab journalists to observe the foreign policy process; see JCL WHCF sf exec., box FO-39, file: FO 5–3, Schecter (NSC) to Brzezinski, 12 January 1978.

[99] JCL Plains file, box 16, file: Accomplishments...ICA, Reinhardt to the President, "Major Accomplishments of USICA during your administration," 16 December 1980, and box 3, Foreign Media Reaction, Middle East Peace, 27 March 1979.

[100] JCL Plains file, box 16, file: Accomplishments...ICA, Reinhardt to the President, "Major Accomplishments of USICA during your administration," 16 December 1980.

In the course of 1979, the ICA launched its Arts America program, which involved a special agreement with the National Endowments for the Arts and Humanities to increase agency access to American cultural materials. With NEA and NEH support and advice, Arts America projects included a major retrospective exhibition of American art in Mexico City, international tours by American folk musicians, international literary events featuring such writers as Susan Sontag and Joyce Carol Oates, and workshops bringing American artists into contact with their peers in the developing world.[101]

With an eye to the "American Learning" agenda, the ICA produced a symposium on "Books and Broadcasting for Children" in cooperation with the Association for Library Services to Children (ALSC) and a television producer from WPBT-TV Miami named Cecily Truett. The event ran from 13 September to 19 October 1979. It was the brainchild of Mildred Marcy, the Director of Institutional Relations in the E bureau, who recognized the potential for synergy between two separate grant proposals submitted to the agency in 1978: a proposal to bring international authors and librarians to America and a proposal for the exchange of educational children's television. The symposium seemed the perfect way to mark the International Year of the Child. Because the project did not fit any particular country plan, funding had to come from the director's discretionary fund. Reinhardt and Bray agreed to release funding provided that the agency also sought private funding.[102] Delegates for the symposium came in pairs from fifteen countries. They ranged from distinguished children's broadcasters, such as the producer of BBC television's *Jackanory* program, to the youth officer from the Syrian Ba'ath Party. For a month they toured libraries (including the Library of Congress) and book fairs and even visited the studios of *Sesame Street*. The symposium created a buzz around the subject of children's books in the television industry, which had been previously cast as the natural enemy of literacy. As a direct result, the project director, Truett, won a commission from the CPB and Kellogg's cereals to create a children's book program aimed at four- to eight-year-olds. *Reading Rainbow* premiered on 260 public television stations across the country in July 1983. Winning eighteen Emmys in its first two decades on the small screen, *Reading Rainbow* helped to engage a generation of young Americans in books. ICA could not have asked for better return on their investment.[103]

*

On 28 March 1979, the Three Mile Island Unit Two nuclear power plant near Middletown, Pennsylvania experienced a partial meltdown of its core. Radioactive gas

---

[101] JCL Plains file, box 16, file: Accomplishments . . . ICA, Reinhardt to the President, "Major Accomplishments of USICA during your administration," 16 December 1980.

[102] In the event USICA provided grants of $35,000 each for WPBT and the ALSC, and $100,000 to pay for international visitor grants for the thirty delegates. The Exxon Corporation kicked in $5,000 to help and WPBT-TV contributed $18,000 in staff and facilities for a workshop session. The Department of Health, Education and Welfare funded three American participants. Other American institutions rallied round to host the visitors.

[103] For a file on the symposium see UoA CU 306/5; the quotation is from Truitt to Marcy, 30 September 1982; ADST oral history, Mildred Marcy. Ari Goldman, "A Series Aims at Turning Young Viewers into Readers," *New York Times*, 10 July 1983, p. H3. On Reading Rainbow see also http://pbskids.org/readingrainbow/family/about_rr.html.

leaked to the outside world. At the Voice of America, Bernie Kamenske realized that the story would be a benchmark for VOA coverage of American news and approached Voice director Peter Straus with a proposal for special programming on the accident beyond the usual news coverage. Appealing to history, Kamenske warned portentously, "People will remember you as the director who didn't if you don't." With Straus's permission, Kamenske assigned three VOA correspondents to surround the story: Al Ortiz, John Paxton, and Sean Kelly. Kamenske cautioned them to be sure that the power company's statements were clearly labeled as quotes and not allowed to slip into the record as fact. The VOA was not about to become an international mouthpiece for the nuclear power industry. Kamenske was intensely proud of the VOA's Three Mile Island coverage, but it did not stop the Soviet spokesman Georgi Arbatov from defending Soviet reluctance to discuss Chernobyl eight years later by citing "Voice of America's Three Mile Island cover-up."[104]

During the summer of 1979, the VOA played an important role in U.S. policy toward the "boat people" refugees expelled from Vietnam, with commentaries condemning Hanoi and information about where the refugees might receive a welcome. In August Straus spoke with pride to the *Washington Post* about the growing credibility of the VOA.[105] His enthusiasm concealed deep reservations over the working of Carter's foreign policy. In September 1979, Peter Straus resigned in order to support Edward Kennedy's bid for the White House in 1980. In remarks to the press, he complained that Carter was "badly served by subordinates" and alluded to the mixed messages arising from the split between Vance and Brzezinski: "conflicting foreign policy makes it difficult for Americans and very hard for foreigners to understand where the country is going."[106] The departure of Straus coincided with growing mood of crisis at the ICA. The summer had seen the fall of the Somoza regime in Nicaragua and the discovery of a Soviet combat brigade on Cuba. The administration responded with a panicked succession of initiatives. Brzezinski ordered the ICA to emphasize Soviet complicity in the human rights abuses of the dictatorships of Amin in Uganda and Macias in Equatorial Guinea,[107] and Carter ordered "a major public relations

104 Interview: Kamenske, 6 December 1995.
105 Henry Mitchell, "Any Day," *Washington Post*, 10 August 1979, pp. D1 & D10; interview: Kamenske. Unfortunately in the same interview Straus offended staff by discussing the new rules for VOA foreign correspondents in terms of their no longer being able to "buy their scotch at embassy commissaries." The remark would be remembered longer than his transmitter construction program or increased broadcast hours.
106 JCL WHCF sf, exec., Box FG 218, file: FG 298–1, Straus to Phillip J. Wise, 12 September 1979 etc., minute by Fran Voorde (Deputy Appointments Secretary) to Wise; Interview: Peter Straus, 3 April 2004. JCL WHCF sf, CF, Box FG 218, file: FG 218/A, Straus to President, 21 September 1979, President to Straus, 28 September 1979. Straus left office on 21 October 1979. Terrence Smith, "Voice of America Director, a Kennedy Ally, Resigns," *New York Times*, 2 October 1979, p. B16; Richard M. Weintraub, "Voice of America Director Quits, Cites Carter's Staff," *Washington Post*, 3 October 1979, p. 3. For a subsequent letter to Straus, intended to mend breaches, see JCL WHCF sf, exec., Box FG 218, file: FG 218–1, President to Straus, 6 November 1979.
107 JCL NSA agency files, box 10, file: ICA, 9–12/79, Brzezinski to SoS/Dir. ICA, "Soviet Union and Human rights in Equatorial Guinea and Uganda," 9 October 1979. He had issued instructions to this end in August 1979.

campaign against OPEC price increases."[108] But the key issue in U.S. public diplomacy that fall was the need to reach out to the Muslim world, and especially Iran and Afghanistan.

4) VALLEY OF THE SHADOW
IRAN AND AFGHANISTAN, 1979–81

Despite the Carter administration's genuine commitment to human rights, there were places in the world where strategic necessity prevailed and America turned a blind eye. This was the case in China, Romania, South Korea, the Philippines, Zaire, Morocco, Indonesia, and above all in Iran.[109] Here the gap between the noble rhetoric of the Carter administration and the tawdry reality of its support for the Shah threw up a shadow-image of the United States as the hypocritical source of that country's ills: "the Great Satan." During the course of 1978 the revolutionary movement against the Shah became increasingly an anti-American movement as well. In January 1979, as street demonstrations multiplied, the Shah cut his losses and fled. On 1 February the religious leader who had inspired the revolution, Ayatollah Ruhollah Khomeini, returned in triumph. The United States now faced a hostile regime in a key strategic area.

In the days that followed the fall of the Shah, the Carter administration launched a rather belated public diplomacy effort in Iran. Obvious needs included a VOA Farsi service. The VOA's Persian language service had been closed down once in 1946 and again in 1960. Giddens had tried in vain to relaunch it in the 1970s but had been overruled by State Department policy concerns. President Carter grew agitated at the long lead time necessary to launch the new service. The delay stemmed in part from the extreme care taken to ensure that none of the new staff employed were agents for the Shah. The VOA's Farsi service began slowly in April 1979 with three and one-half hours a week (half an hour a day). In November 1979 this increased to fourteen hours a week, in January to twenty-one, and by December 1980 it had reached an impressive thirty-five hours a week. Although critics at the NSC questioned whether the Voice had either the transmitter strength or the audience to make a difference, others were delighted by reports – six months into VOA Farsi – of intellectuals in Tehran halting parties at 10 p.m. to listen to VOA news. Significantly the Iranian initiative initially focused on the need to counter Soviet propaganda rather than Islamic fundamentalism. The State Department asked West Germany and – in a remarkable request – its new

---

[108] JCL NSA BM sf, box 10, file: ICA, Brzezinski to SoS/Dir. ICA, "OPEC price increases," 17 October 1979; for an early report of ICA/VOA material in this vein see JCL WHCF sf, exec., box FG 218, file: FG 298, Reinhardt to Brzezinski, 13 June 1979.

[109] For a discussion of Iran and human rights policy in general see John Dumbrell, *The Carter Presidency: A Re-evaluation*, second edition, Manchester: University of Manchester Press, 1995, pp. 149–203. The list of states indulged by Carter is on p. 189, where Dumbrell also notes that after 1979 Pakistan also got a soft line on its human rights abuses.

friends in Communist China to "take account of Soviet propaganda against us in their own Persian language broadcasting."[110]

Alarmed by the lead time for VOA Farsi, Brzezinski asked Reinhardt to review the VOA's entire balance of languages and transmitter time against the emerging priorities of the administration. Reinhardt recommended three new VOA languages: Mongolian, the West African language Lingala, and Azeri (a Turkic language spoken by about a third of Iranians as well as in Soviet Azerbaijan, Georgia, and Dagestan). He also suggested increased English programming to Africa. In the event, the only other new language launched that year was Hausa, to reach out to Muslims in West Africa. Notable absences from Reinhardt's list were Pashto and Dari, the key languages spoken in the country that was already emerging as the scene of the next major crisis: Afghanistan.[111]

In April 1978, a coup in Afghanistan had installed a new Marxist regime led by Noor Mohammad Taraki. The Soviet Union backed Taraki and sent military advisors. In late summer of 1978 the province of Nurestan exploded in rebellion. Other guerrilla risings followed. By the early months of 1979 the Soviets were alleging a U.S.-backed conspiracy to overthrow Taraki, whereas the United States suspected that the Soviets themselves were intriguing against Taraki or elements within his regime. On 14 February 1979, four members of an Afghan opposition group kidnapped the U.S. ambassador, Adolph 'Spike' Dubbs, from his car just outside USIS Kabul. They holed up in a hotel and demanded the release of Islamist political prisoners. Dubbs died of gunshot wounds during an Afghan rescue attempt "supervised" by Soviet advisors. It was one more symptom of mounting chaos.[112]

As the crisis deepened, Brzezinski ordered the ICA to "make a special effort – both in radio broadcasts and in other information output – to publicize the nature of Soviet actions in Afghanistan and to underscore the atheistic and anti-Islamic nature of both the Soviet and Afghan governments." Similar instructions went to the CIA.[113]

---

[110] JCL NSA BM sf, box 10, file: ICA, Reinhardt to Brzezinski, 14 November 1979; Henze to Hunter/Sick, 15 November 1979; JSCL NSA sf box 9, file: BIB, secret, Brzezinski to Vice President, 27 November 1979 and attachment 8D n/d. JCL NSA agency file, box 9, file: ICA, 1–5/79, Inderfurth (White House) to Sick/Henze (NSC), secret, 5 February 1979; Henze to Brzezinski, 6 February 1979.

[111] JCL NSA agency file, box 9, file: ICA, 1–5/79, Brzezinksi to Reinhardt, 9 February 1979; Reinhardt to Brzezinski, 7 March 1979. The VOA hoped that its Persian broadcasts would attract an audience in Afghanistan. For language statistics see RG 306, A1 (1066) box 112, USIA historical collection sfs, file: VOA history 1989, "VOA broadcasting history, 1955–1989"; also JCL NSA SM Henze papers box 3, Henze to Brzezinski, 1 June 1979, recommend Azeri, Pashto, Amharic for Ethiopia. VOA broadcasts in Pashto only began in 1982.

[112] On the Dubs killing see Robert Trumbull, "US Asserts Afghans Ignored Pleas Not to Attack Abductors of Envoy," *New York Times*, 15 February 1979, p. A1. For an account by Dubs's deputy see ADST oral history: Bruce Flattin.

[113] JCL NSA agency file, box 9, file: ICA, 1–5/79, Brzezinski to Dir., ICA, 30 March 1979. ICA's Afghan output to date had chiefly used the VOA and the wireless file. The VOA had broadcast U.S. press and official comment on events into Russia and South Asia and had paid especial attention to the killing of Ambassador Dubbs and the possibility of Soviet culpability in his death. Reinhardt reminded Brzezinski that the effective use of the VOA and the wireless file "depend heavily on publicly available material, including policy statements by U.S. officials." State and the White House needed to pull

September 1979 saw a further change of government in Afghanistan as the Soviet client Taraki died at the hands of supporters of his prime minister, Hafizullah Amin. By this stage the rebellion had broadened into a civil war. On 4 October, Brzezinski sent a secret memorandum to Reinhardt, noting that "There is increasing evidence of growing Soviet involvement in the Afghanistani civil war, and this fact should be publicized. Please report to me on what your various instrumentalities are doing and what they plan to do on this subject."[114]

Then came the thunderbolt. On 4 November 1979, Iranian students invaded the U.S. embassy in Tehran and held its occupants. They released some women and nonofficials on succeeding days but retained fifty-three as hostages, and demanded the return of the Shah, who had entered the U.S. for medical treatment, for trial. The revolutionary regime endorsed the action, while demonstrators rallied in the streets chanting "death to the Americans." The Carter administration correctly saw the problem as much wider than just Iran, but its response remained trapped in a Cold War framework. On 8 November, Brzezinski ordered:

> The Voice of America should begin programming and broadcasting to all Muslim countries information concerning the treatment of Muslims in the Soviet Union. Such programming should include references to the Soviet policy actively discouraging religious belief and practice and specify steps undertaken to the Soviet government to this end.[115]

By return Reinhardt noted that the VOA's output on the subject had recently included a three-part series in Bengali and Urdu on the state of Soviet Muslims and special programming around the 1400th anniversary of the foundation of the faith, which included comment on Soviet Islam. Reinhardt also transmitted warnings from the field. Muslims on the Soviet borders were well aware of conditions in the U.S.S.R. and crude attempts to appropriate the story for political gain could be counterproductive. Reinhardt preferred a more comparative approach in both VOA and ICA programming, documenting Islamic life around the world including that within the United States, confident that the contrast to the Soviet Union would emerge. Brzezinski took the point, and the VOA duly created a series of ten-minute features along these lines for broadcast to Islamic countries in December.[116]

The crisis in Iran was just the beginning. On 21 November, mobs in Pakistan, inflamed by a false radio report of American and Israeli involvement in an attack on the Grand Mosque in Mecca, sacked the American embassy in Islamabad and razed

their weight as well. JCL NSA SM Henze papers, box 3, Reinhardt to Brzezinski, "Soviet activities in and accusations about Afghanistan," 6 April 1979

[114] JCL NSA BM sf, box 10, file: ICA, Brzezinski to Reinhardt, 4 October 1979.

[115] JCL NSA agency files, box 10, file: ICA, 9–12/79, Brzezinski to dir. ICA, "VOA broadcasting," 8 November 1979.

[116] JCL NSA sf, box 9, file: BIB (RFE/RL, VOA), Reinhardt to Brzezinski, "VOA broadcasting," 15 November 1979; for reply see NSA agency files, box 10, file: ICA, 9–12/79, Brzezinski to Reinhardt, 16 November 1979. For follow-up report see NSA BM sf, box 10, file: ICA, Reinhardt to Brzezinski, 26 November 1979.

the USIS cultural centers in Rawalpindi and Lahore. The U.S. government warned Americans to avoid eleven Muslim countries and pulled staff back from the field. On 3 December, as if to emphasize the point, a mob sacked the U.S. embassy in Libya. Attacks on U.S. buildings in India and Bangladesh confirmed an unprecedented crisis.[117]

On 28 November, Brzezinski warned the Vice President that in the matter of broadcasting to the Islamic world "the Soviets are far ahead of us." Still focusing on the Cold War angle, he took steps to strengthen direct broadcasting to Soviet Muslims. The VOA had an Uzbek service, whereas RL carried material in all seven major Muslim languages, albeit with a weak signal and a tiny staff.[118] On 11 December, the Special Coordinating Committee at agreed to invest an extra $2 million in Radio Liberty's Islamic work and a further $1 million in the VOA's Farsi service. They also called for the leasing of relay facilities from other powers in the region. The administration prepared overtures to Egypt, Israel, and Saudi Arabia. A leak of these plans to the press meant that six months later little progress had been made. The ICA resolved to suggest a new transmitter complex in Sri Lanka.[119]

On 12 December 1979, Brzezinski ordered Reinhardt to launch "direct priority efforts toward developing informational and cultural programs in Moslem countries (and those with significant Moslem populations) which will underscore American identification with the authentic values for which Islam stands." He suggested a program of seminars, publications, and academic exchanges. Discussion documents mooted a horizon of one to five years for this work. But the affinity between the American way and Islam would prove a "hard sell." The United States had its support for the Shah to live down, and the American way could not easily be reconciled with a radical Islamic movement that increasingly defined itself in contrast to both the Soviet and American materialist visions of the future.[120]

Reinhardt acknowledged these problems in his response to Brzezinski. He reported feeling in the field that influential Muslims now believed the United States to be hostile to Islam as a whole and unable to differentiate between the militant Shi'ism of Iran and other strains of the faith. Reinhardt asked that all U.S. government pronouncements take care to not to lump all Muslims together. Reinhardt also suggested that the upsurge in radical Islam might be political: an expression of a wider "'Third World' kind of hostility to the developed nations in general and the U.S. in particular." He recommended that the United States seek to engage influential Muslims as

[117] Bernard Gwertzman, "US Asks Americans to Avoid 11 Nations," *New York Times*, 28 November 1979, p. A1.

[118] JSCL NSA sf box 9, file: BIB, secret, Brzezinski to Vice President, 27 November 1979.

[119] JCL NSA BM, sf box 1–9, file: BIB, Henze to Brzezinski, 14 December 1979 etc.; David Binder, "US Wary of Islamic Upheaval to Increase Broadcasts to Muslims," *New York Times*, 17 December 1979. For Henze's disappointed semiannual report see JCL NSA SM Henze, box 5, Henze to Brzezinski, "expanding radio broadcasting," 13 June 1980. NSC discussion of Sri Lanka may be found in JCL NSA sf box 9, file: BIB, Thornton to Denend, 2 January 1980.

[120] JCL NSA agency files, box 10, file: ICA, 9–12/79, Brzezinski to Reinhardt, 12 December 1979; also Rentschler to Brzezinski, "Moslem emotions and anti-American sentiment: Back to Basics," 3 December 1979.

both representatives of "Third World" political identity and a faith that shared some values with the United States. At the NSC, Paul Henze dismissed this advice as revealing "continued addiction in ICA to the 'Third World' orientation – which has been greatly overdone by that agency in this administration."[121]

*

Christmas 1979 afforded ample opportunity for human interest broadcasting about the hostages in Iran, such as the journey of three clergymen to celebrate Christmas services inside the embassy compound. Like an experienced police negotiator, the VOA worked hard to portray the hostages as individuals rather than an undifferentiated mass. The Voice broadcast profiles of particular hostages, including interviews with their families.[122] Then it happened. On Christmas Day the Soviet Union began a massive airlift of troops into Afghanistan. The State Department broke the news on 26 December, estimating that 5,000 troops had already arrived and 50,000 more were massed on the Soviet–Afghan border. The VOA covered the story as it unfolded, with multiple updates on the appointment of the new pro-Soviet president, Babrak Karmal, his appeal for Soviet military aid, and the summary trial and execution of his predecessor, Amin. Brzezinski complimented Reinhardt on the "good work."[123]

On 29 December, the VOA carried its first policy commentary on "The Soviet Intervention in Afghanistan." Quoting from President Carter's condemnation of the Soviet move, the piece compared this action to Hungary in 1956 and Czechoslovakia in 1968. The commentary poured scorn on the Soviet claim that a friendship treaty with Afghanistan entitled them to intervene. Subsequent coverage emphasized the anger and alarm at the Soviet action around the world, and its diplomatic ramifications as all hope of ratifying the hard-won SALT II treaty withered.[124]

On the evening of 4 January 1980, President Carter addressed the American people on television. He announced a package of sanctions against the U.S.S.R, including a substantial embargo on U.S. grain shipments. Other measures included a reduction in the area of cultural exchange. The ICA was well aware that U.S. public diplomacy gained much from the Soviet exchanges and ensured that despite a block on some of the high-level cultural work, academic exchanges continued quietly regardless of the sanctions.[125]

---

[121] JCL NSA agency files, box 10, file: ICA, 9–12/79, Reinhardt to Brzezinski, Communication with Muslim Countries, n/d and Henze to Brzezinski, 8 January 1980.

[122] JCL WHCF sf, exec., box FG 219, file: FG 298–1, Reinhardt to Brzezinski, 28 December 1979 and 4 January 1980 (with sample profile of the teacher William Keough broadcast on 2 January 1980). Broader themes in VOA coverage included U.S. support for President Carter's handling of the crisis, international sympathy for the United States, and the administration's commitment to use "all peaceful and legal means" to resolve the crisis.

[123] JCL WHCF sf, exec., box FG 219, file: FG 298–1, Brzezinski to Reinhardt, 28 December 1979 and WHCF OA: 8496.

[124] JCL WHCF OA: 8594, Commentary 0–0084, "The Soviet Invasion of Afghanistan," 29 December 1979.

[125] JCL Plains file, box 16, file: Accomplishments . . . ICA, Reinhardt to the President, "Major Accomplishments of USICA during your administration," 16 December 1980.

The VOA carried the President's 4 January speech live in English. Other special broadcasts included live coverage in English and Russian of the United Nations Security Council session on the crisis. Commentaries warned that the United States would fight to repel any Soviet attempt to gain control of the Persian Gulf. But even more eloquent were the correspondent reports from the field. The Voice carried eyewitness testimony from Doug Roberts in Peshawar, Pakistan, where refugees were gathering, and from the VOA's India correspondent Fred Brown in Kabul. Brown left Afghanistan in mid-January the day before the Afghan government issued an order expelling him.[126]

The main body of the ICA had rather more difficulty in responding to the crisis. Reinhardt recognized the invasion of Afghanistan as "an extraordinary opportunity... to dramatize Soviet military and cultural imperialism, to enhance our psychological posture in Muslim minds, and to erode Soviet identification with the non-aligned countries."[127] But the resource management system in the Bureau of Programs did not lend itself to a rapid response. As Afghanistan did not figure in the agreed upon "Program Design" for the year, posts could not request materials on the subject, such as film or video for placement on local TV stations. The agency had a contingency mechanism – a so-called "Issues Agenda" – but Afghanistan was only added to the agenda some days after the Soviet invasion. Even then the materials had to be requested by the field and could not be shipped or even offered on the assumption that a post would consider them relevant. It was not until March that Reinhardt's regular crisis reports to the NSC went beyond his usual summary of the VOA and the wireless file to include news of the placement of an ICA video on the invasion and visits by speakers on the subject.[128] Diminishing resources exacerbated the problem. Despite the return to the Cold War, the ICA faced a budget cut of $13.1 million and 200 positions in the coming year.[129]

The President used his State of the Union address on 23 January to enunciate the "Carter doctrine" that any power's attempt to gain control of the Persian Gulf would be met by military force. The President also argued that in view of the Soviet action in Afghanistan the Moscow Olympics scheduled for that summer should be relocated, postponed, or cancelled outright. It seemed increasingly likely that U.S. athletes would boycott the games if they went ahead in Moscow, though this was not confirmed until late April. From the end of January onward the ICA worked to build international support for this. Tactics included coverage of boxer Muhammad Ali's visit to five African nations as "Special Envoy for the Olympic Boycott" and the circulation of highlights from a Communist Party primer for the games entitled *Little*

126 JCL WHCF sf, exec., box FG 219, file: FG 298-1, Reinhardt to Brzezinski, 8 January 1980 and 16 January 1980; Bray to Brzezinski, 25 January 1980; JCL NSA BM sf, box 1–9, file: BIB, Reinhardt to Brzezinski, 18 January 1980.

127 JCL NSA agency files, box 10, file: ICA, 9–12/79, Reinhardt to Brzezinski, "Communication with Muslim Countries," n/d, c. 7 January 1980.

128 JCL NSA SM Henze, box 4, Henze to Brzezinski, "ICA performance," 21 January 1980 with anonymous attachment.

129 JCL NSA SM Henze, box 5, Reinhardt to Brzezinski, 20 June 1980.

Handbook for Party Activities. The VOA broadcast a history of politicization of the Olympics and commentary in support of the President's position.[130]

Contrary to expectations, the return to the Cold War did not immediately mean a resumption of Soviet jamming of the VOA. This time Moscow sought to reply in kind with English language broadcasts. Radio Moscow launched a World Service in English (using both British- and American-accented announcers) which in obvious homage to the VOA approach included disco music in its programming as a lure to listeners. In April, this moved to twenty-four hours a day. Favorite themes included CIA supply of chemical weapons to Afghan guerrillas and US–Chinese plots to undermine the "people's revolution" in Afghanistan. Similarly, Cuba stepped up broadcasts in the Caribbean, including English language programs on the medium-wave band. The Cuban transmitters also relayed Radio Moscow, which could therefore be heard in the United States for the first time on ordinary radio sets.[131]

*

While the crisis raged around Iran and Afghanistan, the administration worked to find a new VOA director. Brzezinski pressed for fellow Polish-American John A. Gronouski from the Board for International Broadcasting as a sop for Slavic voters at home who resented "Black and Hispanic appointments."[132] The eventual nominee was a real departure for the Voice: its youngest and first woman director, thirty-five-year-old Mary Bitterman.[133]

Mary Gayle Foley Bitterman was born in California in 1944. She studied at the Dominican College in San Rafael, California, the School of Foreign Service at Georgetown, and Santa Clara University before entering the graduate program in history at Bryn Mawr. In 1971, she completed a Ph.D. on "Early Quaker Literature of Defense" in seventeenth-century England, noting that small media could have a powerful impact. It was an admirable lesson for the VOA. After working at the University of Hawaii, Bitterman won appointment as executive director and general manager of the Hawaii Public Broadcasting Authority. Committed to cultural exchange in the Asia/Pacific region, she chaired the board of the East–West Center and sat on the television

---

[130]   JCL WHCF sf, exec., box FG 219, file: FG 298–1, Reinhardt to Brzezinski, "USICA activities supporting US policy on 1980 Summer Olympics," 7 February 1980, and Reinhart to Brzezinski, 22 February 1980; JCL WHCF sf, exec., box FG 11, file: FG 1–2/CO 1–1, Louis Martin to President, 11 February 1980 (on Ali tour).

[131]   JCL WHCF sf, exec., Box FO 38, file: FO 5–3, Memo "Cubans and Soviets target the US...," 18 March 1980; JCL NSA SM Henze, box 5, ICA press release, Radio Moscow, 29 May 1980; also Chalmers M. Roberts, "New Image for Voice of America," *New York Times*, 13 April 1980, Sunday Magazine, pp. 27 et seq.

[132]   JCL BSA BM, sf box 1–9, file: BIB, Brzezinski to Jordan, 3 October 1979. See also JSCL NSA sf box 9, file: BIB Henze to Brzezinski, 1 and 2 October 1979. Gronouski had came under attack in the press and the NSC was looking for a way to move him on and appease Polish-American votes.

[133]   The press reported a move to nominate PBS executive Chloe Aaron, wife of Brzezinski's deputy David Aaron, which, as Senator Daniel Inouye of Hawaii pointed out, raised a potential conflict of interest. Judith Cummings and Laurie Johnston, "Notes on People," *New York Times*, 19 December 1979, p. B4. JCL handwriting file, box 157, file: 4 December 1979 [1], Aaron to President, 3 December 1979.

subcommittee of CULCON (the US–Japan Cultural and Educational Cooperation Commission). She also served a term as vice chair of the Democratic Party of Hawaii. Two groups recommended her for the directorship of the VOA: a meeting of Japanese and American television executives and the National Women's Political Caucus. President Carter announced her nomination on 29 January 1980.[134]

Bitterman's first hurdle was the Senate confirmation hearing and specifically Senator Jesse Helms (R-NC). Helms had worked in broadcasting in the 1950s and 1960s and seemed unlikely to be fobbed off with wooly answers. Bitterman prepared carefully. She took the stand on 19 February. Helms' questions were probing and to the point. Would she use broadcasting to encourage a rebellion in Afghanistan? No. Would she hire a certain Cuban émigré from Miami to upgrade propaganda to Cuba? No. At the end of her first session on the stand Helms asked her to be prepared to answer further questions before the vote in two days. The following afternoon Helms' office sent over a list of sixty questions. The first twenty were philosophical, but the remainder dealt with the minutia of international broadcasting, along the lines of "how many hours does Radio Moscow broadcast in Creole for Haiti?" Bitterman immediately began the task of compiling the responses and her colleagues offered to help fill in the blanks. She stayed up all night typing the response, and completed the job by 8 a.m. on the morning of the Senate Foreign Relations Committee's vote. In the committee Helms was gracious and announced that although he did not agree with her in all matters, she had been forthright, and he would endorse her candidacy because she had stood up to him. She was approved by a vote of 11 to 0. As Reinhardt recalled, Helms finally told her, "only thing I have against you is that you are younger than my daughter!" Helms proved a surprising asset during her tenure at the Voice, mobilizing the political muscle to build a new antenna in Greenville, North Carolina. In later years he became the USIA's nemesis.[135]

The VOA staff universally remembered Bitterman's time at the Voice as a brief golden age sandwiched between the difficulties of the Nixon/Ford era and the renewed trouble of the Reagan period. Peace had broken out and the staff came together in common purpose. Even the Serbs and the Croats, who had been known to come to blows in the Voice canteen, seemed to get along while Mary Bitterman was in charge. It helped that Bitterman worked to improve the lot of the language broadcasters. She made her respect for their work far clearer than her predecessors had and reformed inequities in their rates of pay to create a career pathway to match their English language colleagues. They reciprocated her respect. At the same time, external pressures on the Voice were minimal. John Reinhardt even had a promise of respite from Brzezinski's pressure on the VOA. When he took the new VOA director over to the White

---

134 Interview: Mary Bitterman, 6 January 1998. For Bitterman's cv see JCL NSA SM Henze, box 4, attached to Henze to Brzezinski, 9 November 1979. For other documents on the appointment see JCL WHCF sf, exec., box FG 218, file: FG 298, Arnie Miller to President, 23 January 1980.

135 Interviews: Kamenske, Heil, Haratunian, Reinhardt, and Bitterman. JCL WHCF sf, exec., box FG 218, file: FG 298, Senator Daniel Inouye to Frank Moore (WH congressional liaison), 23 February 1980.

House to be sworn in by the President on 7 March, Carter pulled him aside as they were leaving and said, "I'm aware that you get calls from the White House. If any of these ever give you trouble, you have my telephone number, give me a call." Reinhardt and Bitterman never called on Carter to intervene but appreciated the thought.[136]

Bitterman and her deputy director, Bill Haratunian, worked hard to keep the transmitter construction projects on schedule and successfully managed the emergency expansion of VOA programming to the Islamic world. During the course of 1980 the VOA began broadcasting half an hour a day in Dari to Afghanistan. Bitterman maintained the traditional close links with the BBC – commissioning joint research projects – but also worked closely with Deutsche Welle and Radio Netherlands. Her tenure also saw the first exchange of personnel between the VOA and broadcasters of Radio Beijing. The three Chinese visitors particularly enjoyed their contact with ordinary American people. Their thank-you letter mentioned particularly Mrs. Edith Cheek of Battle Creek, Michigan, the elderly mother-in-law of Bernie Kamenske, whom they met at a party in their honor at the News Director's home in Bethesda. Mrs. Cheek had charmed the visitors by demonstrating that one could eat breakfast cereal directly from the individual packets served in hotels by pouring milk right into the box and trusting to the watertight qualities of the wax paper liner. For the VOA, the highlight of contact with the Chinese was their estimate of the Voice's audience in their country. The Vice Minister of Culture informed a VOA delegation that their audience in China "cannot be measured in the tens of millions but in the hundreds of millions."[137]

The fate of the fifty-three hostages in Iran continued to feature prominently. The VOA maintained its coverage of the families at home, many of whom lived in Washington, DC. In early April, the Voice gave prominent coverage to President Carter's imposition of major financial sanctions against Iran and the rupture of diplomatic relations. Then, at 1:30 a.m. on 25 April, Eastern time, the VOA broke into its morning broadcasts to South Asia with a special report from White House correspondent Philomena Jurey. U.S. Special Forces had attempted to rescue the hostages, but their equipment had failed and eight Americans were dead. The VOA covered the story in depth. At 7 a.m. President Carter broadcast to the nation, accepting full responsibility. The VOA extended its Farsi broadcasting by two extra hours to cover this statement live. The Current Affairs Division created a half-hour documentary of reactions from around the administration, emphasizing the search for a peaceful alternative. The VOA also carried reactions from overseas and from the hostages' families. Radio Moscow claimed that the mission had been a coup attempt to overthrow the Ayatollah. In the days that followed, Secretary of State Cyrus Vance, who had opposed any attempt at a military solution, resigned. From this point on the hostage story became a story of American impotence.[138]

136 Interviews: Reinhardt, Haratunian, Kamenske, Heil, and Bitterman.
137 Interview: Bitterman, 6 January 1998.
138 JCL WHCF box FG 219, FG 298–1 exec; Reinhardt to Brzezinski, 25 April 1980; Interview: Bitterman, 6 January 1998. For the script of the VOA's announcement of this see JCL WHCF OA: 9426; see also JCL NSA SM Henze, box 5, ICA press release, Radio Moscow, 29 May 1980.

Although the hostage crisis loomed large, the VOA still had domestic news to report, and some of it was bad. The VOA was frank and thorough in its treatment of the scandal around the relationship between the President's brother Billy and the Libyan government in the summer of 1980. Bitterman's equivalent of Three Mile Island was news of three days of race rioting that blazed through Miami's Liberty City in May 1980, leaving fifteen dead. For Senator Helms this was America's dirty laundry and not for display overseas, but Bitterman insisted that the Voice of America cover the story in depth. Radio Moscow, she noted, never reported a bad harvest. The Voice discussed the political context of the riots: black American anger at police violence and an influx of refugees from Cuba in the so-called Mariel boatlift. The Voice went on to show American community politics in action as the city's religious and political leaders came together to search for answers.[139]

The Voice gave international coverage to the wider story of Cuban refugees that summer. From April, when thousands of refugees crowded into the Peruvian embassy in Havana, to the last sailing of a refugee boat from Mariel in September, VOA correspondents within the United States and sixteen stringers throughout Latin America gathered news and poignant interviews. Mary Bitterman considered their broadcasts to be the best work she had heard at the Voice. On 16 April, the VOA scooped the world with the first report of more Cuban refugees leaving the island, flying in two airliners to Costa Rica. The VOA correspondent phoned in his report from a public telephone box, into which he squeezed a succession of on-the-spot interviewees including the Costa Rican president, Rodrigo Carazo Odio.[140]

The Miami riots focused Republican political interest in the politics of the Cuban-Americans and their desire for a U.S. government-funded surrogate radio station, along the lines of RFE, to broadcast to Cuba. In June Senator Helms introduced a bill to transform the existing VOA Spanish language service into an anti-Castro station (with no additional funds). Mary Bitterman disliked the idea of cannibalizing the VOA's Spanish broadcasts and discouraged advocates from naming the station *Cuba Libre*, since this was the name of a cocktail (rum, cola, and a slice of lime). At the NSC, Henze recommended that Bitterman stall for time by suggesting an inquiry. The issue would reemerge in Reagan years.[141]

*

Early in 1980, the VOA's Russian service came attack from Aleksandr Solzhenitsyn in an article for *Foreign Affairs*. He complained of "trite and inconsequential drivel" and "frivolous" Americana instead of solemn readings of his own books. Bitterman had no difficulty refuting his claims – and RL's research continued

---

[139]　Interview: Bitterman, 6 January 1998. On Billygate see author's collection: Mary Bitterman, National Press Club, "newsmaker breakfast" transcript, 23 July 1980, pp. 5–6.

[140]　For VOA and USICA coverage of the Mariel boatlift see JCL WHCF sf, exec., box FG 220, file: FG 298–1, Reinhardt to Brzezinski, 13 June 1980 & 25 July 1980.

[141]　Interview: Bitterman, 6 January 1998; JCL WHCF sf, exec., box FO 38, FO 5–3, Henze to Brzezinski, "Radio Free Cuba?" 17 June 1980.

to suggest a weekly VOA audience of around fifteen percent – but the VOA director agreed to an external review of the service.[142] The VOA's news became increasingly anathema to the Kremlin as the year unfolded. On 20 August 1980, the USSR recommenced its jamming of the VOA for the first time since 1973. The jamming covered Russian, Ukrainian, and Armenian services and also extended to the BBC and *Deutche Welle*. Jamming of other Soviet language services followed. NSC staffer Steve Larabee noted that the inclusion of British and German broadcasts hinted at more than a response to VOA coverage of Afghanistan. He suspected that a Soviet desire to stifle news of the unrest in Poland radiating out from Gdansk lay at the root of the new policy. The United States issued an immediate protest and resumed its well-tried countermeasures.[143] It was not until the mid-eighties that Radio Liberty researchers noticed a substantial decline in the Soviet audience for Western broadcasting.[144]

Cold War conditions produced Cold War laws, and the autumn of 1980 also saw an ill omen for the future integrity of ICA. An amendment to a new "CIA secrecy bill" crafted to prevent the publication of the names of serving CIA agents also removed the prohibition inherited from the USIA against ICA positions being used as cover for CIA agents. The ICA fought the plan but lost. Although this piece of legislation bogged down in November, the Intelligence Oversight Act successfully passed that year apparently gave the authority to the President necessary to order the ICA, AID or the Peace Corps to provide cover for a CIA agent.[145]

The final months of the Carter administration saw increasing international ferment. In September, war broke out between Iran and the regime of Saddam Hussein in Iraq. VOA Arabic and Farsi mounted extensive programming about the President's speech of 24 September stressing the need to ensure free navigation of the Gulf.[146] Given the world situation, Reinhardt was astonished to receive the Foreign Affairs

---

[142] JCL WHCF sf exec., box FO 38, file: FO 5–3, Reinhardt to Brzezinski, "VOA broadcasts to the Soviet Union," 14 April 1980; JCL WHCF sf exec., box FG 220, FG 298–1, Reinhardt to Brzezinski, "VOA Broadcasts to the Soviet Union," 30 April 1980. For listener research see Parta, *Discovering the Hidden Listener*, Sections 2.1 and 7. Parta has compared RL's data to studies done in the U.S.S.R. at the time and found roughly the same results.

[143] JCL NSA BM sf, boxes 1–9, file: BIB, Larabee to Aaron, "Jamming of VOA," 20 August 1980, etc.; Reinhardt to Brzezinski, "Status of Soviet Jamming . . . ," 19 September 1980.

[144] Parta, *Discovering the Hidden Listener*, Section 2.3.

[145] During the course of 1979 the Senate had enacted legislation (S. 2525) to limit the activities of U.S. intelligence. Over protests from the CIA, Reinhardt worked to add clauses to the bill to prohibit the CIA from recruiting participants in educational or cultural exchanges or staff working for the VOA. Reinhardt argued that such safeguards were essential to the future willingness of other nations to participate in the exchange program and the desired image of the United States as "open and nonmanipulative." The eventual text of the bill compromised by requiring the CIA to seek the ICA's permission before making such an approach, and stipulated that any refusal by the ICA could be appealed to the President. JCL WHCF sfs, exec., box ND 7, file: ND 6, Reinhardt to Brzezinski, S. 2525 regulating US intelligence activities, 1 May 1979. On the 1980 initiative see George Lardner Jr., "Plan to Provide Cover for CIA Operatives Stirs Concern," *Washington Post*, 16 September 1980, p. A13; George Lardner Jr., "Kennedy Committee Votes 8–6 to Ease CIA Protection Bill," *Washington Post*, 18 September 1980; Charles Mohr, "New Action Likely on CIA Legislation," *New York Times*, 10 November 1980, p. A19; Charles Mohr, "Casey Suggests Reagan Backs Laws to Improve Secrecy," *New York Times*, 8 April 1981, p. A 14. An Intelligence Protection Act prohibiting the publication of CIA names passed in 1982.

[146] JCL WHCF sf exec., box FG 220, FG 298–1, Reinhardt to Brzezinski, 26 September 1980.

Budget Review with strict limits on expenditure not only for the ICA but throughout the foreign policy apparatus. He wrote to Secretary of State Edmund Muskie,

> The United States is a great power. We have an inescapable obligation to history. We should find it disturbing that we are reduced to haggling over relatively small budget sums when we should be addressing the questions of how to persuade the country to support a foreign policy budget commensurate with our great power responsibilities.[147]

It was an argument that would appeal to the incoming administration of Ronald Reagan.

The Carter administration ended in an air of defeat and missed opportunities. The hostages remained hostages. As the year ended, the VOA and ICA memorialized the first anniversaries of the seizure of the hostages and invasion of Afghanistan and disseminated the administration's warning to Moscow that dire consequences would follow military intervention in Poland. Wireless file material included a telling piece by Afghan editor Afzal Nasiri from the *Indian Express* describing the Afghan war as a "Soviet quagmire." It seemed possible that the U.S.S.R. had bitten off more than it could chew.[148]

*

John Reinhardt retired from the Foreign Service at the end of the Carter years and joined the senior staff of the Smithsonian Institution. From 1984 to 1987 he ran the institution's Directorate of International Activities. He later taught at the University of Vermont in Burlington. VOA director Peter Straus worked on Edward Kennedy's unsuccessful campaign for the Democratic nomination and was a major backer of Gary Hart's ill-fated presidential campaign in 1984. In February 1998, Straus' name returned briefly to the newspapers when he married author Marcia Lewis, and thereby became the stepfather of Monica Lewinsky. Mary Bitterman later directed the Institute of Culture and Communication at the East–West Center and was president and CEO of KQED, the public broadcasting station in San Francisco. A foundation president, she remains an advocate for the VOA and U.S. public diplomacy. In 2005/6 she chaired the board of the Public Broadcasting Service.

Looking back on the Carter years, Reinhardt's staff could draw satisfaction from a number of important longer-term projects including the creation of the Arts America program, the Hubert Humphrey Fellowships, and the ICA's successor generation work in Europe. Important single-country initiatives included work to buttress the transition to civilian rule in Nigeria and a major effort in South Africa to open discussion about a new future for that country.[149] The VOA had begun a much-needed modernization.

---

[147] WHCF sf exec., box FI 12, file FI4, Reinhardt to Muskie, 10 November 1980.
[148] JCL WHCF sf exec., box FG 220, FG 298–1, Reinhardt to Brzezinski, 12 December 1980.
[149] JCL Plains file, box 16, Reinhardt to the President, "Major Accomplishments of USICA during your administration," 16 December 1980. The Carter years saw over 100 U.S. speakers tour South Africa, visitor grants for 75 black and 100 white South Africans to view racial progress in the United States, and USICA-funded training for over 1,000 young black people. USICA premises served as among the few venues in the country where all races could gather as equals and discuss politics freely.

By January 1981 the Voice had four new transmitters under construction in the United Kingdom; two further transmitters scheduled for construction in the Philippines that summer; a medium-wave transmitter under construction in Botswana; and a site and funds secure to construct six high-powered transmitters in Sri Lanka. The Voice had added Farsi, Dari, and Hausa broadcasts and expanded its programming in Urdu, Turkish, Bengali, and English to the Near East and South Asia. Azeri to Iran and Azerbaijan was scheduled to begin in January 1981.[150]

Like every director, Reinhardt had his critics within his own agency. Some staff felt that he had emphasized the long term rather than the short and questioned his emphasis on the programs aimed at key opinion makers in the target countries rather than mass audiences. Some felt that the agency had drifted away from the business of advocacy in support of U.S. foreign policy. Even so, the ICA had played an important role in advancing the major themes of the Carter presidency – such as human rights – and in managing the information aspects of the crises of the later years over Iran and the invasion of Afghanistan. But there was a limit to what public diplomacy could achieve.[151]

Carter left office amid images of weakness: Soviet tanks in Afghanistan; the charred wreckage of the failed hostage rescue; his own exhausted frame staggering into a collapse while running a ten-kilometer road race in September 1979. No one at the time would have claimed his administration had anything to teach about international image making or communication. Yet in retrospect Carter's public diplomacy policy should not be lightly dismissed. The administration had taken the plunge, reformed the whole U.S. information and exchange program, and begun essential capital investment in the VOA. Just as Reagan's America would have been physically weaker without Carter's investment in the MX missile program, it would have been much harder to deploy U.S. public diplomacy for the final battle of the Cold War without the Carter-era reforms. More than this, the idealism of the early Carter years, although cut short by the return to Cold War crisis, produced a model of public diplomacy for the era of global interdependence when that final Cold War battle had been won. The early Carter years saw an emphasis on two-way exchange and dialogue rather than one-way lecturing and ideology, and humility about the cultural position of the United States rather than boasting. Such may yet prove to be the formula for success in U.S. public diplomacy in the twenty-first century.

---

[150] JCL Plains file, box 16, Reinhardt to the President, "Major Accomplishments of USICA during your administration," 16 December 1980; also NSA SM Henze papers, box 5, Henze to Brzezinksi, 28 October 1980.

[151] For a sustained example of anonymous criticism of the NSC see JCL NSA BM sf, box 10, file: ICA, Thornton to Henze, 13 December 1979 with memo "The State of USIA – What needs to be done."

10 "Project Truth"

THE FIRST REAGAN ADMINISTRATION, 1981–84

> We are determined to stop losing the propaganda war.
>
> Ronald Reagan, 11 January 1982.[1]

He was the ultimate image professional. Sports announcer, turned Hollywood actor, turned politician, Ronald Reagan displayed an almost clairvoyant grasp of political communication. It was only to be expected that as President he would attend to the projection of the United States to the world. He had pledged as much on the campaign trail.[2] In March 1980, on the eve of the Illinois primary, Reagan promised to launch a massive campaign to "convince the world of the superiority of the American system."[3] On 19 October, in a televised address rebutting Carter's record in foreign policy, he pledged to strengthen the USICA, the VOA, and RFE/RL: "What we need most," he concluded, "is conviction; the conviction that in carrying the American message abroad we strengthen the foundations of peace."[4] In January 1981, the ICA let the world know that a new kind of President had taken office. Its guidance to posts emphasized the "assertion of decisive, new leadership; strengthened U.S. military capabilities, and an emphasis on ideas of individual liberty, family, and the need to limit government." Tools included a clutch of brochures with titles such as "The New Conservatism" and a half-hour film biography of the new President.[5]

---

[1] Ronald Reagan Presidential Library (hereafter RRL), handwriting file, President's letter to Barton L. Hartzell, 11 January 1982.

[2] At a Lincoln Day dinner in Worcester, Massachusetts in February 1980, Reagan declared, "It's time to expand dramatically the Voice of America, Radio Free Europe and Radio Liberty. We have a message of peace and hope and nothing to be ashamed of in the examples we set for the world. Millions upon millions of people look to us as a beacon of freedom in a world that is fast losing freedom. We can convey our own deep convictions to the world to combat the hostile and ceaseless communist propaganda that distorts everything we stand for." Lou Cannon, "Reagan's Foreign Policy: Scrap 'Weakness, Illusion,' Stress Military Strength." *Washington Post*, 16 February 1980, p. A3.

[3] Steven V. Roberts, "Reagan, in Chicago Speech, Urges Big Increases in Military Spending," *New York Times*, 18 March 1980, p. B8.

[4] "Excerpts from Reagan's Televised Speech," *New York Times*, 20 October 1980, p. D10. Reagan endorsed the modernization of the VOA and RFE/RL in numerous speeches in office, especially those around the annual Captive Nations resolution. See *Public Papers of the Presidents, Ronald Reagan (PPP RR) 1982*, Vol. II, p. 937; *1983*, Vol. I, p. 255 and Vol. II, p. 1054; *1984*, Vol. II, p. 1048.

[5] RRL WHORM sf FG 298, 8100085, draft cable to all posts 27 January 1981, Tyson (NSC) to Shirley, 2 February 1981.

Reagan was not the only determined communicator committed to spreading his message in the troubled world of the 1980s. With the war in Afghanistan and rising dissent in Poland, Moscow had thrown its international propaganda machine into overdrive. The CIA estimated that the Soviet Union now spent $2.2 billion on foreign propaganda against the $480 million budget of the ICA. The stage was set for an epic confrontation. But world opinion did not need Moscow to prompt it in anti-American directions in the 1980s. An upsurge in Western Europe of grassroots hostility to American nuclear policy brought the toughest challenges to the U.S. information machine since the darkest days in Vietnam. The President himself was not always an asset overseas. The self-confidence and humor that played well at home terrified many Europeans. The European media routinely joked about the President as half-witted, mocked his former career, and scorned his countrymen for being taken in by him. Reagan's description of the U.S.S.R. in March 1983 as an "Evil Empire" also played poorly in Europe.[6] The President did not improve matters when during a microphone test on 11 August 1984 he remarked, "My fellow Americans, I'm pleased to tell you that I've just signed legislation that will outlaw Russia forever. We begin bombing in five minutes." The VOA's Russian service took care to carry the story immediately, lest audiences hear it first with Moscow's spin.[7] But Western Europe was only one audience, and so long as opinion permitted the weapons deployments necessary to maintain pressure on the Eastern bloc, it was sufficient to the administration's purposes. In the Communist world Reagan's uncompromising message of confrontation carried hope.

The Reagan administration arrived with a zeal and ideological self-confidence not seen since the days of Kennedy. Yet it soon became apparent that Reagan's camp could be as divided as any other, with the radical "Reaganaut" right at war with the more traditional Republican center. Despite the President's ability to reconcile these differences, the battles produced their toll of casualties. The era saw a succession of National Security Advisors, competing factions within the White House, and two Secretaries of State. The U.S. information machine would not be immune from disputes, but there would be only one director of the USIA during Reagan's two terms: Charles Wick. He would animate the USIA as no director had before him.

1) THE ARRIVAL OF CHARLES Z. WICK

He was born Charles Zwick in Cleveland, Ohio, on 12 October 1917, son of a successful venture capitalist. Although raised Jewish, he had little time for organized religion.[8] Educated in the public school system, he earned degrees in music from the University of Michigan (1940) and law from Western Reserve University (1943). He

---

[6] For discussion of the "Evil Empire" remark see RRL WHORM sf CO 165 USSR box 11, 237899, Wick to McFarlane, 14 May 1984.

[7] "President's Joke about Bombing Leaves Press in Europe Un-amused," (AP) *New York Times*, 14 August 1984, p. A8. Interview (telephone) Mark Pomar (VOA Russian), 11 October 2004.

[8] Wick to author, 29 September 2004.

paid his way though college by working as a bandleader in Ann Arbor and then at the Carter Hotel in Cleveland, where he caught the eye of the nation's premiere bandleader, Tommy Dorsey. Dorsey would fly him to New York to arrange his music, paying the young man as much for a weekend as most people earned in a month. When he graduated, Dorsey employed him in California as his business and legal advisor. By this point he had changed his name to "something easier" on Anglo-Saxon ears: Charles Z. Wick.[9]

In 1944, Wick joined the New York-based William Morris talent agency as a radio and recording agent. He married Mary Jane Woods in 1947. By 1949, he had his own business offering legal and theatrical representation in New York and London. His clients included Winston Churchill, for whom he handled the American sales of his *History of the English Speaking Peoples*. Wick's other enterprises included the revival of Twickenham Film Studios in west London.[10] In the mid-1950s, he returned to California, where, with outboard motor mogul Ralph Evinrude, he founded the United Convalescent Homes chain. Wick also ran his own venture capital film, Mapleton Enterprises. By the end of the decade, he had five children and had earned his first million. Those meeting him were struck by the energy coiled like a spring in his compact frame and a smile that revealed the sort of perfect teeth found only in California. To colleagues at the USIA he seemed to have the dynamism and bite to personally chomp through the Berlin Wall.[11]

Although proudly conservative, Wick was no ideologue. He believed in serving his President, invigorating his agency, and getting the job done. He was charming and used humor to disarm his interlocutors, but was also quick to anger, sometimes dressing down colleagues in public. Wick frequently fired staff and especially the political appointees imposed by the White House Office of Personnel. One officer managed to be fired several times on the same day. One staffer noted, "he went though executive assistants like salted peanuts." Many at the agency had never encountered anyone quite like him before. Wick's natural habitat – Southern California – was a world as remote from the USIA as the far side of the moon. Life in Los Angeles was larger than life in Washington, DC. There was an inevitable period of mutual adjustment, but Wick eventually developed excellent relationships with his senior foreign service officers, founded on mutual respect.[12]

---

[9] Interview: Charles Z. Wick, 8 January 1996.

[10] There he made television series, including *Fabian of the Yard*, which played on both sides of the Atlantic and in Australia in 1954–5.

[11] Interview: Charles Z. Wick, 8 January 1996; Elizabeth Bumiller, "The Wick Whirlwind: Reagan's ICA Chief Brings Hollywood Hustle to Washington," *Washington Post*, 11 May 1982, p. B1; John A. Barnes, "Show Biz Flair Makes USIA's Wick a Veteran of Controversy, Limelight," *Washington Times*, 30 December 1983, p. A2; and entry for Wick in *Current Biography Yearbook, 1985*, pp. 449–53, as filed in RRL WHORM sf FG 298, 70064.

[12] Interviews, esp. Tuch; ADST oral history, esp. Stanton Burnett; Gifford Malone; Jock Shirley; James P. Thurber. Len Baldyga to author, 26 August 2004. Mike Schneider to author, 26 August 2004. As a symptom of teething troubles in May 1982, the *Washington Post* ran a leaked memo of instructions for handling the director on tour; see Elizabeth Bumiller, "Minding Manners at ICA: The Staff Memo on How to Treat 'the Director,'" *Washington Post*, 12 May 1982, pp. B1, B13. Wick's staff relations

Wick knew that the only way to do his job was to see the agency at work in the field. He spent 177 days of his first two years in office overseas. In transit, he demanded the best hotel suites (for which he paid from his own pocket) and first class plane seats. He traveled in armored limousines with bodyguards and, at their request, wore a heavy bulletproof overcoat, which he detested. These were not a vanity, for following the attempt on Reagan's life in March 1981 he too received death threats. Wick did, however, expect to be recognized and complained when a guard at the Belgrade embassy asked him for ID. The complaint did not have to be repeated. Wick was not at his best when asked to speak off the cuff on policy, but he had other ways of winning over a crowd. He could not pass a piano without playing it, and his engagements on the road frequently included a few tunes from the director. During the Williamsburg Summit in 1983 he surprised delegates by emerging through the stage floor playing the piano at an evening reception.[13]

Ideas flew off Wick like sparks from a Catherine wheel. Throughout the day he would record his ideas on a Dictaphone and fire them off to staff in a steady stream of memos, nicknamed "Z-grams." He labeled the more significant messages "hot" or "very hot." He also took to taping his important phone conversations, a practice that backfired in due course. Although some of Wick's ideas were excellent, others were not, and staff steered him accordingly. His best ideas – such as his use of satellite television – made a real difference. He brought the USIA one gift above all others: his friendship with Ronald Reagan.[14]

The Reagans and the Wicks had been friends since the mid-1950s. Nancy Reagan and Mary Jane Wick met when their children attended the same school in Brentwood.

are noted in David Binder, "Wick Finds a High Profile Need Not Be a Target," *New York Times*, 2 June 1988, p. B10. Wick's willingness to dispose of senior staff was legendary; less well known was his loyalty to those he appreciated. In his memoir, Assistant Director W. Scott Thomson (*The Price of Achievement: Coming Out in Reagan Days*, Cassell: London, 1995, p. 152) records that Wick resisted powerful lobbying for his dismissal for being gay by figures including his influential father-in-law, Paul Nitze.

13   Interviews, esp. Tuch; ADST oral history, esp. Burnett, Malone, Shirley, and Thurber. Len Baldyga to author, 26 August 2004. Mike Schneider to author, 26 August 2004. There is a detailed treatment of Wick's tenure at the USIA in a memoir by his head of TV: Alvin A. Snyder, *Warriors of Disinformation: American Propaganda, Soviet Lies, and the Winning of the Cold War*, New York: Arcade, 1995. See also Howard Kurtz and Pete Earley, "Hollywood Style Diplomacy: Wick Adds Flair to U.S. Story," *Washington Post*, 13 July 1983, p. A1.

14   Howard Kurtz, "As USIA Brews List of Achievements, Wick Ferments Controversy," *Washington Post*, 1 January 1984, p. A2; George Archibald, "House Committee Probing USIA Chief's Secret Taping," *Washington Times*, 29 January 1983, p. A2, in which the USIA's public liaison director, James Bryant, notes that he alone had received as many as 40 Z-grams in a day. For a sample of the style and content of Z-grams see Howard Kurtz, "Re: The Wick Files, for the USIA Chief the Memo Is the Message," *Washington Post*, 20 February 1985, p. C1. In his memoir W. Scott Thompson, *The Price of Achievement*, p. 80, his Assistant Director for Programs, claims that in order to block the wilder notions "we spent much time distracting Charlie" but cites an operation that actually went ahead. The blocking of Wick's ideas by staff was noted with horror by some political appointees and became a subject of comment in the conservative press. Robert Reilly of the E-bureau recalled his anger watching Jock Shirley dissuade Wick from an idea about running a landline to Solzhenitsyn's home in Vermont to allow the author to broadcast on the grounds that Solzhenitsyn's views were discredited and he was unpopular in Russia. Interview: Bob Reilly, 18 December 1995 and 3 January 1996.

They would both arrive early to pick up the kids after class, and took to sitting in each other's cars discussing politics and current events. Soon the two families became close, sharing the joys and trials of family life in a land of plenty. When, following Ronald Reagan's election to the governorship of California, the Reagans moved to Sacramento, Ron Jr. stayed with the Wicks to complete high school. The two families had a tradition of dining together every Christmas Eve, which continued throughout the White House years and after. By the late 1970s Wick had become convinced that Reagan was the "ideal presidential candidate to restore the image of America." Wick raised vast sums of money for the Reagan campaign, roping in corporate top brass and their families through direct mail and glamorous events that showed the Reagans at their best. On 27 June 1979, he inaugurated the "Ground Floor Committee," a gathering of wealthy Californians dedicated to the nomination of Reagan for the presidency. In November 1979 he mounted a similar event at the Hilton Hotel in New York, launching Reagan as a candidate on the East Coast. In the wake of the election victory he was the obvious man to coordinate the lavish inaugural celebrations. Working with Robert K. Gray, he created an unprecedented $80 million spectacle. Frank Sinatra and Elizabeth Taylor led off the festivities. But even as he planned the biggest party in Washington's history, members of the transition team raised the possibility of Wick taking over the USICA.[15]

Reagan wanted his friend to have a job in his administration and the idea of the ICA job appealed to Wick, who had met and admired Ed Murrow. It was not the only job mooted for him, and he was not the only person considered. Other runners included former USIA filmmaker Bruce Herschensohn, the diplomat and former child star Shirley Temple Black, and the conservative editor Norman Podhoretz, but on 6 March the President nominated Wick for ICA director. In the meantime Jock Shirley served as acting director of the ICA (he went on to play a key role supporting Wick in the new post of agency counselor). Because everyone in Washington knew that Wick had access to the President if he needed it, he generally did not need it. Bigger budgets and a role in policymaking followed. Yet the relationship that made Wick a success "within the beltway" made him a marked man in the national press. He was an easy target for journalists seeking to score points at Reagan's expense.[16]

15   Interview: Charles Z. Wick, 8 January 1996; Wick to author, 29 September 2004. On the inaugural see Megan Rosenfeld, "The Inaugural Spectacular," *Washington Post*, 9 January 1981, p. E1. Wick dubbed the inaugural "the biggest show in history" but later conceded that the wedding of Prince Charles and Princess Diana was probably bigger.

16   Interview: Charles Horner (Reagan transition team) 15 December 1995; RRL WHORM sf FG 298-USIA, 100428, Khachigian to James Baker, 27 January 1981; 001757 Carol Grossman (Women's Equity Action League) to President, 5 February 1981; R00031 SS, Reagan to Shirley, 20 January 1981. For papers on the confirmation process see RRL alpha file: Wick, Wick to Senator Percy, 4 May 1981; for press coverage see "Californian Wick Nominated as Head of Communication Agency," *Washington Post*, 7 March 1981, p. A3. On Podhoretz see Charles Fenyvesi, "I Hear America Mumbling," *Washington Post*, magazine, pp. 21 et seq. During the period of his nomination Wick attracted criticism for his founding, with Justin Dart, of "the Coalition for a New Beginning," a committee to promote Reagan's economic program. Businessmen objected to high-pressure fund-raising techniques, and the committee was disbanded, noted in John A. Barnes, "Show Biz Flair...." *Washington*

Once in office, Wick worked hard to raise awareness of the agency around Washington and in the country as a whole. Whereas his predecessors had channeled their correspondence to the Secretary of State and/or National Security Advisor, Wick's memos were much more widely circulated. His announcement of a new editorial system at the VOA was sent to nine people, including the counselor to the President, Ed Meese, the White House Chief of Staff, James Baker, his deputy, Michael Deaver, and the White House personnel staff.[17] Wick and Reagan regularly exchanged notes and also sent each other press cuttings.[18] Wick had more access to the foreign-policy-making process than almost all his predecessors. He worked especially well with Secretary of State George Shultz. Under Shultz, either Wick or his deputy not only attended the Secretary of State's daily morning meeting but also gave the meeting a five-minute briefing on the state of opinion around the world.[19] Wick was invited to participate in NSC meetings whenever ICA/USIA matters were on the agenda, and both he and the U.S. Advisory Commission on Public Diplomacy repeatedly argued that the agency director should become a member by statute. Shultz and others, although respecting Wick, felt that it would be inappropriate for the ICA/USIA director to be a cabinet or mandatory NSC seat. Senior NSC staff considered the case on several occasions early in the Reagan years, but recommended against amending the law. An opportunity had been lost.[20]

Wick worked more closely with the White House press office than any of his predecessors. White House spokesman Larry Speakes recalled, "there were only two people other than the president for whom I'd always jump. One was Mrs. Reagan and the other was Charlie Wick." Wick and Speakes spoke regularly on the phone and ICA/USIA officials participated in Speakes' working lunches at the White House each Thursday, along with spokesmen from the State Department, Pentagon, and CIA. The agency helped inject an awareness of international opinion into White House press operations, broadening the target audience beyond the domestic political press. This brought changes such as a shift in the timing of White House press briefings from

Times, 30 December 1983, p. A2; see also Steven R. Weisman, "White House Kills Budget Lobby That Reagan Friends Had Set Up," *New York Times*, 20 March 1981, p. A1. Also *PPP RR, 1981*, p. 213.

17 RRL WHORM sf FG 298, 092766, Wick to Meese et al. New VOA editorial system, 2 July 1982.

18 For an example see RRL WHORM sf FG 298–01, 051989, Wick to President, 8 December 1981 with *Dallas Morning News* editorial, 20 November 1981.

19 Interview: Charles Z. Wick, 8 January 1996; Mike Schneider to author, 26 August 2004; interview (telephone): John Hughes, 14 September 2004. Shultz's memoirs include a story about a day when noise from building work interrupted Wick's briefing and the director caused much amusement by asking what time the conference room was scheduled to land at La Guardia. George Shultz, *Turmoil and Triumph: Diplomacy, Power, and the Victory of the American Ideal*, New York: Charles Scribner's Sons, 1993, p. 678. Wick also worked well with Secretary of Defense Caspar Weinberger and his under secretary Fred Ickle at the Pentagon, and Ambassador Max Kampelman and the U.S. team at the negotiations with the Soviet Union on nuclear and space arms in Geneva.

20 Interview: Walter Raymond, 12 December 1995; John Hughes, 14 September 2004. On the NSC membership question see RRL Lord files, box 90,051 ICA (2), Carnes Lord to Richard V. Allen, etc., and box 90, 267 USIA (1), Robert Kimmitt to Bud McFarlane, 1 October 1982. For discussion of a revised role for Wick see RRL WHORM sf FG 298, 190852, Raymond to McFarlane, 1 December 1983.

midday to nine in the morning to catch the early evening news in Western Europe. The agency also provided essential support with personnel and country-specific know-how during international summits.[21]

Wick's efforts to regenerate the ICA received essential support from Edwin J. Feulner, the new chairman of the President's Advisory Commission on Public Diplomacy. President of the conservative Heritage Foundation, Feulner believed that ideas had consequences and saw public diplomacy as a crucial dimension of U.S. foreign relations. He maintained the tradition, established during Stanton's tenure at the helm of the commission, of arranging for members to meet a significant figure in Washington on the evening before their monthly meeting, and introducing them to some of the issues around U.S. public diplomacy. He remained in the post until 1991.[22] Other energetic appointees to the commission included former Nixon/Ford legislative aide Tom Korologos.[23]

Wick saw the private sector as an essential partner in the ICA's work. The agency established or reestablished a network of advisory committees to draw private (and mainly conservative) talents into the agency's work and thereby promote awareness of the agency on the home front. Committees drew on expertise in the fields of publishing, public relations, marketing, film, labor, and sports. Distinguished Americans recruited ranged from actor Charlton Heston to philosopher Michael Novak. Norman Podhoretz chaired a "New Directions" committee. AFL-CIO president Lane Kirkland chaired the Labor Committee. Leo Jaffe of Columbia Pictures chaired a Film Acquisition Committee. The CEO of Madison Square Garden, David "Sonny" Werblin, chaired the Sports Committee, which raised nearly $1,000,000 in private sector funds to help African athletes prepare for the Los Angeles Olympics. The Books and Library Advisory Committee brought together the leaders of America's greatest publishing houses. A steady supply of cheap or even free books flowed as a result. Wick knew the value of this help. In June 1984, he mounted a gala event to honor over 100 USIA private sector volunteers.[24]

---

21   Interview (telephone): Larry Speakes, 18 December 1995. On the Williamsburg Summit see Snyder, *Warriors of Disinformation*, pp. 40–41. Speakes personally noticed the difference when he started to get fan mail from elderly women in the United Kingdom and was picked out and greeted by the Queen of Spain from a line of people three deep, but his personal notoriety meant that the European media were getting direct and immediate access to U.S. views on the need to site cruise missiles on the continent.

22   Interviews: Bruce Gregory, 22 November 1995; Ed Feulner, 10 January 1996. In 1987, guests included the chargé from the Soviet embassy, who turned out to be a great fan of the VOA. The power of international exchange had been made plain to him at an early age. In 1953, when he was twelve, his family had hosted an Austrian exchange student from the Russian zone. Feulner well recalled that student's excitement at seeing piles of oranges and bananas stacked in a Chicago grocery store.

23   *PPP RR 1981*, announcement 7 July 1981, p. 599.

24   Interview: Walter Raymond, 12 December 1995; RRL Ryan, Fred files, CF OA 753, USIA private sector committee, 21 June 1984; for further correspondence on potential private helps see RRL Alpha file: Wick, Wick to Meese, 6 January 1983. VOA benefited from the Marketing Committee chaired by Leonard Matthews, president of the American Association of Advertising Agencies, which helped create advertisements for use in the Voice's audience relations survey; from the Radio Engineering Advisory Committee which assisted with VOA modernization; and from a Radio Program Advisory Committee, whose members included the executive producer of CBS radio's Mystery Theatre.

Wick also looked to business to fill a number of key posts in the agency, especially as the administration pushed the boundaries of political appointments. Now political noncareer appointees could be found in such posts as the ICA's Associate Director for Programs.[25] Wick's choice for his deputy director was Gilbert A. Robinson, a New Yorker, whose background included the chairmanship of his own public relations firm and a term as head of corporate communications for Gulf and Western Industries. He had helped to coordinate the American National Exhibition in Moscow in 1959 for the Commerce Department. He was ardently conservative, and the longer-serving VOA staff noted with alarm that he was an associate of Roy Cohn. For VOA director Wick selected his friend James B. Conkling. Born in 1915, Conkling was a director of the media conglomerate Bonneville International. He had sung professionally, presided over several record companies, and founded the Grammy awards.[26]

Despite his friendship with Reagan, Wick suffered some early disappointments. Just weeks into his tenure the administration hit the exchange program with a fifty-five percent budget cut. Press leaks prompted a wave of outrage outside the agency. A bipartisan group of senators led by Lowell P. Weicker (R-CT) rallied in the autumn of 1981 to make the countercase for a nine percent budget increase for cultural work. Senator Pell added an amendment to the agency's appropriation to protect the exchange budget. With this support the exchanges survived and prospered. Wick successfully built up the agency's budget. Appropriations for financial year 1984 totaled $659.7 million – over $201.9 million more than the budget in 1981 – and by the end of Reagan's first term Wick could boast that funding for exchanges had increased forty-six percent over levels inherited from Carter.[27]

Wick's first legislative initiative was to change the agency's name back to the USIA. He estimated the cost of this at $150,000 but had no doubt of its necessity.[28] He also worked to locate larger premises for the agency, raising the matter with the President over a weekend at Camp David. Reagan told Wick that if he could find a suitable building "then you've got it."[29]

[25] Appointees to his post in the first Reagan administration were John Hughes (1981–2), W. Scott Thompson (1982–4) and finally an FSO, Charles (Sam) Courtney.

[26] RRL WHORM sf FG 298, 482673, Willa Ann Johnson (WH) to E. Pendleton James (WH), ICA, 8 April 1981; White House press releases 6 and 18 May 1981. Interview: Kamenske. Rival candidates for the VOA directorship included historian Allen Weinstein. See RRL Lord papers, box 90,051, ICA (1), Lord to Allen, 13 March 1981. John Hughes, Associated Director of Programs at ICA, recalled Robinson once offering him the use of Roy Cohn's private plane to fly down to Florida for a break. He declined. Interview: John Hughes, 14 September 2004.

[27] Interview: Henry Butterfield Ryan, 27 November 1995; Barbara Crossette, "Budget Cuts Threaten Cultural Exchange Projects," New York Times, 34 October 1981, p. A3; Murrey Marder, "US Sharpening Information Policy Overseas," Washington Post, 10 November 1981, p. A1; RRL WHORM sf FG 298, 257944, "USIA initiatives since June 9, 1981," 26 June 1984, p. 1.

[28] In a letter outlining his plans to the OMB, he stressed the confusion that the name had brought, including a report from the ICA hostages in Iran that "their captors were very troubled by the initials and name, believing them to be CIA employees." RRL WHORM sf FG 298, 032656, Wick to Frey (OMB), 7 July 1981; Lenz (NSC) to Peterson, 9 July 1981.

[29] RRL WHORM sf FG 298, 043655, Wick to President, 16 October 1981 and 2 December 1981; 106227, Wick to President, 21 October 1982.

*

The election of Reagan energized plans to establish a radio station aimed at Castro's Cuba. Their driving force was a tough Cuban American businessman and activist named Jorge Mas Canosa. On 8 November 1980, Mas presented a formal proposal for "Radio Free Cuba" based on evidence of unprecedented dissent collected from the Mariel refugees. Mas suggested launching a news-based station staffed by Cuban exiles to provide the facts denied by Castro's censorship. At the same time Mas founded the Cuban American National Foundation (CANF) with a powerful lobbying arm. The station would be their prime cause.[30] On 23 March 1981, National Security Advisor Richard V. Allen announced that the United States was planning to establish a station called Radio Martí after the Cuban liberator José Martí, and had formed a presidential commission to consider logistics.[31] Allen imagined that the station would be funded through RFE/RL's Board for International Broadcasting, but political and budget difficulties required it to be part of the VOA. The VOA staff and their public supporters were appalled by the prospect of this new bedfellow.[32]

During the spring of 1981, the ICA determined its key themes for the coming year. These broke down into six areas: leadership for the 1980s (the promotion of private enterprise and small government); U.S. political and security policies; the U.S. economy and the world economic system; solving the energy problem; American society in a changing world (including an emphasis on spiritual values); and a catchall category: arts, humanities, and sciences in America. The subthemes for U.S. political and security policies led off with opposition to the U.S.S.R. but also included calling for human rights in "totalitarian countries," opposition to terrorism, the promotion of democracy, and "a comprehensive international effort to cut both the supply of and demand for illegal drugs." Regional priorities included illegal immigration in Latin America, the deployment of theater nuclear forces in Europe, and opposition to Communist adventurism in Africa and Central America. Central America would be a particularly important theater of agency operation throughout the Reagan years.[33] The agency also had to confront the dam-burst of propaganda from the U.S.S.R.

The Soviets distributed their propaganda through front organizations, agents of influence, and contacts with the world's media in activities that they termed "active measures" (*aktivnye meropriyatiya*). The most troubling of the "active measures" was the oldest in the book: the rumor. The KGB had transformed "disinformation" into an art. Intelligence officers working for Service A of the KGB's First Directorate crafted stories to play on the suspicions of their audience and planted them in the press of the developing world – newspapers such as *Blitz* and the *Patriot* in India – or fed them out

30 RRL Lord files, box 90,051, Radio Free Cuba (4), Mas memorandum, 10 November 1980. On Mas' background see RRL WHORM sf FG 298, 218147 SS, White House press release, 31 May 1984; also Larry Rohter, "Jorge Mas, 58, Dies," *New York Times*, 24 November 1997, p. B7.
31 "US Radio Station to Send "Information" to Cuba" *Baltimore Sun*, 24 March 1981.
32 RRL Lord files, box 90,051, Radio Free Cuba (2), Fontaine/Lord to Richard V. Allen, 25 June 1981.
33 RRL Carnes Lord papers, box 90051, file: ICA Feb–March 1981 (3), USICA global and regional themes, FY 1982.

through the official Soviet news agencies TASS and Novosti. They then sat back and watched as the rumors spread, even leaking into the mainstream press in the West, undermining the United States as they traveled. The rumors could be deadly. The State Department learned that the KGB had been behind the rumor of American complicity in the Mecca terror attack, which sparked a murderous riot in Pakistan in November 1979. A favorite approach included a forged document to confirm the rumor. Between 1945 and 1975 the United States detected some three or four forgeries a year. During the Carter years this doubled. It would leap again in the 1980s. The ICA also assumed the existence of "silent forgeries," fake documents that circulated but never became public and hence could never be refuted.[34] Sometimes the attacks were even cruder. On 21 February 1981, a bomb blast ripped through RFE/RL headquarters in Munich. It was a backhanded testament to the power of international radio.[35]

During the summer of 1981, Wick became convinced of the need for "a massive counter-offensive to cope with Soviet propaganda and disinformation." When visiting Europe he noted that "within six minutes of landing and every six minutes thereafter" he had been made aware of the crisis of faith in themselves and the United States that left Western Europe vulnerable to Soviet mischief. He called for the administration to mobilize with "wartime urgency" to counter Soviet distortion. The ICA alone could not address the problem. The agency could not speak domestically, and key expertise lay in other agencies. He suggested, "The administration's best speakers and thinkers should assemble to urgently shape a coordinated strategy to enable the United States *to speak with one voice* persuasively and with sensitivity to Soviet engendered disinformation." "The time," he concluded, "is now."[36]

Wick circulated his proposal in the first week of August. On 9 September 1981, President Reagan signed the authorization for an interagency counterpropaganda initiative to be led by the ICA, which Wick, with shades of Truman, dubbed "Project Truth." The President's directive required the State Department, Pentagon, and CIA to work with the ICA gathering raw material to support the project and to join the ICA in implementation. The core plan was the rapid rebuttal of Soviet propaganda and especially disinformation circulated by the KGB. On 15 October, the ICA launched a newsletter called *Soviet Propaganda Alert* for circulation to U.S. diplomats, newspapers, and other contacts, to highlight such distortions before they could take hold. As Project Truth developed, its themes broadened to include Afghanistan, as well as the

---

34   RRL NSA agency files, USIA Vol. 1, file 3, box 91,377, quoted in proposal attached to Wick to Richard V. Allen, 7 August 1981; Barbara Crossette, "US Starts 'Project Truth' in Bid to Counter Soviet," *New York Times*, 4 November 1981, p. A7. Interview: Herbert Romerstein, 17 November 1995. There is an outline of a fake-based "active measure" operation in Cambodia in a Soviet defector's book: Aleksandr Kaznachev, *Inside a Soviet Embassy*, Philadelphia: Lippincott, 1962, pp. 176–7. For an overview see *Active Measures: A Report on the Substance and Process of Anti-US Disinformation and Propaganda Campaigns*, Department of State, August 1986, pp. 43–6.

35   RRL Lord files, box 90051, ICA (1), Kaminsky to Allen, 27 February 1981, and following. Interview: Gene Pell, 30 March 2004. The Munich bomb was eventually attributed to the freelance terrorist known as Carlos the Jackal. Around the same time the staff found poison in the canteen salt shakers.

36   RRL NSA agency files, USIA vol. 1, file 3, box 91,377, Wick to Richard V. Allen, 7 August 1981, with attached proposal. Emphasis in original.

common values that the United States shared with its allies. Materials flowed through all ICA outlets.[37]

The supporting bureaucracy for Project Truth included an interagency think tank called the Policy Group, which focused on long-term strategy. A series of interagency working groups, chaired by the State Department, served each priority area of Project Truth. A year into Project Truth these areas included Afghanistan, Poland, Cuba, Nicaragua, Soviet chemical–biological warfare, Central America, and U.S. peace initiatives. An executive committee brought representatives from these groups, the policy group, and the Public Affairs and Human Rights staff of the State Department together each month to implement the initiatives suggested by the working groups. Particular challenges from Soviet propaganda included claims that the United States had used germ warfare against Cuba and had been behind the massacre in the Sabra and Shatila refugee camps in Lebanon in September 1982.[38]

*

In September 1981, Wick traveled to China to sign a new cultural exchange agreement. It was, however, clear that Sino–American exchange was not progressing smoothly. The Chinese attempted to prevent thirteen abstract paintings, including works by Jackson Pollock, from being shown in the ICA's exhibition in Beijing. When the Chinese demanded cuts Wick threatened to pull the entire show. The Chinese government relented. Wick also criticized the imbalance in student exchanges and restrictions on American journalists in China. Chinese officials were shocked by his insensitivity, but their feelings were not his concern, and Wick's tough line did not prevent the VOA getting a Beijing bureau in 1982.[39]

In surveying the weapons in his own arsenal, Wick was particularly impressed by the potential of satellite television and ordered a number of experiments to test the viability of deploying the medium more widely. In September 1981, the ICA relayed Defense Secretary Weinberger's press conference launching a report called "Soviet Military Power" to stations in all NATO member states. The event and document were well discussed in the European media as a result. The agency also mounted big presidential hookups. An estimated 200 million viewers across fifty countries, including China, watched President Reagan propose the elimination of all intermediate nuclear

37 Barbara Crossette, "US Starts 'Project Truth' in Bid to Counter Soviet," *New York Times*, 4 November 1981, p. A7; Murrey Marder, "US Sharpening Information Policy Overseas," *Washington Post*, 10 November 1981, p. A1; RRL WHORM sf FG 298, 8608614, USICA an overview, tab D, "Project Truth," n.d., circa early 1982. Project Truth was implemented within the agency by the Bureau of Programs under Associate Director John Hughes.
38 RRL WHORM sf FG 298, 128779, Project Truth progress report September to December 1982, with sample agenda and issues of *Soviet Propaganda Alert*. For an early endorsement of the efficacy of the work against disinformation see RRL WHORM sf CO 165 USSR box 5, 088015, Haig to Wick, 14 June 1982. On the Falklands see RRL WHORM sf CO 165 USSR, box 4, 070373, "Soviet Propaganda Alert," 26 April 1982.
39 James P. Sterba, "China and U.S. Sign Pact on Cultural Exchanges," *New York Times*, 6 September 1981, p. A3; "American Art Goes to China," *New York Times*, 19 August 1981, p. C16. The exchange imbalance was on the order of six thousand Chinese going to America against under three hundred Americans traveling to China.

forces on 18 November; such broadcasts allowed the ICA's message to reach audiences "directly, without distortion or filtering."[40]

On 13 December, the new leader of the Communist government in Poland, General Wojciech Jaruzelski, declared martial law in a bid to control the dissent and head off any Soviet military intervention. The VOA's Polish service leapt from four and one-half hours a day to seven. Despite jamming, the VOA estimated its audience to be in excess of eleven million, more than forty percent of the adult population.[41] But Wick wanted to mark the escalation of the Polish crisis with a counterblow in the medium of satellite television. He came up with the idea of a spectacular mix of politics and entertainment, pulling together world leaders and Hollywood royalty to air on the "Day of Solidarity with Poland" scheduled for 30 January. He called the program *Let Poland Be Poland* from the Solidarity anthem "Żeby Polska była Polską." Wick worked with Marty Pasetta, the impresario best known for mounting the annual Academy Awards. Pasetta donated his services. With producer Eric Leiber assisting, he put together the show in under three weeks. Wick received pledges of $500,000 from corporate donors to fund the program. Pasetta brought together footage of pro-Solidarity demonstrations around the world, messages of support from Ronald Reagan, Margaret Thatcher, and Helmut Kohl, and contributions from American, Polish, and international stars. Charlton Heston, Glenda Jackson, and Max von Sydow hosted. Poles featured included the poet Czeslaw Milosz and the newly defected ex-ambassador to the United States, Romuald Spasowski. The Swedish pop group Abba recorded a statement, and submitted a bill for SK 4,740 (around $350) in recording and shipping expenses. Everyone else had donated his or her contribution. The idea alone attracted plenty of detractors. Before the broadcast gruff British Labour politician Denis Healey condemned "Hollywood razzmatazz," arguing "The show will be intensely embarrassing to everyone outside the United States." Some of Wick's staff agreed, but he was unrepentant. "Show people have always been a vanguard of causes," he told the *Los Angeles Times*. "When you want to convey a message, you'd better have an audience."[42]

Let Poland Be Poland opened dramatically. Images of Poland enjoying new freedoms set to the music of Chopin's Polonaise suddenly froze. The music slurred. Color

---

40 RRL NSA, agency file, USIA, vol. 1, file 3, box 91,377, Wick to Richard V. Allen, 22 December 1981. See also RRL WHORM sf FG 298, 054032, Foreign Media Reaction to President Reagan's foreign policy speech, 19 November 1981. For a summary of these and subsequent hook-ups in the first Reagan administration see RRL WHORM sf FG 298, 257944, "USIA initiatives since June 9, 1981," 26 June 1984, pp. 14–15.

41 RRL WHORM sf FG 298, 257944, "USIA initiatives since June 9, 1981," 26 June 1984, p. 17.

42 Bernard Gwertzman, "Now, the Star of the Show: Poland," *New York Times*, 20 January 1982, p. A24; Peter W. Kaplan, "The Poland Production: Pasetta's Planning for TV's Show of Solidarity," *Washington Post*, 29 January 1982, pp. D1, D3; "Support Snowballs for Special Satellite Message to Poland," *New York Post*, 26 January 1982; Betty Cuniberti, "Critics Aim Barbs at U.S. TV Spectacular on Poland," *Los Angeles Times*, 29 January 1982; Michael Getler, "ICA Plans Poland TV Spectacular," *Washington Post*, 28 January 1982, p. A20. The Abba correspondence was filed in the USIA historical branch file on *Let Poland Be Poland*, now available at NA RG 306 A1 (1066) USIA historical collection, box 158. Skeptical colleagues included Wick's senior FSO, Jock Shirley. Shirley later considered that his doubts were "wrong in retrospect." Interview: Shirley, 29 July 2002.

drained and a grinding sound was heard. Still images of repression flashed onto the screen, ending with a picture of a corpse in the snow. In darkness Charlton Heston spoke: "The light of freedom has been extinguished in Poland. It continues to burn in the hearts of the Polish people." Heston lit a candle and emerged from the gloom. "Tonight we are lighting a candle for the people of Poland. . . ." As the program unfolded, statements from international leaders and scenes of protests around the world alternated with artistic contributions. Bob Hope demonstrated what radio jamming sounded like, Frank Sinatra sang a Polish folk song, Kirk Douglas spoke movingly about the country from which his family had emigrated, and Orson Welles growled through John Donne's "No Man is an Island." The ninety-minute show ended with a choir singing "Let Poland Be Poland" and a montage of contributors speaking that phrase over images of the pro-Solidarity demonstrations.[43]

Let Poland Be Poland aired on Sunday, 30 January 1982. The agency estimated that 184 million people in fifty countries had seen at least minutes of the program. PBS broadcast the program within the United States in the following days. The *Washington Post* quipped that "a bit more Hollywood tastelessness would actually have *helped*." European responses were mixed, and many countries screened excerpts only in the context of news, but *Le Soir* in Paris called it "serious . . . and heart rending." "It was a picture," one West German commentator noted, "of America's unbroken capability to be sympathetic to freedom." Soviet TV responded with an improvised special called *The Hypocrisy of Washington*, featuring lurid tales of CIA intrigue from around the Warsaw Pact. For Wick the greatest compliment came in later years when Lech Walesa personally confirmed how much the broadcast had meant to him and his movement. Wick's enthusiasm for satellite television was undiminished.[44] Other ICA satellite projects included the TV Satellite File (TVSF), a weekly half-hour compilation of news footage covering American life and politics. Posts, the foreign press centers, and the world's leading TV news agencies, Visnews and UPI-TN, all received the material and integrated it into their output.[45]

43 RRL audio visual: *Let Poland Be Poland*.
44 Seventeen more nations screened highlights of the show to a further 200 million people, including 100 million Chinese. An audio version broadcast by the VOA and RFE/RL reached 165 million. Interview: Wick; RRL WHORM sf PR16–01, 058660, Robinson (Acting Dir.,) to Baker et al., 2 February 1981; President to Kirk Douglas, 1 March 1982; 069630, McFarlane to Robinson 2 March 1982 with draft letter; RRL WHORM sf FG 298, 257944, "USIA initiatives since June 9, 1981," 26 June 1984, p. 14. The special legislation was HJ Res 382 of 28 January 1982. For comment see Tom Shales, "International Tribute to Poland," *Washington Post*, 1 February 1982, p. B1; "TV Program on Poland Criticized by Many," (Reuters) *New York Times*, 2 February 1982, p. A8; "Soviets Pan Poland Show," (AP) *Chicago Tribune*, 2 February 1982. For post usage reports see NA RG 306 A1 (1066), USIA historical collection, box 158.
45 ICA also found a cheap way to approximate the impact of satellite interviews. The Bureau of Programs developed a technique called televised electronic dialogue (TED) by which the agency videotaped the U.S. end of international telephone interviews and shipped the tape to the interviewer's home country, where it would be cheaply intercut with footage of the other end of the conversation for a fraction of the cost of a satellite circuit. Typical costs per hour were $56 for the long distance phone call and $60 for a high-quality videocassette against nearly $5,000 for an hour on the satellite. Conventional triumphs for the agency's film and television unit included the launch in 1982 of *Science World*, a new series of documentaries on U.S. science. The program found an eager audience in eighty-three

Wick had no doubt that the early work of the agency made a difference. In October 1981, he sent Reagan an agency research report on Western European opinion indicating that opposition to the deployment of medium-range missiles was reduced when framed with information about Soviet missile strength and the U.S. willingness to participate in arms reduction talks. Neutralism and pacifism were minority views. Wick saw "a base on which our information campaigns can build," but acknowledged that Europeans still showed "limited concern for the Soviet threat." There was much more work to be done.[46]

2) THE CRISIS AT THE VOICE OF AMERICA, 1981–82

For the Voice of America the Reagan years began with a series of journalistic scoops. On inauguration day, the VOA was able to confirm the exact moment that the plane carrying the hostages took off from Tehran airport, thanks to a stringer in Iran, Anne Francis, who had located herself, phone in hand, in a villa with a view of the runway.[47] Sixty days later the Voice covered a very different story. Around 2:30 pm on 30 March the newsroom received a frantic call from correspondent Mallory Saleson to say that she had just seen shots fired at the President and he might have been hit. Bernie Kamenske ordered a story written and held pending confirmation. Confirmation came all too soon. The VOA carried the story at 2.39. The third scoop followed the shooting of Pope John Paul II on 13 May. A member of the Turkish service identified the assailant from his photograph as fellow Turk Mehmet Ali Hagca, and the Voice went on the air with Hagca's name and background.[48]

Scoops notwithstanding, it was only to be expected that the activist approach of the Reagan administration would collide with the news values of the Voice of America. In May 1981, the newsroom a senior duty editor named Mark Willen launched an internal newsletter called *Room News* to document policy pressures on his colleagues. The first big clash came on 24 July when VOA English and Dari carried a story by Defense Department correspondent Mark Hopkins (based on a Carl Bernstein story in the *Atlantic Monthly*) that arms were being manufactured in Egypt and Israel with Russian markings for discreet supply to fighters in Afghanistan. All saw the hand of

countries, including China. Productions themed around Project Truth included *Solidarnosc*, a ten-minute montage of images that told the story of the movement; a half-hour documentary produced in English, Arabic, French, Spanish, and Portuguese called *Human Rights: The Universal Struggle*; and a film exploring the involvement of the Communist bloc in the attempted assassination of Pope John Paul II. See RRL WHORM sf FG 298, 257944, "USIA initiatives since June 9, 1981," 26 June 1984, pp. 2, 3, 7; RRL WHORM sf FG 298, 128779, Project Truth progress report September to December 1982: USIA television and film services, productions, and acquisitions supporting Project Truth.
[46] RRL WHORM sf FG 298, 045946, Wick to President, 29 October 1981, with ICA report "European public opinion more upbeat than media reports," 26 October 1981.
[47] Interview: Bernie Kamenske; Alan Heil, *Voice of America*, pp. 196–7.
[48] Interview: Bernie Kamenske (6 December 1995); Jurey, *A Basement Seat to History*, pp. 216–19; Mark Willen to author, 31 August 2004. Usually the VOA waived its two-source rule when one of its own correspondents was a witness, but Saleson's view of the Reagan shooting was partial and the VOA could not afford an error.

the CIA. The NSC complained that "many VOA types envision themselves as a sort of international *Washington Post*/CBS news" and endorsed an appeal from CIA director Bill Casey for closer cooperation in "reporting on sensitive areas." National Security Adviser Richard Allen raged against the VOA management.[49]

As the months rolled by, Mark Willen's list of attempted policy interventions grew longer. On 4 August, the U.S. embassy in Manila called for control of the VOA's coverage of the Vietnamese boat people, lest the Voice encourage the exodus. On 17 August, the U.S. embassy in Moscow objected to the rebroadcasting of an ABC interview with Soviet spokesman Georgi Arbatov. Also on 17 August, an ICA policy official pressed the VOA never again to describe the Afghan *mujahideen* as "rebels" or "anti-government" guerrillas. Willen bemoaned the return of self-censorship among his more timid colleagues. In the Arbatov case, staff were unnerved by the news that VOA director Conkling had asked the acting Program Manager, Cliff Groce, to identify who had authorized the broadcast. Groce refused, recalling the role that "naming names" had played in the McCarthy era, and was transferred to the film branch for his trouble, but news of the pressure on the VOA broke in the *Baltimore Sun*.[50]

Liberal concern for the VOA was matched by conservative outrage at the bias they perceived in the VOA's output. Key critics included Robert Reilly, a conservative writer with links to the Heritage Foundation. Disgruntled VOA staff, especially from the Eastern European Language Services, forwarded partisan copy to Reilly, who passed this material to Wick. His first consignment of material included a VOA World-wide English profile of the new President, which stressed such negatives as Reagan's alcoholic father and his being the first divorced President. Furious, Wick summoned Reilly to his apartment at the Watergate and pledged to fire the writer concerned. Shortly thereafter Reilly joined the ICA's E-bureau as a political appointee. He continued to pass scripts and a weekly report to Wick until Conkling became VOA director, whereupon Reilly suggested that Conkling commission a colleague in the ICA public affairs office to review the VOA's operations. Conkling duly approached Philip Nicolaides, a former advertising executive, conservative speechwriter, and journalist. His name would become synonymous with the turmoil of the early Reagan-era VOA.[51]

49 Interview: Haratunian, 15 December 1995; Mark Hopkins, May 1996; RRL NSA agency files, USIA vol. 1, file 3, box 91,377, Casey (CIA) to Richard V. Allen, 5 August 1981; deGraffenreid (NSC) to Allen, 21 August 1981; Interview: Kamenske. Haratunian papers, memo "Call Pat Simien...," 10 August 1981 and "Courtesy call on Mr Wick...," 8/81, in which Wick suggests that Conkling obtain the same sort of oversight as editor in chief that Ben Bradlee has at the *Washington Post*. Wick got a further sense of the issues around the VOA when in a meeting on 31 July he suggested that Solzhenitsyn be invited to broadcast regularly on the Voice. The VOA staff recoiled at the idea and suggested that Solzhenitsyn was seen as a traitor by the majority of Soviet listeners. Author's collection: Robert R. Reilly to Wick, 14 August 1981.
50 Interview: Kamenske, Alan Heil, *Voice of America*, pp. 201–3. Haratunian papers, memo, "potential violations of public law 94–350, the VOA charter and other complaints which inhibit an honest presentation or analysis of the news. July–Aug. 81"; Jurey, *A Basement Seat to History*, p. 223. The "preferred terms" for the Afghan forces were "freedom fighters," "resistance movement," "guerrillas," "nationalists," "insurgents," or "patriots" and, the NSC noted, "the addition of the adjective Afghan and/or Muslim...adds considerably to their effect."
51 Interview: Bob Reilly, 18 December 1995 and 3 January 1996. Author's collection: Reilly to Wick, 14 August 1981.

On 21 September, Nicolaides submitted his suggestions to Conkling. He pulled no punches, calling the usual output of VOA "mush." He argued that the Voice should "portray the Soviet Union as the last great predatory empire on earth." He scorned the agency's preferred terminology, noting that

> The professor at Tufts who dreamed up the expression "Public Diplomacy," was looking for a bland, sanitized substitute for *propaganda*, a word that had fallen into disrepute because some of its most gifted practitioners had put it to the service of odious ideologies. But the fact is that propaganda has more in common with advertising and public relations than with "diplomacy."

He saw the ICA as an international advertising agency and imagined an active role for the VOA:

> We must strive to "destabilize" the Soviet Union and its satellites by promoting dissatisfaction between peoples and their rulers, underscoring lies and denials of rights, inefficient management of the economy, corruption, indifference to real wants and needs of the people, suppression of cultural diversity, religious persecution, etc. We should seek to drive wedges of resentment and suspicion between the leadership of the various Communist bloc nations.

Nicolaides predicted that a tougher tone on the VOA would be controversial but urged Conkling to steer into the storm regardless: "And when we finally get to the point that the only criticism of VOA is howling from the Kremlin, antiphonal ululation from the U.S. hard left, and even greater Soviet efforts at jamming, we can crack open the champagne."[52]

Conkling was slow to act on Nicolaides' suggestions. First he and Wick instituted a new personnel structure at the Voice that gave the director greater autonomy with regard to staffing issues.[53] On 10 November, the bombshell hit. Conkling announced that Nicolaides would be joining the VOA full time as its first deputy program director for commentary and news analysis. The announcement coincided with news that the VOA's respected deputy director, William Haratunian, would be moved to other duties. He had effectively been fired. In a stark farewell memo, Haratunian spoke of his deep concern for the future of the VOA. Conkling compounded fears of politicization by announcing the creation of a set of senior policy jobs within the Voice to oversee the production of combative editorials. He also proposed giving greater leeway to the language services in their choice of news. As VOA staff petitioned to block the appointment of Nicolaides, an unknown person passed his September memorandum to the *Washington Post*. It ran on the front page three days later.[54]

52 Author's collection: Nicolaides to Conkling, 21 September 1981; Murrey Marder, "Propaganda Role Urged for Voice of America," *Washington Post*, 13 November 1981, p. A1.
53 Interview: Alan Heil, 29 November 1995. The structure was suggested by the chief of News and Current Affairs, Alan Heil, who had no idea at the time of the use to which Conkling would put his increased powers.
54 Interviews: Henry Butterfield Ryan, 27 November 1995; Alan Heil, 29 November 1995; Bernie Kamenske, 6 December 1995; Janie Fritzman, 7 December 1995. Murrey Marder, "Propaganda Role Urged for Voice of America," *Washington Post*, 13 November 1981, p. A1; Murrey Marder,

Meanwhile, conservatives increasingly saw the VOA as a relic of détente bent on appeasing Moscow. On the Hill, Representative John LeBoutillier (R-NY) complained that an excerpt from Solzhenitsyn's new novel, *October 1916*, had been pulled from repeat broadcasts of the VOA's "World of Books" program. The conservative journal *Human Events* cataloged other horrors, from slights against the government of Taiwan to a VOA book review that explored the erotic power of Elvis.[55] In December, as the crisis flared in Poland, Conkling attempted to strong-arm the newsroom into allowing a State Department report on the mounting Cold War to be read straight on the air. For News Director Bernie Kamenske this was the final straw. Increasingly disillusioned, Kamenske mentioned to a friend outside the Voice that he might soon be seeking other employment. On 21 December, Bernie Kamenske resigned to take up the post of senior news editor at the Washington Bureau of a new venture called Cable Network News. When breaking the news to colleagues, he wept. Kamenske's career at CNN was cut short by a heart attack, but in forced retirement he remained an advocate of the VOA charter. He haunted historical commemorations of the Voice lest complacency creep into the record. When he died in 2003, his influence was still palpable in the VOA newsroom.[56]

By the end of the year, the Voice seemed in the grip of a full-scale political purge. More senior figures were transferred into oblivion, while others took early retirement.[57] But the forces of revolution did not have it all their own way. Nicolaides was also sidelined. Conkling denied him extra staff and as of January 1982 only one of his scripts had actually been broadcast. Wick moved Nicolaides back to the ICA, officially to contribute to Project Truth.[58] In fact, Nicolaides was assigned no work. He stuck a sign on his door that read "Gorky" (the Soviet City where the dissident Andrei Sakharov was exiled) and waited. Fifty days later Wick "requested" that Nicolaides leave the agency altogether. The conservative *Washington Inquirer* complained

"Appointment of 'Propaganda' Advocate Defended by VOA Chief," *Washington Post*, 14 November 1981, p. A15; "Selling the Sizzle," *Washington Post*, 16 November 1981, p. A14; Barbara Crossette, "Voice of America Announcers May Get More Choice in News," *New York Times*, 14 November 1981, p. 5. For a press clip from the *Dallas Morning News* in defense of Nicolaides as sent by Wick to Reagan see RRL WHORM sf FG 298–01, 051989, Wick to President, 8 December 1981 with *Dallas Morning News* editorial, 20 November 1981. The entire crisis was documented in Robin Grey, "Inside the Voice of America," *Columbia Journalism Review*, May/June 1982, pp. 23–30.

55 "Voice Spikes Solzhenitsyn Excerpts," *Human Events*, 31 October 1981. "...VOA Still Needs a Thorough House Cleaning," *Human Events*, 13 March 1982.

56 Interviews: Bernie Kamenske, 6 December 1995; Janie Fritzman, 7 December 1995; Alan Heil, 29 November 1995. Barbara Crossette, "Voice of America Loses Key Official," *New York Times*, 22 December 1981, p. A7. For an account by Kamenske see *Voice of America at the Crossroads: A Panel Discussion on the Appropriate Role of the VOA*, Washington, DC: The Media Institute, 1982.

57 Conkling moved Haratunian's deputy Bill Read out of the agency, bounced the head of Worldwide English, Hal Banks, to the VOA's New York office, and reassigned Mark Willen to New Delhi. Willen quit rather than move. Alan Heil moved from the helm of News and Current Affairs to a specially created limbo in "program development." Other casualties included the head of the VOA USSR division, Barbara Allen. Interviews: Groce, Kamenske, Fritzman, Heil; ADST Groce; Heil, *Voice of America*, pp. 206–9. Willen to author, 31 August 2004.

58 John M. Goshko, "Controversial Nicolaides Is Leaving Post at VOA," *Washington Post*, 20 January 1982, p. A9; "... VOA Still Needs a Thorough House Cleaning," *Human Events*, 13 March 1982.

not only about his sacking but also that Conkling had found his new deputy directors from the Foreign Service rather than the ranks of loyal Reaganites.[59]

Conkling filled several key vacancies with appointees from the world of commercial broadcasting, including two journalists from NBC, Frank Scott and Gene Pell, who joined as director of programs and chief of News and Current Affairs, respectively. Pell had been NBC's Moscow correspondent and made no secret of his conservative politics. Scott and Pell endorsed the charter but also believed that the VOA needed considerable reform to match commercial standards. Pell was astonished by the hostility of his writers to any editorial oversight. When one particular science writer objected to being edited, Pell had his piece edited again by five other news organizations: NBC, the *New York Times*, the *Washington Post*, the *Chicago Tribune*, and the *Christian Science Monitor*. All recommended some editing and some suggested that it needed more than the edits made by Pell. Over the months that followed, staff came to accept that the editorial process strengthened their work.[60]

On 24 February 1982, Reagan visited the Voice to mark the station's fortieth birthday.[61] But Conkling remained in the firing line. By late March the intensity of criticism from both left and right had become too much. A particularly savage dressing-down in his own office from Representative LeBoutillier left Conkling sobbing. He duly resigned. Although some conservatives clamored for Nicolaides to fill the post, Wick astutely transferred in John Hughes, a former editor of the *Christian Science Monitor*. Born in Wales in 1930, Hughes joined the ICA in 1981 as Associate Director of Programs to run the agency's printed output. As an experienced journalist, Hughes had been a confidant for Conkling and already knew something of the Voice's difficulties. He immediately sought to close down the leaks to the press. Speaking at one of his first morning meetings Hughes informed staff that life would become very difficult for anyone who spoke to the outside world about the Voice, be it to *Human Events* or the *Washington Post*. He had no time for gripes about freedom of speech.[62]

Hughes saw reforming the Voice's editorials as a priority. Listening to hours of tapes, he had become convinced that the listener he pictured tuning in by "a dim and flaring lamp" in Bangladesh would be utterly confused as to where the news stopped and official comment began. With Wick's approval, on 1 June Hughes introduced a new editorial system at the Voice, removing the ambiguous category of the VOA

59 "Another Reaganite Bites the Dust," *Washington Inquirer*, 19 March 1982, pp. 1, 3. For an account by Nicolaides see *Voice of America at the Crossroads: A Panel Discussion on the Appropriate Role of the VOA*, Washington, DC: The Media Institute, 1982. The new deputy directors were Sam Courtney and Terrence Catherman.

60 Interview: Gene Pell, 30 March 2004; Heil, *Voice of America*, pp. 207–9. Frank Shakespeare and the Heritage Foundation had nominated Pell to be VOA director in 1981; see RRL WHORM sf FG 298, 482673, Willa Ann Johnson (WH) to E. Pendleton James (WH), ICA, 8 April 1981.

61 Interviews: Diane Doherty, Janie Fritzman.

62 Interviews: John Hughes, 14 September 2004, also Pell, Kamenske, Heil, Fritzman; John M. Goshko, "Propaganda Controversy: VOA Chief Conkling Resigns," *Washington Post*, 23 March 1982, p. A17; Jon Parles, "James Conkling, 83, Executive Who Helped Begin Grammys," *New York Times*, 17 April 1998, p. D.21; RRL WHORM sf FG 298, 082593 SS, press release re: John Hughes, 23 March 1982. Hughes was born in 1930.

news analyses, which had been prepared by individuals with minimal policy oversight, and focusing wholly on daily VOA editorials crafted "to communicate our position on international issues and to persuade listeners of the validity of our point of view." The first such editorial denounced Soviet hypocrisy in its arms policy on the eve of a UN session on disarmament. Seeking to build the sort of firewalls that separate news from comment in a printed newspaper, Hughes insisted that the editorials be even more clearly buffered at both ends and flagged "Next/That was a VOA Editorial reflecting the views of the U.S. government." The head of the editorial section was Seth Cropsey, a conservative journalist from *Fortune* who had written speeches for Caspar Weinberger. The NSC staffer with responsibility for public diplomacy, Carnes Lord, noted, "We can expect to see some intelligence and hard-hitting material."[63]

On 15 July, a policy statement on broadcasting – NSDD 45 – endorsed the new editorial policy. It also affirmed the news values of the charter and committed the administration to a multiyear program of transmitter modernization at both RFE/RL and the VOA.[64] The tension between news and policy was not easily resolved, and both sides felt compromised during the years that followed. Editorials were at least buffered from VOA news programs by music and an announcement, and some services even broadcast them after they had signed off. Wick noted that staff had difficulty identifying actual distortions of the news in the name of policy. This was not due to the lack of trying on the part of the political appointees but to the tenacity of the journalists in sticking to their principles.[65]

With the editorials now clearly defined, Wick ordered an expansion of the news content of the VOA to an estimated fifty-five percent of all programming. The VOA began a program called "American Viewpoints" to showcase editorial opinion around the country, created a Department of Audience Relations to answer mail, and started to advertise programs and to publish a monthly listener magazine. The Voice also upgraded its output on American life and culture and planned to deploy a mobile van to travel within the United States to draw "portraits in sound" of American rural life.[66] The VOA carried more religious material. Early in 1983 President Reagan proudly told a convention of religious broadcasters that the VOA's Christian and Jewish broadcasting was being "expanded and improved" and for the first time in 1982 VOA had broadcast a Christmas Eve service from National Presbyterian Church.[67]

The VOA stepped up its broadcasting to Afghanistan. The long-overdue Pashto service began on 4 July 1982. Four months later the Soviets began trying to jam the

63 Interview: Hughes, 14 September 2004. RRL WHORM sf FG 298, 092766, Wick to Meese et al. New VOA editorial system, 2 July 1982; RRL WHORM sf FG 298–01, 084442, Hughes to James A. Baker, 11 June 1982; 102338, Lord to Clark, 10 August 1982. On the international placement of VOA editorials in newspapers see RRL WHORM sf FG 298–01, Lord to Clark, 4 May 1983 etc. Interview: Wick.
64 NSDD 45, 15 July 1982, on line at http://www.fas.org/irp/offdocs/nsdd/nsdd-045.htm. Interview: Wick.
65 See Wick's response to Bernie Kamenske in *Voice of America at the Crossroads*. Interview: Heil.
66 RRL WHORM sf FG 298–01, 104916, Robinson (Acting Dir. ICA) to James A. Baker, 15 September 1982.
67 *PPP RR 1983*, Vol. I, p. 154.

service. By the summer of 1983, the Voice carried three hours of programming a day
for Afghanistan, evenly split between Dari and Pashto. The VOA also added special
Afghan programs to its Farsi and Urdu services, knowing that many Afghans spoke
those languages also.[68] VOA Russian carried the signs of a tougher political position,
broadcasting sermons from the celebrated dissident pastor Georgi Vins, then resident
in Indiana. In answer to the criticism from Solzhenitsyn, Wick established a panel of
Russian émigrés to advise the Russian service, chaired by the cellist Rostropovich. The
VOA also began announcing each day that it was the "nth consecutive day of the
jamming of our transmissions to the Soviet Union."[69] By RL's estimation, the VOA's
audience in the Soviet Union grew steadily during this period, exceeding 15 percent
per week, though similar trends in listening to the BBC and Radio Liberty suggest
that it was the call of political circumstances rather than fine-tuning of formats that
kept Russians listening.[70]

There were also certain covert uses of the VOA. In the course of 1982, Frank Scott
asked Pell to arrange for the playing of any song from the Rod Stewart album *Foolish
Behaviour* on the VOA's World Wide English service at a particular time. Scott did
not expand on the request but staff assumed that it came from "another agency" and
related to some aspect of cloak and dagger. In April 1985, Pell passed a similar request
to the VOA Georgian Service. When a disgruntled former member of the Georgian
service named Nodar Djindjihashvili made the story public in 1988 it did not reflect
well on the VOA's claims to objectivity. Pell had no regrets, noting that messages to
the underground had been staples of the wartime BBC.[71]

In mid-June the hard right took steps to mend bridges with Wick. On 16 June,
Roy Cohn and Congressman LeBoutillier hosted a lunch for the ICA director at the
Madison Hotel. Guests included columnist Pat Buchanan and senior figures from
Human Events, *National Review*, and *Conservative Digest*. The lunch became a three-
hour question and answer session on Wick's plans for the ICA. On 28 June, Cohn called
on Wick with Nicolaides and Dick Birshirjian, who had served as Associate Director
for Educational and Cultural Affairs in 1981. Wick noted with palpable relief, "We
had a fine 'make-up session.' A consensus was reached that the agency was on the right
track." At the NSC Carnes Lord adjudged that Wick had overestimated the good will.
Further storms lay ahead.[72]

[68] RRL WHORM sf FG 298–01, Wick to James A. Baker, 4 November 1982; also FG 298, 257944, "USIA initiatives since June 9, 1981," 26 June 1984, pp. 18–19.
[69] RRL WHORM sf FG 298–01, 084790, Vins to President, 11 May 1982; Pipes (NSC) to Vins, 23 June 1982; RRL WHORM sf UT 001–01, 101553; Jonathan Friendly, "Voice of America to Broadcast More Opinion," *New York Times*, 11 July 1982, p. A4.
[70] Parta, *Discovering the Hidden Listener*, sections 2.3 and 2.4.
[71] Interview: Pell; Carolyn Weaver, "When the Voice of America Ignores Its Charter," *Columbia Journalism Review*, November–December 1988, pp. 36–43. The story broke in the February/March 1988 issue of *Mother Jones*.
[72] RRL WHORM sf FG 298, 086288, Memo to White House from Wick, "Conservative Wing," received 30 June 1982. Also Niles Lathem, "Bureaucratic Monster Defies Reagan's New-Right Knights," *New York Post*, 21 June 1982, p. 47. For Lord's skepticism see RRL WHORM sf FG 298–01, 102338, Lord to Clark, 10 August 1982.

The appointment of George Shultz to be Secretary of State brought an unexpected blow to the VOA. Shultz offered director John Hughes the post of Assistant Secretary of State for Public Affairs and spokesman for the Department of State. Hughes accepted the job.[73] On 15 September, President Reagan announced the third director of the Voice of America to serve in 1982: Kenneth Tomlinson, a thirty-seven-year-old foreign correspondent and senior editor from *Reader's Digest*. Born in 1944, Ken Tomlinson had grown up poor in the Virginia mountains. He never forgot the wonder of the world that came to him as a child through broadcasting. He joined the *Digest* in 1968, only a year after graduating from Randolph Macon College, and rose swiftly through the ranks. While overseas as a foreign correspondent, he became a fan of the BBC World Service. He recalled longing to twist the dial to hear programs of equivalent quality from the VOA. As an active Republican, he had the chance of a role in the Reagan administration and indicated interest in joining the Advisory Commission on Public Diplomacy. When John Hughes moved to State, White House staff recalled Tomlinson's interest in international broadcasting and offered him the VOA job.[74]

Voice personnel understood Tomlinson to be a candidate to please the conservative right. The *Washington Post* reported that Roy Cohn had thrown a party in his honor at the Madison Hotel. But Tomlinson would be his own man. He urged the *Post* to stay tuned and judge him by the output of the VOA.[75] Tomlinson had two core priorities at the Voice. The first was to hold undue political influence at bay. Under Secretary Eagleburger at State, in particular, needed regular reminding of the VOA charter. His other priority was to lift the sound of the VOA to match the BBC. Tomlinson noticed that VOA programs still tended to avoid actuality and he challenged staff to give the world the "*voices* of America," recording interviews on location or bringing newsmakers into the studio. Voices captured included those on Capitol Hill. Tomlinson succeeded in obtaining permission from the executive board of the Congressional Radio and Television galleries for VOA correspondents to cover legislative affairs on the same basis as commercial correspondents.[76]

For the rest of the USIA, 1982 was a year of satisfactory progress, although along the way Wick had to cope with the exit of his former ombudsman – one Arthur Imperatore – who, on being denied promotion in the agency, resigned and raged against

73 Interview: Hughes; RRL WHORM sf FG 298–01, 099484, Wick to President, Voice of America, 3 August 1982.
74 Interview: Ken Tomlinson, 28 September 2004; RRL WHORM sf FG 298, 09836355, Press release, 15 September 1982, nomination sent to Senate, 19 November 1982.
75 Interview: Tomlinson; Haynes Johnson, "Voice: For VOA Employees, Black Tie Back Evokes Disquieting Feelings," *Washington Post*, 6 February 1983, p. A3. In an apparent allusion to Cohn's support for Tomlinson, Cohn's friend William Safire later wrote that Roy Cohn relished the "ironic symmetry" that enabled the man vilified for his attack on the USIA in 1953 to "put his man in as head of USIA's Voice of America" thirty years later – William Safire, "About Roy Cohn," *New York Times*, 4 August 1986, p. A17. Cohn was a key referee in the USIA's search for a new director for its office of public liaison; see RRL WHORM sf, FG 298, 178515, Wick to Liebman, 2 August 1983.
76 Interview: Tomlinson; RRL WHORM sf FG 298, 257944, "USIA initiatives since June 9, 1981," 26 June 1984, p. 19.

mismanagement, waste, and even fraud at the agency.[77] The agency opened a new Foreign Press Center in Los Angeles in preparation for the Olympics in 1984.[78] In May, the President announced a new International Youth Exchange Initiative to expand the exchange of young people by 15,000 over three years, to be administered by Wick. The government pledged $10 million in funding, with a further $10 million to be raised from the private sector.[79] The Youth Exchange Initiative exceeded expectations, arranging more than 22,000 exchanges in its first three years. Youth exchanges became a major element of the ICA's exchange work.[80] Finally, even in the midst of a renewed Cold War, some cultural exchanges with the Soviet Union continued. On 4 July 1982, jazz musicians Chick Corea and Gary Burton played a concert at the House of Composers in Moscow. The VOA's Willis Conover acted as master of ceremonies.[81]

In the second half of 1982, Wick realized two of his key goals for the agency. He won back the old name and got the agency into new, consolidated premises. In August 1982, Congress approved the bill restoring the name USIA. The change was accomplished by executive order 12388, signed by the President on 14 October 1982.[82] News of the new building broke about the same time. It had been a fight largely because the USIA's landlord at 1776 Pennsylvania Avenue hired five teams of lobbyists to torpedo the move. On the eve of the election recess, the House Public Works Committee approved Wick's plan to move to a newly constructed building at 400 C Street South West, just across the street from the VOA. In relief Wick wrote thanking the President for his support and noting that it had taken the Department of Energy four years to move into their building after a presidential "OK." For the USIA to be on the verge of moving just one year after the "OK" was a minor record.[83]

[77] RRL WHORM sf FG 298, 068941, Imperatore to Wick, 27 & 30 April 1982; 099803, Robinson to Attorney General et al., 29 April 1982, with Imperatore to Wick, 15 April 1982. For an analysis of Imperatore's claims, absolving Wick, see 112843 CU, "Report of USIA general counsel on Arthur Imperatore's allegations," 14 December 1982. For press coverage see Hendrick Smith, "Ex-Aide Is Charging Corruption in a U.S. Agency," *New York Times*, 15 May 1982, p. 3; Barbara Crossette, "A Volunteer Ombudsman Tells His Unhappy Story," *New York Times*, 19 May 1982. p. B6.

[78] RRL WHORM sf FG 298, 257944, "USIA initiatives since June 9, 1981," 26 June 1984.

[79] RRL WHORM sf PR 007–01, CF 129871, Wick to Clark (WH), 22 April 1982; RRL WHORM sf FG 298, 257944, "USIA initiatives since June 9, 1981," 26 June 1984, pp. 26–7. Themes within the exchange initiative included exchanges for future political leaders and young people in labor and agriculture. Wick planed to expand to include a program of business internships. Other changes to the exchange program included the transfer of the Fulbright Teacher Exchange program and supporting staff from the Department of Education to the USIA, p. 55. For public statements see *PPP RR 1982*, Vol. 2, p. 1626 and *PPP RR 1983*, Vol. 1, pp. 78–9. On private sector contributions see RRL WHORM sf FG 298, 387632, Wick to President, 26 March 1986.

[80] Allen C. Hansen, *USIA: Public Diplomacy in the Computer Age*, 2nd edition, New York: Praeger, 1989 p. 159.

[81] RRL WHORM sf FG 298–01, 096495, Robinson to Clark, "VOA effectiveness," 17 August 1982.

[82] RRL WHORM sf FG 298; 106797, Wick to President, 13 August 1982 etc., 0921445; Darman to President, 12 October 1982 with executive order attached. The change was effective from 24 August 1982. See *PPP RR 1982*, Vol. II, p. 1318.

[83] Phil Gailey and Marjorie Hunter, "Washington Talk: Briefing, USIA on the Move," *New York Times*, 8 October 1982. RRL WHORM sf FG 298, 106227, Wick to President, 21 October 1982.

3) FROM "PROJECT DEMOCRACY" TO WORLDNET

CONFRONTING COMMUNISM IN 1983

On 8 June 1982, in an address to a joint session of the Houses of Parliament in the United Kingdom, President Reagan proposed a new global crusade to promote democracy. Officials explained that the core of his policy would be a "new and generous program of grants to aid anti-Communist political institutions, labor unions, and newspapers in the third world." The idea was a reworking of the CIA's old 1950s policy of funding of the center-left, but this time the mechanism had to be overt.[84] Cabinet discussions honed Reagan's concept into a comprehensive interagency program. Known initially as "the Democracy Initiative," the program aimed to "launch an aggressive worldwide effort to strengthen the political, intellectual and social infrastructures that make democracies function worldwide." For reasons of credibility the CIA took no part. The lead agency would be Wick's USIA.[85]

The new initiative prompted a revised infrastructure for U.S. information work. On 15 January 1983, President Reagan signed National Security Decision Directive 77 to strengthen public diplomacy. The directive built the USIA into the core of decision-making. It established a Special Planning Group (SPG) at the NSC to oversee the planning and implementation of all public diplomacy, chaired by the National Security Advisor and including the secretaries of State and Defense, the directors of the USIA and AID, and the White House communications assistant. Four standing subcommittees reported to the SPG, including a public affairs committee co-chaired by NSC and the White House communications staff to coordinate foreign policy speeches at home and an International Information Committee chaired by the USIA to take over responsibility for Project Truth. NSDD 77 also set up an International Broadcasting Committee, chaired at NSC, to coordinate planning, antijamming, and transmitter modernization. The task of implementing the Westminster speech – now known as Project Democracy – lay with an International Political Committee chaired by State.[86]

---

84   Interview: Walter Raymond, 12 December 1995. For press coverage see R. W. Apple Jr., "President Urges Global Crusade for Democracy, Revives Flavor of 1950s in Speech to Britons," *New York Times*, 9 June 1982, pp. A1, A17. Raymond (whose home agency was the CIA) noted that Reagan hoped that all the G7 countries meeting in France would organize parallel structures. Although the President omitted to raise this formally at the conference, Britain, Canada, and West Germany all created similar initiatives. See also U.S. GAO, "Report to Senator Malcolm Wallop: Events leading to the establishment of the National Endowment for Democracy," 6 July 1984 (copy filed at NA RG 306 A1 (1061), USIA historical collection, box 6, misc. files, 1940s–1990s, NED).

85   For a summary of the cabinet discussion see Jeff Gerth, "Problems in Promoting Democracy," *New York Times*, 4 February 1983, p. A14. Wick seized on this project as the crux of his appeal against an OMB clampdown on the USIA budget; see RRL Harper files, BRB appeals, USIA ... (1), OA 7891, Wick to Meese, Baker & Stockman, 10 December 1982; Wick imagined an ultimate cost of $100 million for the whole project.

86   Interviews: Raymond & Schneider (5 December 1995). For USIA background on Project Democracy from early 1983 see NA RG 306 A1 (1066), USIA historical collection, box 207, subject files, "Project Democracy, 1981–2" and "...1983." For an online copy of NSDD 77 see

In February 1983, Congress began hearings on Project Democracy. In the House, Dante Fascell was both skeptical of the $85 million budget and hostile to the prominent role planned for the USIA. The Senate also had its doubts. Paul Tsongas (D-MA) scoffed at "Project Right-Wing Democracy" and the committee trimmed the plan severely.[87] Fast work behind the scenes created a compromise plan based around a National Endowment for Democracy (NED), which would be independent of the federal bureaucracy in all matters but its budget. The endowment would award grants to struggling democratic political groups, newspapers, schools, and trade unions, focusing especially on the developing world. The NED operated chiefly through four "core grantee" institutes managed by the U.S. Chamber of Commerce, the AFL-CIO's Free Trade Union Institute, and the Republican and Democratic National Committees. The first director of the NED was Carl Gershman, an aide to Jeane Kirkpatrick and former executive director of Social Democrats, U.S.A.[88]

The NED distributed tens of millions of dollars during the Reagan years. Its grants restored schools and trained teachers in rebel-held areas of Afghanistan, furnished election monitors in Haiti, helped opposition groups in South Korea, funded the moderate Social Democratic and Labor Party in Northern Ireland, and maintained pro-democracy groups in South Africa. The anti-Sandinista newspaper *La Prensa* in Nicaragua received $100,000 from the endowment in 1985. More controversially, in 1984 the NED funded the Panamanian army's candidate in that country's election. In 1985 the American Association of Publishers objected to Gershman's attempts to influence the choice of books for their stand at the Moscow International Book Fair, and the French press was outraged to find that the NED had subsidized two right-wing opposition groups in their country.[89] The NED's credibility took a further blow when Oliver North used the term "Project Democracy" to describe his secret

---

http://www.fas.org/irp/offdocs/nsdd/nsdd-077.htm. The document defined public diplomacy as "those actions of the U.S. government designed to generate support for our national security objectives." For early meetings of the International Broadcasting Committee see RRL WHORM sf FG 298–01, 150814, Tomlinson (VOA) to McFarlane, 20 May 1983. The system included a Senior Planning Group, chaired at NSC by Raymond, with Schneider representing the USIA, Craig Alderman (Deputy Under Secretary of State for Defense) from the Pentagon, Gerald Helman from the State Department, and a representative from the USAID.

[87] On the debate see Bernard Gwertzman, "Skeptics Pelt Shulz with Queries on Reagan's 'Project Democracy,'" *New York Times*, 24 February 1983, p. A6; Patrick E. Tyler, "USIA Chief Questioned on 'Project Democracy,'" *Washington Post*, 3 March 1983; Mary McGrory, "Promoting the 'Infrastructure of Democracy,' with Charts," *Washington Post*, 3 March 1983, p. A3; Howard Kurtz, "As USIA Brews List of Achievements, Wick Ferments Controversy," *Washington Post*, 1 January 1984, p. A2.

[88] Ben A. Franklin, "Project Democracy Takes Wing," *New York Times*, 29 May 1984, p. B10; Ben A. Franklin, "Pro-West Project Blocked by House," *New York Times*, 1 June 1984, p. D15; Rep. Hank Brown (R-CO), "A Tax Supported Endowment for Mischief," *Wall Street Journal*, 20 June 1983; "Senate, 51–42, Vote to Back Plan to Promote Democracy," *New York Times*, 29 June 1983, p. A13; Walter Goodman, "Congress Assails Democracy Group," *New York Times*, 15 August 1983, p. A21. On the budget for the NED see RRL WHORM sf FG 999, Raymond to McFarlane, 5 June 1984.

[89] For a survey of NED work see NA RG 306, A1 (1066), USIA historical collection, box 207, subject files, "Project Democracy, 1984–5," Joel Woldman, "The National Endowment for Democracy," Library of Congress Congressional Research Service, 19 July 1984; NA RG 306, A1 (1061), USIA historical collection, box 6, misc. files, 1940s–90s, NED, NED annual report, 1984; NA RG 306 A1, (1070) USIA historical collection, reports and studies, box 7, including "The Democracy

war in Central America. North's private backers deepened the confusion by establishing a National Endowment for the Preservation of Liberty. Even so, the NED survived.[90]

Project Democracy was not the only piece of terminology abused during the Reagan years. The White House took the phrase "public diplomacy" in vain. Though practitioners and scholars had spent many years arguing that public diplomacy was more than a synonym for propaganda, in 1983 the Reagan administration named its State Department propaganda unit seeking to generate domestic support for U.S. policy in Central America the "Office of Public Diplomacy for Latin America and the Caribbean." It was as if the perpetrators of the Bay of Pigs invasion had taken the codename "Fulbright Program."[91] In a similar vein, the Assistant Secretary of Defense for Public Affairs, Henry E. Catto, who headed the USIA under George H. W. Bush, recalled that during his weekly meetings at the White House to discuss looming problems and coordinate a response, the words "public diplomacy" were used "deliberately and with malice-a-forethought" to refer to the administration's entire approach to domestic public opinion, giving a "totally different meaning to the phrase" from its USIA meaning.[92]

Meanwhile, the Soviet Union denounced Project Democracy as a conspiracy to meddle in the domestic affairs of others. The KGB attempted to undermine the campaign by circulating a faked State Department memo entitled "Democratization in Communist States," which spoke of infiltrating CIA-trained émigrés and covertly "eliminating" Communist parties in allied countries. *Pravda* gave details of recent media training given to the regimes in Chile, Guatemala, Haiti, and El Salvador. Just in case Project Democracy sounded like a good idea, Radio Moscow noted that Lenin himself had invented "public diplomacy" in 1917 when his decree on peace lifted

Program" and "The American Commitment to Democracy: A Bipartisan Approach," 30 November 1983; Joel Brinkley, "US-Backed Group Donates $100,000 to Nicaragua Paper," *New York Times*, 26 March 1985, p. A11; Ben A. Franklin, "Democracy Project Facing New Criticisms," *New York Times*, 4 December 1985, p. A28; David K. Shipler, "Missionaries for Democracy: U.S. Aid for Global Pluralism," *New York Times*, 1 June 1986, p. A1; "Stormy History of Endowment," *New York Times*, 15 June 1988, p. A14. The South African groups were the Institute for a Democratic Alternative for South Africa and the Black Consumers Union; the French groups were *Force Ouvrière*, an anti-Communist trade union, and the National Inter-University Union (UNI) a student group with ties to the banned right-wing paramilitary group *Service d'Action Civique* (SAC).

90   Interview: Raymond. "The Good Democracy Project," *New York Times*, 13 March 1987, p. A34.

91   This office, under Otto Reich, sent out speakers, published pamphlets, and mailed materials to editorial writers. The Comptroller General ruled that the office had violated prohibitions against the use of federal funds for propaganda purposes by conducting "prohibited covert propaganda activities" without Congressional authorization. In 1987 a White House Office of Public Diplomacy for Central America assumed these functions. Interview: Raymond. 100th Congress, 1st session, H. Rept. 100–433/S. Rept. 110–216, *Report of the Congressional Committees Investigating the Iran Contra Affair*, November 1987, p. 34. For summary of these activities see Thomas Blanton (ed.,) *Public Diplomacy and Covert Propaganda, the Declassified Record of Ambassador Otto Juan Reich*, National Security Archive briefing book, http://www.gwu.edu/~nsarchiv/NSAEBB/NSAEBB40. The Office included staff seconded from the USIA. Romerstein briefed the group on Soviet disinformation regarding Central America – major stories included Soviet denials of aid to El Salvador. Interview: Romerstein.

92   Interview: Henry Catto, 26 March 2004.

"the cover of secrecy surrounding policies made behind the people's back." As ever, this was a sign that the plan had found its mark.[93]

*

In the closing months of 1982, Wick developed a new method to harass the Soviet Union. Taking his lead from the President's use of anti-Soviet jokes, he hit on the idea of using humor as a weapon. USIA posts in the Communist bloc collected political jokes from their local contacts and forwarded them to Washington for inclusion in an anthology for discreet distribution throughout the world. The jokes were a wry comment on the inability of communism to deliver on its promises and evidence of popular opposition to Communist rule. Material included a story about a Muscovite who goes to buy sausages from the butcher, waits in line in vain, and in despair curses the Marxist–Leninist system. A policeman hears his remark and cautions him, "Comrade, a few years ago you would have been shot for saying that." Back at home the man confides to his wife that he now knows the depth of the economic crisis. "No sausages in the shops?" she asks. "Worse than that," he replies, "no bullets for the police." Other jokes turned on the political repression in the Communist world: "Question: What is the difference between an Eastern European journalist and his Western counterpart? Answer: An Eastern European journalist is free to say what ever he wants, but his Western counterpart is free the next day as well."[94]

Although embarrassed staffers in Washington soft-pedaled the anthology, some posts reported considerable success in placing these jokes around the world. The Seychelles considered the publication to be the "one of the best ever" put out by the agency. Journalists in Nepal, Burma, and Barbados happily worked the material into their output. In Brazil the conservative São Paulo daily *Jornal da Tarde* translated the entire packet and agreed to publish it as a feature with specially commissioned cartoons. Many posts merely issued the anthology to staff for use in small groups and one-to-one conversation. Brussels noted dryly that Belgians were well aware of the Soviet Union's economic weakness and requested jokes addressing Soviet aggression. One Middle Eastern post was unamused and wired back noting that jokes about sausages were not thought funny in the Muslim world. Wick duly forwarded the anthology and feedback to the President, together with the highlights of the second edition, focusing on "true" stories (or urban myths) of Soviet life.[95]

93 RRL WHORM sf, CO165 USSR box 8, 147992, Robinson to William P. Clark, 22 April 1983 with attachments.
94 RRL WHORM sf CO 165, USSR, box 7, 134465, Wick to President, 25 March 1983, with anthology "Political Humor in the Soviet Union and Eastern Europe."
95 On the soft-pedaling see Scott Thompson, *The Price of Achievement*, p. 80. RRL WHORM sf CO 165, USSR, box 7, 134465, Wick to President, 25 March 1983, with collection of responses from posts. One of the best "true stories" concerned a Soviet women who in 1981 found a metal tube inside a frozen chicken informing her that she had purchased the ten millionth chicken exported by a French company and had won a Peugeot car and should contact the nearest French consulate. Being a good Communist, she first approached the Soviet Ministry of Foreign Trade in Moscow to ask about her prize. With some embarrassment they offered her a Soviet car (a Zhiguli). When she complained, an official eventually explained that the chicken had originally been exported to Somalia in 1975 and sold

*

In the course of 1983, Wick engaged the Soviet rumor mill, hiring Herbert Romerstein (at Ken Tomlinson's suggestion) to lead the Disinformation Response Team. A teenage Communist who had grown gray fighting Soviet subversion as a Hill staffer, he became one of the great characters of the Reagan-era USIA. Romerstein brought energy and an encyclopedic knowledge of the world of propaganda to his post at the USIA. Romerstein investigated Soviet claims and briefed the press (especially in Europe) and U.S. government agencies. He was a key member of the interagency Active Measures Working Group, chaired at State by Dennis Kux.[96] The group's cases included a new crop of KGB forgeries, including a "speech" by UN ambassador Jeane Kirkpatrick on the U.S. plan to use world hunger as a political weapon, a pair of "cables" from the U.S. embassy in Rome revealing a U.S. plot to smear Bulgaria with the attempted assassination of the Pope, and a "letter" by a Danish general informing elderly and handicapped Copenhageners that the U.S. army planned to requisition their homes during a forthcoming NATO exercise. Romerstein would be busy.[97]

*

The year 1983 saw a number of USIA initiatives to promote better transatlantic relations. In West Germany, efforts were themed around the tricentennial

on to the U.S.S.R. The Ministry begged her not to raise the matter with the French government, as it would embarrass the Soviet Union were it known that its government was buying and distributing old frozen chickens. The source knew she eventually got a car but was unsure whether it was a Zhiguli or whether the Ministry of Trade bought her a Puegeot.

96 Interview: Herb Romerstein, 17 November 1995. Born in 1931, Romerstein had actually joined the Communist Party in Brooklyn as a teenager. This experience and service in the Korean War made him a zealous foe of Communism. In the mid-1950s (and again in 1964) he worked as an investigator for the New York State Legislature's investigation into Communist summer camps and charities. In 1959 he worked as a young volunteer at an émigré clandestine radio station called Radio Free Russia that broadcast an extreme anti-Communist line from mobile transmitters mounted on the back of two trucks in West Germany. The organization also smuggled leaflets and tiny copies of banned books into the U.S.S.R. using merchant seamen. In 1965, he moved to Washington and became an investigator for the House Committee on Un-American Activities, initially probing the KKK. In 1969 the committee changed its name to House Committee on Internal Security. In 1971, Romerstein became chief investigator for the Republican minority. In 1978, he became a professional staff member for the House Intelligence Committee. In 1979 and 1980, when the house held hearings on Soviet "active measures," Romerstein helped to produce two major reports highlighting the scale of the Soviet effort. On the House Intelligence Committee Romerstein held the highest level of security clearance, above top secret, which he considered "an indication that the U.S. doesn't persecute people for teenage stupidity." For profile see Jacob Weisberg, "Cold War without End," *New York Times Magazine*, 28 November 1999. Also Herbert Romerstein and Eric Breindel, *The Venona Secrets: Exposing Soviet Espionage and America's Traitors*, Washington, DC: Regnery Publishing, 1999. The Active Measures Working Group (AMWG) (founded under the chairmanship of State in 1981) produced a steady stream of reports and notes on Soviet Active Measures, including front groups, human rights, and fakes, beginning in October 1981 with its very first report: *Forgery, Disinformation, Political Operations*. It comprised personnel from State, the USIA, the CIA, the FBI, the DIA, the FBIS, the JCS, and the office of the Secretary of Defense.

97 RRL WHORM sf CO 165 USSR, box 9, 174478, Wick to William P. Clark, 22 July 1983 with attachment; *Active Measures*, Department of State, August 1986, pp. 47–8, 57–9, 73–80. On the origins of the AIDS story see United States Department of State, *Soviet Influence Activities: A Report on Active Measures and Propaganda, 1986–87*, August 1987, pp. 33–4.

of the founding of the first German settlement in North America in 1683. Tricentennial events looked to build on long-term links and especially to cultivate the so-called
"successor generation," but the United States had short-term goals also.[98] Above
all, the Reagan administration wished to deploy its cruise and Pershing II missiles to
counterbalance the Soviet deployment of the SS20 missile. In the face of continued
European public opposition, the administration established a special interagency committee to coordinate public diplomacy to support deployment of these intermediate
nuclear forces (INFs). Peter H. Dailey, Reagan's advertising manager in the 1980
election and ambassador to Ireland, returned to Washington serve as the committee's chair. The initiative needed merely to reduce opposition, because key European
leaders, including Kohl in West Germany and Thatcher in Britain, were willing to support deployment despite internal opposition.[99] This work was closely related to Project
Democracy. Wick's brief within Project Democracy included responsibility for recruiting donors from the private sector to bankroll the plan and, where possible, disseminate
its ideas through their own channels. The key message fed into those private channels
was the need to support INF deployment. Wick put together a small group of David
Rockefeller, the major conservative funders Dwayne Andreas and Henry Savatori, the
British financier Sir James Goldsmith, and two media moguls, Rupert Murdoch and
Joachim Maitre (of Axel Springer Publishing in Hamburg). On 21 March the group
met the President for lunch and received a detailed briefing from Dailey on the INF
issue.[100]

The real masterstroke was the selection of a new U.S. ambassador to NATO, David
M. Abshire. As the founder of the Center for Strategic and International Studies (CSIS)
in Washington, DC, Abshire already had a special relationship with the European think
tank circuit and defense journalists. He also knew senior people in the European peace
movement. He recruited an experienced USIA man, Stanton Burnett (then PAO in
Rome), and a colleague from the CSIS, Mike Moody, to run his campaign and began
to call in favors and rekindle old relationships in the cause of deployment. The core
of his argument was that the Soviet deployment of the SS20s in 1975 was the true
disruption to peace, rather than America's plan. Abshire was not averse to branching

[98] This initiative was directed by a German Tricentennial Commission that included Wick. Wick chaired
an interagency "Steering Committee on US–German Contacts," which launched youth exchanges,
a tricentennial postage stamp, a traveling National Park Service exhibition, a clutch of heart bypass
operations for German patients at a leading U.S. clinic to open tricentennial medical exchanges, and
a visit to Germany by Vice President Bush. In Bonn the PAO, Hans N. Tuch, ran a vibrant program
of reaching out to German schoolteachers and universities teaching American studies, which like the
youth exchange played into the long-term strategy of building links with the "successor generation."
Participants in visitor programs in these years included the young Gerhard Schroeder. Interview:
Tuch. RRL Joanna Bistany papers, box 1, OA 7887, file: USIA (1), Wick to Gergen, 6 May 1983.
For Presidential statements see *PPP RR 1983*, Vol. I, pp. 55, 826.
[99] RRL NSA, BOX 91,377, USIA Vol. 1, file: 1/81–12/83, (2), Shirley to William P. Clark, 29 Decem-
ber 1982 with attached minutes of meeting, 27 December 1982; Bernard Gwertzman, "Reagan
Intensifies Drive to Promote Policies in Europe," *New York Times*, 20 January 1983, p. A1. Interview:
Walt Raymond, 12 December 1995. For comment see Hans N. Tuch, *Communicating with the World:
U.S. Public Diplomacy Overseas*, New York: St Martin's Press, 1990, p. 161.
[100] RRL WHORM sf PR 130946, William Clark to Sadlier (presidential appointments), 15 March 1983.

off into just war theory or talking about real peace – he liked to use the Hebrew *shalom* – being more than the absence of war, but an international system based on real respect between countries. To Abshire's satisfaction, the European national security elite readily accepted the arguments for deployment and made the case to their own countrymen.[101]

For Walter Raymond, the NSC staffer responsible for the INF project, the whole operation worked well. Despite ongoing protests, during his European tour in June 1983 Vice President Bush received the necessary commitments to allow deployment to go ahead.[102] It proved difficult to persuade the general public on the continent of the wisdom of this move. In August, Wick transmitted a USIA report on European opinion and the INF that found that feeling remained strongly negative in four of the six countries slated to be bases for the missiles. Wick noted that Europeans seemed "either unaware or unwilling to accept a number of the basic assumptions inherent in our INF policy." Europeans did not know that the Soviets had both a monopoly on INFs at that time and missile supremacy in Europe in general. Only the British believed that cruise missiles would act as a deterrent. On the positive side, Europeans seemed to believe that the administration had a genuine commitment to arms reduction, preferred Reagan's proposal to Moscow's, and rated the missile issue as a low priority when set against social and economic problems.[103] The wider point was that with the help of sound public diplomacy the missiles had been deployed. A step had been taken that compelled the Soviets to return to the negotiating table and in retrospect looks like the critical winning move in the Cold War confrontation. David Abshire received the Distinguished Public Service Medal for his role in the deployment.

During the course of the INF campaign, President Reagan moved the nuclear weapons issue into a whole new dimension. On 23 March, he proposed the Strategic Defense Initiative (SDI) to develop a space-based antimissile shield to protect the United States from Soviet attack. Senator Ted Kennedy derisively nicknamed the program "Star Wars." SDI was expensive, but that was all part of its significance. As Walt Raymond at the NSC put it, "SDI sent a loud message to the Soviets: 'we will spend you into poverty.'" For SDI to work as a gambit, it had to be credible. The USIA played an important role in publicizing the "science" behind the concept and keeping the initiative in the international public eye. The Soviets mobilized their propaganda machine to respond. Just a month after Reagan proposed SDI, General Secretary Andropov suggested a meeting of Soviet and U.S. scientists to discuss its consequences. In the following months, Communist Parties and front organizations around the world scrambled to denounce SDI. The idea had clearly hit a nerve.[104]

101 Interview: David M. Abshire, 23 October 2006.
102 Interview: Walt Raymond, 12 December 1983.
103 RRL WHORM sf PR 015, 178676, Wick to David Gergen. 9 August 1983.
104 Interview: Walter Raymond, 12 December 1995; *Active Measures: A Report*, Department of State, August 1986, pp. 18–19. The USIA's support for SDI and the Pentagon's use of rigged tests and technological hoaxes is dealt with in Snyder, *Warriors of Disinformation*, pp. 121–5.

*

In April 1983, the USIA established its "Artistic Ambassador" program.
The agency sought out the best adult pianists who had yet to find management or
play a major debut and then sent them on international tours. The first four tours took
place in the spring and summer of 1984. Dean Kramer of Oregon played in Hungary,
Romania, Malta, and Egypt; Nancy Weems of Texas gave concerts in Scandinavia and
the U.S.S.R.; Steve Warzycki of California and Michael Caldwell of New Mexico both
toured South America. The critics and audiences raved. The USIA also commissioned
five American composers to create music especially for the ambassadors. The scores
were later presented to the Library of Congress.[105]

During this period the USIA also established a task force dedicated to Afghanistan.
Activities included the mounting of "Afghanistan Weeks" at USIS posts around the
world, a regular video program, *Afghanistan Digest*, and a visit by Kirk Douglas to
Afghan refugee camps in Pakistan, covered in a moving film created by Ashley Hawken,
Thanksgiving in Peshawar, which was screened in seventy countries.[106] The USIA also
drew together material filmed by thirteen broadcasters around the world to create
Afghanistan: The Hidden War, an hour-long documentary that included actual scenes
of combat between the *mujahideen* and the Soviet Army, of devastation in Afghan
villages, and of Afghan children maimed by Soviet "toy" bombs.[107]

In summer 1983, Congress had moved forward on the question of broadcasting
to Cuba. In order to save money, it had voted to establish Radio Martí within the
Voice of America, effectively replacing the VOA's Spanish service to Latin America
with the Cuban station. The President's Advisory Commission on Public Diplomacy
expressed alarm in a letter to the President. Replying to chair Ed Feulner, National
Security Advisor William P. Clark essentially endorsed his worries and encouraged the
commission to keep a close eye on the Martí project. "We must insure," Clark noted,
"that the Voice of America mission is not compromised." Reagan signed the Radio
Broadcasting to Cuba Act on 4 October 1983.[108]

The USIA worked to provide general support for U.S. policy in Central America
and the Caribbean. This included the secondment of one of the agency's most experienced Latin Americanists, Don Mathes, to serve in the White House as deputy to

---

[105]   NA RG 306 A1 (1066), USIA historical collection, box 168, subject files, "Artistic Ambas-
        sador Program"; RRL WHORM sf FG 298, 257944, "USIA Initiatives since June 9, 1981," 26
        June 1984, pp. 22–3. The composers commissioned were Lee Hoiby, Robert Muczynski, George
        Rochberg, Ross Lee Finney, and Ernst Bacon. For later coverage see David Saltman, "Negotiat-
        ing the Keyboard: USIA's Mission of Diplomatic Harmony," *Washington Post*, 25 August 1986,
        p. D7.
[106]   RRL WHORM sf FG 298, 257944, "USIA initiatives since June 9, 1981," 26 June 1984, p. 48.
[107]   RRL WHORM sf FO 0005–03, 5606, Wick to William P. Clark, 5 August 1984.
[108]   RRL WHORM sf FO 005–03, 169242, Clark to Feulner, 11 October 1983. *PPP RR 1983*, Vol. II,
        p. 1441, announcing the measure on 11 October, the President noted, "I would have preferred to
        place Radio Martí under the Board for International Broadcasting instead of the Voice of Amer-
        ica . . . nevertheless I am satisfied this legislation will permit the new Cuba service to broadcast pro-
        grams that promote freedom in Cuba, while maintaining the high standards of the Voice of America
        for accuracy and reliability."

spokesman Larry Speakes for Latin America.[109] Central America figured prominently in the USIA's antidrug work. The Assistant Secretary of State for International Narcotics Matters, Dominick DiCarlo, later noted that the single most important development in U.S. international drug policy in 1983 had been the USIA's increased output on the subject.[110]

*

In the midst of the INF initiative, the USIA ran into a scandal over unusual hiring practices at the agency. The *Washington Post* revealed that not only had the number of political appointees grown from a previous peak of 43 to 150 under Reagan (and at a time when the Federal Government was operating under a hiring freeze), but also a number of these appointees were children of Reagan administration officials. The scandal became known as "Kiddiegate." The Kiddiegate appointees included Caspar W. Weinberger Jr., son of the Secretary of Defense; Monica Clark, daughter of the National Security Advisor; and Barbara Haig, daughter of the former Secretary of State. The daughters of Bud McFarlane and VOA director Jim Conkling and the nephew of presidential assistant David R. Gergen had worked as interns at the USIA. But the appointments that really angered USIA staff were the selection of a public relations executive named Anne Collins, a family friend of the National Security Advisor, to serve as Cultural Affairs Officer in London and of Catherine Smyth, a friend of Vice President Bush and former vice chair of the Texas Federation of Republican Women, as CAO in Ottawa. Jobs that career officers worked twenty years to secure were becoming political wampum.[111] The final straw came when Caspar Weinberger Jr. received one of only five performance bonuses awarded in 1982. Deputy Director Robinson made the award without the knowledge of Weinberger's line manager and despite his rather patchy record. A press leak followed.[112] On 15 April, Senator Edward Zorinsky (D-NE) of the Foreign Relations Committee formally requested clarification of hiring policy and queried plans to promote Weinberger and Daniel Wattenberg, the son of a BIB member, to serve as Assistant Cultural Affairs Attaches in Bonn and Paris, respectively, and for a political appointee whose previous employment was as manager of a New York deli to serve as CAO in Port-au-Prince,

---

[109] Interviews: Don Mathes, 12 December 1995, and Larry Speakes.

[110] The USIA maintained its own Narcotics Working Group. In 1982 the agency gave priority to publicizing the Federal Strategy for Prevention of Drug Abuse and Drug Trafficking. In August 1982 Wick assigned a USIA officer named John Keller to serve on the staff of Carlton E. Turner, special assistant to the President on drug abuse. Keller designed a domestic and international communications strategy for the White House drug education initiative, launched on 25 April 1983. He then moved back to the USIA to coordinate the agency's narcotics work. RRL WHORM sf HE 006–01, 113534, Turner to Robinson, 2 December 1982; RRL WHORM sf, JL 003, 163319, Wick to William P. Clark, 22 July 1983 with attachment; RRL WHORM sf FG 298, 202183 PD, Turner to Wick, 1 February 1984, also RRL Alpha file: Wick. Turner to Wick, 27 April 1983.

[111] RRL Fred Fielding (White House Counsel) files, box 16 OA 10566, (USIA), Robinson to Zorinsky, 19 April 1983; Gene Gibbons, "USIA Showering Administration Children with Plum Positions," *Washington Post*, 17 April 1983, p. A3; Marjorie Hunter, "Some Well-Known Names at USIA," *New York Times*, 19 April 1983, p. B6.

[112] "Weinberger Son's Raise Questioned," *Atlanta Constitution*, 30 March 1983.

Haiti.[113] Wick, speaking from Thailand, dismissed the whole story, noting, "this happens . . . everywhere. Everybody knows somebody."[114] His deputy Gil Robinson defended the appointment of Collins, noting that she had sat on the National Council of the Metropolitan Opera, but his letter left many allegations unanswered.[115] Zorinsky added evasiveness to his list of concerns and wrote to the Comptroller General suggesting that the USIA had become "an agency financially out of control."[116] The scandal required scalps. On 13 May, Deputy Director Robinson resigned. Caspar Weinberger Jr. followed.[117]

Although Wick weathered Kiddiegate, he was back in the newspapers in July for spending $32,000 of taxpayers' money on a security system for his two-acre home in northwest Washington. After a word from the White House, Wick repaid $22,000 of this bill, but the press now had the USIA director in their sights.[118]

*

At 18:26 GMT on 31 August 1983, Soviet fighter planes destroyed a Korean 747 airliner – KAL Flight 007 – off course over the Sea of Japan. Two hundred sixty-nine people perished. News broke on 1 September and the USIA immediately created a task force composed of the area and media directors and chaired by the agency counselor, John Hedges. The task force's brief was to reinforce world reaction against the outrage; to inform those who, because of censorship or poverty, would not otherwise learn of the incident; and to present the shootdown as of concern to all nations.[119] The story became the lead in all forty-two VOA languages. The Voice immediately added an hour to its Russian service and doubled the number of transmitters carrying the broadcast to blast through jamming. Soviet reticence about the story at home gave the USIA a golden opportunity to undermine Moscow's credibility at home as well as abroad. As Reagan noted later that month,

---

[113] RRL Fred Fielding (White House Counsel) files, box 16, OA 10566, (USIA).

[114] Quoted in *Los Angeles Times*, 18 April 1983. President Reagan made much the same point at his press conference on 17 May 1983 (*PPP RR 1982*, Vol. I, pp. 724–5): "Well, isn't almost everyone that you appoint to a position in government someone that you either know or you know through someone? Because, how else do you find the kind of people that you want for the jobs? Nepotism, in my mind, would be if the person in charge was hiring his own relatives. And there's been nothing of that kind going on."

[115] RRL Fred Fielding (White House Counsel) files, box 16, OA 10566, (USIA), Robinson to Zorinsky, 19 April 1983.

[116] RRL Fred Fielding (White House Counsel) files, box 16, OA 10566, (USIA), Zorinsky to Bowsher (Comptroller General), 12 May 1983. Zorinsky also noted conflict of interest among recipients of certain USIA grants and consultant fees being paid to people for days when they did not actually show up to work.

[117] RRL WHORM sf FG 298, 125257 SS, Robinson to President, 13 May 1983; President to Robinson, 18 May 1983. "USIA Hiring Dispute Leads Weinberger's Son to Resign," *New York Times*, 17 May 1983, p. A11.

[118] "USIA Chief Repays $22,000," *New York Times* 8 July 1983, p. A11.

[119] RRL WHORM sf FG 298, 175007, Wick to Meese, 28 September 1983, with chronology. On 2 September Wick took part in the special NSC meeting on the crisis. The initial NSC meeting is described in Seymour M. Hersh, *"The Target is Destroyed": What Really Happened to Flight 007 and What America Knew about It*, New York: Random House, 1986, p. 137. USIS posts collected local media's identification of victims and transmitted them to the State Department to build up a master list for release to the world's press.

Every Soviet statement and misstatement, from their initial denials, through all
the other tortured changes and contradictions in their story – including their UN
representative still denying they shot down the plane, even as his own government
was finally admitting they had – was given full coverage by the Voice and other
USIA outlets.

VOA director Ken Tomlinson encouraged broadcasters around the world to follow
the VOA's example. The Voice carried President Reagan's addresses on the crisis on
5 and 10 September live in English, and relayed a Russian translation an hour later.
Reagan used the second speech to ask American citizens to lobby Congress for the
necessary funds to upgrade the VOA and RFE/RL and launch Radio Martí.[120]

All sections of the USIA went into overdrive to cover the crisis, but the film and
television branch had a special impact, transmitting news of the UN debate by satellite
and creating video packages of domestic news programs for use on local television
or in embassy briefings around the world.[121] Their crowning glory was an eleven-
minute videotape documenting the last minutes of the Korean airliner, which formed
the backbone of Jeane Kirkpatrick's presentation to the UN Security Council on 6
September. The tape comprised an introduction with map graphic and 273 panels of
text from the transcript of radio traffic between the Soviet pilots and their base, as intercepted by Japanese intelligence. At the State Department, John Hughes had persuaded
Under Secretary Lawrence Eagleburger that the political impact would more than out-
weigh the cost of revealing that the United States had access to this sort of material.
Eagleburger took a chance. Although the tape actually revealed confusion rather than
malice, the world was ready to think the worst. It destroyed Soviet denials as surely as
the Russian MiGs had destroyed the Korean plane. *Izvestia*'s Alexander Shalnev privately called it America's most devastating propaganda blow of the entire Cold War.
The tape and transcripts of the Soviet radio traffic were distributed around the world
by USIS posts.[122] Faced with the evidence, the Kremlin finally acknowledged that its

[120] "Voice of America Is Telling Russians of Plane Incident," *New York Times*, 5 September 1983, p. A4;
RRL WHORM sf FG 298, 257944, "USIA initiatives since June 9, 1981," 26 June 1984, p. 51;
RRL WHORM sf FO 005.03, 147072 SS, William P. Clark to President, 7 September 1983; RRL
WHORM sf PR011, 160701, Fielding to Elliott (WH speechwriting), "draft presidential remarks for
30th anniversary of USIA," 20 September 1983. For 10th September broadcast see *PPP RR 1983*,
Vol. II, pp. 1250–51.
[121] RRL WHORM sf FO 005.03, 147072 SS, William P. Clark to President, 7 September 1983; RRL
WHORM sf FG 298, 175007, Wick to Meese, 28 September 1983, with chronology.
[122] Interview: Hughes. RRL WHORM sf FG 298, 257944, "USIA initiatives since June 9, 1981," 26
June 1984, p. 51; RRL WHORM sf FG 298, 175007, Wick to Meese, 28 September 1983, with
chronology. The State Department requested this tape on Saturday 3 September for use on Tuesday 6
September. The first version was screened at the State Department on Monday morning and reedited
soon thereafter to be longer and "more visual." For a full account of this making of the tape see Snyder,
Warriors of Disinformation, pp. 43–72. Snyder here claimed to have detected a five-minute gap in
the tape, suggesting that some U.S. government agency had doctored the tapes, but the complete
Soviet transcript released in 1993 contained incriminating material. Hersh, *The Target is Destroyed*,
pp. 165–7. USIA Associate Director Scott Thompson later told Hersh that he doubted at the time
that the tape proved much. Both Hersh and Snyder note that problems in creating the transcription
included the translation of the pilot's oath Елки-Палки/*yolki palki*. The USIA settled on the gentle
"fiddlesticks" rather than fruiter alternatives, but the term is benign enough to now be used as the
name of a chain of Russian restaurants.

planes had shot down the airliner. The Soviet media retreated into allegations that the flight was being used for espionage. The level of distortion was so crude that USIA analysts concluded, "Support of the armed forces appears to have been given precedence over the U.S.S.R.'s credibility and image as a country devoted to peace. . . ."[123]

On 24 September, President Reagan delivered the final blow of the KAL 007 campaign with a major address on the theme of peace, carried over live VOA Worldwide English, with simultaneous translation in Russian, Ukrainian, Lithuanian, Romanian, Bengali, Hindi, and Hausa. Wick assured Reagan that he had "hit the Soviets where they are most sensitive – their credibility with their own people" and cited examples of the Soviet scramble to denounce the speech as evidence of its effectiveness. Research by Radio Liberty into Soviet audience reactions to the whole incident bore this out, demonstrating a high correlation between exposure to Western broadcasting, disbelief in the Kremlin's version of events, and disapproval of the Kremlin's actions in shooting down the plane. Wick concluded the affair with a gentle reminder to the President of the need for his continued support in modernizing VOA's facilities. Reagan responded with a presidential order to all agencies to support Wick in this work. It was tangible recognition of a job well done.[124]

*

October 1983 brought two shocks. On 24 October, a devastating double suicide bomb attack against U.S. and French installations in Beirut killed 241 Americans and 56 French. Even as that news broke, the administration was pondering its response to a coup on the Caribbean island of Grenada, where Cuban troops already had a foothold. Early on the morning of 25 October, troops from the United States and six Caribbean countries landed on that island. The President justified the move on three counts: to protect lives, including the lives of 1,000 Americans; to forestall further chaos; and to restore order by wresting power from "a brutal group of leftist thugs."[125] The VOA carried Reagan's words and a statement by the chair of the Organization of Eastern Caribbean States, Prime Minister Eugenia Charles of

[123] RRL WHORM sf CO 165, 183689, Wick to William P. Clark, 7 October 1983 with *Soviet Propaganda Alert*, no. 16, 7 October 1983.

[124] *PPP RR 1983*, Vol. II, pp. 1342–3; RRL WHORM sf SP 601–66, 167830 SS, Wick to President, 7 October 1983; RRL WHORM sf FG 298–01, 188955, Wick to William P. Clark, with "a sampling of VOA presidential coverage '83." For Reagan's interagency order (supporting NSDD 45, of 15 July 1945), see RRL NSA agency files, USIA vol. 1, file 1, box 91,377, President to Wick, 28 November 1983, etc. For the RL study see Parta, *Discovering the Hidden Audience*, Section 5.3. The survey (of 274 Soviet travelers) estimated that although 62 percent of Soviets had learned of the shootdown from special Agitprop meetings to promulgate the Kremlin's line, 45 percent had some exposure to Western radio coverage (compared to 48 percent for Soviet TV and 44 percent for Soviet radio). Of these listeners, 30 percent were uncertain and 52 percent believing of the Western version (making a total of 82 percent), and 31 percent were uncertain and 47 percent disapproving of the Kremlin's action in shooting down the aircraft (making a total of 78 percent).

[125] RRL WHORM sf ND 016, Grenada, 180933, Statement by the President, 9.00, 25 October 1983. For comments by the Secretary of State see RRL NSA, AP, RCDS, Country file, "Grenada invasion, Oct. '83" file: 5, George Shultz, press conference, 25 October 1983.

Dominica, live, and repeated them throughout the first day. The Voice also increased its English broadcasts in the Caribbean to twenty-one hours a day and its Spanish to Latin America to six-and-a-half hours a day.[126]

The Pentagon maintained tight control over media coverage over the Grenada operation, applying the lessons of British press management during the Falklands War.[127] With even U.S. correspondents initially excluded, the USIA played a vital role in feeding information about the operation to the world's press. Pentagon camera crews interviewed liberated Grenadans and filmed Soviet arms caches; then the USIA edited these images and transmitted them to the outside world. USIA officers also served in interagency strategy meetings, monitored world reaction, traveled with the naval task force, and provided advice to the airborne units on their use of psychological operations. They expanded USIS press operations in Barbados to cope with the media demands of the crisis. After the landing, VOA technicians worked with the U.S. army to establish a radio station on Grenada. A USIA film crew and VOA team covered the aftermath of the operation on the ground.[128]

The USIA worked with the Pentagon to publicize the evidence of Soviet intrigue in the Caribbean uncovered by the invasion. By 3 November, the Pentagon team on the island had created a leaflet giving a chronology of the invasion, presenting key administration statements, and showcasing evidence of Soviet, Cuban, and even North Korean aid. The USIA distributed this leaflet to the world and, no less significantly, to UN delegates in New York. On 10 November the Pentagon opened an exhibit of 440 tons of captured Communist military hardware at Andrews Air Force base. In four days, 17,000 people, including 20 foreign correspondents, viewed the haul. The USIA filmed the exhibit.[129] U.S. forces on Grenada also recovered a quantity of Soviet documents, and, in the Soviet embassy, instructional films on the art of sabotage. Although the USIA's television unit was shy of using "ill-gotten" film in its own productions, in the USIA's Disinformation Response Unit, Herb Romerstein used them to illustrate presentations on Soviet subversion and supplied videotapes to interested foreign journalists. Romerstein also co-edited an anthology of documents

[126] USIA transmitted images of the joint press conference in English and Spanish to Latin America, and in English to East Asia. Videotapes of this and Secretary Shultz's conference followed. Other statements distributed internationally in text or video form by the USIA included speeches by Jeane Kirkpatrick, Eugenia Charles' address to the Organization of American States on 26 October, and a press conference that same day by Caspar Weinberger and the Chairman of the Joint Chiefs of Staff, General John W. Vessey Jr. Other USIA activities included the rapid rebuttal of Soviet and Cuban propaganda claims; see RRL WHORM sf FG 298, 183019, Wick to Baker et al., "USIA programs and activities in support of Grenada," 3 November 1983.
[127] For the debate over media relations and Grenada see "Should the press have been with the military on Grenada?" (articles for and against by Harry Summers and Caspar Weinberger), *Los Angeles Times*, 13 November 1983, pt. VI, p. 1, and RRL WHORM sf ND 016, Grenada, 168198 SS, Kimmitt (NSC) to Stanford (exec. Sec. DoD), 23 November 1983 with attachments.
[128] RRL WHORM sf FG 298, 183019, Wick to Baker et al., "USIA programs and activities in support of Grenada," 3 November 1983.
[129] RRL WHORM sf FG 298, 183019, Wick to Baker et al., "USIA programs and activities in support of Grenada," 3 November 1983; RRL WHORM sf ND 016, Grenada, 168340 SS, McFarlane to President, 29 November 1983 with leaflet.

revealing Soviet and Cuban intrigue in the Caribbean, published in September 1984.[130]

Grenada provided the first opportunity for the USIA to unveil its new capability in satellite television broadcasting, WORLDNET. It began with the linking of five European embassies with USIA facilities in the United States to allow live interactive video discussions between senior journalists in their host country and guest leaders from American political and economic life in Washington. WORLDNET was developed and named by the director of USIA television services, Alvin Snyder. Snyder, a veteran of CBS, NBC, the Nixon White House, and the Ford-era USIA, first proposed such programs in October 1982. He imagined that selected correspondents would be cultivated by cigars and whiskey in the build-up to the sessions and that programs made in this way could then distributed over the network for still wider dissemination or excerpted for use on local TV news. On 27 October, the USIA tested this system with a briefing to the Foreign Press Center by the head of the "public diplomacy" office at the State Department, Ambassador Otto J. Reich.[131]

The inaugural WORLDNET broadcast on 3 November was a two-hour press conference bringing together European editors with Jeane Kirkpatrick in New York, Deputy Assistant Secretaries of State Craig Johnstone and James Michel in Washington, and Prime Ministers Sir John Compton of St Lucia and Tom Adams of Barbados in Bridgetown "to dispel misconceptions" about the Grenada incident. Kirkpatrick savaged a German reporter who compared the Grenada mission to the Soviet invasion of Afghanistan and reminded her audience that "a good many governments and peoples were rescued from tyranny by force" in World War Two. She made the evening news across Europe. Still more successful was a WORLDNET hook-up between the President, West German Chancellor Helmut Kohl, and U.S. and German astronauts orbiting aboard Skylab on 5 December. Twenty million Germans watched the program. *Die Welt* hailed it as "a technical masterpiece."[132]

Snyder planned WORLDNET around five regional systems. Euronet – as launched in November – served Western Europe. Arnet, for the American Republics, began in January 1984. Pacnet, for East Asia and the Pacific, and Afnet, for Africa, followed. USIA also planned Mednet for the Middle East for the future. Charles Wick noted that many PAOs initially hated the idea until they noticed the effect that it had on their ambassadors. When ambassadors started coming into the USIS post to take part

[130]   Interview: Romerstein, 17 November 1995; Michael Ledeen and Herbert Romerstein, *Grenada Documents: An Overview and Selection*, U.S. Departments of State and Defense, September 1984; Romerstein to author, 1 September 2004; Snyder, *Warriors of Disinformation*, p. 80.

[131]   Snyder, *Warriors of Disinformation*, pp. 40, 78, 82; RRL WHORM sf FG 298, 183019, Wick to Baker et al., "USIA programs and activities in support of Grenada," 3 November 1983.

[132]   Snyder, *Warriors of Disinformation*, p. 80; "News over the Atlantic" (editorial), *Wall Street Journal*, 27 December 1983; RRL WHORM sf FG 298, 183019, Wick to Baker et al., "USIA programs and activities in support of Grenada," 3 November 1983; Wick to Deaver, 29 August 1984; also 257944, "USIA initiatives since June 9, 1981," 26 June 1984, pp. 9–14. On 24 May 1984, WORLDNET marked the 35th anniversary of the founding of NATO with a two-hour special linking representatives of all the NATO members. Entitled "Peace: The Atlantic Promise" and anchored by British journalist Sandy Gall, it included Secretary of State Shultz among its guests.

in WORLDNET events, they felt that they had risen a notch within the embassy. Wick himself fell in love with the project. But even as he unveiled WORLDNET, the USIA director sailed into a new storm.[133]

4) WICK UNDER FIRE
THE USIA IN 1984

Charles Wick could never resist a joke. On 3 December, he quipped to the California Press Association that Margaret Thatcher had only objected to the Grenada intervention "because she is a woman." The story was soon on the AP wire. Eighteen Democrats in the House of Representatives, led by Barney Frank of Massachusetts, demanded that Wick resign. "When the appointee who engages in this bizarre behavior is the person in charge of our information policy abroad," they noted, "we have a situation equivalent to the appointment of a pyromaniac as a fire warden." Critics also noted Wick's readiness to send senior Republicans overseas as speakers on the "American Participation Program" and to award grants to conservative organizations. Cases in point included a $162,000 grant to teach South American governments how to manage the U.S. press.[134] Wick's enemies scented the moment to settle old scores.

In the run up to Christmas, Wick was alarmed by calls from a succession of *New York Times* reporters regarding his practice of taping phone conversations without notifying the people to whom he was speaking. Although an everyday part of the Johnson presidency, this was now against federal regulations and illegal in thirteen states, including Florida and California.[135] The key accuser was conservative columnist William Safire. On Monday, 26 December, Wick threw Safire and reporter Jane Perlez out of his home, enraged by their probing. Wick attempted to preempt their story through a statement to the press on 27 December, but when the story by Perlez and Safire hit the front page of the *New York Times* the next day it included gleeful citations of inconsistencies between Wick's statement and their information. Wick seemed especially vague about the date on which taping began. Leaks and a Freedom

133 Interview: Wick. RRL WHORM sf FG 298, 221557, Wick to James A. Baker, 6 April 1984 with WORLDNET Briefing book; also 218279, Wick to Motley (ASoS Inter-American Affairs), 27 January 1984.
134 "Thatcher Stance on Grenada Attributed to Being a Woman," *New York Times*, 4 December 1983, p. A19; RRL WHORM sf FG 298, 8400340 NB, Frank et al. to President, 20 December 1983; Harvey (USIA Cong. Liaison) to Frank, 2 February 1994, and for Wick's later statement on Grenada see Rod Townley, "This Is One Show That's 'Driving the Russians Crazy,'" *TV Guide*, 22 December 1984, pp. 40–42; Howard Kurtz, "As USIA Brews List of Achievements, Wick Ferments Controversy," *Washington Post*, 1 January 1984, p. A2. Wick claimed that the remark was intended to be "laudatory not only to Mrs. Thatcher but to all women," but later admitted that her reaction to Grenada had emphasized the challenge facing the USIA in Europe.
135 RRL Fred Fielding (White House Counsel) files, box 16, OA 10566 (Wick); for White House notes and legal opinions see Walter Raymond Jr. to McFarland (NSC), 29 December 1983; John G. Roberts to Fred Fielding, 23 December 1983. This pre-dates Safire's story and was presumably stimulated by an enquiry to the White House from the paper during its research. Also Roberts to Fielding, 30 December 1984, with "Outstanding questions on Wick recording." For NSC correspondence see RRL WHORM FG 298, 185583.

of Information request exposed the scale of his habit. He had taped half of all his calls since taking office. His "victims" included James A. Baker at the White House, actor Kirk Douglas, and philanthropist Walter Annenberg. His future hung in the balance.[136]

On 27 December, Wick called President Reagan to offer his resignation. Reagan would have none of it. "Don't you recognize," the President said, "that they're trying to get to me through you?" On 28 December, Larry Speakes emphasized that the President did not expect Wick to resign and deftly managed questions of Reagan's views on taping by quipping, "He doesn't do it himself. It's not done at the White House – not since 1974." But press stories multiplied and an attorney in Florida prepared a suit against Wick for tapes made in that state. On 6 January, the President personally defended Wick's taping as a way of ensuring that suggestions made in the phone calls could be transmitted to his staff. "I don't think that Charles Wick is a dishonorable man in any way," Reagan told reporters. "He has done a splendid job. I think the Voice of America, the whole United States Information Agency is far superior to anything that has ever been and he's going to continue there."[137]

As Safire's stories continued, observers assumed that the columnist had an informant with an inside knowledge of the USIA and swiftly recalled the long-term friendship between the columnist and Wick's disgruntled ex-deputy Gil Robinson, dating back to both men's work at the American Exhibition in Moscow in 1959. Despite Robinson's denials, the story seemed to be his revenge for being the fall guy over Kiddiegate.[138] Safire would not allow the story to drop, and developed his theme by suggesting that Wick's calls revealed illegal political fundraising from a federal office. Column followed column in what the *Wall Street Journal*'s Suzanne Garment called the daily spectacle of Safire rolling "his *New York Times* delivery truck backward and forward over the helpless body" of Wick.[139] In the *National Review*, William F. Buckley Jr. judged that, although the taping was wrong, "there is no need . . . to hang

136 Jane Perlez (with William Safire), "USIA Director Acknowledges Taping Telephone Calls in Secret," *New York Times*, 28 December 1983, p. A1; also Stuart Taylor Jr., "Opinions Differ on Law in Taping Phone Calls," *New York Times*, 28 December 1983, p. D17; William Safire, "The Wick Tapes (I)," and Jane Perlez, "White House Inquiring into Taped Telephone Calls," *New York Times*, 29 December 1983, both p. A20; William Safire, "The Wick Tapes (II)," and Jane Perlez, "Agency to Give Panel Transcripts of Secretly Taped Phone Calls," *New York Times*, 30 December 1983, both p. B12; Jane Perlez, "Officials Say Wick Got '81 Warning on Taping," *New York Times*, 31 December 1983, p. A9; William Safire, "And Used against You," *New York Times*, 1 January 1984, p. B13; William Safire, "'Limited Hangout Route," *New York Times*, 12 January 1984, p. A31; William Safire, "Wick Making History," *New York Times*, 27 April 1984, p. A27.

137 Interview: Wick; Lou Cannon, "Wick Informs Reagan of His Secret Taping," *Washington Post*, 29 December 1983, p. A3; RRL Fred Fielding (White House Counsel) files, box 16, OA 10566, (USIA), "Remarks of the President upon departure for Camp David," 6 January 1984. For press response see Howard Kurtz and David Hoffman, "Reagan Defends Wick, Will Keep Him on Job." *Washington Post*, 7 January 1984, p. A1.

138 "TRB: Holy Mackerel, Safire," *New Republic*, 30 January 1984, pp. 4, 25.

139 *Wall Street Journal*, 30 December 1983, as quoted in "The Wick–Safire Caper," *Wall Street Journal*, 9 January 1984, p. 18, noting that Wick had just hired this columnist's husband, Leonard Garment, as an attorney. For a refutation of the fund-raising story (Safire, "The Wick Tapes (II)," *New York Times*, 30 December 1983), see George Gallup, "A Wick Parley with No Hint of Party Politics" (letter), *New York Times*, 10 January 1984, A22.

Charles Wick on the sour apple tree," whereas the *New Republic* noted that whereas Wick had merely taped the calls, Safire had actually published their contents.[140]

On 9 January, Wick published an apology for the taping and his "misinformation" on the first day of the crisis. He handed eighty-one transcripts and four cassette tapes to the Senate Foreign Relations Committee and House Foreign Affairs Committee to aid an investigation. The White House and General Services Administration also mounted investigations.[141] But with the President's support clear, the media frenzy abated. In January, a Florida district attorney declined to prosecute a case against Wick. The Senate committee concluded that although a serious lapse of judgment, the transcripts did "not reveal any abuse of the director's official position." Safire still periodically chewed at the old bone. In April he mocked Wick's defense that he needed the tapes to write his memoirs, because he was part of history. Safire noted that as the furor had inspired a bill to make undisclosed taping by a federal official a federal crime, Wick certainly was making history.[142]

Just as Wick began to find his feet, a new scandal broke. On 8 February, the *Atlanta Constitution* revealed that the USIA had maintained a "blacklist" of ninety-five Americans considered unsuitable to speak overseas in its American Participants (Amparts) program. The list included novelist James Baldwin, poet Allen Ginsberg, journalists Elizabeth Drew, Ben Bradlee, and the iconic Walter Cronkite, activists Betty Friedan, Ralph Nader, and Coretta Scott King, economist J. K. Galbraith, and figures in U.S. foreign policy such as McGeorge Bundy and Madeline Albright. In this case Wick was not to blame. He was "appalled" when the list surfaced during an audit in late January 1984. He immediately ordered an end to the practice and a full investigation. "I am sure we all agree," he wrote to senior staff, "that a 'blacklist' is repugnant to the very foundation of our democracy." This did not prevent a leak. The press had yet another field day at Wick's expense.[143]

The internal USIA investigation revealed that the "blacklist" had been begun informally in the summer of 1981 by John Hughes at the P-bureau at the suggestion

140 William F. Buckley Jr., "On the Right," *National Review*, 10 February 1984; "TRB: Holy Mackerel, Safire," *New Republic*, 30 January 1984, p. 25.
141 RRL Fred Fielding (White House Counsel) files, box 16, OA 10566, (Wick), Statement by Wick, 9 January 1984, and USIA fact sheet, 9 January 1984; "Wick's Job Seems to Be Safe Despite 'Unethical' Recording," *Washington Times*, 5 January 1984, p. A3.
142 Joel Brinkley, "Florida Official Explains Decision Not to Prosecute Wick on Taping," *New York Times*, 25 January 1984; Howard Kurtz, "Panel Report Criticizes Wick for Recording Calls," *Washington Post*, 4 February 1984, p. A3. William Safire, "Wick Making History," *New York Times*, 27 April 1984, p. A27.
143 RRL WHORM sf FG 298, 206078, Wick to McFarlane, 23 February 1984, with copy of "blacklist"; Wick to associate directors et al., 16 February 1984. Other inconsistencies included the presence of Drew, Ambassador Mort Abramovitz, and Lester Thurow on lists of approved speakers. For coverage see Howard Kurtz, "USIA Blacklisted Liberals from Speaking Engagements Abroad," *Washington Post*, 9 February 1984, p. A2; Howard Kurtz, "Democrats Blast USIA on Blacklist," *Washington Post*, 10 February 1984, p. A9; Howard Kurtz, "USIA Aides Dispute Blacklist Allegations," *Washington Post*, 15 February 1984, p. A3; Art Buchwald, "Let's Play List-o-mania," *Washington Post*, 21 February 1984, p. D1; Joel Brinkley, "USIA Asks Advice on Destroyed List," *New York Times*, 2 March 1984, p. A15. Journalists asked Reagan if Wick planned to resign on 10 and 13 March. The President denied the story and endorsed his friend. *PPP RR 1984*, Vol. I, pp. 321, 339.

of Deputy Director Gil Robinson as a "working tool" to pool ideas and track responses to nominations for speaking trips, and was only available to a small number of staff. The list arose following reports from the field that some speakers had been insufficiently supportive of White House policy. Not all names were nominees. The journalists were included as a reminder that if invited they would decline for professional reasons. Congress began its own inquiry and the story then developed into a question of who knew about the list and when. Testimony from Associate Director for Programs W. Scott Thompson implicated Acting Deputy Director Les Lenkowsky as someone who had known of its existence. Lenkowsky, former head of the conservative Smith Richardson Foundation in New York, denied this. But he did not endear himself to colleagues by blaming "mindless gnomes in the bureaucracy" for creating the list, or to one particular senator by correcting his English during hearings on the case. Lenkowsky's defiant cry, "I stand by what I intended to say," entered the folklore of the agency. On 15 May, following three days of hearings on the blacklist, the Senate Foreign Relations Committee voted 11–6 not to confirm Lenkowsky as Deputy Director.[144] Lenkowsky served as the necessary blood sacrifice and, appeased, the mob moved on. In June a grand jury in California declined to prosecute Wick over the telephone taping.[145] He had survived both crises, but Wick now had much to live down. He tightened internal review procedures and set about rebuilding his relationship with the U.S. press by entertaining the publisher of the *New York Times*, Arthur O. Sulzberger, at USIA headquarters. Over a drink the USIA director took great delight in fixing Sulzberger with a theatrical stare and launching a faux tirade: "Oh the things you've written about me . . . and so much of it is true."[146]

　　　　*

Throughout the troubled early months of 1984, Wick maintained the agency's wider support of U.S. foreign policy. Tasks that year included management of European alarm at the U.S. decision to mine Nicaraguan ports in April, coverage of President Reagan's announcement of the withdrawal of U.S. troops from Lebanon, and responding to the Soviet boycott of that summer's Los Angeles Olympics.[147] Soviet assaults on the Los Angeles Olympics included the anonymous mailing to twenty African and Asian Olympic committees of faked Ku Klux Klan leaflets threatening

---

144　For the USIA and Senate report (19 March 1984) and associated material see RRL Fred Fielding (White House Counsel) files, Box 16, OA 10556, USIA blacklist. Also RRL WHORM sf FG 298, 206078, Wick to McFarlane, 23 February 1984; Culpepper (IO) to Everson (D), 17 February 1984; Raymond to McFarlane, "Confirmation hearings," 19 April 1984; Raymond to McFarlane, 15 May 1984; Joel Brinkley, "USIA Critical of Its Moves in Inquiry over the 'Blacklist,'" *New York Times*, 30 March 1984, p. A18; Joel Brinkley, "Panel Rejects a Reagan Nominee after 3-Day Hearing on Blacklist," *New York Times*, 16 May 1984. A1. For W. Scott Thompson's account see Scott Thompson, *The Price of Achievement*, pp. 105–8. Interviews: Hughes.

145　"Grand Jury Decides Not to Indict Wick," *New York Times*, 26 June 1984, p. A11.

146　Interview: Charles Z. Wick, 8 January 1996. On tighter procedures see RRL WHORM sf FG 298, 260030, Wick to President, 24 December 1984.

147　RRL WHORM sf PR 016, 227115 PD, Foreign Media Trends paper, ". . . mining of Nicaraguan ports," 25 April 1984.

nonwhite athletes who attended the games. The USIA's response included a ninety-minute WORLDNET session featuring the games organizer Peter Ueberroth and the mayor of Los Angeles, Tom Bradley, who happened to be black, answering questions from African journalists. The USIA followed up with a half-hour film called *Hello, Los Angeles*, which touted the professionalism of the Los Angeles police department. None of the nations targeted by the Soviet campaign withdrew from the games.[148]

Wick's own priorities included the massive program to modernize the VOA. The administration budgeted $1.2 billion over an assumed two terms of the Reagan White House. The OMB objected and took the matter to the budget appeals board in the autumn of 1983, but when Wick produced Reagan's campaign pledge to restore the radios, budget director Dean Stockman crumbled. In 1983, Wick concluded the long-sought agreement to build a VOA relay station in Sri Lanka. In March 1984, he signed an agreement with Morocco to upgrade the Tangier relay station (unfortunately, the site chosen for the new transmitter was prone to seasonal flooding, and so construction took a decade, millions of extra dollars, and vast quantities of landfill). In May 1984, four new studios opened at VOA headquarters. Bureaucratic reforms included a new personnel system to facilitate the hiring of foreign language broadcasters. Potential hiccups in the modernization included a Senate budget freeze, but the VOA successfully dodged its impact.[149]

The VOA stabilized under Tomlinson's leadership. A new head of the Russian Service, a professor of Russian literature from the University of Vermont named Mark Pomar, brought energy and bite to broadcasts. Guests on the air included Rostropovich and his wife, diva Galina Vishnevskaya. The writer Vassily Aksyonov gave weekly talks on life in the United States. Solzhenitsyn thought the service so much improved that in 1984 he offered the VOA the exclusive right to broadcast readings from the second volume of his novel cycle *The Red Wheel*. Pomar recorded the novelist's first international interview in years and ten hours of the master reading his work for serialization in fifteen-minute segments.[150] Innovations in the VOA's Worldwide English in 1984 included "Talk to America," a phone-in show of a type already being piloted by the BBC World Service.[151]

148 Interview: Romerstein; Snyder, *Warriors of Disinformation*, pp. 108–11; *Active Measures*, Department of State, August 1986, pp. 22–4, 54–6. TASS also reported that security in Los Angeles would include surveillance by Israel's MOSSAD.

149 RRL WHORM sf FG 298, 257944, "USIA initiatives since June 9, 1981," 26 June 1984, p. 17; *PPP RR 1984*, Vol. I, pp. 281–82; RRL WHORM sf FI 004, 241325, Raffensperger to Tomlinson and Levitsky, 24 May 1984; Ken Tomlinson, "Putting VOA at Risk," *Washington Times*, 22 September 1986, pp. 1D, 2D. On the VOA's problems in Morocco see Snyder, *Warriors of Disinformation*, pp. 190–91, 273.

150 Author's collection, Tomlinson to Wick, "Solzhenitsyn readings for VOA broadcast," 17 July 1984; RRL WHORM sf CO 165, box 14, 268033, Wick to Baker et al., "VOA Russian Language Programs," 20 September 1984. Although USIA documents identify the novel as *August 1914*, this had been published in 1971. The novel was *November 1916*, published in the United States to disappointed reviews in 1999. Nina Khrushcheva, "Solzhenitsyn's History Lesson," *The Nation*, 15 April 1999, pithily termed the full cycle "sadly little more than a crank's mausoleum within which his Nobel Prize-worthy talent has been interred."

151 RRL WHORM sf FG 298–01, Wick to Deaver and Speakes, 15 May 1984. "Talk to America" became a daily feature of VOA English and a large part of other services during the Clinton years.

In April 1984, the VOA opened a news bureau within the United Nations compound in Geneva. Its correspondent, Andre de Nesnera, caused a stir when he took advantage of a flying visit by Yasir Arafat to interview the PLO leader. This was his own idea, and given the tight time frame, he did not consult his editor in Washington. His action broke the unwritten rule about interviews with controversial figures requiring special approval and opened the old wound about VOA contact with the PLO. The fallout was substantial. The State Department issued multiple messages denying that the interview had been authorized and that U.S. policy toward Arafat was changing. However, de Nesnera continued to take full advantage of his strategic location and soon aired interviews with other controversial figures, including the Soviet arms control negotiators, without pressure to change or edit the content. When officials complained, he merely referred them to the VOA director. Voice journalists seemed, at last, to have real autonomy.[152]

In July 1984, VOA director Tomlinson unexpectedly announced his decision to return to *Reader's Digest*. The magazine had made him an offer "too generous for a poor mountain boy" to refuse. He went on to serve on the Board for International Broadcasting, overseeing RFE and RL, and later returned to oversee all U.S. international broadcasting in the era of George W. Bush as chairman of the Broadcasting Board of Governors. Wick nominated Gene Pell, by this time Deputy Director for Programs, as Tomlinson's successor. Pell took over as acting director in September 1984, but because of the legislative calendar, was not confirmed until June 1985. He spent half his time managing the VOA's modernization, which now included transmitters in Puerto Rico and Costa Rica for broadcasting to Nicaragua. He began computerization at the Voice, installing the System for News and Programming, or SNAP – at the time the world's largest multilingual word processing system – able to cope with translating central news or originating copy in languages as diverse as Amharic, Georgian, and Mandarin, and spent many hours testifying and lobbying on Capitol Hill.[153]

The USIA's coverage of that autumn's presidential election was enhanced by Wick's investment in television. The USIA's weekly Satellite File, now seen in ninety countries, carried a story on the campaign each week that year. WORLDNET relayed all three debates live to twenty-two countries. Embassies around the world hosted audiences of journalists and government officials to view the foreign policy debate on 21 October and follow-up programming. In Beijing, 230 invited guests watched at a special breakfast at the Great Wall Hotel. When election night came, posts in thirty-six countries, including China and Yugoslavia, received live feeds of U.S. domestic news coverage and hosted viewing events. The networks donated the feeds and local chambers of commerce raised money to pay for downloading. WORLDNET followed

---

[152] Interview: Andre de Nesnera, 16 May 1996; Bernie Kamenske, 6 December 1995.
[153] Interviews: Tomlinson, Pell, also RRL WHORM sf FG 298, 243088, Wick to Herrington (Assistant to the President for Personnel), 19 July 1984. Pell had served as the VOA's director of News and Current Affairs from February to September 1982, whereupon he moved to WCVB-TV in Boston and the post of chief correspondent (producing a nightly news commentary). Tomlinson called Pell several times a week for advice and eventually prevailed on Pell to return to the VOA in September 1983 to the specially created post of deputy director (programs).

up with a series of interactive press conferences featuring experts from across the political spectrum.[154]

At the end of the first Reagan administration, Wick drew pride from a budget that now stood 74 percent above that which he inherited in 1981. To celebrate the rebirth of the agency, Wick organized a series of gala "Salute to the USIA" fundraising lunches at cities around the country. The first took place on 20 September in New York's Madison Hotel, with former agency directors Frank Shakespeare and Leonard Marks as co-chairmen. Administration luminaries, including George Shultz and James A. Baker, paid tribute to Wick. In a recorded video message, President Reagan praised the "clarity of vision and purpose that is the most important attribute of the new USIA." The President concluded, "I salute and thank your director, Charlie Wick, for these achievements, and I salute all of you at USIA. Together you have written a proud chapter not just in the annals of your agency, but in American diplomatic history itself."[155]

[154] RRL WHORM sf FG 298, 268324, Wick to James A. Baker, 26 October 1984; 260474, Wick to President, 9 November 1984.

[155] RRL WHORM sf PR 011, 253883 SS, "Tribute of Charles Wick, 14 September 1984." Wick collated tributes to USIA made at these lunches and published a commemorative brochure at his own expense. For sample see RRL WHORM sf FG 298, 272957, Wick to President, 17 January 1985; for press comment see RRL David B. Waller files, subject file, Oct '84 – second series, tab 26, OA 12682, Waller to Fielding, 19 December 1984. Critics noted that the research budget was cut during the first Reagan term and doubted the effectiveness of Wick's broadcasting strategy; see John Spicer Nichols, "Wasting the Propaganda Dollar," *Foreign Policy*, Vol. 56, Fall 1984, pp. 129–40.

11 Showdown

THE SECOND REAGAN ADMINISTRATION, 1985–89

I believe that our public diplomacy represents a powerful force, perhaps the most powerful force at our disposal, for shaping the history of the world.

Ronald Reagan, 16 September 1987.[1]

On 20 January 1985, Ronald Reagan took the oath of office for his second term as President of the United States. His inaugural address highlighted both his commitment to the Strategic Defense Initiative and his openness to continued negotiation with the Soviet Union.[2] No one watching could have predicted how swiftly events would move. The second Reagan administration saw a revolution in the relationship between the United States and the U.S.S.R. The USIA played a vital role in managing the public relations aspects of the round of summits and making the most of the new opportunities for international cultural exchange, on one hand, and maintaining the war of words against Soviet disinformation, on the other.

Charles Wick was now well established at the helm of the USIA and soon had the benefit of excellent appointments to the two key supporting positions at the agency. First Marvin Stone, editor of *U.S. News and World Report*, joined the USIA as deputy director and then a broadcaster from Southern California, Richard W. Carlson, became the VOA director.[3] They brought experience and continuity to posts that had been unstable in the first administration. The agency was now in top condition to deliver its message to the world. In 1987, Reagan credited the USIA with shaking off the "malaise and self doubt" of the 1970s, projecting a vision of a better, freer world, and clearly asserting the moral differences between the U.S. and Soviet ways of life.[4]

All of Wick's resources were integrated into the climactic confrontation with the Soviet Union. Although unprepared to indulge Moscow, Reagan was plainly attracted to the idea of building peace and, whether by technology or diplomacy, moving

---

[1] *PPP RR 1987*, Vol. 2, p. 1036, remarks marking the 40th anniversary of the U.S. advisory commission on public diplomacy.

[2] RRL WHORM sf FG 298, 288130, Wick to President, 29 January 1985 with attachments.

[3] For the nomination of Stone on 14 May 1985, see *PPP RR 1985*, Vol. 1, p. 612. Born in 1924, Stone was eminent enough to be a USIA director in his own right, prompting press speculation that he might replace Wick. Such talk underestimated Wick's commitment to the job and his relationship with the President. Howard Kurtz, "US News Editor Reported in Line for No. 2 USIA Post," *Washington Post*, 17 January 1985, p. A21.

[4] *PPP RR 1987*, Vol. 2, p. 1036.

America out from under the shadow of nuclear oblivion. The health of Soviet leaders and unforeseen events such as the destruction of KAL 007 had prevented any major breakthrough in his first term. His landslide election victory in 1984 gave him political security. His place in the White House was secure. His place in history had still to be determined. Like the lawman in one of his old television westerns, Reagan prepared for one last confrontation with the old enemy: the showdown.

Yet the Cold War would not be the only challenge. In the Middle East Libya sponsored terrorism against American targets, while in Central America the second Reagan administration faced the continuing challenge of hostile regimes. In November 1984, the left-wing Sandinistas won the election in Nicaragua. On 10 January 1985, with Fidel Castro looking on, Daniel Ortega took the oath as that country's new President. It was a humiliation for American foreign policy. The USIA's response included a documentary film, *Focus on Nicaragua*, that set out flaws in the election process.[5] In late 1986 the Reagan administration's covert response to the Sandinista government – its illegal backing for the Contra rebels – spawned a major crisis with implications for the international image of the administration: the Iran–Contra scandal. As during Watergate, the USIA found itself working to turn the crisis into a lesson on the ability of the U.S. system to police itself.[6]

1) FACING GORBACHEV, 1985

On 25 January 1985, Wick wrote to Leonid Zamyatin, head of the International Information Department of the Central Committee of the Communist Party, with a radical proposal. Wick suggested that to "further mutual understanding," the U.S. and Soviet Union might exchange television broadcasts. Journalists could question each other's leaders in a WORLDNET interactive satellite broadcast. Might not President Reagan address the Soviet people on television and a Soviet leader speak to the American people in the same way as Nixon and Brezhnev? Wick also suggested that each side allow the other to transmit radio programs over the medium wave to the other's population. He did not receive a reply. But Moscow was on the brink of a change that would open the way to such innovations.[7]

During the first Reagan administration, the Soviet leadership had typically been ailing. Leonid Brezhnev finally died in November 1982, to be succeeded by Yuri Andropov, who survived only until February 1984. As the health of his successor Konstantin Chernenko deteriorated, Muscovites joked that the undertaker no longer showed a pass to enter the Kremlin, but a season ticket. A wry British diplomat observed

---

5   RRL WHORM sf PR 011, 325354, McFarlane to Wick, 3 June 1985. Longer-term plans included a new exchange initiative to divert Central American students from Soviet exchanges. Keith Richburg, "US to Woo Latins with Scholarships," *Washington Post*, 8 July 1985, pp. A1, A14.

6   For White House talking points on the scandal see RRL WHORM sf CO 071, 448022 SS, 15 December 1986.

7   This proposal was reported by Wick in an interview (see Penny Pagano, "TV Goes Global on WORLDNET," *Los Angeles Times*, 2 March 1985, p. 1) and by the White House (see Bernard Weintraub, "Reagan Wants to Voice Views on Russian TV," *New York Times*, 4 September 1985, A1).

that the Soviets had developed a new form of diplomacy: the working funeral. On 10 March 1985, Chernenko died. The following day Mikhail Gorbachev became General Secretary of the Communist Party. He brought a new challenge to the USIA. For the first time since the fall of Khruschev, the USIA faced a Soviet leader with charisma. Gorbachev and his foreign minister Eduard Shevardnadze were younger, warmer, and more media-savvy than their predecessors. Soviet Foreign Ministry spokesmen adopted a relaxed approach at their press conferences, even mingling informally with journalists. By 1986, the western press was using the Russian word for this new openness – "*glasnost*" – but for the time being the revolution was in style rather than content. The Soviet message remained the same, the volume of Soviet propaganda increased, and Western Europe seemed susceptible.[8]

As Soviet–American arms negotiations reconvened in Geneva on 12 March 1985, the Kremlin launched a major initiative to portray itself as the fount of peace, while accusing the United States of an aggressive quest for military superiority. Gorbachev stole the headlines by announcing a unilateral moratorium on the deployment of medium-range missiles in Europe until November. He called on the United States to reciprocate and end space-based weapons research.[9] Soviets engaged a New York public relations firm to distribute press releases that emphasized highpoints in U.S.–Soviet friendship, such as the joint space mission in 1975 or the meeting of armies on the Elbe in 1945.[10] Wick responded by working with the new White House Assistant to the President for Communications, Patrick Buchanan, to create a rapid response mechanism so that "same day" denials, repostes, and rebuttals of Soviet attacks identified by the USIA could be devised by Buchanan's staff, delivered by the White House press spokesman, and then distributed swiftly over USIA media. "If we can blow some of the cobwebs off the speed and rhetorical style of America's world debate with the Soviets," Wick wrote, "our modern communications can provide a dynamic system for delivering it to a worldwide audience."[11] The Foreign Broadcast Intelligence Service agreed to fast-track the distribution of stories out of Moscow requiring an immediate response with a "USIA alert" label.[12] The USIA also sought to increase awareness of Soviet activity by supplementing the bimonthly *Soviet Propaganda Alert* with a weekly digest of Soviet propaganda highlights. Recipients included the White House Chief of Staff and the National Security Advisor.[13] The system was slow to get going, but it represented a significant improvement.

[8] RRL WHORM sf C0 165, box 19, 356242, Wick to McFarlane, 1 November 1985, with *Soviet Propaganda Alert*, 9 October 1985. For a detailed USIA report on *glasnost* see RRL WHORM sf FO 005–03, 526690, Marvin Stone to Colin Powell, 17 July 1987, with USIA Office of Research, R-3–87, "Gorbachev, *Glasnost*, and reform," July 1987.

[9] RRL WHORM sf C0 165, box 16, 303504, Wick to Donald Regan, 25 April 1985.

[10] RRL WHORM sf CO 165, box 18, 344371, Raymond to McFarlane, 8 August 1985.

[11] RRL WHORM sf CO 165, box 17, Wick to Buchanan, 31 May 1985, also Wick/Buchanan to Chief of Staff, 31 May 1985.

[12] RRL WHORM sf CO 165 box 20, 400336, Marvin Stone to Larry Speakes, 14 November 1985. On 26 October, Wick met with Dan Rather of CBS news, who stressed the need for the "same day response."

[13] RRL WHORM sf CO 165, box 17, Wick to Buchanan, 2 July 1985.

Moscow prepared for the first meeting of Reagan and Gorbachev in Geneva in November with a major charm offensive. Gorbachev gave a major interview to *Time* magazine in which he blamed the United States and its fixation on SDI for the deterioration in relations. His visit to France, accompanied by his stylish wife Raisa, won positive comment in the European press. Then, in a well-crafted speech to the United Nations, Foreign Minister Shevardnadze contrasted Moscow's proposal for demilitarized use of space, which he dubbed "Star Peace," with America's Star Wars. The USIA feared a propaganda coup in the making.[14] The USIA's response focused on publicity for America's hopes for and concerns about the Geneva meetings. Initiatives included an "SDI" study tour of the United States for leading NATO journalists and a round of speaker tours and electronic conferences featuring SDI experts. The USIA also arranged a round of interviews with Reagan – among his first after his cancer surgery earlier that summer – for British, French, Indian, and Soviet journalists (the first Presidential interview granted to a Soviet journalist since 1961).[15]

On the eve of the Geneva meeting, the Soviets let loose a new salvo from the old guns of KGB rumor. In October the weekly magazine *Literaturnaya Gazeta* alleged that the AIDS virus had been created by the U.S. government as a biological weapon. The story had been road tested before. Back in July 1983, the KGB outflow pipe in India – *The Patriot* – printed an anonymous letter from New York claiming that AIDS had actually been created at Fort Detrick, Maryland, home to the United States Army's germ warfare laboratory since 1943 (though since 1969 the laboratory had worked only on cancer research and defense against biological weapons). No one paid much attention at the time, but in 1985 the story took off. It filled the need for an explanation of the terrifying spread of the disease and played to anti-American sentiment. By the end of the year, versions of the AIDS libel had run in twelve other countries. Soon a major campaign was under way in the Soviet domestic media, while TASS and Novosti sent the story round the world.[16]

Soviet propagandists supplemented the AIDS story with general allegations of American chemical and biological warfare activity. The U.S. was allegedly supplying chemical grenades to the *mujahideen* in Afghanistan, spreading dengue fever on Cuba and yellow fever in Pakistan, and, most imaginatively of all, developing an ethnic weapon that could lock onto particular genes to kill black Africans, Arabs, or Asians,

14 RRL WHORM sf C0 165, box 19, 356242, Wick to McFarlane, 1 November 1985, with *Soviet Propaganda Alert*, 9 October 1985.
15 RRL WHORM sf FO 006–09, 363372, Wick to President, 11 December 1985. On the Soviet interview see Eleanor Clift, "Rare Exchange Today: Reagan to Be Interviewed by Soviet Media," *Los Angeles Times*, 31 October 1985, p. 22.
16 "AIDS May Invade India: Mysterious Disease Caused by U.S. Experiments," *Patriot* (New Delhi), 16 July 1983, p. 2, as forwarded to Romerstein by USIS New Delhi, 2 July 1987. USIA paper, "Soviet disinformation claims AIDS made in USA (chronology of campaign as of 3/31/87)" contains a history of Ford Detrick – home to the Frederick Cancer Research Facility, U.S. Army Medical Research Institute for Infectious Diseases (AMRIID), and the head quarter of U.S. Army Medical Research and Development Command (USAMRDC), which researched countermeasures against bio-weapons. Measures against the AIDS story included journalist visits to Fort Detrick. Department of State, *Soviet Influence Activities*, pp. 33–49.

but leave "whites" unharmed. First seen around 1980, the ethnic bomb story went into overdrive in 1985. Like Hollywood producers tweaking a screenplay to maximize audience, Moscow's disinformers now added two fiendish accomplices to the tale – South Africa and Israel – who were supposedly testing the bomb on black and Arab prisoners. The USIA's Herb Romerstein used humor to squash the story in meetings with journalists in Western Europe, wondering that the U.S.–Israeli bomb could tell the difference between two Semites based on their religion, but the story rattled around the Third World press like a well-flipped pinball. As Reagan and Gorbachev prepared to speak of peace, the USIA's anti-disinformation unit worked harder than ever.[17]

As the summit approached, Reagan delivered a number of important speeches emphasizing his readiness to negotiate with the Soviets. On 9 November, he addressed the world over the VOA and WORLDNET, speaking about elements in his background that might appeal to the Soviet bloc: his upbringing in the American heartland and his leadership of a trade union. He stressed the commonalities between East and West, the shared effort in World War Two and admiration for each other's literature, and appealed to the Kremlin for more dialogue. The use of WORLDNET struck the Soviets. To Wick's delight, they denounced the channel in a front-page article in *Isvestia* as "USIA's Trojan Horse."[18]

WORLDNET proved its value during the summit. The channel produced over eighteen hours of programming around the meetings. Highpoints included George Shultz's interactive press conference with 100 journalists in the International Press Center in Geneva and "remote" guests in Britain, West Germany, Japan, and France. Scenes from the WORLDNET conference made the evening news in the first three countries and the broadcast formed the core of an Agence France Presse story. Over the entire conference period, WORLDNET staff estimated that they won a total of nine-and-a-half hours of prime time news placement around the world. By adding together the audience figures for the various relays and national bulletins that included WORLDNET material, the USIA estimated that over a billion people had seen some portion of WORLDNET's conference coverage.[19]

The Soviets had dominated the pre-summit war of words, fielding two able propagandists, Zamyatin and Yakovlev, the Communist Party propaganda chief. Alexander N. Yakovlev knew North America well, having been an exchange student at Columbia University in 1959 and served as ambassador to Canada from 1973 to 1983.[20] But once the summit was under way, the USIA clawed back the Soviet advantage. Press

---

[17] Department of State, *Soviet Influence Activities*, pp. 51–5.

[18] For the text of Reagan's VOA/WORLDNET speech see *PPP RR 1985*, Vol. 2, pp. 1362–4. RRL WHORM sf FO 006–09, Wick to Buchanan, 15 November 1985, citing Aleksandr Palladin, "USIA's Trojan Horse," *Isvestia*, 18 October 1985, p. 1, which called WORLDNET "the child of Charles Wick, born with the king of yellow journalism Rupert Murdoch in the role of midwife."

[19] RRL WHORM sf FG 011, 361024, Kordek (EU) to Wick, 15 November 1985, and RRL WHORM sf FO 006–09, 353176, "WORLDNET, Geneva November 19–20 1985, A Report of Television Activities."

[20] William J. Eaton, "Soviets Lead Pre-summit War of Words," *Los Angeles Times*, 18 November 1985, p. 1. On Yakovlev see Gary Lee, "Key Gorbachev Aide Named to Politburo," *Washington Post*, 29 January 1987, p. A27.

relations at the conference were a cooperative effort between the USIA and the White House press office. The agency supported 3,000 journalists and, between 14 and 21 November, generated such a volume of transcripts, fact sheets, and background information on the American position that the Soviet delegation complained. The Swiss hosts ruled that none of the sixty-two USIA documents created for the conference could be considered propaganda. This support was particularly significant given that much of the conference took place under a news blackout. The VOA sent twenty-one journalists and technicians to Geneva. They provided round-the-clock multilingual coverage over specially extended schedules and cooperated with National Public Radio and Mutual Broadcasting to operate a pool for current news of the summit. Key statements and presidential speeches were carried live in English or broadcast in translation (often simultaneously) in the forty-one VOA languages. The USIA's Research and Media Reaction Office monitored responses throughout and provided the White House with reports twice a day.[21]

Reviewing the agency's performance at the end of the conference, the P bureau noted that world opinion seemed to have accepted the U.S. "agenda and rationale" in thinking about the key issues of the conference. The SDI issue had not dominated in the way the Soviets hoped. The world's press portrayed Reagan as "firm, forceful and constructive," and his sober assessment of the difficulties ahead was well understood, yet even the Soviets repeated the President's assessment of the summit as a "fresh start" in East–West relations. The USIA had facilitated this positive outcome by steering a steady course with the world's media, maintaining a clear sense of the U.S. agenda, rallying the principal figures in the U.S. camp to deliver timely comment, and coordinating the message across all of the agency's channels of communication.[22] The Soviet successes, in contrast, had been minimal. As USIA analysts looked to the year ahead, they noted that for all his flair, Gorbachev could still expect difficult questions over his country's human rights record.[23]

The agreement reached at Geneva had immediate implications for the USIA. Reagan and Gorbachev agreed to resume the sort of high-profile cultural exchanges suspended in 1980. Negotiations had been in progress to this end for fifteen months. The agreement was wide-ranging, authorizing exchange not only in education and the arts but also in medicine, the professions, sports, and television, and including a mandate "to find as yet undiscovered avenues where American and Soviet citizens can cooperate fruitfully for the benefit of mankind."[24]

21 RRL WHORM sf FO 006–09, 363372, Wick to President, 11 December 1985.
22 RRL WHORM sf FO 006–09, 418968, Schneider to Wick, 12 December 1985. For a USIA report on European opinion following Geneva see 356102, Wick to McFarlane, 18 December 1985. National Security Advisor Admiral Poindexter singled out Michael Braxton, the USIA's representative to the NSC chaired group on arms control and SDI, for particular praise: 380854 Poindexter to Wick, 19 December 1985.
23 RRL WHORM sf FO 006–09, 365012, Wick to President, 27 December 1985, with USIA report "Assessing Soviet Public Diplomacy for the Reagan-Gorbachev meeting," 16 December 1985.
24 Carla Hall, "Cultural Exchanges: The Format," *Washington Post*, 23 November 1985, p. G1; Irvin Molotsky, "Kirov and Bolshoi Set Exchange Visits to US," *New York Times*, 23 January 1986, p. C25;

*

The Reagan administration knew that one of the best ways to weaken their Soviet opponent was to strengthen his enemies in Afghanistan. The USIA had its role in aid to the *mujahideen* through what became known as the Afghan media project. In the summer of 1985, Senator Gordon J. Humphrey (R-NH) amended the USIA appropriation, making $500,000 available to teach the *mujahideen* the basics of modern news gathering. The USIA awarded a substantial grant to Boston University to teach journalism at an Afghan Media Resource Center (AMRC) in Peshawar, Pakistan, and an even larger grant to the Hearst Corporation and King Features Syndicate to advise the AMRC and help it produce, market, and distribute media materials created by Afghans. The combined school and news agency opened for business in February 1987. Soon Afghan fighters crossed the border armed not only with Stinger missiles but also with USIA video cameras and the skills to use them. The astonishing combat footage they brought back played on television news at home and abroad. Still photos and written copy also circulated widely, as when Reuter's picked up an AMRC report that the Soviet Union had fired SCUD missiles in their defense of Kabul and Jalalabad. The Afghan struggle had never been so visible.[25]

Gordon Humphrey also sponsored legislation to establish a Radio Free Afghanistan as a surrogate station broadcasting under RFE/RL's Board for International Broadcasting. The station began slowly in 1985 with just six hours a week in Dari and added Pashto language broadcasts in 1987. Although the VOA already broadcast a total of twenty-eight hours a week divided between Dari and Pashto, the Voice was increasingly seen by conservatives as overly bound by its charter and federal staffing regulations. They saw the BIB as both more maneuverable and better able to play rough. It was an ill omen for the future of the VOA.[26]

*

The year 1985 brought a measure of stability to the VOA. Early in the year the Voice had weathered yet another round of inquiries into its alleged liberal bias. The U.S. embassy in Managua took exception to the reporting of Voice correspondent Sean Kelly on Nicaragua. In January 1985, acting VOA director Gene Pell compiled a full dossier for the NSC of Voice coverage of Nicaragua, demonstrating that "coverage had been accurate, balanced, and comprehensive in accord with the mandate of the VOA's Congressional charter."[27] The VOA still needed massive investment.

Irvin Molotsky, "Moiseyev to Visit U.S. in Exchange Program," *New York Times*, 24 January 1986, p. C4; also Barbara Gamarekian, "Swapping Culture with Moscow," *New York Times*, 1 May 1986, p. B10.

25 NA RG 306 A1 (1061) box 1, USIA historical collection, misc. files, 1940s–1990s, file: Afghan Media Project, Lindburg (USIA acting gen. counsel/cong. liaison) to Cooper (Dept. of Justice), 18 February 1987; Burnett to Raymong (NSC), 12 August 1986; Lionel Barber, "Afghan Rebels Financed for Propaganda War," *Washington Post*, 7 August 1985, p. A17. For a narrative of the project see Snyder, *Warriors of Disinformation*, pp. 202–19.

26 "Radio Free Afghanistan to Air in Pashto," *Washington Post*, 1 September 1987, p. A18.

27 RRL executive secretariat, NSC system files, folder 8500733, Pell to Raymond (NSC), 22 January 1985. Interview: Gene Pell, 30 March 2004.

As of 1985, 80 percent of the VOA's transmitters were fifteen years old, and more than thirty-five percent were over thirty years old. The VOA managed to broadcast just under one thousand hours a week in its forty-two languages, but Radio Moscow topped two thousand hours in eighty-one languages. The VOA came in fifth in terms of hours on the air in Africa and Latin America, and sixth in Eastern Europe and East Asia. Much hung on the $1.5 billion VOA construction program. As of 1985, this included shortwave construction in Morocco, Thailand, and Sri Lanka, medium-wave construction in Botswana, shortwave negotiations in Israel, and negotiations for medium-wave relay stations in Costa Rica and Belize. Progress was slow. India and some Sri Lankan politicians opposed construction on that island, and the presence of two hundred squatter-fishermen on the chosen site posed major problems for construction. In June 1986 the entire project had to move to a new site fifty miles away. In September the Democratic Congress threatened the VOA modernization program. Former Voice director Tomlinson and others successfully lobbied the White House to break the logjam. Work continued with $44 million earmarked for financial year 1987.[28]

The Reagan administration's highest profile radio initiative – Radio Martí for Cuba – was not faring well either. Frustrated by delays, in the autumn of 1984 Wick hired a Los Angeles-based radio consultant named Paul Drew to crack the whip and get Martí ready to air by Jose Martí's 132nd birthday, 28 January 1985. Drew found staff shortages, an absence of prepared material, and a lack of understanding of the methods or standards of the VOA. Members of the Martí staff were reportedly traumatized by his abrasive methods and he resigned. In desperation, Wick persuaded former VOA director Ken Giddens to return to the USIA as acting director of Martí. Giddens provided the necessary balm and, although the January deadline passed, the station was approaching readiness.[29]

At the start of May 1985, National Security Advisor Admiral Poindexter attempted to block the launch of Radio Martí, arguing that it was too provocative. Wick refused to be cowed and pointed out that his oath of office required him to uphold the laws of the United States, including the Broadcasting to Cuba Act. Wick insisted that the matter be decided by the President. On 18 May, the NSC gathered for an emergency session in the map room at the White House, around a large map of Cuba mounted on an easel. Wick had ensured that Secretary of Defense Weinberger and Secretary of Defense Shultz understood what was at issue. The President invited Wick to speak first. Wick stressed that the launch was scheduled; he explained the input of engineers from the VOA and the private sector to overcome jamming. The Chairman of the

28 James Reston, "The Other Star Wars," *New York Times*, 20 March 1985, p. A27; Rone Tempest, "Regional Politics Cause Static over Voice of America Relay Station," *Los Angeles Times*, 19 July 1996, p. 5; RRL WHORM sf FG 298–01, 439855, Tomlinson to Pat Buchanan (White House), n.d., with Ken Tomlinson, "Putting VOA at Risk," *Washington Times*, 22 September 1986, pp. 1D, 2D; RRL Alan Kvanowitz files, box 1, OA 16797, USIA file 1, Morris (USIA) to Tuck (WH), 4 November 1986.

29 For a summary see Tom Miller, "Radio Martí: Another Mission to Cuba Minus Air Support," *Wall Street Journal*, 31 January 1985, p. 28.

Joint Chiefs of Staff expressed concern that the radio station might spark an escalation in jamming. Reagan then ruled, "Charlie . . . you go on the air with Radio Martí on Monday." Turning to the rest of the meeting, he said, "I don't want you guys to come up with any ideas and stall this project, because I'm a stubborn bastard." At 5:00 a.m. on 20 May, Radio Martí began broadcasting on the 1180 AM wave band. Wick was delighted to learn that the signal was coming through loud and clear. Reportedly any taxi radio in Havana could pick up Radio Martí.[30]

Castro condemned the launch of Radio Martí and suspended an emigration agreement in protest. In the summer of 1986 the Cubans offered to restore emigration and accept the station in return for access to America's airwaves. U.S. negotiators knew that this could never happen – neither the existing radio stations broadcasting on the Cuban's desired band nor the Cuban-American lobby would tolerate such a deal – so they broke off the talks. Castro had constructed two enormous 500-KW transmitters, ten times more powerful that any commercial American station and capable of broadcasting on the medium wave as far as Alaska. The United States now faced the possibility of a radio war in the Caribbean. Officials made it clear that they would see retaliatory broadcasts by Cuba as a "hostile act" and spoke about "surgical strikes" to remove the transmitters if necessary.[31]

Martí's programming included news, music, and readings of dissident literature. In early 1986, Wick expanded broadcasts from fourteen and one-half to seventeen and one-half hours daily.[32] Programs included *Puente Familiar* (Family Bridge), in which personal messages from Cuban exiles in the United States were collected from calls made to a toll-free phone line and broadcast back into Cuba.[33] Martí was not universally welcomed. In November 1987, Representatives Dante Fascell (D-Fl) and Daniel Mica (D-Fl) raised legal concerns over the audibility of Martí in the United States. News gathered through government channels was now available to Spanish-speaking listeners in Florida on the medium wave. Commercial channels complained about being scooped at government expense.[34]

In the early autumn of 1985, VOA director Gene Pell received a phone call from an executive recruitment consultant in New York City inviting him to consider the presidency of Radio Free Europe and Radio Liberty in Munich. RFE and RL had prospered during the Reagan years. Pell was especially taken by the quality of the Board for

---

30   Interview: Charles Z. Wick, 8 January 1996. For the supporting decision, NSDD 170 of 20 May 1985, see RRL Executive Secretariat NSC, box 91,294, NSDD 170 (1). For concerns over delays in the launch see RRL Executive Secretariat NSC, file 8590096, Wick to Hawkins (Senate Foreign Relations Committee, 22 January 1985, file 8501679, Raymond to McFarlane, 4 March 1985. For reaction to the launch see file 8504883, LaSalle to Kimmitt (NSC), 11 June 1985 on world media and Platt (State) to McFarlane, 14 June 1985 on domestic reaction.

31   RRL Executive Secretariat NSC, file: 8508089, Pell to Wick, 1 October 1985; and re possible countermeasures see file 8590326, "contingency press guidance," n.d.; John Spicer Nichols, "Word War Broadcast over Voice of America," *Los Angeles Times*, 4 January 1987, p. 2.

32   RRL WHORM sf FG 375, 382987, Wick to Poindexter, 10 January 1986.

33   Hansen, *USIA: Public Diplomacy in the Computer Age.* 2nd ed., p. 120.

34   RRL WHORM sf PR 16–01, 545077, Fascell and Mica to Frank Carlucci (National Security Advisor), 3 November 1987.

International Broadcasting. Assembled by Frank Shakespeare and chaired by Malcolm "Steve" Forbes, the board included Michael Novak, Ben Wattenberg, Lane Kirkland, and Ed Ney (CEO of Young and Rubicam). He was impressed by a visit to the RFE/RL facility in Munich and drawn to the idea of playing a key role in the coming final act of the Cold War. When offered the post, he accepted. The job brought many challenges, from Russian jamming to German labor unions, but his most immediate challenge was to break the news of his departure to Charles Wick. Pell submitted his resignation on 3 October 1985. Incandescent at the news, Wick saw Pell's departure as the height of disloyalty and checked to see whether any of the discussions relating to the recruitment had been conducted at the USIA's expense. They had not. Reluctantly Wick began yet another search for a VOA director.[35]

The other major radio project that autumn was the launch of VOA Europe, an English language service aimed at wooing the "successor generation" away from anti-Americanism. Launched in October 1985, operating initially from Washington and then from Munich, VOA Europe blended news with music and features about American life. Frank Scott directed the operation. Its signal – broadcast around the clock on the medium wave – could be heard as far away as Scandinavia, Britain, and Italy. VOA Europe was also relayed over FM radio in Paris and Berlin and could be heard on cable in six West German cities. The VOA planned expansion on FM in Brussels, Amsterdam, Geneva, and Milan.[36] But VOA Europe lacked the political support that sustained Radio Martí. Indigenous radio stations offered much the same music with local announcers. After just eleven months the USIA announced its imminent closure. In the House, Dante Fascell suspected that Wick was cutting a high-profile initiative to dramatize the impact of recent budget laws and persuaded the director to continue the service with restructured programming.[37]

Wick continued to invest in WORLDNET. In 1984, he proposed that the system expand to mount as much as fifteen hours of programming per week. He speculated that as the satellite footprints stretched into Soviet territory, the VOA could broadcast instructions on how to build a receiving dish and WORLDNET material could be recorded and circulated on videotape.[38] In April 1985 the network inaugurated a

35 RRL WHORM sf FG 298–01, 401623, Pell to Wick, 3 October 1985; Interview: Pell, 30 March 2004. Pundits predicted a feud between Wick and Pell, but the anticipated sparks never flew. In later years Pell and Wick met socially and Pell made RFE/RL research available to help with a post-USIA initiative to train Eastern European broadcasters.
36 RRL WHORM sf FG 298–1, 415394, Wick to Nancy Reagan, 14 April 1986, with Charlie Bowden, "VOA Broadcasts America to Europe," *The Stars and Stripes*, 24 February 1986, p. 9; RRL WHORM sf FO 005–03, 417125, Raymond to Poindexter, 16 May 1986. See also "New Voice of America Sets Sights on European Youth," *Los Angeles Times*, 14 October 1985, p. 2, and John M. Goshko, "Broadcasts to Europe by VOA May Resume: Informing New Generation Is Goal," *Washington Post*, 13 July 1985, A6.
37 ""Voice" to Go Silent in Europe," *Los Angeles Times*, 26 September 1986, p. 2; Jeffrey Yorke, "Europe's Youth to Lose VOA," *Washington Post*, 19 September 1986, p. D7; Jeffrey Yorke, "Reprieve for VOA Europe," *Washington Post*, 28 November 1986, p. B7. For a restructuring proposal with private sector help see RRL FO 005–03, 477797, Larry Taylor (USIA) to Rodney McDaniel (NSC), 28 November 1986.
38 Rod Townley, "This Is One Show That's 'Driving the Russians Crazy,'" *TV Guide*, 22 December 1984, pp. 40–42.

daily schedule of two hours of English language programming to U.S. embassies, private cable subscribers (via the Belgian-based World Public News channel), and certain hotels in Western Europe using the ESC-1 satellite. Content included news on *America Today*, talk on *Almanac*, and features on *Arts America, Sports Machine, Cine Showcase*, and *Science World*. Wick trumpeted "a turning point in USIA's efforts to tell America's story to the world" and promised that WORLDNET would not ignore the country's "warts."[39] Meanwhile, the USIA began the process of installing TVRO (television receive only) dishes at Eastern European embassies and looked forward to developing programs for local rebroadcast.[40]

Wick also worked to launch a television arm of RIAS – Radio in the American Sector – the USIA's radio station in West Berlin. He knew that its programs would be watched in much of East Germany and its content could be more pointed than that of the existing West German channels. The idea was first suggested to Wick in April 1984 by Berlin's Mayor Eberhard Diepgen during the director's visit to the city. Early supporters included German media magnate Axel Springer. By 1986, Congress approved $12 million for the project. The station went on the air in August 1987. Its audience soon dwarfed that of both East and West German stations in the city. An MTV-style rock music video show on Saturday mornings proved a particular hit. The East German attempt to produce their own version served only to point up the gulf between the free culture of the West and the gray world of the East.[41]

Wick's third visual initiative was to expand the agency's use of videotape. Walking in the streets of Jordan in May 1984, he had noted the abundance of videocassette players and ordered an immediate ten-country pilot project for agency home video libraries. In 1985 the USIA introduced free video libraries at most posts, each equipped with up to 850 tapes, ranging from documentary series such as *Alistair Cooke's America* to such Hollywood hits as *Raiders of the Lost Ark*. It all helped.[42]

The USIA continued to play a role in the U.S. government's anti-drug campaign. In 1985 the agency distributed a pamphlet entitled *Illegal Drugs: An International*

39 RRL WHORM sf PR 011, 311905, Wick to Deaver et al., 19 April 1985; Peter W. Kaplan, "US Agency Transmits TV Programs to Europe," *New York Times*, 23 April 1985, p. C18. The new service was profiled in "Mission to Explain," *TV World*, May 1987, p. 92, and Simon Baker, "The World Network," *Cable and Satellite*, n.d., filed in RRL WHORM sf FG 006–012, 540281.
40 RRL Executive Secretariat, NSC system files, folder 8704772, Snyder to Wick, WORLDNET expansion in Eastern Europe, 16 June 1987, reviewing progress since 1985; also RRL Executive Secretariat, NSC records, PA files, file: 8890395, Powell to Shultz, Webster, Wick, and Odom, 5 July 1988. The TVRO network carried a major bonus. It could also be used to receive the wireless file, and so speedily that transmissions that once took hours to receive could now be received in just a few seconds; see Allen C. Hansen, *USIA: Public Diplomacy in the Computer Age*, 2nd edition, pp. 86, 90–91.
41 RRL Alan Kranowitz files, box 1, OA 16797, USIA file 1, Morris (USIA) to Tuck (WH), 4 November 1986. For an account of RIAS TV see Snyder, *Warriors of Disinformation*, pp. 126–42, and for documentation Alvin Snyder papers (c/o Center on Public Diplomacy, Annenberg School for Communication, University of Southern California), file: RIAS, 1984. Memorandum of Conversation, participants inc. Wick and Diepgen, 17 April 1984.
42 RRL WHORM sf PR 011, 358667, Wick to Buchanan, 19 September 1985. Snyder, *Warriors of Disinformation*, pp. 144–6.

Crisis, which emphasized the anti-drug activities of First Lady Nancy Reagan.[43] The agency also provided full overage for the "First Ladies Conference" in Washington and Atlanta in April 1985 and at the United Nations in October 1985, at which Nancy Reagan brought together the wives of leaders from around the world to showcase the problem of drug abuse.[44] The VOA broadcast a Christmas special on the rehabilitation of drug addicts for Latin America, and WORLDNET made the White House assistant for Drug Abuse Policy, Carlton Turner, a regular guest, while the USIA also made good use of its own anti-drugs film, *A Trip*. Produced in the mid-1970s by Ashley Hawken, it remained relevant, displaying the impact of drug trafficking on individuals and their families in Colombia. The film was particularly sought after by drug educators in Latin America.[45] In July 1987, the director used the in-house magazine *USIA World* to survey the Agency's drug work. Sixty-four posts now listed drugs as a priority. "USIA is at the international crossroads of the War on Drugs," Wick concluded, "and I believe we are building worldwide cooperation in eradicating drug producers and suppliers and reducing demand."[46]

It was an uphill struggle, but the USIA's involvement in the issue served to demonstrate the agency's relevance to issues beyond the Cold War. As tensions eased with Moscow, such relevance would become critical to the survival of the agency.

2) THE ROAD TO REYKJAVIK, 1986

The year 1986 began with a dramatic sign of progress. Reagan and Gorbachev sent brief New Year's television messages to each other's populations.[47] In mid-January, Wick and his exchange administrator, Stephen Rhinesmith, spent ten days in Moscow negotiating with the Soviet ministry to enact the deal agreed to at Geneva. Wick returned fired up with possibility. He promised imminent visits to the U.S. from the Kirov ballet, Bolshoi ballet and opera, Leningrad Symphony orchestra, and Moiseyev folklore ensemble, whereas major U.S. art exhibitions featuring Thomas Eakins and the Wyeth family would visit the U.S.S.R.[48] Wick's conciliatory tone raised eyebrows. The

43   RRL WHORM sf HE 00601, 344813, Stone (acting dir., USIA) to Nancy Reagan, 21 August 1985.
44   RRL WHORM sf FG 298, 361989, Wick to Nancy Reagan, 14 November 1985 and RRL WHORM sf PR 016–01, 371485 PD, VOA editorial, c. 30 October 1985.
45   RRL WHORM sf PR 016–01, 371520, Araujo to Barun (Office of the First Lady), 30 October 1985. RRL WHORM sf FG 298, 397534 PD, McGuire (USIA) to Turner, 23 December 1985, also RRL Donald Ian MacDonald files, CI 079, USIA WORLDNET (3), OA 16,759, Burke (WORLDNET) to Turner, 4 November 1986 including script etc. Allen C. Hansen, *USIA: Public Diplomacy in the Computer Age*, 2nd edition, p. 104.
46   RRL WHORM sf HE 006–01, 512552, Wick to Nancy Reagan, 15 July 1987, with Charles Z. Wick, "USIA Is Waging a 'War on Drugs,'" *USIA World*, July/August 1987.
47   Michael Wines, "Reagan and Gorbachev to Exchange TV Talks," *Los Angeles Times*, 28 December 1985, p. 1.
48   "US Information Aide Is to Confer in Moscow," *New York Times*, 11 January 1986, p. 3; Irvin Molotsky, "Kirov and Bolshoi Set Exchange Visits to US," *New York Times*, 23 January 1986, p. C25; Irvin Molotsky, "Moiseyev to Visit U.S. in Exchange Program," *New York Times*, 24 January 1986, p. C4; also Barbara Gamarekian, "Swapping Culture with Moscow," *New York Times*, 1 May 1986, p. B10.

press gasped to hear the man who once called the Soviet Union "the last great predatory empire on earth" publicly describe Moscow as "a fascinating Winter Wonderland." Wick even passed on Soviet objections to red-baiting in American films such as *Rambo* or *Rocky IV*. A hysterical editorial in the *Washington Times* on 27 January opined, "If we had 'understood' Hitler in the way that some people want us to 'understand' Mr. Gorbachev, Radio Moscow's North American service would be broadcasting in German and Japanese." Wick's rebuttal noted that exchanges with the Soviet Union were now U.S. foreign policy and that he had not spared the Soviets from criticism of their jamming and other barriers to free communication.[49]

The wheels of this "President's United States–Soviet Exchange Initiative" turned swiftly. Even as Wick negotiated, a children's theater from Albany, New York wowed Moscow. Within a matter of weeks, art lovers in Leningrad were viewing an exhibition of forty French impressionist paintings loaned by the National Gallery in Washington.[50] In June the two governments announced an exchange of ten school children with interests in space exploration.[51] Existing programs such as the Fulbright exchanges, scholarly contacts overseen by the International Research and Exchanges Board (IREX), student exchanges, and the teacher exchange run by the American Council of Teachers of Russian expanded. American visitors in the first year of the exchange initiative included the Russian-born pianist Vladimir Horowitz, a Sister City delegation from Tallahassee, Florida to Krasnodar in the Caucasus, a delegation of newspaper editors, and literary critics for a comparative symposium on Faulkner and Sholokhov. The Soviets reciprocated.[52] In line with the new spirit, WORLDNET helped a Soviet television crew to film on the streets of New York. Although distressed that the Soviets "abused this hospitality" and filmed homeless people, the USIA had the last laugh. Audiences back in the U.S.S.R had seen poverty before but were simply delighted by glimpses of the latest American cars and the stores along 5th Avenue.[53]

Throughout 1986, the Soviet Union maneuvered for the high ground of peace. Gorbachev suggested total abolition of nuclear weapons and the whole Soviet media machine assailed the SDI. Even the loss of the American space shuttle *Challenger* elicited pointed comments about space weapons. *Pravda* noted,

---

[49]   RRL WHORM sf FG 298, 359239, Wick to Arnaud de Borchgrave (*Washington Times*), 27 and 28 January 1986; Wesley Pruden, "Lighting a Wick in the Dark," *Washington Times*, 24 January 1986; Irvin Molotsky, "Wick Has Met the Enemy," *New York Times*, 24 January 1986, A16.

[50]   Serge Schmemann, "US Art Show Opens in Leningrad," *New York Times*, 4 February 1986, p. C11.

[51]   "US and Soviet Set '86 Youth Exchange," *New York Times*, 27 June 1986, p. A12.

[52]   RRL WHORM sf FG 006–01, 485438, Nancy Starr (USIA) to Linda Faulkner (WH), 20 March 1987 with press release, fact sheet, profile of Rhinesmith, and first-year anniversary report. The Soviet response included sending a delegation from the Lenin district of Moscow to Trenton, New Jersey and dancers to the International Ballet Competition in Mississippi. Festivals of Soviet films proved a sellout success in New York, Washington, Los Angeles, and San Francisco. In the summer of 1986 Russia's Ganelin Jazz trio toured twelve U.S. cities. The United States replied in 1987 with tours by Miles Davis and the Dave Brubeck Quartet.

[53]   Philip Taubman, "Through a Soviet Lens: Gomorrah on the Hudson," *New York Times*, 7 April 1986, p. A2. Snyder, *Warriors of Disinformation*, p. 111.

If this could have happened to a relatively well-tuned and proven spaceship, how can one expect faultless performance by the multiplicity of ultra-complicated systems . . . which are to be "suspended" above the globe in accordance with the SDI program? Is this not the way to world catastrophe?[54]

USIA reports charted a surge in Soviet cultural propaganda in all regions.[55]

*

But the Reagan administration faced a more immediate challenge than Moscow's charm offensive: the rogue regime of Colonel Moammar Qadhafi in Libya. The crisis had really begun with the burning of the U.S. embassy in 1979. In 1981, Reagan closed the Libyan embassy in Washington in protest over assassination squads at large on U.S. soil. American and Libyan aircraft exchanged fire over the Gulf of Sidra. By 1985 the hand of Libya could be discerned in terrorist incidents including a car bomb at a U.S. base in Wiesbaden, Germany in August and attacks on airports in Rome and Vienna in December. In January 1986, Reagan initiated economic sanctions. Naval and terrorist incidents multiplied, culminating on 2 April in a bomb on a TWA plane that killed four and the 5 April bomb attack on a West Berlin disco frequented by American servicemen. On the night of 14 April 1986, the U.S. bombed Libya.[56]

The USIA was fully integrated into the NSC's follow-up to the bombing. The VOA delivered President Reagan's message to the Libyan people in both English and Arabic translation and the agency distributed guidance cables with suggested questions and answers on the strike to all posts. The agency compiled evidence of world reaction for the NSC. WORLDNET swiftly scheduled interactive television press conferences, starting with the White House spokesman on the Middle East, Ed Djerejian, and eventually featuring Secretaries Shultz and Weinberger. On 18 April, the agency convened an interagency task force to oversee a public diplomacy drive against terrorism. Wick was generally satisfied with the performance, but noted problems arising from the conflicting needs of domestic and international presentation of the attack on Libya. Wick wished that at least one major administration figure had been available for a WORLDNET interview in the early stages of the crisis. All his preferred speakers were preoccupied with domestic morning news programs. "In the future," he concluded, "I believe there should be one prominent U.S. spokesman who has the foreign audience as his first priority."[57]

54   RRL WHORM sf CO 165 box 21, 414848, Wick to Poindexter, 7 March 1986 and *Soviet Propaganda Alert* no. 40.
55   RRL WHORM sf CO 165 box 22, 419228, Wick to Donald T. Regan, 14 May 1986, with attachment re Middle East and North Africa and 419229, Wick to Regan, 13 May 1986, with attachment re South Asia; RRL WHORM sf CO 165 box 21, 413422 PD, USIA report, Soviet Cultural and Information activities in South Asia, 1985, 10 May 1986.
56   RRL Howard Teicher papers, "Libya Sensitive," file 1, Gibson (White House) to David Chew, chronology of terrorist attacks/U.S.–Libya relations (for White House staff), 24 April 1986.
57   RRL WHORM sf CO 089, 390518, Wick to Donald T. Regan, 17 April 1986, with attachment.

The Libyan strike did not enhance America's standing among its European allies. USIA follow-up surveys of public opinion in France, Germany, and Britain found that, despite hostility to Libyan terrorism, only the French would support future retaliation (by fifty-six percent to twenty-eight percent). Some 60 percent of Britons and 70 percent of West Germans disapproved of the raid. Europeans believed that a military response would merely escalate terrorist violence.[58] As the dust settled, some commentators conceded that the strike had clipped Qadhafi's wings, but the USIA still had difficultly selling the tough anti-terrorist line.[59] The Libyan threat remained. The second anniversary of the U.S. raid brought presumed Libyan attacks on the USIA's binational centers in Columbia, Peru, and Costa Rica.[60]

*

Wick had problems replacing Gene Pell as director of the VOA. In February 1986, his choice of candidate, Bill Sheehan, met with a group of conservatives led by Roy Cohn for a two-hour lunch at the Ritz Carlton hotel in Washington, DC. They winced to hear Sheehan describe himself as a centrist pledged to uphold the Voice charter. They listened aghast as he dismissed concerns about liberal bias in the domestic media. They nearly fell off their chairs when he declined to say whether he had voted for Reagan in 1984. The White House received a loud message that Sheehan was not an acceptable candidate.[61] Wick found an ideal substitute in Richard W. Carlson, a moderate Republican journalist and businessman from southern California who had attracted the attention of the Reagan administration through a gallant but unsuccessful campaign to be mayor of San Diego. Born in 1941, Carlson had worked as a journalist from 1966 until 1980, serving as a three-time Emmy Award-winning television reporter, writer, and producer. In 1985, Carlson joined the USIA to head the Office of Public Liaison. His broadcasting experience fitted him for the VOA and, being married to the niece of ex-Senator Fulbright, he had excellent Democratic Party connections on the Hill. Fulbright testified on his behalf. Carlson took up his duties in March 1986.[62]

58 RRL WHORM sf PR 015, 415296, Wick to Donald T. Regan, 24 April 1986, with USIA foreign opinion note, 23 April 1986. The murder of British and American hostages in Beirut on 17 April lent weight to this argument.

59 RRL James Stark, "Strike on Libya file," Cobb to Poindexter, 25 July 1986, with "The Effect on Libya," *Toronto Globe and Mail*, 24 July 1986.

60 Robert Pears, "US Again Reports Libyan Role in Terrorism," *New York Times*, 19 January 1989, p. A11.

61 RRL WHORM sf FG 298–01, 377654, Buchanan to Chief of Staff, 25 February 1986, with "Wick's VOA Choice Concerns Conservatives," from *Human Events*, c. 25 February 1986; also "Acting Director Is Appointment at Voice of America," *Washington Post*, 12 March 1986, p. A21.

62 Interview: Dick Carlson, 6 April 2004; Bob Coonrod, 3 January 1996. For USIA press release on Carlson see NA RG 306 A1 (1066), box 112, USIA historical collection subject files, file: VOA history 1983–5, announcement no. 46, 14 March 1986. For White House nomination see *PPP RR 1986*, Vol. 2, p. 970. He was political editor at KABC-TV in Los Angeles in the early 1970s and anchorman for KFMB-TV in San Diego from 1975 to 1977. Along the way he had also won four "Golden Mikes," a Peabody, and a National Headliner's Award.

Carlson's first priority was to maintain the integrity of the VOA charter. Wick supported this, but pressure came from elsewhere. He received periodic telephone calls from the NSC urging the VOA to cover this or avoid that or objecting to the treatment of the other story in a language service. He became adept at humoring the NSC staff and found that a sympathetic "we'll look into that" generally did the trick. He never passed the NSC's concerns on to his staff, though he accepted that the language services could be erratic and maintained the system of surprise inspections and back translations to keep staff on their toes. It did not take long for Carlson to become acquainted with the multiple factions at the VOA. Each service seemed to have its share of nationalists, monarchists, socialists, and/or separatists, all at daggers drawn, even before he addressed relations between the various services. The internecine struggles were sometimes taken up by audiences. Carlson realized the problem when Soviet dissident Yelena Bonner summoned him to a secret meeting during her visit to Washington and quizzed him about a recent demotion in the Russian branch. Some VOA services included out-and-out Communists. It was a mark of the importance of broadcasting in the last years of the Cold War that the Voice became a target for enemy infiltration as never before. Carlson referred some forty or fifty cases each year to the FBI's counterintelligence experts. Penetrated services included those aimed at Nicaragua and Afghanistan. One agent was identified only after turning up in Havana denouncing American imperialism at a press conference.[63]

*

Moscow wanted to keep it quiet. In 1957, a major nuclear accident had hit the Soviet installation near Kasli in the Urals. The Kremlin said nothing and the name Kasli remained obscure. When, on 26 April 1986, an accident rocked the aging power station at Chernobyl, Moscow hoped to repeat the trick. It failed. Western broadcasters carried the story to the people who lived in the path of the billowing cloud of radioactivity. The disaster at Chernobyl marked the coming of age of satellite technology in news gathering and dissemination. Although ground-based detection equipment raised the alarm, military and civilian satellite photographs provided proof and the USIA then used satellites to relay the full story to the world over the VOA and WORLDNET. WORLDNET's breaking news on Chernobyl was picked up by Austrian and West German news and hence became part of broadcasts seen by audiences in Hungary and East Germany. RFE estimated that nearly half of Eastern Europeans heard of the disaster through one or another of the Western radio channels. RL estimated that – despite ongoing jamming – 36 percent of Soviets first heard of the disaster from a Western station, and 18 percent from the VOA. In contrast, they estimated that only twenty-eight percent had heard the news first from Soviet television and fifteen percent by word of mouth. "This," Wick declared, "is the end of the Soviet monopoly on telling people what they want to tell them." Within days a Soviet representative

---

[63]   Interview: Dick Carlson, 6 April 2004.

was on Capitol Hill discussing the crisis. It took significantly longer for the Kremlin to fully brief its own people.[64]

Between 29 April and 30 May, USIS posts surveyed reactions to the disaster in 175 editorials and 310 commentary pieces in 107 newspapers across thirty-nine countries. Gorbachev's policy of openness seemed a sham. His television speech eighteen days after the incident could hardly make amends for his silence. The Soviet Union suddenly seemed both technologically backward and so bound by dogma that it could not even warn its own people of disaster. Many papers extrapolated that Moscow could not be trusted to abide by disarmament agreements without rigid verification procedures. Above all, as the USIA report put it, "The disregard for human life, both Soviet and foreign, in the path of the unannounced radioactive cloud, shows that the health of human beings must be subordinated to the progress, prestige and ultimate triumph of the Communist system."[65] Soviet citizens felt exactly the same way. At Chernobyl the mask of benevolent and technologically advanced socialism finally crumbled to reveal the decaying husk behind.[66]

The summer of 1986 demonstrated the persistence of tension in the Soviet–American relationship. On 30 August, the Soviet government arrested an American journalist, Nicholas Daniloff, on spying charges in obvious retaliation for the arrest of Gennadi Zakharov, a Soviet physicist employed by the United Nations in New York. It took a month to negotiate the journalist's release. The USIA worked to lift the case out of the realms of Cold War "tit for tat" to stress its human rights implications and American outrage. Wick noted that the world's press read the exchange of the innocent Daniloff for the obviously guilty Russian as a diplomatic defeat for the United States.[67] Tensions over the affair marred the reporting of a "town meeting" between 250 Americans and 2,000 Soviets held in Riga that month as part of the President's Exchange Program.[68]

Meanwhile, the KGB's disinformation campaign remained in full swing. Fake documents now surfaced at the rate of twenty-five per year, the all-time peak. Targets included the Strategic Defense Initiative. Forgeries included an NSC paper that spoke

---

[64] Irvin Molotsky, "USIA: Chernobyl and the 'Global Village,'" *New York Times*, 8 May 1986, p. B22; Michael Nelson, *War of the Black Heavens*, pp. 167–8; for case study see Parta, *Discovering the Hidden Listener*, Section 5.4.

[65] RRL WHORM sf CO 165, box 23, 436195, Wick to Poindexter, 22 May 1886, with attached USIA report "Chernobyl: World Press Questions Gorbachev's Credibility," 20 May 1986. According to the quantitative analysis, almost all papers surveyed condemned Soviet media policy; 90 percent said that the cover-up had greatly damaged the reputation of the Soviet Union; 85 percent condemned Moscow's callous disregard for human life, and 70 percent questioned Gorbachev's credibility as a more open leader.

[66] For discussion see Michael Nelson, *War of the Black Heavens*, pp. 167–8.

[67] RRL Judy Mandel files, box 91,721, USIA actions re Daniloff case, Wick to Poindexter, 16 September 1986.

[68] The Kremlin denied a visa to the VOA correspondent assigned to cover the event. In protest, Wick withdrew the VOA's Latvian and Russian correspondents as well. RRL WHORM sf FG 006–01, 485438, "US–Soviet Exchanges, The First Year Anniversary, November 1986" press release; James Gerstenzang, "Soviets Bar Voice of America Reporter," *Los Angeles Times*, 14 September 1986, p. 14.

of SDI as a first strike weapon.[69] In August 1986, the KGB created a letter to a U.S. senator, "signed" by the USIA's disinformation expert Herb Romerstein himself, in which he revealed a USIA plot to exaggerate the casualties of Chernobyl. Romerstein had no difficulty exposing the fraud as a clever piece of Xeroxing, cut, and paste.[70]

The AIDS libel received a major boost in September 1986 from a "scientific" report that appeared mysteriously at the Non-Aligned Movement Summit in Harare. In this report a retired East German professor (born in Leningrad) named Jakob Segal, his wife, Dr. Lilli Segal, and one Dr. Ronald Dehmlow advanced a "hypothesis" by which U.S. scientists could have manufactured AIDS. Segal was transformed into a French expert in many Soviet versions of the story to boost his credibility. By the end of the year, newspapers in forty-eight other countries had run the "U.S. made AIDS" story, including such reputable outlets as London's *Sunday Express*.[71] The USIA worked with the World Health Organization and scientists around the world to counter the claim, sending letters of protest to journals that printed the story. Because of improved access to the Soviet elite, they were able to cite Eastern bloc

69 The State Department upgraded its capability to respond to disinformation at this time, creating an Office of Active Measures Analysis and Response within its Bureau of Intelligence and Research. *Active Measures: A Report*, Department of State, August 1986, pp. 18–19; United States Department of State, *Soviet Influence Activities: A Report on Active Measures and Propaganda, 1986–87*, August 1987, p. 30. The twenty-five year figure comes from John M. Goshko, "For Forgery Specialist a Case Close to Home," *Washington Post*, 19 August 1986.

70 Goshko, "For Forgery Specialist a Case Close to Home," *Washington Post*, 19 August 1986; *Soviet Influence Activities*, pp. 30–31, 79; Romerstein to author, 1 September 2004. Romerstein's signature had been taken from a letter to U.S. General Robert Schweitzer dealing with a forgery in the general's name that Romerstein had submitted to Congressional hearings on disinformation in September 1985. When the Czech press attaché in Washington requested a copy, Romerstein had provided one, having first added an identifying mark to his signature against exactly this eventuality. The Czech signature appeared on the fake letter, allowing Romerstein to neatly instruct the American press and foreign governments and journalists on the methods used in Soviet active measures. The Czech, Vaclav Zluva, later apologized and explained that the forgery had happened after he forwarded the note to Prague. The KGB had targeted the USIA before. In 1984 they mailed out a fake questionnaire to Asian journalists on USIA stationary with some questions hinting at sinister American designs. Posts discovered the document when some dutiful journalists began to return completed forms, and were able to head off negative stories in the local press. Questions included, "Do you prefer the guarantee of human rights or insuring your well-being . . . Do you think your country should take part in creating the special armed forces within ASEAN to suppress rebellions and international terrorism?" *Active Measures: A Report*, Department of State, August 1986, pp. 68–70.

71 Department of State, *Soviet Influence Activities*, pp. 33–49; Jakob Segal et al. *AIDS – Its Nature and Origin*, c. September 1986, (provided to author by the USIA); "AIDS 'Made in Lab' Shock" *Sunday Express*, 26 October 1986. For comment on the AIDS campaign see Christopher Dobson, "AIDS: How the Russians Smear the Americans," *Sunday Telegraph* (London), 9 November 1986; Roy Godson, "Commie Bigs Say AIDS Is U.S. Plot for Control," *Washington Post*, 25 January 1987, pp. B1–B4. On 17 March 1992, after the end of the Cold War, the head of Russian intelligence, Yevgeny Primakov, boasted about KGB responsibility for the campaign during a student recruitment drive. He could not resist adding a further deception, claiming that the U.S. retaliated by alleging KGB complicity in the attack on Pope John Paul II (which actually long pre-dated this). "Russian Spy Chief Admits KGB Cooked Up AIDS–CIA Link," Reuter's, 18 March 1992, and reported in *Izvestia*, 18 March 1992. FBIS-USR-92-118, *Commonwealth Affairs*, 16 September 1992, p. 8, reprints an interview – Yevgeniy Dodolev, "The Lies of General Kalugin," *Moskovskaya Pravda*, 12 August 1992, p. 6, in which General Oleg Danilovich Kalugin credited "the American Section in the A directorate" with the AIDS story and also noted that the U.S. Senate's study "Active measures in Soviet Intelligence" was 95% correct and he considered publishing a Russian translation.

sources to support their case, including the president of the U.S.S.R. Academy of Medical Sciences and Segal's old colleagues at Berlin's Humboldt University. In June 1986, a member of the audience at the Second International AIDS conference in Paris asked the Soviet AIDS expert Viktor Zhdanov whether the United States had created the virus. "That is a ridiculous question," he snapped back, "perhaps it was the Martians."[72]

*

In October 1986, Reagan and Gorbachev met in Reykjavik. USIA polls in the run up to the summit noted that although Gorbachev's proposal for a ban on nuclear testing was popular, Europeans suspected Soviet motives and accepted America's demand for verification. Unfortunately, the USIA also detected a decline in support for the SDI and opposition to wider U.S. arms policies.[73] Soviet spin gained early advantages at Reykjavik with four press conferences before the arrival of the U.S. team and subsequent flouting of the media blackout. Soviet leaks hinted at a "historic proposal of enormous dimensions" in the apparent hope of raising media pressure on the President to abandon the SDI. The USIA noted that the Soviets were treating the European media as their key audience and urged the U.S. delegation to do the same.[74]

Agency press analysis conducted after the conference revealed disappointing results. Europeans were crestfallen at results but still hoped that an arms agreement might be brokered in the ongoing Geneva talks.[75] The conference had been a roller-coaster. Negotiations swung between Reagan's astonishing proposal for the total abolition of nuclear weapons and deadlock, but both leaders sensed that real progress was possible. Reagan held fast to the SDI as America's insurance policy and left Reykjavik bitterly disappointed that Gorbachev had not accepted a deal. Wick, in contrast, was upbeat. He reassured the President, "Ronnie, you have just called the bluff of one of the world's master strategists." He had complete confidence that the SDI would force the Soviet Union to fold its hand.[76]

During the course of negotiations, Reagan raised the vexed issue of radio jamming. Gorbachev responded by complaining that because so many people in the U.S.S.R owned shortwave radios, the United States could broadcast to Soviet citizens, whereas the United States, with its limited shortwave ownership, was closed

[72]   Department of State, *Soviet Influence Activities*, pp. 33–49. VOA editorial, "FEAR: The Enemy of Just Solutions," October 1987 (document provided by USIA).

[73]   RRL WHORM sf PR 015, 440490, Marvin Stone to Donald T. Regan, 10 October 1986 with USIA report 7 October 1986.

[74]   RRL WHORM sf CO 165, box 24, 452433, USIA "interim report on Soviet public diplomacy at Reykjavik," 14 October 1986. The USIA provided its usual support to the 3,000-strong press corps. The VOA reported in English, Russian, and Ukrainian and gave major play to Reagan's post-summit address on 13 October. VOA editorials explained the American position in the aftermath of the conference. RRL WHORM sf FO 0006–11, 445109, Wick to President, 14 October 1986 with attachments including VOA editorials.

[75]   RRL WHORM sf CO 071, 473288, USIA foreign media analysis, 21 January 1987.

[76]   Interview: Wick.

territory to foreigners. Gorbachev presented jamming as a measure to level the playing field and proposed that the Soviet Union cease jamming in return for access to
the domestic airwaves of the United States. Reagan pledged to consider the idea.[77]
The same proposal figured in a "freewheeling" two-hour meeting between Charles
Wick and the Communist Party's propaganda chief, Aleksandr Yakovlev, held on the
evening of 11 October in the Saga Hotel. When Wick noted that he was prepared to
trade Soviet access to a U.S. frequency for "VOA access to a local Soviet radio facility,"
Yakovlev rose to the proposal and suggested that the Soviets might broadcast from
a "nearby country" (Cuba). After Wick had enthusiastically announced "you've got
a deal," Yakovlev noted that he was only talking about the VOA, implying that RFE
and RL would still be jammed. Yakovlev then complained about the limited availability of Soviet books, plays, and films in the USA. Wick simply noted that Moscow was
"free to rent an American theater" and show whatever films they wished. The director doubted that he would be given any such right in the U.S.S.R.[78] As the Reagan
administration considered how best to open U.S. airwaves to the U.S.S.R., they hit a
snag. U.S. law prohibited foreign ownership of or substantial influence in a U.S. radio
station. Any quid pro quo would require an arrangement with an existing domestic
broadcaster. Wick immediately began to sound out potential partners.[79] In the meantime the administration faced a new crisis, but this time it was of its own making:
Iran–Contra.

3) IN THE SHADOW OF IRAN–CONTRA, 1987

On 5 October 1986, Nicaraguan soldiers shot down a plane resupplying the rebel
Contra army and captured an American called Eugene Hasenfus. Given that Congress
had forbidden U.S. aid to the Contras, the incident rang alarm bells. Less than a
month later, the Lebanese newspaper *Al-Shiraa* reported that the United States had
secretly sold arms to Iran. Allegations mounted. On 25 November 1986, the White

[77] John M. Goshko, "US Offered to Assist Soviet Radio Propaganda," *Washington Post*, 24 October 1986,
p. A34; Bernard Gwertzman, "US and Soviet Weigh Exchange of Broadcasts," *New York Times*, 29
October 1986, p. A8; the issue of Soviet jamming had been placed on the agenda for Reykjavik by
a Concurrent House Resolution, 391, passed on 30 September 1986. For correspondence see RRL
WHORM sf FO 006–11, 451396, Rep. Dick Armey to President, 7 October 1986.
[78] RRL WHORM sf CO 165, box 23, Wick to President, 14 October 1986, with transcript. Yakovlev also
complained bitterly about the VOA, comparing Russian service reports of splits in the Politburo to Nazi
propaganda forgeries used to encourage the purges. Wick pointed proudly to the VOA charter and
promised to correct any inaccuracy that Yakovlev might identify. For his part Yakovlev challenged Wick
to cover the next round of successful exit applications by Soviet Jews and send a VOA correspondent
to inspect Soviet mental hospitals to establish that they were not full of political detainees. For criticism
of these negotiations see William Safire, "You've Got a Deal," *New York Times*, 10 November 1986,
p. A23; Charles Horner and John Kordek, "No Summit 'Deal' Was Made on Radio Jamming," *New
York Times*, 20 November 1986, p. A30. See also Jim Hoagland, "The Ministry of Truth," *Washington
Post*, 17 October 1986, p. A2, which also included an attack on WORLDNET.
[79] RRL WHORM sf CO 165, box 23, 426613 SS, Wallison (Counsel to the President) to President, 30
October 1986; John M. Goshko, "US Offered to Assist Soviet Radio Propaganda," *Washington Post*,
24 October 1986, p. A34; Bernard Gwertzman, "US and Soviet Weigh Exchange of Broadcasts,"
New York Times, 29 October 1986, p. A8.

House confirmed that the administration had both sold arms to Iran and diverted the money raised to fund the Contra rebels. On 1 December, President Reagan appointed a commission headed by Senator John Tower (R-TX) to probe the matter. Attorney General Ed Meese appointed an independent counsel to investigate, and both the House and Senate formed Iran–Contra committees.

The USIA saw massive foreign policy problems arising from the affair. A digest of newspaper reports completed on 21 January 1987 noted that "Almost all papers questioned the ability of a 'weakened' President to maintain strong leadership of both the U.S. and the West. Most were concerned that the Iran affair might paralyze U.S. foreign policy." They saw an obvious opportunity for Soviet gain. The decline in the President's personal standing was especially noticeable. Europe sensed "panic and confusion" in Washington. "Where," Europeans were asking, "is the triumphant, self-assured Reagan with the smile of the eternal winner?"[80] The USIA found some comfort in a telephone poll conducted in France, Germany, and Britain on 19–22 January. The poll revealed that although large majorities believed that Iran–Contra had damaged the international credibility of the United States, the level of confidence in American leadership remained steady and certainly ahead of confidence in the Soviet Union.[81]

A survey of the VOA's coverage of Iran–Contra in late 1986 published in *National Journal* on 24 January 1987 found that the VOA had "covered the most critical aspects of this multi-faceted story with persistence." But the Voice did not stay free from controversy. In late January the Senate Select Committee on Intelligence disclosed that on 25, 26, and 27 September 1986, the VOA's Farsi service had carried a special editorial written by Oliver North's staff at NSC. The editorial praised Iran for refusing to allow a Pan Am plane hijacked in Pakistan to land on their soil. Immediately after the VOA transmitted the message, Iran deposited $7 million in the secret Swiss bank account set up by Oliver North. North had declined to approach the VOA himself and asked the new State Department anti-terrorism tsar Paul Bremer to do the job. Bremer's staff paid a call on the head of the VOA Farsi service, William Royce, at his home, but found him unprepared to accept an editorial through the back door, as was the senior editorial writer at the Voice, Kenneth Thompson. Bremer then tracked down Wick in a restaurant and pitched his request as of "great importance to national security" and "from the highest levels." Wick resolved to take Bremer at his word and, after confirming that the editorial was factually accurate and not in violation of the VOA charter, agreed to transmit the text. Carlson concurred. Even so, the revelation embarrassed the administration. The VOA was also embarrassed that a page from Oliver North's notebook emerged bearing the name of the head of the VOA's Current Affairs Unit,

80 RRL WHORM sf CO 071, 473288, USIA foreign media analysis, 21 January 1987.
81 RRL WHORM sf PR 015, 502187, Wick to Donald T. Regan, 4 February 1987 with USIA research memorandum "Iran Affair and European public opinion," 6 February 1987. When asked, "Some people say that U.S. credibility has been damaged as a result of the stories surrounding US-Iranian arms shipments. Others say U.S. credibility has not been damaged. Which view is closer to yours?" 78% of Britons, 75% of Germans, and 60% of French said that U.S. credibility had been damaged.

former *Time* writer, Ed Warner. Some VOA insiders noted that whereas VOA news had been objective, the VOA's current affairs features had reflected a clear pro-Contra, anti-Sandinista agenda, and assumed that Warner had been taking orders from North. Warner left the helm of VOA's Current Affairs Division under a cloud in August 1988.[82]

In June 1987, the deputy director of the USIA, Marvin Stone, felt it prudent to remind the NSC staff and the State and Defense Departments that "neither USIA management nor other agencies of the government should attempt to influence what VOA reports through approaches to program personnel." Stone pointed other agencies to Carlson or his deputies, noting, "*Approaches to subordinate personnel on program matters must be avoided because they may be interpreted as efforts to circumvent the VOA charter.*" The VOA's Office of Policy Guidance, then headed by Philip Arnold, was designated to consult across the executive branch to obtain the necessary guidance to generate two VOA editorials each day.[83]

The White House strategy for international presentation of Iran–Contra emphasized a "two track procedure." Reagan would manage business as usual while a full investigation would be conducted, coordinated within the White House by Ambassador David Abshire.[84] The White House emphasized the multiple inquiries underway. President Reagan swiftly brought in new personnel to replace the casualties of Irangate, including Frank Carlucci as the new National Security Advisor. WORLDNET mounted interactive broadcasts about the Tower report and a special program to introduce Carlucci. On 4 March Reagan presented his house cleaning in an address to the American people. The Voice of America carried the statement live. It is a testament to the reach of the Voice that the Secretary of State was able to tune in while on a visit to China. "We held a small portable radio up to the window of our train," he wrote to the President, "and heard your statement coming in over the Voice of America as our railroad car rolled across the North China plain today. The message came in loud and clear. It unmistakably conveyed that mark of leadership which you have made your own." But George Shultz was not the audience that Reagan needed to win.[85]

The Iran–Contra hearings made Colonel Oliver North a hero to some at home. The USIA noted that foreign newspapers thought that he mounted a better defense of the Contra cause than did the President. The USIA reported that the world's media were palpably relieved to hear the testimony of the disgraced Admiral Poindexter

82 John M. Goshko, "Wary VOA Praised Iran in Broadcast Following Administration Request," *Washington Post*, 31 January 1987, p. A16; Carolyn Weaver, "When the Voice of America Ignores Its Charter," *Columbia Journalism Review*, Nov/Dec, 1988, pp. 37–42; the split between news and current affairs position on Nicaragua is confirmed (from a different political perspective) in "The VOA Made Gains under Reagan, but Still Needs Improvement," *Human Events*, 11 February 1989, pp. 10–11.

83 RRL WHORM sf FG 298–01, 506826, Stone to Powell (NSC), Armacost (USoS), and Ickle (USoD), 17 June 1987. Emphasis in original.

84 RRL WHORM sf CO 071, 483992, Abshire to Gibson, 18 February 1987.

85 RRL WHORM sf FO 005–03, 509572, Wick to Carlucci, 27 March 1987 (re WORLDNET to South America on 5 March 1987). RRL WHORM sf FG 011, 472376, Shultz to President, 5 March 1987. On WORLDNET see also "Mission to Explain," *TV World*, May 1987, p. 92.

distancing the President from the illegal diversion of funds to the Contras, but also detected "a continuing sense of the decline of presidential power and authority."[86] The USIA responded with an initiative to "strengthen the U.S. leadership image abroad," including hard-hitting speeches on subjects as diverse as arms control and the bicentennial of the Constitution. The agency also proposed a series of carefully planned "conversational interviews" for the President with sympathetic TV and print journalists from Britain, West Germany, France, and Italy. The chosen journalists included Sir Alistair Burnett of Britain's ITN, Fritz Wirth of *Die Welt*, and Indro Montanelli, editor of *Il Giornale* of Milan. The White House approved and promised to build "foreign media opportunities" into the fall agenda.[87]

In May 1987, at the height of Iran–Contra, Wick presented Reagan with a new idea to enhance U.S. public diplomacy: a bipartisan "International Council of distinguished opinion makers" who would be brought to Washington to meet senior administration figures. The first International Council conference was scheduled for 8 and 9 October 1987. Although Wick noted that the conference would "provide us with an opportunity to better explain our role in the world," he also intended that the International Council members would provide valuable advice on "vital issues such as arms control, protectionism, trade issues and perceptions of the United States." The plan was all the more interesting for this strand of mutual exchange. It could be seen as an attempt by the USIA to establish a gathering along the lines of the shadowy muster of the European and American great and good known as the Bilderberg Group that could be directed to the administration's needs. Wick had road-tested a small-scale mobilization of foreign opinion makers back in 1983 at the time of INF deployment, but the dual gathering and guiding of foreign opinion makers in a conference setting had really begun at an International Conference on Private Sector Initiatives, held in Paris in November 1986, under the auspices of the White House Office of Private Sector Initiatives and its director, Frederick J. Ryan. Many of the Paris delegates were invited to join the international council. Wick always understood the value of a headline name and invited Rupert Murdoch to act as co-chair of the council. Alexander Papamarkou accepted the vice chairmanship. Honorary co-chairs would be Henry Kissinger, David Rockefeller, Robert Strauss, and Jeane Kirkpatrick. The White House promised to lend full support, mounting a lunch and making senior officials available to participate. The President, Vice President, White House Chief of Staff,

[86] RRL WHORM sf FO 005–03, 526690, Marvin Stone (deputy director USIA) to Colin Powell, 17 July 1987, with Foreign Media Reaction Special Report, Iran–Contra hearings, 16 July 1987.

[87] RRL WHORM sf FG 298, CF, 509198, Dean (NSC) to Carlucci, 22 June 1987, filed with memos containing USIA suggestions for speeches and content; RRL WHORM sf PR 014–08, 583644, Stone to Colin Powell/Thomas C. Griscom, 31 July 1987; RRL WHORM sf PR 014–08, 518580, Griscom to Stone, 3 August 1987. Other USIA initiatives that summer included an emergency tour by Stanton Burnett, Agency Counsellor, to see "key political figures and journalists" in London, Brussels, Bonn, and Paris. See RRL WHORM sf FG 298, 537788, Dean (NSC) to Powell, 11 August 1987, and for Burnett's digest of British opinion see RRL Speechwriting Office: Research Office, file: WORLDNET [2] OA 18108, Burnett to Wick, 7 July 1987.

and National Security Advisor and the Secretaries of the Treasury, Defense, and State all addressed delegates.[88]

The first USIA International Council Conference took as its theme "US policies and foreign perceptions." The delegate list read like a conspiracy theorist's dream. Wick assembled 103 senior media and business figures from thirty nations. They included French television CEO Patrick LeLay, ebullient British press baron Robert Maxwell, and Hisanori Isomura, executive controller general of the Japan Broadcasting Corporation, as well as CEOs from companies as varied as Swarovski of Geneva and Agfa–Gevaert of Belgium, and international businessmen such as Rupert Hambro and Sir James Goldsmith. U.S. delegates included a number of serving and distinguished former ambassadors, including Walter Annenberg, and business leaders such Dwayne Andreas, CEO of the agricultural giant Archer Daniels Midland and chairman of the U.S.–U.S.S.R Trade and Economic Council. Given the prominence of businessmen within the International Council, it was not surprising that feedback collected from the delegates included concern over the rise in protectionist feeling in the United States. Small group discussions about issues including *Glasnost* and public diplomacy endorsed the work of the USIA and noted the inherent difficulty in competing with a dictatorship for public opinion. Delegates emphasized the need for the USIA to focus on the rising generation in its European information work especially. The overall reaction was encouraging. The official report noted that the feedback would help the USIA and that "the conference revealed an impressive level of support among opinion leaders abroad for U.S. leadership in world affairs." Although staff found the level of pampering expected by the international great ones exhausting, Wick felt it would be well worth repeating.[89]

*

The great game of Soviet–American negotiation continued apace. On 24 May 1987, the U.S.S.R. stopped jamming all VOA broadcasts, but jamming of RFE and RL intensified. As there was no arrangement yet in place for Soviet radio broadcasts within the United States, the U.S.S.R simply began medium-wave transmissions from Cuba on the 1040 band, which violated international broadcasting agreements and disrupted a number of Florida's radio stations. The United States welcomed the first move and complained about the rest in the strongest terms.[90]

88 RRL WHORM sf PR 007, 546277, Wick to President, 13 May 1987; for the text of the President's remarks see *PPP RR 1987*, Vol. 2, pp. 1160–1162.

89 RRL WHORM sf FO 006, 527373, Wick to Howard Baker, 19 October 1987; the final report is filed at RRL WHORM sf FO 006, 540710, The Gallup organization polled delegates before and after the meeting. For Presidential briefing documents see RRL WHORM sf PR 007–01, 559009, and (for press briefing documents) CF OA 877.

90 Philip Shenon, "Years of Jamming Voice of America Halted by Soviet," *New York Times*, 26 May 1987, p. A1. Jamming of the BBC Russian service ended in January 1987; also Bill Kellers, "American Outraged by Soviet Article," *New York Times*, 6 June 1987, p. 5, and Janet Hemming (letter to editor), "US–Soviet Radio Deal Is Denied by Wick," *New York Times*, 13 July 1987, p. A16. Also William Tuohy, "Soviet Charges of 'Ethnic Warfare' Anger U.S. Aide," *Los Angeles Times*, 6 June 1987, p. 1.

Exchanges flourished. In June 1987, Wick traveled to Moscow to open *Information USA: Linking People and Knowledge*, the first major exhibition in the U.S.S.R. since 1979. Muscovites waited in line for two hours or more to view the latest American home computer technology, cell phones, supermarket checkout systems and a trolley full of processed food, a Plymouth Voyager mini-van, and a host of other devices produced by American ingenuity. In a recorded message of welcome. President Reagan expressed his hope that visitors gain "a better idea of how this 'Information Revolution' has indeed transformed American life." Rock and sports videos played on large screens. One hundred thirty corporations donated their wares to the show, and the agency spent $14 million to pull the whole thing together. Technical problems in setting up the exhibit included managing the famously volatile electrical current in Moscow. Some visitors presented Bulgarian-made floppy disks in the hope that they might be allowed to pirate the latest software; others quizzed the Russian-speaking guides on how they might be able to construct their own TV satellite dishes. They went away disappointed. Most visitors were simply dazzled by the rage of technology available in the West. Materials given away included stacks of surplus magazines donated by the USIA's magazine committee. Associate Director for Programs Charles Horner recalled that some of the glossier titles were selected simply to make the Soviets "feel terrible" about their standard of living. Samples included *Harpers* and *Yachting* magazine. The show rolled on to eight more cities including Leningrad, Kiev, Minsk, and Tashkent.[91]

*

The USIA still wrestled with Soviet disinformation, encountering ten to fifteen presumed Soviet fakes each year. Moscow had launched a new campaign targeting the CIA, alleging agency complicity in the assassinations of Olof Palme and Indira Gandhi, the attempted assassination of the Pope, a coup in Fiji in 1987, and the mass suicide of the Jonestown cult in Guyana in 1978.[92] They also circulated a grisly story linking American citizens to an illegal trade in the organs of children for use in transplants. The "baby parts" story first emerged in Honduras in January 1987 as a "rumor" repeated in an ill-considered interview by the former Secretary General of the Honduran Committee for Social Welfare, Leonardo Villeda Bermudez. The story grew from there. In April 1987, *Pravda* gave the story an encouraging shove and off it spun through the media of the Soviet bloc and the developing world as

---

91 Felicity Barringer, "US Exhibit in Moscow Draws High-Tech Crowd," *New York Times*, 6 June 1987, p. 6; William Tuohy, "Muscovites Gawk as U.S. Opens High-Tech Exhibit," *Los Angeles Times*, 5 June 1987, p. 5; Garry Lee, "The Soviets' Americana: Exhibit of U.S. Images Opens in Moscow," *Washington Post*, 5 June 1987, p. B1. Interview: Horner, 15 December 1995.

92 In the course of 1987 the House Appropriations committee commissioned the USIA to report on "Soviet active measures in the era of Glasnost." On 8 March 1988, Wick presented the findings to a Congressional hearing: Wick, "Soviet Active Measures in the Era of Glasnost," presented to the House Committee on Appropriations, 8 March 1988, published Washington, DC: USIA, July 1988. Vehicles for the CIA stories included a book, *Army of the Night*, published in Moscow in February 1988 in an edition of 200,000.

evidence of American corruption. The USIA investigated and publicized the total lack of supporting evidence.[93]

Countering the Soviet rumors at the USIA, Herb Romerstein now worked with a young assistant, named Todd Leventhal. They found that Gorbachev's charm offensive opened a new dimension in the USIA's counterdisinformation work. By exposing Soviet lies (and especially the crude lies used in the developing world, which shocked European audiences), Romertstein and Leventhal not only cut off a significant Soviet line of attack, but also disrupted the image of Glasnost. Leventhal realized that "discrediting the strategic adversary" should be the core objective of counterdisinformation work. He and Romerstein did not publicize the insight around the bureaucracy, as they suspected that some enthusiasts for détente might consider their work overly aggressive. As glasnost advanced, so the USIA's leverage against Soviet disinformation increased. At last it became possible to apply real pressure on the Kremlin to shut down its rumor mill.[94]

In the spring the U.S. government sought to finally end the AIDS libel by tackling the problem at its source, threatening to end all AIDS research collaboration with the U.S.S.R. unless the disinformation campaign stopped. The U.S. delegation to the eighth session of the US–U.S.S.R. Joint Health Committee delivered the ultimatum in April 1987. On 15 July 1987, Wick wrote to Carlucci and Shultz suggesting that all U.S.–Soviet science and technology exchange be suspended. Shultz opposed this but Carlucci agreed to review cooperation in the "health and bio-medical fields." "Above all," he asserted, "we must make clear to Soviet leaders that we draw political conclusions about them from activities of this sort." From August on the USIA noted a sharply reduced use of the AIDS story within the U.S.S.R., but it still popped up from time to time overseas. The story, like a virus, now had a life of its own.[95]

The USIA also engaged wider Soviet rumors, especially the "ethnic bomb" story. Countermeasures included a State Department seminar for journalists from Africa and Latin America in April 1987 called "Disinformation, the Media and Foreign Policy."

93 Wick, "Soviet Active Measures in the Era of Glasnost"; also USIA, *The Child Organ Trafficking Rumor: A Modern Urban Legend*, report to UN special rapporteur, December 1994. The story was a variation on the "urban myth" about the man who wakes after a night out in a foreign city to find that a kidney has been stolen. It drew credence from grisly reports from India of organs for sale and from China of executed criminals being effectively recycled for spare parts, but also echoed ancient stories variously told against Jews, early Christians, eccentric old maids, and the nobility whereby child abductions were in fact the harvest of blood or body parts for a barbaric religious rite or to restore a wounded leader.
94 Interviews: Todd Leventhal, 28 November 1995, 30 September 2004. In a symptom of the leverage identified by Leventhal, during a conference in Moscow in October 1987, Gorbachev expressed real irritation to George Shultz over the State Department report *Soviet Influence Activities: A Report on Active Measures, 1986–87*, waiving a copy at the Secretary of State. Shultz confessed that he had not seen the document before. Don Oberdorfer, *The Turn: From the Cold War to a New Era*, New York: Simon and Schuster, 1991, pp. 249–52.
95 RRL WHORM sf CO 165, box 26, CF, 509511, Carlucci to Wick, 12 August 1987 and Shultz to Wick n.d. (from which the content of Wick's memo can be deduced); Department of State, *Soviet Influence Activities*, pp. 33–49.

USIA also collected and circulated expert opinions from top American medical scientists at the NIH to emphasize the absurdity of the "ethnic weapon" story, Finally, Charles Wick himself took up the issue in a meeting on 5 June 1987 with the chief negotiator for the media exchanges, the head of the Novosti news agency, Valentin M. Falin. When Wick complained about the ethnic bomb story, Falin insisted that such a report was quite consistent with America's track record of massacring Indians and abusing Japanese-Americans. Wick walked out of the meeting in protest. The battle against disinformation had entered a new phase.[96]

*

In 1987, the USIA mounted a substantial program to mark the bicentennial of the U.S. Constitution. In addition to circulating the Constitution in an annotated sixty-page edition in eleven languages, the USIA translated thirty-five key textbooks about the document, sent a small library of books on the Constitution to all posts, and circulated a fifty-panel poster exhibit called "We the People" to cultural centers, universities, and law schools around the world. The USIA sponsored conferences on the subject in Islamabad, Bologna, Dakar, Buenos Aires, and, in a sign of the times, Warsaw. The VOA commissioned a twenty-six-part documentary series also called "We the People." One thousand two hundred agency-sponsored international visitors passed through Philadelphia, where the Philadelphia Council for International Visitors presented a special program on the Constitution. AmParts lecturers included the chairman of the Pennsylvania Democratic Party, who spoke on Martin Luther King and the U.S. Constitution to audiences in Africa. The USIA's Television Service circulated such appropriate classic films as *Mr. Smith Goes to Washington* and hosted Chief Justice Warren Burger on WORLDNET. Finally, the agency hosted legal scholars from Brazil, Chile, Hong Kong, South Africa, and Venezuela, who were interested in reforming their own constitutions, and provided expert advice to the framers of the new constitution for the Philippines. Yet the most eloquent testament to the Constitution that year was the spectacle of the Iran–Contra investigation, laid open to the world though USIA channels, performing a public house cleaning unthinkable in all but a handful of countries.[97]

96   Department of State, *Soviet Influence Activities*, pp. 51–5. Key stories include "South Africa Researches Ethnical Weapon," TASS, 13 August 1984 (with New York byline). For illustration see *Al Qabas*, 29 January 1987. Also: USIA notes, "Soviet Disinformation on the 'Ethnic Weapon,'" c. June 1987. Other Soviet disinformation campaigns at this time included the leak of a fake letter from CIA director Bill Casey to Ed Feulner of the Heritage Foundation revealing a plot to oust Rajiv Gandhi, which ran in *Blitz* magazine on 28 July and 1 August 1987. Leventhal (USIA Policy Officer on Soviet Disinformation) to Ambassador Barry (New Delhi) 11 August 1987. *Blitz* printed the letter on 8 August 1987 on the front page with the headline, "Forgery? Here's the Final Proof." All documents provided to author by the USIA. Wick's confrontation with Falin is reported in Bill Kellers, "Americans Outraged by Soviet Article," *New York Times*, 6 June 1987, p. 5, Celestine Bohlen, "USIA Head Cuts Short Stormy Meeting with Soviet Official," *Washington Post*, 6 June 1987, p. A17, and William Tuohy, "Soviet Charges of 'Ethnic Warfare' Anger U.S. Aide," *Los Angeles Times*, 6 June 1987, p. 1.
97   NA RG 306 A1 (1066) USIA historical collection subject files, box 142, file; USIA policy, Bicentennial, 1976 [sic], USIA fact sheet, March 1987. Experts sent by USIA to the Philippines included Professor A. E. Dick Howard of University of Virginia.

*

The VOA flourished under Carlson. Although the production of editorials
remained highly politicized by the convictions of the political appointees to that office,
Carlson eased regulations on their use. From April 1987, the VOA's smaller language
services were no longer required to broadcast an editorial every day. Instead they
worked to a formula requiring one editorial a week for every fifteen minutes of daily
airtime. The VOA policy office retained the right to insist that services carry regionally
specific editorials and the key policy editorials designated "MUST," but otherwise
the services now had a degree of choice.[98] Resentments eased, but Carlson had other
headaches. In June 1987 the *Washington Post* revealed that two VOA producers had
been running a gold-trading business from the office. When caught they admitted to
making "a very bad mistake."[99]

In June 1987, the USIA and RFE/RL finally concluded a deal to build a radio
relay site in Israel to improve signals reaching Western and Central Asia and East Africa,
an initiative begun in the Carter years. Certain Israeli politicians resisted the scheme,
fearing that it would slow Jewish migration from Russia. Carlson and BIB chairman
Steve Forbes pleaded their case directly to the Knesset. Unfortunately the designated
site in the Negev desert was not ideal, being below sea level and directly in the path
of a major bird migration route. After sinking $64 million into preparing the site, the
U.S. government abandoned the entire plan in 1991.[100]

In July 1987, the Senate Foreign Relations Committee delivered a major attack
on the USIA's budget, taking aim at VOA modernization and recommending cutting
the budget for WORLDNET and other agency film and television projects from a
$44 million request for 1988 to just $15 million. Senator Claiborne Pell questioned
whether anyone was actually watching WORLDNET and pointed out that the audience figures used by the USIA often referred to the numbers capable of receiving the
signal rather than those who actually tuned in. Wick vigorously defended WORLD-
NET, its audience estimates, and his conviction that satellite broadcasting was the
wave of the future.[101] Wick appealed to the White House for a presidential statement
of continued commitment to the modernization program. In reply, Frank Carlucci
assured Wick "of the importance the Administration attaches to bringing VOA, RFE,
and RL up to date" but declined to arrange any presidential statement on the grounds
that one special appeal during delicate budget negotiations could open a floodgate

98 Author's collection, VOA/G, Ken Thompson to all language services and division chiefs, "Usage of Editorials," 9 April 1987. Under this deal the half-hour Greek service was required to use at least two editorials, the forty-five minute Georgian service three, and the ninety-minute Khmer service six.
99 Ted Gup, "VOA Offices Used for Gold-Selling Business," *Washington Post*, 28 June 1987, p. A6.
100 For the signing ceremony on 17 June 1987, see RRL FO 005–03, 504341 SS. For a summary of the problems in the Negev see Snyder, *Warriors of Disinformation*, pp. 194–7.
101 "At $30 Million, Is Anyone Watching?" *New York Times*, 14 July 1987, p. A22. Some on the Hill feared that Wick indulged WORLDNET at the expense of the more effective VOA; see Bill McAllister, "Fiscal Laryngitis Lowers the Voice," *Washington Post*, 31 March 1987, p. A19. For criticism of VOA modernization see Bill McAllister, "Executives Blamed for Delays at VOA," *Washington Post*, 22 September 1987, p. A19.

to such requests from others.[102] The budget crisis required other desperate measures. In the course of 1987, USIA management extended a measure by which all agency employees could be placed on involuntary unpaid furlough for up to twenty-two work days every year in order to save money. Though Wick never used this power, the measure hung heavily over the agency.[103]

Although parsimonious with funding, Congress did at least devote a measure of attention to the future organization of the USIA. In the course of 1987 Congress amended the VOA charter law to include WORLDNET and the agency's other film and television services, and wrote a new mission statement requiring the USIA to

> Strengthen foreign understanding and support for United States policies and actions;
>
> Counter attempts to distort the objectives and policies of the United States;
>
> Advise the President, the Secretary of State, members of the National Security Council, and other key officials on the implications of foreign opinion for present and contemplated U.S. policies;
>
> Promote and administer educational programs in the national interest in order to bring about greater understanding between the peoples of the world;
>
> Cooperate with the American private sector to enhance the quality and range of America's overseas information and cultural efforts;
>
> Assist in the development of a comprehensive policy on the free flow of information and international communications;
>
> Conduct negotiations on information and educational and cultural exchanges with other governments[104]

The emphasis in the second point on the mission to counter disinformation was a new addition, but the emphasis on a policy role for the USIA was all too familiar. As ever, there would be a gap between the role the USIA sought and the role afforded by the architects of U.S. foreign policy.

*

In July 1987, the USIA ran into difficulty with an exhibition of paintings from the National Portrait Gallery in Washington, scheduled to visit China. Beijing objected to pictures of Golda Meir and Douglas McArthur, which they argued would offend "third countries." Wick was unprepared to negotiate and cancelled the entire exhibit. "There is just no other alternative," he told the U.S. press; "we can't be fighting for democracy and be intimidated to oppose democracy with censorship." The tactic had worked in 1981, but this time the Chinese did not back down.[105]

---

[102] RRL WHORM sf FO 005–03, 540322, Carlucci to Stone, 29 October 1988, with attachments.
[103] Allen C. Hansen, *USIA: Public Diplomacy in the Computer Age*, 2nd edition, p. 55.
[104] NA RG 306 A1 (1070) box 3, USIA historical collection, reports and studies, 1945–94, *Transition U.S. Information Agency, March–April, 1991*, pp. 1–2.
[105] Irvin Molotsky, "US Cancels Show in Beijing over China's Demand to Cut It," *New York Times*, 16 July 1987, p. C19; John M. Goshko, "Art Exhibit Scuttled by Chinese 'Sensitivities' to 2 Portraits," *Washington Post*, 16 July 1987, pp. A1, A21.

The USIA also encountered legal problems at home. The class action against
Agency gender bias in employment, filed in 1977 as Hartman v. Reinhardt, had now
become Hartman v. Wick. In 1984, the court found for Hartman, identified a culture of bias at the agency, and ruled the USIA liable. In 1988 the district court
established the framework for compensation. The case now concerned all women
who had suffered employment discrimination at the USIA between 1974 and 1984.
Apparently, Hartman's original suit had not prompted certain members of staff to
mend their ways. It seemed that thousands of women could be eligible for compensation. The USIA spent $2 million notifying potential claimants of the situation
while still appealing against the ruling.[106] But this was not the USIA's only legal
headache.

In December 1985, a group of filmmakers filed suit in California against the USIA
on the grounds that its administration of the international distribution of documentary
films violated the Constitution. The case of Bullfrog Films, Inc. v. Wick arose from the
Beirut Agreement of 1948, which allowed that audiovisual materials whose "primary
purpose or effect is to instruct or inform" could be exported duty free. The USIA
issued licenses under the agreement. Alone among the seventy signatories, the U.S. and
Canada previewed films and denied certification to documentaries that they considered
unsuitable. The review process was low-key and conducted by a single career employee.
In its peak year for nay-saying, 1975, the USIA blocked nearly 100 documentary
films and approved over 4,000. Ten years later the agency approved nearly 8,000
films and blocked less than 20, but the makers of 6 of these cried foul.[107] The six
documentaries cited in the case were *In Our Own Back Yards: Uranium Mining in
the US*, an environmental horror story; *Ecocide: A Strategy of War*, on defoliation
in Vietnam; *Whatever Happened to Childhood?* which included scenes of youth drug
abuse; *Save the Planet*, a polemic against nuclear weapons; and a pro-Sandinista film
from 1981 called *From the Ashes... Nicaragua Today*. The plaintiffs noted that the
USIA had approved such apparently biased titles as *To Catch a Cloud: A Thoughtful
Look at Acid Rain* and *The Family: God's Pattern for Living*. As the case dragged
on, the agency drafted and redrafted its regulations, first to require balance in any
certified films and then to allow the USIA to declare a film "propaganda." Appeal
Judge A. Wallace Tashima struck these measures down as well. In May 1988, the
Ninth Circuit Court of Appeals upheld Tashima's ruling, denying the USIA the right
to evaluate documentaries on the basis of content. Despite Wick's threat to withdraw
from Beirut, the exchange continued without the intervention of the agency. The
case finally ended in 1993 with courts finding for the filmmakers and affirming their
entitlement to recover their costs.[108]

---

106 Documentation on the case may be found online at http://caselaw.lp.findlaw.com/cgi-bin/getcase.
     pl?court=dc&navby=case&no=955030a.
107 For summary history (1988), and texts of the Beirut Agreement and the USIA's regulations see NA
     RG A1 (1066) box 155, USIA historical branch, subject files, file: Motion Pictures, 1988.
108 Katherine Macdonald, "Filmmakers Sue USIA: Politics in Distribution Alleged," *Washington Post*, 6
     December 1985, p. A13; Deborah Caulfield, "Producers Sue: USIA Called Censor of Film Exports,"

*

For much of 1987, the world suspended judgment on Reagan, doubting the
wisdom of his line at Reykjavik and the viability of his leadership as Iran–Contra
unfolded. USIA polls taken in September 1987 in France, Italy, West Germany, and
Britain suggested a mounting favorable opinion of Gorbachev's U.S.S.R. (around forty
percent and climbing) and a steady decay in opinion of Reagan's America (around sixty
percent and falling). If the trends had continued, Europeans would have been equally
favorably disposed to both powers around the spring of 1990.[109] Then came the
breakthrough. On 18 September 1987, Secretary of State Shultz and Soviet Foreign
Minister Shevardnadze announced that they had reached an "agreement in principle"
to conclude the long-sought treaty on intermediate nuclear forces. The two delegations
set to work drafting a treaty. USIA posts noted a welcome surge in international
support for Reagan. The liberal *Observer* in London went so far as to ask, "Is the Cold
War over at last?"[110]

With international opinion on the move, the USIA's Office of Research conducted
an in-depth analysis of its polling in Europe since 1985 and formulated "Four themes
likely to strengthen Western European confidence in the US." These were stressing
that the United States is protecting European interests through arms negotiations
with the U.S.S.R; emphasizing the commitment and reliability of the United States
as an ally; emphasizing the commitment of the United States to negotiate and abide
by arms control agreements with the U.S.S.R; and asserting that "President Reagan,
personally, is an effective world leader who can be trusted." The agency noted that neither the European estimate of the U.S.S.R nor favorable attitudes toward U.S. society
as a whole had much bearing on European confidence in U.S. foreign policy. Their
suggested angle for criticism of Gorbachev was not his human rights policy, which
seemed a low priority for Western Europe, but Afghanistan. On 4 November 1987,

Los Angeles Times, 3 October 1986, p. 1; Jay Mathews, "Denial of Movie Certification Overruled,"
Washington Post, 25 October 1986, p. A24; Kim Murphy, "USIA Threatens to Back out of Treaty
in Row on Export of Films," *Los Angeles Times*, 27 July 1987, p. 3; Bill McAllister, "After 90,000
Movies, Court Ended Career of USIA's 'Film Critic,'" *Washington Post*, 2 October 1987, p. 21; Bill
McAllister, "Reviewing USIA's Role as Reviewer," *Washington Post*, 30 December 1987, p. A21; Bill
McAllister, "USIA Labels U.S. Film "Propaganda," *Washington Post*, 17 January 1988, p. 23; Matt
Lait, "USIA Loses Film Appeal," *Washington Post*, 19 May 1988, p. C4; Elizabeth Kastor, "Wick,
Heating Up Film Battle," *Washington Post*, 27 July 1987, p. C1; Joe O'Connell, "USIA Has Never
Engaged in Censorship," *Washington Post*, 1 September 1988, p. A22; David Cole, "The USIA and
Censorship (con'td.)," *Washington Post*, 14 September 1988, p. A22; Bill McAllister, "Court Pans
USIA's Case on Rating Film Exports," *Washington Post*, 17 March 1992, p. A19; note in "Attorneys'
Column," *LA Times*, 13 April 1993 re: Bullfrog Films v. Catto, USDC (Cent Dist. Cal.), no. 85–7930,
1 March 1993, Tashmia, J., p. 4533 of *Daily Appellate Report*.
109 RRL WHORM sf PR 015, 547491, USIA research memorandum "Western European opinion of the
U.S. remains more favorable but Soviets have closed the gap in recent years," 13 November 1987. For
further poll on European opinion and Gorbachev see RRL, Judy E. Mandel papers, box 92141, file:
USIA, foreign opinion note, "Mikhail Gorbachev's impact upon Western European Public Opinion,"
20 May 1988.
110 RRL WHORM FG 298, 514318, Wick to President, 22 September 1987 with USIA foreign media
reaction special report, 21 September 1987. See also RRL WHORM sf FG 298, 524947, USIA INF
chronology attached to Griscom to Rodota, 2 November 1987.

Reagan broadcast to the people of Western Europe over WORLDNET, outlining his hopes for an INF settlement.[111]

As Washington prepared to host the summit, National Security Advisor Carlucci convened one of the occasional Special Planning Group meetings mandated by NSDD 77 of January 1983 to direct U.S. public diplomacy. At the meeting on 5 November, Wick proposed the establishment of a White House office for telecommunication policy. He also noted that the integrated committee structure envisioned by NSDD 77 no longer operated and proposed re-creating it. Carlucci declined any substantial revision, preferring that the NSC continue "coordinating, advising, and being ready to bring together interagency groups as the situation warrants." The thinking behind Wick's bid to increase NSC input into public diplomacy was betrayed by his later contributions to the meeting: he called for some kind of "affirmation" of the administration's commitment to VOA modernization and some way to "institutionalize" WORLD-NET. As the budget squeeze tightened, the USIA needed as much help from the top as it could get.[112]

The year 1987 ended with the summit between Gorbachev and Reagan in Washington, DC, which ran from 8 to 10 December. Gorbachev's gambits in the days before the meeting included the publication of his book *Perestroika*. The USIA prepared facilities for nearly 7,000 accredited journalists and established a press center in Marriott Hotel and briefing facilities at the Department of Commerce. Officers marked a path through the labyrinthine corridors of the building with yellow tape, evoking merry allusions to *The Wizard of Oz*. During the summit, Wick broached the subject of disinformation with Gorbachev and a three-man media negotiation team led by Falin. Wick stressed his outrage at the anti-CIA, AIDS, and baby parts stories. Responding, Gorbachev personally assured Wick that there would be "no more lying. No more disinformation." Encouraged, Wick spoke to the press of a major breakthrough, but added, "It may all be like putting love letters in a hollow log."[113]

From 12 to 21 December 1987, VOA director Richard Carlson visited the Soviet Union. He opened the *Information U.S.A.* exhibit in Tbilisi and met Soviet media officials. He found his Soviet interlocutors "hell bent on demonstrating that they were pleased with the results of the summit." The deputy chairman of Gosteleradio, Ivars Kezbers, was open to further contact with the VOA and conceded in the course of

111 RRL WHORM sf PR 015, 547489, USIA briefing paper, "Four themes likely to strengthen Western European confidence in the US," 16 October 1987. For Reagan's speech see *PPP RR1987*, Vol. 1, p. 1269.
112 RRL Executive Secretary, NSC filing system, file 8708249, Dean to Carlucci, "Items for consideration from SPG meeting on public diplomacy, November 5, 1989," 9 November 1989.
113 NA RG 306 A1 (1070) box 31, USIA historical collection, reports and studies 1945–94, Washington Summit, U.S. Advisory Commission on Public Diplomacy, "Public Diplomacy: Lessons from the Washington Summit," March 1988 (praising USIA's advance planning and the even-handed treatment of foreign journalists as against the U.S. press and emphasizing the need for public diplomacy planning to be an essential element of summit planning). Also Don Oberdorfer, "US, Soviets to launch 'Battle of the Briefings,'" *Washington Post*, 29 November 1987, p. A38; Eleanor Randolph, "Reporters Follow the "Yellow Tape Line" to Summit News," *Washington Post*, 6 December 1987, p. A33; Don Shannon, "USIA Chief Presses Drive on Soviet Disinformation," *Los Angeles Times*, 11 December 1987, p. 28; and Wick, "Soviet Active Measures in the Era of Glasnost," March 1988.

the meeting that "Radio Moscow had erred in publicizing that AIDS was man made rather than a natural-occurring virus."[114] His visit bore immediate fruit. On 1 January 1988, Carlson announced that the Soviet Union had ended jamming of VOA and RFE broadcasts to Poland. Only VOA broadcasts to Afghanistan and RL's broadcasts to the U.S.S.R. remained subject to jamming.[115]

4) THE HOME STRETCH, 1988–89

On 1 January 1988, Gorbachev and Reagan exchanged televised New Year's greetings. Wick noted that this, together with Reagan's other television appearances and a recent interview in *Izvestia*, had sparked a full-fledged "Reagan phenomenon" in the U.S.S.R. The U.S. embassy in Moscow reported that the Soviet public perceived the President as "sincere, straight-forward and humane," a "moderate man and likeable." Given the scale of anti-Reagan propaganda in previous years, Wick considered this a remarkable testament to Reagan and the power of direct communication.[116] Wick's sense of accomplishment was dulled by the fact that the USIA now faced a major budget crisis. His appeal to the budget review board had failed and so, as a last resort, on 14 January he wrote directly to the President, warning that "the disallowed [budget] appeal for USIA will seriously reduce our overall capability in the war of ideas." Neither Reagan nor his Chief of Staff, Howard Baker, felt able to help. Wick's charmed life before the budget committees had ended. It was a sign of a post-Cold War mentality on Capitol Hill.[117]

The year 1988 brought further progress in U.S.–Soviet media relations, including a project to review each other's school textbooks and remove distortions. At the American team's request, the Soviets cut a passage from the standard eighth grade world history textbook that reported nineteenth-century Americans using blankets infected with smallpox to kill Indians and noted that this anticipated U.S. germ warfare in the modern period.[118] But Gorbachev lacked either the ability or the will to turn off the disinformation rumors as easily. The ethnic bomb and AIDS libel remained in circulation. Wick complained in two personal letters to Yakovlev that also urged further negotiations.[119]

---

[114]   RRL WHORM sf FO 008–01, Carlson to Wick, 29 December 1987.
[115]   Wayne King, "Soviet Halts Jamming of Broadcasts to Poland," *New York Times*, 2 January 1988, p. 5.
[116]   At New York in 1987 Reagan and Gorbachev failed to exchange messages owing to Soviet obstruction. Reagan broadcast directly over the VOA. See *PPP RR 1986*, Vol. 2, p. 1655, 31 December 1985; RRL WHORM sf CO 165, CF, 53616 SS Wick to President, 14 January 1988. In a further testament to Russia's rising enthusiasm for things American, *Amerika* magazine sold out for the first time since the invasion of Afghanistan. The embassy also found that back numbers returned as unsold or unwanted in previous years were eagerly snapped up by visitors to the *Information U.S.A.* exhibit; see RRL WHORM sf CO 165, 544219, Wick to President, 10 February 1988.
[117]   RRL WHORM sf FI 004, 538810 SS, Wick to President, 14 January 1988.
[118]   Wick, "Soviet Active Measures in the Era of Glasnost"; Don Shannon, "USIA Chief Presses Drive on Soviet Disinformation," *Los Angeles Times*, 11 December 1987, p. 28.
[119]   Despite the fine words spoken to Carlson in December, the AIDS story surfaced on Radio Moscow, whereas the ethnic bomb featured in TASS, the Novosti Military bulletin, and a Radio Moscow broadcast to South Africa. Other stories alleged that the head of the U.S. delegation to the UN

From 20 to 22 April, Wick and a delegation mixing government and, for the first time, the private sector met Soviet officials met for an intensive round of bilateral information talks. Panels considered books, print journalism, broadcasting, films, and government-to-government exchanges. The print panel discussed improved access (especially within the U.S.S.R.) and agreed to address mutual stereotyping. In government-to-government talks Wick raised concern about Soviet disinformation and jamming of RL, whereas Moscow complained that U.S. media coverage "does not adequately reflect the level of debate taking place" within Soviet society. Both sides agreed that the "importance of ongoing talks raise issues of concern and to dispel misunderstanding." Wick considered the whole enterprise a resounding success.[120]

The USIA continued its program of initiatives for "strengthening the U.S. leadership image abroad" and played a key role in publicizing the U.S. agenda for both the Toronto summit and the fourth Reagan–Gorbachev summit in Moscow. National Security Advisor Colin Powell noted that public diplomacy was now a core concern of all U.S. summit preparation.[121] The Moscow summit ran from 29 May to 2 June. Organizing media coverage in the heart of the U.S.S.R. caused plenty of headaches for the USIA. The conference brought 5,365 journalists and technicians (including over 1,000 Americans) to a city with only eleven phone lines to the United States. Each of the major U.S. networks requested twenty- two lines. The satellite link proved temperamental; Moscow's electricity caused the USIA's massive Xerox machine to explode like a Fourth of July party, and Japanese journalists were found substituting their chairs for those of the White House press corps in the front row of the press center. Wick, in Moscow for his third visit, refused to be downhearted. "I think it's working out really well," he told the *Los Angeles Times*.[122]

At the summit the streets proved as eloquent as the Soviet negotiators. While taking an early morning walk along the Moscow river embankment, Wick came upon two young boys wearing blue jeans and fishing. He assumed they were American. As he

human rights conference had committed terrorist acts against Cuba. See RRL WHORM sf FG 298, 55813, Wick to Howard H. Baker, 22 March 1988 with attached documents; also David B. Ottaway, "US Links to Soviet Disinformation," *Washington Post*, 17 January 1988, p. 23; "Soviets Said to Renew 3rd World Disinformation Drive," *Los Angeles Times*, 18 January 1988, p. 18; USIA, *The Child Organ Trafficking Rumor: A Modern Urban Legend*, report to UN special rapporteur, December 1994 noted that in May 1988 the weekly journal *Jeune Afrique* ran a hybrid story in which South Korean fetuses were being used to create a U.S. ethnic weapon.

120 RRL WHORM sf CO 165, box 29, CO 165, 561343 SS, Powell to President, 10 May 1988, Wick to President, 29 April 1988, with attachments. Private sector panel chairs were Nicholas Veliotes, the president of the Association of American Publishers, Jack Clements, the president of Mutual Broadcasting, Jack Valenti of the Motion Picture Association of America, Joseph Judge, senior associate editor of *National Geographic*, and Loren Ghiglione, president of ASNE for 1989. Other members included James Billington, the Librarian of Congress, communications lawyer (and ex-USIA director) Leonard Marks, Tad Szulc, the foreign editor of *Parade Magazine*, and the deputy director of the VOA, Robert L. Barry.

121 RRL WHORM sf FG 298, CF, 562342, Powell to Wick, 5 May 1988 with attachments. There were problems with White House plans for Moscow. Wick arrived in Moscow to find that he had not been initially scheduled for cultural meetings. See RRL WHORM sf FG 298, 593170, Stone to Howard H. Baker, 24 May 1988.

122 Nikki Finke, "The Moscow Summit for Media, Glasnost Does Not Mean End to Moscow Glitches," *Los Angeles Times*, 30 May 1988, p. 13.

drew close he realized that they were Russians and in that moment the enormousness of the changes happening in the Soviet Union suddenly became real. Pizza had come to Moscow and McDonald's had just announced plans to open its first burger restaurant in the city. Wick warned the press corps against equating superficial Americanization with real political change. "We have much more responsibility," he noted, "to have the Soviets understand our values and our concepts of democracy."[123] Highlights of the summit included Reagan's announcement of a new youth exchange initiative. The Soviet press accentuated the positive, reporting the conference as "truly a landmark" marking the beginning of serious nuclear disarmament and the "dying of the Cold War." Europe seemed to agree.[124]

*

The AIDS and baby parts libels rumbled on. In August 1988, a Reuter's story from Paraguay carried the baby parts rumor into the heart of the world's media. After a speedy briefing from the USIA, Reuter's ran a corrective piece including a history of baby parts stories, but the agency noted that a known Soviet front organization, the International Association for Democratic Lawyers, kept the story going.[125] Around the same time the USIA encountered a pamphlet circulating in Spain at a time of tension over U.S. bases, carrying the World Health Organization's AIDS logo. Inside the reader was invited to fold together two sides of a translucent page marked with Rorschach-test blobs to "see clearly the agents that transmit this terrible disease." When held up to the light the blobs formed a crude, pornographic silhouette of three male GIs in full battledress energetically engaged in an orgy beneath the stars and stripes. The USIA had no way of proving the Soviet origins of the leaflet, but noted that the production was too sophisticated for amateurs, the English, Spanish, and German language used inside was so stilted as to rule out any native speaker of those languages, and the U.S.S.R. clearly had most to gain from stirring opinion against the U.S. bases in Spain.[126]

AIDS, however, presented greater problems for the USIA than just the KGB's disinformation. The new disease had developed into a global public health problem requiring U.S. leadership, and one that could be helped to an astonishing extent by accurate information about transmission. Set against this obvious role for the USIA was the danger perceived by some that the United States might become too closely

---

[123] Nikki Finke, "Americanizing Moscow, Reagan–Gorbachev Summit Triggers an Influx of Distinctly Western Flavors," *Los Angeles Times*, 31 May 1988, p. 1.

[124] RRL WHORM sf CO 165, box 31, 585644, Wick to Powell, 28 June 1988 with advance copy of *Soviet Propaganda Trends*, 30 June 1988. Agency polls in June revealed that European opinion had responded well to the Moscow summit, approving of the pace of START talks. French and German opinion endorsed President Reagan's criticism of Soviet human rights. A narrow majority of Britons disapproved. RRL WHORM sf PR 015, 593782, Wick to Griscom, 15 June 1988, with "Post-Moscow flash survey," 13 June 1988.

[125] John M. Goshko, "Nailing Disinformation: The Slum Child Tale," *Washington Post*, 26 August 1988, p. A19.

[126] Interview: Todd Leventhal (28 November 1995), sample leaflet, and Leventhal to Linda Cheatham, 4 August 1988 (documents provided by USIA).

associated with HIV/AIDS. International AIDS policy was now handled by an interagency AIDS Working Group chaired at the State Department's Bureau of Oceanic and
International Environmental and Scientific Affairs. The group brought together personnel from State, AID, USIA, CIA, Defense, Immigration, and Health and Human
Services. A paper on AIDS and U.S. foreign policy from November 1987 identified
four objectives: (1) protection of U.S. citizens, (2) "Assisting other governments to
deal with the public health, social and political problems associated with the AIDS epidemic," (3) Supporting U.S. and international medical responses, and (4) "To ensure
that AIDS does not become a political problem which damages the relationships which
the U.S. government had with other nations." It was a start.[127]

Although some at the USIA, such as Mike Schneider in the P-bureau, saw AIDS
as an important issue for the USIA, others spoke against the subject. Although the
VOA had regularly carried AIDS stories since the disease was first identified in 1981, in
1987 senior staffer Janie Fritzman and others encountered resistance when the VOA
planned a call-in program on HIV/AIDS. At an emergency USIA policy meeting,
Fritzman insisted that the USIA could not censor the VOA, only to be told that the
charter related to news and not features. Fritzman went ahead with the program over
the objections of some USIA staff. The show included instructions from a surgeon on
how to sterilize a needle. Following the expected complaints from the field, Carlson
asked Fritzman to justify the program in writing and sent her defense back to the posts.
Subsequent highlights in the VOA's HIV/AIDS related programming included the
delivery of safe sex instructions in "Basic English" and similar programs that challenged
some of the cultural taboos of the more traditional language services.[128] By 1988,
the USIA regularly carried AIDS material on its wireless file for global distribution.
The USIA's in-house science writer, Jim Fuller, wrote much AIDS copy, charting
developments in public health and drug research.[129]

---

[127] AIDS working group, "Foreign Policy Implications of AIDS," draft, 13 November 1987 (document
provided to author by the USIA). Constructive policy responses included aid from USAID to the
World Health Organization and investment in two major AIDS programs: AIDSCOM, a global public
health communications program to educate the world away from high-risk behavior, and AIDSTECH,
a program to develop better screening methods and testing procedures. The U.S. government also
began testing U.S. military personnel assigned overseas and incoming immigrants and refugees for the
protection of populations abroad and at home.

[128] Interview: Fritzman, 7 December 1995. AIDS was first covered on the VOA in science reports by
Brian Cislak of an unusual infection coming in from Haiti at the same time as the story broke in the
New England Journal of Medicine. Interview: Ira Bergner, 29 November 1995.

[129] Interview Jim Fuller, 7 December 1995. Wireless file stories in 1988 included "Ten-Point AIDS
Program Announced by Reagan" (2 August); "US Congress Approves Major AIDS Bill" (14 October);
by Jim Fuller, "US Government Mails AIDS Pamphlet to Every Home" (4 May); "Global Effort
Probes Secrets of AIDS Virus" (24 June); "President's Commission Calls Term AIDS 'Obsolete' "
(27 June); "US Researchers Develop New Blood Test for AIDS" (1 August); "US Researchers Begin
Human Tests of New AIDS Drug" (10 August); "AIDS Drug Trials Expanded to Community Level"
(22 November); and during the transition,: "Coalition Calls on Bush to Make AIDS Top Priority"
(21 December). The file also carried Thomas Eicher, "Simple, Low Cost AIDS Blood Test Developed."
(22 July 1988). Fuller's subsequent stories included "Researcher Says New Drugs Check Spread
of AIDS Virus" (3 February 1989) and "Study Seeks Expanded Effort to Track AIDS Epidemic"
(8 February 1989).

*

Wick maintained his work with the private sector. The second International Council ran from 15 to 17 June 1988, with the theme "Facing the 1990s – Foreign Views of U.S. Policies," with much attention given to issues raised by the march of reform in the U.S.S.R. Once again the President himself addressed the gathering.[130] In a wider range of small group discussions than in 1987, the ninety-four or so financiers, publishers, and men of the world present expressed support for the free market, opposition to protectionism, concern for the "rich–poor gap," and concern over both Third World debt and the growing U.S. deficit. They suggested that the United States might be emphasizing its bilateral relationship with the U.S.S.R. at the expense of attention to North–South and Middle Eastern issues. They worried about terrorism, drugs, and exactly how the U.S.S.R. and China could be integrated into the world economy. They stressed the degree to which emerging technologies would shape the future for better and worse and predicted that "the information revolution will produce wealth, stimulate democracy, and increase interdependence." Wick informed Reagan that although members often thought the United States "inconsistent and disorderly in domestic and foreign affairs," they admired American values and credited the administration with the remarkable rapprochement with the U.S.S.R.[131]

On 27 July 1988, the Senate passed the USIA appropriations bill, assigning $881 million for the coming year. Controversies during the debate included lobbying by labor groups against USIA's au pair program as a source of cheap childcare rather than a serious international educational enterprise. Senator Pell questioned $7.5 million in the budget to start TV Martí, but suspended his objections pending hearings in September, which authorized test broadcasts using a transmitter suspended from a "tethered aerostat" blimp at Cudjoe Key Air Force Base in Florida.[132] The Senate authorization bill for 1989 imposed a limit on WORLDNET, insisting that the channel demonstrate a daily audience of at least two million in Europe before it expanded noninteractive programming any further. As the network only averaged 234,000 European viewers, WORLDNET had to temporarily suspend programs in October, missing the chance to transmit the second presidential election debate and the vice presidential debate. In its defense the USIA noted that programming now targeted Africa, Asia, and Latin America. The Senate relented with temporary funds in time to allow WORLDNET to cover election night.[133]

[130]   RRL WHORM sf FO 006, 592417, Wick to President, 12 September 1988, with attachments. For the President's remarks see *PPP RR 1988*, Vol. 1, pp. 789–91, 17 June 1988. The White House private sector office organized its third binational conference, a British–American Conference on Private Sector Initiatives, in London in May 1988, RRL WHORM sf FO 006, 541107, Ryan to President, 5 February 1988, etc.

[131]   RRL WHORM sf FO 006, 583038, Wick to President, 24 June 1988. For member opinion polling see RRL WHORM sf FO 005–03, Wick to President, 15 June 1988.

[132]   RRL Alan Kranowitz, box 1, OA 16797, USIA file 1, Raymond (deputy dir., USIA) to Kranowitz (WH), 29 July 1988; for follow-up see Raymond to Kranowitz, 23 September 1988, 30 September 1988 and 7 October 1988; Bill McAllister, "TV Martí: A High-Flying Propaganda Plan," *Washington Post*, 29 September 1988, p. A19.

[133]   John Carmody, "The TV Column," *Washington Post*, 5 October 1988, p. C12, 14 October 1988, p. B8 and November 1988, p. B10; Eleanor Randolph, "Lack of Viewers Forces USIA's

The end of September saw another round of U.S.–U.S.S.R. Bilateral Information Talks in Moscow. From 26 to 28 September, Wick and sixty-seven American officials and private sector leaders met Soviet representatives in plenary session and specialist panels, which now included an additional panel on concerts and exhibits. Private sector figures involved in Moscow talks included the preeminent entrepreneur in U.S. radio broadcasting, Norm Pattiz. Founder and chairman of the Westwood One radio network, Pattiz had an empire that included not only the music stations that made his name but most of the nation's traffic news services and the radio news divisions of CBS, NBC, and CNN. There was something incongruous about the intense Californian billionaire closeted with an earnest Soviet bureaucrat, Vladimir Posner. One was arguing the need for exchange to avoid nuclear war and the other trying to sell a Van Halen concert. But Pattiz was soon seized by the historical moment. He made a dramatic offer to counter the longstanding Soviet complaint of being excluded from America's airwaves, offering Radio Moscow time on the Westwood One chain if they could produce appropriate programs, and if such a deal would facilitate further U.S. access to Soviet airwaves. Moscow appreciated but never accepted the offer. Enthused by the potential of public diplomacy, Pattiz began to provide Westwood One programming free of charge to VOA Europe. He played a central role in U.S. international broadcasting at the turn of the millennium.[134]

At the end of the Moscow negotiations, Valentin Falin, head of the Soviet delegation, announced that the VOA could open a bureau in Moscow and that Andre de Nesnera had been accepted as its correspondent. The film panel, led by Jack Valenti, agreed to a protocol protecting copyright. The book panel arranged for the translation and publication of a series of classic American novels, beginning with Herman Wouk's *The Caine Mutiny.* The concert and exhibit panel agreed to open links between regional museums. The press panel agreed to an exchange of journalists. The government-to-government panel resolved to open talks toward the exchange of cultural centers, to increase briefings for each other's media, and to establish a mutual "early warning system" to correct misunderstandings and head off disinformation.[135] On 22 November 1988, the Kremlin stopped its last jamming operation, allowing the free reception of Radio Liberty's services for the first time since that service went on the air in 1953. It rapidly became the most listened to Western broadcasting in the U.S.S.R., reaching

WORLDNET off the Air," *Washington Post*, 7 October 1988, p. A21; and Joe O'Connell, "Who's Watching WORLDNET," *Washington Post*, 26 October 1988, p.A22. In November WORLDNET increased programming through an experimental deal for content with C-SPAN to run use their public service material when not airing WORLDNET content. In December the network began to screen the U.S. Chamber of Commerce weekday program *Nation's Business Today*; see "U.S. Network to Transmit Business News," *Washington Post*, 19 December 1988, p. BF8.

134   Interview: Norm Pattiz, 15 April 2005. On a visit to Paris he got an immense kick from tuning into VOA Europe on a mini radio while walking down the Champs-Élysées with his wife (Westwood One host Mary Turner) and hearing her on the air doing her signoff.

135   RRL WHORM sf CO 165, box 32, 599560, Stone (acting dir.) to Powell, 11 October 1988, with attachments; "Voice of America Is Granted Permanent Moscow Bureau," *New York Times*, 29 September 1988, p. A11; also RRL alpha file Wick, Wick to Duberstein, 8 December 1988 with "Report of Director Wick's Trip to Moscow, Leningrad, Helsinki, Ankara, Istanbul, and Madrid, September 23–October 8, 1988," 16 November 1988.

around 15 percent of the audience (around thirty-five million people a week).[136] Having delivered a long-sought concession to Washington, the Soviet information team paid a return visit to the United States in December. Wick acted as host.[137]

*

The presidential election in which Vice President George Bush battled Massachusetts governor Michael Dukakis provided the usual scope for the USIA to demonstrate the spectacle of U.S. democracy at work. In the course of the election year, fifty-three AmParts lecturers toured sixty-seven countries, speaking on aspects of the context. The USIA's International Visitor Program ensured that 400 grantees took part in special election events. The IVs included journalists, some of whom filed reports on the spectacle of the election to home audiences as they traveled. On the election night of 8 November, the VOA expanded its schedules to allow sustained coverage in English and thirteen other languages. New dial-in technology allowed 170 radio stations in the Middle East and 192 stations in Latin America to pick up VOA material over phone lines. Fifteen thousand radio or television stations around the world used VOA coverage in their election news. WORLDNET used seven Intelsat satellites to transmit round-the-clock election coverage to the world, carrying a feed from ABC news and supplementing it with interactive dialogues and its own programming once that channel had signed off. U.S. embassies and USIS posts and cultural centers hosted election-watch parties. Six thousand guests attended the event in Madrid and USIS Rome reported "a media extravaganza: possibly the largest, most ambitious event ever sponsored by USIS or this embassy." The morning after, the USIA set to work introducing the new administration to the world.[138]

As the Reagan administration drew to a close, Wick reported with satisfaction the many positive assessments of his President's achievement. The *Sydney Morning Herald* quipped, "Ronald Reagan has had the luck of the Irish. But we've all shared in it."[139] Domestic commentators recognized what Wick had accomplished at the USIA.[140] Reagan himself took steps to ensure that Wick's work was appreciated, speaking at a grand dinner held in Wick's honor at the Organization of American States Building in Washington on 17 November, with guests from the glittering roster of USIA private sector volunteers, including Rupert Murdoch. "We've accomplished great things these past eight years," the President declared. "Under Charlie's inspired leadership and with your strong support, USIA has undergone a rebirth of vision that will guide it well into

[136]   Serge Schmemanns, "Soviet Union Ends Years of Jamming Radio Liberty," *New York Times*, 1 December 1988, p. A1; Parta, *Discovering the Hidden Listener*, Sections 2.3 and 2.6.

[137]   RRL WHORM sf FG 298, 605758, Wick to Duberstein, 13 December 1988. For Wick's public summary see Charles Z. Wick, "Talking to Moscow about Cultural and News Issues," *Washington Post*, 29 October 1988, p. A27.

[138]   RRL WHORM sf FG 298, 605485, Wick to President, 29 November 1988 with report "US Information Agency and Election '88."

[139]   RRL FG 001, 601171 SS, Wick to President, 16 September 1988, with attached USIA foreign media reaction special report, "President Reagan's image," 15 September 1988.

[140]   See for example David Binder, "Wick Finds a High Profile Need Not Be a Target," *New York Times*, 2 June 1988, p. B10.

the next century and for which America is truly grateful."[141] In October Wick tendered his resignation, but asked to serve until the last day of the administration. Reagan's reply concluded, "you're going to be missed here in Washington – and remembered for truly distinguished services to our country's cause. Again, and from the bottom of my heart, thank you for a job well done."[142]

Out of office, Wick joined the board of Murdoch's News Corporation. "It is exciting to me," he wrote in a letter to President George H. W. Bush, "to participate in Rupert Murdoch's worldwide media giant."[143] In December 1989, Wick led a delegation of News Corporation executives to Moscow, discussing a host of joint commercial ventures in the realm of publishing, filmmaking, and even satellite broadcasting. The private sector now seemed poised to move into the territory opened by the public diplomacy of the Reagan years, though their victory would not be as complete as they imagined.[144] Wick also continued to work closely with Reagan. In 1989, he negotiated a $2 million fee for the former President to speak in Japan. Following the ex-President's diagnosis with Alzheimer's disease, Wick and his wife joined Nancy Reagan in her campaign to promote the use of human stem cells in medical research. Wick also lobbied on behalf of American public diplomacy. At Reagan's funeral in June 2004, Wick was one of five honorary pallbearers. Some journalists had forgotten about Wick's role in the administration and spoke of him only as the President's friend. When others asked about his time at USIA, he merely quipped, "Some of the people didn't like me, and they had to stand in line."[145]

141 *PPP RR, 1988*, Vol. II, pp. 1519–20; Elizabeth Kastor, "For Wick: Cheers from the Chief," *Washington Post*, 18 November 1988, pp. C1, C11.
142 RRL WHORM sf FG 298, 700064, President to Wick, n.d.
143 George Bush Presidential Library (GBL) WHORM sf FG 128, 58055, Wick to Bush, 18 July 1989.
144 Jeremy Gerard, "Murdoch Looking for Ventures in Moscow," *New York Times*, 1 December 1989, p. D11.
145 William Safire, "Recruiting Reagan," *New York Times*, 11 May 1989, p. A29; Martin Kasindorf, "Reagan's Fall from Grace . . . ," *Los Angeles Times*, 4 March 1990, p. 11; Richard Fausset et al., "The Reagan Legacy," *Los Angeles Times*, 7 June 2004, p. A1; Grant Segall, "Pallbearer, Old Pal, Says Reagan Was Smart, Hid It." *Cleveland Plain Dealer*, 9 June 2004.

EPILOGUE

Victory and the Strange Death of the USIA, 1989–99

Everywhere those voices are speaking the language of democracy and freedom, and we hear them and the world hears them, and America will do all it can to encourage them.

George H. W. Bush, 24 May 1989.[1]

In the months following Wick's departure, the staff at the USIA saw the work of two generations come to fruition. As the Soviet Union struggled to restructure its ailing economy, Moscow's foreign policy changed. In February, Gorbachev completed his withdrawal of troops from Afghanistan. In June, Solidarity swept to victory in Polish elections. In September, Hungary opened its border with East Germany. On 9 November, the Berlin Wall came down. By the year's end, the dissident playwright Vaclav Havel had been elected president of Czchoslovakia, Bush and Gorbachev had met on Malta and spoken of the Cold War ending, and the crowd had disposed of the Romanian dictator Nicolae Ceaușescu. A new era had begun.

It is moot to consider the role of U.S. public diplomacy in bringing these changes. Eastern European leaders paid repeated tribute to the role of radios in sustaining the hope of freedom and spreading news of the changes that permitted its return. Soviet citizens had seen enough at exhibitions and heard enough over the air to understand the abundance of the West. Their aspirations drew the Kremlin into a race it could never win. Audience research in the U.S.S.R. before and after the political change revealed weekly audiences of around twenty-five percent for all Western broadcasters and a strong correlation between politically moderate or liberal views and Western radio listenership in the U.S.S.R., and although this probably means that Soviet audiences sought information sources to match their political outlook, providing that information presumably helped along the way.[2]

The behavior of the governments reinforced the messages on the air. By attempting to block Western information through jamming and censorship, the Eastern Bloc governments betrayed their fears, undermined their own credibility, and wasted billions of rubles. Conversely, U.S. public diplomacy had been an important tool for minimizing disasters like Watergate, managing relationships with allies, blocking the

---

[1] *Public Papers of the Presidents, George [H. W.] Bush, 1989*, Vol. 1, Remarks at the U.S. Coast Guard Academy Commencement, New London, Conn., 24 May 1989, p. 601.

[2] For analysis see Parta, *Discovering the Hidden Listener*, Sections 3 and 6.

enemy's ability to win, and holding the imagination of the developing and nonaligned world until the American system had decisively passed the Soviet. There was an irony in the victory of the free market system in the Cold War. Although the end of the Cold War certainly made the world safe for the free market, the battle had been fought by state-subsidized media going to places and showing things that afforded no short-term profit.

*

The freedom within American culture – as represented by jazz on the VOA or opinion on CNN – seemed everywhere in 1989. In June, the Soviet spokesman Gennadi Gerasimov drew on U.S. popular culture to explain his government's new policy to its neighbors, telling German foreign correspondents that the Soviet Union had traded the Brezhnev doctrine of intervention for "the Frank Sinatra doctrine: 'I do it my way'[sic]."[3] On the other side of the world, students in Tiananmen Square, Beijing, erected a goddess of democracy that echoed the Statue of Liberty and relayed VOA coverage of their protests over giant loudspeakers out across the crowd. The stock of U.S. public diplomacy could hardly have been higher.

At Harvard, political scientist Joseph Nye hit on the idea of "soft power" as a way to counter Yale historian Paul Kennedy's auguries of America's impending "relative decline." Nye noted that the attractiveness of American life and values had played a core role in the recent past and represented a resource that meant that the United States was, as the title of his 1990 book had it, *Bound to Lead*.[4] Such ideas should have set the agency up for a prime role in the post–Cold War world, but it was not to be. The end of the Cold War robbed the agency of its most potent argument in appropriations hearings. The USIA was not without blame. Rather than fight for the argument that public diplomacy was an essential element in the regular foreign relations of a state, the USIA fell back on talk of crisis and the strategic battle with Communism. The USIA cast itself as a Cold War agency and became an obvious target for senators in search of budget cuts to fund the "peace dividend."

The USIA died by stages. There were opportunities missed, as when the USAID won the place of lead agency in the democratization of Eastern Europe. There were wounds inflicted from within, as when the ancient struggle between the VOA and USIA flared in the public clash between VOA director Dick Carlson and Wick's successor, Bruce Gelb. There were blows from the right, as Senator Jesse Helms sought to wring the fat out of the foreign affairs machinery. There were blows from the left, as President Clinton himself traded the agency's future to secure Republican signatures on a chemical weapons treaty. Neither the USIA's Cold War record, nor its distinguished performance in the Gulf War, nor innovative responses to the world of

---

3 "Glasnost Innovation: Jokes," *New York Times*, 13 June 1989, p. A12. He repeated the remark on the U.S. TV show *Good Morning America* on 25 October 1989; see Michael Simmons, "Shevardnadze approves the Sinatra doctrine," *Guardian* (London), 26 October 1989.

4 Joseph S. Nye Jr., *Bound to Lead: The Changing Nature of American Power*, New York: Basic Books, 1990.

new media under the leadership of Carter's old Assistant Secretary of State, Joe Duffey, nor even a bid to demonstrate relevance by serving the ends of American business overseas could save the agency.[5]

At midnight on the night of 30 September 1999, the USIA slipped silently into history. Most of its functions passed to the State Department and a purgatory of reduced budgets and a hostile institutional culture. Outside the USIA's headquarters at 4th and C street Northwest in Washington, DC, workmen had already removed the identifying sign with its motto, "Telling America's story to the world." In its place they erected a stark designation: Department of State, Annex 44. The Voice of America staff popped champagne to celebrate their independence under the newly created Broadcasting Board of Governors.[6] Their celebrations proved short-lived. The board designed to shut caprice and political influence out in effect seemed to lock it in. The VOA was sailing into the greatest challenge in its history.

It is difficult to overestimate what was lost with the merger of the USIA into State. Agency hands with decades of field experience took early retirement, young people with an eye to career prospects avoided public diplomacy work; budgets withered and skills grew rusty. The folly of neglecting the public dimension became clear all too soon. On 11 September 2001, America awoke to the need to do something to rebuild both its relationships with ordinary people around the world and the realization that the key mechanism to accomplish this – its public diplomacy – was in disarray. "Why do they hate us?" became the question of the season. Polls accumulated up showing the extent to which America, or more specifically American policy, was, indeed, hated. Reports stacked up bemoaning the errors of the past and calling for a major investment in the future of public diplomacy. Insiders who remembered the sensitivity of George H. W. Bush to world opinion wondered that a son could be so different from his father. The Bush administration was slow to respond and, as in Vietnam, the positive images and messages spun out by the public diplomats seemed feeble compared to the power of the negative images flowing from America's policy: its detention facility at Guantanamo Bay or the conduct and development of its war in Iraq.[7]

The crisis has not been without its encouraging signs. One of the most interesting is the emergence of a private sector lobby for better public diplomacy in the form of the group Business for Diplomatic Action, led by advertising executive Keith Reinhard.[8] The tourist industry also produced a group – the Discover America Partnership – to work for better public diplomacy through better hospitality for visitors to the country.[9] In academia, public diplomacy emerged as a major field of study, with a lively literature,

---

[5] This story will be the subject of a monograph by the present author. For a survey see the final chapter of Dizard, *Inventing Public Diplomacy.*

[6] Al Kamen, "Abracaember, a Month to Count On," *Washington Post,* 6 October 1999, p. A31.

[7] For comment see William Rugh, *American Encounters with Arabs: The "Soft Power" of American Diplomacy in the Middle East,* New York: Praeger, 2005; Nancy Snow, *The Arrogance of American Power: What U.S. Leaders Are Doing Wrong and Why It's Our Duty to Dissent,* Lanham MD: Rowman & Littlefield, 2006; Carnes Lord, *Losing Hearts and Minds? Public Diplomacy and Strategic Influence in the Age of Terror,* New York: Praeger, 2006.

[8] For background see http://www.businessfordiplomaticaction.org/.

[9] For background see http://www.poweroftravel.org/.

specialist research centers, and even a crop of public diplomacy-related master's degree programs. All of these developments auger well for the long-term future of U.S. public diplomacy.

This book began with a sketch of one memorial to the USIA – the Family of Man exhibition in Luxembourg. A better memorial is to be found elsewhere: in the diffusion of democratic ideas around the world, in the spread of an understanding of the best of American life and culture, and in the stubborn persistence of a few hardy souls within the U.S. foreign policy machine of the idea that international opinion and the human dimension – public diplomacy – matter.

CONCLUSION

Trajectories, Maps, and Lessons from the Past of U.S. Public Diplomacy

This book has told a complex story spread across a forty-six-year span. Stepping back from the details of the year-by-year development, it is worth reconsidering the whole in search of the broader patterns of narrative, the big geographic sweep of USIA history, and the lessons that may be derived for those who practice public diplomacy today.

1) FIVE TRAJECTORIES

The preface to this work identified five core elements of public diplomacy – listening, advocacy, cultural diplomacy, exchange diplomacy, and international broadcasting. Each has – to a greater or lesser extent – been woven into the fabric of this history, but considered in isolation the individual trajectory of each is instructive.

I. The USIA and Listening

The core of the USIA's engagement with world opinion was its network of posts in the field, which continually fed back evidence and assessments of the international mood into the agency system. The USIA's career as a listening agency was further advanced at the time of its foundation by the appointment of Henry Loomis as special assistant to the director. Late in 1954, Loomis founded the USIA's Office of Research and Intelligence. The ORI's specialized research and public opinion analysis reports informed the agency's engagement with the key issues of the day and were of considerable use in alerting the wider administration to the scale of particular problems. It was ORI reports that Eisenhower waived at Dulles to remind him of the "P-factor" that charted the scale of the negative reactions to the launch of Sputnik and the crisis in Little Rock, Arkansas, and that, when revealing the decline of America's global prestige, became an issue in the election of 1960.

For the listening function to work in public diplomacy, it requires an attentive bureaucracy, and the Eisenhower administration proved an eager consumer of the USIA's formal advice, incorporating the USIA director into the cabinet and the National Security Council. Yet if there was a golden age in the listening function at the USIA, it was the Kennedy era. The Kennedy archives reveal that many agency reports reached the highest level of policy-making and carry the President's hand annotations to prove it. Kennedy was a particular fan of the USIA's digest of world editorials on any key issue and would read these as one of his first jobs on any day. He took a lively interest in the USIA's running world prestige poll, launched in 1963. It is harder to find archival evidence of any particular piece of the UISA evidence changing a Kennedy policy, but its presence in the mix is easy to find. In contrast, JFK's successor took an especial dislike to this world opinion survey. Johnson ordered a halt to the poll in the fall of 1965, apparently fearing that the publication of negative polls would have domestic political consequences. LBJ also cut the USIA's weekly achievement report to a bimonthly bulletin. Nixon went still further and requested that he receive USIA reports only when they directly concerned opinion about him. USIA polling and analysis never again attracted such attention in the White House. The input of USIA feedback into the highest levels of policy-making was not helped by the absence of the post-Johnson USIA directors from the National Security Council, which necessarily made it harder for agency listening to be injected into the highest levels of U.S. foreign policy making.

The Carter years saw the famous flirtation with a radically restructured public diplomacy by which the USIA (or the USICA, as it became for a season) was not merely listening but providing a channel for foreign voices to be expressed within the United States through the so-called "reverse mandate." The experiment was never properly funded and it foundered on the shoals of the renewed Cold War. During the Reagan years, USIA research was an important part of Project Truth. All quarters of the Reagan administration received copies of the USIA's bulletin that monitored Soviet activities, *Soviet Propaganda Alert*, but Wick was denied the ultimate assurance of a permanent seat at the NSC table.

Throughout the whole period the Voice of America maintained its own listening system in the form of audience research and shared information back and forth with fellow international broadcasters including the BBC, the CIA's Foreign Broadcasting Information Service, and – the acknowledged masters of Eastern European research – Radio Free Europe. VOA audience research always felt itself a neglected element within the whole and Voice staff repeated an adage that if you compared the BBC and the VOA you would find that only two things were bigger at the BBC, the audience and the audience research department, but it was better than nothing.

Taken as a whole, the USIA emerges as an agency that was good at using research internally but frustrated in its attempts to pass that expertise higher in the bureaucratic chain. The U.S. government conceived of the agency as a way to address the world rather than a mechanism for understanding it.

II. The USIA and Advocacy

From the Eisenhower era onward, the advocacy function dominated the U.S. government's approach to the USIA. The agency was justified in appropriations hearings primarily as a mechanism for short-term communication of policy in a Cold War context. Although the agency's advocacy included both policy-intensive products such as the anti-Communist films of the 1950s and "soft policy" products such as its presentation of American life, purported interracial tolerance, and undoubted material abundance, the softer approach had a difficult time in the early years especially.

The mechanism for transmitting the policy that the administration wished to advocate to the USIA apparatus was twofold. In the field, each PAO served under an ambassador as part of his country team, generally doubling as the embassy spokesman. At headquarters, policy was transmitted across from the State Department through the USIA's Office of Policy and Plans. Typically the director of this office was a foreign service officer who attended daily State Department briefings. This relationship functioned fairly well until 1972, when Frank Shakespeare rebelled against the policy direction of Secretary of State William Rogers over the question of missiles in Egypt, noting that he too was directly appointed by the President. Equilibrium was later restored with the USIA director or his deputy remaining regulars at the Secretary of State's daily morning staff meetings.

The USIA evolved in parallel with the National Security Council apparatus, and in the early days had its own advocate at the White House in the shape of special advisor C. D. Jackson, who collided head-on with Secretary of State John Foster Dulles. Jackson did not endure long, and his successors, Nelson Rockefeller and William Jackson, fared little better. The role of National Security Advisor grew in stature from the tenure of McGeorge Bundy onward, but with no special provision to manage the USIA within the White House National Security structure. Arthur Schlesinger Jr. did some "hand holding" but was certainly not a C. D. Jackson tasked to pull the rest of the bureaucracy into an awareness of public diplomacy. Bundy's successors had mixed expectations of the USIA's advocacy role. Rostow drew the agency into a prominent role in Vietnam, whereas Kissinger held it at arm's length. Brzezinski had great expectations and sought to utilize the agency in the big initiatives of his era. The Reagan years saw Charles Wick able to use his relationship with the President to maximize his connection into the highest levels of policy-making and working well with both Secretary of State Schultz and Defense Secretary Weinberger to ensure the optimal relevance of the USIA's output to the issues of the day.

The USIA played a sustained role in large-scale integrated advocacy campaigns. The Atoms for Peace and People's Capitalism of the Eisenhower years gave way to a campaign of support for the Alliance for Progress under Kennedy. The agency did much around the theme of civil rights and Vietnam and worked hard to turn Watergate into a civics lesson for the world. It shone during the Bicentennial and delivered the Carter-era message of human rights before its sterling service in the Reagan-era Project Truth, or its campaign of support for the "freedom fighters" in Afghanistan.

The core methods of the USIA's advocacy remained surprisingly consistent across the four decades of its Cold War career, but the relative emphasis shifted over time. The USIA began with heavy investment in libraries and information centers overseas, many of which were inherited from the wartime or Marshall Plan publicity. They famously became a favorite target for anti-American rioters in the 1960s. By the 1980s, the expense of such capital-intensive operations was talking its toll and it was clear that the future was not in the big real estate end of public diplomacy. The agency also drifted away from its use of magazines and other publications. Film had its golden age in the 1960s, to be eclipsed by television, and by the 1980s the agency had begun to use satellite broadcasting and associated interactive technology. Computers were not a tool of advocacy in the Cold War per se but were an excellent subject for advocacy, from the exhibition of the vast IBM machine in Brussels in 1958 to the compact home computers that dazzled Soviet exhibition-goers at Information USA in the 1980s.

The price of this emphasis on advocacy was strained relationships with the other elements in public diplomacy – international broadcasting, exchange, and cultural work – all of which bridled against the requirement to demonstrate their relevance in crude policy terms. The strain of managing these centrifugal forces sometimes brought the USIA to its knees and, arguably, underpinned the body blows of the early 1990s that set the agency on the road to its ultimate demise.

III. The USIA and Cultural Diplomacy

Cultural diplomacy was perhaps destined for a rough ride in American foreign relations, if only because the astonishing reach of American popular culture around the world throughout the twentieth century made it seem unnecessary on first glance. It also faced intolerance toward high culture in some quarters of the legislature, where congressmen knew that more votes lay in affirming the tastes of the common man than playing for the hearts of the foreign intelligentsia. The working of cultural diplomacy was further hobbled by its bureaucratic context. The USIA sat ambiguously off to the side of the structure, thanks to Senator Fulbright's demand that both exchanges and culture remain at State in order to protect "his" fellowships from the taint of propaganda. The State Department's cultural apparatus remained small and subcontracted the USIA to represent its interests overseas through a network of cultural affairs officers. The CAOs became a band apart among USIA staff, with a deep attachment to the idea of cultural projection for its own sake and a frequently expressed desire to maximize their distance from policy.

Culture rose and fell on the usual political tides. The Eisenhower years brought special White House funding for cultural diplomacy and initiatives such as the Family of Man, the jazz tours by Dizzy Gillespie and Duke Ellington, and big budget exhibitions of American art and culture. This level of investment and enthusiasm was never repeated in the USIA's history. The Kennedy administration's approach to cultural diplomacy included the creation of the new office of Assistant Secretary of State for Cultural Affairs at the Department of State, and the great opportunity came in 1965, when Johnson appointed Charles Frankel to fill the post and spoke of his personal commitment to the field of cultural diplomacy. Hope of bold new initiatives flourished, only to be crushed as the President turned on the cultural program as a way to punish Fulbright for his opposition to the Vietnam War. In the 1970s, the USIA and the State Department's Cultural Bureau worked together to prepare for the Bicentennial, putting particular investment into the promotion of American studies as a discipline around the world. The Reagan years saw a challenge to expenditure on cultural diplomacy – an early function of the right/left culture wars – followed by an effective counterattack and an unexpected revival of cultural work with programs including the arts ambassadors.

The cultural component of the USIA's work included strategic translations of works that market forces alone would not have provided in key target languages; the operation of cultural centers, some of which were imbedded within their host populations as binational operations, run in conjunction with the local community; and cultural activities in realms as mutually distant as sport, music, and art. The USIA's relationship to American popular culture was somewhat bipolar. At some points – the 1970s especially – the USIA justified itself on the Hill as correcting the biases of and filling the gaps left by commercial U.S. popular culture. USIA directors, including Murrow and Shakespeare, criticized Hollywood's portrait of American life. At other times the USIA worked closely with the popular culture industry and especially Hollywood to extend its reach overseas. Under the Informational Media Guarantee program established during the Marshall Plan era, the U.S. government underwrote the conversion of otherwise soft currencies to speed the path of American books and movies in priority countries. The USIA and other agencies also worked closely with Hollywood to ensure that its biggest pictures did not offend overseas audiences. Cultural figures were welcome partners of U.S. public diplomacy, especially during the Eisenhower and Reagan years when the agency had special committees to structure private sector support for its work.

In 1978, the USIA finally acquired dominion over all cultural work. Yet culture never sat well within the advocacy-driven USIA, and elements in the cultural outlook, such as its readiness to look only to long-range impact rather than a short-term fix, were at odds with the drive for results on Capitol Hill. As the debate around the time of the Stanton Commission made clear, some insiders looked enviously across the Atlantic to the scope available to the British Council as an independent agency and hoped that the United States might someday establish an equivalent to allow cultural diplomacy to reach its full potential.

IV. The USIA and Exchange Diplomacy

When asked to name the most effective tool of public diplomacy at their disposal, veterans of embassy level public diplomacy are near-unanimous in identifying exchange diplomacy, yet the USIA's encounter with exchange diplomacy was as troubled as its engagement with cultural diplomacy.

Exchanges sat awkwardly beside (and from 1978 within) the agency's approach to world opinion. Exchanges were usually two-, rather than one-way; exchanges were hard to target to particular short-term objectives and showed results over a much longer time frame. Moreover, exchanges relied to a large extent on links to the private sector. The USIA needed exchange organizations such as IREX, the Institute for International Education, or Meridian House to deliver the necessary programs for their visitors – bidding for contracts for this work as a builder might to construct a bridge. In addition to the contractors, there were the universities that served as partners in the educational exchange activity and the international visitor councils that hosted visitors in diverse communities around the country. Overall exchange diplomacy frequently took the form a people-to-people activity, with the government playing the role of coordinator or facilitator, a dynamic that may yet prove a model for the future of public diplomacy.

America's exchange diplomacy had its origins in nongovernmental charitable foundation work in the early twentieth century and sprang from a philosophy that international relations should be based on mutual learning and reciprocity. This distinctive two-way exchange approach was dominant in the State Department's Cultural Department as founded in 1938 and restrained the tendency of cultural diplomacy to descend into boastful self-promotion, which was readily detectable in the cultural diplomacy of the other great powers of the age. The experience of World War Two changed this as the Executive Branch added new agencies to address public opinion in Latin America, the United States, and the world with no thought to learning in the process but with the sole objective that American ideas might prevail. The original objective of exchange diplomacy was eclipsed by the drive for advocacy and a preoccupation with the ends of American power. Exchanges were treated not as a mechanism for mutual knowledge but as just another way to convince a foreigner of the superiority of the American way. Exchanges were especially prominent in the attempt to woo the postwar political generation in West Germany. Although it is outside the scope of this study, there was also a parallel network of exchanges specifically for military personnel through which the Defense Department built links and laid foundations for "interoperability" with allied or potentially allied militaries.

Although the USIA was denied control over the exchange program on its creation in 1953, agency staff in the field ran the exchanges set up under the Fulbright Amendment, or those begun during the occupation of enemy countries. Key initiatives taken forward by USIA personnel overseas included the Foreign Leader Program. Launched in 1950 and later known as the International Visitor Program, this brought over 100,000 rising stars to the United States in its first half-century of operation, including nearly 200 heads of government or heads of state at an early stage of their careers. The development of public diplomacy in the 1950s brought new opportunities, including major initiatives in the developing and newly decolonized world and, no less significantly, the exchange agreements with the Soviet Union. From 1958 the Soviet–American exchanges opened the U.S.S.R. to penetration by material evidence of U.S. prosperity in the cycle of American exhibitions. The Soviet public eagerly seized all that the agreements made available. In contrast, the reciprocal Soviet exhibitions in the United States with their Sputniks, sculptures of steel workers, and odd fashions attracted little attention.

The 1960s saw exchanges gain momentum with the Fulbright–Hays act of 1961. A number of America's exchange partners – including Germany and Japan – developed bilateral structures with mutual funding for their exchanges with the United States.

Although the era proved frustrating for administrators such Lucius Battle or Charles Frankel with high hopes for a major rethinking of American cultural diplomacy, the recipients of the era's exchanges were a resource in waiting for the future. The 1970s saw new relationships, including Sino–American exchanges, and new structures as exchanges were brought into the integrated structure of the International Communication Agency. The 1980s saw a renewed interest in exchanges, albeit in the context of the new Cold War, first with the "successor generation" strategy, as the USIA worked to build relations with the youth of Western Europe, and then as part of the process of opening the Soviet Union to new ideas.

Although the advocates of exchange in public diplomacy felt underfunded, neglected, or bruised in the name of policy, their discomfort paled beside the running battle between the USIA and the Voice of America.

V. The USIA and International Broadcasting

Whatever the views of staff in the field, every director interviewed for this book named the Voice of America as the most potent tool at the agency's disposal. Despite, or arguably because of, this recognition of the VOA's power, the relationship between the USIA and international broadcasting was especially troubled. The VOA spent much of the Cold War working for its independence.

From international broadcasting's origins in the 1920s, the world's broadcasters have pursued a range of strategies to the ends of public diplomacy, including varieties of advocacy and cultural diplomacy. However, in Western practice, news swiftly acquired a special status. The ethical foundations of journalism mark it apart from other elements of public diplomacy. The emphasis on news was accompanied by pressure for editorial independence. Britain's BBC led the way, recognizing the importance of balanced reporting for its credibility, and the VOA pressed for the same. The VOA would have doubtless encountered more opposition in its push for objectivity had not the CIA established its own Radio Free Europe system to play propaganda hardball against the Eastern bloc. The two systems developed in tandem, often rivals yet ironically interdependent because of their complementary roles.

The VOA charter of 1960 strengthened the hand of the journalists at the Voice against attempts by the USIA policy office, the State Department, or the White House to skew its broadcasts, but did not settle the issue. In 1976, sympathetic legislators tried to further stack the deck in favor of the broadcasters by giving the VOA charter the force of law, and perhaps managed to deter the some of the pressure from diplomats to massage the news to please allies, but political pressure remained a fact of life throughout the Cold War life of the Voice.

Although the reading of the charter within the Voice always emphasized the rights of journalists to present a balanced story, successive administrations and USIA directors focused on the responsibilities also embedded in the VOA charter for the Voice to present the policies of the U.S. government to the world. This function of the VOA loomed especially large in the minds of the legislators who voted for the budget. They consistently reflected concern that the Voice be of value to U.S. foreign policy. Through most of the history of the VOA the station's advocacy value lay in its commentaries. These were short opinion essays written within the VOA but subject to guidance from the USIA and on important stories to approval from the Department of State. During the Carter years, as the VOA distanced its self from the foreign policy bureaucracy, director Peter Straus initiated a system of editorials, to be carried in all VOA languages and to reflect the immediate concerns of U.S. foreign policy. The editorials were much resented within the Voice, especially during the Reagan years, when they became a daily feature of Voice output. Pressure for politicization seemed especially intense. One of the achievements of Richard Carlson as VOA director was to take much of the heat out of the issue.

The dream of independence extends through the history of the VOA from its foundation to the present. The very term "public diplomacy" has a context in the USIA's struggle to assert continued dominion over the Voice and head off its push to be free. The high tide came in 1976 when the VOA came within a few votes of its goal. The USIA's victory had its price. The tensions in the relationship with the USIA were a drain on both the agency and the Voice. Although the excellent relationship between Charles Wick and Richard Carlson held the forces in check, the clash between Carlson and Wick's successor, Bruce Gelb, weakened the agency at a critical moment and arguably set the USIA back for the duration of the 1990s.

The 1980s saw auguries of the future, including the shift away from shortwave to medium-wave or FM with the VOA Europe project. There was also the worrying trend for the VOA of the creation of niche broadcasters with agendas to focus on particular targets. Radio Martí to Cuba in the 1980s prefigured Radio Free Asia in the 1990s and Radio Sawa in Arabic and other projects in the 2000s. These new stations were conceived on the assumption that the VOA was too bound by its traditions and obstructive working practices to advance U.S. public diplomacy where it was needed most. They raised the prospect of the VOA being closed down service by service and replaced by advocacy-driven mission-specific stations.

2) THREE MAPS

Beside the trajectories of the five elements of public diplomacy, the story of the USIA saw movement across three distinct maps: first, the East–West map of the role of the USIA in waging cold war against the Soviet Union, China, and their satellites; second, the West–West map, which saw the USIA sustaining and developing relationships within the Western alliance; third, the North–South map, which had the USIA reaching out to the developing world. Each map tells its own story of USIA's shifting priorities and achievements.

I. East–West

The East–West dynamic was essential to the creation of the USIA. The true founder of U.S. postwar public diplomacy was Josef Stalin, for without the immense Soviet propaganda effort around the world, the skeptics on Capitol Hill would never have endorsed the Smith–Mundt Act of 1948. The need to maintain opposition to the Soviet Union further necessitated the creation of the USIA in 1953 and provided its sustaining logic throughout the Cold War.

The Voice of America was the USIA's single most significant mechanism for directly addressing the East, with output ranging from news to the jazz broadcasting of Willis Conover. The VOA found ways to minimize the impact of Soviet jamming and by the 1960s had the authority to mount massed broadcasts to punch though the noise and deliver news of key developments that the Soviet government wished to withhold from their own population, such as the resumption of nuclear testing. Other news coups for the VOA and the other Western international broadcasters included Khrushchev's denunciation of Stalin, the KAL 007 shoot-down, and the disaster at Chernobyl. All made their mark.

The obvious restrictions on American activity in the Soviet bloc at the time of the USIA's founding did not last long. Traffic across the boundary in Berlin before the wall gave valuable scope, the reforms of 1956 opened new opportunity in Poland, and the treaty of 1958 brought the Soviet Union itself into the picture. Communist China took rather longer to open to agency activity. As the agency's work hit its stride, touring exhibits, student exchanges, and publications such as *Amerika* magazine abounded. The Eastern bloc's ability to represent the West according to its own dogma suffered accordingly.

The key moment in the Soviet–American propaganda duel came in 1975 and initially seemed like a Soviet success. The signing of the Helsinki Accords recognized Soviet power in Eastern Europe. Yet the concession had its price. Moscow agreed to international standards of human rights that gave new ammunition to its dissidents and Western public diplomacy alike; moreover, it agreed to an expanded round of international exchanges, setting the stage for the denouement of the drama.

The 1980s saw rapid political change, and historians will probably never agree on the proportion of credit due to international voices and cultural incursions as against internal factors in bringing about the collapse of Communism. It should mean something that the ordinary people who lived through the events, like their leaders, believed that international broadcasting had played an important part. Apart from helping sustain dissent locally, American public diplomacy also played a role in keeping each pocket of dissent informed of its fellows and charting the march of reform once it began. Yet this role of U.S. public diplomacy is more than matched by the role the agency played in building and maintaining America's alliances.

II. West–West

Although the USIA's self-description always emphasized its Cold War context, its operations, for most of its history, fell disproportionately into the realm of maintaining relations with America's allies. Arguably its true achievement lies here also. The agency began with massive forces in Western Europe, having inherited the infrastructure of the Marshall Plan publicity machine. It also took over the reeducation apparatus in West Germany and Japan. Although the 1950s saw a steady redeployment of forces to other areas, the allied nations retained a perceptible center of gravity in Europe. This was by no means a redundancy. Inter-allied relationships are notoriously prone to tension and misunderstanding, especially when one of the allies is disproportionately powerful and easily accused of flooding the world with its popular culture.

The USIA was part of the mechanism by which Washington managed the centrifugal forces within the Western alliance and encouraged developments such as European integration. Although it failed to sell the Vietnam War effort to allies, it managed many moments when faith in Washington wavered, winning friends by its honesty about civil rights difficulties and turning Watergate into a civics lesson. It worked hard to ensure a transition of the war and postwar relationships forged in one generation to the next "successor generation." In 1983, public diplomacy was critical in bringing European opinion to the point at which it became possible to deploy the intermediate nuclear forces necessary to bring Russia to the table for the final round of Cold War negotiation.

III. North–South

It has often been said that the tragedy of American Cold War foreign policy was its tendency to regard its North–South relations through an East–West lens: seeing nationalists as Communists, and missing opportunities to build coalitions. The USIA was part of this effort and this failure. The opening of USIS posts and information centers in Africa, Latin America, and East Asia is an indication of the shifting emphasis within American foreign policy. The USIA was part of the Alliance for Progress, worked in parallel with the Peace Corps, and, through activities such as the Special English broadcasts on the VOA, found new ways to speak to the global South. Its concern also included contemplation of the best term to use for these areas. Murrow instructed agency staff to drop such terms as "under-developed" and "backward countries" from their lexicon and use positive terms such as "developing countries" or "modernizing countries" instead.

The agency's most spectacular failure was in Vietnam. Here the USIA was swept up in the spirit of can-do-ism that drove the military and political architects of the war. Although their blunders of strategy and tactic loom largest, the USIA contributed blunders of its own. These ranged from USIS Saigon's creation of the term "Viet Cong," which inadvertently affirmed the nationalist credentials of its enemy, to its assumption of more and more of the communication duties of the Saigon government, which undermined the nationalist credentials of its ally. Its successes, such as the *Chieu Hoi* appeals for enemy defections, made little difference in the long run, and in some cases, as with the introduction of a television service that showed the remotest corners of the country images of America's corruption of Vietnamese culture, it made things more difficult. At the key moment when the agency should have counseled Lyndon Johnson to limit America's involvement, based on existing indicators of the strength of the enemy's hold on the countryside, director Carl Rowan advised a greater effort for the sake of American credibility in the world.

The 1970s saw the USIA learning to engage the South in its own terms. Tighter budgets meant a search for more cost-effective methods, and the agency increasingly focused on the cultivation of elites on the assumption that their attitudes would radiate out to the wider population. This strategy worked well so long as the elites retained the confidence of their own masses. In one region in particular the approach laid the foundation for later problems. This was also one area in which the Cold War continued to distort America's diplomacy, public and otherwise: the Islamic world. The USIA was slow to react to the emergence of a new map for its activities quite distinct from its North–South, East–West, or West–West activities: the West–Middle East map. The USIA had no obvious interface with Islamism and no ready response. The VOA was not able to launch its Persian service until after the fall of the Shah, and Brzezinski's direction of diplomacy, including public diplomacy, treated the Gulf as a sunnier version of the Fulda Gap, of relevance because it might provide an avenue of Soviet attack. As the U.S.S.R. bogged down in its own crisis in Afghanistan the agency assisted the *mujahideen* in their propaganda war and continued to build own relationships with the elites and autocrats of the Middle East. These networks served America well during the Gulf War of 1991 but left a growing weakness for the post-Cold War.

3) SEVEN LESSONS

Surveying the stories and maps generated by this forty-four-year sweep of history, the reader may be struck not so much by the changes in the working of U.S. information overseas as by the persistence of certain core issues. Seven basic lessons emerge.

I.   Public Diplomacy Does Not Exist in a Vacuum

At its creation, the term "public diplomacy" built a necessary bridge between the realms of communications and foreign policy. Its founders argued that information had to be recognized as a subfield of diplomatic practice. Successive administrations have, however, fallen into the trap of overemphasizing the distance between public diplomacy and regular diplomacy and ignoring the degree to which public diplomacy is inextricably tied to the whole. Public diplomacy is a dimension of the foreign policy process; it is not a "magic bullet" to – in the jargon of Washington in the first years of the twenty-first century – "move the needle" of international opinion. As the Vietnam War demonstrated, the best and most skilful public diplomacy in the world cannot save a flawed policy, but a flawed policy can compromise the best-established public diplomacy. The history of U.S. public diplomacy is characterized not only by cycles of need – the great crises of the Cold War, the Vietnam Era, the second Cold War, and today's global war on terror – but also by cycles of confidence in the power of communications. Every decade seems to produce its enthusiast for the power of public diplomacy – its equivalent of the original prophets of the practice, such as Bill Benton or C. D. Jackson. It is important to separate arguments for the significance and value of public diplomacy from overinflated claims of its short-term influence.

One way of boosting the power of public diplomacy is to recognize its role in the wider foreign policy process and include public diplomats at the planning stage. The USIA would have been far more effective if it had been granted a consistent role in the formation of U.S. foreign policy, feeding the perspective and priorities derived from a close reading of world opinion into the policy process. Opinion research is a crucial element in any effective structure of public diplomacy. The senior public diplomat – whether Under Secretary of State for Public Diplomacy, USIA director, or ideally, perhaps, a presidential assistant within the NSC structure – needs both authoritative feedback and input into policy making. Successive USIA directors craved a mandated seat on the National Security Council. Although a fortunate few were invited to participate at the President's pleasure, most found themselves condemned to watch in dumb silence and dutifully clean up what Edward R. Murrow dubbed "the crash landings" of U.S. foreign policy.

II. The Term Public Diplomacy Has Historical Context

The term "public diplomacy" should not be taken for granted. Although the United States developed the term, it did not invent its constituent practices of listening, advocacy, cultural diplomacy, exchange diplomacy, and international broadcasting. These practices have precedents and even antiquity. The modern age brought a special emphasis on such practices in the United States and elsewhere, and the term "public diplomacy" contributed a linking concept to facilitate thinking about, arguing for, and coordinating this work. The United States should not assume that its way of organizing its mechanisms of international information is the only way of accomplishing the task. In fact, the American centralizing approach embodied by the history of the USIA has tended to conceal the extent to which each activity is distinct.

The term "public diplomacy" was the product of a specific time and place. It fitted the need of the United States to have a way of speaking about international information that sidestepped the dreaded word "propaganda" (leaving it free to be used exclusively to describe the activities of America's enemies). It also fitted the wish of the USIA staff to be seen as a variety of diplomat and thereby worthy of professional respect, rather than a subspecies of ad man. Finally, use of a single term for all U.S. information work tended to bolster arguments that a single agency should oversee this work: The term "public diplomacy" would help the USIA's case for absorbing the cultural and exchange elements remaining at the State Department. The term was seldom used outside the United States until the 1990s. But the historical meaning of the term should not limit its future. By the turn of the century it had become clear that to be meaningful the practice of public diplomacy had shifted from the top-down model of the high Cold War to a new horizontal form in which networks form between peers and the role of the public diplomat is to facilitate such connections and maybe to pass useful information along them, using an array of digital and Internet-based technology that would have bewildered the generation of 1965. To differentiate the twenty-first century reality from what was, at its inception, a euphemism for propaganda, scholars now speak of the "new public diplomacy." The future of public diplomacy will look very different from its past.

III. The Constituent Elements of Public Diplomacy Are Often Incompatible

Throughout its history the USIA's work in advocacy, international broadcasting, and cultural/exchange diplomacy regularly clashed. Relations between the media elements and area elements were also characterized by recurrent tension, and the field always pulled against headquarters. Such tensions arose not only from human nature but also from inherently contradictory functions. Voice of America journalists saw their role as that of balanced disseminators of news; the USIA information staff had a sense of mission to spread a particular "take" on American life and policy, whereas the USIA's cultural/exchange experts were much more open to notions of "exchange" and sought to facilitate a learning process within the United States as well as overseas. The political appointees at the helm of the agency and authorities seeking to direct U.S. diplomacy – public or otherwise – from the State Department and National Security Council have also clashed with all three missions. The VOA has been especially divided, with the news agenda of journalists striking sparks against country-specific political agendas in the language branches and wider diplomatic agendas of foreign service officers and the administration. These tensions were regularly fought out in the pages of America's newspapers and on Capitol Hill.

Although there is something to be gained from understanding the joint interests and common goals of the constituent elements of the public diplomacy process, it should also be borne in mind that news, advocacy, and cultural work can harm each other. The danger is yet more severe when – as in Vietnam – psychological warfare is added into the mix. Both news and advocacy are vulnerable to any loss of credibility, and cultural work is plainly held back by any hint of politicization. Psychological warfare must be completely insulated from civilian communications machinery.

One of the most fundamental tensions arises from the very different horizons of time employed in public diplomacy as against conventional diplomacy, and in the various elements of U.S. public diplomacy. Listening functions operate in both the short and long term; advocacy work uses personal networks created over time, but is most obviously of the moment and requiring the closest connection to the mainstream of the foreign policy process. In the age of real-time news, rebuttals of enemy propaganda stories have to be instant to prevent those stories gaining hold. International broadcasting work is longer-term, seeking and sustaining audiences over years. Cultural and exchange work bears fruit only decades later. Each strand of activity has to be insulated from the time scales of the others.

The best answer to this problem is that which was learnt over time by the VOA: the firewall. Whatever their grouping at the strategic level, the individual elements of public diplomacy need protection one from the other by firewalls similar to the VOA charter of 1960. Once a charter is in place, the temptation to push one public diplomacy element into the territory or to subject it to the priorities of another is much reduced. By this logic, under the post-1999 structure for U.S. public diplomacy, the Bureau of Educational and Cultural Affairs should have been separated into a quasi-nongovernmental organization along the lines of the British Council in the United Kingdom. Logical brandings for such a bureau would have been to take such internationally respected names as Fulbright or Smithsonian or the name of an American icon such as Mark Twain or Benjamin Franklin. By the same token, it would seem logical to raise the profile of the listening function of public diplomacy to bureau status, perhaps in partnership with an expanded incarnation of the CIA's Open Source Center, or even create a quasi–private sector public opinion analysis and policy advice unit along the lines of the RAND corporation.

In the twenty-first century, as U.S. embassies become impenetrable compounds, the need for direct points of contact between the United States and foreign publics has never been greater or harder to achieve. Distance from policy would create greater freedom of action for cultural work in moderately hostile locations and head off questions about the motivation of exchanges. It should also be noted that public diplomacy work is increasingly being done through nongovernmental organizations. The National Endowment for Democracy, though hardly insulated from political influence, has effectively channeled millions of dollars to grassroots operations around the world. The credibility of NGO partners is easier to sustain if the point of contact with the U.S. government is itself bounded by a firewall and insulated from the drives of party politics or diplomatic priorities.

IV. The United States Is at Its Heart a Skeptical Participant in Public Diplomacy, and the Development of the Practice Was Contingent on the Anomalous Politics of the Cold War

The United States has a longstanding and pervasive suspicion of government information and an associated reluctance to spend money on such work. The American people have always seemed more comfortable with the operation of commerce or private philanthropy. Public diplomacy has been justified only in an emergency when the call of "national security" has trumped natural reticence. With the exception of the early National Committee for a Free Europe days, the practices of public diplomacy and international broadcasting have generally lacked a major domestic constituency and hence relied on individual enthusiasts such as William Fulbright, Dante Fascell, or more recently Joseph Biden or single-issue ethnic lobbies. The story of broadcasting to Cuba has demonstrated the potential for such lobbies to distort U.S. public diplomacy. The

USIA gained much from the existence of its advisory commission and future activity will certainly require similar support.

Although short of friends, U.S. public diplomacy has had plenty of natural predators. The domestic media have always been suspicious of a government presence in communications, and the danger – real or imagined – of public diplomacy materials leaking back into the domestic media market has been used to limit the growth and in the later Clinton years the interagency coordination of U.S. public diplomacy. It is noticeable that from the days of Truman and Benton to those of Reagan and Wick, overseas information was used as the soft underbelly of an administration's foreign policy. It was a soft target for critics and hence became a venue for domestic struggles rather than an issue debated only in its own terms. While providing no absolute guarantees, clear legislative mandates – such as the VOA charter – diminish the scope for the cheaper political potshots at public diplomacy.

The organs of U.S. public diplomacy were born out of World War II and were, in their turn, suffused with the ideals of New Deal liberalism and the notion that the government could and should work to fix the world. These organs only became permanent elements in the U.S. foreign affairs apparatus because of the perceived challenge of international Communism. They were never fully accepted on Capitol Hill, and rather than fighting the battle to establish public diplomacy as an essential dimension of U.S. foreign relations, the agency sold itself as a crisis tool, and was hence hostage to the end of the Cold War and a victim of its own success. Although the global war on terror provides an obvious logic for a new expansion of U.S. public diplomacy, practitioners should avoid arguments based solely on the needs of the moment. The so-called "long war" offers a second chance to build on the best practice and an opportunity to get the structure of U.S. public diplomacy right for the long term. Arguably, had more resources and attention been devoted to long-term information in the 1990s, the United States might not have faced a war on terror on quite such a scale in the first place.

There is no substitute for a serious and sustained debate over the role of public diplomacy in international relations and for scholarship and civic engagement to support this debate. The recent currency gained by concepts such as "soft power" and its cognate "smart power" (the effective integration of "hard" and "soft" power in a manner that seems to have been second nature to C. D. Jackson) is an excellent beginning, and this book is offered as a contribution to the process.

Perhaps the most tangible consequence of the domestic landscape in which the USIA operated was the budget that Congress handed on to the agency. Funds were almost never adequate to the task in hand, and laughably tiny when compared to the sums lavished on the military during the Cold War to much less result. One less aircraft carrier or a couple of fighters here or there would not have been missed by the Pentagon but their cost, if diverted to public diplomacy, would have contributed to a different sort of strength and enhanced a no less necessary resource against future conflict: understanding of and sympathy for the United States around the world. Doubling the resources currently devoted to public diplomacy would be a good start.

V. U.S. Public Diplomacy Is Especially Dependent on Its Leader

Public diplomacy bureaucracies, Ministries of Information, and their like around the world have generally suffered as newcomers to their local bureaucratic hierarchies. They start from a position of weakness in the scrabble for resources and influence. Their responsibilities necessarily cross boundaries within government and beyond, and they necessarily "tread on toes." When these toes are in the commercial media, a powerful domestic enemy is called forth. Such problems call for a special sort of leader. Globally, the great ministers of information have been close friends of their respective premiers. The obvious example is Brendan Bracken, British Minister of Information and friend of Winston Churchill, during the later part of the Second World War. In the same way, the most effective periods of U.S. public diplomacy have been when the leader had a direct link to and personal connection with the President. Charles Z. Wick is the prime example of this. Budgets and bureaucratic clout followed. Staff inside the agency swallowed their initial discomfort with the Wick way and by the end of his tenure had rallied to perceived success. The USIA got things done. Conversely, periods when the White House has been distant from the leader have been difficult. Wick's successor, Bruce Gelb, was largely unsupported by the White House, and his tenure saw a crucial drift in the fortunes of the USIA. Key responsibilities for democratic development in the former Soviet Bloc focused on the USAID rather then the USIA. The agency never recovered.

The system inaugurated in 1999 robbed U.S. public diplomacy of an obvious leader. The Under Secretary of State had a voice only within the State Department and a severely limited management capacity. There was no forum for the interagency direction of public diplomacy such as the USIA had been able to provide at critical moments in its past. There was little or no hope of the Under Secretary of State's voice being heard in the higher echelons of U.S. foreign policy making. Although the USIA director seldom actually shaped the formation of U.S. foreign policy, the new system made such influence even less likely. The appointment of President Bush's close associate Karen Hughes in 2005 offered a unique chance for effective leadership in the field of U.S. public diplomacy. In her two-and-a-half years in office Hughes was able to use her clout to knock some of the rough edges off the structure created in 1999. Inevitably she left much undone. She could do little to offset the wave of international antipathy that flowed in response to the Iraq War. One Karen Hughes could never be enough. Future administrations would do well not only to seek out someone with the standing to get the job done, but also to avoid sinking them with unsellable policies.

One problem with the issue of leadership is that the constituent parts of public diplomacy each call for a different kind of leader. Cultural and exchange work would benefit especially from leadership across a longer cycle than that afforded by the four-year rhythm of Washington's political calendar. The National Endowment for Democracy has benefited from a single chairman throughout its twenty-year history, a feat made possible by its abstraction from the hurly-burly of partisanship. The leadership issue thus contains a further argument for subdivision of public diplomacy functions into firewalled components, but with a powerful leading presence tightly connected to the advocacy element and present in the highest circles of foreign policy–making.

VI. Public Diplomacy Is a Specialist Pursuit

In her speech at the time of the merger of the USIA into the State Department in 1999, Secretary of State Madeline Albright spoke of agency staff bringing their perspective and expertise into the mainstream of U.S. foreign policy and thereby making all U.S. diplomacy at some level public diplomacy. Those who advocated such a line underestimated the disdain of the old school State Department types for their new colleagues. The USIS was routinely known as "useless" in State Department slang. The advantage of the USIA was that it provided a life-support system for a distinct and fragile approach. The USIA's original staff was recruited from a variety of professions at midcareer, including many journalists. The agency learned to promote a remarkable range of skills, including the linguistic and cultural fluency to reach out to opinion makers and audiences around the world. By the end of the 1960s, the agency had developed its own career path leading to ambassador rank and a system of honors and distinctions to ensure that its specialists did not feel like second-class citizens but valued specialists.

While it endured, the USIA served as a repository for two generations of local knowledge. Many agency staff in the field famously knew all the key intellectuals, editors, and writers in their host countries. They had found the way to get America's message across what Murrow called "the last three feet." The value of their unique range of skills was not really acknowledged until such skills were lost in the wake of the changes of 1999.

Any rebuilding of the U.S. public diplomacy capacity will require intense professional development in the field, supporting educational programs in leading U.S. universities, and a cultural shift among colleagues in the Department of State.

VII. Public Diplomacy Is Everyone's Business

The dedicated public diplomacy structure created by Eisenhower suited a world in which foreign relations were the monopoly of a relatively small group within any state or society. Such is not the case today. In the twenty-first century, public diplomacy is practiced by a diverse range of international actors, including global corporations, nongovernmental organizations, international organizations, and any terrorist with access to a live Internet connection. Even within the state structure, all of the major federal agencies have an interest in foreign policy. By the 1990s, some U.S. missions overseas included more personnel from the Treasury and Justice Departments than from the USIA. Moreover, in the age of the Internet, the distinction between the domestic and the international news sphere has been removed. A causal word to a domestic audience can resonate around the world as never before. To be effective, the public diplomacy goals of the United States should be known throughout the federal bureaucracy and factored into decision-making accordingly. Although it is unreasonable to presume that the entire federal government should bend its working to meet the needs of public diplomacy, the interests of world public opinion should be one factor in the decision-making process – a line in everyone's account ledger – for public diplomacy operates in a world of effects and not intentions. Careful public diplomacy can be negated by the high deeds of the U.S. government – such as its refusal to join the international criminal court system – or by such mundane things as humiliating visa procedures.

This same principle extends to the individual citizen. The behavior of one American – whether a tourist, businessman, or service person overseas or a waitress, motorist, or passer-by encountering a foreigner at home – plays a part in U.S. public diplomacy. The small kindnesses that are the currency of American life can make a big difference, whereas the thoughtlessness and arrogance that lurk at the edge of America's interactions with the world can destroy much. Experience of life within the United States is no guarantee that the participant will be won over to the American way. Notable failures in this regard include Japanese foreign minister Matsuoka Yosuke, whose seven years of schooling in Oregon did not dissuade him from bringing his country into alliance with Hitler's Germany, or the Egyptian scholar Sayed Qtub, who was so appalled by the decadence he perceived as an exchange visitor in postwar Colorado that on returning to his country he energized the radical Muslim Brotherhood to halt the encroachment of Western culture, and became the intellectual grandfather of al-Qaeda.

In the wake of the terrorist attacks of 2001, a number of commentators noted the irony of the date of the attack. The date 11 September – the newly minted emblem of American victimhood – was the anniversary of the U.S.-backed coup against Salvador Allende in Chile, and hence a date charged with symbolism of the dark side of American foreign policy. The date had another significance. In a speech on 11 September 1956, President Dwight D. Eisenhower launched the People to People program and initiated what became a flood of grassroots connections between ordinary Americans and communities around the world. The date 11 September 1956 speaks of hope that the citizens on whom the ultimate success of American public diplomacy depends can rise to the challenge.

In the final analysis one is struck by the limits of public diplomacy. The best public diplomacy in the world cannot make a bad policy good, although, if properly empowered, public diplomats might know enough to prevent a bad policy from being enacted in the first place. In the short term, public diplomacy cannot make an arrogant country respectful. A nation's public diplomacy can reveal the best and contextualize the worst, but it cannot present a fiction. However, in the longer term, public diplomacy can contribute to fundamental changes of attitude – as the myriad postwar bilateral exchanges between France and Germany rolled back centuries of hostility. The key concept in cultural diplomacy has always been "mutuality." If the goal of a nation is to improve its relationship with another country, it stands to reason that both parties should be able to speak and listen in that relationship. Individuals would not long tolerate interaction with someone who entered an interaction convinced that they had nothing to learn and closed to any possibility that they might themselves be changed by the encounter. The United States needs not only to improve its own public diplomacy but also to facilitate and encourage the public diplomacy of other nations in their attempts to reach and engage the people of the United States. In the sixty years since 1945 the United States has learned to speak. Truly effective public diplomacy will also require that America learn to listen.

SELECTED BIBLIOGRAPHY

ARCHIVAL SOURCES

Library of Congress
  Edward Bernays papers
  Averell Harriman papers
  Neil Sheehan papers
  Robert A. Taft papers

National Archives II, College Park, MD
RG59, Department of State
  Records relating to International Information, 1938–55
  Files of Assistant Secretary of State for Public Affairs, 1945–50
  Records of Assistant Secretary of State William Benton, Memoranda 1945–47
  Records of Assistant Secretary of State for Public Affairs, 1949–53
  Bureau of Public Affairs, Office files of Edward W. Barrett, 1950–51
  IIA records relating to Project TROY
  CPF 1960–63, 1964–6, Culture and Information
RG306, United States Information Agency
  Cultural Subject files (75–0016)
  Office of Administration, 1952–5
  Director's Office Subject Files, 1957–8
  Director's Chronological Files, 1953–64
  Director's Subject Files
  Director's Chronological File, 1969–70
  USIA Historical Branch Papers
  USIA Historical Collection
  USIA Historical Collection, Misc. Files, 1940s–1990s
  USIA Historical Reports and Studies, 1945–94
  USIA subject files, IOP/C
Central Intelligence Agency
  Declassified documents CD-ROM

University of Arkansas, Special Collections
  State Department Bureau of Educational and Cultural Relations
  William Fulbright papers

University of Chicago Joseph Regenstein Library
  William Benton papers

Lilly Library, University of Indiana, Bloomington
John Ford papers

Fletcher School, Tufts University
Edward R. Murrow Papers

USIA Historical Branch,/State Department Public Diplomacy Historical Collection
Various files

Harry S. Truman Library, Independence, Missouri
Democrat National Committee
Official File (OF) 20E, Office of International Information and Cultural Affairs
Official File (OF) 74, Office of War Information papers
President's Personal File (PPF)
President's Secretary File's (PSF)
Staff Member and Office Files (SMOF) Psychological Strategy Board (PSB)
Dean Acheson papers
George Elsey papers
Charles Hulten papers
Howland Sargeant papers
Charles Thayer papers
Charles W. Jackson papers
Oral History Collection

Dwight D. Eisenhower Library, Abilene, Kansas
Dwight D. Eisenhower papers as president (Ann Whitman file)
Office of Special Assistant for National Security Affairs, NSC/Subject Files
Office of Special Assistant for National Security Affairs, OCB Files
Operations Coordinating Board (OCB) Secretariat series
President, Administrative Files
President's Advisory Committee on Government Organization
Records of President's Committee on International Information Activities (Jackson Committee)
U.S. Committee on International Information Activities (Sprague Committee),
White House Central Files (WHCF) Official File (OF) 133
White House Central Files OF 153
White House Central Files OF 230
White House Central Files OF 247
White House Central Files, Confidential File, Subject files
C. D. Jackson papers
John Foster Dulles papers
Oral History Collection

John F. Kennedy Library, Boston, Massachusetts
Pre-presidential papers,
National Security Files, Meetings and Memoranda
National Security Files, Countries
National Security Files, Depts. & Agencies: USIA
President's Office Files, Depts. & Agencies: USIA
USIA files

USIA director's files
VOA microfilm
White House Central Files, esp. Subject File: FG296 (USIA)
Roger Hilsman,
Pierre Salinger papers
Arthur Schlesinger Jr. papers
Oral History Collection

Lyndon B. Johnson Library, Austin, Texas
National Security Files (NSF), Agency File, USIA
National Security Files, Country File, Vietnam
White House Central Files, Confidential File, USIA
White House Central Files, Executive File, FG296 (USIA)
White House Central Files, General File, FG296 (USIA)
White House Central Files, Confidential Files, ND19/CO 62, (Dominican Republic)
White House Central Files, Confidential Files, PR 18 (Publicity)
Joseph Califano papers
Leonard Marks papers
Bill Moyers papers
Fred Panzer papers
Lee White papers
Oral History Collection
Presidential telephone tapes

Richard M. Nixon Presidential Materials, National Archives II
White House Central Files, FG230 (USIA)
White House Central Files, Confidential File, FG227 (Advisory Commission on Info.)
White House Central Files, Confidential File, PR 11 (Motion Pictures)
White House Central Files, Speeches
Bruce Herschensohn papers

Gerald R. Ford Library, Ann Arbor, Michigan
Council of Economic Advisors records
Ford Vice President Files
NSC Convenience File
OA 2271, *International Information, Education, and Cultural Relations, Recommendations for the Future* (Stanton Report)
White House Central Files, Subject File FO 5–3 (Publicity-International)
White House Central Files, Subject Files FG230 (USIA) and FG 230–1 (VOA)
White House Central Files, Subject File (confidential) FG354
Richard Cheney papers
Myron Kuropas papers
John Marsh Files
Ron Nessen papers
James B. Shuman papers

Jimmy Carter Library, Atlanta, Georgia
National Security Affairs Agency Files
National Security Affairs Subject Files
National Security Affairs, Staff Material (NSA SM), Paul Henze papers

National Security Council, Brzezinski material (NSC BM)
Plains File
Press (Advance) Files
White House Central Files, Subject Files
White House Central Files, Executive Files
White House Central Files, Confidential Files

Ronald Reagan Library, Simi Valley, California
Alpha File
Executive Secretariat, NSC System Files
Handwriting File
National Security Affairs, Agency Files, USIA
White House Office of Records Management, Subject Files, (WHORM sf) CO 165 (USSR)
White House Office of Records Management, Subject Files, FG 298 (USIA)
White House Office of Records Management, Subject Files, FG 298–01 (VOA)
White House Office of Records Management, Subject Files, FO 005–03 (Publicity-International)
White House Office of Records Management, Subject Files FO 006 (Summits)
White House Office of Records Management, Subject Files, ND 016 (National Defense)
White House Office of Records Management, Subject Files, PR (Public Relations)
Lyndon (Mort) Allin Files
Fred Fielding Files
Alan Kranowitz Files
Carnes Lord papers
Donald Ian MacDonald papers
Judy E. Mandel papers
Fred Ryan Files
James Stark/"Strike on Libya File"
Howard Teicher papers

AUTHOR'S INTERVIEWS (WITH LOCATION OF MAJOR SERVICE AND DATE OF INTERVIEW)

David M. Abshire, U.S. Ambassador to NATO, 23 October 2006
Burnett Anderson, USIA, 14 December 1995
Mary Bitterman, VOA Director, 6 January 1998
John H. Brown, USIA, 21 October 2005
Tim Brown, USIA, 28 November 1995
Joe Bruns, USIA/IBB, 9 April 1995
Ira K. Burgener, VOA, 29 November 1995
Harry Cahill, Department of State, 10 May 2006
Richard Carlson, VOA Director, 6 April 2004
Alan Carter, by telephone, USIA, 29 June 2004
Henry Catto, USIA Director, 26 March 2004
Brian Cislak, VOA, 7 December 1995
Bob Coonrod, VOA, 3 January 1996
Geoffrey Cowan, VOA Director, 3 January 1996
Frank Cummins, VOA, 9 November 1995
Dick Cushing, VOA, 7 January 1998

Walter de Hoog, filmmaker, by telephone, 20 April 1998
Andre de Nesnera, VOA, 16 May 1996
Wilson Dizard, USIA, 7 April 2004
Diane Doherty, VOA, 7 December 1995
Joseph D. Duffey, ASoS, State Dept./USIA director, 2 April and 28 September 2004
Robert Elphick, BBC/Reuters, 24 July 2005
Ed Feulner, Advisory Commission, 10 January 1996
Rich Firestone, VOA, 29 November 1995
Kevin Foley, RFE-RL, 5 December 1995
Janie Fritzman, VOA, 7 December 1995
Jim Fuller, USIA, 7 December 1995
Barry Fulton, USIA, 28 April 2006
Bruce S. Gelb, USIA Director, 18 September 2004
Robert Goldmann, VOA, 26 December 1996
Bruce Gregory, Advisory Commission, 22 November 1995
Clifford Groce, VOA, 30 November 1995
Charles Guggenheim, filmmaker, 27 April 1998
Rosemary Hall, VOA, 29 November 1995
William Haratunian, VOA, 15 December 1995
Ashley Hawken, filmmaker, 17 September 2007
Bruce Herschenson, filmmaker/USIA/White House, 6 January 1996
Alan Heil, VOA, 29 November 1995
Mark Hopkins, VOA, 16 May 1996
Charles Horner, USIA, 15 December 1995
John Hughes, by telephone, VOA Director, 14 September 2004
Bernie Kamenske, VOA, 6 December 1995; 10 April 1998; 9 November 2001
James Keogh, USIA Director, 6 November 2001
Chris Kern, VOA, 5 January 1996
Alex Klieforth, VOA, 7 January 1997
Gene Kopp, USIA Deputy Director, 11 January 1996
Jerry Krell, USIA, 14 April 1998
Dick Krolik, USIA, 21 December 1995
Al Laun, by telephone, VOA, 18 January 2001
Todd Leventhal, USIA/VOA, 28 November 1995, 30 September 2004
Evelyn Lieberman, VOA/USoS State Department, 7 February 2006
David Mack, State Department, 26 December 1996
Leonard Marks, USIA Director, 15 May 2003
Carmen Marrero, USIA, 29 November 1995
Don Mathes, USIA, 12 December 1995
David McAlary, VOA, 7 December 1995
Leonard Miall, BBC, 20 July 1987
Paul Modic, VOA, 6 December 1995
Caroline Nafeih, VOA, 18 December 1995
Joe O'Connell, VOA, 9 November 1995
Meyer Odze, filmmaker, 14 April 1998
Jim Ogul, by telephone, USIA, 27 November 1995
Louis T. Olom, Advisory Commission, 3 April 2001
Steve Munson, VOA, 18 December 1995
Sharon Norman, USIA, 29 September 2004

Norman Pattiz, BBG, 15 April 2005
Gene Pell, VOA/RFE-RL, 30 March 2004
Michael Pistor, USIA, 12 January 1996
Mark Pomar, by telephone, VOA/RFE-RL, 11 October 2004
Walter Raymond, CIA/NSC/USIA, 12 December 1995
Len Reed, USIA/VOA, 12 December 1995
Robert R. Reilly, VOA, 18 December 1995 and 3 January 1996
Bill Reinckens, USIA, 21 December 1995
John Reinhardt, USIA/USICA Director, 10 November 2001
Walter Roberts, USIA, 10 November 2001
Herbert Romerstein, USIA, 17 November 1995
William A. Rugh, USIA, 14 December 1995
Rick Ruth, USIA/Department of State, 27 September 2004
Henry Butterfield Ryan, USIA, 27 November 1995
Michael Schneider, USIA, 14 November 1995
Michael Schoenfeldt, VOA, 4 January 1996
Leo Seltzer, filmmaker, 6 April 1998
Frank Shakespeare, USIA Director, 11 January 1997
Jock Shirley, USIA, 29 July 2002
Larry Speakes, by telephone, White House, 18 December 1995
Elmer Staats, White House, 21 December 1995
Frank Stanton, CBS/Advisory Commission, 28 July 2002
Bill Stetson, VOA, 5 January 1996
George Stevens, Jr., USIA, 14 April 1998
Peter Straus, VOA Director, 3 April 2004
Tad Szulc, by telephone, *New York Times*, 30 October 2000
Ham Taylor, VOA, 7 December 1995
Kenneth Tomlinson, VOA Director/Chair BBG, 28 September 2004
Hans N. "Tom" Tuch, USIA/VOA, 16 November 1995
John Twitty, by telephone, USIA, 15 November 2000
Bill Wade, VOA, 5 January 1997
Abbott Washburn, USIA Deputy Director, 1 December 1995
Wanda Washburn, USIA, 1 December 1995
Carolyn Weaver, VOA, 5 January 1996
Charles Z. Wick, USIA director, 8 January 1996
Donald Wilson, USIA, 2 September 1964
Barry Zorthian, VOA/USIA, 4 December 1995

SELECTED AUTHOR'S CORRESPONDENCE

Richard Arndt, USIA
Len Baldyga, USIA
Paul B. Henze, CIA/White House
Robert Forrey, Bicentennial
Jordan Tanner, USIA
Philomena Jurey, VOA
William Kiehl, USIA
Yale Richmond, USIA
Charles Weiss, VOA
Mark Willen, VOA

SELECTED PRINTED DOCUMENTARY SOURCES

Foreign Relations of the United States., Washington, DC: GPO, various dates.

Public Papers of the Presidents, Washington, DC: GPO, various dates.

United States Committee on Public Information, *Complete Report of the Chairman of the Committee on Public Information 1917: 1918; 1919*, Washington, DC: GPO, 1920.

United States Information Agency, *Review of Operations*, Washington, DC: USIA, 1953–68.

SELECTED BOOKS

Alexandre, Laurien. *The Voice of America: From Détente to the Reagan Doctrine.* Norwood, NJ: Ablex Publishing Corp., 1988.

Amerson, Robert. *How Democracy Triumphed over Dictatorship: Public Diplomacy in Venezuela.* Washington, DC: The American University Press, 1995.

Appy, Christian G., editor. *Cold War Constructions: The Political Culture of United States Imperialism, 1945–1966.* Amherst, MA: University of Massachusetts Press, 2000.

Arndt, Richard T. *The First Resort of Kings: American Cultural Diplomacy in the Twentieth Century.* Washington, DC: Potomac Books, 2005.

Arndt, Richard T. and David Lee Rubin. *The Fulbright Difference.* New Brunswick, NJ: Transaction, 1996.

Benjamin, Curtis G. *U.S. Books Abroad: Neglected Ambassadors.* Washington, DC: Library of Congress, 1984.

Beschloss, Michael R. *The Crisis Years: Kennedy and Khrushchev, 1960–1963.* New York: Harper Collins, 1991.

Black, Jean and Viktoria Schmidt-Linsenhoff, editors. *The Family of Man, 1955–2001: Humanism and Postmodernism, A Reappraisal of the Photo Exhibition by Edward Steichen.* Marburg, Germany: Jonas Verlag, 2004.

Blitzer, Mark and Neil Pickett. *Review of VOA Programming during the Persian Gulf War.* Indianapolis, IN: Hudson Institute, 1991.

Brown, Donald R. *International Radio Broadcasting: The Limits of the Limitless Medium.* New York: Praeger, 1982.

Casey, Steven. *Cautious Crusade: Franklin D. Roosevelt, American Public Opinion and the War against Nazi Germany.* Oxford: Oxford University Press, 2001.

Castle, Eugene W. *Billions, Blunders and Baloney.* New York: Devin Adair Co., 1955.

Caute, David. *The Dancer Defects: The Struggle for Cultural Supremacy during the Cold War.* Oxford: Oxford University Press, 2003.

Chandler, Robert W. *War of Ideas: The U.S. Propaganda Campaign in Vietnam.* Boulder, CO: Westview Press, 1981.

Costigliola, Frank. *Awkward Dominion: American Political, Economic and Cultural Relations with Europe, 1919–1933.* Ithaca, NY: Cornell University Press, 1984.

Creel, George. *How We Advertised America: The First Telling of the Amazing Story of the Committee on Public Information.* New York: Harper & Bros., 1920.

Cull, Nicholas J. *Selling War: British Propaganda and American "Neutrality" in World War II.* New York: Oxford University Press, 1995.

Dadge, David. *Casualty of War: The Bush Administration's Assault on the Free Press.* Amherst: Prometheus Books, 2004.

Daugherty, William E. and Morris Janowitz. *A Psychological Warfare Casebook.* Baltimore: Johns Hopkins, 1958.

Dawson, Alan. *55 Days: The Fall of South Vietnam.* Englewood Cliffs, NJ: Prentice-Hall, 1977.

Deibel, Terry and Walter Roberts. *Culture and Information: Two Foreign Policy Functions.* Washington, DC: Sage, 1976.

Defty. Andrew, *Britain, America and Anti-Communist Propaganda, 1945–1953.* London: Frank Cass, 2004.

Dizard, Wilson. *Inventing Public Diplomacy: The Story of the U.S. Information Agency.* Boulder, CO: Lynne Rienner Publishers, 2004.

Dizard, Wilson, *Strategy of Truth: The Story of the U.S. Information Service.* Washington, DC: Public Affairs Press, 1961.

Dudden, Arthur Power and Russell R. Dynes. *The Fulbright Experience.* New Brunswick, NJ: Transaction, 1987.

Dudziak, Mary. *Cold War Civil Rights: Race and the Image of American Democracy.* Princeton, NJ: Princeton University Press, 2000.

Dumbrell, John. *The Carter Presidency: A Re-evaluation,* second edition. Manchester, UK: University of Manchester Press, 1995.

Duncanson, Dennis, Richard Yudkin, and Barry Zorthian. *Lessons of Vietnam: Three Interpretive Essays.* South Orange, NJ: Seton Hall University/American Asian Educational Exchange, 1971.

Espinosa, J. Manuel. *Inter-American Beginnings of U.S. Cultural Diplomacy, 1936–1948.* Washington, DC: Bureau of Educational and Cultural Affairs, U.S. Department of State, 1976.

Frankel, Charles. *High on Foggy Bottom: An Outsider's Inside View of the Government.* New York, Harper & Row, 1968.

Frankel, Charles. *The Neglected Aspect of Foreign Affairs: American Educational and Cultural Policy Abroad.* Washington, DC: Brookings Institution, 1965.

Franzusoff, Victor. *Talking to the Russians: Glimpses by a Voice of America Pioneer.* Santa Barbara, CA: Fithian Press, 1998.

Fried, Richard M. *The Russians are Coming! The Russians Are Coming! Pageantry and Patriotism in Cold War America.* Oxford: Oxford University Press, 1998.

Gary, Brett. *The Nervous Liberals: Propaganda Anxieties from World War I to the Cold War.* New York: Columbia University Press, 1999.

Gienow-Hecht, Jessica C. E. *Transmission Impossible: American Journalism as Cultural Diplomacy in Post-war Germany, 1945–1955.* Baton Rouge, LA: Louisiana State University Press, 1999.

Goldmann, Robert B. *Wayward Threads.* Evanston, IL: Northwestern University Press, 1997.

Green, Fitzhugh. *American Propaganda Abroad: From Benjamin Franklin to Ronald Reagan.* New York: Hippocrene Books, 1988.

Grose, Peter. *Operation Rollback: America's Secret War behind the Iron Curtain.* Boston/New York: Houghton Mifflin, 2000.

Haddow, Robert H. *Pavilions of Plenty: Exhibiting American Culture Abroad in the 1950s.* Washington, DC: Smithsonian Institution Press, 1997.

Hammond, William M. *Reporting Vietnam: Media and Military at War.* Lawrence, KS: University of Kansas Press, 1998.

Hammond, William M. *United States Army in Vietnam, Public Affairs: The Military and the Media, 1962–1968.* Washington, DC: US Army, 1989.

Hansen, Allen C. *USIA: Public Diplomacy in the Computer Age,* second edition. New York: Praeger, 1989.

Heil, Alan L. Jr. *Voice of America: A History.* New York: Columbia University Press, 2003.

Hilderbrand, Robert C. *Power and the People: Executive Management of Public Opinion in Foreign Affairs, 1897–1921.* Chapel Hill, NC: University of North Carolina Press, 1981.

Hixson, Walter. *Parting the Curtain: Propaganda, Culture and the Cold War, 1945–1961*. New York: St. Martin's Press, 1997.

Hogan, Michael J. *The Marshall Plan: America, Britain and the Reconstruction of Western Europe, 1947–1952*. Cambridge, UK: Cambridge University Press, 1987.

Hunt, Michael H. *Ideology and US Foreign Policy*. New Haven, CT: Yale University Press, 1987.

Hunt, Richard A. *Pacification: The American Struggle for Vietnam's Hearts and Minds*. Boulder, CO: Westview Press, 1998.

Hyman, Sydney. *The Lives of William Benton*. Chicago: University of Chicago Press, 1969.

Jurey, Philomena. *A Basement Seat to History: Tales of Covering Presidents Nixon, Ford, Carter and Reagan for the Voice of America*. Washington, DC: Linus Press, 1995.

Kendrick, Alexander. *Prime Time: The Life of Edward R. Murrow*. Boston: Little, Brown and Co., 1969.

Krenn, Michael L. *Black Diplomacy: African Americans and the State Department, 1945–1969*. New York: M. E. Sharp, 1998.

Krenn, Michael L. *Fallout Shelters of the Human Spirit: American Art and the Cold War*. Chapel Hill, NC: University of North Carolina Press, 2005.

Krugler, David. *The Voice of America and the Domestic Propaganda Battles, 1945–1953*. Columbia, MO: University of Missouri Press, 2000.

Kuisel, Richard. *Seducing the French: The Dilemma of Americanization*. Berkeley, CA: University of California Press, 1993.

Kunczik, Michael. *Images of Nations and International Public Relations*. Mahwah, NJ: Lawrence Erlbaum Associates, 1997.

Latimer, Harry D. *US Psychological Operations in Vietnam*. Providence: Brown University, 1973.

Leffler, Melvyn P. *A Preponderance of Power: National Security, the Truman Administration and the Cold War*. Palo Alto, CA: Stanford University Press, 1992.

Littleton, Taylor D. and Maltby Sykes. *Advancing American Art: Painting, Politics and Cultural Confrontation at Mid-Century*. Tuscaloosa, AL: University of Alabama Press, 1989.

Lord, Carnes. *Losing Hearts and Minds? Public Diplomacy and Strategic Influence in the Age of Terror*. New York: Praeger, 2006.

Lowenthal, Abraham F. *The Dominican Intervention*. Baltimore: Johns Hopkins University Press, 1995.

Lucas, W. Scott. *Freedom's War: The American Crusade against the Soviet Union*. Manchester, UK: Manchester University Press, 1999.

MacCann, Richard Dyer. *The People's Films: A Political History of US Government Motion Pictures*. New York: Hastings House, 1973.

Manheim, Jarol B. *Strategic Public Diplomacy and American Foreign Policy: The Evolution of Influence*. Oxford: Oxford University Press, 1994.

McMurray, R. E. and M. Lee. *The Cultural Approach: Another Way in International Relations*. Chapel Hill, NC: University of North Carolina Press, 1947.

Mecklin, John. *Mission in Torment: The Intimate Account of the U.S. Role in Vietnam*. New York: Doubleday, 1965.

Melissen, Jan, editor. *The New Public Diplomacy*. London: Palgrave, 2006.

Merson, Martin. *The Private Diary of a Public Servant*. New York: Macmillan, 1955.

Mickelson, Sig. *America's Other Voice: The Story of Radio Free Europe and Radio Liberty*. New York: Praeger, 1983.

Mitrovich, Gregory. *Undermining the Kremlin: America's Strategy to Subvert the Soviet Bloc, 1947–1956*. Ithaca, NY: Cornell University Press, 2000.

Nelson, Michael. *War of the Black Heavens: The Battles of Western Broadcasting and the Cold War*. Syracuse, NY: Syracuse University Press, 1997.

Ninkovich, Frank A. *The Diplomacy of Ideas: US Foreign Policy and Cultural Relations, 1938–1950*. Cambridge, UK: Cambridge University Press, 1981.

Nye, Joseph S., Jr. *Soft Power: The Means to Success in International Relations*. New York: Public Affairs Press, 2004.

Osgood; Kenneth. *Total Cold War: Eisenhower's Secret Propaganda Battle at Home and Abroad* Lawrence, KS: University of Kansas Press, 2006.

Page, Caroline. *U.S. Official Propaganda during the Vietnam War, 1965–1973: The Limits of persuasion*. Leicester, UK: University of Leicester Press, 1999.

Paddock, Alfred H., Jr. *US Army Special Warfare: Its Origins*, revised edition. Lawrence, KS: University of Kansas Press, 2002.

Parta, R. Eugene. *Discovering the Hidden Listener: An Assessment of Radio Liberty and Western Broadcasting to the U.S.S.R. during the Cold War*. Palo Alto, CA: Hoover Press, 2007.

Persico, Joseph E. *Edward R. Murrow: An American Original*. New York: McGraw–Hill, 1988.

Pirsein, Robert William. *The Voice of America: A History of the International Broadcasting Activities of the United States Government, 1940–1962*. New York: Arno Press, 1979.

Prevots, Naima. *Dance for Export: Cultural Diplomacy and the Cold War*. Middletown, CT: Wesleyan University Press, 1998.

Price, Monroe E. *Media and Sovereignty: The Global Information Revolution and the Challenge to State Power*. Boston: MIT Press, 2002.

Price, Monroe E. and Mark Thompson, editors. *Forging Peace: Intervention, Human Rights and the Management of Media Space*. Edinburgh: Edinburgh University Press, 2002.

Pronay, Nicholas and Keith Wilson, editors. *The Political Re-education of Germany and Her Allies after World War II*. London: Croom Helm, 1985.

Puddington, Arch. *Broadcasting Freedom: The Cold War Triumph of Radio Free Europe and Radio Liberty*. Lexington, KY: University of Kentucky Press, 2000.

Rawnsley, Gary D. *Radio Diplomacy and Propaganda: The BBC and VOA in International Politics, 1956–64*. London: Macmillan, 1996.

Richmond, Yale. *U.S.–Soviet Cultural Exchanges, 1958–1986: Who Wins?* Boulder, CO: Westview, 1987.

Richmond, Yale. *Cultural Exchange & the Cold War: Raising the Iron Curtain*. University Park, PA: Pennsylvania State University Press, 2003.

Ripmaster, Terence M. *Willis Conover: Broadcasting Jazz to the World*. Lincoln, NE: iUniverse Inc., 2007.

Rosenberg, Emily S. *Spreading the American Dream: American Economic and Cultural Expansion, 1890–1945*. New York: Hill and Wang, 1982.

Rowan, Carl T. *Breaking Barriers: A Memoir*. Boston: Little, Brown, 1991.

Rugh, William. *American Encounters with Arabs: The "Soft Power" of American Diplomacy in the Middle East*. New York: Praeger, 2005

Sandeen, Eric J. *Picturing an Exhibition: The Family of Man and 1950s America*. Albuquerque, NM: University of New Mexico Press, 1995.

Saunders, Francis Stonor. *Who Paid the Piper: The CIA and the Cultural Cold War*. London: Granta, 1999.

Scott-Smith, Giles. *The Politics of Apolitical Culture: The Congress for Cultural Freedom, the CIA, and Postwar American Hegemony*. London: Routledge, 2002.

Scott-Smith, Giles and Hans Krabbendam, editors. *The Cultural Cold War in Western Europe, 1945–1960*. London: Frank Cass, 2003.

Scott-Smith, Giles. *Networks of Empire: The U.S. State Department's Foreign Leader Program in the Netherlands, France, and Britain 1950–1970*. Brussels: Peter Lang, 2008.

Short, K. R. M., editor. *Western Broadcasting over the Iron Curtain*. London: Croom Helm, 1986.

Shulman, Holly Cowan. *The Voice of America: Propaganda and Democracy, 1941–1945.* Madison, WI: University of Wisconsin Press, 1990.

Simpson, Howard R. *Tiger in the Barbed Wire: An American in Vietnam, 1952–1991.* Washington, DC: Brassey's, 1992.

Sorensen, Thomas. *The Word War: The Story of American Propaganda.* New York: Harper & Row, 1968.

Snow, Nancy. *The Arrogance of American Power: What U.S. Leaders Are Doing Wrong and Why It's Our Duty to Dissent.* Lanham, MD: Rowman & Littlefield, 2006.

Snyder, Alvin A. *Warriors of Disinformation: American Propaganda, Soviet Lies, and the Winning of the Cold War.* New York: Arcade Publishing, 1995.

Sperber, A. M. *Murrow: His Life and Times.* New York: Fordham University Press, 1986.

Steichen, Edward. *The Family of Man.* New York: The Museum of Modern Art, 1956.

Taylor, Philip M. *Munitions of the Mind: A History of Propaganda from the Ancient World to the Present Day*, third edition. Manchester, UK: Manchester University Press, 2003.

Tent, James F. *Mission on the Rhine: "Reeducation" and Denazification in American-Occupied Germany.* Chicago: University of Chicago Press, 1982.

Trumpbour, John. *Selling Hollywood to the World, U.S. and European Struggles for Mastery of the Global Film Industry, 1920–1950.* Cambridge, UK: Cambridge University Press, 2002

Tuch, Hans N. *Communicating with the World: U.S. Public Diplomacy Overseas.* New York: St. Martin's Press, 1990.

Tudda, John. *The Truth Is Our Weapon: The Rhetorical Diplomacy of Dwight D. Eisenhower and John Foster Dulles.* Baton Rouge, LA: Louisiana State University Press, 2006.

Vaughan, James R. *The Failure of American and British Propaganda in the Middle East, 1945–1957: Unconquerable Minds.* London: Palgrave Macmillan, 2005

Vaughn, Stephen. *Holding Fast the Inner Lines: Democracy, Nationalism and the Committee on Public Information.* Chapel Hill, NC: University of North Carolina Press, 1980.

Von Eschen, Penny M. *Satchmo Blows Up the World: Jazz Ambassadors Play the Cold War.* Cambridge, MA: Harvard University Press, 2004.

Wagnleitner, Reinhold, *Coca-Colonization and the Cold War: The Cultural Mission of the United States in Austria after the Second World War.* Chapel Hill, NC: University of North Carolina Press, 1994.

Wagnleitner, Reinhold and Elaine Tyler May, editors. *Here, There and Everywhere: The Foreign Politics of American Popular Culture.* Hanover, NH: University Press of New England, 2000.

Wilford, Hugh. *The CIA, the British Left and the Cold War: Calling the Tune?* London: Frank Cass, 2003.

Winkler, Allan M. *The Politics of Propaganda: The Office of War Information, 1942–1945.* New Haven, CT: Yale University Press, 1978.

Woods, Randall B. *Fulbright: A Biography.* New York: Cambridge University Press, 1995.

SELECTED ARTICLES

Cook, Wiesen. "First Comes the Lie: C. D. Jackson and Political Warfare." *Radical History Review* 31 (1984): 42–70.

Cull, Nicholas J. "Auteurs of Ideology: USIA Documentary Film Propaganda in the Kennedy Era as Seen in Bruce Herschensohn's *The Five Cities of June* (1963) and James Blue's *The March* (1964)." *Film History* 10 (1998): 295–310.

Eldridge, David N. "Dear Owen: The CIA, Luigi Luraschi and Hollywood, 1953." *Historical Journal of Film, Radio and Television* 20 (2000): 149–96.

Elliott, Kim Andrew. "Too Many Voices of America." *Foreign Policy* 77 (1989–90): 113–31.

Haefele, Mark. "John F. Kennedy, USIA and World Opinion." *Diplomatic History* 25 (2001): 63–84.

Koppes, Clayton R. and Gregory D. Black. "What to Show the World: The Office of War Information and Hollywood, 1942–1945." *Journal of American History* 64 (1977): 87–105.

Krenn, Michael L. "'Unfinished Business': Segregation and U.S. Diplomacy at the 1958 World's Fair." *Diplomatic History* 20, 4 (Fall 1996): 591–612.

Lunenfeld, Peter. "There Are People in the Streets Who've Never Had a Chance to Speak: James Blue and the Complex Documentary." *Journal of Film and Video* 46 (1994): 21–33.

Needell, Allan. "Truth Is Our Weapon: Project TROY, Political Warfare and Government–Academic Relations in the National Security State." *Diplomatic History* 17 (1993): 399–420.

Nichols, John Spicer. "Wasting the Propaganda Dollar." *Foreign Policy* 56 (1984): 129–40.

Ninkovich, Frank. "The Currents of Cultural Diplomacy: Art and the State Department, 1938–1947." *Diplomatic History* 1 (1977): 215–37.

Palmer, Allen W. and Edward L. Carter. "The Smith–Mundt Act's Ban on Domestic Propaganda: An Analysis of the Cold War Statute Limiting Access to Public Diplomacy." *Communication, Law and Policy* 11 (2006): 1–34.

Vion, Antoine. "Europe from the Bottom Up: Town Twinning in France during the Cold War." *Contemporary European History* II (2002): 623–40.

Weaver, Carolyn. "When the Voice of America Ignores Its Charter." *Columbia Journalism Review* 27 (1988): 36–43.

Zhang, Liqing and Joseph Dominick. "Penetrating the Great Wall: The Ideological Impact of Voice of America Newscasts on Young Chinese Intellectuals of the 1980s." *Journal of Radio Studies* 5 (1998): 82–101.

SELECTED UNPUBLISHED DISSERTATIONS AND PRESENTATIONS

Belmonte, Laura. "Defending a Way of Life: American Propaganda and the Cold War, 1945–1959." Ph.D. dissertation, University of Virginia, 1996.

Corti, Thomas George. "Diplomat in the Cavier, Charles Wheeler Thayer, 1910–1969." Ph.D. dissertation, St. Louis University, 1988.

Leventhal, Todd. "The Illegal Transportation and Sale of Human Organs: Reality or Myth?" Presentation to the International Association of Chiefs of Police, Ghent, Belgium, April 1995.

Nguyen, To-Thi. "A Content Analysis of Voice of America Broadcasts to Vietnam." Ph.D. dissertation, Ohio State University, 1977.

Parry-Giles, Shawn J. "Exporting America's Cold War Message: The Debate over America's First Peacetime Propaganda Program, 1947–1954." Ph.D. dissertation, Indiana University, 1992.

Schwenck-Borrell, Melinda M. "Selling Democracy: The United States Information Agency's Portrayal of American Race Relations, 1953–1976." Ph. D. University of Pennsylvania, 2004.

Wolper, Gregg. "The Origins of Public Diplomacy: Woodrow Wilson, George Creel and the Committee on Public Information." Ph.D. dissertation, University of Chicago, 1991.

SELECTED MAGAZINES, NEWSPAPERS AND NEWSWIRES

BBC Monitoring, World Media
Baltimore Sun
Chicago Daily News
Chicago Tribune
Christian Science Monitor
Cincinnati Enquirer

The Economist
Federal News Service
The Guardian (London)
Honolulu Advertiser
Human Events
The Independent (London)
Los Angeles Times
The Nation
The New Republic
Newsweek
New York Daily News
New York Herald Tribune
New York Post
New York Times
Reuters News Report
The Times (London)
U.S.A. Today
U.S. News and World Report
Village Voice
Wall Street Journal
Washington Post
Washington Star
Washington Times

SELECTED USIA FILMOGRAPHY (FROM NATIONAL ARCHIVES II UNLESS OTHERWISE INDICATED)

Agnew. 1970.
And Now, Miguel. 1953.
Bridges of the Barrios. 1962.
Crimes against Humanity. 1993. [private hands]
Czechoslovakia 1968. 1969.
A Distant Province. 1967.
Eulogy to 5:02. 1965.
Evil Wind Out. 1963.
The Five Cities of June. 1963.
Fragile Ring of Life. 1995.
Invitation to India. 1962.
Invitation to Pakistan. 1962.
Infinite Journey. 1969.
John F. Kennedy: Years of Lightning, Day of Drums. 1964.
Let Poland Be Poland. 1982. [RRL]
Letter from Columbia. 1962.
The March. 1964.
Night of the Dragon. 1965. [LBJL]
Nine from Little Rock. 1965.
The President. 1963. [LBJL]
The School of Rincon Santo. 1962.
Silent Majority. 1969.
U.S.A.: The Seventh Generation. 1967.

Vietnam! Vietnam! 1971.
The Voice. 1992.
The Wall. 1963.

WEB SITES

Center on Public Diplomacy, University of Southern California, http://uscpublicdiplomacy.
   org/
Library of Congress, http://thomas.loc.gov/
Federation of American Scientists (FAS), http://www.fas.org/
National Aeronautical and Space Agency (NASA), http://www.hq.nasa.gov/
National Archives and Records Administration (NARA) Chile declassification project (tranches
   II & III), site at Dept of State, http://foia.state.gov/SearchColls/Nara.asp
National Security Archive, George Washington University, http://www.gwu.edu/~nsarchiv/
Public Diplomacy Foundation, http://www.publicdiplomacy.org/

CD-ROMS

Association for Diplomatic Studies and Training. *The Foreign Affairs Oral History Collection.*
   Arlington, VA: ADST, 2001. (Now accessible on line at http://memory.loc.gov/ammem/
   collections/diplomacy/)

INDEX